THE BODY BROKEN

The Body Broken is a thematic survey of Europe in the late Middle Ages, a period of huge crisis, conflict and religious change that included the Black Death, the Reformation, the Peasants' Revolt and the Renaissance.

This thoroughly updated and revised second edition retains the thematic approach of the first edition, combining sweeping interpretive synthesis with careful attention to recent and revisionist scholarship. It also devotes more attention to the histories of women and religious minorities, Renaissance humanism, politics and government in Italy and eastern Europe, and the religious reformations of the early sixteenth century. Examining late medieval and Renaissance Europe in the context of its place within global history, this book covers all the key areas, including:

- society and the economy – disaster and demography; individuals, families and communities; trade, technology, exploration and new discoveries;
- politics – government and the state; political developments; war, chivalry and crusading;
- religion – the institutional Church; Catholic devotion; religious minorities and dissenting beliefs and practices; religious reformations;
- culture – schooling and intellectual developments; language, literacy and the arts.

Equipped with maps, tables, illustrations, a chronology and an annotated bibliography, *The Body Broken* is an essential and complete student's guide to Europe in the fourteenth to early sixteenth centuries.

Charles F. Briggs is Senior Lecturer in History at the University of Vermont. He has published numerous books and articles on the history of late medieval intellectual and political culture, including the recent edited volume (with P.S. Eardley) *A Companion to Giles of Rome* (2016).

THE BODY BROKEN

Late Medieval and Renaissance Europe,
1300–1525

SECOND EDITION

Charles F. Briggs

Routledge
Taylor & Francis Group

LONDON AND NEW YORK

Second edition published 2020
by Routledge
2 Park Square, Milton Park, Abingdon, Oxon, OX14 4RN

and by Routledge
52 Vanderbilt Avenue, New York, NY 10017

Routledge is an imprint of the Taylor & Francis Group, an informa business

© 2020 Charles F. Briggs

First edition published by Routledge 2011

British Library Cataloguing-in-Publication Data
A catalogue record for this book is available from the British Library

Library of Congress Cataloging-in-Publication Data
Names: Briggs, Charles F., author.
Title: The body broken : late Medieval and Renaissance Europe, 1300-1525 /
Charles F. Briggs.
Description: Second edition. | Abingdon, Oxon ; New York, NY : Routledge,
[2019] | Includes bibliographical references and index. |
Identifiers: LCCN 2019010511 (print) | LCCN 2019010673 (ebook) | ISBN
9780429297090 (eBook) | ISBN 9781138842274 (hardback : alk. paper) |
ISBN 9781138842281 (pbk. : alk. paper)
Subjects: LCSH: Europe—History—476-1492. | Civilization, Medieval. |
Middle Ages.
Classification: LCC D202.8 (ebook) | LCC D202.8 .B75 2019 (print) | DDC
940.2/1—dc23
LC record available at https://lccn.loc.gov/2019010511

ISBN: 978-1-138-84227-4 (hbk)
ISBN: 978-1-138-84228-1 (pbk)
ISBN: 978-0-429-29709-0 (ebk)

Typeset in Times New Roman
by Swales & Willis Ltd, Exeter, Devon, UK

CONTENTS

CONTENTS

FIGURES

MAPS

TABLES

PREFACE TO
THE SECOND EDITION

Every story – and a general history is precisely that – should have a theme. The theme of this story is the Body of Christ. Labelled 'a metaphor of metaphors' in the late medieval context, the Body of Christ became, during the thirteenth century, Latin Christendom's most powerful symbol and organising principle. It was the justification for the Roman Church's claim of universality as the Body of Christ's earthly manifestation. In the liturgical rite of the Eucharist and in the popular feast of Corpus Christi the Body of Christ was made present and worshipped; as sacrifice it offered salvation, broken and distributed in the communion bread it brought peace and strengthened community. Likewise it was the focus of popular devotion, whether in the form of the consecrated host, the cross, the blood relic, or the ubiquitous images of the bruised, bloody and broken Christ of the Passion. The Body of Christ as conceived in the later Middle Ages was also a fiction, a dream, an ideal, a means to power, an occasion for controversy, and a justification for social inequality and exclusion as well as acquisitive expansion.

As such, the Body of Christ is also a useful symbol and organising principle for this book, which tells the story of a society marked by multiplicity, diversity and plenty of competition and hostility between individuals and groups, but which nonetheless believed that it was somehow unified in the Body of Christ. This metaphor was, in short, the ideological basis of a *civilisation*. Christ's broken and yet still whole body also can be taken to represent a Europe that survived the devastations of famine, plague and war, but which was also changed by these forces. One of these changes, indeed, was Europe's abandonment of its long-cherished unifying metaphor.

A good story also has a structure. This story is divided into four thematic parts, the first being devoted to social and economic change, the second to political structures and developments, the third to religion and devotion, and the fourth to cultural change. Three supplemental sections follow. The first is a list of key dates; it and the several tables included throughout the text should be consulted for basic chronological information. Readers wanting to pursue further studies or research are encouraged to peruse the suggestions for further reading and the list of references at the end of this volume. While this edition retains the structure and most of the contents of *The Body Broken*'s first iteration, I have, in addition to incorporating more recent scholarship and filling minor *lacunae*, tried to address what I thought to be several deficiencies in the original. First and most importantly, much more attention has been given to subjects especially connected with the Italian Renaissance (e.g. city-state government and politics, humanism) and with the background to the religious reformations of the sixteenth century. Hence the revised subtitle and slightly altered range of dates of this new version: *Late Medieval and Renaissance Europe 1300–1525*.

Likewise, the histories of women and of religious minorities are less neglected than previously. Finally, substantial material has been added to the political history of what might be called the Angevin complex of Naples, Provence and Hungary in the fourteenth century.

Books, even ones written by a single author, are communal enterprises. Medieval authors were keenly aware of this fact. Since at least the early twelfth century, scholars were wont to liken themselves to dwarfs seated on the shoulders of giants, by which they meant the authors of antiquity. In a similar vein, medieval authors frequently thought of themselves as bees gathering the honey of others' labours, or as compilers picking and choosing from among the fruits of others' wisdom, as when Chaucer said 'I n'am but a lewd [i.e. unlearned] compilator'. As the compiler of this present book, I owe a great debt of gratitude to the assiduous labours and impressive learnedness of the many scholars whose publications I have consulted, and to the faculty and staff of Howe Library at the University of Vermont for their professional and always kind assistance in making this scholarship available. For the preparation of this new edition, I owe special thanks to my students in several classes taught at the University of Vermont since the appearance of the first edition. The changes and (I hope) improvements to the first edition are a direct result of my teaching and students' responses to it. Thanks are also owed to the University of Vermont for the sabbatical leave awarded me for the 2017–18 academic year, which afforded me the time to complete this edition (for the most part) in something other than a state of panic. Conversations with and assistance offered by colleagues have been invaluable in the preparation of this edition. At the University of Vermont, my colleagues in the History Department and in Medieval Studies have been unfailingly supportive, as has the broader community of medievalists and Renaissance scholars in northern New England who participate in the annual Vermont Medieval Summit and Dartmouth College's Medieval Seminar. Special thanks are due to Andy Buchanan, Anne Clark, George Dameron, Sean Field, Miri Rubin and Duncan Hardy for generously having commented on draft chapters or shared the fruits of their scholarship pre-publication, and to John Watts for enlightening conversations on various matters late medieval. This edition also benefited from the perceptive comments offered by the proposal readers commissioned by Routledge. It hardly needs saying that the author takes full responsibility for whatever mistakes of fact and reasoning remain.

From first to last, this book and its author have been the beneficiaries of the encouragement and assistance of the Routledge editorial team. I can only hope that the final product is worthy of their confidence and patience. I literally could not have finished this edition had it not been for Jane Briggs's patient forbearance and material assistance as I made the penultimate changes to the manuscript while having the use of only one foot, thanks to the other being broken.

I originally dedicated *The Body Broken* to my mother, Caroline Triplett Briggs, for her constant support and encouragement, and for the example she set for me to follow. I now dedicate it to her memory.

INTRODUCTION
The Body Broken

In thousands of churches and chapels throughout what we now are accustomed to call late medieval or Renaissance Latin Christendom an identical miracle happened almost every day of the year: food and drink became God. During mass, after the singing or saying of the anthems *Sanctus* and *Benedictus*, the priest consecrated the Eucharistic elements of the communion bread and wine, an act through which they were fully transformed into Christ's true body and blood. The key, indeed crucial, moment of the consecration was the prayer *Qui pridie*, during which the priest picked up the consecrated host in his two hands and raised it above his head so that all might see the Body of Christ:

> Who on the day before he suffered took bread in his holy and venerable hands (*here the priest should raise his eyes*) and with his eyes raised toward heaven, toward you, God, his omnipotent Father, and giving thanks to you, he blessed it, and (*here let the priest take up the host*) broke it, and gave it to his disciples, saying, 'Take and eat from this all of you: FOR THIS IS MY BODY'.[1]

This act, this singular yet infinitely repeatable event was the defining symbol of what has been called the 'myth of Christendom', the idea that all Catholic Christians, living, dead and yet to be born, were united in the mystical Body of Christ, represented on earth, spiritually, by the Church and its clerical hierarchy, and protected, temporally, by secular rulers, chief among them being the Holy Roman Emperor.[2]

The myth of Christendom and its sacramental complement, the doctrine of Eucharistic transubstantiation – that at the moment of consecration the substances of bread and wine are wholly destroyed and replaced by those of Christ's true body and blood – were for the most part creations of the eleventh through thirteenth centuries. Yet only in the fourteenth through early sixteenth centuries did these core ideas fully mature and find widespread popular acceptance, as expressed most dramatically in the cult of the Eucharist, the feast of Corpus Christi, and the cult of Christ's blood. Paradoxically, during these same years several things seriously called these ideas into question. Efforts to revive the kind of imperial power that Frederick II had possessed in the first half of the thirteenth century failed utterly and the papacy's claims to universal authority were challenged by the rise of national churches and badly shaken by the Great Schism that fractured Latin Christendom in the four decades on either side of 1400. Likewise, the doctrine of transubstantiation and the tradition of clerical control over the Church were both subjected to penetrating criticism by the theologians John Wyclif and Jan Hus, and by their respective followers, the Lollards in England, and the Hussites in Bohemia. In the second decade of the sixteenth century this alternative,

1

dissenting tradition was taken up and reworked into a fundamentally new, and non-Catholic, theology by the German Augustinian friar Martin Luther.

There were multifarious reasons why the mystical Body of Christ became Latin Christendom's 'metaphor of metaphors' in the late Middle Ages, not the least of them being its ability to express unity and uniformity in the midst of diversity, and to make the divine and eternal become manifest and present.[3] But surely there must also have been something comforting, or at least familiar, in the Passion's hope-giving story of redemption through suffering, during a time that seems to have been especially troubled by famine, plague, war and insurrection. At the heart of this story was the reassuring mystery of the 'body which is broken for you' (1 Cor. 11:24); Christ's suffering body, like society's own, might have appeared to be broken, but by it, as St Catherine of Siena said, 'there is revealed . . . such generosity that he has torn open his very body, has shed his life's blood, and with that blood has baptised and bathed us'. The very same message is represented pictorially in the image found on this book's cover, the crucifixion scene painted in the 1380s by the Sienese artist and bureaucrat Andrea Vanni. On one level the depiction is clearly unsettling, even frightening, with the shattered, bleeding bodies of the crucified Christ and two criminals, as well as the chaotic crowd gathered about them. But on closer examination it tells a tale of unity and salvation, at least for those who choose to accept its truth and live by its message. Two angels bear aloft to heaven the soul exhaled from the mouth of the criminal who has accepted Christ as saviour, while the blood that drips from Christ's right hand and spurts from his side cures the blindness of Longinus, the soldier whose lance has just wounded him. Salvation is also promised to the 'good centurion', who announces the divinity of Christ ('Truly this was the Son of God!' Matt. 27:54) while placing his right hand over his heart, and to the five haloed figures gathered at the foot of the cross (Mary Magdalene and John, and the recumbent Virgin Mary attended by her sister and Mary the wife of Clopas). Congregants were encouraged to contemplate the Passion each time they attended mass, where the host, although broken into pieces shortly after having been consecrated, was in fact a singularity gathering together all who witnessed it and consumed it:

> When, at last, the sacrament is broken apart,
> Do not waver [in faith], but remember that
> As much is contained within a single bit,
> As is in the whole thing.
>
> There is no division of the thing itself,
> But only a breaking of the sign,
> In which neither the condition nor the size
> Of what is represented is diminished.[4]

For better or worse, in the following pages the history of Europe in the years 1300–1525 is viewed through this metaphor of the broken body of Christ. Corpus Christi was, after all, the master narrative which those who called themselves Catholic during that time used to construct their 'imagined community'.[5] Moreover, for us today, this metaphor reminds us not only of its message of inclusiveness but also of its power to exclude, and at times foment persecution of those whom the majority regarded as 'Other', whether Jews and Muslims, or those labelled 'heretics' and 'pagans'. The metaphor of the body broken also recognises the fractures in that community, some of which eventually turned into the permanent rifts of national identity and religious confessionalism. It also calls to mind the series of harsh blows, chief among them the Black Death, which afflicted late medieval Europe but also helped bring about fundamental changes in its economy, society and culture. Last, though, the metaphor of the body broken adopted here is a conscious effort to decentre the traditional metaphors applied to this period of European history: those either of 'waning' and 'autumn', of 'crisis' and 'calamity', or of 'transition' and 'transformation'. The first pair goes back to Johan Huizinga's brilliant evocation of aristocratic culture in greater Burgundy and northern France during the late fourteenth and fifteenth centuries, *The Autumn* [or *Waning*] *of the Middle Ages*, originally published in Dutch in 1919. For Huizinga, this was the time during which medieval 'forms of life and thought' ripened and then decayed, at which point 'the ebb tide of the deadly denial of life' at the end of the Middle Ages gave way to the 'new flood and stiff, fresh breeze' of the modern age.[6] As for the themes of crisis and calamity, one can easily understand their appeal; the Black Death alone was undoubtedly calamitous and can be characterised as a crisis in so far as its effects were manifold and had short- and long-term consequences. Nonetheless when popular histories like Barbara Tuchman's *A Distant Mirror: The Calamitous 14th Century* (1978) see the entire age as 'tormented', marked by 'a succession of wayward dangers', when 'Violence threw off restraints. . . . Rules crumbled, institutions failed . . . Knighthood did not protect' etc., it is no wonder we all breathe a great sigh of relief when 'at some imperceptible moment' round about 1450, 'by some mysterious chemistry, energies were refreshed, ideas broke out of the mold of the Middle Ages into new realms, and humanity found itself redirected'.[7] Here again, the Renaissance and modernity come to the rescue of benighted late medieval humanity. More neutral and defensible is the theme of transition, and its somewhat more poetic cousin, transformation, seen in such titles as Wallace K. Ferguson's *Europe in Transition, 1300–1520* (1962) and David Nicholas's *The Transformation of Europe, 1300–1600* (1999). Change, after all, has been called the one historical constant, and there is no doubt that Europe was a very different place in the sixteenth century from what it had been in the thirteenth. Yet to emphasise transition and transformation as being qualities more typical of this span of years than others, suggests once again the deeply entrenched narrative of 'the medieval' becoming 'the modern' through the vehicle of the Renaissance.

This, however, is not to say that the organising theme of the body broken is necessarily better than, or for that matter of a different order from those of autumn, crisis and transition. Taken together, my choice of metaphor and my preference for the terminology 'late medieval' and 'late Middle Ages' reveal my own sense that enough elements cohere to lend the Latin Christian Europe of the years 1300–1525 some kind of common identity, and that this identity can best be summed up in an image that is undeniably religious rather than secular. And what of the term 'Renaissance'? When writing this book's first edition I said that it 'is best regarded as a cultural movement rather than as a distinct, though by no means autonomous, historical period'. Since then my views on this have modified somewhat. I now am inclined to think that although the Renaissance can still signify a cultural movement starting in Italy and then ramifying into the rest of Europe over the course of fifteenth and sixteenth centuries, it can also be used to designate a chronological period roughly contemporary with the 'late Middle Ages', but with particular applicability to Italy. The subtitle of this second edition has been modified to express this duality. Other choices could have been made, but as for my choices and the narrative which they inform, I can but hope that readers will find them meaningful and useful.

Notes

1 Beckwith 1992: 74.
2 Saak 2002: 15.
3 Rubin 1991; Bynum 2007.
4 Blume and Dreves 1907: 584–85.
5 Anderson 1991.
6 Huizinga 1996: 397.
7 Tuchman 1978: 578–81.

Part I

SOCIAL AND
ECONOMIC CHANGE

1

THE DEMOGRAPHY OF DISASTER

From plague, famine and war, deliver us, O Lord![1]

At the start of the fifteenth century the population of Latin Christian Europe was just over half what it had been a century before. Wracked by famine, deadly epidemics, war and insurrection, it is no wonder that the fourteenth century has gained the dubious distinction of being the most deadly in recorded history, and of only being equalled, in terms of savagery and misery, by the calamity wrought by the totalitarian social engineering and total war of the first half of the twentieth century. If the fifteenth century offered some improvement, it was not enough to allow the population to rebound in any significant way. Not until the last quarter of the fifteenth century would Europe's population begin to recover, and it would not again achieve its c. 1300-level until the mid-sixteenth century in Germany, and not until the seventeenth in Western Europe, or even perhaps the eighteenth in England.[2] The chief cause of this dramatic demographic decline and persistent trough was the murderous pandemic of pestilence, the Black Death, which swept through much of the eastern hemisphere in the 1340s, and ravaged Europe from the end of 1347 until 1351. Yet this one episode, which was responsible for having wiped out between one-third and one-half of Europe's population, does not, on its own, explain late medieval Europe's long-term demographic malaise. To understand that, one must consider multiple factors which played themselves out over the course of some two centuries, beginning in the latter half of the 1200s.

Population pressure, climate and subsistence crises

After almost three centuries of dramatic growth, Latin Christendom had, by the later years of the thirteenth century, reached and in some ways perhaps exceeded its economic and demographic limits. To begin with, territorial expansion and land reclamation for agriculture had by and large reached their maximum during the 1200s. Moreover, whatever improvements in agricultural technology and practice which the medieval centuries had to offer – e.g. the horse collar, heavy plough, three-field crop rotation, creation of polders, marling and planting of legumes – had already been made and been adopted where they were advantageous. Finally, communications and market networks were as sophisticated and interlinked as they were going to get, prior to the major reorientation of trade that would accompany the Age of Exploration of the fifteenth and early sixteenth centuries. In most of Europe the population had reached its saturation point. Societies can, however, carry on at or just above their saturation point for quite some time. By the early 1300s medieval Europe seems to have done just that for some two or three generations. A possible sign of people making adjustments to population saturation may be found in confessors' manuals from the end of the thirteenth century, which show a sudden heightened interest in counselling against birth-control as a sin, suggesting that the practice had become more commonplace.[3]

But what explains the demographic decline which historians agree affected much of western and Mediterranean Europe, beginning in the second decade of the fourteenth century? The first serious attempt to explain this 'Crisis of the Early Fourteenth Century' came from Michael Postan,[4] who posited an increased death rate, which he called a Malthusian 'positive check', brought on by population growth exceeding food supply. Indeed not only did the food supply cease to keep up with demographic increase, owing to there being no more land to put under the plough, it in fact started to shrink on account of the exhaustion of the poor soils of 'marginal lands'. The problem with this 'neo-Malthusian' explanation is that although it rightly identifies the fact of population saturation at the end of the thirteenth century, it does not account for the situation in those parts of Europe that were under-populated, nor does it identify the underlying social reasons for why population outstripped production.[5] Nor, for that matter, is there certain evidence for a higher mortality rate in the two or three decades prior to the Great Famine of the 1310s. The same holds true for the supposed crisis of marginal lands, for which, it turns out, there is no really conclusive evidence. Perhaps, then, the problem was social. This can certainly be seen in areas where partible inheritance of peasant holdings was the rule, as the repeated subdivision of landholdings, generation after generation, among heirs rendered them too small to sustain their tenants.[6] More generally, it may have been the result of the grossly unequal power relations of lord and villein on the medieval manor. This Marxist position, put forth first and too crudely by Robert Brenner, but argued with considerably more evidence and sophistication by Rodney Hilton and Guy Bois, says that during the decades leading up to the Great Famine the crisis was brought on by landlords putting the squeeze on their peasants in the way of overly oppressive labour services and rents, as a reaction to their own falling revenue thanks to inflation brought on by devalued currency.[7]

This Marxist 'crisis of feudalism' has more to recommend it than the neo-Malthusian position, because it focuses on systemic problems in the mode of agricultural production that not only impeded but actually curtailed the output of foodstuffs. The main problem with it, however, is the insistence on rooting the problem in feudalism, without paying sufficient attention to aspects that might best be characterised as market-related. By the end of the thirteenth century, some cash-strapped landlords, in response to falling revenues, on the one hand, and rising taxation and cost of living, on the other, began to convert arable to pasture and forests.[8] There was, after all, money to be made from the sale of meat, hides and wool, lumber, firewood, charcoal and naval stores to growing towns and acquisitive kings and princes. This combination of a growing market economy and a subsistence level of agriculture contributed to the instability of life at the opening of the fourteenth century.

Nonetheless, such precarious conditions in and of themselves only seem to have slowed population growth; what stopped and then reversed the trend were the natural calamities of appalling weather with its predatory companion, disease, and the manmade one of internecine war. Periodic, localised poor weather and attendant crop failure and famine were nothing new in the early fourteenth century. Northern Europe had, for example, suffered from particularly cold winters during the 1160s, and in 1258 the English monastic chronicler Matthew Paris reported that owing to a long-delayed spring planting occasioned by exceedingly cold weather lasting well into June, 'an innumerable multitude of the poor died'.[9] Overall, however, Europe seems to have enjoyed a relatively agreeable climate during the High Middle Ages. This long-term trend of favourable conditions came to an end beginning in the last decades of the thirteenth century. Cooler temperatures made the farming of arable increasingly difficult at higher elevations and colder arctic temperatures brought about greater storm activity, and with it rising waters and frequent seawater inundation in the coastal zones of eastern England and along the north Atlantic coast of Europe; all this stressed local economies and made agriculture and pastoral activities more costly or impossible.[10] By 1305 there is evidence of food shortages and price rises in the Île-de-France, and the same can be seen in Scotland and Germany at the end of this decade.[11] The next two decades were to witness the most sustained succession of bitterly cold winters of the entire Middle

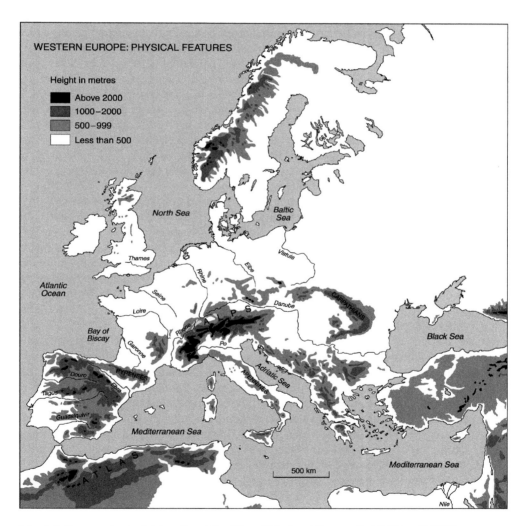

Map 1.1 Europe, physical, taken from *The Atlas of Medieval Europe*, 2nd Edition, © 2007, Routledge. Reproduced by permission of Taylor & Francis books UK

Ages, and generally the weather during the remainder of the Middle Ages was marked by an abnormal level of unpredictability.[12]

However, it was the combination of this exceptional cold with heavy and sustained precipitation that devastated northern Europe and the British Isles in the years 1315–22. Evidence from tree-rings in Ireland and Germany, peat bogs in the north of England and manorial records of the bishops of Winchester all confirm that there was excessive precipitation during the 1310s.[13] Crop failure was, of course, the most immediate consequence of this atrocious weather. Yields were never particularly bountiful in the Middle Ages, ranging from a high of fifteen bushels harvested for every one sown (in Norfolk and Artois) to lows of 2:1 in Scandinavia and parts of Poland. The European norm, however, seems to have been around 4:1 or 5:1 for all grains (wheat, barley and oats). Thus, when the cold lasted well into the spring and came early in the fall, and when heavy precipitation and high humidity persisted through all four seasons, as it did during most of these bad years, not only were the growing seasons drastically curtailed but much of the seed failed to germinate in sodden soils, and much of what did reach maturity was decimated by plant diseases, like moulds and rusts, which flourished in the wet conditions. Moreover, much of what was harvested rotted, while nutrients leeched from soils and thinner soils eroded. Yields, of course, dropped precipitously. Wheat was particularly hard hit, with yields in some cases dropping below 1:1, thus leaving farmers less grain than they had sown and, what is worse, diminishing the seed corn for the next year's growing season. Overall, wheat yields fell to between 15 per cent and 50 per cent below normal during the famine years. But even oats and barley, which are less sensitive to moisture, were adversely affected, with yields on the manors of the abbot of Westminster and the bishop of Winchester as low as 33 per cent for oats and 30 per cent for barley (in 1316); nor did beans and field peas fare any better.

As if things were not desperate enough, the bad weather wreaked havoc on livestock. Sheep froze in the fields and their newborn lambs died from exposure. The incessant rain destroyed fodder for all beasts, who, weakened by hunger, succumbed all the more easily to the epizootic diseases flourishing in the damp conditions. Liverfluke, a parasitic worm, ravaged flocks, while rinderpest, a fatal disease marked by foul stench, explosive diarrhoea and tenesmus (the spasmodic and uncontrollable effort to defecate) afflicted both sheep and cattle;[14] anthrax may also have been at work, particularly during the later years of the famine. The flocks of Bolton Priory, Yorkshire dropped from 3,000 to 913 head in 1316/17; the priory suffered even graver losses of cattle during the sustained murrain of 1319–22, with mortality standing at roughly 75–80 per cent. Finally, wine harvests declined sharply, and the supply of salt dropped substantially in many areas, since abundant sunlight was necessary to evaporate the sea water in the salt pans along the north Atlantic and Baltic coasts. Further complicating things, the heavy rains swelled rivers, caused flooding, and turned roadbeds to muck, thus slowing and sometimes halting the flow of goods to market.

Severe dearth of produce and impeded travel brought elevated and unstable prices in their wake. In Paris grain prices increased four-fold in 1315, and then doubled again the following year.[15] During the 1310s, the estates of the bishop of Winchester and abbot of Westminster sold grain at prices 44 per cent higher than the average for the previous decade. In 1315, the first very bad year in England, the price of wheat from the Winchester and Westminster manors climbed to its highest level, selling for quadruple the norm. On the consumption end of things, matters were even worse, since local demand could bring on extreme price fluctuations, with one English chronicler reporting that in Leicester wheat was selling at 43s. a quarter (eight bushels) on Saturdays, but at 14s. – which was still no bargain – on

Wednesdays. Prices of meat and consumable animal products (dairy, eggs, grease and fat) were also high, owing both to the high mortality of herds and flocks and to the increased demand for foods from animals not affected (pigs, poultry, rabbits and wild game). Higher salt prices also pushed up the cost of butter and cheese, salt-pork and salt-fish. Wine prices fluctuated wildly, rising sometimes to as much as three times their pre-famine levels. As for non-consumables, the price of live animals climbed, as did that of wool. Even after the weather improved, it took quite some time for prices on many items to come down, since it took a few years to restock the decimated herds and flocks, to restore the fertility of soils, and to replant the rootstocks of vines destroyed by cold and flooding.

Southern Europe, although spared the devastation of the Great Famine, nonetheless suffered considerably at times from scarcity, with Italy being struck by severe dearth in 1328–29 and 1339–40, and full-blown famine in 1346–47, Iberia and much of the Mediterranean basin in 1332–33 (killing 20 per cent of the population of Barcelona), and Catalonia, Provence and the Midi in the 1347. Even after the arrival of plague, serious scarcity occasionally struck Europe's much depleted populace. England suffered from famine in 1370 and then more seriously and along with the rest of northern Europe in 1437–38. Famine struck Spain in 1374 and Languedoc in the following year.[16]

Had lower-than-normal yields and animal mortality alone been the problem, especially during the Great Famine, high prices and dearth would have brought misery enough, especially since wages did not keep pace with rising prices. A bad situation, however, was made far worse by the complications of social dislocation, insufficiently integrated markets, the inappropriate or insufficient responses of government and charitable institutions, the ravages of attendant disease and the effects of warfare. Those living in the countryside suffered less in general than town dwellers, since they had more direct access to food, whether cultivated or gathered from forests and fields, and were less densely settled, and thus somewhat less subject to infectious diseases than their urban counterparts. Nonetheless they suffered considerably. Many peasant landowners who took out loans or subleased or mortgaged their farms in the first year of the famine to obtain cash, were subsequently unable to pay off their loans and ended up forfeiting or selling their land to wealthier peasants or landlords. Many abandoned their lands, either owing to flooding along rivers and rising seas in coastal areas, or simply on account of desperate hunger. These rural vagabonds often made their way to cities and towns, thus compounding the crisis of the urban areas. Those who stayed on the land certainly suffered from hunger and malnutrition, and seem often to have resorted to eating unusual or normally unpalatable foods (e.g. bark, leather, grass, insects, rotten animal carcasses), whose ingestion might cause further complications. Few probably starved outright, but severe, long-term hunger and malnutrition weakened immune systems, leading to increased morbidity. Those least able to fight off disease (the elderly and the very young), often perished, and pregnant women were more likely to have suffered miscarriages and still-births. Rates of mortality in the countryside were very uneven, though in general more densely populated areas suffered more than those more sparsely settled. For example, in England's more heavily populated south-central and south-east regions, several Winchester manors and Essex villages lost between 10 per cent and 15 per cent of their population between 1316 and 1318, whereas the evidence suggests much less severe mortality in the less populous south-west. Disease struck the malnourished peasants of densely settled Burgundy in 1316, killing off as many as a third of them. And if the shockingly high number of deaths of heads of (mostly rural) religious houses in the Low Countries between 1315 and 1319 is any indicator of more general-ised mortality, this would indicate mortality rates similar to those in Winchester and Essex.

Matters were categorically worse in the towns, with their crowded, unsanitary conditions and dependency on imported food supplies. Grain prices surged at times to as high as eight times their normal level (Mons in 1316), and food prices in general over the course of the 1310s ran at about double the norm in most towns. But high prices were not the only problem. Sometimes, and especially in 1316, food simply ran out. In these conditions, as many starved, some hoarded food, either to feed themselves or in order to drive up demand and prices. Needless to say, such behaviour was terribly corrosive of social bonds. As for what food there was, it frequently was of inferior quality, with bread, for example, being made out of whatever was available; and, even more so than in the country, people turned in desperation to eating things they would normally find revolting. Malnourishment was certainly one outcome of this combination of starvation and unusual diets, making people weak, lethargic and anaemic; another was illness, and especially severe diarrhoea. More deadly, however, were the attacks of epidemic opportunistic diseases like typhus, which periodically wiped out citizens and the rural poor who huddled outside the walls of many towns. Tournai and Ypres lost something like 10 per cent and Bruges some 6 per cent of their population to malnutrition and disease in 1316; and the language of the chronicles, which speaks, as at Erfurt, of 'innumerable cadavers' or, at Cologne, of a 'great universal pestilence', strongly suggests comparable mortalities in many if not most of the towns of northern Europe, especially in the first three years of the Great Famine.[17]

Cities experienced such acute shortages because they imported almost all their food. For inland towns, the food market was almost entirely local, with agricultural produce coming from farms in the surrounding hinterland. This market system worked perfectly well in good times, but was stressed when local food production fell off and failed entirely when the crisis continued for several years. Port cities relied both on local produce and foodstuffs coming by ship from further afield. But again, the existing trade network of bulk shipments of grain was a northern one, linking north Atlantic and Baltic ports: ports whose agricultural hinterlands had all been affected by the bad weather. Attempts to alleviate the suffering certainly were made by pious and charitable bodies, like religious houses, hospitals, and religious confraternities and guilds, and by municipal and territorial governments. Local charities provided some relief in 1315 but were far less able to do so as the crisis went on. Again, city governments and territorial princes also tried to do their part to bring relief, chiefly in the form of securing grain shipments from south-western and Mediterranean ports. This strategy, however, had very mixed results. First, there was the problem of establishing novel trade agreements. Second, speed of transport was very variable and the kinds of ships 'that were the workhorses of Mediterranean trade' were not well suited to transporting in bulk in the strong currents and winds of the Atlantic.[18] Third, supplies were limited, since agricultural surpluses were modest even in the best of times. And finally, food often went to the highest bidders (and therefore to those less in need), rather than to the most desperate. Governments, moreover, sometimes contributed to the misery by waging war.

War

Organised, large-scale violence between and within states exacerbated scarcity's impact during the Great Famine. This was especially the case in the British Isles, where depredations by soldiers in the Anglo-Scottish war combined with the hardships occasioned by fiscal and provisioning demands of governments and armies. Especially hard hit were areas directly affected by this war. The north of England and southern Scotland were repeatedly buffeted by raids from both sides from the time immediately after the Scottish victory at Bannockburn (23–24 June 1314) until a period of stalemate reached after unsuccessful English invasions of Scotland in 1319 and 1322. War even made itself felt in Ireland, where an army led by King Robert Bruce's brother, Edward, fought the Anglo-Irish from 1315 until Edward's death in battle in 1318. The Welsh also rose up in rebellion in 1315, an uprising which was brought on in part by frustration at crop failure. Invading armies frequently devastated the areas they moved through, since they not only provisioned themselves by living off the land, but also made a point of plundering any material wealth they could lay their hands on and of destroying crops, orchards, livestock and farm buildings, both as a form of psychological warfare and in order to damage the tax-base of their enemy. At times, non-combatants even suffered at the hands of their own soldiers, as was the case in 1319 and 1322, when King Robert ordered his troops to carry out a scorched-earth strategy in the Scottish Borders in order to deny spoils and provender to the armies of Edward II. The war's toll on the northern counties of England can be gauged by the fact that they received a lower tax assessment in 1318. By 1321 things had deteriorated to such an extent that the English government declared an indefinite moratorium on taxation for the border counties of Cumberland, Westmorland and Northumberland, on account of them having been 'devastated by war and a sudden murrain of beasts so that they have no means of sustenance nor of tillage'.[19]

Less violent, but highly disruptive nonetheless, was the heavy taxation required by war. Four of the seven direct lay and clerical subsidies levied by the government of Edward II during his reign (1307–27) occurred during the Great Famine; these four subsidies yielded almost two-thirds of the total amount raised from this form of taxation during a reign of two decades.[20] People in the north and Midlands of England were also often subjected to contribute to the war through purveyance, or 'prise'. Purveyance was the chief means by which armies were supplied with food and transport during campaigns. In theory, purveyors paid their suppliers fair market value for the goods taken; in reality, however, this rarely happened, with purveyors habitually paying only a fraction of what the goods were worth or, even worse, seizing them without any payment whatsoever. This abuse drove the cleric William of Pagula to write a work of protest, entitled *The Mirror of King Edward III* (c. 1330), in which he cries out to the young king, 'in certain deeds you are similar to a leader of robbers, who has under himself many thieves and robbers. . . . And I promise to you, Lord King, as long as such things happen by your authority and with your defense, that unless you amend the aforesaid things reasonably, you will be punished eternally and your son also'.[21] Nor were the purveyors the only ones guilty of corruption, as tax-collectors on the make frequently extorted money from those least able to pay. As if this were not bad enough, those living on the English side of the border very often had to pay tribute to the Scots in return for promises to keep truces. Those further south, although largely spared the worst effects of this war, did nonetheless feel the bite of the baronial revolt against Edward II in late 1321 and early 1322.

War also complicated matters on the Continent. The Scandinavian countries were especially hard hit during the 1310s by civil war, while in the Empire war broke out off and on between the emperor Ludwig of Bavaria and Duke Frederick of Austria. All this, and especially the wars in Scandinavia, had a severely disruptive effect on trade in the Baltic, since resources that might have gone toward famine relief were frequently diverted to provision troops at war. War with France, moreover, added to the woes of the Flemings in the first year of the famine. In all cases, war brought with it refugees, disruption of trade and agriculture, and a greater tax burden. As in the case of modern famine, so was it then: scarcity from bad weather became deadly when joined by war and disease.

Of course, war's contribution to crisis in the late Middle Ages was not limited to the time of and regions affected by the Great Famine. For reasons that will be examined further in Chapter 6, war was endemic to late medieval and Renaissance Europe. During the first half of the fourteenth century alone, in addition to conflicts already discussed, war touched virtually all parts of Latin Christendom. Flemish town militias slaughtered a French army at Courtrai in 1302. Hostilities broke out there again when what began as a peasant insurrection in 1323 soon turned into a fully fledged civil war and then into a war against the French. This terrible internecine conflict raged until 1328, when a French army mercilessly cut down the assembled Flemish militias at Cassel. The Anglo-Scottish war was in full swing before the famine flared up again in 1327 and resulted in two staggering defeats of the Scots at Dupplin Moor and Halidon Hill in 1332–33. Elsewhere, in the German Empire, the militias of the Swiss Confederation inflicted crushing defeats on the Austrians at the battle of Morgarten in 1315 and over an army led by members of the German and Swiss nobility at Laupen in 1339; in Hungary, King Charles-Robert defeated rebelling nobles at Rozgony in 1319 and eleven years later at Posada his army met defeat at the hands of the Wallachians; and in central and northern Italy, frequent warfare was the order of the day between shifting constellations of multiple protagonists rallying under the banners of Guelf and Ghibelline. Some sense of the effects of war on society can be discerned by looking at the misery and devastation meted out during the so-called Hundred Years War, a series of conflicts between England and France and their respective allies that dragged on for 116 years (1337–1453).

The few major spectacular battles of this war, at Sluys (1340), Crécy and Neville's Cross (1346), Poitiers (1356), Agincourt (1415), Verneuil (1424), Patay (1429), Formigny (1450) and Castillon (1453), belie both its tremendous expense and grim impact on the populace. Owing to changes in the composition of armies and improvements in artillery, armour and fortification design, the costs of war rose precipitously, starting in the later thirteenth century. During most of the High Middle Ages armies tended to be on the small side, being composed mostly of heavily armed aristocratic cavalry, along with fairly small contingents of poorly armed levies of infantry and better equipped mercenary infantry and crossbowmen. Tactics very much favoured the mounted knights and casualties were usually light, since the knights preferred taking one another hostage as a way to gain prestige and collect hefty ransoms. All this changed in the decades on either side of 1300, as highly disciplined companies of infantry, protected with body armour and armed either with bows, long pikes, poleaxes or, in the case of the Flemings, short lances, called *goedendags* (for 'hello', in Flemish) held their own against or bested formations of cavalry. It was the skilled use of this infantry that was responsible for the Scottish victories at Stirling (1297) and Bannockburn, the Flemish successes at Courtrai and during the early years of the Flemish Rebellion, and the Swiss victories at Morgarten and Laupen. King Edward III would take the lessons of these battles to heart, and rely on infantry and dismounted men-at-arms when defeating the Scots in 1332–33 and later the French at Crécy. Also used to great effect by the English armies at Crécy, and again at Poitiers and Agincourt was the longbow. When shot *en masse* by skilled archers, these great bows of yew, with their draw of 100 pounds or more, and propelling long 'clothyard' shafts, tipped either with small barbed or case-hardened, armour-piercing 'bodkin' points, could wreak havoc on lightly armoured infantry and disrupt cavalry charges at more than 200 metres. At closer range, not even the skilfully designed plate armour of knights and men-at-arms guaranteed protection against a hail of arrows.

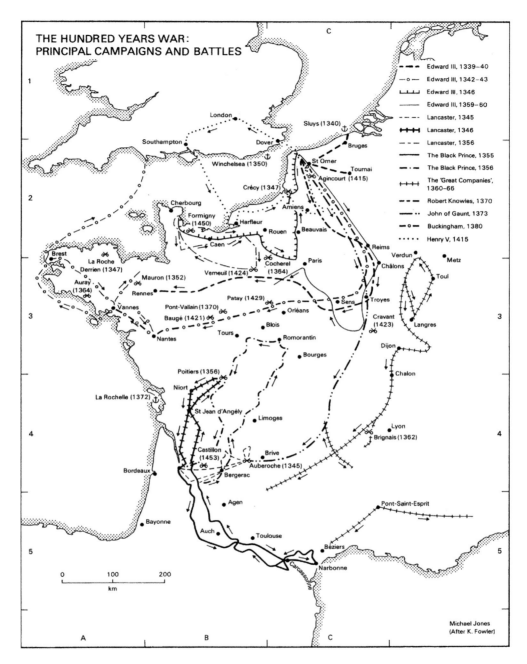

THE HUNDRED YEARS WAR:
PRINCIPAL CAMPAIGNS AND BATTLES

Legend:
- Edward III, 1339–40
- Edward III, 1342–43
- Edward III, 1346
- Edward III, 1359–60
- Lancaster, 1345
- Lancaster, 1346
- Lancaster, 1356
- The Black Prince, 1355
- The Black Prince, 1356
- The 'Great Companies', 1360–66
- Robert Knowles, 1370
- John of Gaunt, 1373
- Buckingham, 1380
- Henry V, 1415

London
Southampton
Dover
Winchelsea (1350)
Sluys (1340)
Bruges
St Omer
Tournai
Agincourt (1415)
Crécy (1347)
Amiens
Cherbourg
Formigny (1450)
Harfleur
Rouen
Beauvais
Caen
Reims
Verdun
Metz
Brest
La Roche Derrien (1347)
Cocherel (1364)
Paris
Châlons
Toul
Verneuil (1424)
Mauron (1352)
Rennes
Auray (1364)
Pont-Vallain (1370)
Sens
Troyes
Langres
Vannes
Baugé (1421)
Orléans
Cravant (1423)
Nantes
Blois
Romorantin
Dijon
Tours
Bourges
Chalon
Poitiers (1356)
Niort
Lyon
La Rochelle (1372)
St Jean d'Angély
Limoges
Brignais (1362)
Castillon (1453)
Brive
Auberoche (1345)
Bordeaux
Bergerac
Agen
Pont-Saint-Esprit
Bayonne
Auch
Toulouse
Béziers
Narbonne
Carcassonne
Patay (1429)

0   100   200
km

Michael Jones
(After K. Fowler)

Map 1.2 The Hundred Years War: principal campaigns and battles, taken from *The Atlas of Medieval Europe*, 2nd Edition, © 2007, Routledge. Reproduced by permission of Taylor & Francis books UK

Infantry and archers were drawn largely from the ranks of commoners and were not nearly as well paid as knights or mounted men-at-arms. Nonetheless, because late medieval armies needed large numbers of them and tended to remain on campaign for extended periods of time, the expense of provisioning, transporting and paying the wages of late medieval armies was considerable. Consequently, the tax burden imposed on the French and English populace, especially after the dramatic population decline of the Black Death, was heavy indeed. Once on campaign, these armies were responsible for inflicting almost unimaginable devastation. There are several reasons for this. First, armies were expected to live off the land and were hardly likely to pay their enemies for provisions. Second, pay was often low, on the understanding that soldiers would supplement their wages with spoils and plunder reaped from the countryside and captured towns of their enemies. And pillage and plunder they certainly did. Also, pay was more often than not in arrears, which only whetted the soldiers' appetite for booty. But even more to the point, visiting wrack and ruin on the non-combatant enemy populace was key to English (as well as Scottish and French, when practicable) strategy throughout much of the war. The war was mostly fought in northern and western France, areas of relatively flat and open countryside (*plat pays*) punctuated by fortified towns and castles. Prior to the advances in gunpowder weaponry of the fifteenth century, the taking of these towns and castles one after another in order to conquer and hold territory was prohibitively expensive and time-consuming. Instead, Edward III pursued a strategy of *chevauchées*, swift moving campaigns of mounted armies whose chief purpose was to devastate a broad swath of the countryside through which they passed, as well as looting and destroying any towns or castles they could easily capture. At the very least, these campaigns, launched in 1339, 1346–47, 1349, 1355, 1356, 1359, 1370, 1373 and (in the reign of Richard II) 1380 destroyed the productive capacity and tax-base of the areas affected, as well as humiliating the French authorities responsible for protecting the Church and people from such depredations. Even the 1339–40 campaign, whose grand strategy of alliances had yielded little for the English besides a massive debt, succeeded in laying waste the countryside around Cambrai to such an extent that Pope Benedict XII sent 6,000 gold florins as disaster relief.[22] Writing of the *chevauchée* of 1359, the Carmelite friar Jean de Venette wrote:

> The loss by fire of the village where I was born, Venette near Compiègne, is to be lamented, together with that of many others near by. The vines in this region, which supply that most pleasant and desirable liquor which maketh glad the heart of man, were not pruned or kept from rotting by the labors of men's hands. The fields were not sown or ploughed. There were no cattle or fowl in the fields. . . . No wayfarers went along the roads, carrying their best cheese and dairy produce to market. Throughout the parishes and villages, alas! went forth no mendicants to hear confessions and preach in Lent but rather robbers and thieves to carry off openly whatever they could find. Houses and churches no longer presented a smiling appearance with newly repaired roofs but rather the lamentable spectacle of scattered, smoking ruins to which they had been reduced by devouring flames. The eye of man was no longer rejoiced by the accustomed sight of green pastures and fields charmingly colored by the growing grain, but rather saddened by the looks of the nettles and thistles springing up on every side. The pleasant sound of bells was heard indeed, not as a summons to divine worship, but as a warning of hostile incursions, in order that men might seek out hiding places while the enemy were yet on the way. What more can I say? Every misery increased on every hand.[23]

These *chevauchées* had another purpose, however, this being to force the French to offer battle, but at a time and place of the invader's choosing. Such was the outcome of the 1346 and 1356 campaigns, when the English slaughtered the flower of French chivalry at Crécy and Poitiers, and, in the latter case, took the French king, John II 'the Good', hostage. A similar strategy drew out the French to equal effect in 1415 at Agincourt and it was advocated again by Sir John Fastolf in 1435, who recommended 'brennyng and distruynge alle the lande as thei pas, bothe hous, corne, veignes, and alle treis that beren fruyte for mannys sustenaunce, and all besteile that may not be dryven, to be distroiede'.[24]

Even in times of truce and 'peace' this war brought misery and destitution to many in France. Thanks to poor pay and provisioning, and, frankly, a sense of entitlement to spoils and respect, English garrisons ran what amounted to protection rackets, extorting money and goods in the form of ransoms and *pâtis* ('collective ransoms') from the unfortunate locals, and enforcing payment through intimidation and outright violence. Likewise, decommissioned soldiers, accustomed to the camaraderie, freedom, profit and power of army life, often continued to practise their craft as mercenaries, freebooters or brigands. In France itself, these *routiers* organised themselves into 'free companies' in the fourteenth century. In the fifteenth century they earned the far less savoury name of *écorcheurs* ('skinners'). They spread fear and wreaked widespread havoc, especially during the lulls in official hostilities in the 1360s, 1380s and 1390s, and in the late 1430s and early 1440s. Sometimes these companies gathered together into 'great companies', like the one that assembled shortly after the Peace of Brétigny in 1360 and made its way to Avignon, where Pope Innocent VI, after first declaring its members excommunicate and then launching an unsuccessful crusade against them, at last had no other option than to buy them off for the princely sum of 100,000 florins. Despite this, mercenary bands continued their depredations in southern France, and this during a vicious outbreak of plague no less, prompting one despairing clerk in the town of Millau to write 'everything is dead, everyone is dead'.[25]

Mercenary companies also moved beyond France into Italy, where during the later decades of the fourteenth century they fought under the command of captains called *condottieri* ('military contractors'). The most famous of these companies formed of veterans of the wars in France was the, predominantly English, White Company, one of whose officers, Sir John Hawkwood, fought in the pay of several employers, including Pisa, Milan, the papacy, and Florence, for which city-state he worked exclusively from 1380 till his death in 1394. Captains and soldiers from the Anglo-French war also made their way to Spain, where, in the 1360s a French company under the command of the Breton mercenary Bertrand du Guesclin supported the forces of Pere IV of Aragon and the Castilian pretender Enrique of Trastámara, while an English/Gascon force under Edward the Black Prince fought for King Pedro I 'the Cruel' of Castile. Here it should be said that the movement into Italy and Spain of soldiers from the Anglo-French war only fanned already burning fires of war in either peninsula. In Italy mercenary companies had long been fighting on the part of city-states and princes, and the problem of roving bands of 'companies of adventure', made up of German, Provençal, Hungarian, and native Italian mercenaries, had already become acute in the aftermath of Louis the Great of Hungary's invasion of Naples in 1347. In Spain, the so-called 'War of the Two Pedros' had been going on since 1356, and the return of the Black Prince and du Guesclin to France upon the renewal of the Hundred Years War in 1369 did nothing to bridle the dogs of war in Iberia. This story of groups of mercenary soldiers on the move does, however, indicate a problem endemic to late medieval warfare: the steady employment and orderly demobilisation of the professional soldier before the days of permanent standing armies.

Figure 1.1 The devastation of war. Paris, Bibliothèque national de France, ms. fr. 250, fol. 215r

Pestilence

The effects and demands of war doubtless had some impact on medieval demography, at least at the local level. Areas laid waste by invading armies could take years to recover their productivity, peasants fled from the countryside to towns and forests, heavy taxation and purveyance depressed the rural economy, and disruption of trade could turn dearth into famine. War, combined with more frequent bad weather and underlying structural problems in the agrarian economy and society, sufficed to halt population growth in the early fourteenth century. In some areas these factors even reversed the trend and contributed to a decline in population, as in Tuscany, eastern Normandy and in parts of Burgundy. Still, there is general historical consensus that things in Latin Christian Europe would have gone on much as they had before, had the catastrophe of pandemic pestilence not occurred. But, of course, it did; and its advent and seemingly malevolent recurrence brought both untold misery and major changes to late medieval society.

> In that year [1348] and the following, there was a general mortality of men throughout the world. It started first in India, then it went through Tarsus, and then to the Saracens, and finally to the Christians and Jews, so that in the space of a single year . . . in those remote regions eight thousand legions of people [i.e. 32 to 48 million], not counting the Christians, died suddenly. . .

But the plague 'became strong among the Christians, just as it had among the other nations' and:

> At Avignon 1,312 people died in a single day, according to a calculation made at the papal court. And on another day 400 or more died there. During Lent 356 Dominicans died in Provence. Of the 140 friars at Montpellier only seven remained; at Magdalen only seven of 160 survived. . . . Of the 150 Franciscans at Marseilles not even one remained who could spread the news to others. . . . At that same time in Corinth and Achaea several cities collapsed and the earth covered them over. Castles and towns were cracked, broken up and swallowed. The mountains in Cyprus were levelled so that rivers were, and are, obstructed and many cities inundated and towns destroyed. . . .
>
> Then the most grievous plague penetrated the sea-coast by way of Southampton and came to Bristol. They died there as if all the healthfulness of the town had been seized in advance as it were by sudden death, for there were few who lasted more than two or three days, or even half a day, once they had taken to their beds. Thereafter cruel death itself burst forth everywhere in the space of a day's time. At Leicester, in the small parish of St Leonard more than 380 died; in the parish of Holy Cross, more than 400; in St Margaret's parish, 700; and so it went, with a great multitude in each parish. . . .
>
> In the same year [1349] there was a great pestilence among sheep throughout the kingdom, and to such an extent that in one place more than 5,000 sheep died at pasture and their bodies were so foul that neither beast nor bird wanted to touch them. And prices were low on everything on account of the fear of death. For there were few indeed who gave a care for riches or anything else. . . . Stray sheep and cattle wandered through the fields and among the crops. And as there was none to drive and gather them in, in every place countless numbers of them perished in

out of the way ditches and hedges. . . . For there was no memory of a mortality so hard and cruel since the time of Vortigern, king of the [ancient] Britons, in whose time . . . there were not enough living to bury the dead.[26]

Although written some four decades after the events it describes, this account by Henry Knighton, an Augustinian canon of Leicester still retains afresh the sense of bleak terror, numbing confusion and profound social dislocation sown by the first attack of the great pestilence. It also points to the fact that the plague came from the East. The Italian lawyer Gabriele de' Mussis, writing immediately after the first outbreak, gave the most detailed account of the plague's origins and passage to Europe. He leaves no doubt that it was a pandemic that originated in Asia and moved westward:

> The scale of the mortality and the form which it took persuaded those who lived, weeping and lamenting, through the bitter events of 1346 to 1348 – Chinese, Indians, Persians, Medes, Kurds, Armenians, Cilicians, Georgians, Mesopotamians, Nubians, Ethiopians, Turks, Egyptians, Arabs, Saracens and Greeks (for almost all the East has been affected) – that the last judgement had come.[27]

That the disease spread via trade routes is likely, for in the first half of the fourteenth century, thanks to the power of the Mongols and the intrepid mercantile activity of the Genoese and Venetians, Europe was closely connected to Asia and North Africa by trade. It would be those Italian merchants who first brought the plague to Europe. In 1347, 'Tartars' besieging Caffa, a Genoese trading post on the Black Sea, passed the sickness to the inhabitants, when 'they ordered corpses to be placed in catapults and lobbed into the city in the hope that the intolerable stench would kill everyone inside'.[28] Once in the city the disease spread rapidly, as 'one infected man could carry the poison to others, and infect people and places with the disease by look alone'. Refugees from Caffa made their way back to Europe:

> Some boats were bound for Genoa, others went to Venice and to other Christian areas. When the sailors reached these places and mixed with the people there, it was as if they had brought evil spirits with them: every city, every settlement, every place was poisoned by the contagious pestilence, and their inhabitants, both men and women, died suddenly. And when one person had contracted the illness, he poisoned his whole family even as he fell and died, so that those preparing to bury his body were seized by death in the same way.[29]

De' Mussis' narration accords well with contemporary accounts from Asia and with the findings of modern scholarship. Beginning in central Asia, probably in 1331–32, the plague made its way to China and India, and then westwards through Transoxania north along the Silk Road to infect the Kipchak Khanate of southern Russia by the mid-1340s. It may also have moved southwest from Samarkand to infect Armenia and Azerbaijan. The Tatars of de' Mussis' account were the forces of the Kipchak Khan Janibeg. The refugees from Caffa infected Constantinople as well as Italy in 1347. Likewise, Italian merchants probably were the principal transporters of the disease throughout the Mediterranean basin, infecting Cyprus, the Near East and North Africa as well as Mediterranean Europe in the course of 1347–48. In 1348 it had crossed the Alps into Austria and southern Germany, and moved north from Marseilles to Avignon by the spring, and to Toulouse, Paris and Bordeaux by the summer of 1348. From Bordeaux the infection made its way to England that same summer, probably arriving at several ports there, including Bristol, Melcombe Regis and Southampton. Soon after this the plague was in London, and from there it made its way to Norway in the spring of 1349. Where infected people, and perhaps goods moved, so moved the pestilence, so that eastern and northern Iberia were infected in 1348, and Portugal, the remainder of Britain and Ireland, northern Germany and the Low Countries in 1349. It had reached the remainder of Scandinavia as well as Poland by 1350. Not surprisingly, some locales were stricken more than others. Among the hardest hit, Bremen lost up to three-quarters of its inhabitants, and Genoa and Hamburg some two-thirds. Urban losses of roughly 50 per cent, as at Givry and Albi in France, and Florence and San Gimignano in Italy, were not uncommon. Some areas, on the other hand, were largely spared, as seems to have been the case in Milan, and in most of Bohemia and Poland. The old view that parts of the Low Countries (especially Hainault and Brabant) escaped the first visitation of plague with light losses has recently been questioned; rather one should say that the Black Death struck there but with less savagery than in the hardest hit areas.[30] Thanks to its relative isolation, Iceland managed to avoid infection throughout the fourteenth century. It paid a heavy price, however, in the fifteenth, when its population declined by roughly half.[31] Death also stalked small towns and villages in the countryside. In England, where the most detailed local studies have been done, Essex appears to have lost roughly 45 per cent of its population and the townships of County Durham just over 50 per cent. In the Durham countryside, more than 60 per cent of Durham priory's tenants succumbed, and in the Midlands the estates of the bishop of Worcester lost over 40 per cent of their tenants, with some manors losing as much as 80 per cent (Aston) and 76 per cent (Bibury). One village in Cambridgeshire suffered losses of 70 per cent and frankpledge dues dropped by 55 per cent in Somerset. Deaths among the English clergy that can likely be assigned to the plague stand at about 45 per cent, with some deaneries losing as much as 75–77 per cent of their beneficed clergy. Taken as a whole, the evidence of urban, rural, clerical and monastic deaths points to an English mortality of something like 45 to 50 per cent.

In its first wave, the Black Death was no respecter of persons. It carried off men and women, rich and poor, noble and commoner, cleric and lay person alike. The one preference it may have had was for children and the elderly. In the parish of Walsham-le-Willows, Suffolk, 64 per cent of the children died, 90 per cent of the elderly and more than 50 per cent of the plus-fifties. Compare this to a 14 per cent and 20 per cent death rate for working men in their twenties and thirties respectively. At Halesowen in the West Midlands, a little over 20 per cent of young adults died, whereas some 60 per cent of the elderly were carried off. Deaths among children there are reckoned to have been quite heavy as well.[32] If, then, the overall mortality in places like Walsham-le-Willows and Halesowen hovered around 50 per cent in 1349, a substantial number of those in their prime were spared. Thus, despite the undoubted shock, horror and temporary social dislocation brought on by the advent of the Black Death, it is very likely that Europe would have recovered much of its population over the course of the next couple of generations, had the plague been a one-time event.

Of course, it was not. It struck again in 1357–58 in Italy, the north and south of France, Flanders, Spain, northern Germany, Hungary and Denmark, and in 1363–64 in Italy and Germany. Second and third pandemic waves swept through Europe in 1361–63 and 1369. After the third pandemic it struck again and again, sometimes throughout Europe and

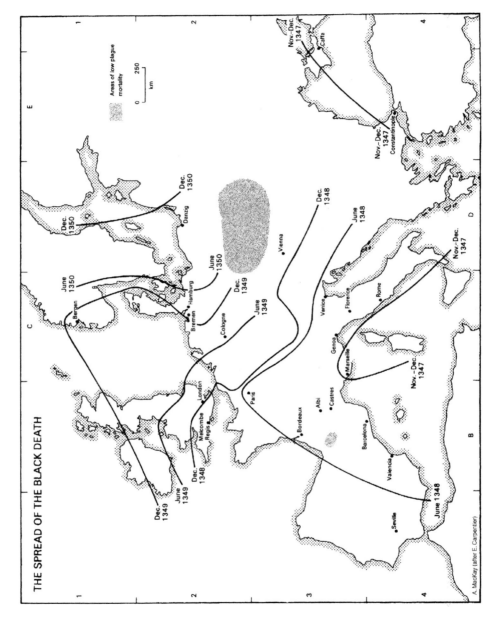

THE SPREAD OF THE BLACK DEATH

Areas of low plague mortality

0   250
km

Nov.–Dec. 1347 Caffa

Nov.–Dec. 1347 Constantinople

Dec. 1350 Danzig

Dec. 1350

June 1350

Dec. 1350

Vienna

Dec. 1348

June 1348

June 1350 Bergen

Hamburg
Bremen

Dec. 1349

Cologne

June 1349

Venice

Florence

Rome

Genoa

Marseille

Nov.–Dec. 1347

London

Mecombe Regis

Paris

Dec. 1348

June 1349

Bordeaux

Albi
Castres

Dec. 1349

Barcelona

Valencia

June 1348

Nov.–Dec. 1347

Seville

A. MacKay (after E. Carpentier)

Map 1.3 The spread of the Black Death, taken from *The Atlas of Medieval Europe*, 2nd Edition, © 2007, Routledge. Reproduced by permission of Taylor & Francis books UK

sometimes more locally, sometimes with more, sometimes with less force during the next eighty years:

1373–78	nearly everywhere
1382–83	nearly everywhere
1385–93	localised outbreaks throughout most of Europe
1399–1401	nearly everywhere
1405	Padua
1409	Bologna
1411	Florence and central Italy
1413–14	nearly everywhere
1417	Florence and central Italy
1418	Paris
1419	nearly everywhere
1423–24	Italy
1426	Tournai
1430	Florence and central Italy
1433	Paris (?)
1438	Paris, central Italy
1448	Trent, Montpellier
1450	Florence and central Italy

Striking on average every 11–12 years in the fourteenth century, and every 13 years in the first half of the fifteenth, the plague's deadly grip on children became even more pronounced. Several chroniclers from throughout Europe remarked this during the second great wave of plague in 1361, calling it the 'plague of children' (*mortalite des enfauntz*). Perhaps even more depressing, after 1361 the plague's disproportionate killing of the very young ceased to be remarkable. In England, the *Anonimalle Chronicle* reported that the plague of 1369 was 'particularly fatal to children' as was the fourth attack of 1373–75.[33] This was also the case during the fifth pestilence, when, in 1390, according to the St Alban's chronicler, Thomas Walsingham, 'it especially attacked adolescents and boys, who died in incredible numbers in towns and villages everywhere'.[34] At Camporeggio in Siena less than 9 per cent of burials in 1348 were of children; these increased to over a third in 1363, to over half in 1374, and to 88 per cent in 1383. Records of the gravediggers of Florence identify some 65 per cent of burials in 1400 as being of children, rising to 69 per cent in 1423–24.[35] Males too may have been more susceptible to death from plague in the visitations after 1347–51. This was the opinion of the continuator of Ranulf Higden's *Polychronicon*, who claimed the mortality of 1361 was 'particularly of men'.[36] More solid evidence for this, however, comes from the burial records from Tuscan cities. Men accounted for 57, 55, 58, 58 and 57 per cent of burials at Camporeggio in Siena in the plague years of 1363, 1374, 1383, 1400 and 1411. In Arezzo burials of men significantly outnumbered those of women during the plague months of 1390, and the same was the case in Florence in 1400.[37]

Plague, however, was hardly the only epidemic killer of the late Middle Ages. Smallpox, tuberculosis, influenza, typhus, malaria, cholera, dysentery, whooping cough and an illness called 'the sweat' (which may have been influenza) were all major instruments of mortality. At Christ Church Priory, Canterbury, for example, roughly a third of the monks succumbed to plague during the course of the fifteenth century; but just about the same number died from tuberculosis and another 21 per cent from 'the sweat'. Frequently one or more of these diseases ravaged the populace along with plague, adding to the overall mortality. What with frequent visitations of plague, the disproportionate killing of the young, and the admixture of other fatal or seriously debilitating illnesses, it is little wonder that Europe's population failed to begin its slow and halting rebound to pre-plague levels prior to the second half of the fifteenth century. Florence in 1427 had 69 per cent fewer residents than it had had in 1338; nor had its denizens taken up permanent residency in the countryside, as the population in its *contado* had also fallen by some 62–67 per cent. Flanders' population, already shrunken by the first visitation of plague, declined by a further third between 1365 and 1424. Poor Normandy, wracked by plague, famine and war, was devastated. After losing 50 per cent of its population between 1347 and 1374, it partially recovered over the next forty years, only again to suffer a 50 per cent drop between 1415 and 1422, and a 30 per cent decline between 1436 and 1442. Normandy would remain depopulated until the sixteenth century.[38] England, largely spared the devastation of war, except in the north, had a population in the second half of the fifteenth century that was about the same as it had had at the time of the Norman Conquest.

Owing to its ferocity and novelty, the Black Death stunned Europe during its first visitation. Thomas Walsingham, who, writing several years after the fact, reckoned that the plague wiped out half of humanity, reported that at the time of the first plague 'it was calculated by several people that barely a tenth of mankind remained alive'. More desperate was the assessment of the chronicler of Louth Park Abbey in Lincolnshire who said that 'so great a pestilence had not been seen, or heard, or written about, before this time. For it is thought that so great a multitude of people were not killed in Noah's Flood'.[39] The most eloquent, though somewhat rhetorically contrived, evocation, however, comes from Giovanni Boccaccio, in the introduction to his *Decameron*:

> In the face of its onrush, all the wisdom and ingenuity of man were unavailing. Large quantities of refuse were cleared out of the city by officials specially appointed for the purpose, all sick persons were forbidden entry, and numerous instructions were issued for safeguarding people's health, but all to no avail. Nor were the countless petitions humbly directed to God by the pious, whether by means of formal processions or in any other guise, any less ineffectual. . . .
>
> Against these maladies, it seemed that all the advice of physicians and all the power of medicine were profitless and unavailing. Perhaps the nature of the illness was such that it allowed no remedy; or perhaps those people who were treating the illness (whose numbers had increased enormously because the ranks of the qualified were invaded by people, both men and women, who had never received any training in medicine), being ignorant of its causes, were not prescribing the appropriate cure. At all events, few of those who caught it ever recovered, and in most cases death

occurred within three days from the appearance of the symptoms . . . some people more rapidly than others. . . .

But what made this pestilence even more severe was that whenever those suffering from it mixed with people who were still unaffected, it would rush upon these with the speed of a fire racing through dry or oily substance that happened to be placed within its reach.

Boccaccio went on to observe that the plague not only passed from person to person but that the contagion could be spread by means of infected clothing. Fear of contagion gripped the people of Florence, making them take 'a single and very inhuman precaution, namely to avoid or run away from the sick and their belongings. . . .' The normal social bonds and practices broke down. Some people withdrew 'to a comfortable abode where there were no sick persons . . . locked themselves in and settled down to a peaceable existence, consuming modest quantities of delicate foods and precious wines and avoiding all excesses'. Others, he said, engaged in heavy drinking and riotous merrymaking. But throughout the city, 'In the face of so much affliction and misery, all respect for the laws of God and man had virtually broken down and been extinguished. . . . For like everybody else, those ministers and executors of the laws who were not either dead or ill were left with so few subordinates that they were unable to discharge any of their duties'. The terror, coupled with a breakdown of public authority, was so great that 'brothers abandoned brothers, uncles their nephews, sisters their brothers, and in many cases wives deserted their husbands. But even worse, and almost incredible, was the fact that fathers and mothers refused to nurse and assist their own children, as though they did not belong to them'.[40]

Also deeply troubling was the subversion of gender roles and the 'never before heard of' social practices occasioned by the plague: 'when a woman fell ill, no matter how gracious or beautiful or gently bred she might be, she raised no objection to being attended by a male servant, whether he was young or not. Nor did she have any scruples about showing him every part of her body as freely as she would have displayed it to a woman . . . and this explains why those women who recovered were possibly less chaste in the period that followed'. Not only that, but women for the most part abandoned the time-honoured custom of gathering in the homes of dead men to mourn them and then accompanying the deceased in solemn funeral processions. Now men died 'without having many women about them', and 'more often than not bereavement was the signal for laughter and witticisms and general jollification – the art of which the women, having for the most part suppressed their feminine concern for the salvation of the souls of the dead, had learned to perfection'.[41] This lack of respect for the dead extended to the rest of society, as the old practice of large, well-attended funeral processions for those of more elevated social status was replaced by a far less elevated one wherein the bodies were borne away 'by a kind of gravedigging fraternity . . . drawn from the lower orders of society', who 'demanded a fat fee for their services, which consisted in taking up the coffin and hauling it swiftly away, not to the church specified by the dead man in his will, but usually to the nearest at hand'.[42]

More immediate and pathetic than Boccaccio's literary rendering, however, are the heart-rending words of Agnolo di Tura:

And in many places in Siena great pits were dug and piled deep with the multitude of dead. And they died by the hundreds, both day and night, and all were thrown in those ditches and covered with earth. And as soon as those ditches were filled, more were dug. And I, Agnolo di Tura, buried my five children with my own hands.

> And there were also those who were so sparsely covered with earth that the dogs
> dragged them forth and devoured many bodies throughout the city. There was
> no one who wept for any death, for all awaited death. And so many died that all
> believed it was the end of the world.[43]

Fears of the impending end of the world were indeed widespread. Millenarian expectations
were nothing new in 1347–48, as belief in the imminent Last Days with the coming of
Antichrist, the Second Coming of Christ and Last Judgement went back to the early Church.
They became particularly popular, however, starting in the thirteenth century, thanks to the
writings of the Cistercian monk Joachim of Fiore (d. 1202) and the propagation of his millenarian doctrines by means of the preaching of the Spiritual Franciscans during the later thirteenth and early fourteenth centuries. Given the popularity of this strain of Christian thought,
it is little wonder the Black Death confirmed many people's worries and hopes of the Last
Days. Rumours were rife that the boy Antichrist was preparing to reveal himself and the
Emperor of the Last Days (usually identified as a resurrected Frederick II of Hohenstaufen)
was about to return. The most dramatic expression of millenarian fears came in the guise
of the penitential flagellant movement, whose participants claimed to be the 'race without
a head' mentioned in an apocalyptic prophecy on the 'Cedar of Lebanon' which had been
floating around since the thirteenth century.[44]

> They are called flagellants because of the whips [*flagella*] they were seen using
> when doing penance. The whip itself was a rod from which three thin cords hung;
> at the end of each of these cords was a large knot, through the middle of which two
> bits of needle-sharp iron were driven cross-wise, so that all four points poked out
> about as far as an ordinary grain of wheat, or perhaps a bit more. With these whips
> they struck and scourged their uncovered torsos so that these became disfigured by
> swollen bruises, while blood ran down onto their lower bodies and defaced nearby
> walls with its spray.[45]

'Flocking together from every region', groups of flagellants would go from town to town. In
each they would strip to their waists, sing hymns, beat themselves, fall on their faces in the
form of a cross and pray. These exhibitionist displays were accompanied by calls for public
penance and sermons, which frequently took on an anti-clerical and anti-Semitic tone.

Anti-Semitic preaching likely helped foment the murderous pogroms that erupted
throughout Latin Christendom, but especially in Germany and the Low Countries, during
1348–49. Ever since the time of the First Crusade, European Jews had been labelled as
enemies of Christ, and over the course of the twelfth and thirteenth centuries an anti-
Semitic discourse had developed which included several charges. The first was that Jews
were child-killers, a belief that had surfaced it seems in England in the mid-twelfth century, when the murder in 1144 of a twelve-year-old boy named William in Norwich was
blamed on the Jews there. Such allegations, which included reports of torture and crucifixion, and sometimes sexual abuse, were oft repeated during the remainder of the twelfth
century, and then were reinforced in the thirteenth by charges of host desecration and even
cannibalism, when Jews were alleged to have eaten Christian children in a perverse mock-
ery of the Eucharist and to have used their blood for ritual magic.[46] Another charge against
the Jews, surfacing in the early fourteenth century, was that they mocked the Virgin Mary.
Other more practical and political motivations also lay behind attacks on Jews, however.

The Church's condemnation of usury marked Jewish money-lenders as offenders of canon law, despite the fact they were exempt from its restrictions and that their services as money-lenders and money-changers was in fact welcomed and encouraged by public authorities, including the papacy. In the later thirteenth century the uncomfortable situation of the Jews became even more precarious and, indeed, dangerous. First, there was the inexorable pressure from the mendicant friars, who made a point of preaching against usury and of insisting that the Jews convert. Second, monarchs hard-up for cash, like Edward I of England and Philip IV of France, took advantage of anti-Jewish feeling and expelled the Jews from their realms – in 1290 and 1306 respectively – fleecing them of all their cash and property in the process. Third, the economic stagnation and instability of the late medieval crisis led to many a Christian being indebted to Jews. When Christian resentment at being beholden to people they believed to be not only their inferiors but also their enemies combined either with anger at public authorities – be that the local bishop, city council or prince – or with the perceived support of those same authorities, pogroms were the result. The Jews of Mainz were persecuted in 1283, and then more widespread violence broke out against the Jews of Germany in 1287–88, 1298, 1309 (mostly in Brabant) and 1336–38. To the west, Jews in the towns of the Loire valley (some Jews had been re-admitted to France in 1315) were lynched in 1317 on charges of child-murder. But far more deadly persecutions were on the way in France, Navarre and the Crown of Aragon in 1320, when fear and anger brought on by the Great Famine and frustrations over a promised but stalled crusade resulted in the popular movement known as the Pastoureaux (named for the shepherds who participated). The Pastoureaux, who initially set out as volunteers for the crusade, quickly turned to slaughtering Jews. This movement had hardly been dispersed when a rumour circulated in France in 1321 that Jews, working as agents for the Saracens, had induced lepers to poison wells. Again, angry mobs in several French towns rounded up Jews and murdered them.

Given this terrible recent history, it is perhaps hardly surprising that the terror and social dislocation of the Black Death resurrected the rumours of Jewish well-poisoning, although this time the Jews' accomplices were said to be poor beggars, strangers and, in one case, a friar. There is something chilling in the objective certainty expressed by the castellan of Chillon in Savoy, who reported to the city council of Strasbourg on the confessions extracted from Jews arrested on suspicion of poisoning:

> I am writing to tell you that the people of Bern have a copy of the inquisition and confession of the Jews dwelling in their neighbourhood who were involved in putting poison into the wells there and in several other places, and that that copy contains a detailed account of the truth of the matter. Many Jews have been tried after being put to the question or, in some cases, making confession without it, and have been condemned to be burnt. Some Christians, to whom the Jews gave poison for use against Christians, have also been put on the wheel and tortured. For the burning of Jews and the torturing of Christians has gone on in numerous places within the county of Savoy. May God keep you.[47]

Such cool language obscures the burning hatred, fuelled by fear that raged, especially in German-speaking lands, over the course of a year, beginning in the autumn of 1348. These sentiments are evident in this passage from the account of the persecutions by a canon of Constance, Heinrich Truchess von Diessenhoven:

they were burned and killed in Lindau on the feast of St Nicholas [6 December], in Reutlingen on 8 December and in Haigerloch on the 13th. On the 20th, in Horw, they were burned in a pit; when the wood and straw had been burned up and a few of the young and old Jews remained half-alive, the strongest among them grabbed clubs and stones, and with these they dashed out the brains of those wanting to crawl from the fire, thereby consigning those trying to avoid the fire to the eternal flames of hell. And thus the curse seemed to have been fulfilled: 'His blood be on us and on our children!' [Mt. 27.25]. . . . And thus within a year's time . . . all the Jews from Cologne to Austria were burned, and in Austria they await the same [fate], since they are accursed by God. And I would believe that the end of the Jews was upon us, had the time prophesied by Elijah and Enoch reached its conclusion; but since it has not, it is necessary that some Jews be preserved so that 'the hearts of the children will turn to their fathers and those of the fathers to their children' [Mal. 4.5]. Where they shall be preserved, I do not know, but I reckon that rather than being among these Jews here, Abraham's seed resides somewhere in Ultramare [i.e. the Holy Land]. Here, therefore, let me make an end of the Jews.[48]

The appalling death from plague and pogroms, the savagery of persecutions, and the seeming overturning and confusion of the social order and of conventions must indeed have signalled to many the end of the world. But Heinrich von Diessenhoven was right about one thing: the time had not yet come. Throughout the first attack of plague, governments continued to function and local authorities, despite what Boccaccio tells us, did manage to limp along and keep some measure of public order. Physicians still visited and treated the dying and clergy still offered them their last rites. Masses were said, graves were dug, albeit often common ones, and funeral rites were observed, for the most part. Bishops ordered intercessory processions and granted indulgences to those who participated. And when it was all over, heirs inherited the property of their dead parents, and the living purchased the land of the dead; the young married, widows remarried and couples had children. The pope, for his part, declared 1350 a jubilee year. But then the pestilence returned, remorselessly, again and again. Yet these later visitations were perceived and treated differently from the first. Physicians explored ways to treat plague victims; and municipal authorities, with the advice of physicians, developed policies for guarding against and containing the contagion, principally by limiting contact with those who had been infected and stressing sanitary measures, like the washing of hands, covering the nose and mouth, and burning the personal effects of the deceased.[49] This is not to say that these strategies were very effective (although likely they had some positive result), but it does show that plague began to be treated rationally and with some degree of hope in cure and containment.

Considerable attention was also given to determining the cause of the pestilence. Certainly the initial response was that it was the wrath of God, aroused by mankind's sinfulness. As for which sins (or sinners) precisely brought it on, that was open to interpretation, some saying it was loose sexual behaviour and the sporting of revealing clothing, others the spoiling of children by their parents. The Scots said the plague was sent to punish the English, and the English in their turn were certain God was wreaking vengeance on the Scots. But as the plague abated and then became a cyclical occurrence, it was frequently portrayed as a sign of God's *mercy*, drawing sinners to penance so that they might avoid eternal damnation. If plague had a divine cause, then surely prayer and penance were called for. Likewise, and in a more personal vein, it could be countered by the power of the holy, that is by the invocation and veneration of saints especially noted for their ability to avert or cure the pestilence, the favourites being St Rock and St Rose of Viterbo.[50] More natural causes were also suggested. It was widely agreed that air corrupted by pestilential vapours – here rotting corpses were considered the chief culprit – played a signal role. Thus the near cause was to be removed by means of better sanitation and proper burial practices. Still, there was general acceptance that the first incidence of plague had also required a catastrophic release of fouled air; thus the insistence by the chroniclers that the first plague was preceded by massive, vapour-releasing earthquakes. Also, because corrupted air could enter the body through the pores, excessive perspiration, owing to too strenuous physical exercise, bathing, eating and drinking or sexual intercourse, was to be shunned. But this pestilential miasma needed more than the material cause (in the Aristotelian sense) of rotting matter, it also required some action on the part of heavenly bodies to set it off, since the influence of the planets brought about imbalances in the four elements (earth, water, fire and air) and their complementary humours (phlegm, black and yellow bile and blood). One physician, observing the way plague seemed to spread from person to person tried to explain this by saying that the disease could be spread by sight. While this was certainly incorrect, it was a sensible response to a weakness in the corrupted air theory: that not everyone exposed to the vapours was infected, but virtually everyone who came into close contact with plague victims did end up with the contagion. As he put it: 'and the greater strength of this epidemic is such that it kills almost instantly, as soon as the airy spirit leaving the eyes of the sick man has struck the eye of a healthy bystander looking at him, for then the poisonous nature passes from one eye to the other'.[51]

Despite their limited knowledge, primitive techniques, mistaken assumptions and lack of access to the tools and pharmacopoeia of modern medicine, medieval physicians did a fair job of identifying and describing plague, even if they did not know what caused it. They also had a decent understanding of how plague spread, even though they did not know why. Today, thanks to the results of DNA sequencing from the remains of numerous historical plague victims, we can confidently say that the microorganism responsible for the medieval bubonic plague is the same as that which caused the great 'Justinianic Pandemic' of 541–750, as well as modern-day bubonic plague, that is, the bacillus *Yersinia pestis*. The plague bacillus is endemic in certain rodent populations, where it is spread by fleas (two species, *Xenopsylla cheopis* and *Oropsylla montana* have so-far been verified, though the human flea, *Pulex irritans* may also be a vector). Modern-day plague takes three forms. The first, bubonic, takes its name from the swollen lymph node or *bubo*, forming close to the site of the flea bite, which is the characteristic sign of plague. It is largely fatal and the victim dies within a few days of infection. Because bubonic plague often attacks the lungs, it can take on a secondary pneumonic form, with the bacillus being coughed out and spreading through the air from person to person. This form is virtually always fatal and can kill in one or two days. Finally, if the plague bacillus infects the blood stream, this always deadly septicaemic form kills within a day.

However, if in many respects the medieval plague appears to have behaved much like its modern-day counterpart, several features of its symptomology and epidemiology seem to differ.[52] First, medieval descriptions of the plague's symptoms, while they certainly mention buboes, also say that victims usually suffered from several buboes (rather than the characteristic single bubo of modern plague), that the buboes frequently appeared in the upper part of the body (rather than from the abdomen down), and that the victims suffered from terrible pain (unlike the fairly painless modern version). Moreover, sufferers from the medieval plague also ended up covered with small black, red or green freckles, pustules and/or bruises:

a symptom entirely absent from modern plague. As far as medieval plague's epidemiology is concerned, its virulence, lethality, frequency of activity, climate preferences and preference of victims look very little like those which have been observed in modern-day outbreaks of *Yersinia pestis*. Simply put, although there can no longer be any doubt about the germ responsible for the Black Death, there is still much we have to learn about the context of plague in the Middle Ages and the early modern period.[53] Faced with this admission of our own ignorance, and given our own fears of future pandemics, we should perhaps be less keen to lay too much blame for the Black Death's deadliness on the perceived stupidity and filthy habits of medieval people.

Popular rebellion

It will be left to later chapters to examine the myriad social, cultural and political effects of the three-fold curse of famine, war and plague. Suffice it here to discuss one of the more dramatic social responses which they inspired: popular rebellion. First, however, a word of caution is in order. The causes, character, participants and aims of these rebellions varied considerably. Some were urban insurrections aimed at toppling a corrupt oligarchy. The instigators of such rebellions might be urban artisans and workers looking for better working conditions and better political representation, like the Bruco of Siena in 1371 or the Ciompi of Florence in 1378. Other rebellions drew their participants largely (though by no means exclusively) from the countryside, as was the case of the French Jacquerie of 1358, the English Peasants' Revolt of 1381, the Catalonian *remensa* movement in the first half of the fifteenth century, or the periodic German *Bundschuh* of 1439–1517. Some, indeed, took on a sort of national character, as did the Flemish revolt of 1323–28, the Hussite wars of 1420–34, and the wars fought on again off again by the cantons of the Swiss Confederation from 1291 until the 1470s. Religious motivations are also apparent in several rebellions, including that of the Hussites and the English rebels of 1381, but also among the participants in the Hungarian Revolt of 1514 and the German Peasant War of 1525. Others look on the surface to have been pogroms against the Jews but, when examined more carefully, show signs of having been political rebellions against the state, as in the Spanish persecution of 1391 and the attacks on the Jews and *conversos* (converted Jews) of Castile between 1449 and 1473. Likewise it must be remembered that urban and rural insurrections occurred both before and after the late Middle Ages: witness, for example, the communal rebellions of the cities of Lombardy and northern France during the eleventh and twelfth centuries, or the Swiss Peasants' War of 1653.

This being said, however, there is good reason to assert that Latin Christendom suffered from a veritable 'plague of insurrection' from the late thirteenth through the early sixteenth century, with the most intense period occurring in the latter half of the fourteenth century in western and southern Europe and during the fifteenth and early sixteenth centuries in central Europe. It is also fair to say that certain common elements can be discerned. First and foremost in importance were political tensions created on the one hand by the fiscal demands of increasingly centralised states, and, on the other, by the growing political consciousness and involvement of the 'lower' orders of society, that is, of rural peasants and labourers, and urban artisans and workers. Social and economic factors were also involved, however, like the long-term underlying problems of seigneurial exploitation of peasant labour in the countryside and of low wages and unfavourable working conditions for workers in towns. Nor can the influence of certain religious ideals, like those of apostolic poverty, the equality of all believers and expectation of the millennium be ruled out. No doubt these elements alone would have been enough to bring about several uprisings and rebellions in town and country.[54] Nonetheless, it was the conjuncture during these years of the sparks of famine, war and plague with the tinder of these underlying political, socio-economic and religious tensions that gave to the late Middle Ages its character as 'the age *par excellence* of "popular revolutions"'.[55] This intersection is particularly apparent in the succession of peasant and urban revolts that rocked France and Flanders during the second half of the fourteenth century, the explosion of revolts in central Italy during the 1370s, the massacre of Jews and *conversos* in Andalusia in 1473, and the English Peasants' Revolt of 1381.

The spectre of the Hundred Years War was never far removed from the many rebellions that rocked France and Flanders. Both the Jacquerie in the countryside and the uprising by the Paris commune against royal government in 1358 were direct results of the French defeat at the battle of Poitiers in 1356 and the subsequent power vacuum and political strife resulting therefrom. The abasement of French chivalry at Poitiers, the subsequent depredations of the countryside by English soldiers and *routiers*, and the royal and seigneurial exactions upon peasants and townsmen – greatly increased in order to pay the extravagant ransom on King John II and falling heavily on a populace reduced by plague and devastated by war – inflamed commoners against a nobility whom they now believed to be worse than useless. Their exasperation is apparent in this cry of the Jacques's leader, Guillaume Cale: 'Who set them in such high estate, these men who pump out our sweat and labour, wretches that we are?'[56] Such sentiments were shared by the Tuchins, those peasants and townsmen of Languedoc and the Massif Central, who from the 1360s to the 1380s took to the hills and forests and launched attacks on *routiers*, nobles and clerics alike as a response to the violence and destruction of war and pillage. Heavy taxation occasioned by the war also led to the urban rebellions in Rouen and Paris in 1382. In central Italy, war and the fiscal exactions to pay it, as well as disputes over wages and working conditions brought on a veritable explosion of urban and rural violence and insurrection from 1355 until 1378. One year, 1375, saw at least sixty cities rebelling against the rule of the papacy. Nearly 1,600 villages followed their lead over the next two years.[57] The papacy's effort to return from Avignon to Rome, under Pope Gregory XI, as well as the war (the War of Eight Saints) which this had precipitated between papal forces and Florence sparked off much of this rebellion. One town, Cesena in the Papal States, only 'rebelled' (in February 1377) after mercenaries in the papal army to which it was playing host murdered several prominent citizens. When the townspeople responded by killing a number of mercenaries, the leader of the army, Cardinal Robert of Geneva (who would soon become Pope Clement VII) encouraged the mercenaries, including the company led by Sir John Hawkwood, to butcher some 4,000 to 8,000 of Cesena's inhabitants. And, in the summer of 1378, following on three years of this ruinously expensive war, the low-paid and politically disenfranchised wool workers of Florence, the Ciompi, rebelled, cast the urban oligarchy there from power and established their own, short-lived government.

Sometimes anger and frustration with the state and nobility stirred up hatred of foreigners (the English rebels of 1381 hunted down Flemings and other foreigners) or 'outsiders', especially the Jews. A powerful strain of anti-Semitism is apparent in the many urban insurrections targeting Jews and *conversos* that broke out in Castile in the third quarter of the fifteenth century. Yet, if one looks beneath the surface of these rebellions, one finds a complex set of motivating factors, including: ruinous visitations of plague; dramatic price rises brought on by disastrous harvests and the government's debasement of the coinage to pay for war; increased taxation, also resulting from the financial demands of warfare and to pay for imported grain during subsistence crises; and resentment of royal and municipal offi-cials. Since Jews frequently acted as tax farmers, and *conversos* occupied some of the most important posts in royal government, their actions on the part of government were resented and their success envied by Christians.[58]

Novel taxation, heavy-handed labour legislation, an unsuccessful war, religious zeal and a combination of social dislocation and frustrated expectations in the aftermath of the Black Death all had a hand in precipitating the great rebellion that broke out in the south-east of England at the beginning of June 1381. Both contemporary chroniclers and modern-day historians agree that the catalyst for the Peasants' Revolt was the attempt on the part of royal government to collect a poll tax. The poll tax was a recent innovation, born of the high costs of waging the war against France and the frustration of the boy king Richard II's councillors with the insufficient sums collected by the traditional property tax. Had the war been going well for the English, then perhaps the three poll taxes granted by Parliament from 1377 to 1380 would not have been so resented. Unfortunately things had been going very badly indeed, for not only had English armies fared poorly since the renewal of hostilities in 1369, but the south coast had been subjected to repeated seaborne raids by France's Castilian ally. In addition to being novel – and thereby annoying to a society wedded to custom – the poll tax was profoundly regressive. Moreover, the third poll tax, of 12*d.*/head, was far heavier than either the 1377 poll tax of 4*d.*/head or the grad-uated poll tax of 1379.

It seems likely, however, that rustics and urban workers were already in a dangerous mood by the 1370s. First, the great and ongoing mortality destabilised both rural and urban communities. At the manor of Thaxted, Essex, for example, less than a quarter of the hold-ings of 1393 belonged to the same families as had occupied them in 1347. It may well be that things had been even more fluid in towns, where devastated populations were replaced by newcomers, who resented being denied the franchise or access to public office while still being required to provide money and services, especially in relation to defence.[59] They also were angered by repeated attempts by the government to deprive them of the higher income and more favourable land-tenure arrangements that had been a direct consequence of the drastic decline in population resulting from repeated visitations of plague. The buoyant effect of population decline on wages was grasped by members of Parliament immediately after the first attack of plague, prompting them in June 1349 to promulgate the Ordinance of Labourers, a temporary act which was made permanent when the Statute of Labourers of 1351 set wages at their pre-plague level. That the statute was resented by workers cannot be doubted. For a long time, however, it appears that employers and landlords, desperate for scarce labour, found ways around the letter of the law either with under-the-table payments of additional wage or by offering generous non-monetary compensation in the way of food and shelter (as well as reduced rent and labour services for villeins). But these years during which agriculturalists and workers became accustomed to improved working conditions and standards of living came to an end in the mid-1370s when grain prices dropped precipitously. Employers reacted to declining income by cutting back on pay and fringe benefits while also demanding enforcement of statutory wages. Even more galling for the many English peas-ants who still had villein status, landlords insisted on maintaining customary rents and labour services in the face of falling land values.[60] Had they been free men, they would have been able to negotiate more favourable terms, but as villeins they were bound by law, enforced through manorial courts, to keep providing what to their eyes were patently inflated rents and overly burdensome services. No wonder the rebels of 1381 demanded an end to villeinage.

Moreover, the heavy hand of the law was felt by free men as well, who according to the Statute of Labourers could be forced to work against their will.[61]

It seems likely the flames of resentment were fanned further by moral outrage at a ruling lay and ecclesiastical order who offended against God's law. Certainly we see this sentiment in the calls for moral regeneration in *Piers Plowman* – a poem evidently known to the leaders of, and to many of the participants in the Peasants' Revolt – and in the heretical Oxford theologian John Wyclif's demands for the secularisation of all Church property owing to the ecclesiastical hierarchy's scandalous sinfulness.[62] Likewise, preaching associated with the popular liturgical feast of Corpus Christi played an important role in forming the rebels' ideas regarding the equality of all believers. In his book of model sermons, the *Festial*, the Augustinian canon John Mirk (fl. 1400) encouraged parishioners on Corpus Christi Day to think:

> How the Father of heaven had but one Son that he loved beyond measure. And yet to deliver man from the Devil's thralldom, He sent Him into this world, that He might with his own heart's blood write a charter of freedom, which made man free forever unless it should be that he forfeits this charter.

Similar language is found in John Ball, one of the rebels' leaders, when he preached 'that all bond men may be made free'; and his call that 'we [rebels] may be all united together' also reflects the central message of Corpus Christi: Christian unity.[63] That the rebels converged on London on 12 June, the eve of Corpus Christi, also appears not to have been a coincidence.

All this anger and anxiety need not have led to rebellion, of course. Popular discontent with the third poll tax might have been nothing more than that, had royal officials been willing to accept the poor returns resulting from widespread tax-evasion. They, however, were not. According to the author of the *Anonimalle Chronicle*:

> the royal council appointed certain commissions to make inquiry in every township how they [the poll tax] had been levied. Among these commissions, one for Essex was sent to one Thomas [*recte* John] de Bamptoun, a lord's steward, who was considered a king or great lord in that country because of his great state. One day before Whitsuntide [2 June 1381] he sat in the town of Brentwood in Essex in order to make an inquisition; and he displayed the commission sent to him to raise all the money in default and to inquire how the collectors had raised the aforesaid subsidy. He had summoned before him the townships of a neighbouring hundred and wished to levy from them a new subsidy. . . . Among these townships was Fobbing, where all the people replied that they would pay nothing at all because they had an acquittance from himself for the said subsidy. On which the said Thomas threatened them violently; and he had with him two of the king's serjeants-at-arms. For fear of his malice, the people of Fobbing took counsel with those of Corringham; and the people of both townships rose and assembled, instructing those of Saniforth [Stanford-le-Hope] to rise with them for their common profit. Then the people of those three townships gathered to the number of a hundred or more and with one assent went to the said Thomas de Bamptoun and told him outright that they would not deal with him nor give him any money. On which the said Thomas commanded the serjeants-at-arms to arrest these people and put them in prison. But these commons rose against the royal officers, would not be arrested and were ready to kill the said Thomas and the two serjeants.[64]

Something similar happened in Kent, according to Henry Knighton:

> A certain John Leg with three colleagues asked the king to give him a commis-
> sion to investigate the collectors of this tax in Kent, Norfolk and other parts of
> the country. They contracted to give the lord king a large sum of money for his
> assent; and most unfortunately for the king his council agreed. One of these com-
> missioners came to a certain village to investigate the said tax and called together
> the men and women; he then, horrible to relate, shamelessly lifted the young girls
> to test whether they had enjoyed intercourse with men. In this way he compelled the
> friends and parents of these girls to pay the tax for them; many would rather pay for
> their daughters than see them touched in such a disgraceful way. These and similar
> actions by the said inquisitors much provoked the people. And when the commons
> of Kent and the neighbouring areas suffered such evils and the imposition of new
> and almost unbearable burdens which appeared to be endless and without remedy,
> they refused to bear such injuries any longer.[65]

And so the men of Essex and Kent rose up and, after some activity in their separate counties, converged on London. Insurrection also erupted in the counties of East Anglia and in the south-west. Discontent, then, was geographically widespread. But it was also socially broad. A great many of the rustics who participated in the rebellion were hardly destitute, but were, rather, those better-off peasants who had grown accustomed to improved working conditions and standards of living. Nor was the rebellion an affair of peasants alone, for it included a large number of urban artisans and labourers, members of the lower clergy, and even some knights and gentry. Moreover, the commoners of several towns in the south-east and East Anglia, as well as of the capital, London, supported the rebels, while uprisings inspired by the revolt broke out in the Yorkshire towns of York, Beverley and Scarborough.

Despite the tendency of the chroniclers – who all were hostile to the rebels – to charac-
terise the participants in the rebellion as senseless and bestial, their actual descriptions of what happened tell a very different story. To begin with, the rebels organised themselves and coordinated their efforts, even going so far as to send cryptic letters (using the language of *Piers Plowman*) to one another. Also, they did not kill, burn and pillage indiscriminately, but rather chose political targets: men like the archbishop of Canterbury and Chancellor of England, Simon Sudbury, the Treasurer, Sir Robert Hales and the Chief Justice of King's Bench, Sir John Cavendish, who they believed were guilty of corrupt governance, unfair exercise of the law and the institution of oppressive policies. Indeed, and not surprisingly, they did not see themselves as being rebels at all, but rather called themselves the 'true commons', faithful subjects of King Richard who were going to loose him from the bonds of his evil councillors and expose the traitors of the realm. As such, when they met Richard II in London, they petitioned the king for the abolition of villeinage and an end to the provisions of the Statute of Labourers. But, if the *Anonimalle Chronicle* is to be believed, their demands went even beyond this:

> Then the king asked him [Wat Tyler, one of the leaders of the rebels] what were the
> points which he wished to have considered. . . . Thereupon the said Wat rehearsed
> the points which were to be demanded; and he asked . . . that no lord should have
> lordship in future, but it should be divided among all men, except for the king's
> own lordship. He also asked that the goods of Holy Church should not remain in

the hands of the religious, nor of parsons and vicars, and other churchmen; but that clergy already in possession should have a sufficient sustenance and the rest of their goods should be divided among the people of the parish. And he demanded that there should be only one bishop in England and only one prelate, and all the lands and tenements of the possessioners should be taken from them and divided among the commons, only reserving for them a reasonable sustenance.[66]

Neither Richard nor the politically mighty had any interest in making good on his promise to accede to these demands, however. Indeed Wat Tyler was seized and killed at this very meeting, and the rebels everywhere were soon dispersed and their leaders hunted down and executed. Rebellion, which was itself a response in part to the pressures exerted on society by famine, plague and war, was also regarded as a threat to the body politic. In the case of the Peasants' Revolt, it was also seen as an assault on the mystical Body of Christ because of the rebels' appropriation of Corpus Christi and the suspicion that the rebellion had partly been inspired by Wyclif's heretical views, including his denial of orthodox teaching on the Eucharist. On the anniversary of the rebellion, during the days leading up to Corpus Christi, the new archbishop of Canterbury, William Courtenay ordered public processions and sermons preached against Wyclif's heresy.[67]

Notes

1 Litany of the Saints (my translation).
2 Scott 2002: 57; Smith 1991: 48–50.
3 Biller 1998.
4 Postan 1966: 548–70.
5 Goldsmith 1995.
6 Rösener 1994: 66–67.
7 Aston and Philpin 1985.
8 Fossier 1988: 186–93; Harvey 1991: 13–15.
9 Jordan 1996: 17; Barber 2004: 15.
10 Bailey 1991.
11 Fossier 1986: 40; Aberth 2001: 13.
12 Jordan 1996: 17; Fossier 1986: 40.
13 Le Roy Ladurie 1972: 45–48.
14 Jordan 1996: 36.
15 Fossier 1986: 40.
16 Leguay 2000: 107.
17 Jordan 1996: 142–45.
18 Epstein 2009: 163.
19 Aberth 2001: 44.
20 Ormrod 1991: 153, 161.
21 Nederman 2002: 84, 89.
22 Allmand 1998: 271.
23 Birdsall and Newhall 1953: 93–94.
24 Allmand 1998: 264.
25 Fowler 2001: 32–38.
26 Lumby 1895: 58–62 (my translation).
27 Horrox 1994: 18.
28 Horrox 1994: 17.
29 Horrox 1994: 18–19.
30 Blockmans 1980.
31 Karlsson 1996.

32 Platt 1996/1997: 15.
33 Horrox 1994: 88.
34 Horrox 1994: 91.
35 Cohn 2002: 212–15.
36 Horrox 1994: 85.
37 Cohn 2002: 210–11.
38 Aberth 2001: 130–31.
39 Horrox 1994: 66–67.
40 McWilliam 1972: 50–54.
41 McWilliam 1972: 54–55.
42 McWilliam 1972: 55.
43 Aberth 2001: 109.
44 Lerner 1983: 109–12.
45 Potthast 1859: 281 (my translation).
46 Orme 2001: 103–6; Müller 2004: 247–48.
47 Horrox 1994: 211–12.
48 Böhmer 1868: 69–71 (my translation).
49 Cohn 2002: 233–38.
50 Herlihy 1997: 79–80; Cohn 2002: 76–77.
51 Horrox 1994: 182.
52 Twigg 1984; Karlsson 1996; Cohn 2002; Scott and Duncan 2004.
53 Little 2011: 289–90.
54 Fourquin 1978.
55 Mollat and Wolff 1973: 272.
56 Leguai 1982: 54.
57 Cohn 2006: 226.
58 MacKay 1972.
59 Butcher 1984.
60 Hatcher 1994.
61 Harding 1984.
62 Hudson 1994.
63 Aston 1994: 19–20.
64 Dobson 1983: 124.
65 Dobson 1983: 135–36.
66 Dobson 1983: 164–65.
67 Aston 1994: 38–39.

2

INDIVIDUALS, FAMILIES AND COMMUNITIES

> For just as the hand cannot truly be a hand unless it be attached to a man, so a man is not really a man if he does not live in a community. Wherefore Cicero said that we were not born for ourselves alone, but for our lineage, our city and our country.[1]

This comment by the Parisian theologian Nicole Oresme in his French translation of Aristotle's *Politics* (1374) sums up the late medieval attitude toward the place of the individual in society. It is at once organic and communitarian, seeing the individual as part of a body, and the body as being somehow prior to the individual in importance. For intellectuals like Oresme, it certainly was convenient that Cicero's and Aristotle's views agreed in a fashion with the Church's teaching that each Christian is a member of the Body of Christ. This mystical body of the Church was complemented by a political body, first fully articulated in the twelfth century in John of Salisbury's *Policraticus*, in which the clergy functions as the body's soul, the prince its head with the various 'organs' of his government making up the senses and viscera, the knighthood and lesser royal officials the hands, and peasants and others of servile condition the feet.[2] Each part depended upon the other, and yet there was a clear hierarchy, with the prince and clergy at the top, the aristocracy (acting as counsellors, soldiers and bureaucrats) in the middle, and the peasantry at the bottom. John of Salisbury's body politic was itself an attempt to fit the functions of the state within the dominant ideology of the time, which conceived of Christendom as a society of three orders – those who prayed (*oratores*), fought (*bellatores*) and worked (*laboratores*) – which three orders corresponded to the clergy, the knighthood and all those peasants, merchants and artisans who laboured in the countryside and cities.[3] These ideologies of the organism, hierarchy and order should not be mistaken for the social reality they attempt both to describe and influence. They do nonetheless give us a place to start when trying 'to understand the interrelationship between social structures and their "notion of themselves"'. This interrelationship is predicated on three components, these being social reality itself, the views people have of it and 'the behavior of people that results from this image, which in turn creates and shapes reality'.[4]

In his book of political advice, *De regimine principum* ('On the Rule of Princes', c. 1280), dedicated to the future king of France, Philip the Fair, the Augustinian friar and former student at the University of Paris, Giles of Rome, makes several interesting observations about individuals and their relationships with one another. At the very start, Giles lays out what was then becoming the standard university doctrine, based on Aristotle, of the symbiotic, but nonetheless hierarchical and unequal, relationships of individuals, families and communities.

Therefore be it known that we intend to divide this whole book into three partial books: in the first it will be shown how the royal majesty, and consequently how each and every man should rule himself; in the second it will be made clear how he ought to govern his family; and in the third it shall be declared how he is to rule the city and realm. . . . And this order is reasonable and natural. It is rational because those things which pertain to another derive their origin from those things which pertain to us as well. Whence it is written in the ninth book of [Aristotle's] *Ethics* that feelings of friendship seem to have arisen from that which one feels for oneself. For that man is seen to be a friend who loves his friend as he loves himself. . . . And this order is not only rational, it is also natural, for nature always proceeds from imperfect to perfect, just as he who is naturally imperfect and a boy then becomes perfect and a man.[5]

Giles goes on to state several of his other views on social reality. About the different types of men (by which Giles exclusively means males) within society, he agrees with Aristotle that there are two main types, those who live as men, that is politically and in association with one another, and those who live outside society. In the second category, of asocial beings, there are those who are worse than men and live a bestial life, e.g. as criminals, outcasts, madmen, and those who are better than men and hence sharing something with the angels, by which he means contemplatives, e.g. monks.[6] Among those men of the first category, who live politically, there are three divisions: the rich, those of middling wealth and the poor. Men, moreover, are distinguished by their age – that is, young, middle aged and old – while the earliest stage of life can itself be subdivided into the three phases of babyhood (*infantia*), childhood (*pueritia*) and youth (*adulescentia*). Each social condition and age, moreover, is associated with certain emotional and moral tendencies. The rich, for example, are given to overweening pride and contempt for those beneath them, while the poor tend to hate the rich, so that a stable society needs a large number of people of middling wealth. This is not to say, however, that men of middling means are better than men of high estate, since Giles makes it quite clear that men of noble birth tend to be more virtuous than men who have become rich through fortune or commerce (i.e. merchants), and that these noble men are the prince's natural counsellors.[7] Men of middle age are also more stable and inclined to virtue than youths and old men:

> For those who are in the middle state between the old and young, as the Philosopher says in the second book of the *Politics*, have those traits which are praiseworthy in the old and the young. They are neither as hotheaded as youths nor as slow to move as the old, nor are they as bold and headstrong as the young or fearful and pusillanimous as the old. Instead they maintain a middle course between the two extremes, having fear when it is right to be fearful and being bold when boldness is required. Likewise they are not so inexperienced as the young nor have they been so frequently deceived as the old, so that they are not overly credulous like callow youths nor so quick to disbelieve as the old, but they hold themselves in the middle, judging things according to truth. Furthermore, because they occupy the mean between old men and young, they are not intemperate, like youths, nor fearful and weak, like old men, but are instead manly with temperance and temperate with manliness. So, in a word, whatever is praiseworthy in the old and young is found in men of middle age, and whatever is damnable in them is wholly missing in men of middle age.[8]

38

Men who live as men, then, are meant to live sociably, in a community, and the most funda-mental community is the household:

> it will appear that the community is fourfold, namely household, neighbourhood, city and realm. For just as a household is made up of several persons, so is a neigh-bourhood from many households, a city from many neighbourhoods and a realm from many cities. . . . And in this way the community of the household is ordained to the other communities, because all these others presuppose it and it is in such a way part of all the others.[9]

This same idea was taken up a few years later by Giles's younger contemporary at Paris, Marsilius of Padua, who, in his *Defensor pacis* ('Defender of the Peace', 1324) wrote that:

> the first and minimum combination, from which all others have arisen, is that of male and female, as the best of philosophers [Aristotle] says in *Politics* I, chapter 1, and further apparent from his *Economics*. This combination produced more human beings, who first of all filled one household; and then as further combinations of this type occurred, the multiplication of human beings was so great that one house-hold was insufficient for them and it was necessary to set up several households. A plurality of these is called a village or neighbourhood, and this (as Aristotle also writes, as earlier) was the first community. . . . Finally, man's reason and experi-ence made up the full range of things that are necessary to living and living well, and that perfect community was established which is called the city, with the dif-ferentiation of its parts.[10]

The constituent parts of this state are, according to Marsilius:

> agriculture, manufacture, the military, the financial, the priesthood and the judicial or councillor. Three of these, viz. the priesthood, the military and the judicial, are parts of the city in an unqualified sense, and in civil communities they are usually called the notables. The others are called parts in a broad sense, in that they are functions necessary to the city according to the opinion of Aristotle in *Politics* VII, chapter 7. And the multitude of these is usually called plebeian.[11]

Marsilius's two-fold, hierarchical division of society into the notable class and common plebeian mass reflects to some extent the reality of the social division between the *popolo grosso* and *popolo minuto* in the cities of central and northern Italy, a division also found in most northern cities. In contemporary France, however, the theoretical division of soci-ety into three orders not only continued, but gained some political force in the structure of provincial and general 'Estates', or representative assemblies called by the king in order to approve grants of taxation. This structure was, in fact, instituted by the French 'people' itself, according to King Philip VI's secretary Philippe de Vitry in 1335:

> The People, in order better to evade the evils which it sees upon it, thus formed itself into three parts. One was formed to pray to God, the second to trade and work the land, and then, to keep these two groups from harm and injury, knights were created.[12]

Seven decades later, the keen social observer and professional author, Christine de Pizan, borrowed the structure of the three orders and of John of Salisbury's body politic for her own *Livre du corps de policie* ('Book of the Body Politic', 1404–07). Yet hers is no slavish repetition, but rather a clever adaptation, which reconfigures the schema of the three orders into a hierarchy of princes (the head), of knights and nobles (the arms and hands), and of the common people (the belly, legs and feet). By princes, she meant not only kings and their eldest sons, but all the greatest men of the realm. Her most interesting adaptation, however, occurs in her discussion of the common people, which she subdivides into three ranks, of clerics – among whom the foremost are university scholars – of 'burghers and merchants of the cities', and of artisans and labourers.[13]

Largely missing from these theoretical treatments of the constituent elements of society was any discussion of women; and when women were mentioned, it was almost exclusively in the context of the family and household. So Giles of Rome consigns almost all considera- tion of women and girls to the second book of *De regimine principum*, whose subject is the rule of the household, and where woman's role is limited to that of wife, mother and daugh- ter. According to nature, says Giles, the community of the household requires a husband, wife and servants,

> for the community of husband and wife is ordained to generation and the commu-
> nity of lord and servant to conservation. Wherefore if generation and conservation
> are natural in some way, a household is also natural. . . . And that the community
> of husband and wife is ordained for generation is not hard to discern, since the
> company of male and female is principally ordained to the production of children.

Following this logic, 'if the household is to be complete it must be endowed with a third community, namely that of a father and son'.[14] After Giles devotes eighteen chapters to the upbringing and education of boys, he admits that 'not only sons and male children are engen- dered from the use of marriage but daughters and female children can also arise'. So follow three chapters consecrated to the upbringing of girls, whose basic message is that girls should be kept from wandering about and associating with men, in order to keep their purity intact, that they should be kept occupied with licit and honourable activities like weaving, spinning and working with silk, and that they should be taught to keep their mouths shut. Giles's distrust of the female tongue extends to princes' wives, whose counsel, he warns, should not be sought out (unless the prince be in haste, for women are good at giving swift, if shallow, counsel) and who must not be privy to any secrets of the realm, unless the husband has had many years' proof of her ability to guard her tongue.[15]

Giles rules out any more public role for women, deriding Plato's teaching in the *Republic* (by way of Aristotle's refutation of it in the *Politics*) that women should be trained for war. Interestingly, one of his contemporaries, the Dominican friar Ptolemy of Lucca, in his own work of the same name, *De regimine principum* (1301–03), seems to take this passage from Plato seriously enough to devote considerable space to arguments both in favour of and opposed to it. In the end, however, he agrees with Aristotle, Giles and, indeed, the Bible:

> Therefore, I must say simply that a woman ought not to be exposed to matters of
> war, but ought to live in the home and take care of household matters. . . . Solomon
> commends a woman's fortitude in a song that he composed using each of the letters
> of the Hebrew alphabet, in which he attributes all of her fortitude to domestic action.

[handwritten: women — quiet + domestic duties]

And what is domestic action?

> The first is the art of spinning. . . . Further on, Solomon added other womanly acts refer-
> ring to the domestic home, such as taking care of children, running the household, pro-
> viding for her home, honoring the friends of her husband, and making up for his defects.
> These are proper things for a wife to do, and they pertain to the good of marriage.[16]

About women, Marsilius simply agreed with Aristotle that they, like children, slaves and
aliens, cannot be citizens, and expressed suspicion of the relationship between women and
their confessors: 'because they are easy to seduce, especially the young ones, whether they
are virgins or even married . . . a corrupt priest will easily corrupt their morals and their
chastity'.[17] Such views were hardly unique to these three university-educated intellectuals,
but were more widely shared, as is clear from the extensive anti-feminine literature produced
throughout the Middle Ages. The essential case against women was that they were weak,
physically, morally and intellectually. One needed to look no further than the authority of the
Bible and Aristotle to prove this. Eve, after all, was the original human sinner and temptress,
while, according to Aristotle, woman's weakness began *in utero*, since the female foetus
was merely an imperfect male. This weakness made her passive, in the sense of her role in
procreation being merely that of an incubator of male semen, and yet perniciously active, as
a sexual predator looking to ensnare men with her wiles and allures.

   This dismal discourse, while certainly dominant in the late Middle Ages, did not go wholly
unchallenged, however. Giovanni Boccaccio, who on the one hand wrote the viciously
anti-feminine *Corbaccio* (c. 1355) – 'A woman is an imperfect creature excited by a thousand foul passions, abominable even to remember, let alone speak of' – also wrote *The Elegy
of Lady Fiammetta* (c. 1345), a psychological novel narrated by its female protagonist, and
a book *On Famous Women* (c. 1355).[18] Geoffrey Chaucer also exhibited this ambivalence,
especially in the persona of the Wife of Bath in his *Canterbury Tales*. The Wife is a powerful and independent personality who makes a strong case against the stupidity and errors of
misogynist literature. Yet there can be no doubt that Chaucer satirises her as well, as a kind
of bullying, man-eating philistine. Chaucer's contemporary John Gower took up the case for
women in his *Confessio Amantis* ('Lover's Confession', late 1380s), defending them against
charges of leading men sexually astray:

> There is no deception on the part of the woman, where a man bewilders himself: if
> he deludes his own wits, I can certainly acquit the women. Whatever man allows
> his mind to dwell upon the imprint his imagination has foolishly taken of women,
> is fanning the flames within himself – and, since the woman knows nothing about
> it, she is not to blame. For if a man incites himself to drown, and will not restrain
> himself, it is not the water's fault.[19] *[handwritten: lets Go! Chaucer good]*

   It was, however, left to Christine de Pizan to make the most concerted and learned
defence of women. To the charge that Eve deceived Adam, she replied in her *Epistre au dieu
d'amour* ('Letter of the God of Love', 1399):

> I can assure you that she never did deceive Adam, but innocently swallowed and
> believed the words of the devil, which she thought were sincere and true, and with
> this conviction she went on to tell her husband. There was therefore neither trickery
> nor deceit in this.[20]

indeed the entire discourse of woman's moral weakness, especially in the realm of sexual desire, is a great slander perpetrated by generations of lascivious men, going back to the biblical kings David and Solomon, and the Roman poet Ovid 'who lusted after so many women', and continued by medieval clerks who were 'maddened with lust not for just one, but for thousands of them!'[21] As for women not being physically as strong as men, she is not troubled 'that women's nature and character are not conducive to their waging war, killing people, or kindling tinder to start fires, or committing similar acts', but rather judges it a good thing 'that their hearts are not predisposed to such behaviour nor to committing acts of cruelty. For woman's nature is noble, very compassionate, timid, and timorous. She is humble, gentle, self-effacing, and full of charity, loveable, devout, and quietly modest'.[22] Yet if Christine is no advocate for women waging war themselves, she herself was not averse to giving advice on how to do so, writing a manual of military strategy, *Le livre de fais d'armes et de chevalerie* ('The Book of Deeds of Arms and Chivalry'), in around 1410.

Her belief that women could advise men on military matters and politics, as well as on love and morality stems from her conviction that women were every bit as intelligent as men. This was so because, contrary to woman being an 'imperfect' man, she was in fact created perfect, in the image of God, from the noble substance of Adam's rib,

> signifying that she should stand at his side as a companion and never lie at his feet like a slave, and also that he should love her as his own flesh. If the supreme craftsman was not ashamed to create and form the feminine body, would Nature then have been ashamed? It is the height of folly to say this![23]

She drives home the point of woman's intellectual equality in her *Livre de la cité des dames* ('Book of the City of Ladies', 1405), with the (albeit fabulous) story of the Roman lady, Carmentis, who invented Roman law and the Latin language:

> she worked and studied so hard that she invented her own letters, which were completely different from those of other nations; that is, she established the Latin alphabet and syntax, spelling, the difference between vowels and consonants, as well as a complete introduction to the science of grammar. She gave and taught these letters to the people and wished that they be widely known. . . . thanks to the subtlety of this teaching and to the great utility and profit which have since accrued to the world, one can say that nothing more worthy in the world was ever invented.[24]

And, of course, Christine lived according to what she believed, being herself a great poet and author of several treatises. Still, it must be said, that although Christine believed women were men's equals, she nonetheless insisted upon their difference, and thus did not challenge women's social roles but only men's denigration of women and the roles they performed.

Marriage, family and the household

With the exception of those dedicated early on to a life of celibacy in the clergy or religious orders, it was rare indeed for an adult to remain unmarried in the late Middle Ages. More than 95 per cent of women could expect to marry in late fourteenth- and early fifteenth-century Tuscany, with the percentage of marrying men there having been slightly lower, owing to the greater likelihood of men being married multiple times.[25] North of the Alps, marriage rates seem to have been slightly, but probably not appreciably, lower. So common in fact was the married or widowed state for adults in late medieval England that the terms 'wife' and 'husband' in Middle English referred to adult women and men, regardless of their actual marital status.[26] During the course of the High Middle Ages, and especially in the twelfth century, the Church had elaborated a theology of marriage that stressed mutual consent between the partners, spoken in the present tense, as the only necessary component of a valid marriage. More, however, was needed in the eyes of the Church to make a marriage licit, including the publishing of banns prior to the wedding, the blessing by a priest 'in the face of a church' and the handing over of a dowry by the bride's family to the husband.[27] Likewise, secular custom demanded some sort of betrothal before the wedding, with the consent of the future couple's parents or legal guardians, as well as that of a feudal lord, in the case of a vassal, and of the landlord, in the case of serfs. The wedding itself would be concluded with a public celebration of some kind, followed by the sexual consummation of the marriage.[28] According to both Church doctrine and social practice, the normative marriage in late medieval Christendom was exogamous, monogamous, indissoluble and consensual. In reality, of course, there were transgressions. Marriages were sometimes contracted (and frequently pardoned by ecclesiastical authorities) between parties who were related within the minimum four degrees of kinship stipulated by the canons of the Fourth Lateran Council of 1215, and although in theory marriages could not be dissolved, they could be annulled by ecclesiastical courts, owing to, or on the pretext of, non-consent by one or both parties, consanguinity, non-consummation or bigamy. Moreover, it was not unheard of for couples to separate or, if their marriage had been of a somewhat less formal nature to begin with, simply to dissolve the union and agree to go their separate ways. None questioned the rule of monogamy, although men whose careers required a considerable degree of travel, especially merchants and sailors, seem not infrequently to have kept more than one conjugal household, whether with women they recognised as wives or with concubines.[29] This practice, however, was universally condemned. Interestingly, the one sacramental absolute of Christian marriage, the free consent of the married partners, came to be construed as consent of parents as well as their children; indeed, sons and even more so daughters not infrequently bent to the will of their parents when it came to marriage. There was, after all, too much at stake in a marriage, in the way of lineage, property, business, communal peace and politics. Likewise, lay people's insistence on consummation being a requisite confirmation of marriage led to its being expected in practice by ecclesiastical authorities as well, despite its not being doctrinally necessary.[30]

The canons of the Church also set a minimum age for marriage, twelve years for girls and fourteen for boys. This minimum was not a problem in the case of boys, since rarely, if ever, did they marry before their fourteenth year. However, there certainly were cases where the Church offered dispensation for marriages of girls below the twelve-year minimum, especially among the nobility and, in southern Europe, in wealthier urban families. The custom of marrying off very young brides was so common in Mediterranean Europe that it prompted the Dominican St Antoninus of Florence (1389–1459) to remark, when commenting on Albert the Great's assertion that a nine-year-old girl had been impregnated and given birth at age ten, that 'the natural philosophers say that some are born . . . who are apt for intercourse more quickly than others. And I believe that these things vary according to hot and cold places, just as impregnation and bodily growth varies'.[31] His point here was that girls from southern climes matured earlier than those further to the north. Women normally entered first marriages there in their mid- to late teens, with girls from wealthy urban families marrying on average a bit earlier than their poorer or rural counterparts. Likewise southern men tended to marry fairly late, in their late twenties, so that the age difference between couples was on average between ten and twelve years. It comes as little surprise that scholars from Italy and Spain approved of Aristotle's recommendation in the *Politics* that men not marry until their mid-thirties, since this would allow their semen time to mature, resulting in better children.[32] Or, as the humanist man of letters and architect Leon Battista Alberti, in his *Libri della famiglia* ('On the Family', c. 1435–40), put it, 'to our modern minds it seems to be practical for a man to marry at twenty-five. . . . The youthful seed, moreover, seems faulty and frail and less full of vigor than that which is ripened. Let men wait for solid maturity'.[33] In stark contrast to this, the age difference of couples in first marriages in northwestern Europe – below the rank of the nobility, whose marital practices in this regard were similar to those in the south – was only some two to four years, with women entering marriage in their early to mid-twenties and men in their mid- to late twenties. The reasons for this disparity are complex and disputed, but seem to have something to do with differences in attitudes to family shame and honour, and different kinship and inheritance practices. According to the 'southern model', families were intensely patriarchal and patrilineal, but also predicated a considerable portion of the kinship group's honour on the reputation for sexual purity of their women. Thus they kept their girls particularly well-protected and married them off early, so as to avoid the scandal that might arise from premarital sexual relations, since women, in the words of the fifteenth-century Florentine merchant Giovanni Morelli, 'become full of vices when they do not have what nature requires'.[34] Men, for their part, waited to marry late, so that they might be able to establish the material base for their own households, through a combination of business and inheritance. Because girls themselves could not inherit from their fathers, their families provided them with dowries, both in lieu of an inheritance and to make them more attractive to prospective mates. By the latter half of the fifteenth century the dowries in central and northern Italy had become so large that mothers and members of the extended family frequently joined fathers and older brothers in contributing to the dowries of young females. Contributions to dowry funds also became a form of pious bequest, while in Florence the commune established a municipal fund, the *Monte delle doti*, to help defray the high costs of dowries. Women in northwestern Europe generally enjoyed somewhat more favourable inheritance arrangements. They also tended, like their male counterparts, to spend their teenage years working as servants in other families' households. This allowed both men and women to build up some wealth prior to marriage, so that when they did marry, they could establish autonomous households. In southern Europe, to the contrary, kinship groups tended to stay closer together and be more financially dependent on one another.

Marriage's primary functions were procreation and production. In Alberti's words, 'In the family the number of men must not diminish but augment; possessions must not grow less, but more'.[35] As to the former activity, it is apparent that the average conjugal union tended to be quite fertile, especially in wealthier and urban households. In the early fifteenth century, Florentine women from wealthier households who married in their late teens and remained married into their mid-thirties could expect on average to give birth every twenty-one months. The fecundity of some marriages was really quite staggering. For example, a woman from the city of Arras in northeast France became a widow in 1461 at the age of twenty-nine.[36] In her thirteen years of marriage she had given birth twelve times. Cecily Neville, duchess of York (d. 1495), was the eighteenth child of her father, Ralph, earl of Westmorland and the tenth from his second marriage, to Joan Beaufort (who went on to have four more children).

Cecily's union with Richard, duke of York (d. 1460) was nearly as fecund as her parents', as she bore twelve children between 1439 and 1455.[37] The Florentine merchant Gregorio Dati recorded in his secret diary that his mother, Ghita, had borne seventeen children to his father, Stagio, and then lived on to the ripe old age of roughly seventy-five.[38] Admittedly, the fertility rate in less-elevated households was a bit lower, probably more on the order of one birth in every thirty months.[39] The reasons for this are not hard to find. First, the wealthiest households could better afford large numbers of children, whereas middling and poorer families had correspondingly fewer children based on what they felt they could afford. Another important factor was nursing, since it generally delays renewed fertility. Also there were strong taboos in the Middle Ages against engaging in sex while nursing. Women in wealthier households turned their newborn infants over to the care of wet nurses, thus shortening the span of infertility between births. As for other methods of birth control, while there is some evidence of the use of abortifacients, the far more common method was *coitus interruptus*. If one believes the evidence of confessors' manuals and sermons, the 'sin of Onan' was commonly practised, especially it seems during the period of extraordinarily high population pressure in the early fourteenth century.[40]

High fertility, however, did not often result in large families. The culprit here was the extraordinarily high mortality rate, especially during times of plague. Mean household size in late medieval England was roughly four persons per household, while the size of households in Tuscany tended to be a little higher, at just over four per household, of whom only two were children. These small households were primarily caused by extremely high infant mortality, with an average of one of every two children born to a family never reaching adulthood.[41] But death also stalked parents. Late medieval marriages lasted roughly two decades on average, meaning that the vast majority of those who married could expect to remarry or spend time in the state of widowhood.[42] Husbands, especially in southern Europe, but also among the nobility and urban patriciates of northern Europe, tended to precede their wives to the grave, owing to their being so much older. And everywhere women were subject to death, permanent injury or lingering ill health owing to complications during pregnancy or in childbirth. One-third of Florentine women who died before their husbands succumbed to the perils of pregnancy and childbirth. King Henry V of England's mother, Mary de Bohun, died in 1394 after giving birth to Henry's youngest sister, Philippa; and although Henry VII's mother, Margaret Beaufort survived the birth of her only child at age thirteen, the difficulty of her labour left her unable to bear any more children.[43] Men who lost their wives rarely remained unmarried for long. Women, on the other hand, were much more likely to remain widows for the long haul, especially in southern Europe. Women in northwestern Europe fared a little better because they were able by law to inherit or have more control over their and their dead husband's property. Many northern widows preferred to remain thus, and those who desired remarriage had better luck doing so than their southern counterparts; there is even evidence from England that it was not unusual to find widows marrying men younger than themselves.

The perils of childbirth and childhood are poignantly laid bare in the pages of Gregorio Dati's secret diary. During a life that stretched 73 years (1362–1435), Gregorio married four times, kept a slave concubine, and had 26 children and at least two miscarried babies. Death claimed three of his wives and eighteen of his children before he stopped keeping his diary in 1431, at the time of the birth of his last child when Gregorio was 69. The table that follows lists Gregorio's wives, concubine and children (including known miscarriages). Those family members who still survived in 1431 are given in boldface.

Table 2.1 Gregorio Dati's immediate family

1st Wife: Bandecca: m. 1388; d. 15 July 1390 (from nine-month illness caused by miscarriage in fifth month of pregnancy)

Child*

Miscarriage after five months of pregnancy, 15 July 1390

Concubine: Margherita (Tatar slave in Valencia)

Child

1) **Tommaso**: b. 21 December 1391 (in Valencia)

2nd Wife: Isabetta: m. 22 June 1393; d. 2 October 1402 (cause of death not given)

Children

2) Bandecca: b. 17 May 1394; m. 1414; d. 1 August 1420 (plague)
3) Stagio: b. 17 March 1396; d. 30 July 1400 (plague)
4) Veronica Gostanza: b. 12 March 1397; d. July 1420 (plague)
5) **Bernardo Agostino**: b. 27 April 1398
6) Mari Piero: b. 1 July 1399; d. 22 August 1400 (plague)
7) Filippa Giovanna: b. 22 June 1400; d. 1 August 1420 (plague)
8) Stagio Benedetto: b. 13 July 1401; d. 29 September 1401 (cough)
9) Piero Antonio; b. 5 July 1402; d. 2 August 1402 (cause of death not given)

3rd Wife: Ginevra: m. 1403; d. 7 September 1419 (from childbirth after long suffering)

Children

10) Manetto Domenico: b. 27 April 1404; d. January 1418 (very sick)
11) Agnolo Giovanni (girl): b. 19 March 1405; d. 19 March 1405 (premature birth at 7 months)
12) Elisabetta Caterina: b. 8 June 1406; d. 21 February 1414 (after long illness)
13) Antonia Margherita: b. 4 June 1407; d. 5 July 1420 (plague)
14) Sandra: b. (unknown but probably 1408–10); d. 1 July 1420 (plague)
15) Niccolò: b. 31 July 1411; d. 22 October 1411 (dysentery)
16) **Girolamo Domenico**: b. 1 October 1412
17) Filippo Jacopo: b. 1 May 1415; d. 2 August 1419 (cause of death not given)
18) **Ghita**: b. 24 April 1416 (after a painful and almost fatal labour)
19) **Betta**: b. (unknown but probably 1417–18)
20) Lisa: b. 17 July 1419; d. 1419 (shortly after birth?)

4th Wife: **Caterina**: m. 29 March 1421 (at age 30 with no wedding ceremony)

Children

Miscarriage after four month's pregnancy, August 1421

21) Ginevra Francesca: b. 4 October 1422; d. 6 October 1431 (dies same day as Lionardo; some sort of sickness)
22) **Antonio Felice**: b. 7 January 1424
23) Lionardo Benedetto: b. 20 March 1425; d. 6 October 1431 (dies same day as Ginevra; in perfect health just 24 hours before)
24) **Anna Bandecca**: b. 26 July 1426
25) Filippa Felice: b. 28 August 1427; d. 19 October 1430 (cause of death not given)
26) **Bartolomea Domenica**: b. 2 June 1431

If Gregorio's long-lasting sexual appetite and prolific progeny (at least 27 pregnancies in 37.5 years of marriage) were hardly typical, the fates of his women and children were more so. Each of his wives spent the majority of her married life pregnant, and at least two died from complications brought on by miscarriage or childbirth. Moreover Ginevra almost died during the birth of her ninth child, Ghita; it was her eleventh labour that finally killed her. Of the children who we know predeceased Gregorio, only three reached adulthood, and of those, only Gregorio's firstborn legitimate daughter, Bandecca had married before dying. Six of his children died in infancy. Nor is it certain that all his surviving children managed to reach adulthood, since at the time he stopped keeping his diary, only three had passed the age of eighteen. As for cause of death, in the fifteen cases when it is given, seven were the result of the two great outbreaks of plague in 1400 and 1420, one dysentery, one a cough in early infancy, and the remainder some sort of illness, one of which struck very quickly and killed two siblings on the same day.

The story of the Dati family lays out in harsh relief three of the demographic realities of the late Middle Ages: high fertility (and the attendant threats to women's health and longevity), high infant and child mortality, and high mortality from the pestilence. In Chapter 1 we discussed the effects of the death rate on population, and in this chapter some words have been said about fertility, but what about fertility's concomitant, nuptiality? Death, the great equaliser, affected late medieval Latin Christendom fairly uniformly. But the reproductive end of the system could to some extent be adjusted to respond to population pressure or deficit, either through the practice or avoidance of birth control (fertility) or by changing the age of marriage and the number of women in marriage (nuptiality). What evidence there is suggests that changes in the fertility rate were barely affected by the Black Death. Nuptiality, however, was another matter. Marriage age in Tuscany, for example, does seem to have been lowered somewhat, for both men and women, owing to the devastation of plague. Then, when the ravages of the disease eased off in the second half of the fifteenth century, marriage ages rose slightly. Still, the practice of marrying off very young daughters had already been in place prior to the plague, so that the downward adjustment does not seem to have made much of a difference in the number of children born to couples. Moreover, the undesirability of widows in southern Europe largely remained in force during the years of pestilence, leaving these women, many of whom were still of child-bearing years, out of the marriage market. Things were rather different in northwest Europe. Immediately after visitations of plague there is evidence of an increase in marriages of young couples; but this was only temporary, and things would settle back to normal within a few years. In some areas the average marriage age of women may have even increased during the century following the first onset of the Black Death, as was certainly the case in Champagne, where women's age at first marriage rose from 18 to 24 years.[44] Widows also were more likely to marry in the north, frequently choosing men younger than themselves as mates. Still, it is also undeniable that marriage opportunities for widows declined with the amelioration of the death rate in the later years of the fifteenth century. So, although some adjustments in nuptiality did take place, neither in the south or north were these changes sufficient to alter dramatically the reproductive end of the equation. Prior to the late fifteenth century, demographic recovery was held in thrall to King Death.

Individuals, social hierarchy and communities

No longer credible is the old notion that the birth of the individual in Europe had to await the dawning of modernity. Medieval people were very much conscious of themselves as individuals. They had individuated souls for which they alone were, in the end, responsible, and, if anything, penitential practices increased and further articulated this sense of the individuated soul in the late Middle Ages. This soul was embodied, moreover, meaning that the individual was both soul and body. And although the soul might leave its corruptible earthly body at the time of death, it nonetheless received a new, incorruptible and personal body in the afterlife. Still, it is fair to say that one's social status and place in the community did play a profound role in the formation of an individual's identity and self-consciousness. One need only look at the new organising principle that informs several confessors' manuals, beginning in the latter half of the thirteenth century, which instead of proceeding from one sin to the next, as they had formerly done, now treated types of sinner, according to their status and profession.[45] Although, not surprisingly, the elements of social structure differed somewhat according to region and locale throughout medieval Europe, it is fair to say that in general people in the late Middle Ages thought of society as being divided into three orders (or estates) of clergy, nobility and commons, and that there was not only a horizontal division between clergy and laity and a vertical hierarchy among these orders, with clerics and nobles occupying the upper and the commons the lower register, but that each order of society was itself hierarchically structured with the stability of the hierarchy being maintained through limited social mobility. The structure and personnel of the clerical hierarchy will be the subject of a later chapter. Suffice it for now to say of this group, that clerics and religious started out their lives as lay people, and thus throughout their lives remained to some degree tied to and influenced by their origins in lay society.

The nobility

Nobles derived their primary identity and legitimacy as an order from a combination of noble lineage, the profession of arms, the exercise of lordship and service to princes or other nobles. Here at the start one sees that this social group very much defined itself according to masculine functions, since men alone could bear arms, and lordship, although it could be exercised by women in default of a male, was normally the province of men. But this order was hardly uniform. There was, to begin with, great regional diversity: 'The Polish nobility was not that of Germany, nor was that of France Italian'.[46] Nobles engaging in mercantile activities were, for example, quite common in northern and central Italian cities, whereas by the fifteenth century in Germany, a clear formal division had been created between urban merchant patricians and rural nobles.[47] Likewise within each region's nobility there were substantial differences in both wealth and power, between the exalted estate of great territorial princes, like the three lay electors of the German Empire or the fifteenth-century Burgundian dukes, on the one hand, and that of humble knights, on the other. In between these, moreover, were the titled hereditary nobility of dukes and counts (called earls in the British Isles), as well as those sporting other assorted designations, such as marquis and viscount, below whom were the barons or castellans. In the fourteenth century a further subclass emerged, called esquires and gentlemen in England, *écuyers* and *escuderos* in France and Spain, and *Knechte* in Germany, whose military duties as men-at-arms and whose practice of minor lordship over the peasants of one or two manors gave them some claim to nobility and, eventually, to a coat of arms, but whose modest means made them more akin in lifestyle to urban merchants and the wealthier rural peasantry. In England, this lower grade of nobility joined the knighthood, to form an aristocratic class called the gentry, which occupied a social register below the upper, or political nobility of the Parliamentary peerage of titled nobles and barons, and above the thoroughly non-noble rural yeomen and husbandmen.

Plague and changes in inheritance practices, as well as changing political and economic conditions also had their effect on the composition and functions of the nobility over the course of the fourteenth and fifteenth centuries. Noble families, like all others, were subject over time to extinction in the male line, a process which accelerated during the years of the plague. In England between 1300 and 1500 roughly one quarter of families in the upper nobility became extinct in the male line every twenty-five years. The rate was little different in France and Scotland. Families of the lower nobility suffered an even higher rate of failure, since they were no more likely than the greater nobles to produce viable male heirs, and were subject as well to the diminution of their considerably smaller estates through partition among younger sons and widows. Various legal innovations were concocted to protect the landed possessions of a lineage, the most important of which was the entail in tail male, which restricted the inheritance of the patrimony to the eldest direct or, failing that, the eldest patrilineal collateral male heir. However, the force of the entail was frequently undercut by legal devices which guaranteed land to younger sons, daughters, and widows, thereby breaking up the patrimony. Even efforts to guarantee the livelihood of the heir, like the jointure in England, which granted use of the estate to a widow during the heir's minority, could go awry if the widow remarried. Plague also affected the fortunes of the lower nobility in another way, since the rising agricultural wages, lower rents and falling corn prices that came in its wake drastically lowered the income of landed estates. It even seems that a growing anxiety about death and the sufferings of Purgatory exacerbated by the plague prompted nobles to dispense considerable and sometimes onerous sums on pious bequests, and that these too ate into already shrinking inheritances. Once a noble family's fortunes sank to such a state that it could no longer maintain an 'honourable' lifestyle of liberality, courtliness and service, it typically ceased to be regarded as noble. 'If an individual is reduced to poverty or engages in demeaning tasks, he cannot be called or be considered noble', wrote the fifteenth-century Veronese Bartolomeo Cipolla.[48] It must here be pointed out, however, that what was considered demeaning in one setting, was not necessarily so in another. Thus one finds knights in the kingdom of Castile working as cobblers, blacksmiths, tailors and even butchers, activities that would surely have disqualified lesser nobles in England, northern France or Germany.[49]

Of course, as noble lineages died out, others came into being, so that the nobility constantly recruited new members. This is not to say that noble lines were always replaced. The size of the English peerage, for example, shrank from 147 to 73 between 1360 and 1450.[50] This was due in part to the overall population decline occasioned by the plague; but it also was a function of English royal policy, since new peerages could only come into being at the king's pleasure. On the other hand, the principal means of entry into the nobility and social advancement for those already in it was service, military and civil, to princes and great lords. War of course both extinguished and created nobility, with bad fortune killing off an heir or wasting a captive knight's estate in ransom payments, and good fortune (not to mention prowess) advancing a soldier through the material gains of ransoms and plunder and the acquisition of honour through exceptional military service. One need only look at the meteoric rise of the humble Breton knight Bertrand du Guesclin who attained the constableship of France, or at the *condottiero* ('military contractor') Sir John Hawkwood who rose to become the Captain General of Florence, whose grateful populace buried him in their cathedral in a tomb decorated with a memorial plaque painted immediately after his death in 1394 by Taddeo Gaddi and Giuliano d'Arrigo, and then for a second time, in 1436, and with even greater magnificence, by Paolo Uccello.[51] Less striking perhaps, but still notable are the scions of minor gentry families Robert Knowles (or Knolles), Hugh Calverly and John Norbury, all of whom became successful knights fighting in the Anglo-French wars (and as mercenaries) during the 1360s and 1370s.[52] Service of a more civil kind could also ennoble, however, as kings and princes began to grant nobility as a reward for the loyal service of lawyers, administrative officials and even merchants.[53] This willingness to serve the state needs to be seen in the context not only of a desire for social advancement but also of their declining seigneurial revenues, brought on by rising agricultural wages, falling rents and grain prices, which compelled nobles to seek income in return for service to the state. These came either from the wages and other financial benefits of office-holding, from princely grants of land and privileges, or from mortgages in return for loans. Lesser nobles also frequently entered the service of the greater nobility, serving as household staff, legal advocates and military retainers.

One further aspect of the late medieval nobility needs to be mentioned here: the growing formality of its practices. This expressed itself particularly in the increasingly articulated intricacies of heraldry and the science of blazon (i.e. the rules governing the colours, symbols and arrangement of elements on coats of arms), which was overseen by an international brotherhood of heralds, who 'were well on their way to becoming a kind of secular priesthood of chivalry' by the later 1300s.[54] There can be no doubt of the heralds' need for erudition and experience, thanks to the profusion of coats of arms among not only the upper but also the lower nobility, as well as the other demanding duties of heralds, which included acting as messengers between enemy combatants, giving advice on points of honour and rendering judgements on knightly prowess, identifying and registering the deeds of participants in tournaments (which themselves were growing increasingly ritualised), writing up genealogies and even, as in the case of Berry Herald, histories. Little wonder then that heraldry became a true profession in the late Middle Ages, with heralds being classified according to their expertise and accomplishments as apprentices, known as 'pursuivants' of arms, then, once they had mastered their craft, marshals of arms and, finally, kings of arms. Another major contributor to this formalism was the birth of a new kind of association of knighthood, the secular 'orders' of chivalry. The first of these, the Order of St George, founded by King Charles-Robert of Hungary in 1325, was soon followed by several others, all centred on a princely court, the most notable being Alfonso XI of Castile's Order of the Band (1332), the English Order of the Garter, founded in or shortly before 1349 by Edward III, King John the Good of France's Order of the Star (1351), and the Burgundian Order of the Golden Fleece (1431). There can be no denying the baldly political nature of these orders, designed to create bonds of service and loyalty between a state's nobility and its prince, and to enhance the international prestige and influence of the monarch. Yet if the chivalric orders can be seen as instruments of state power, membership in them also conferred the favours of improved reputation and political pull upon their noble fellowship, whose mutual bonds were cultivated by elaborate ceremonial and who bore distinctive insignia as marks of their enhanced status.

Whatever diversity is observable among the nobility – and as we have seen, it was considerable – it pales in comparison with the variety of occupations, social groupings and levels of wealth and status of the so-called third order, the non-noble laity. Indeed, the complexity of its composition had already destabilised medieval intellectuals' neat tri-functional ordering of society, so there is no need for us to try to fit these people into such a straightjacket. Suffice it to say that if clergy and nobility were recognisable, albeit artificial, social

Figure 2.1 Monumental painting of Sir John Hawkwood, by Paolo Uccello, Florence Cathedral.
Photograph: The Picture Art Collection / Alamy Stock Photo

groups in the last centuries of the Middle Ages, the only quality that unified the third order was negative, i.e. 'not-clergy' and 'not-noble'. Here, then, it makes sense to shift our terms of discussion from that of social groups to that of the social and economic environments of countryside and city.

Rural communities

There is a great deal of truth in the truisms that the society and economy of medieval Europe were overwhelmingly rural and that the denizens of the countryside were by and large peasants. As to the first of these truisms, some 80 per cent of the late medieval populace lived and worked in the countryside; and although some regions, like northern Italy and the Low Countries, had as much as a third of their population living in cities and towns, other areas, like Scandinavia and Ireland, had no sizeable cities to speak of and some 95 per cent of their populace living in the countryside. Agriculture, then, formed the base of the medieval economy, and those who practised it were indeed the muddy feet of the body politic. The great majority of these country dwellers were, moreover, peasants, whom Rodney Hilton defines as members of a 'stratum of cultivators and herdsmen' who: (1) possessed, even if they did not own, the means of agricultural production by which they obtained a livelihood; (2) worked their holdings as a family unit and did so primarily with the labour of family members; (3) normally associated beyond the family in larger units of villages or hamlets, which had, to a greater or lesser extent, elements of common property and collective rights; (4) might engage in ancillary economic activities, as agricultural day-labourers, artisans or builders; and (5) supported super-imposed social strata and institutions, such as lay and ecclesiastical landlords, churches, cities and territorial states, which lived off and were enriched by their surplus.[55] Less true is another truism, that peasant life was bound by tradition and custom, and was thus resistant to change and innovation. Although tradition and custom surely guided peasants and were in turn sometimes used by them to advantage, especially when asserting ancient liberties against the encroachments of landlords, the late Middle Ages was, in fact, a time of considerable flux for European peasantries, who, along with their landlords, were affected by changing circumstances and sought ways to adjust to and profit from these changes.

Any attempt to generalise about the lives and working conditions of medieval peasantries immediately runs up against the impediment of a dizzying variety of climate zones, soil types, crops planted, farming and inheritance practices, and tenurial arrangements. Agriculturalists working the vast, open grain-growing zones of northern France, the English Midlands, the Spanish Meseta, central Sicily and much of central and northeast Europe, worked under very different conditions from pastoralists engaged in transhumant herding in Provence and the Pyrenees, grape growers in the hills of Tuscany or along the Rhine, dairy herdsmen in southern Denmark or flax farmers in Swabia. The wheeled plough equipped with iron coulter and mouldboard (which, respectively, cut the soil and turned it over), and drawn by a team of six to eight oxen (or, increasingly, by heavy horses) used by husbandmen to plough the heavy soils of long strips in the great open fields of Oxfordshire, was very different from the light scratch ploughs employed by peasants scoring the light, dry soils of Mediterranean lands. Crop rotation practices differed as well, with a three-cycle rotation of winter corn, spring corn or legumes, and fallowing generally having been adopted in regions of richer, heavier soils and good rainfall, and a two-cycle system of planting and fallowing in more arid lands with lighter soils. Grain yields, almost universally quite low by modern standards, at about

3.5 to 5 grains harvested per seed planted, could be raised substantially with proper care and fertilising, as was done on the estates of St Denis in the Paris basin, which obtained yields of 8:1 to 10:1, or in the fields of Artois, where harvests in a good year could reach fifteen-fold what was sown.[56] Inheritance practices varied considerably, though there was a tendency toward impartible inheritance (either primo- or ultimogeniture) in northern Europe and partible inheritance in the south.

As for the conditions of land-holding, Hilton is right to say that late medieval peasants normally 'possessed', rather than outright owned, their land. Certainly there were some peasants who owned their land outright and others whose obligations to their landlords were either so ill-defined or based on the old Roman law of usufruct that they were owners in fact, if not in law. The great majority nonetheless 'held' and worked the land of a landlord (the seigneur) in return for some form of rent. This rent took three forms: labour service, payment in kind or a money rent. By the late Middle Ages, money rents were far more common than those paid in crops, although in the share-cropping economies which predominated in some parts of northern Italy (*mezzadria*) and southern France (*métayage*) a payment of up to half the harvest was made in return for use of the landlord's land and equipment. Labour services too tended to be relaxed in favour of increased money leases as more landlords parcelled out lands they had formerly exploited directly (their 'demesne') among peasant tenants. If landlords, for their part, derived the lion's share of their income from rents, they also received income from fines levied through their manorial courts, the fees peasants had to pay to grind their grain at the lord's mill, and, in some areas, the exclusive right to buy up and vend their tenants' produce and to charge bridge and road toll fees. Lords of unfree tenants (serfs, villeins) also derived some income from entry fines imposed and a payment in cattle ('heriot') at the time of inheritance, a marriage fine when a daughter married ('merchet'), and a fine for an unmarried daughter's fornication or pregnancy ('leyrwite'). Still, it must be said that few peasants remained in bondage by the late Middle Ages. Prior to the Black Death, in England, where serfdom was most common, roughly a third of peasants were of servile status in the fourteenth century, whereas very few serfs could be found on the Continent. In the decades following the Peasants' Revolt serfdom largely disappeared in England, while to the contrary, in the fifteenth century landowners in Catalonia, southwest Germany, Bohemia and Poland attempted with some success to impose serfdom on their peasants. The same began to happen at the end of the fifteenth century in Denmark and in some of the Baltic principalities of Germany.

Peasant households throughout Europe tended to consist only of the conjugal family unit of a husband, wife and their children. All members of the family who could work had tasks to do. Women's work was confined largely to the 'inner economy' of childrearing, housework (cooking, cleaning, spinning and weaving), tending to the livestock, gardening and brewing – although this last was increasingly the province of male brewers as hopped beer replaced ale in the fifteenth century.[57] Wives and their teenage daughters were also expected to help out during the harvest. The 'exterior economy' of fieldwork (ploughing, mowing, sowing, reaping, threshing) was the husband's province. Men also frequently engaged in specialised crafts, as carpenters, tailors, bakers, potters or blacksmiths, or sought to supplement the family income by earning a wage as day labourers or, if among the better-off peasants, as manorial officials. Women too could earn extra income as brewsters and spinsters. A family's children spent their earliest years at play, but starting at about age six they began contributing to the household economy, with the younger ones fishing, helping gather wood, fruits, berries, nuts, herbs (or shellfish along coasts), or looking after younger siblings and, especially the boys, tending flocks. At roughly age thirteen girls' and boys' tasks began more to resemble those of their parents, so that by the time they entered their twenties they could carry out gender appropriate work with some expertise. Teens, of both sexes, also frequently left the family to spend time in service, either to wealthier peasants or, very frequently, in the households and shops of nearby towns.[58]

Although some peasant families lived on isolated farmsteads or worked as charcoal burners in the forests, and some, especially in more urbanised areas, might even live in towns or their suburbs, the overwhelming majority lived in villages and hamlets. These villages, which might be nucleated or axial in plan, and could be open or fortified depending on the degree of peace and security in their locale, would be surrounded by fields, which typically were of three kinds: individual peasant household's strips or plots, the lord's demesne (if this had not been leased out), and common waste and pasture. A forest or wood of some kind might also be nearby, where peasants could gather firewood, nuts and berries, leave their pigs to root for mast and mushrooms, and engage in trapping of smaller game (or poaching larger prey, normally reserved to the lord). In the village itself, peasant dwellings usually had a small yard for growing vegetables and herbs and keeping fowl; especially in the case of better endowed households, there might be outbuildings for livestock. There might well be a parish church in the village, as well as a mill and, perhaps, the lord's manorial court. Here, however, it needs to be made clear that villages were often not identical with manors, as the peasants in a village might be tenants of more than one landlord, and several villages or parts of villages could make up a single manor. Nor should it be imagined that landlords necessarily dwelt in the countryside, 'lording it over' their peasants. In fact, absentee landlords were common, and becoming increasingly so during the course of the fourteenth and fifteenth centuries, leaving the day-to-day management of estates to stewards and bailiffs.

The manorial officials were themselves more often than not peasants, whose dual identity as custodians of the interests of both landlord and the village elite could raise the ire and contribute to the resentment of their less well-off neighbours. This stratification of the peasantry into an upper, middle and lower class of tenants, with the wealthier peasants tending to acquire larger holdings, is one of the signal developments of late medieval rural societies. Those at the top end of the scale – the English yeomanry and French *gros fermiers* – possessed some 40 hectares (99 acres) or more of land, with middling peasants farming anywhere between 10 and 20 hectares, and smallholders fewer than 10. As little as 4 hectares could adequately support a family, if the quality of land was good and their rent not too onerous. Still, it must be said that in order to make ends meet, smallholders often had to supplement their incomes through crafts and work as day-labourers, often in the fields of their wealthier neighbours. Moreover, prior to the demographic decline of the mid-fourteenth century, nearly half the peasantry farmed less than the four-hectare minimum. Little wonder, then, that peasant households tended to be small and periods of scarcity had such serious consequences for rural dwellers. Disparities of wealth and power in the village could also fray the bonds of communal solidarity, both in the land-hungry times of overpopulation prior to the Black Death and during the decades of dislocation and instability brought on by rapid population decline, the depredations of war and the grasping demands of Church, state and landlords. Still, on the whole, peasants maintained a remarkable degree of communal peace and solidarity, resolving property disputes in court, protecting common rights and customs, celebrating religious festivals and belonging to parish confraternities and rural guilds, sharing work, animals and tools, and enjoying games, entertainments and drinking bouts together.

In some ways peasant life was characterised by stability, with life being lived according to the seemingly eternal round of the agricultural and liturgical year, and with only very minor developments in farming practices and technology. Yet the rural economy also changed considerably during the fourteenth and fifteenth centuries. Most profound was the impact of growing commercialisation. Simply put, the late medieval rural economy became increasingly monetised and integrated with urban business interests and activities. This process was already under way at the beginning of the fourteenth century, with cash-hungry landlords reforesting arable to provide lumber for buildings, ships and mining operations, firewood for heating and charcoal for iron-working, shifting from grain-growing to pasturing livestock to satisfy the growing demand of cloth manufacturers, parchmenters and leather workers, while also growing cash crops for the cloth trade, like flax, and madder and woad (for red and blue dyes). Demographic decline only accelerated this trend. Fewer mouths to feed meant less grain was needed; eventually this decreased demand also lowered the price of grain. Meanwhile workers demanded, and got, higher wages and lower rents, while expanding governments demanded higher taxes from a shrinking tax base. Even land had become a commodity, with landlords and peasants buying, selling and mortgaging land, either to make a profit or to pay off debts. Higher labour costs and lower grain prices prompted landlords to turn even more of their land over to fishponds and pasturage and the growing of dyestuffs, wine grapes, and barley and hops for beer; likewise, the rising wages of peasants meant they had more money to buy meat and dairy products, beer and ale, as well as clothing and manufactured household goods. And just as rural dwellers provided ever more commodities to meet urban demand, so too did the towns intrude into the countryside. Many urban patricians got involved in the rural land market, thereby becoming landlords. Even city governments got into the act, with urban communes, especially in northern Italy, the Low Countries and Germany buying up and managing farmland. Industry too made its way to the countryside, with townsmen building fulling mills, ironworks and paper-making factories and organising piece-work by rural spinners and weavers.[59]

Urban communities

If late medieval Europe's population was overwhelmingly rural and its economic base lay in the countryside, much of its cultural and economic dynamism was generated in its cities and towns. Few cities were large by modern standards. Paris, which remained the largest European city throughout the late Middle Ages, had a population of roughly 200,000 prior to the Black Death. The next six largest cities in the early fourteenth century, Florence, Genoa, Milan, Naples, Palermo and Venice, all with populations of roughly 100,000, were located in Italy and Sicily. North of the Alps, only London, with its 80,000 or slightly more inhabitants, was of comparable size. The other great urban centres of northern Europe, the Flemish cities of Ghent and Bruges, had respective populations of roughly 65,000 and 46,000 before the plague. Yet if Europe was short of large cities, it was hardly lacking in medium-sized and small cities and towns. Besides the urban centres already mentioned, some 25 with populations of 20,000 or more, 80 or 90 cities of 10,000 or more, as well as hundreds of towns with between 1,000 and 10,000 inhabitants were liberally scattered about early fourteenth-century Europe. Plague, as well as, in some cases, famine, war and economic depression, drastically reduced the populations of many of these cities and towns. Paris in the early fifteenth century had half as many residents as it had had just over a half century earlier, while London already by 1377 had only some 40,000–45,000 inhabitants. Even more striking was the fate of Toulouse, whose population of nearly 50,000 in 1335 had plummeted to 19,000 in 1405 and Ypres, a city of some 28,000 souls in 1311–12, but of only 10,782 a century later.[60] Florence too saw its population drop from a high of nearly 120,000 before the Black Death to a low of some 40,000 in 1427, while Winchester, a thriving small city of around 12,000 in 1300 was only one-third that size in 1524.[61] If, however, most medieval towns and cities saw their population contract, and if virtually no new towns or cities were founded after 1350, this is not to say that urban life and vitality declined in any significant way. Immigrants from the rural hinterlands continued to replenish the populations of urban centres and market towns so that the proportion of people living in cities and towns in the early sixteenth century was no less and perhaps somewhat greater than it had been two centuries earlier. Some cities, like Venice, Milan and Naples had populations in 1500 that were little different from what they had been prior to the arrival of the pestilence. Others, like Lisbon, Nantes, Bayonne, Antwerp and Rome, grew significantly during the fifteenth century owing to economic or political fortune. The urban vitality of the late Middle Ages is perhaps best exemplified by the explosion during these years of urban voluntary associations (guilds and confraternities), charitable institutions (hospitals and almshouses), parish and mendicant churches, and universities. Indeed, the fact that the overwhelming majority of surviving medieval urban buildings and monuments are products of the late fourteenth and fifteenth centuries is tangible evidence of their citizens' confidence and ingenuity.

With their mazes of narrow streets and alleyways, houses and buildings crowded together (some as tall as five storeys or with projecting storeys often further obscuring the sunlight), bustling activity, noise, clutter, filth and stench, the larger towns and cities offered little in the way of privacy, peace or quiet. The cramped quarters were largely a function of city walls, which owing to their cost expanded far more slowly over the course of the thirteenth and early fourteenth centuries than did burgeoning urban populations. Most of Paris's populace of 200,000 was crowded into the mere 275 hectares encompassed by walls built in the time of Philip II (d. 1223). In around 1320, the university scholar and provost of the Collège de Navarre, Jean of Jandun, described houses teeming with craftsmen and packed so tightly that they were like 'the hairs on the heads of hairy persons, or the stalks in a great field, or the leaves of a gigantic forest'.[62] Conditions could not help but have improved when in a time of declining population kings Charles V and Charles VI undertook an expansion of the city's fortifications, to enclose another 125 hectares. Somewhat more spacious were Ghent, Louvain and Cologne with 500 hectares each, and Genoa and Milan, which in the later fourteenth century expanded their walls to include some 800 hectares. Still, with average densities of some 125 persons per hectare, Ghent, Genoa and Milan were still crowded by modern standards, and Paris c. 1400 with its 250 persons/hectare was even more so (though a paradise compared to the pre-plague average density of 727 persons/hectare). And, of course, people were not distributed evenly throughout the urban space. For instance, in depopulated mid-fifteenth-century Winchester the average density was only 46 per hectare but reached 199 along the central High Street.[63] Nor was the population of medieval cities confined to the area within the city walls, as suburbs clustered along the principal streets leading out of practically all large and medium-sized towns. The population of late fourteenth-century London, for example, was complemented by those of Westminster, Southwark and the congeries of industrialised settlements in the East End.[64] Writing in 1403, the Florentine humanist Leonardo Bruni spoke of his city as a set of concentric circles:

[T]he city is the first, placed at the center in the middle of all. The city is surrounded by walls and by lovely suburbs, and the suburbs themselves are encircled by villas. These enclose more distant villages and fortified places. And all this is surrounded, as in a larger circle, by outlying regions.[65]

It is unlikely that most suburbs were lovely, since municipal governments usually banished the most noisome trades – butchers, tanners, dyers and lime-burners, for example – to suburban locations. Urban governments might also strive to keep 'foreigners', disreputable elements like prostitutes, and prisons beyond the city walls. City squares and streets were not only crowded with inhabitants but with folk from the suburbs and hinterland, in town on business or pleasure. Likewise, much business was conducted by city-dwellers moving without the walls.

Late medieval cities brought together the worst and best of what life had to offer. On the one hand, they were crowded, filthy and violent. Living and working in close proximity, neighbours not only looked out for one another, they also practised 'a widespread voyeurism'.[66] It is little wonder that wealthier burghers were keen to purchase country estates, for they not only brought in extra income but also provided a place of retreat from the noise, congestion and prying eyes of neighbours; those less fortunate could look for no such relief. At the best of times, the state of urban hygiene was hardly admirable. Well water often became contaminated and streets filled with animal as well as human and household waste. Still, under normal circumstances householders were directed by municipal authorities to keep waste from blocking the streets in front of their homes; sometimes city governments employed street and public latrine cleaners as well. However, in times of crisis or civic disorder waste could pile up, making life barely tolerable and encouraging the spread of disease. Interestingly, the severity of plague outbreaks encouraged many cities to enact public works and hygiene legislation, piping in fresh drinking water, paving streets, establishing street drainage systems and controlling the dumping of liquid sewage and human waste.[67]

The city's 'dense sociability' brought with it high rates of crime and violence that were roughly twice that found in the countryside.[68] Historians have suggested several reasons for this. Burglary and petty theft were encouraged by the large numbers of vagrants and small-time crooks attracted by the multitude of targets and anonymity offered by towns, while violence was the order of the day in a society where honour was highly valued, drink flowed liberally in ubiquitous taverns (fourteenth-century Avignon alone had 66), family and neighbourhood ties encouraged strong affinities, knives and other weapons were always close at hand, and public policing and provision of justice were inefficient and often arbitrary. Most violence was unpremeditated and the product of 'a sequence, which might start in some pushing or rudeness, progress to insult and punching, and finally result in bloodshed'.[69] A London jury gave testimony in 1421, in the case of Arnald van Harsill's killing of John Bene:

[T]hat the said Arnald and John were sitting together on a seat in a tavern called 'The Moyses', when abusive words, begun by John, arose between them concerning John's concubine, and that John drew a dagger and attacked Arnald, who did his best to flee, whereupon John pursued him to a wall behind the inn-door, and threw him down and fell on him repeatedly striking him with his dagger, and that Arnald, being in great danger of death and unable to escape unless he defended himself, drew a knife and struck John in the left part of the breast, of which John died.[70]

In another case from England, this one from early fourteenth-century Oxford, the noise of a wake that in the wee hours of morning had spilled out into the street, so angered a clerk, Gilbert de Foxlee, that he seized a sword and violently accosted the participants, who, in their turn killed him with blows from sword, dagger and axe.[71] In each case local justice was served, as the killers were deemed innocent, having acted in self-defence.

When, however, local authorities were unable to or not sufficiently interested in imposing public order, initial insult or violence could escalate into riot or vendetta. At Oxford in 1355, for example, 'there came Walter Spryngeheuse, Roger de Chesterfield, and other scholars to the tavern called Swyndolnestok and there took a quart of wine and threw the said wine in the face of John Croidon, taverner, and then with that quart pot beat John without reason'. When the town's bailiffs demanded the offenders make amends, they took up bows, arrows and other weapons and made their way to the central market at Carfax 'ready for ill-doing', whereupon the bailiffs again intervened, seizing the students' weapons. Normally in such a case municipal authorities would have arrested the malefactors and brought them to trial, but this, after all, was a case involving university scholars, who had benefit of clergy and were thus exempt from secular jurisdiction. So Oxford's municipal authorities made their way to the chancellor of the university, demanding he take some action. When he did nothing the emboldened students came 'armed in the manner of war, and they beat and assaulted the mayor, bailiffs, and sergeants, and wounded some of them, whereby they despaired for their lives, and then [the students] slew a child of about fourteen years and threatened to set the town on fire'. Fondly enough, the university officials' account of what followed the initial fracas in the tavern credits the townsmen with initially gathering up arms, and shooting at the chancellor, who had come to 'appease the tumult'. Before order was restored shops as well as university halls were broken into and looted, fires were set, and several scholars met their deaths, some even apparently being scalped.[72] In late thirteenth-century Pistoia, a long-standing feud broke out between the Amadori and Rinieri when some youths from each family 'were gathered at a shop where wine was sold, and, having drunk to excess, a dispute arose among them as they gambled. They exchanged words, then blows, and the Rinieri lad had the better of the Amadori lad'. Violence between the two families quickly escalated: 'And this was the beginning of the division of the city and *contado* of Pistoia, from which followed killings, the burning of houses, castles, and villages, and the emergence of the faction names Black and White.'[73]

Gang rape, of both women and men, as well as child molestation, were also not uncommon crimes. Women rape victims in late medieval Florence had often been attacked by gangs of three to six men. In three reliably documented cases, Florentine women had been raped and sodomised by thirteen, fourteen and thirty men respectively. Adolescent boys also were on occasion gang-sodomised. Between 1495 and 1515, more than a third of the documented victims of convicted rapists in Florence were girls between the ages of six and twelve, and each year on average four boys aged twelve and under were brought to court as the victims of sodomisers. In contemporary Venice pimps regularly offered clients pre-pubescent girls to sodomise.[74] In response to such crimes, and owing, frankly, to a growing 'sodomophobia' and desire to police and control their populations, Venice in the mid-fourteenth century established the sex-crimes commission of the 'Lords of the Night', and in 1432 Florence instituted its 'Office of the Night', whose remit was confined to rooting out and punishing sodomy. Fears about the sexual criminality of young men drove the town councillors of Massa Marittima in 1444 to enact a statute 'That all those men who are twenty-five years of age and have not taken a wife are to be punished'![75]

But cities also had considerable appeal. There were more plentiful job opportunities and higher wages than those available in the countryside, and those wages could go to buy food and drink, whose variety and quality were superior to what could be found in most rural districts. Indeed, in the wake of the Black Death medieval townspeople became accustomed to eating white bread and large quantities of meat and fish, and to drinking plentiful beer, ale and wine of high quality. There was even a considerable trade in 'fast food', roasted meats and meat pies vended by cooks and pasty-makers. They also had greater access to other consumables and commodities, as well as to entertainments of various sorts. A sense of this comes through from the anonymous fifteenth-century poem 'London Lickpenny':

> Then to London I did hasten;
> Of all the land it bears the prize.
> 'Hot pea pods!' one began to cry;
> 'Ripe strawberries and cherries on the stem!'
> One bade me approach and buy some spices;
> Pepper and saffron then they offered. . . .
> Then on to Cheapside I did go,
> Where many people stood about.
> One offered me velvet, silk and linen;
> Another took me by the hand:
> 'Here is Paris thread, the finest in the land!'
> Then I went forth past London Stone,
> And all along Candlewick Street,
> Drapers immediately offered me cloth.
> Then one came up to me and cried, 'Hot sheep's feet!'
> One cried, 'Mackerel!' another 'Rushes green!'
> One invited me to buy a hood to cover my head. . . .
> Then I rushed on to Eastcheap;
> One cried, 'Ribs of beef and many a pie!'
> Pewter pots they clattered in a heap.
> There was harp, pipe and minstrelsy;
> 'Yea, by Cock! Nay, by Cock!' some began to cry. . . .
> Then I wandered into Cornhill,
> Where many stolen garments were;
> And there among them I saw my own hood,
> That I had lost among the throng.
> To buy my own hood, I thought it wrong. . . .[76]

And if living in such close quarters had its downside, it also brought considerable advantages in the way of neighbourliness and community. The centre of an urban dweller's existence was the neighbourhood. Extended family groups, as well as immigrants from the same region, and people working in the same craft often formed the demographic nucleus of a neighbourhood, while the parish church and its cemetery served as its spiritual centre and key gathering place. Denizens also gathered at taverns (mostly men), the well and bake-oven (women), and, generally, out in the street. Many artisans and shopkeepers also worked out of their homes (though this was far from universally the case), the front room on the ground floor having a shutter that opened horizontally to form a table from which wares or comestibles could be displayed and sold. The late Middle Ages, especially after the onset of the plague, saw the rise of urban parish churches to a very high level of prominence. They not only functioned as centres of religious devotion and commemoration, but wealthier denizens of the parish often established chantry chapels in them, while they and humbler heads of households joined the parish confraternity. Beyond the neighbourhood, townspeople worked and shopped at central and suburban markets, participated in guilds and religious confraternities associated with mendicant churches, and, with their neighbours and fellow parishioners, got swept up in carnival, May Day celebrations and religious processions. Given the intense sociability of the late medieval city, a certain Fra Paolino spoke well when he said of the urban dweller, 'Teach him the skill of living among many'.[77]

Such multi-layered community ties did not preclude hierarchical and professional divisions among the urban populace. Town government was in the hands of wealthy merchant patricians, who intermarried, looked after one another's interests and ruled as oligarchs. Lesser merchants and master craftsmen formed the next tier. These men acted as officers in their guilds and in some towns acted as officials in city government. Living with and working under them were their apprentices, who laboured in the hope of one day becoming masters themselves. Lower on the scale were the journeymen artisans and, finally, the petty hawkers and the poor labourers who provided the muscle for textile and other manufacturing. Cities also had their clerks, notaries and lawyers, physicians, barber surgeons and herbalists, and, where there were universities, teaching masters and students. Women too engaged in work. In northern Europe wives of merchants and artisans either assisted their husbands in the family business or managed their own enterprises. Silk textile manufacturing was a particularly feminine occupation. Paris had five women's guilds of silk workers, Cologne four. Several women also acted as entrepreneurs in the silk industry. Other women in northern cities brewed ale, baked bread, worked as midwives and even surgeons, ran taverns and inns, and sold food at market stalls. Some widows were admitted to their deceased husbands' guilds, although this practice admittedly became less common and virtually ceased during the fifteenth century. Business opportunities were far less abundant in Mediterranean Europe, though here too women worked with silk, as well as with cotton and linen. Everywhere men impeded or excluded women from the more lucrative specialisations of wool cloth manufacturing, only giving them access to the poorly paid jobs of washers, carders and spinners. Everywhere too girls and young women worked as servants, though this seems to have been more common in the north.[78] In short, the city was a place of activity, where businessmen and women, workers and professionals plied their trades. This diversification and specialisation of labour was to have a profound impact on the way people conceived of the individual. Such a diversity of useful and productive activities gave the lie to the old conception of society as composed of three orders and challenged the old predominance of clergy and nobility.

Less easy to accommodate into this new model of the individual and community were those living on the margins of urban life, the beggars and vagabonds, prostitutes and Jews. Grinding, widespread poverty was endemic to late medieval cities, making them 'hell for the poor'.[79] Many gainfully employed artisans and labourers were poor enough to be exempt from paying municipal taxes. But then there were the armies of the unemployed. On the one hand, were the 'worthy beggars' whom ecclesiastical and municipal authorities sought to help, although with limited success, by means of hospitals and almshouses; on the other, were the 'sturdy beggars' and vagabonds whose presence frightened and disgusted the better off. Victims of economic contraction, natural disaster and war, or wilful slackers and career thieves, the disparate members of this group were frequently shunned by citizens and increasingly subject to surveillance and persecution. Laws were passed in several countries authorising enforced labour for all able-bodied beggars and demanding that beggars and vagabonds register with municipal authorities. In fifteenth-century France, beggars and vagrants could be imprisoned, branded and banished. In contemporary Genoa all beggars were subject to expulsion.[80]

Like beggars, prostitutes were both tolerated and subject to control or removal by urban governments. On the Continent, there was a general tendency to become more lenient toward prostitution, especially after around 1350. Indeed many cities licensed brothels and bath-houses, or designated a given street, usually at the edge of or just outside the city walls, as a red light district (although in Siena the 'place of the prostitutes' was located right behind the City Hall); and in southern Europe especially, prostitution even began to be seen as a public good, since it gave young bachelors and 'professional celibates' (monks and priests) another target for their sexual energy besides hopeful brides-to-be, or for that matter married women and widows. In the words of Giordano of Pisa (1305–06), 'Do you see that in cities prostitutes are tolerated? This is a great evil, but if it were to be removed a great good would be eliminated, because there would be more adultery, more sodomy, which would be much worse'.[81] Bologna, with its large complement of university students, who were regular customers of brothels, even listed prostitution as an occupation in its tax survey of 1395. Official tolerance of prostitution was not forthcoming in England, however, although this did nothing to dampen its practice; public authorities there treated it as an 'offence of common nuisance'.[82] It was not unheard of for poor unmarried women labourers to engage in prostitution in order to supplement their meagre wages. Even impoverished married women occasionally engaged in prostitution, with their husbands sometimes acting as their pimps.[83] Doubtless many women entered the sex trade of their own volition, but others were duped or kidnapped into the white slave trade. This was the case of one Johanna, a young woman who in 1385 sought work in London with one Elizabeth, who:

> under color of the craft of embroidery, which she pretended to follow took in and retained Johanna and diverse other women as her apprentices and bound them to serve her after the manner of apprentices in such art. Whereas, the truth of the matter was that she did not follow that craft, but that, after retaining them, she incited Johanna and the other women who were with her, and in her service, to live a lewd life and to consort with friars, chaplains, and all other such men as desired to have their company, as well in her own house . . . as elsewhere, she retaining in her own possession the sum so agreed upon.[84]

In late fifteenth-century Burgundy, a fourteen-year-old girl named Jehanne, having just lost her mother, was put into service by her father with the proprietor of a roast meat shop in Dijon. After being raped she was induced by another young woman to lodge with a woman named Jambe de Fer (Iron Leg), who gave them employment working in the vineyards. Unknown, apparently, to Jehanne, however, Jambe de Fer's female lodgers were also expected to perform sexual services, so that one day when she

> went down from the city and over the moat . . . she was immediately hunted by the young men of the city, who pursued her so that she began to give them the pleasure of her body. And she could not name them except for a carpenter who she said was the son of Mongin the Carpenter, who brought with him other companions by night to the house of Jambe de Fer . . .[85]

While prostitution was viewed as a kind of necessary evil by both secular and ecclesiastical officials, prostitutes were nonetheless despised and 'subjected to humiliating laws', like having 'to wear eye-catching items of clothing such as red hats, ribbons on the sleeves or sleeves of contrasting colour to their robes'. And although they could attend church services, they were kept separate from other parishioners.[86] By the very end of the Middle Ages, however, official attitudes toward prostitution began to harden. Early signs of this can be seen in the puritanical (and very likely Lollard) legislation enacted by Coventry's city council in the 1490s, that not only banned all prostitutes from the city but also all tapsters (barmaids) and other women of ill repute. Municipal authorities all over Europe began to restrict prostitution after 1500, and by the mid-sixteenth century, under the influence of Protestantism, most cities shut down their brothels altogether.[87]

Like prostitutes, Jews too were restricted to certain areas of late medieval cities and increasingly were forced to wear identifying markings of various kinds (e.g. yellow badges, hats or circles, or, for women, yellow veils or hooped earrings).[88] Unlike prostitutes, however, they were not infrequently the victims of murderous violence. Yet between these outbursts of violence Jews lived and worked in many medieval cities, acting as money-changers and money-lenders, pawn brokers, petty merchants, and physicians. It must be said, however, that from around the beginning of the fifteenth century municipal, royal and ecclesiastical authorities increasingly either expelled their Jewish communities or segregated them, whether by banning all interaction between Christians and Jews or forcing them to live in an enclosed quarter.[89] In the eyes of these officials, Jews, like prostitutes threatened the moral health of Christian society. Hence the language used by the magistrates of Brescia in northern Italy when they ordered the expulsion of their Jewish community in 1494:

> While the Christian Church may tolerate the Jews, it has in no way decreed that they have to be tolerated in Brescia; they should be treated as public prostitutes, who because of their filth are tolerated [only] while they live in a brothel. In like manner should those Jews live their stinking life in some stinking place, separate from Christians.[90]

Notes

1 Menut 1970: 49 (my translation).
2 Nederman 1990: 67.
3 Duby 1980.
4 Oexle 2001: 94.
5 Fowler, Briggs and Remley 1997: 7–8 (my modernisation).
6 Fowler, Briggs and Remley 1997: 12–13, 291–92.
7 Fowler, Briggs and Remley 1997: 150–57, 386.
8 Fowler, Briggs and Remley 1997: 148–49.
9 Fowler, Briggs and Remley 1997: 164.
10 Brett 2005: 15–17.
11 Brett 2005: 22–23.
12 Fourquin 1978: 45.
13 Forhan 1994.
14 Fowler, Briggs and Remley 1997: 170–73.
15 Fowler, Briggs and Remley 1997: 206–8, 245–49.
16 Blythe 1997: 234.
17 Brett 2005: 67, 345.
18 Blamires 1992: 167.

19 Blamires 1992: 249.
20 Blamires 1992: 284.
21 Blamires 1992: 281.
22 Blamires 1992: 285.
23 Blamires 1992: 292.
24 Blamires 1992: 295–96.
25 Klapisch-Zuber 2000: 143.
26 Bennett 1987: 8.
27 Herlihy 1985: 80–81.
28 Bennett 1987: 91–95; Ribordy 2004.
29 Biller 1992.
30 Ribordy 2004.
31 Biller 1992: 67.
32 Biller 1991.
33 Watkins 1969: 114.
34 Klapisch-Zuber 1990: 298.
35 Watkins 1969: 110.
36 Klapisch-Zuber 1990: 298.
37 Ross 1974: 5–7: Ward 2002: 52.
38 Brucker and Martinas 1967.
39 Bennett 1987: 115.
40 Biller 1992: 70–75.
41 Smith 1992: 39–40; Klapisch-Zuber 1990: 301.
42 Bennett 1987: 143.
43 Allmand 1992: 9; Orme 2001: 17.
44 Fossier 1986: 56.
45 Le Goff 1980: 118–19.
46 Contamine 1998: 95–96.
47 Morsel 2001.
48 Contamine 1998: 91.
49 Contamine 1998: 103.
50 Harriss 2005: 97.
51 Keen 1984: 231–32; Fowler 1998: 131.
52 Harriss 2005: 177–78, 411–12.
53 Contamine 1998: 103.
54 Keen 2000: 117
55 Hilton 1975: 13.
56 Fossier 1986: 43.
57 Bennett 1996.
58 Hanawalt 1986.
59 Dyer 1998: 114–15.
60 Leguay 2000: 108; Prevenier 1983: 259.
61 Herlihy and Klapisch-Zuber 1985: 69; Dyer 2002: 300.
62 Herlihy 1990: 130.
63 Harriss 2005: 298.
64 Harriss 2005: 309.
65 Herlihy and Klapisch-Zuber 1985: 28.
66 Rossiaud 1990: 159.
67 Leguay 2000: 108; Harriss 2005: 299.
68 Rossiaud 1990: 156.
69 Dean 2001: 23; Leguay 2000: 112.
70 Dean 2001: 1–2.
71 Kowaleski 2006: 309.
72 Rashdall 1936: vol. 3, 96–99; Leff 1968, 90–91.
73 Dean 2000: 185–87.
74 Rocke 1998: 163–64.

75 Mormando 1999: 158–60.
76 Tyrrell and Nicolas 1827: 266–67 (my modernisation).
77 Rossiaud 1990: 141.
78 Herlihy 1990; Howell 1986.
79 Fossier 1986: 100.
80 Mollat 1986: 291.
81 Rocke 1998: 159.
82 Rees Jones 2001: 129.
83 Herlihy 1990: 157–58.
84 Kowaleski 2006: 231–32.
85 Kowaleski 2006: 346–47.
86 Shahar 2003: 206–10.
87 Goldberg 2001: 105–7; Rocke 1998: 160–61; Otis 1985: 40–45.
88 Hughes 1986.
89 Fossier 1986: 451; Mormando 1999: 200–8; Haverkamp 1995: 13–28.
90 Hughes 2004: 117–18.

3

TRADE, TECHNOLOGY AND EXPLORATION

Working only six hours a day, perhaps you may think they cannot produce enough of the necessaries of life. But, on the contrary, it is more than enough to provide abundance of necessities and comforts. You will realize that this is so, if you consider for a moment how many people in this country are idle. . . . Altogether you will find that it is the labour of much fewer people than you thought which produces the necessary supplies for the whole nation.

Again, consider how few workers are providing necessities. Where money is plentiful many profitless and superfluous occupations must needs be encouraged, to cater to profligate waste and wanton pleasure. If all the present workers were restricted to necessary occupations. . . . [and if] to the number of those now profitably employed you add all those who are at present idle – each of whom wastes more than two workers do – you easily perceive how few hours daily would be required to produce the national store of necessities and comforts.[1]

Through these words of the imaginary Portuguese explorer/philosopher Raphael Hythlodaeus, Thomas More in his *Utopia* (1516) expresses some fundamental truths of the late medieval economy: that it was fully commercialised and driven by the demand for luxury goods as well as the need to produce 'all the articles that mortals require for daily use'. More's fictional satire also exemplifies, in its setting and subject, some important developments in trade and exploration. The purported meeting of More and Hythlodaeus occurs during an English diplomatic mission to Bruges and Antwerp, the fading and rising commercial stars of northern Europe, and close trading partners with England. Hythlodaeus (whose name means 'dispenser of nonsense'), appears to be one of those members of the Portuguese lesser nobility who so often participated in the fifteenth- and early sixteenth-century Atlantic voyages. We are told, moreover, that he accompanied the Florentine merchant explorer in at various times Castilian or Portuguese employ, Amerigo Vespucci, 'in three voyages of the four that are now in print, and in everyone's hands'.[2] Electing to remain in Brazil during the final voyage, Hythlodaeus and some companions explored the more southerly reaches of South America and then took to sea, sailing with the prevailing westerlies they made their way, like Vasco da Gama in 1497–98, through the South Atlantic, around the Cape of Good Hope, and then on to southwest India. Somewhere in the South Atlantic, however, they took a detour from reality and visited the island commonwealth of Utopia. But Utopia itself, although fantastic, reflected a long-held desire on the part of Europeans in general, but of Englishmen even more particularly, to discover the legendary island of Brasil. Although by the time More wrote *Utopia* few probably still held out hope of finding Brasil, that very hope had played a large part in stimulating the merchants of Bristol to launch a series of expeditions into the north Atlantic between 1480 and 1498, the last of which, with the backing of King Henry VII, were led by the Venetian merchant John Cabot.

No doubt real European noble and merchant explorers, bent on finding gold and making reputations, would have disputed Hythlodaeus' raillery against money and pride; even More, at least in the persona he adopted in *Utopia*, objected that the absence of money 'alone utterly overthrows all the nobility, magnificence, splendor, and majesty which are, in the estimation of the common people, the true glories and ornaments of the commonwealth'.[3] Their attitude was likely much closer to that of the merchant of Ragusa (Dubrovnik), Benedetto Cotrugli who, in his *On Commerce and the Perfect Merchant* (1458), provides a pretty fair description of the activities and relationships involved in trade during the late Middle Ages:

> The dignity and office of merchants is great and exalted in many respects. . . . First, with respect to the common weal. For the advancement of public welfare is a very honorable [purpose]. . . . The advancement, the comfort, and the health of republics to a large extent proceed from merchants; we are always speaking, of course, not of plebeian and vulgar merchants but of the glorious merchant of whom we treat [and who is] lauded in this work of ours. . . . Through trade, that ornament and advancement [of republics], sterile countries are provided with food and supplies and also enjoy many strange things which are imported from places where [other] commodities are lacking. [Merchants] also bring about an abundance of money, jewels, gold, silver, and all kinds of metals. They bring about an abundance of gilds of various crafts. Hence, cities and countries are driven to cultivate the land, to enlarge the herds, and to exploit the incomes and rents. And [merchants] through their activity enable the poor to live; through their initiative in tax farming they promote the activity of administrators; through their exports and imports of merchandise they cause the customs and excises of the lords and republics to expand, and consequently they enlarge the public and common treasury.[4]

An economic crisis?

Over the past few decades historians have spilt considerable quantities of ink debating whether or not the late Middle Ages amounted to a gloomy time in the history of the European economy. For those who agree that it was a bad time, there is still plenty of disagreement over when things declined and why, and when and why they got better. The problem with these arguments is that they are based even now, after extensive research on everything from prices and wages to manufacturing processes and trade routes, on limited and spotty data; these data, moreover, not only lend themselves to widely different interpretations, their import is frequently contradictory or simply incomparable. Moreover, trying to make blanket assertions about the economy of all Latin Christendom, with all its tremendous diversity, smoothes over or ignores the considerable differences in local economies as well as rates and kinds of change in different locales. Still, the fact remains that for all their differences, the localities of Latin Christendom all participated at some level in a highly integrated trade and communications network, and this network extended beyond Europe to Asia and Africa. Thus before describing this trade and its development over the late Middle Ages, it seems prudent to establish a general chronological framework and identify the basic factors and forces at play.

There is now a general consensus supporting the view that after a period of tremendous growth over the course of the twelfth and thirteenth centuries (the so-called Commercial Revolution) the European economy contracted in the late Middle Ages. Not surprisingly, the chief cause of this contraction was the precipitous population decline and long-term demographic stagnation occasioned by epidemic disease. Population decline not only diminished the production and trade of bulk goods, most especially grain, but also, at least temporarily, the expenditure of elites on luxuries, owing to a decline in their landed income from lower rents and higher wages. The spices and silks which were the most highly coveted of luxuries from the East also became more expensive with the collapse of the Mongol empire, with its relatively liberal trade policies, over the course of the 1330s and 1340s and the takeover of the Levant by the Mamluk sultanate, and of Asia Minor by the Ottoman Turks, whose rulers imposed stiff trade tariffs. Within Europe itself the endemic warfare of the fourteenth and early fifteenth century also took its toll on trade. For warfare not only disrupted agricultural production, it also raised the cost of doing business by disrupting trade routes, forcing merchants to protect their cargoes from pirates and brigands, and causing warring states to resort to all sorts of fiscal measures, like debasement of coinage, forced loans and high taxes. There is also every reason to believe that the amount of money – that is, of gold and silver in currency – was virtually stagnant, and may even have shrunk somewhat, from the 1370s, until just after the middle of the fifteenth century.

It is not necessarily the case, however, that this decades-long contraction of trade was attended by widespread and severe economic depression. What contracted, after all, was the total volume of trade. What is less clear is whether or not per capita consumption declined, rose, or remained steady. After all, we have already seen that after the Black Death, and particularly from the 1370s until the mid-fifteenth century, living standards, and thus consumption, generally improved for rural and urban labourers. Also, as we shall see below, impediments to the eastern trade in high-quality silk and cotton textiles encouraged the growth of domestic substitution industries. And even war had its upside for certain sectors of the economy like mining, arms manufacturing and even banking. Nor did the stagnation of the money supply necessarily entail a depressed economy, since the effects of a limited supply of precious metals were partly offset by adjustments in the value of specie, the decline in volume of trade, and the development and use of various banking techniques and credit instruments. Therefore although economic growth and commercial activity suffered a temporary setback in the middle decades of the fourteenth century, the attendant quantitative changes in production and consumption also caused qualitative changes in the patterns of supply and demand. The years of contraction, then, were a time during which there was, on the one hand, considerable modification, innovation and refinement in the way business was done and, on the other, a growing demand on the part of consumers for more and better goods. Eventually, starting in about the 1460s, thanks to the cumulative effects of these changes combined with technological improvements and the discovery of new sources of silver and gold, the period of contraction gave way to one of renewed expansion. And this expansionary phase proved to be more than economic, since it included the discovery and exploitation of new sources of wealth and power which were the fruits of overseas exploration.

Trade and technology

If we can detect three separate phases in the history of trade in the late Middle Ages, this in no way implies that the discontinuities outweighed the continuities. First, throughout the late Middle Ages the principal motivator of trade was consumer demand, and the consumers who most influenced trade belonged to the lay and clerical elites, acting both as individuals and as the directing forces of the institutions of Church and state. The elite's taste for luxuries, whether food and drink, clothing, furnishing and ornamentation, or buildings, and the demands of governments, both secular and ecclesiastical, to fund wars and fuel their ostentatious displays of power and patronage, drove production and unleashed huge sums of capital. Second, Latin Christendom participated in a highly integrated and interdependent trade and commercial network, whose chief routes, products, basic technologies and business practices were already in place in 1300. The story of the late medieval economy, then, is not one of revolutionary (or catastrophic) change, but rather of a gradual evolution and transformation in response to changing circumstances. These developments, however, led, over the course of more than two centuries, to a far more 'modernised', capitalised and muscular economy poised to exploit and eventually to dominate world trade.

The European trade network at the start of the fourteenth century comprised many regional trade networks, in each of which goods were produced for both regional and interregional consumer markets. Likewise, local markets sold locally produced goods as well as a selection of commodities obtained from a distance. The bulk of regional commerce was, of course, conducted in market towns and at regional fairs, which centres of commerce were themselves connected either directly or through intermediaries to the great international commercial cities and fairs where goods of European, Asian and African origin were bought and sold, and financial services conducted. Although closely interlinked, this trade network was principally built to serve a densely settled urban band, shaped somewhat like a banana, which stretched from central Italy in the south to London in the north, and encompassed the cities of Lombardy, southwest Germany and the Rhône valley, the Rhineland, Flanders and Brabant. Paris, as the largest city in western Christendom, constituted the most important outlier of this band, while the cities of northern Italy and Flanders formed its magnetic poles. A secondary urban band ran along the edge of the Mediterranean from Genoa through Provence, Languedoc and Catalonia, and terminated in Valencia.[5]

Although most local trade moved overland, the poor condition of roads, frequency of tolls, threat of brigandage and limited payloads of carts, made overland travel slow, hazardous and prohibitively expensive for long-distance shipping of low-value bulk goods. The seas, therefore, became the preferred routes for long-distance and bulk trade; and Europe, being bounded by water on three sides, was especially conducive to seaborne travel. The Mediterranean was the busiest of the water routes, owing to the comings and goings of large bulk traders, chiefly operated by the Genoese and Venetians, supplying grain and other foodstuffs to the populous and hungry cities of northern Italy, and engaging in the Black Sea, Levantine and North African trade in search of spices, silks, ivory, gold and, increasingly, slaves. This busy commerce was reflected as in a glass darkly by the movement of goods in the Baltic, where, by one estimate, the volume of trade was between one-fifth and one-tenth as great as that of the Mediterranean.[6] The Atlantic and North Sea belong to the third and final zone, where a vigorous trade in wool was maintained between England and Flanders, and in wine between Bordeaux and England. The Baltic and Atlantic trade zones were, not surprisingly, closely interlinked, especially via the Flemish city of Bruges. But by the close of the thirteenth century, a considerable amount of seaborne trade also was being conducted between the Mediterranean and Atlantic, thanks to a combination of technological improvements in shipbuilding and the kingdom of Castile's wresting from Muslim control the Iberian Atlantic ports of Seville (1248) and Cadiz (1265). Here again, Bruges became the chief

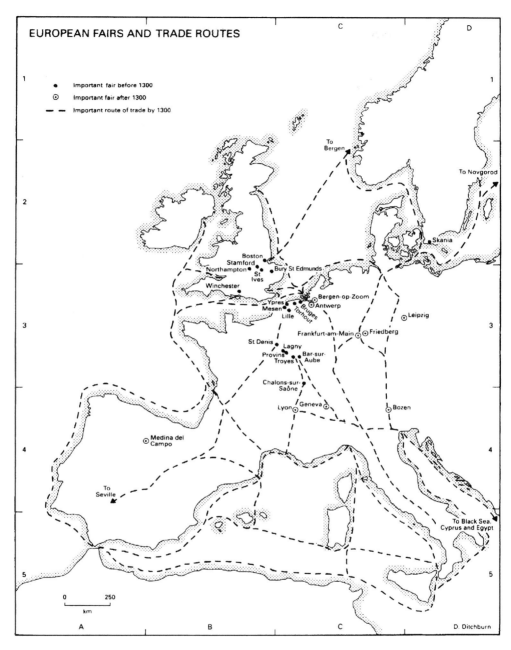

Map 3.1 European fairs and trade routes, taken from *The Atlas of Medieval Europe,* 2nd Edition, © 2007, Routledge. Reproduced by permission of Taylor & Francis books UK

entrepôt for trade between north and south, taking the place of the old Champagne fairs as the centre of trade and banking for all northern Europe.

Bulk goods made up most of the tonnage carried in ships' holds. Grain was the chief foodstuff of Mediterranean trade, especially prior to the great mortality of the mid-fourteenth century. Genoese ships moved grain grown in southern Italy and Sicily, as well as from Andalusia, Greece, North Africa and the Black Sea to the crowded urban centres of Tuscany and to Genoa itself.[7] This trade was so considerable and so regular that the four Florentine 'super-companies' of the Bardi, Peruzzi, Acciaiuoli and Buonaccorsi, whose activities ranged from woollen textile production to international banking, nonetheless made most of their profits from the grain trade. Likewise the disruption of this trade from the many bad harvests of the late 1320s through the 1340s deserve most of the blame for the spectacular collapse of these great enterprises in the 1340s, although Edward III of England's decision to renege on paying off his enormous debts to the Bardi and Peruzzi also had something to do with these companies' demise.[8] Although the Mediterranean grain trade contracted after the Black Death, it continued to be important, as northern Italians still needed imported wheat for their bread and pasta. Like Tuscany, the cities of densely populated Flanders relied on grain shipped by German Hanseatic merchants from the eastern Baltic (the Hanse was a commercial confederation). Although population decline decreased the need for imported grain for bread, the growth of the brewing industry in the Netherlands in the later fourteenth and fifteenth centuries kept demand high for imported grain. Beer made its way from the breweries of Hamburg and Bremen to the Netherlands; and once the cities of Holland had developed their own brewing industry in the early fifteenth century, casks of beer were shipped from Holland to Flanders, Brabant and England. As the fifteenth century wore on, Brabant and England became major beer producers as well.

Despite the growing popularity of beer in northern Europe, wine remained the most sought-after beverage in France, southern Germany and the Mediterranean countries, while considerable quantities of wine continued to be shipped to Britain, northern Germany and the Low Countries. From its principal port of Bordeaux, Gascony sent out approximately 80,000,000 litres of wine per year during the first third of the fourteenth century.[9] And although the Gascon wine trade suffered terribly from the depredations of English and French armies during the Hundred Years War, the vineyards of the Loire valley and Burgundy more than replaced this deficit for the French, while the English and Flemings turned to Andalusian, Portuguese and Rhenish wines. In the Mediterranean, the chief wine exporting centres, in addition to Seville in Andalusia, were Naples and Genoa, in the west, and Candia on the island of Crete, in the east. In the second half of the fifteenth century, moreover, the new fortified wines of Jerez (sherry) became popular, as well as the malmseys being cultivated on the newly settled island of Madeira. Here two things about the wine and beer trade need stressing. First, the growing demand for wine and beer contributed substantially to the shift from the cultivation of food to cash crops in the late Middle Ages – grapes, of course, in the case of wine, and hops for beer. Second, this demand not only affected the quantities produced, but also quality and portability. We see this with Duke Philip the Bold of Burgundy's efforts to produce better wines, beginning c. 1395, and in the displacement of locally brewed ales by imported and long-lasting hopped beers and the growing popularity of fortified Candia, Jerez and Madeira wines.[10]

The demands of food preparation and preservation guaranteed a flourishing and consistent market for salt and olive oil. Although salt for purely local use was obtained from salt marshes and brine wells throughout Europe, the need for salt as a preservative for fish and meat, and in the preparation of butter and cheese drove a vast international salt trade. In the Mediterranean the Venetians collected enormous quantities of salt from salt pans along the Adriatic coast, which they sold to the cities of Lombardy. Their efforts were matched by the Genoese who vended salt from Ibiza, Sardinia and the south French coast to the Papal States, Naples and Savoy, and even threatened the Venetian monopoly in Lombardy. Along the Atlantic coast, vast salt pans in the Bay of Bourgneuf satisfied demand in western and northern France, England and even the Low Countries. Nor were eastern France and the German-speaking lands inadequately supplied, since they drew on the prolific salt mines and brine wells at Salins in Franche-Comté, Hall and Hallein in Austria, Halle and Lüneburg in northeast Germany, and Wielicza in Poland. Lüneburg salt was intimately connected to another important bulk food commodity, salted fish. From Lüneburg, the salt made its way by barge to Hamburg and Lübeck (indeed the latter city built a thirty-mile long canal just for this purpose), whence it travelled in Hanseatic cogs to Bergen in Norway for the preparation of salt-cod and to Scania in southern Sweden for pickling herring. At times the salt-fish industry demanded so much salt, that despite Lüneburg's annual production of some 15,000 tons, additional salt had to be obtained from the Bay of Bourgneuf.[11] In the Mediterranean, olive oil performed much the same role as salt for preserving barrels of tuna. In fact, olive oil was used for everything from cooking and food preservation to the making of highly prized hard white soap, the oiling of washed wool and the tawing of leather. Nor was the demand for olive oil confined to southern Europe. The English, for example, not only used old olive oil for industrial applications but evinced a strong preference for new olive oil in cooking.[12]

As far-ranging and impressive as was the trade in bulk foodstuffs and related commodities, the textile industry constituted the most complex and interconnected sector of the late medieval economy. In terms of volume and complexity, the woollen textile industry held pride of place. At the beginning of our period, the Flemish cities of Ghent and Ypres, in the north, and Florence, in the south, were the dominant manufacturers of both fine and cheap woollens. England was the chief source of high-quality raw wool, while Spain provided the bulk of cheap raw wool. Over the course of the fourteenth century, however, the English developed a native wool cloth industry, largely in response to heavy export duties imposed on raw wool by King Edward III. Another important change occurred when, in the later fourteenth century, Spanish shepherds began raising merino sheep, imported from North Africa. The extremely fine quality of merino wool rivalled that of England's flocks, and gave Florentine textile producers a new source of supply as they shifted the balance of their capacity to the manufacturing of high-quality woollens, leaving more of the production of cheap cloth to the cities of Lombardy. The Low Countries remained the centre for wool textile manufactures in the north, but dominance passed from Flanders to the Brabantine cities of Brussels, Louvain and Antwerp in the middle of the fourteenth century, and then increasingly to smaller towns in Flanders and Brabant, as well as the cities and smaller towns of Holland. The English wool industry was almost entirely confined to small towns and even rural villages. By far, then, the vast preponderance of cloth made for export as well as high-quality cloth came from the Low Countries, northern Italy and England (from the late fourteenth century), although consumer demand for cheaper cloth was also met by manufactures from Perpignan at the eastern edge of the Pyrenees and Wrocław (Breslau) in Silesia.

From bleating sheep to finished cloth, woollens manufacturing involved many steps, each of which was performed by specialists. When it arrived at the warehouse, raw wool first had to be sorted, beaten, cleaned and then, frequently, re-oiled (usually with old olive oil). From there it went out to be combed or carded, depending on the grade of wool; this wool then was distributed to countless numbers of women, often in the countryside, to be spun (hence the expression 'spinster'). By the fourteenth century, most wool was spun on mechanical spinning wheels, although the finer quality wools continued to be spun on the distaff and drop spindle. The yarn was then distributed to weavers, who were almost universally men, and who owned, or hired to purchase, their looms (and looms were quite expensive). A weaver and his assistants (who might well be his wife and children) produced on average one cloth between 30 and 40 metres long over the course of about two weeks. The cloths then made their way to the fullers, where they were soaked in a mixture of water and fullers' earth, and then beaten, usually by the trip-hammers of a water-driven fulling mill, although, in the case of the finest woollens, by hand (or feet). Once fulled, the now damp and felted cloth had to be stretched (tentering), dried and rolled. These unfinished cloths would then normally be finished through a process of napping and shearing, to produce a smooth cloth. It was usually at this stage that cloths were dyed, although some cloths were made from already dyed wool, and patterned cloths were woven from dyed yarns. Owing to the high level of skill required and the cost of materials (dyes and mordant), this was the most costly phase in the manufacturing process. Some dyes, like woad (a blue dye), did not need to be fixed with mordant (alum), but most did, including madder, for red, and 'grain' (derived from a kind of louse), for the whole range of expensive 'scarlets', from brilliant vermilions to browns and even blue-blacks.

The production of woollen textiles, then, involved multitudes of workers of both sexes (women not only spun but did most of the carding and combing), many of whom were highly skilled specialists. So labour intensive was it, that during the 1330s the merchant and chronicler Giovanni Villani reckoned nearly one-third of the population of Florence was involved in wool cloth production. If this seems an exaggeration, we know from recent studies that a quarter of Salisbury's inhabitants were engaged in wool cloth manufacturing in the 1370s, 39 per cent of Bruges's in 1316, and a clear majority in both Ghent and Ypres, with 59 per cent in the former in 1356–58 and between 48 and 64 per cent in Ypres in 1412.[13] The organisation of all these disparate activities was in the hands of the wool merchants, entrepreneurs who bought the raw wool, saw it through all stages of production, and then sold the finished and dyed product. Given their profit motive, these entrepreneurs tried to keep production costs to a minimum while at the same time keeping a close eye on maintaining quality. The move in both the Netherlands and England to small town and village sites was likely a cost-cutting measure, since this helped entrepreneurs keep wages lower and avoided strikes or more violent actions organised by urban workers. Mechanisation, where feasible, also helped keep operating costs down. But notice here that when high quality was the goal, the preference was still for work done by hand (as in spinning and fulling). Also, despite the fact that some workshops were fairly large (some weavers, for example, had multiple looms) and workers increasingly were expected to work by the clock, we are still a long way from any kind of factory system here. Finally, every effort was made to minimise the cost of dyes and alum. The most common dyes, woad and madder, were grown in Europe, and thus relatively cheap, although they fetched their growers a much higher price per hectare than any type of grain. Other dyes, however, like Brazil wood, indigo and 'grain' (a derivative of the insect *Kermes vermilio*), were very costly, the first two because they came from India and Ceylon and the last because it was labour-intensive to gather and prepare. Alum – a commodity over which the Genoese had a near monopoly – was expensive because it had to be shipped in bulk from the mines at Phocaea in Asia Minor. To lower costs the Genoese used larger and larger ships, with the largest three-masted carracks reaching 800 to 1,000 tons in

Figure 3.1 Dyeing fabric. Photograph: Arterra Picture Library / Alamy Stock Photo

the fifteenth century. The Ottoman seizure of the Phocaea mines in 1455 raised the price of alum considerably, but fortunately temporarily, since a new source was found at Tolfa near Rome in 1460.

If wool was the king of late medieval textiles, the fourteenth and fifteenth centuries witnessed a growing, indeed accelerating, trade in silk, cotton, linen and the linen-cotton blend 'fustian'. Behind this growth one can perceive several trends. The first was an increase in per capita consumption of both luxury and more modestly priced goods, much of which was clothing, but also tapestries, carpets and other furnishings. The late Middle Ages was a time of lavishly conspicuous consumption and display: one need only look at the sumptuous dress and furnishings depicted in manuscript illuminations and paintings, as well as the surviving artefacts themselves, to see this. But the improved living standards of middling sorts in the wake of the plague also spurred their consumption of more and better goods. Thus, just as merchants and better-off artisan masters began to ape their 'betters', sparking off sumptuary legislation in some cases, so too did a new taste for creature comforts, like cotton and linen undergarments, play into this trend. On the production side of things, landowners were only too happy to convert land to the growing of cash crops, whether flax cultivated in Swabia, northern France and the Low Countries, cotton in Sicily and southern Italy, Malta, Cyprus and Crete, or mulberry bushes in Sicily, southern Italy and Andalusia. Finally, in the case of cotton, and more especially silk, growing demand and rising costs of raw and finished material from Asia and Egypt promoted substitution production, whether that meant growing cotton, practising sericulture, or setting up or expanding cotton and silk textile industries.

Although Europe never lost its taste for imported silk textiles, a thriving silk industry had already established itself in Lucca during the thirteenth century. By the start of the fourteenth century Lucchese silk workers (many of them women) and merchants had established the industry in Bologna and Venice. By the early 1500s, each city boasted some 25,000 workers employed in the industry. The same development occurred in Florence in the first half of the 1300s, and by 1462 the value of its annual silk production amounted to 300,000 florins.[14] On a lesser scale, but still important, were the silk industries in Paris and Cologne. Although European-made silks were imitations of Middle Eastern and Chinese models, they attained an extremely high level of quality and beauty, eventually rivalling those of imports. Already in the thirteenth century Lombardy had established itself as the centre of cotton textile production, and throughout the fourteenth and fifteenth centuries it would continue to be, along with neighbouring cities in the River Po basin, in Emiglia, the Romagna and the Veneto; moreover many of these same cities manufactured linen and fustian cloths as well. Linens and fustian also became a specialty of the cities of Swabia, while linen textiles were churned out in a broad swath of cities and towns running from Artois through the southern Low Countries and on into Westphalia. The very finest linens, however, were those of Champagne which, with the best quality woollens, were the only commodities that European merchants regularly exported to the Levant. These industries were organised much like the woollen industry, with entrepreneurs 'putting out' the material with specialists at each stage of production. In the case of silk and cotton, there was also some effort to lower costs through mechanisation, as in the case of the water-powered silk-throwing machine, one of which, in Lucca, employed 480 spindles driven by an undershot waterwheel.[15] Likewise the spinning wheel was universally employed for the making of cotton thread, since its use did not compromise the quality of cotton cloth. Linen's growing popularity, moreover, had an added fringe benefit in that a healthy trade in used and discarded linen clothing fuelled an ever-expanding paper industry, beginning in northern Italy in the 1200s, then spreading into France, Swabia and the southern Low Countries in the fourteenth century, and continuing on to Austria and England in the fifteenth (see Chapter 10).

Hungry for precious metals with which to make specie and luxury objects, lead for pewter and building supplies, and, above all, iron and copper for weapons and tools, Latin Christendom devoted considerable energy and ingenuity to finding, extracting, and fashioning metals. The staggering amount of gold and silver required to compensate for Europe's trade imbalance with the Muslim world and China, and to satisfy the fiscal demands, chiefly arising from warfare, of centralising states, compelled the never-ending search of merchants and princes for seams of precious-metal bearing ores. The bullion shortages of the first half of the fifteenth century also spurred advances in mining technology, with the application of horse- and water-driven water pumps and ventilation bellows, and of new, more efficient ways to remove silver from lead and copper ores. Even the invention of the moveable-type printing press by the goldsmith Johannes Gutenberg and his associates in Mainz c. 1450 can be regarded as a byproduct of advances in metalworking expertise. War demanded iron and bronze (from copper and tin) for artillery and projectiles, and steel for edged weapons, crossbows and armour. Despite iron ore being plentiful and widespread in Europe, war's insatiable thirst drove the development of the mechanised ore-crushing mill, the blast furnace (1384), to make cast iron, and the tilt-hammer forge, for wrought iron. Much of this iron made its way to the armourers of Lombardy who fashioned both mass-produced armour for foot soldiers and men-at-arms, and expensive fitted suits of articulated plate armour and chain mail for well-to-do knights; by the end of the fourteenth century, demand for arms and armour was so heavy that a thriving industry grew up in the cities of Swabia, and especially in Nuremberg. Bronze casting improved in response to demands for better cannon, and orders flooded in to the bronze casters of Dinant (until its destruction in 1466), Namur and Mechelen.

Metalworking also responded, however, to growing consumer demand for table- and housewares. Thanks to their access to copper and propinquity to mines of zinc-bearing calamine, Dinant, Namur and Mechelen were also major producers of brassware. And if cheap pottery was manufactured for local use wherever clay was to be found, the deluxe tin-glazed majolica ware of Majorca, Andalusia and Faenza found its way to wealthy purchasers throughout Christendom. Liberally endowed with high-silica sand and graced with a virtual monopoly on the importation of the finest soda ash from Syria, the Venetians also monopolised the production of high-quality glassware throughout the late Middle Ages. From their glassworks on the island of Murano, they exported not only the very finest glassware to points throughout Europe, and even to Egypt and the Levant, but also clear glass for the making of spectacles (invented in the 1280s) and mirrors, and, starting in the fifteenth century, crystal. Bohemia also became a leading exporter of fine glass, starting in the second half of the fourteenth century, and served markets throughout central and northeastern Europe.

All this trade and industry devoured wood at an alarming rate. Timber was, of course, needed for shipbuilding and for the superstructures of buildings and fortresses. Wooden beams shored up mines and formed the skeletons of all manner of machines as well as the engines of war; and wine, beer, pickled herrings and innumerable other items were shipped in wooden casks. But wood was consumed most prolifically in the form of fuel. Firewood heated homes, evaporated brine, and fired soap vats, baker's ovens, breweries and pottery kilns. Even more frightful, however, was the toll taken by the insatiable hunger for charcoal. For every 50 kilos of iron produced, some 25 cubic metres of wood had to be burned; 'Let us imagine a furnace repeating this action every day in a forested countryside furnishing 100 cubic metres per hectare: in 40 days all the wood for a kilometre all round would be exhausted'.[16] Armourers went through vast quantities of charcoal, but glassmakers consumed even more. Little wonder, then, that Venice managed to strip the forests not only of its own hinterland but also of Dalmatia.[17] Pit-coal, although too full of impurities for the forging of steel, did begin during the late Middle Ages to see heavy use in home heating, iron forging and several other industrial applications. Still, its use was confined to northwest Europe, since only the coalfields of Newcastle and Liège were situated close enough to water for cost-effective transport, and then only along the North Sea and – although only secondarily – Baltic routes. Peat was another fuel, but had limited uses owing to its low burning temperature. It also was used only in the vicinity of peatbogs, since it, like coal, was far too heavy to be worth transporting over any distance.

If bulk goods like grain, wine and beer, wool, timber, metals and alum filled the holds and gave ballast to the great cogs and carracks that plied the seas around Europe, what made long-distance trade so profitable were the super high-value items whose price far exceeded their dimensions and weight: furs, silks, tapestries, spices, gems and pearls, gold, ivory and slaves. Most furs came to Europe from Russia by way of the Baltic and Black Sea, although Ireland too was a major source for marten skins and Bougie in North Africa exported the prized black lamb fleeces, called 'budge'. Silks and tapestries from the East continued to be sought-after items throughout the late Middle Ages, although a considerable part of this demand was met increasingly by output from domestic substitution industries. When medieval people spoke of spices, they meant not only the culinary spices we think of today, but many other foods, chief among them sugar and dried fruits, as well as medicines (e.g. rhubarb root and borax) and aromatics (e.g. camphor and frankincense), and even cotton, alum, dyestuffs and gems. Of the culinary spices, pepper and ginger – although still quite expensive by weight – were the cheapest and most used. Sugar also was in great demand and therefore was shipped in considerable bulk; and unlike the culinary spices, almost all of which had to be bought from Muslim merchants in Alexandria and the ports of the Levant, sugarcane cultivation and sugar refining became a preoccupation of European entrepreneurs. Because sugarcane requires a full twelve-month growing period, it could only be cultivated in the far southern reaches of Latin Christendom. The Venetians controlled much of the sugar trade in the fourteenth century, bringing sugarcane from Cyprus and Crete, and refining it in Venice. The Genoese also got in on the act, growing sugarcane in Sicily and, then, southern Portugal, but really striking it rich as partners with the Portuguese in Madeira. By the last two decades of the fifteenth century so much sugarcane was being cultivated on Madeira and the Cape Verde Islands, and by the Genoese and Castilians in the Canaries, that the price of sugar collapsed and it became a common household sweetener, replacing honey.[18]

Like culinary spices, ivory, precious and semi-precious gemstones and pearls originated in Asia (and most of these from India and Ceylon). So valuable were they (and easy to transport) that Italian merchants were willing to travel overland to India to procure them during the early fourteenth century. The collapse of the Mongol empire resulted, however, in more restricted and mediated access to these riches, most of which made their way to Europe by way of Venetians who had purchased them in Alexandria. By the end of the fourteenth century, ivory was so hard to obtain (due in part to the depredations of the central Asian conqueror Timur/Tamerlane in the 1390s), that ivory carving largely ceased.[19] Gold was both a precious commodity used in jewelery, decoration and artwork, and one of the two materials out of which high-value specie was minted. And while mined in Europe, it continued throughout the late Middle Ages to be obtained through trade with North Africa. The gold itself originated in sub-Saharan Africa, and then made its way by caravan across the Sahara to the ports of Tunis, Tangier and Ceuta, where it was sold to Italian and Catalan merchants in return for European textiles and silver. Here was the one case where the balance of trade favoured Europeans, since the textiles fetched a very high price and the gold-silver ratio there played to the Europeans' relative advantage. Much of this gold in turn flowed out of Europe to Asia, where the balance of trade was decidedly unfavourable to the former.

Some merchants from southern Europe even embarked on the caravans themselves, seeking more direct access to the sources of African gold. One, Anselme d'Isalguier, also traded in the other major commodity of the trans-Saharan trade, slaves, and in 1413 brought a harem of black women from Gao to Toulouse.[20] Although human chattels fit uncomfortably into the category of imported luxuries, this was indeed how they were regarded by those late medieval Europeans who vended and purchased them. Slavery, which had been common in early medieval Europe, largely died out in Latin Christendom during the eleventh and twelfth centuries, probably owing to a combination of Church canons forbidding the enslavement of Christians, the abundance of cheap labour from freemen and serfs, and the relative poverty of Europe, compared to Byzantium and Islam. By the early fourteenth century, however, a revival of slavery in Mediterranean Europe was one of the less savoury fruits of the Commercial Revolution. This trade accelerated in the aftermath of demographic collapse in the mid-fourteenth century, perhaps owing to rising wages of domestic help; at the same time the war and civil unrest that broke out in central Asia after the break-up of the Mongol empire and ongoing internecine conflict in West Africa assured plentiful supply. Prior to the exploding demand for slaves to work the sugar plantations of the Mediterranean and eastern Atlantic islands, beginning in the middle of the fifteenth century, most slaves purchased by Genoese and Venetian merchants for sale in Europe were girls bound for domestic service (of the 2,059 slaves listed in Genoa's tax records for 1458, only fifty-four were men), and the vast majority of these girls came from central Asia, eastern and southeastern Europe.[21] Slave girls were clearly regarded as a status symbol and fetched a high price, costing as much as or more than 80 florins.[22] Many also were used as concubines, as in the case of Gregorio Dati's Tatar slave, Margherita, whom we met in the preceding chapter. And just as Dati recognised, baptised and considered free-born the child he had by Margherita, so too was this practice observed by other male slave owners in regard to their issue from such unions. Consequently, and just as in Islam, there was an ongoing need in southern Europe for freshly imported slaves. Male slaves were not, however, unheard of. Used by the Genoese to row their war galleys and sent to work in the salt pans of Ibiza and the alum mines of Phocaea, and in the fields of Sicily as agricultural labourers, their lot was hardly enviable. Then, in the 1460s, a Genoese merchant, Antonio da Noli, hit upon the idea of using a workforce entirely made up of slaves to work the sugar plantations in the Cape Verde Islands, which had recently been acquired by the Portuguese off the west coast of Africa.[23] This became the labour model for sugar cultivation from then on, and thus exponentially increased the European trade in slaves, who from this time forward would be drawn almost exclusively from sub-Saharan Africa. Genoese and Venetian merchants also actively engaged in the Islamic slave trade, selling boys from central Asia and the Balkans (most of the latter indeed were Christians), as well as from the slave markets of Tunis to the Mamluks and Ottomans, who relied on them to swell the ranks of their conquering armies.

Faced with all the vicissitudes of fortune, from the high cost and limited availability of imported luxuries to the drastic decline in total consumption brought on by demographic collapse, late medieval merchants, artisans and agriculturalists proved themselves mightily adaptable and innovative when it came to imitation of desirable products and efficient methods of production. Likewise, merchants were constantly on the lookout for new potential sources of wealth and, especially in southern Europe, displayed a particular ruthlessness when it came to exploiting these sources. Merchants also, however, made real headway in advancing managerial practices and improving transport. Although most management practices employed by medieval merchants originated in the time of the Commercial Revolution, late medieval merchants continued to refine and modify them in keeping with changing circumstances. To avoid the risk and expense of transporting large quantities of specie over long distances and to make low-interest credit available to facilitate business transactions, a system of international merchant banking had already been established by northern Italian companies during the twelfth and thirteenth centuries. These banks developed the practice of book transfers between current accounts in the same and different company bank branches, as well as between different banks, and of using bills of exchange to avoid carrying cash and facilitate exchange between two or more types of currency. Because these merchant-banks were able to make a profit from their companies' trading activities, from interest and fees charged on bills of exchange and loans, and from capital investments of various kinds, they were able at one and the same time to pay their shareholders and depositors healthy interest and to offer loans at reasonable rates of between 7 and 10 per cent. The late Middle Ages also saw the establishment of local banks in cities throughout Europe, which offered interest-bearing accounts to depositors (most often these were religious houses and orphanages), and safe-keeping of money and the convenience of book transfers to their current account holders. Increasingly these local bankers, who in northern Europe were usually money-changers or innkeepers, worked out arrangements with bankers in other cities, so that a merchant from Bruges, for instance, could transfer payment and credit from his local bank to a banker in Antwerp. For those of more modest means, or indeed for hard-up nobles and princes, pawn brokers were always ready to offer high-interest short-term loans in return for suitable security. In the late fifteenth century, the outcry (often tinged with anti-Semitism) of the reformed Observant mendicant orders against these usurious loans led to the creation of eleemosynary institutions, called *monti di pietà* in Italy and *monts de piété* in France, which lent money to the poor at the low interest rate of 5 per cent annually. The overall effect of these banks was to facilitate business by increasing the velocity of money exchange and, especially in times of currency shortage, by extending the money supply, both in reality by encouraging investment rather than hoarding, and artificially through credit.

Company structures developed in the thirteenth century remained consistent throughout the late Middle Ages. In northern and southern Europe the typical company was made up of managing partners and 'silent' investor partners. In northern Italian companies it was also typical for the difficult and risky business of being the company's travelling agents to be entrusted to 'sweat-equity' partners, usually younger men who invested their time and labour, rather than money, in the venture in return for a lesser share of the returns (an arrangement known as the *commenda* or *colleganza* contract). Larger companies also used salaried employees in both their home office and foreign branches. The spectacular bankrupt-cies of the Florentine super-companies in the 1340s, as well as the uncertainty and instability brought on by high mortality and political turmoil in the decades thereafter, encouraged mer-chants, first in Italy but later in southern Germany, to set up their companies in such as way as to minimise the liability of the partners. Companies could decentralise, like the Alberti partnership of Florence, which first went into business in 1302, then split into two branches, the 'Alberti antichi' and 'Alberti nuovi', in 1347, each of whose branches continued to split throughout the remainder of the century, creating a loose confederation of independent com-panies, 'connected through family relationships, trust, and linked investments rather than through corporate control'.[24] The Alberti association of companies survived plague, war and even exile from Florence, only going into decline in the 1430s. Another strategy was for an individual or group to set up and maintain managing control of several autonomous part-nerships. This was done with great success by Francesco Datini of Prato, who after being orphaned by the Black Death, had established himself as a successful arms merchant in Avignon in the 1360s and went on from there to become the dominant partner in a group of companies located throughout the western Mediterranean. Later, in the fifteenth century, the Medici family of Florence combined international banking (it had branches in Geneva, Bruges, Avignon, London, Rome, Milan, Venice and Pisa) with wool and silk textile man-ufacturing, and, from 1466 to 1476, a monopoly on alum mining at Tolfa. The Medici minimised risk, in part by acting as a holding company with controlling ownership of each of its disparate companies and branches. At the same time it maximised opportunity by engag-ing in varied but mutually reinforcing business enterprises. A similar approach was taken by the Fugger family of Augsburg at the end of the fifteenth century. Involvement in banking and the import-export business had, by the 1490s, extended to oversight of fustian manufacturing and, even more importantly, the capital-intensive, but highly profitable mining and metallurgy industries. By 1520, the Fugger company commanded such vast resources that it was able to secure the capital sum of 500,000 golden gulden necessary to get the Habsburg Charles V elected Holy Roman Emperor.[25]

Late medieval merchants also went to considerable lengths to minimise risk to goods in transit. Since storms, piracy, government-ordered seizures and brigandage were all-too-common perils, merchants typically parcelled out their consignments to different ships and organised ships into armed convoys. For precious cargo the Venetians continued to use expensive-to-operate galleys, since their manoeuvrability and large crews made them less vulnerable to seizure. Still, because the best laid plans oft go awry, Italian merchants, beginning in the first half of the fourteenth century, also began to take out insurance policies on their cargo. By the end of the century a system of underwriters and brokers had developed, and cargoes were regularly insured for premiums of between 3.5 and 10 per cent of the total estimated value of goods. Much more rarely, shippers too insured their vessels, at rates varying from 8 to 12 per cent on large vessels engaged in long-distance commerce, to 20 to 30 per cent on small, vulnerable craft.[26] Nor was insurance confined to marine transport as, from 1382 at the latest, policies could be taken out on merchandise travelling overland.[27] Premiums themselves were determined according to a sophisticated calculation of distance, time of year, type of ship, value of cargo, and whether or not war was being waged or pirates or brigands were active anywhere along the route travelled.

Besides managing risk, medieval merchants managed information; indeed the whole edifice of late medieval business was built on a foundation of elaborate accounting, correspondence and record keeping. Business, in other words, was a highly literate and numerate undertaking, and required merchants to be well, if very practically, educated. To satisfy the need for an educated class of merchants, towns throughout northern Italy hired grammar masters and teachers of commercial arithmetic (*abbaco*); by 1338, according to Giovanni Villani, the city of Florence had established six schools of accountancy and management; and a similar education in business could be got in several other cities, both in northern and southern Europe, by the first half of the fifteenth century.[28] As in most business practices, the northern Italians led the way, having adopted Arabic numerals in the thirteenth century and invented double-entry bookkeeping by the mid-fourteenth. The Italians Francesco Pegolotti (c. 1330–40), Giovanni da Uzzano (1442), Benedetto Cotrugli (1458) and Luca Paciolo (1494) also wrote the first business 'textbooks'.[29] The use of Arabic numerals and double-entry bookkeeping eventually spread to northern Europe, although it took well into the fifteenth century for the latter to make its way north of the Alps. Regular and swift correspondence was also a necessity, since managers needed constantly to send out bills of exchange and give directions to their branch agents, who in turn provided news and information (e.g. commodity prices, rates of exchange, safety of routes) to the head office and other branches. From the mid-fourteenth century, in an effort to ensure an uninterrupted flow of correspondence, the merchants in northern Italian cities established courier services, called *scarselle* from the leather pouches in which correspondence was carried. Certainly the speed of these courier services seems slow in our own age of instantaneous communication by phone and the Internet, but there is nonetheless something impressive about the 50 kilometres per day normally traversed by these couriers, not to mention the 150 kilometres per day they could cover when pressed. To be of use, accounts and correspondence had to be recorded and kept for comparison and future consultation. Tuscan businessmen became so habituated to record keeping, that they obsessively kept *libri di ricordanze*, or books of memoranda, in which they not only jotted down notes about business affairs but also kept personal information, like that found in the secret diary of Gregorio Dati.

In their quest for greater control and efficiency, merchants even subjected time itself to regimentation. Merchants wanted to minimise the duration of time required for the transfer of correspondence. Moreover time was a primary factor governing the accumulation of interest, price of commodities and relative value of currencies. There was also the need to control labour time, in order rationally to measure and predict production output while simultaneously controlling costs through maximising worker productivity. In the first quarter of the fourteenth century, textile towns like Arras and Ghent set up bells to chime the beginning and end of the work day; and in 1335 Philip VI of France granted to the mayor and aldermen of Amiens,

> that they might be permitted to issue an ordinance concerning the time when the workers of the said city and its suburbs should go each morning to work, when they should eat and when return to work after eating; and also, in the evening, when they should quit work for the day; and that by the issuance of said ordinance, they might ring a bell which has been installed in the Belfry of the said city, which differs from the other bells.[30]

Time was money for the merchants who controlled the city councils of Arras, Ghent and Amiens, and in order to regulate time they demanded that workers submit to regimented, normal and certain hours 'rather than the *uncertain* clerical hours of the church bells' which rang out the seasonally flexible 'hours' of the old monastic daily office.[31] Merchants were not the only ones who in the early fourteenth century had developed an interest in measuring and controlling time. So too had astrologers, physicians and some 'natural philosophers' at the universities of Paris and Oxford. And because princes sought counsel from both men of learning and merchants, it comes as no surprise that they too wanted to domesticate time. The interests of all parties converged with advances in engineering to create the first mechanical clocks, like the one installed at Milan in 1335,

> which strikes a bell twenty-four hours of the day and night, and thus at the first hour of the night gives one sound, at the second two strokes . . . and so distinguishes one hour from another which is of the greatest use to men of every degree.[32]

Three years later, a Venetian ship exported one of these new mechanical wonders to the East, and by 1370 at least thirty had been installed in cathedrals, palaces and city halls throughout Europe.[33] By the second quarter of the fifteenth century, further advances (namely the invention of the mainspring and fusee) made possible smaller and more accurate timepieces for home use, and by 1488 the 'timepiece had reached the human neck, if not the wrist'.[34] 'From Normandy to Lombardy, the sixty-minute hour was firmly established; at the dawn of the preindustrial era, it replaced the day as the fundamental unit of labor time.'[35]

Concern over minimising transit time, keeping down costs and managing risk all played a role in the quest for better overland and maritime transport. Towns and principalities, largely at the behest of merchants, built more and better bridges, dug canals, improved roads and routes over mountain passes (even digging the first road tunnel, through Monviso in the

Figure 3.2 Mechanical clock, Old Town Hall, Prague. Photograph: B. O'Kane / Alamy Stock Photo

Alps, to facilitate the transport of salt from Provence to Milan), and built and maintained ports. Venice and Florence both subsidised the building of galleys, and Florence even went so far as to build fortified townships along the important trade route to Bologna, to help protect merchants from brigands and predatory rural nobles.[36] Along with better and wider roads came bigger and better wagons, with iron-shod spoked wheels, mobile front axles, suspended carriages and carrying capacities of more than a ton and a half, if the goods were bulky, and as much as four tons of stone. Thanks to these improvements, and with the end of the Hundred Years War and a decline in warfare in northern Italy coupled with the rise of mining and industry in southern Germany, more goods began to flow along the roads of Latin Christendom during the second half of the fifteenth century. Also spurring on this movement was the parallel development of increased danger to Mediterranean shipping, owing to the rise of Ottoman sea-power in the eastern Mediterranean and the depredations of Barbary pirates between Italy and the Iberian Peninsula.[37]

Ship design and navigational aids underwent ongoing improvements and modifications as well. Until 1300, for purposes of long-distance trade (there were also countless small tramp-ers, barges and fishing boats), three main types of ship plied the open seas of northern and southern Europe: the cog in the north, and the buss (or *bucius*) and galley in the south. Both the cog and buss were sail-powered, round-hulled ships designed for bulk transport, while the galley was powered by both sail and oars, with the smaller light galley designed for war, and a heavier version for transport of both high-value goods and passengers. Increased seaborne trade between the Mediterranean and northern Europe encouraged southern shipbuilders first to imitate certain features of the northern cog, leading to the creation of the *cocca*, and then, after the mid-century, to combine the greater size of the buss with the design advantages of the cog – including rigging with square sails and steering by stern rudder (rather than oar) – into a new kind of ship, called the carrack. In an effort to keep down transport costs after the onset of the Black Death, ship designers throughout the remainder of the late Middle Ages sought to build larger, and yet faster and more manoeuvrable, ships. Northern cogs and hulks (a ship much like the cog) rejected their age-old reliance on clinker-built hulls, with their overlapping planking, and opted instead for the edge-to-edge planking and frame construction of carvel-built ones (the method long preferred by Mediterranean shipbuilders). The number of masts on bulk carriers increased from one to three, with the large main mast often sporting two to three square sails, with a square sail on the foremast and a lateen on the mizzen; and by the end of the fifteenth century some ships added a spritsail to the bow. The fifteenth century also saw greater specialisation in ship design. In 1441 at the latest, the Portuguese, needing a ship which could sail very close to the wind for their explorations into the eastern Atlantic and along the coast of West Africa, adopted the low-sided and shallow-drafted caravel. Originally a smallish fishing vessel, the caravel was enlarged to give it more capacity for sailors and their supplies, equipped with three masts, and given a square mainsail to complement its traditional lateen rigging. Meanwhile the Dutch devel-oped a large three-masted fishing vessel equipped with facilities for salting and packing fish on board, called the herring buss, in order to exploit the North Sea herring fisheries and thereby successfully compete with the Hanse. Another Dutch ship, the *hoeker*, used for cod fishing far out in the Atlantic, kept the cod alive by bathing them in seawater which entered the hull through small holes.[38] At the end of the fifteenth century, guns began to make their way onto the decks of warships, and although modifications in hull design to accommodate large cannon would have to await the third decade of the sixteenth century, already in 1513 the first ship sank its enemy with gunfire.[39]

Although the period is not characterised by any stunningly sudden inventions in the way of navigation technology, nonetheless navigation instruments, aids, techniques and knowledge improved steadily and markedly over the course of the fourteenth and fifteenth centuries. Already by 1300, the magnetic compass had taken the form of a free-swinging needle set above a card calibrated either with a wind-rose or degrees. In the first decades of the fourteenth century, Mediterranean sailors had begun to use the compass along with 'portolans' (charts drawn to scale describing the coastline and port locations) and an hour-glass, to calculate speed. By 1400 they supplemented their portolans with tables that allowed them to determine position while tacking. Portuguese exploration in the lower latitudes of the Atlantic near the equator during the fifteenth century necessitated substituting a calculation of the sun's declination at midday for the traditional method of doing so according to the Pole Star. Sailors in northern Europe relied very little on the compass and never used portolans, preferring to navigate according to the declination of the sun and the position of celestial bodies, while the treacherously shallow and shifting sea bottom of the Baltic compelled them to devote considerable attention to measuring depth by means of line and lead. Still, in an effort to improve navigation, northerners had started using tide tables by 1400, and combined this information with descriptions of currents, depth-soundings and routes in books called rutters or *routiers*.[40]

Exploration

Robert Fossier has said that at the end of the Middle Ages, merchants, both in economic and political terms

> were now the State's leading men. Because they controlled both ends of the chain of production, raw materials and distribution; because they controlled the various states of the intermediary work by their power to lend or not lend money for wages and equipment; because they even controlled production at the family level by providing their only means of distribution, and finally because the State was their leading customer and servant (even if they did not necessarily appear at its head), the merchants . . . were the new masters of society.[41]

Although perhaps a trifle overstated (the nobility, surely, were still hardly a spent force), this Marxist interpretation of merchant power goes a long way toward explaining why late medieval rulers increasingly came to patronise, rely upon and try to control commerce. This relationship is apparent in everything from Edward III of England's creation of the Calais staple, to Charles VII of France's reliance on the industrialist banker of Bourges, Jacques Coeur, to the Venetian Republic's granting of patents to attract and retain the services of inventors and commercial innovators.[42] Perhaps nowhere, however, is it better exemplified than in the close connection between trade and princes found in the fourteenth-century Arago-Catalonian 'empire' and in fifteenth-century Portugal. But because these rulers and their nobles injected their own predilections for chivalric deeds, conquest and crusading into this relationship, and because in each case the object of their desires lay beyond the seas, their political interests led them to promote sea-going commerce and Atlantic exploration. One final ingredient prompted and facilitated this movement, this being the mercantile interests of the Genoese, whether acting as competitors or companions of the Iberians.

The roots of the 'Age of Exploration' lie in the thirteenth century, when the Aragonese conquered the islands of the western Mediterranean and the Genoese set up shop in the ports of Andalusia and Portugal. Despite the crusading rhetoric employed by King Jaume I of Aragon, when in 1228 he launched the first round of conquest, against Muslim-held Majorca, the initial and principal motivation was commercial; moreover, 'strictly commercial rewards' seem also to have been what 'justified such widespread adhesion to the king's enterprise', and 'the conquest was determined and the subsequent colonisation shaped by cupidity for commerce and land'.[43] King Jaume's hopes for Majorca were indeed realised and it became a great emporium for commerce in all manner of commodities, including slaves, olive oil, iron and salt, as well as a centre of ship-building and textile production. And thanks to the 'paucity of their patrimony' at home in Aragon and Catalonia, the commercial interests of the Crown of Aragon only grew as the thirteenth century wore on, encouraging further conquests, in Ibiza, Sicily and Malta, and in the fourteenth century, Sardinia. After trade began moving easily through the straits of Gibraltar in the later thirteenth and early fourteenth century, seafaring Majorcans explored the Canary Islands in 1342 and in 1346 attempted, unsuccessfully, to find the source of West African gold. Yet, Arago-Catalonian success in the western Mediterranean, including securing African gold via the safer and surer means of favourable trading relations with Tunis, sated the hunger that might have led them to continue exploring the Atlantic in the second half of the fourteenth century. Instead, during these years the Canaries were left to the missionary activities of Majorcan and Catalan friars.

If the Arago-Catalonian monarchs pursued commerce for political ends, the Genoese did so for commercial ones. Perhaps in response to a papal ban on trade with Egypt in 1291, the Genoese brothers Ugolino and Vadino Vivaldi set off in two galleys to seek a direct route to India. The fact that they never returned hardly dissuaded later Genoese voyages of exploration, especially because members of several Genoese merchant families installed themselves in Iberian Atlantic port cities during the later thirteenth and early fourteenth centuries. Thus the Canary Islands were first spotted by the Genoese Lanzarotto Malocello, probably when he was sailing in the service of Portugal in 1336. Genoese leadership is also probable for the Portuguese expeditions of 1341 that first discovered Madeira and the eastern islands of the Azores.[44] Events in the late fourteenth and fifteenth centuries further compelled the Genoese to seek their fortunes in the Atlantic. The loss to Venice at the battle of Chioggia in 1380 weakened Genoa's presence in the eastern Mediterranean and the conquests of the Ottoman Turks in the fifteenth century diminished and finally cut off their trade both in the eastern Mediterranean and in the Black Sea. Yet in the Atlantic the Genoese worked not only for themselves but for their hosts, whether that was the Portuguese royal family or the monarchs of Castile and England.

Already in the 1340s, the monarchs of both Portugal and Castile, like those of Aragon, had expressed some interest in Atlantic colonisation and the economic benefits that would accrue therefrom. It was only in the fifteenth century, however, that this process began in earnest, at first haltingly and at arms-length in the case of the kings of Castile, but early on and with considerable energy by the Portuguese. Prior to Columbus, Castilian interest in Atlantic exploration and colonisation was largely confined to the Canaries. The origins of this interest, however, came not from the Castilian monarch but from two noble French adventurers, Jean de Béthencourt and Gadifer de la Salle, who, probably with the encouragement of some family connections among the Genoese of Seville, set out to conquer the Canaries in 1402. Although they had initially intended to claim the islands for France, a series of misadventures led to Béthencourt giving his allegiance to King Enrique III of Castile. If, however, Castile gained the Canaries almost by accident, interest in its sugar-producing capabilities, fear of Portuguese intrusion and a desire to extend the 'Reconquest' (*reconquista*) into the Atlantic induced the monarchs Ferdinand and Isabella to establish direct control over the islands.[45]

Sparsely populated, poor in arable land and natural resources, under a new but still unsteady royal dynasty, threatened by its larger and wealthier neighbour of Castile, and stuck out on the western edge of Latin Christendom, Portugal in 1400 hardly seemed a likely candidate for global empire. Yet these very disadvantages were indeed the factors that impelled it on that course; for Portugal's poverty, shaky dynasty and fear of Castile made it acquisitive, while its being poised at the eastern edge of the mid-Atlantic had not only long acclimated its people to sea-going commerce, but also placed them in a particularly advantageous location for exploiting the ocean's winds and currents. King João I of Avis, who usurped the throne in 1383 and reigned until his death in 1433, sought, like his Lancastrian cousin Henry V in England, to cement the legitimacy of his parvenu dynasty through military conquest. In João's case, the target was Morocco in North Africa, and the first step was the taking of the port city of Ceuta in 1415. If Ceuta gave the Portuguese a toehold in North Africa, and with it some commercial advantages and some land to grant out as fiefs to the nobility, it did very little to gain access to the trans-Saharan gold trade. It was left to João's youngest son, Dom Henrique, dubbed 'Prince Henry the Navigator' in Anglophone scholarship, to pursue a path to his own, as well as to his family's, wealth and glory, by means of Atlantic conquest. Control of the Canaries, and thus, he hoped, of the gold trade, were his main motives, with the colonisation of Madeira and the Azores being of secondary interest. Frustrated in his ambitions for the Canaries, his patronage of voyages along the coast of Africa was an effort to outflank the Castilians. He and his older brother, the *infante* Pedro, patronised several explorers, drawn both from the Portuguese nobility and the Genoese, whose successive voyages further and further down the West African coast finally began bringing rewards, in the form of gold and slaves (in one instance, Henrique helped himself to 46 of the 230 captive Africans shipped back by a voyage in 1444), and in land. Madeira, whose colonisation began in the 1440s, was already producing cane sugar by the mid-1450s, while the Azores, in addition to beginning to yield a harvest of wheat, had become an essential staging post for the return journey from the bulge of Africa (the *volta da Guiné*). After Henrique's death in 1460, sugar plantations were established by the Genoese Antonio da Noli on the Cape Verde Islands, while at the same time Genoese entrepreneurs on Madeira began turning a substantial profit from both sugar and wine. Continued expeditions between 1469 and 1475, under the patronage of the Lisbon merchant Fernão Gomes not only pushed exploration to 2 degrees south of the equator but started bringing back wealth in the form of ivory and malaguetta pepper.

After 1475 exploration was under the direct patronage of the Portuguese *infante* Dom João, who became king in 1481 and reigned until 1495. Under his watchful eye, the Portuguese started bringing back large quantities of gold from their fortress of São Jorge da Mina, between the Volta and Niger estuaries, and to engage in serious missionary activity, especially among the people of the Kingdom of Kongo. As understanding of Atlantic winds and currents advanced among Portuguese sailors, so too did mathematicians and cartographers affiliated with King Joao's court make improvements to navigational tables and charts. Once the voyages of Diogo Cão (1486) and Bartolomeu Dias (1487–88) confirmed a passage around the tip of Africa, and reports from the Portuguese agent Pero da Covilha provided intelligence about trade routes in the Indian Ocean and about Christians in India and Ethiopia, Portuguese acquisitiveness and crusading zeal combined in a quest for spices and the legendary African kingdom of the Christian Prester John. The culmination of all this was Vasco da Gama's expedition of 1497–99, which, despite the loss of two out of four ships, proved the feasibility of such a voyage and brought back a large enough haul of precious spices to attest to its profitability. Repeating the wide westward sweep into the south Atlantic made by da Gama on his outgoing voyage, a Portuguese expedition to India under the command of Pedro Alvares de Cabral fortuitously made landfall on the coast of South America in 1500, thereby initiating what was to become the Portuguese colony of Brazil.

Other than wanting to assure their benefits from the lucrative sugar business of the Canaries, the rulers of the now united crowns of Aragon and Castile, Ferdinand and Isabella, had little interest in exploration. When, after ten years of war, the last Iberian Muslim stronghold, at Granada, fell in January 1492, the Spanish monarchs were more amenable to entertaining the prospect of an exploratory overseas commercial venture proposed to them by the Genoese merchant Christopher Columbus. A consummate businessman and social climber, Columbus (1451–1506) began life as the eldest son of a weaver from the Ligurian hinterland. After some schooling in Genoa and several years spent as a merchant's apprentice and sailor, he settled in Lisbon in 1476 (after having shipwrecked on the Portuguese coast), whence until 1485 he participated in several overseas mercantile ventures – to England, Ireland and, perhaps, Iceland, to Madeira and São Jorge da Mina – and where he ran a business selling books and maps. While in Portugal he also contracted a very favourable marriage to Felipa Moniz Perestrelo (d. 1485), whose noble father, Bartolomeu, had been a hero of African coastal exploration as well as governor of Porto Santo in Madeira. His reading during this time of such works as Marco Polo's *Travels*, *The Travels of Sir John Mandeville*, and Pierre d'Ailly's *Imago Mundi* ('Image of the World'), as well as correspondence with the Florentine cosmographer Pietro Paolo Toscanelli convinced him of the likelihood of a narrow Atlantic passage between Europe and Asia. Thus he began to hatch his plan to sail westwards to China and the Indies. King João II, on the advice of his better-informed experts in cartography and navigation, rejected overtures by Columbus in 1484, as did Ferdinand and Isabella, Henry VII of England and Charles VIII of France in 1487; João again rebuffed Columbus in 1488. Still convinced he was right, and now with the backing of some of the Genoese and Florentine merchants of Seville, Columbus secured the Spanish monarchs' backing of his voyage in April 1492. In addition to ennobling him and granting him the hereditary offices of 'Admiral of the Ocean' and 'Governor' of whatever lands he should happen to find, his original commission makes clear the commercial nature of the expedition:

> You [Ferdinand and Isabella] wish him [Columbus] to have and take for himself one-tenth of all and any merchandise, whether pearls, precious stones, gold, silver, spices, and any other things and merchandise of whatever kind . . . that is bought, exchanged, found, acquired, and obtained within the limits of the admiralty . . . deducting all the relevant expenses incurred, so that, of what remains clear and free, he may take and keep one-tenth for himself . . . reserving the other nine-tenths for Your Highnesses. . . .
>
> Of all vessels outfitted for trade and business, each time, whenever, and as often as they are outfitted, Sir Christopher Columbus, if he wishes, may contribute and pay one-eighth of all that is spent on the outfitting and likewise he may have and take one-eighth of the profits that result from such outfitting.[46]

Using two caravels and a small carrack, called a *nao*, navigating by means of compass and dead reckoning, armed with the knowledge of Atlantic winds and currents obtained from some two centuries of Atlantic commerce and exploration, and taking advantage of the Canaries as a staging post, Columbus crossed the Atlantic in a mere 32 days. What he found and what he would continue to explore, exploit and conquer on that expedition and three more, was not China, or Japan (Cipangu, as he called it), or the 'Indies', but rather the Caribbean Islands and the mainland of Central and South America. Convinced until his dying day that he had been mere days from finding the empire of the 'Grand Khan', a personage who had not existed since the days of Marco Polo, Columbus died a man who after having discovered a New World, stubbornly remained committed to a world view dating from the fourteenth century. Nonetheless he laid the foundation for the Spanish colonial adventure in the New World; one that by 1520 was already bearing considerable fruit in the form of sugar, and would two decades later unleash a flood of silver.

Columbus's world view was shared by the Venetian of Genoese parentage John Cabot, who, with the backing of several Bristol merchants and King Henry VII of England, tried on two voyages in 1496–98 to find a North Atlantic route to China. Like Columbus, he found instead a new continent. Unlike him, however, Cabot's discoveries elicited very little excitement and succeeded only in convincing the English to abandon such nonsense, until the time of Elizabeth I. For the foreseeable future, the English, and their chief competitors, the Dutch, directed their seafaring acumen to trade in the Baltic and along the European side of the Atlantic. In the north, it was left to humanists like Thomas More to dream of the wonders of the West.

Notes

1 Paget 1908: 114–16.
2 Paget 1908: 7.
3 Surtz 1964: 151.
4 Lopez and Raymond 1990: 416–17.
5 Spufford 2000: 157.
6 Spufford 2002: 379–80.
7 Spufford 2002: 286.
8 Hunt and Murray 1999: 116–20.
9 Spufford 2002: 294.
10 Fossier 1986: 80.
11 Spufford 2002: 300–1.
12 Spufford 2002: 304.
13 Harriss 2005: 277; Prevenier 1983.
14 Franceschi 2004: 128–30.
15 Gies and Gies 1994: 179.
16 Wolff 1986: 125.
17 Spufford 2000: 161.
18 Spufford 2002: 309.
19 Spufford 2002: 280.
20 Fernández-Armesto 1998: 190.
21 Epstein 2009: 258–59.
22 Spufford 2002: 340.
23 Fernández-Armesto 1987: 200–2.
24 Hunt and Murray 1999: 155.
25 Hunt and Murray 1999: 222–23.
26 Wolff 1986: 138–39.
27 Spufford 2002: 33.
28 Denley 1990; Fossier 1986: 99.
29 Wolff 1986: 272–73; Epstein 2009: 271–74.
30 Le Goff 1980: 46–47.
31 Le Goff 1980: 48.
32 Gies and Gies 1994: 213.
33 Cipolla 1993: 210.
34 White 1962: 126–28.
35 Le Goff 1980: 49.
36 Spufford 2002: 216.
37 Spufford 2002: 407–8; Fossier 1986: 421.
38 Unger 1980: 206, 212–17.

39 Unger 1980: 234.
40 Unger 1980: 174–75, 215; Childs 1998: 150.
41 Fossier 1986: 431.
42 Ashtor 1989.
43 Fernández-Armesto 1987: 15–18.
44 Phillips 1998: 149.
45 Fernández-Armesto 1987: 203–17.
46 Symcox and Sullivan 2005: 60–62.

Part II

POLITICAL DEVELOPMENTS

4

THE THEORY AND
IDEOLOGY OF GOVERNMENT

Politics is that which sustains the care of the republic and, by the industry of its prudence, the balance or weight of its justice, the constancy and firmness of its fortitude, and the patience of its temperance, gives medicine for the health of all; and thus Politics can say of itself: 'By me kings reign, and through me those who make the laws discern and determine which things are just' [Prov. 8:15]. . . . Thus of all the worldly sciences this is the most principal, worthy and profitable, and it is the one most appropriate for princes. Consequently it is called 'architectonic', that is to say, Princess over all.[1]

By the time Nicole Oresme made his translation of Aristotle's *Politics* in the 1370s, few in Europe would have disputed his insistence on the primacy of political science in the sphere of worldly affairs. Knowledge of this science and conformity to its principles, it was believed, should guide the wills of those responsible for the governance of states and control their passions in such a way as to ensure their assiduous cultivation of the common good. It was only in the last decades of the thirteenth century that a science of politics had come into its own in Latin Christendom. That it did so had as much to do with innovations in the curriculum of the nascent universities as with profound changes in the political complexion of Europe. The translation from Greek into Latin of Aristotelian moral philosophical works, the *Nicomachean Ethics*, *Economics* and *Politics*, during the 1200s gave scholars full access to that branch of ancient knowledge they called 'moral philosophy', that is the philosophy of this-worldly human activity. Just as importantly, however, the newly translated text of Aristotle's *Rhetoric* instructed them in the mode of discourse appropriate to the contingent and emotionally charged arena of political activity.[2]

The incorporation of Aristotle's moral philosophy into the universities' curriculum coincided with the beginning of a distinct phase in the political history of Europe: the age of the 'germination' of what has been termed the 'modern European power state'.[3] The 'universal' governing bodies of Empire and Church whose power and prestige had been such distinctive features of the High Middle Ages, and whose competition with one another had so influenced its politics, began to lose ground to increasingly centralised and unified city-states and dynastic monarchies. The political elites of these states, as well as those of a Church and Empire on the defensive, sought the help of intellectual 'experts', with their training in philosophy, theology and law; and the experts, for their part, were only too happy to comply. This relationship brought about that 'confrontation with political reality' that was responsible for the late Middle Ages being 'the most productive and profound' period in medieval political thought.[4]

Political ideas, beliefs and ideologies both condition and are shaped by the realities of political structures and events. Historians have argued over whether mentalities precede and cause political reality or are a result and *ex post facto* expression thereof, but most now agree that there is a subtle interplay of ideas and facts. That I have chosen to begin a treatment of political developments with a discussion of theory and ideology is because, like Bernard Guenée, I think 'politics are the work of men who do not submit passively to facts, but react to them according to the character and requirements of their own minds'.[5] This chapter opens with an examination of the political 'languages' of the intellectuals, as revealed in the treatises of lawyers, philosophers and theologians. These 'men of learning', as Jacques Verger calls them, wrote in response to real political problems and in order to assist and curb the ambitions of political leaders.[6] Being themselves members of the political elite, moreover, they frequently sought to put their ideas into practice. These same intellectuals, however, also engaged in an enterprise of *haute vulgarisation* in the form of translations, like those of Oresme, or of 'mirrors of princes', works that instructed their princely and noble patrons in the science of politics and art of governance. Despite, or perhaps because of, their dry, didactic tone, several of these works gained considerable popularity with their target audiences, and influenced political discourse and action. Finally, there were the ever-present displays of state power and normative political attitudes through such media as art, architecture and insignia, and the performance of the same in the rituals of the court, speeches, sermons and such public events as processions, coronations, entries and funerals.

Intellectuals and the 'languages' of political theory

The seemingly abstruse commentaries, disputations and *summae* produced in the medieval universities and the elegant treatises of the humanists should not blind us to the fact that higher education in late medieval Europe had distinctly practical aims. 'What good is knowledge that cannot be applied, that is not useful for one's salvation and for society at large?' asked Jean Gerson in 1405.[7] Clerks with university training and laymen who studied civil law or the notarial arts were all convinced of the utility of their education, and especially of the habits of study and methods of discourse they had learned.

> In the Middle Ages an educated person was recognized by his mastery of a whole disciplinary field, by his ability to reason, solve problems, analyze texts, conduct a discussion, and derive universal principles that made him capable . . . of assuming a variety of related social roles.[8]

Those social roles included being a servant (and occasionally a critic) of the state. The education of these intellectuals equipped them with several 'languages', by which are meant distinct vocabularies, each derived from separate bodies of authoritative texts. These languages can be characterised as theological, 'native', legal, classical or Aristotelian.[9]

Theological and native political languages already had long histories by the start of the fourteenth century. In a society so infused with the Christian religion and in which ecclesiastics fulfilled so many administrative functions, the employment of theological language was a ubiquitous feature in politics. Kings and kingship were legitimated with reference to the Old Testament kings Melchizedek, David and Solomon. Biblical language and imagery and the wisdom of the Fathers of the Church were the stock-in-trade of polemicists, whether seeking to limit the power of kings or to argue in their favour. So, in the conflict between

King Philip IV of France and Pope Boniface VIII at the start of the fourteenth century, Giles of Rome in *De ecclesiastica potestate* ('On Ecclesiastical Power', 1301–02) privileged the pope's spiritual over the king's temporal power:

> But because . . . it has been said on the authority of Genesis that the body was formed first and received the breath of life subsequently, so that the formation of the body seems to have preceded the infusion of the soul in time, we can reply that in *De Genesi ad Litteram*, Book 7, Augustine appears to assert that the soul of our first parent was created before the body, or before the formation of the body. For he says: 'It may permissibly be said that, in His first works, by which He created all things together, God seems also to have created the human soul which, in His own time, He breathed into the members of the body formed from the slime.'[10]

Countering Giles was the pro-royal John of Paris, who wrote:

> if the word "priesthood" is accurately understood, then it can be said that the kingdom preceded the priesthood in time. For as Augustine recounts in the *City of God* the first of the kingdoms was that of the Assyrians which began before the giving of the Law.[11]

Those seeking to instruct princes made heavy use of this sort of language. The anonymous author of a mirror of princes written in the 1430s for England's young King Henry VI, entitled *De regimine principum ad Regem Henricum Sextum*, structured his work according to an elaborate allegorisation of the throne of Solomon:

> For it is written . . . that King Solomon made a great throne of ivory and covered it with yellow gold. The top of the throne was round on the back side and there were two hands holding the seat on one side and on the other. And he commanded that six steps be built for the purpose of ascending to the throne. But because no virtuous man will be able to reach up to the height of this throne by any means other than by ascending the aforementioned steps, I likewise have begun with a description of these steps, so that their stations stay fixed in your virtuous memory.[12]

Moreover, just as theological language could exalt kingship, as it did in service of the 'royal religions' of the kings of Naples and of France, so too could it serve as a rallying cry for radical populism, as when the priest John Ball inspired the English rebels of 1381 by preaching, 'When Adam delved, and Eve span, who was then the gentleman?'[13]

The rebels also made use of native language, that is the language of 'national' custom, when they demanded through their leader Wat Tyler that there be no law but the law of Winchester, by which they seem to have meant the provision for self-policing and the right to bear arms laid out in the Statute of Winchester of 1285.[14] By the end of the thirteenth century, all the peoples of Europe could draw on the language of customary law, enshrined in texts like Henry de Bracton's *De legibus et consuetudinibus Angliae* ('On the Laws and Customs of England'), Philippe de Beaumanoir's *Coutumes de Beauvaisis*, Eike von Repgau's *Sachsenspiegel*, Alfonso X's *Siete Partidas* and the northern Italian *Libri feudorum* ('Books of Fiefs'). Such language could be called upon to enforce the power of central government, as happened in France during the fourteenth century with the expansion of northern French customary law into the Midi, or it could be used by localities to resist imperial intrusions, as was the case with the *Libri feudorum*.[15] Likewise the language of native custom served to strengthen national identities in the last centuries of the Middle Ages, as can be clearly seen in a text like Sir John Fortescue's *De laudibus legum Angliae* ('In Praise of the Laws of England', c. 1470). Not infrequently historical writing also contributed arguments to 'native' positions, as when, for example, the Parisian chronicler Jean de Saint-Victor, in his *Memoriale historiarum* ('Memorial of Histories', 1309–22) to discredit the universal authority of the German emperor and 'prove' that France had always been a separate and autonomous realm.[16]

If customary law had its political uses, however, far more influential was the language of Roman and canon law. The foundational text of Roman, or civil law was the *Corpus iuris civilis*, a codification of Roman law sponsored by the Byzantine emperor Justinian in the sixth century. Serious study of this text – or, really, four texts, the *Institutes*, *Digest*, *Codex* and *Novels* – in the Latin West began at Bologna c. 1100, where in the course of the next century and a half scholars like Azo (d. 1230) and Accursius (d. 1263) wrote what became the standard commentaries, or glosses of civil law. Several important principles of governance were derived from civil law. Most statements favoured strong imperial (or royal) power, like 'what pleases the prince has the force of law' or 'the prince is not bound by the law'; but some could be read as placing limits on the monarch, like the principle of 'what touches all should be approved by all'. During the late Middle Ages, the so-called Postglossators, among whom the most important were Bartolus of Sassoferrato (d. 1357) and his student Baldus de Ubaldis (d. 1400), weighed in on matters ranging from the legitimacy of popular sovereignty, the autonomy of city-states and kingdoms, and the distinction between a king and a tyrant.

The origins of canon law lay in papal decrees and the decisions of Church councils. These had been collected and organised at Bologna c. 1140 by Gratian in a work that came to be known as the *Decretum*. Although the chief province of canon law was religious faith and practice, and ecclesiastical discipline and governance, it also frequently played a role in politics. Not only was canon law itself strongly influenced by civil law, but scholars often took degrees in both civil and canon law (*in utroque iure*). Moreover, in an era when the affairs of Church and state were so closely intertwined, the language of canon law found its way into all manner of political developments and debates. The principle of papal 'fullness of power' (*plenitudo potestatis*) and statements from canon law like 'the king is emperor in his own realm' and 'the king does not recognise a superior' were frequently drawn upon by kings in their disputes with pope and emperor. In the late Middle Ages, the experts in canon law who made the most important contributions to the political arena were Johannes Andreae (d. 1348), Franciscus Zabarella (d. 1417) and Nicholas de Tudeschis (Panormitanus, d. 1445).

The legacy of Roman antiquity made itself known also in the writings of classical authors, among whom Cicero, Seneca and Valerius Maximus were the most important for late medieval politics. These authors take it for granted that the political life is something good and natural to humankind, rather than being a result of the primordial sin of Adam and Eve. They also stress the indissoluble connection between the ethical conduct of individuals, especially those belonging to the political elites, and the achievement of the state's ultimate goal, this being the common good. Four virtues in particular were required for the political life: prudence, justice, fortitude and temperance. Derived from the teachings of Plato and the Stoics, these four 'cardinal', or 'civic', virtues were transferred to the Middle Ages by way of Cicero's *De officiis* ('On Duties') and Seneca's 'Moral Letters', as well as in the writings of Ambrose and Gregory the Great, but they were most fully treated in the treatise of a sixth-century Spanish bishop, Martin of Braga. His *Formula vitae honestae* was tremendously popular in the late Middle Ages, normally circulating under the title *De quattuor virtutibus cardinalibus* ('On the Four Cardinal Virtues') and mistakenly ascribed to Seneca.[17] The four cardinal virtues were a commonplace of art, of confessional and pulpit, and of didactic literature of all kinds. They were also ubiquitous in all manner of political discourse, from Nicole Oresme's translation of the *Politics*, quoted at the beginning of this chapter, to the anonymous English translation of Claudian's *De consulatu Stiliconis* presented to Richard Duke of York in the mid-fifteenth century.[18] Moreover, in early fourteenth-century Italy, the Paduan notary Albertino Mussato began experimenting in his play, the *Ecerinis*, with a form of political language that sought not only to use the lessons of the Roman classics but also to emulate their literary style and form (in this case, the tragedies of Seneca).[19] By the end of the century, his 'humanist' successors Coluccio Salutati of Florence and Antonio Loschi of Milan crafted highly wrought humanist political propaganda for their respective (and mutually antagonistic) city-states.[20]

Interestingly, the body politic, that image ascribed to classical antiquity which was to become late medieval Europe's most important intellectual tool for thinking and talking about the structure and functions of the state, was, in fact, not antique at all. It originated, rather, in John of Salisbury's *Policraticus*. This twelfth-century scholar and bishop gave his creation the authority of antiquity by presenting it as part of a work he claimed was by Plutarch, the *Institutio Traiani* ('Instruction of Trajan'), when in fact this ersatz classic was almost certainly the work of John himself. In a society already accustomed to thinking of itself in organic terms as the mystical Body of Christ, and which had developed the notion that collective entities could exist as 'fictive persons' or corporations in the eyes of the law, it made compelling sense that the state should be a kind of body in which

> those who direct the practice of religion ought to be esteemed and venerated like the soul in the body. . . . The position of the head in the republic is occupied, however, by a prince subject only to God and to those who act in His place on earth. . . . The place of the heart is occupied by the senate. . . . The duties of the ears, eyes and mouth are claimed by the judges and governors of provinces. The hands coincide with officials and soldiers. Those who always assist the prince are comparable to the flanks. Treasurers and record keepers . . . resemble the shape of the stomach and intestines. . . . the feet coincide with peasants perpetually bound to the soil. . . .

And just as a correctly ordered human body is healthy, so too does the properly regulated body politic strive for the common good, under the direction of its head, the prince, who is 'the minister of the public utility and the servant of equity'.[21]

As important as all these languages were, however, it was that relative late-comer, Aristotelian, which was to become the master political discourse of the late Middle Ages. This was partly the outcome of the curriculum of the universities' arts course being based almost entirely on the works of Aristotle; but it also resulted from the utility of Aristotle's concepts and vocabulary and their applicability for theorising and making sense of contemporary political structures and events. Like the Romans, Aristotle taught that the political life was natural to man or, as he put it, 'man is a political animal', whose natural abode is the state (*polis*).

Life in the state, moreover, is a necessary precondition for living a full and sufficient human life, a life in which humans can achieve their end, which is happiness. Furthermore, 'happiness is a certain activity of the soul according to perfect virtue' (*Nicomachean Ethics* I.13). This perfect virtue, however, can only be achieved by having a virtuous character, which is the result of habituation to virtuous behaviour from an early age. Aristotle also made it clear that the form of discourse appropriate for political life was rhetoric, an art whose real utility lay not so much in the specific rules governing public speaking but rather in understanding emotions and developing prudence, the virtue by which one evaluates and makes the best choices in given situations.

Aristotle's political language also derived force from the high esteem accorded him in the Middle Ages. He was, after all, *the* Philosopher, 'the wisest and truest philosopher that ever was'.[22] Moreover, he was the teacher of the greatest of all ancient kings, Alexander the Great. If Aristotle's lore worked for Alexander, should it not also bring success and happiness to contemporary rulers? For medieval political elites, the answer was, clearly, yes.

The intellectuals confront political reality

To our eyes the curriculum of the medieval universities can seem abstract and impractical. This, however, is a misconception. In fact, the universities answered 'a practical need for clear, authoritative solutions to practical questions about collective "governance"' by teaching a way, a method, of analytical thinking and interpretation and the skills of persuasive debate.[23] When it came to engagement with political events and problems, scholars took what they had learned and put it to use either in learned polemical tracts or those books of princely instruction called mirrors of princes. The authors of these works usually had spent at least some time studying in one of the universities' three higher faculties – law, medicine or theology – and these higher studies tended to influence how they approached political issues. Nonetheless, they all shared a foundation in the arts curriculum, where they were exposed to the corpus of Aristotle's moral philosophy. By the first years of the fourteenth century, moreover, these difficult texts had been rendered more 'user-friendly' through the medium of commentaries, the most important and influential of which were by Thomas Aquinas, Peter of Auvergne, Giles of Rome and Bartholomew of Bruges. The early fourteenth century was also the time during which several scholars began preparing questions for disputation with their colleagues (*quaestiones disputatae*) regarding various statements in these texts. These questions helped them find ways to enlist the material in these texts for practical ends. Those who moved on to the higher faculties continued to draw concepts and language from their engagement with Aristotle. Nor should it be thought that scholars in the higher faculties were ignorant of the texts of their colleagues in other faculties, since lawyers and physicians frequently show an easy familiarity with theological material and theologians with that of law and medicine. Here it should be mentioned that although the university curriculum did not require them to, these intellectuals were familiar with such classical Roman authorities as Seneca, Cicero, Valerius Maximus and Sallust.

The chief political problem occupying the minds of late medieval intellectuals was that of legitimate jurisdiction. Although this problem was not new, its nature changed in the face of new political realities and aspirations. Since the end of the fifth century, when the idea was first given expression by Pope Gelasius I, the rule of the Christian community had been conceived as being shared between two powers, the spiritual and the temporal, the former exercised by the clergy and the latter by secular authorities. Yet if those two powers were distinct, Gelasius left no doubt that the spiritual took precedence over the temporal, since 'of the two [powers] that of the priesthood is a greater burden, in so far as they must also render account before God for the very kings of men'. During the controversy over episcopal appointments (the so-called Investiture Controversy) waged between the German emperors and popes in the late eleventh and early twelfth century, the political order of Latin Christendom came to be seen as being divided between Empire and papacy, with each claiming authority over the other. To the old Gelasian language was added the striking new analogy, derived from Luke 22:38, of two swords: the one spiritual and wielded by the papacy; and the other temporal and in the hands of the emperor. This analogy was used by apologists for both sides in the Investiture Controversy, with the pope's supporters claiming that the emperor's sword had only been delegated to him by the priesthood, and the emperor's countering that 'the sacerdotal sword would be used to encourage obedience to the king on God's behalf, whereas the royal would be employed for expelling the enemies of Christ without, and for enforcing the obedience to the priesthood within'.[24]

During the first half of the thirteenth century, the earthly power of the two competitors reached its apogee, especially since the emperor, Frederick II of Hohenstaufen had also inherited the kingdom of Sicily. In the 1260s, however, the long-standing conflict between popes and emperors was brought to a violent end with the defeat of imperial forces and the obliteration of the Hohenstaufen line. Yet the papacy had little time to savour its victory, since the destruction of its nemesis merely cleared away the last serious obstacle to the accretion of power by ascendant dynastic territorial states, on the one hand, and central and northern Italian city-states, on the other. Thus, by the turn of the thirteenth and fourteenth century the new political dynamic in Latin Christendom was that between a papacy trying to maintain its power, an Empire trying to reassert itself and the states negotiating their power between pope, Empire and one another. The first salvos were exchanged between Pope Boniface VIII and King Philip IV of France. In July 1301 Philip, in what may have been an act designed to provoke Boniface, arrested Bernard Saisset, the bishop of Pamiers in southern France, on charges of treason, blasphemy and heresy. In contravention of the long-established principle of clerical immunity from secular jurisdiction, Philip's judges went on to find Saisset guilty of all charges, depose him from his see and cast him into prison. In the bitter dispute which ensued, the papacy found its most eloquent advocate in Giles of Rome (who sided with the pope in spite of having earlier dedicated his *De regimine principum* to Philip). His lengthy treatise, *De ecclesiastica potestate* used theological, legal and Aristotelian language in order to make the most thorough and extreme claims ever for papal power, asserting the right of the pope not only to wield both swords, spiritual and temporal, but even his universal *dominium*, meaning both his lordship over all Christians – 'the faithful are Catholic . . . because they must be universally subject and subservient to the Church' – and over their property – 'the Church has a greater lordship over the possessions of the faithful, and over temporal things as such, than the faithful themselves have'.[25]

Philip also had his own learned supporters. Two anonymous tracts produced during this conflict, *Rex pacificus Salomon* ('Solomon, the Peaceable King') and *Quaestio in utram-que partem* ('Both Sides of the Question') took the Gelasian idea of spiritual and temporal spheres and argued for a complete separation of their functions. Using organic imagery, *Rex pacificus Salomon* said that although the political community may be regarded as a kind of body composed of both a temporal substance or authority and a spiritual substance or author-ity, nonetheless unlike a human body it can still function should the institutional Church and the pope be destroyed. On the contrary, the Church needed the protection of the state, meaning that in a practical sense the temporal authority was more essential than the ecclesiastical.[26] The Dominican theologian John of Paris, in *De potestate regia et papali* ('On Royal and Papal Power') accepted the greater dignity of the spiritual order but stressed that it was *purely* spiritual, thereby exercising no authority over temporal affairs. Such affairs were instead the province of secular government, which John, adapting Aristotle's *Politics* I.1–2, concluded was instituted according to natural law in order to promote the common good.[27] John also took Giles of Rome's principle of ecclesiastical *dominium* to task, saying that the property of lay people belonged to them alone and that the Church had no jurisdiction over it. Indeed, the pope did not even have jurisdiction over ecclesiastical property, since this belonged to individual ecclesiastical communities.[28]

In the end, this particular dispute was resolved through the exercise of raw force when a band of Philip's agents and some of Boniface's Roman enemies seized him at the papal palace of Anagni in 1303, the shock of which seems to have precipitated the elderly pontiff's death shortly thereafter. Still it should not be thought that the learned disquisitions of the intellectuals were mere window dressing. Both prelates and princes believed in the rule of law as did the communities over which they ruled. Actions in and of themselves were not sufficient, and those who advocated and carried them out felt the need to legitimate their desires and acts. Moreover, these theoretical arguments had real force in their own right, because they alone could convince other university-educated men, who, after all, staffed the administrations of both Church and state.[29] Furthermore it was principally through such disputations that the concept of the medieval state was articulated.

Giles of Rome and his opponents raised two other issues that were to take centre stage in the political debates of the next several decades: the power of the emperor and the poverty of Christ. At the start of the fourteenth century, a student of Aquinas and fellow Dominican, Ptolemy of Lucca, completed a treatise begun by his teacher, the *De regno* ('On Kingship'), which circulated as a combined work under the title *De regimine principum*. In it Ptolemy made a case for universal rule by the papacy as the best means for ensuring that virtuous city-states, like Lucca, could operate free of interference by an empire whose only legitimate acts were conducted as the pope's political agent.[30] Both John of Paris and the *Rex pacificus Salomon* made sure to assert the independence of the kingdom of France in relation to the Empire; this case was taken up in the *Tractatus de potestate papae* ('Treatise on Papal Power', 1316/17) of the Paris Dominican Pierre de la Palud, who used (or rather misused) historical evidence to claim French freedom from both imperial and papal power, while asserting papal dominance *over* the Empire.[31] At the same time as this was happening, lawyers like the Neapolitan civilian Andreas de Isernia and the Avignon canonist Oldradus de Ponte deployed legal arguments to release the Angevin kings of Naples from any jurisdictional obligation to the emperors.[32] If Ptolemy and the apologists of monarchs viewed the Empire as an obstacle to the consolidation of state sovereignty, some intellectuals from the communes of central and northern Italy, on the contrary, turned to it both as a peacekeeper in the volatile and competitive world of city-state politics and as a defence against an overly intrusive and authoritarian papacy. Most avid was the Florentine exile Dante Alighieri, who composed his *Monarchia*, probably in 1317–18 as a response to John XXII's attack on the legitimacy of the imperial vicariates that had recently been granted by Emperor Henry VII to several central and northern Italian *signori*.[33] Aimed at a learned and largely clerical audience, the *Monarchia* drew heavily from a wide array of biblical, classical, legal and Aristotelian authorities to argue that the universal peace necessary for humankind's reaching its highest potential could only be attained under the rule of the Roman emperor, whose power was derived directly from God. Any effort on the part of the papacy to interfere with or negate this power was contrary to nature, God's law and Christ's example:

> Thus he himself left the form of his life on record in *John* when he said: 'I have given you an example that as I have done to you, so you do also.' And indeed he specifically said to Peter, after he had entrusted the office of shepherd to him, as is recorded in the same gospel: 'Peter follow me.' But in Pilate's presence, Christ denied exercising any such directive power over our mortality: 'My kingdom is not of this world. If my kingdom were of this world, my servants would certainly strive that I should not be delivered to the Jews. . . .'[34]

At Paris a few years later, another Italian, the physician and arts master Marsilius of Padua, took up the imperial banner in his *Defensor pacis* (1324). For Marsilius the papacy's illegitimate meddling in temporal affairs was the world's greatest source of discord and violence. By rights the Church and its clergy had no jurisdictional authority whatsoever, but rather had a duty within the commonwealth 'to teach the commands and counsels of the evangelical Christian law in those things that must be believed, done or avoided with view to the status of the world to come'. As such, priests, including the bishop of Rome, were only officers of the state, along with soldiers and judges.[35] As for jurisdiction, it is founded upon laws made either by the universal body of citizens or by its 'prevailing part', and its proper exercise should be in the hands of a prince, 'be it one man or several', whose power is itself subject to the law.[36] So far all this sounds like a defence of civic republicanism, and so it was. But Marsilius, like Dante before him, also advocated the need for a universal and Christian authority who could stand above localised disputes and maintain universal order and peace. This 'defender of the peace', this 'faithful human legislator who lacks a superior', had, since the time of Constantine the Great, been the Roman emperor. When Marsilius wrote the *Defensor pacis*, the current claimant to the imperial title, Ludwig IV of Bavaria, was locked in conflict with Pope John XXII over the question of imperial jurisdiction in northern Italy. According to the pope, Ludwig's claims to jurisdiction were invalidated on the grounds that he had not yet received papal confirmation of his imperial title. Marsilius meant the *Defensor pacis* to serve as a radical rejection of such arguments.

In 1326 Marsilius fled to Ludwig's court and became one of his principal learned advisors. He was joined there in 1328 by a group of Franciscans who had fallen afoul of the papal curia over the issue of whether or not Christ and the apostles had been absolutely poor. This issue of absolute poverty had opened a rift within the Franciscan order between the radical Spirituals who advocated for absolute poverty within the order, in imitation of Christ, and the Conventuals, who favoured a moderate position whereby the order could enjoy the use of goods without claiming their ownership. John XXII, who had taken the side of the Conventuals, promulgated a number of bulls against the Spirituals, culminating in *Cum inter nonnullos* (1323), which declared their position heretical. The anathematised Franciscans, led by the general of their order, Michael of Cesena, and including among their number the English theologian William of Ockham, found a willing host in Ludwig, who delighted in adding yet more antipapalists to his stable of intellectuals.

John was right to fear the Spiritual Franciscan position, since the apostolic poverty they advocated for their own order could easily apply by extension to the clergy as a whole. This was, in fact, precisely what Marsilius argued in *Defensor pacis*, saying the whole clergy was bound by their vows to follow the example of Christ and the apostles, who practised perfect poverty:

It is a vow, I say, further, by which he wills, for the sake of Christ, to be deprived of and to lack, both as proper to himself or in common, all power, disposition, and handling or use of [riches] superfluous to what is sufficient for him at the present moment, both in quantity and in quality. Nor is it his will to have such goods, however licitly they may come to him, all at once in order to supply many future needs or wants, either for himself or in common. . . . Rather, his will is to have them only for a single need at once, for example the immediately pressing and almost present want of food or covering.[37]

Ockham too attacked the pope over the matter of property and poverty, saying that the Franciscans, like Christ and the apostles, exercised their natural right to *use* goods sufficient to survival, but that neither they nor indeed the Church had any power of *dominium* over property or people. This power was, rather, the preserve of temporal rulers, like Ludwig's ally King Edward III of England, who could, in support of his righteous war against France in 1338 tax the clergy of his realm without papal permission, since

it can clearly be seen that by human law, namely, that of the king, the possessions of the clergy are possessed by them from the lordship of the king of England. . . . God did not give to the ministers of the new law any special possessions, but ordained only that the lay people provide for their needs. Therefore, everything they have, especially the surplus, is conferred on them by kings and those subject to kings.[38]

Ockham's learned support of temporal rulers had motivations profoundly different from those of Marsilius, for whereas the latter desired peace and civic autonomy in his native Italy, the former sought to restore Christian society to a state of evangelical purity. Perhaps no late medieval intellectual evinced greater fervour for fundamental reform, however, than Ockham's countryman John Wyclif (d. 1384), who, during the 1370s, proved perfectly willing to serve the interests of secular princes when they agreed with his own. The expenses of renewed hostilities with France brought forth calls in England for expropriation of ecclesiastical property in aid of the war effort. Such sentiments accorded well with Wyclif's developing theories of reforming a Church hopelessly mired in sin. He believed this could only be achieved if secular rulers, who alone had rightful *dominium* in cases of sin, seized the possessions of the Church, thus forcing the clergy to return to a life of apostolic purity: 'Kings, princes, and temporal lords can lawfully and very meritoriously take riches away from any ecclesiastical person or community habitually abusing them'.[39]

Wyclif published his treatises on *dominium* in 1378. Shortly thereafter his own heretical views on the Eucharist lost him the support of his aristocratic supporters, chief among them Richard II's uncle John of Gaunt, duke of Lancaster, while his evangelical and anticlerical teachings found favour with the leaders of the Peasants' Revolt of 1381 and with a growing body of devout puritans whose enemies labelled them Lollards. The year 1378 also witnessed the opening of a rift in the seamless mystical Body of Christ when a dispute between the papal curia, recently returned to Rome after seven decades in the south of France, and the Roman commune led to the election of two popes. The ensuing Great Schism (1378–1415) further damaged the reputation of the papacy and compelled the competing claimants to garner the support of secular princes. This and the final recognition, enshrined in the Golden Bull of Charles IV in 1356, of the efficacy of election by the seven imperial electors to make an emperor without papal approval, together changed the terms of political debate at the end of the fourteenth century. From here on the sphere of politics stood apart from claims of universal sovereignty, whether exercised by pope or emperor. Debates about the governance of the Church continued but now the intellectuals focused on the issue of internal reform; meanwhile the apologists of territorial and city-states asserted the identity of their polities as fully autonomous, sovereign entities.

Informing the prince: works of instruction and advice

Intellectuals lent their talents to rulers not only in the form of learned polemics designed to be read by other men of learning but also in the guise of texts of political instruction. Although a few of these works were intended for a broader readership of politically active citizens, most had a princely recipient in mind, hence the generic name 'mirror of the prince'. In an age when political power was largely the preserve of aristocratic elites and monarchical rule was the norm, these works were no mere exercises in personal pedagogy but performed the vital task of mediating sophisticated and complex ideas about governance for the benefit of both rulers and ruled. Although works of princely instruction did not originate in the late Middle Ages, there can be no doubt that this was the era in which they proliferated and reached their mature form. The chief expectations and values expressed in the mirrors were: (1) that rulers should be wise, knowledgeable, virtuous and tireless promoters of the common good; (2) that these qualities could be learned; and (3) that a prince properly educated in the art of governance was the best guarantor of a strong (albeit regulated), fortunate and long-lasting rule. These works also presented themselves as a special kind of counsel, one that embodied the wisdom and knowledge of the ages (and of the learned individuals who composed them) and that could be internalised through diligent study. A prince so schooled not only became a political 'expert' but was, or so it was hoped, far less likely to veer off down the path toward tyranny.

Like the polemics discussed earlier, the mirrors were by and large products of the new learning of the universities. Their authors were, for the most part, university graduates; and even those who were not, were well versed in the principal texts of the arts curriculum. The mirrors, however, also express a new model of the lettered, technically competent ruler, whose immediate precursors were philosopher-kings like the Hohenstaufen Frederick II (d. 1250) and his son Manfred of Sicily (d. 1266), and Alfonso X 'the Wise' of Castile (d. 1284). Moreover, these texts evince a desire on the part of both the intellectuals and their prospective audiences to make the learning of the universities available to a public beyond the confines of the classroom. The earliest examples of this new kind of text of princely instruction were composed, starting in the second half of the thirteenth century, by mendicant friars schooled at the University of Paris and associated with the Capetian court. What distinguished these mirrors from earlier works of political instruction was not only their mendicant authorship but also their clearly didactic tone and a desire to vulgarise the sophisticated, and mostly Aristotelian, moral philosophical learning of the university curriculum.

The masterpiece and 'best-seller' of this genre was Giles of Rome's *De regimine principum* (c. 1280). In *De regimine* Giles made available the most up-to-date 'political science' of the university curriculum, making liberal use of Aristotle's *Ethics*, *Politics* and *Rhetoric*, Thomas Aquinas's *Summa theologica*, and several classical authors, including, most importantly, the late Roman military manual of Flavius Renatus Vegetius, *De re militari*. Giles's message found a large and diverse audience in the late Middle Ages, as evidenced by some 300 surviving Latin copies and another eighty copies in vernacular translations into French,

Italian, Castilian, Catalan, Flemish, Low German, High German and English; there is even a Hebrew translation, and a Portuguese translation was made but subsequently lost. The popularity of such a text cannot be credited only to its early dissemination via the Capetian court and University of Paris, although this doubtless played a role. It was also broadly useful, whether to university scholars and learned ecclesiastics, to kings, princes and the greater nobility or to country gentry and urban merchants. And if Giles's preference for hereditary kingship and prerogative rule must have appealed to monarchs and their supporters, his insistence on rule according to virtue and directed to the common good, and the necessity of good, broadly based counsel surely attracted the favourable attention of nobles like the English Thomas, Lord Berkeley, an opponent of Richard II's absolutist rule, who in the 1390s patronised the English translation by John Trevisa.[40]

Academics used *De regimine principum* as a means better to understand and apply the teaching of Aristotle on moral philosophy, and both they and the mirror's lay readers appreciated the political efficacy of Aristotle's doctrine, since they knew he had tutored Alexander the Great. Little wonder then that these same readers also applied themselves to the study of a work calling itself the *Secretum secretorum* ('Secret of Secrets'), which purports (falsely) to be a letter of instruction from Aristotle to his former pupil. Never mind that it was in fact a Latin translation of a multi-authored Arabic compilation of the ninth through eleventh centuries, its ascription to the Philosopher and the similarities of some of its passages to those found in the *Ethics* was enough to convince its medieval European translators and readers of its authenticity.[41] Part mirror of princes and part manual on health, hygiene and various forms of divination, its popularity is attested by roughly 600 Latin copies in several versions and scores of copies in assorted vernacular translations (as well as fifteen printed editions by 1520).

The *Secretum secretorum* and *De regimine principum* were the base texts of what amounted to a kind of Aristotelian political vernacular in the last centuries of the Middle Ages. Conjoined to this were works of advice for rulers which drew to a considerable extent from the Roman classical tradition of the four cardinal/civic virtues, but almost invariably combined this with Aristotelian material and a liberal admixture of biblical citations. Early examples of this genre were the *De quattuor virtutibus cardinalibus* ('On the Four Cardinal Virtues') of Henry of Rimini, the *Speculum virtutum* ('Mirror of the Virtues') of Engelbert of Admont and Luca Mannelli's *Compendium moralis philosophiae*. The Dominican Henry of Rimini probably wrote his treatise at the time he was resident in Venice at the beginning of the fourteenth century. Although its intended audience is unknown, the work's praise of Venice's mixed form of government, in which Aristotle's three good forms of government – monarchy, aristocracy and democracy – are combined, suggests a member of the Venetian ruling elite.[42] Between 1306 and 1313, the Austrian Benedictine abbot Engelbert of Admont combined elements from Giles of Rome's mirror of princes with heavy borrowings from classical Roman sources; he dedicated his work to the dukes of Austria, Albert II and Otto of Habsburg.[43] During the 1340s, the Florentine Dominican Mannelli prepared his *Compendium* in Latin for the soldier, poet and would-be *signore* Bruzio Visconti of Milan, and then translated it into Italian.[44] Despite their differences in emphasis and intended audience, all these works stressed the political efficacy of rule based on the exercise of the four cardinal virtues.

Not surprisingly it took no time for the Aristotelian mirror and Roman cardinal virtues strains to become inextricably blended, as they are in most books of princely advice from the fourteenth and fifteenth century. Nor did the popularity of these texts abate, since books of princely advice proliferated in all corners of Latin Christendom. Several were composed in France, the heartland of the mirror of princes, among which the most interesting was Christine de Pizan's *Livre du corps de policie* ('Book of the Body Politic'), written between 1404 and 1407 and dedicated to Charles VI and his eldest son, Louis of Guyenne. In it she blended elements of the *Policraticus*, the *De regimine principum* and various classical authors, but in such a way as to create a strikingly original work.[45] Across the Channel in England, books of instruction for princes flourished beginning in the late 1300s, when John Gower made the seventh book of his *Confessio amantis* into what amounts to a mirror; over the next century several more mirrors were written, including Thomas Hoccleve's *Regiment of Princes*, dedicated in 1411 to the future Henry V. In Bohemia, Michael the Carthusian of Prague compiled his *De quatuor virtutibus cardinalibus pro eruditione principum* ('On the Four Cardinal Virtues for the Instruction of Princes', 1387) in the form of a dialogue between himself and its intended reader, Rupert, duke of Bavaria, and Smil Flaška prepared his Czech *Nová Rada* ('New Counsel'), a blend of mirror of princes and fables on the cardinal virtues for Wenceslas IV during the 1390s.[46] In the 1340s in Castile, a Franciscan, who may have been Juan García de Castrojeriz translated, abridged and then attached a lengthy commentary to Giles's *De regimine principum* for the instruction of the heir to the throne, Pedro 'the Cruel'. *De regimine principum* influenced at least three other Castilian mirrors of princes, the *Libro de los estados* of Juan Manuel (1320s), the *Castigos e documentos* (in the expanded version of 1369) and the *Rimado de palaçio* of Pedro López de Ayala (1380s). The cardinal virtues also had plenty of currency in Castilian mirrors and were used by Juan de Mena as the framework upon which he built his poem of political advice for King Juan II, the *Laberinto de Fortuna* (1444).[47] In fifteenth-century Italy complicated city-state politics made their mark on the books of political instruction written by the humanists. The Sienese Francesco Patrizi wrote two versions of a treatise during the 1470s, one called *De institutione reipublicae* ('On the Education of the Republic') and the other *De regno et regis institutione* ('On the Kingdom and the Education of the King'); similarly, the Vatican librarian Bartolomeo Platina dedicated a treatise *De principe* ('On the Prince') to the marquis of Mantua, Federico Gonzaga, in 1471, and then, a few years later, presented a reworked and re-titled version, *De optimo cive* ('On the Best Citizen') to Lorenzo de' Medici 'the Magnificent', the *de facto* ruler of ostensibly republican Florence.[48]

But whether they were stressing the advantages of republican or monarchic government, and despite their growing respect for Plato's *Republic*, these humanist authors continued to hold to the basic Aristotelian and classical Roman principle of good government being predicated on an active life of virtue dedicated to the common good. Still, certain aspects of more pragmatic and hard-headed counsel start to be found in the books of advice written in the fifteenth century. Christine de Pizan, for example, in her *Livre des trois vertus* ('Book of the Three Virtues', 1406), a kind of mirror of princes for ladies, advises that a princess should feign unknowing when in the presence of her enemies, despite knowledge of their plots:

> The wise lady will use this prudent device of discreet dissimulation, which should not be considered vicious but rather a great virtue when employed for the common good. . . . Not only will she escape trouble but she will also achieve great benefit if she pretends not to notice conspiracy against her.

She later counsels that 'expedient hypocrisy is not unworthy for others desiring honor, as long as they practice for worthy ends'.[49] Hoccleve's *Regiment*, long regarded as the fairly

derivative and jejune work of a mediocre talent, has more recently been read as 'a calculated act of self promotion' by the chancery clerk and his scheming patron Prince Henry.[50]
Indeed what looks on the surface to be very traditional political language may, in works like
John Lydgate's *Fall of Princes* (1430s), be fundamental reconfigurations of meaning. So,
for example, the traditional relationship between fortune and the cardinal virtues, wherein
the well-counselled virtuous man better avoids bad fortune and maintains a stoic resolve in the
face of both good and ill fortune – as in the *Fall of Princes*' source, Boccaccio's *De casibus
virorum illustrium* ('On the Fall of Famous Men') – becomes in Lygate's re-working a kind
of fortune-proofing whereby the poet's patron, Humphrey, duke of Gloucester, exercises
pre-emptive foresight:

> Eyed like Argus with reason and foresight;
> Of his learning, I dare also say of him,
> And truly do believe he does surpass
>
> In understanding all others of his age,
> And greatly enjoys communing with scholars.
> And no man is more expert in language,
> As he continues always stable in study,
> Setting aside all changes of Fortune.[51]

Lydgate goes so far as to defy Fortune, asserting:

> A man who is armed with virtue
> In order to resist your [Fortune's] power,
> And puts his trust, by grace, in Jesus Christ,
> And gives heartfelt attention
> To Justice, Fortitude and Prudence,
> And their sister called Temperance,
> Has a safe-conduct against your changeableness![52]

In Lydgate's 'virtue' we begin to see a new usage of the terminology of the cardinal virtues,
one that looks a bit more like Niccolò Machiavelli's *virtù*.[53] Still, it must be said that the *virtù*
of Machiavelli's *Il Principe* ('The Prince') has taken on a distinctly harder edge and flexibil-
ity, meaning 'whatever range of qualities the prince may find it necessary to acquire in order
to maintain his regime and achieve great things'.[54] Lydgate's Prince deftly rode Fortune's
wheel; Machiavelli's tamed Fortune herself. In some ways, *Il Principe* conforms to the genre
of the mirror of princes. Machiavelli (1469–1527), exiled from his native Florence, where he
had served as chancery secretary in the republican government until its dissolution in 1512,
dedicated *Il Principe* in 1515 to the currently reigning strongman, the young Lorenzo de'
Medici. It purports, like other mirrors, to be a form of counsel, offered in hopes of instructing
the prince in the knowledge and skills necessary for successful rule. But unlike other mirrors,
which demand unbroken moral rectitude of their audience, Machiavelli advises his prince that
the good man must be willing to be bad when being bad secures desirable ends. And rather
than adopting the tone of calm didacticism of other mirrors, Machiavelli's has an immediate
and pressing purpose, the restoration of a strong Florentine republic under a politically canny
and ruthless leader who can unify Italy and drive out the barbarians, whether French, Spanish
or German, who for so long have disturbed the peace and curtailed Italian liberty:

So you should not let this opportunity slip by. Italy, so long enslaved, awaits her redeemer. There are no words to describe with what devotion he would be received in all those regions that have suffered from foreign invasions which have flooded across the land. No words can describe the appetite for revenge, the resolute determination, the spirit of self-sacrifice, the tears of emotion that would greet him. What gates would be closed to him? What community would refuse to obey him? Who would dare be jealous of his success? What Italian would refuse to pledge him allegiance? Everyone is sick of being pushed around by the barbarians. Your family must commit itself to this enterprise. Do it with the confidence and hope with which people embark on a just cause so that, marching behind your banner, the whole nation is ennobled.[55]

Finally, whereas the authors of mirrors typically *appealed* to the authority and example of the ancients, Machiavelli *used* ancient and recent history to teach real-life lessons about effective action in contingent circumstances. Given *Il Principe*'s debt to humanism and its appropriation of the late medieval mirror of princes genre, on the one hand, and its striking innovation, on the other, it is no surprise that modern-day medievalists and Renaissance scholars tend to see him as standing at the end of an era, whereas early modern and modern historians and political theorists regard him as the harbinger of modernity.

Performing and displaying the state

The authors of mirrors and related works of political advice and instruction wrote in response to perceived needs: they and, one presumes, their audiences believed in the *utility* of these texts. But the mirrors' utility went far beyond the particular teachings they expressed. To start, the authors of mirrors were always motivated by their own particular, and immediate, political agendas and programmes. Thus mirrors usually offered at one and the same time a plea on the part of the author to be taken into the target audience's confidence, a legitimation of a ruler or a particular kind of government, and an implied (or occasionally overt) critique of that ruler or government. Beneath their calm, contemplative façade one can, at times, perceive a desperate effort to ameliorate a crisis, as one can see with the several mirrors produced during the calamitous reign of Charles VI of France (1380–1422). More importantly, however, the mirrors were crucial contributors to and manifestations of political ideologies and mythologies, operating as vehicles of what might be called 'propaganda'. As such they participated in a much larger and varied field of political communication which included not only other literary and rhetorical forms, like history, prophecy, speeches and sermons, but also ceremonies, symbols and iconography. This broader field included many more participants than that of the audience of works of political theory and political instruction. Indeed, it included all members of society, whose involvement and perceptions certainly varied: after all, a political sermon on the virtues of a good citizen would make a slightly different impression on an alewife than on a noblewoman or a chantry priest. This broader group can be termed the 'public' and their collective attitudes constituted 'public opinion'.

Here we would do well to define a few key terms. *Ideologies* are 'collective belief systems that are often inconsistent with the "facts", but no less powerful or historically significant for those inconsistencies'.[56] Every ideology has its own 'vocabulary', constructed partly of *myths* – that is 'powerful stories that organize experiences, aspirations, fears and memories into more or less coherent accounts of how the world is perceived to be and how it ought to be'[57] – and partly of sentiments, images and ideas, the most powerful and influential of which are often those 'soundbites, buzz-words, strings of interrelated terms and pre-packaged sections of argument' that 'exist, and flourish, and propagate themselves principally in the words which constitute them'.[58] Ideologies are cultivated and promoted principally by means of *propaganda*, a term which usually carries a negative connotation in today's common usage, but which will be used here in the neutral sense of any means by which political actors and agents of the state communicated a political message or projected an image or version of the state in order to mould public sentiment and 'generate allegiances'.[59]

The nineteenth-century Swiss scholar Jacob Burckhardt spoke of the Renaissance state as a 'work of art', in the sense of princes legitimating their power by means of works of art and festivals.[60] Conceived rather more broadly, both chronologically and geographically, and taking into account the manifold rituals and occasions by which political power and authority expressed themselves, this notion of the state can be useful. It can indeed be argued that every state is a work of performance art and that in the late Middle Ages, when the institutions of state power were still relatively weak, the various means of propagating political ideology did more 'to shore up the unsteady trusses of the state than any institutions'.[61] Propaganda, to be effective, needs an audience, so the best place to find it at work is during public occasions. Public assemblies were excellent opportunities for such performances. Meetings of the English Parliament, for example, began with a sermon by the Chancellor (who was usually a cleric). In particularly charged circumstances the ideological programme might be quite baldly put, as in Bishop Edmund Stafford's sermon to the Parliament of 1397, in which Richard II exacted his revenge on those nobles who nine years previously, in the so-called 'Merciless Parliament', had appealed several of his friends for treason. Its theme, taken from the prophecy of Ezekiel, was 'There will be one king ruling over all':

> In [it] he always came to the same conclusion, that the king's power was united, attached and entire in him, and that those who removed, impeded or disturbed it would rightly suffer the punishment of the law. And so the present parliament had been ordained for fulfilling that purpose, first, by inquiring who disordered the power and royal state of the king, and second, by determining which penalties were to be meted out to those who had done so. Third, a remedy was to be arranged in order that in future nothing further would perturb the king.[62]

Normally, however, the sermons dressed themselves in the calm, didactic garments of the mirrors of princes, like the sermon of John Stafford, bishop of Bath and Wells, to Parliament which opened in January 1442, whose structure and language were very similar to those found in a contemporary mirror entitled *Tractatus de regimine principum ad Regem Henricum Sextum* (see above in this chapter) or those composed by Bishop John Russell of Lincoln in 1483–84, which through the use of body politic imagery and the repeated emphasis on the 'common weal' and 'our republic' stressed the notion of government as a collective responsibility of citizens under the direction of the monarch.[63] Similar performances were given on occasions of state by Guillaume Hugonet, chancellor of Charles the Bold of Burgundy, who, like his contemporary Russell, had a fondness for discussing the cardinal virtues and citing Cicero's *De officiis*. That kings were marked out by their superabundance of virtue was insisted upon by both the chancellor of France and the speaker of the estates in speeches given during the meeting of the French Estates General in 1484.[64]

Even kings themselves at times weighed in, as both Pere IV (1336–87) and Marti I (1395–1410) of Aragon did on occasion by preaching to meetings of the *Cortes*.[65] And occasions for royal preaching sometimes extended beyond legislative assemblies. Take for example the case of King Charles II 'the Bad' of Navarre. One evening in 1355 this ally of the English and future *bête noire* of the kings of France had been dining in the city of Rouen in Normandy with the dauphin Charles, duke of Normandy, and some members of the Norman nobility. King John, who suspected that the king of Navarre and some of the Normans were plotting against him, surprised them as they dined and arrested them. He proceeded forthwith to throw Charles of Navarre into prison and summarily executed four of the Normans, publicly displaying their heads impaled on stakes and their bodies suspended from gibbets. When Charles of Navarre obtained his release from prison at the end of 1357, he immediately began to exact revenge on the Valois. Instead of resorting to violence, however, he employed a combination of oratory and ceremony. First he preached to an enormous crowd at Saint-Germain-des-Prés on the outskirts of Paris in order to gain favour with the citizens there. Shortly thereafter he travelled to Rouen, scene of his earlier arrest. There, as recompense for what he and many others thought had been a gravely unjust act on the part of King John (who by then was himself a hostage of Edward III of England after the French defeat at Poitiers in 1356), Charles combined preaching and elaborate ritual in an impressive bit of political theatre:

> [H]e had the bodies [of the executed Normans] which were affixed to the gibbet . . . taken down on Innocents' Day [28 December, although in fact this occurred on 10 January 1358] and borne in procession with great lighted candles and a great multitude of people to the cathedral of Saint Mary at Rouen. There, after the bells had been rung and masses solemnly celebrated and a sermon delivered by the king on the text 'The innocent and righteous have cleaved to me: because I have expected thee', the bodies were buried honorably in the chapel of the Innocents to the no small wonder of all the people.[66]

Another king, Robert of Naples, even went so far as to make royal preaching a fundamental aspect of policy, composing and delivering hundreds of sermons during his reign (1309–43). Robert gave these sermons, which bear all the marks of the learned homilies of university masters, in all kinds of venues, whether formal state occasions, religious rites or academic ceremonies. In so doing, he distinguished himself as a king noted for wisdom and learning, and reinforced the sacral character of his kingship.[67] He even had his corpse depicted on his tomb attended by personifications of the seven liberal arts.

As the two preceding examples illustrate, religious language and symbolism were never far from political performances; nor was the ideology of mirrors of princes, with their stress on princely learning, civic virtues and the common good. One distinctive feature of the late Middle Ages was the tendency of these pieces of political theatre to become increasingly sophisticated and elaborate, whether in formal occasions at court, in meetings of assemblies, or during coronations, funerals and ceremonial processions. Monarchies promoted themselves on the basis of their sacredness, exemplified in the anointing ceremonies included in many dynasties' coronations. The Capetian and Valois kings took this a step further with the legend of the Holy Ampulla, brought down from heaven by a dove for the anointing of the first king of the Franks, Clovis, and miraculously refilled with chrism for each new coronation of a French king. Perhaps feeling outdone by their rivals across the Channel in this regard, the English in the 1300s confected their own legend of a miraculous oil which had been delivered by the Virgin Mary to St Thomas of Canterbury, and which, although subsequently lost, would, when found, bring to the king anointed therewith the restoration of lands lost, the first of which would be Normandy and Aquitaine.[68] When Henry of Lancaster seized the English throne from Richard II in 1399, it seems he had the good fortune to discover the miraculous oil, which the archbishop of Canterbury, Thomas Arundel, used forthwith to anoint him. Still, whatever benefit Henry IV may have received from this oil was clearly open to question, as the chronicler Adam of Usk relates that 'as a result of his anointing . . . his head was so infected with lice that his hair fell out'.[69] Other sacred aspects played up in the coronation ritual might be the identification of the body of the king with the Body of Christ – as clearly symbolised by the image of King Alfonso II of Naples riding to his coronation under a canopy in imitation of the procession of the consecrated host during the feast of Corpus Christi – the equation of the king with the episcopate, as adopted in the coronations of the Angevin kings of Naples and by King Charles V of France, and the singing of the *laudes regiae*, taken up by the kings of Castile in the late Middle Ages and used at the coronation of Edward IV of England in 1461.

Ritualised processions, inspired by the *adventus* (imperial entry) of Roman antiquity, were not new to the late Middle Ages, but what had been relatively simple ceremonies

Figure 4.1 Tomb of Robert of Naples, Santa Chiara, Naples. Photograph: Alinari

became increasingly complex vehicles for propaganda. In France, during the later decades of the fourteenth century, royal entries into the more important towns became elaborate affairs indeed. It was during this time that the king first began to ride under a canopy in imitation of the Body of Christ and that local confraternities and guilds began to stage *tableaux vivants* along the procession route. During the next century these 'mystery plays' multiplied and frequently presented a strongly pro-royal message, so that 'by the end of the fifteenth century a royal entry had become a grand spectacle in which the king's advisers adeptly developed all the themes of monarchical propaganda'.[70] English royal entries also became involved affairs in the fifteenth century, as when Henry V returned to London on 23 November 1415 after his victory at Agincourt just over a month earlier. Greeted by the mayor, aldermen and representatives of the city's guilds, lauded by choirs dressed as Old Testament prophets and angels and by maidens crowned with laurels and blowing gold leaf upon the king from golden goblets, he was acclaimed as 'flower of the English and of the world, knight of Christ!' and 'Henry ye fifte, Kynge of Englond and of Fraunce'. As for the king himself, he played his part well, as a humble servant of God, eschewing crown and sceptre but nonetheless robed in imperial purple and leading a group of French noble prisoners. According to one observer, 'from his quiet demeanour, gentle pace, and sober progress, it might have been gathered that the king, silently pondering the matter in his heart, was rendering thanks and glory to God alone, not to man'.[71] The royal demeanour also impressed the royal clerk Pierre Salmon in the case of Charles V of France, who when riding in public in royal array was seen 'not as a man but as the exemplar of justice and model of good character, and as a mirror of all honours'.[72]

Kings, then, in their *public* persona functioned as a sort of central organising metaphor or symbol. They represented the royal 'majesty', a term that gained ever greater currency during the fourteenth and fifteenth centuries, and that majesty was the guarantor of peace, order, justice and true religion. This was true, whatever the personal foibles or failures of the king as a *private* person. In other words, the king really had two bodies, one personal, private and mortal and the other formal, public and deathless. It was in this second sense – that sense that frequently was termed the 'crown' or 'dignity' – that the king *was* the state. No wonder, then, that more and more the symbols of monarchy, crown, sceptre and throne could stand in for the king, and why kings demonstrated the charisma of their office through the practice of their healing touch to those suffering from scrofula. This also explains why the symbolism of deathless royalty took on such significance in late medieval funerals. Funeral corteges, like royal entries, became elaborate performances as well, with the deceased monarch's catafalque topped by an effigy of the living king in royal habit and sheltered under a canopy. Likewise, royal successors no longer dated their accession to their coronation but rather to the very moment at which the old king died, so that by the end of the fifteenth century, at least in England and France, the phrase, 'the king is dead, long live the king!' was proclaimed.

Courts, too, became scenes for the articulation of elaborate ritual which amounted to a kind of 'civil liturgy'.[73] This is reflected in the growing expenditure and personnel of courts, as well as by the elaboration of decoration and ceremonial, all with the aim, as Pierre Salmon responded to Charles VI, of assuring that when the king was seated on his throne he might 'shine among and above all those of his realm through virtues and wisdom, by grace and through all good habits'.[74] Formal meals became a sacralised secular counterpart to the Eucharist, wherein every object and action was pregnant with meaning (for example,

Figure 4.2 Triumphal entry of Charles VII into Rouen, 1449. Paris, Bibliothèque nationale de France, ms. fr. 2679, fol. 322v

an object placed upon the prince's table called the *nef*, which looked like a boat, represented the prince in the same way as the monstrance represented the Body of Christ) and, in a tendency mirroring the ceremonial entry, elaborate decorations and *tableaux vivants* combined in a dazzling display of magnificence and majesty.[75] During the fifteenth century it was frequently non-royal courts like those of Burgundy and several of the Italian *signori* which took the lead in this expansion of courtly ostentation, perhaps in an effort to compete with the better-established symbolic practices of kings. Public assemblies also exploited the potential of symbolism, as for example when the Speaker of the Commons, Sir Arnold Savage, in a speech during the Parliament of 1401 narrated an extended analogy comparing that legislative body to a mass.[76] In France, meetings of the *Parlement* of Paris dealing with especially serious cases or legislation were held in the presence of the king himself, bearing the symbols of his office and seated upon a kind of raised and canopied throne called the *lit de justice* ('bed of justice'). Thus enthroned, the king emanated the awesome power of his divine office, holding justice 'in his person, sitting in his majesty'.[77] Similar symbolic strategies were employed by the Valois's princely competitors, the Montfort dukes of Brittany, who asserted the independence of their duchy from French jurisdiction through the use of their own royal vestments, crown, sceptre and *main de justice* ('hand of justice') during the ducal *parlements* over which they too presided in majesty.[78]

Rituals of political power found their own particular expressions in the republics and *signorie* of central and northern Italy. Both Venice and Rome (after the end of the Great Schism) practised elaborate coronation rituals for their elected rulers, the doge and the pope. But whereas royal coronations stressed dynastic continuity, those in Venice and Rome put the emphasis on *discontinuity*. Upon the Venetian doge's death, all emblems associated with his rule were ritually destroyed, and a new silver emblem depicting a stereotyped doge with the symbols of his office was struck for the newly elected doge, but with a space left blank where the doge's name should appear. This was done to symbolise 'the theory of the two doges', one being the perpetual office of the doge, and the other the mortal, elected one, who 'is tied by the laws in a way that his position is not at all different from the other positions of any magistracy'.[79] At a pope's death, his ring of office was removed from his finger and then broken, after which ritual defacement or destruction of public statues bearing his image often occurred. Once a new pope was elected, he first was presented with a newly fashioned ring of office and crowned in order to symbolise his accession to spiritual lordship over the Church. But then he performed the *possesso*, a ritual which symbolised his assumption of rule over the city of Rome, during which he rode to the Capitol on a white mule, an animal whose sexual sterility signified the celibate pope's inability to produce a legitimate heir and successor.[80]

All Italian cities had their patron saints, and their feast days were accompanied by elaborate civic rituals. So, for example, in Siena, whose patron saint was the Virgin Mary, the government, in the early fourteenth century, established the feast of the Assumption of the Virgin (15 August) as the city's chief civic and religious holiday. One ritual established in connection with this holiday was the procession of all citizens before the painted image of the Virgin in Siena's cathedral (Duccio di Buoninsegna's *Maestà*). Solemn entries too were a common form of political performance in the city-states. *Signori* marked their arrival in towns subject to their lordship with ritualised entries freighted with the symbols of their power. And in 1515, three years after the return to power of the Medici, the proud former republic of Florence performed its submission to its new ruling dynasty with a triumphal entry of the Medici pope Leo X (Giovanni de' Medici), in which the pontiff rode through a series of arches, each depicting one of the three theological and four cardinal virtues.[81]

The visual arts re-presented these performances through the media of illuminated books, illustrated pamphlets, mural paintings etc., thereby reinforcing their message and broadening their public. Artwork propagated the ideology of states in other ways as well. Many kings and dynasties exploited the sacred charisma of national patron saints and saintly ancestors. Particular stress was laid on saintly ancestors by the Angevin rulers of Naples in the late thirteenth and fourteenth century and by the Luxemburg kings of Bohemia during the second half of the fourteenth and early fifteenth century. The founder of the Angevin dynasty, Charles I, initiated this strategy by campaigning hard during the late thirteenth century for the canonisation of his older brother Louis IX of France, motivated by the desire to associate his own line with his sibling's saintly virtues. It even seems likely that he chose the spouse of his son and heir Charles II, Mary of Hungary, partly because the blood flowing in her veins was that of the Árpád dynasty, which boasted several royal saints: Stephen, Emeric, Ladislas and Elizabeth. With so much holiness in the blood, little wonder then that Charles II's heir, Louis of Toulouse, rejected worldly temptations, passing his claim to the throne on to his younger brother, Robert, joining the Franciscan Order, becoming bishop of Toulouse, caring for the poor, comforting the sick, and then dying (in 1297), all by the age of twenty-three. Robert and his queen Sancia played up Louis's saintliness for all it was worth, pushing hard, and successfully, for his canonisation in 1317, and patronising several works of art depicting this second St Louis (as well as other members of the dynasty's stable of saints). One of the finest and most arresting of these is Simone Martini's painting of Louis, enthroned as though a king, clothed in episcopal vestments bordered with the Capetian *fleurs de lis* (a reference to the Angevin dynasty and his great uncle Louis IX) and a Franciscan habit, bearing in his right hand his bishop's crozier and in his left a crown, which he places on Robert's head. Two angels place a similar crown on Louis's own mitred and haloed head, thus symbolising the divine origin of his and his brother's royalty.[82]

The king of Bohemia and Holy Roman Emperor, Charles IV of Luxemburg, employed a similar policy, sponsoring artworks in which he is associated with the relics of Christ's Passion, and in which he and his heir, Wenceslas, are depicted with Bohemia's patron saint, Wenceslas and the Luxemburg dynastic saint, Sigismund. In the votive painting (1370s) commissioned by one of the dynasty's most avid supporters, Archbishop John Očko of Vlašim, the upper register depicts Sts Sigismund and Wenceslas presenting Charles, in all his imperial regalia, and the young Wenceslas, crowned king of Bohemia, to the Virgin and Christ Child.[83] This scene may well have inspired Charles IV's son-in-law Richard II of England and the (perhaps Bohemian) artist responsible for the so-called Wilton Diptych (c. 1395–97). The two panels of the Wilton Diptych depict John the Baptist and the English patron saints King Edward the Confessor and King Edmund Martyr presenting a youthful looking Richard, crowned and wearing his personal symbols of the broom-cod collar and white-hart badge, to the Virgin and Christ Child, who are surrounded by eleven angels also wearing white-hart badges and broom-cod collars. One angel carries the banner of another English patron saint, George. Historians have argued over the meaning of the Diptych, asserting messages as diverse as supporting a crusade against the Turks to the more domestic political ones of English hegemony over the British Isles or Richard's revenge over his enemies in the Parliament of 1397. Whatever its specific import, there can be no doubt of

Figure 4.3 Charles IV and Wenceslas with Bohemian patron saints. Photograph © National Gallery in Prague 2008

Figure 4.4 Portrait of Richard II of England, Westminster Abbey. Photograph © Dean and Chapter of Westminster

Figure 4.5 Ambrogio Lorenzetti, *Allegory of Good Government*, Sala dei Nove, Palazzo Pubblico, Siena. Photograph: Heritage Image Partnership Ltd / Alamy Stock Photo

the Wilton Diptych's expression of divine sanction for Richard's rule. This message is also forcefully stated in the iconic portrait commissioned by the king for display in Westminster Abbey. In it, Richard, enthroned, crowned and bearing the orb and sceptre of his office, fixes the viewer with a serene but intimidating gaze, 'the secular reflection of Christ in majesty'.[84]

Monarchies had no monopoly on iconographic propaganda. The two frescoes executed in 1366–68 by Andrea di Bonaiuto in the chapter hall of the Dominican convent of Santa Maria Novella in Florence, although ostensibly depicting an allegory of the Church and Dominican Order, on the east wall, and the triumph of St Thomas Aquinas and an allegory of the sciences, on the west, also put contemporary viewers in mind of the legitimacy of the ruling oligarchic elite.[85] A generation earlier in the Hall of the Nine, in nearby Siena's Palazzo Pubblico, Ambrogio Lorenzetti painted his allegories of good and bad government, which asserted the instrumentality of the civic virtues, and especially justice, in the maintenance of peace, public order and prosperity.[86] Depictions of the cardinal virtues also were painted on the walls of churches in Ferrara and Padua in the fourteenth century and in the Sala Vecchia degli Svizzeri of the Vatican in the mid-1450s; some two decades before this, the new façade of London's Guildhall was adorned with statues representing these virtues.[87]

Conclusion: the king's body

In his *Memoirs*, the courtier and diplomat of Burgundian dukes and French kings Philippe de Commynes wrote of the death of King Charles VIII in April 1498. This young king, who had inspired such awe and fear during his invasion of Italy a few years before, took his queen, Anne of Brittany, to watch a game of tennis played in the dry moat of his castle at Amboise. He chose as the best vantage point a gallery, which was 'the filthiest place in the castle, for everyone pissed there and it was all broken down'. Entering the gallery he struck his head and a short time later 'he fell backwards and lost his speech'. He never left that filthy gallery alive, spending the next nine hours 'lying on a miserable straw mattress' until he expired:

> And so this great and powerful king died, and in such a miserable place, when he possessed so many magnificent houses and was building such a fine one, and he could not choose anything but a poor chamber to die in at the end. . . . How plainly . . . can we realize that the power of God is great . . . and our miserable life is a very little thing . . . and kings cannot resist it any more than a laborer.

Having spent so long as an intimate companion of kings, Commynes was unimpressed by the sacred charisma of royalty: kings, for him, 'are men like us'. When it came to performing the state, however, Charles VIII's sacred body was 'given very sumptuous funeral ceremonies', which 'never ceased by day or night' for about a month, 'and everything was richer than for any other king. . . . and it cost forty-five thousand francs, as I was told by people in charge of the finances'.[88] Government is very much a flesh and blood affair, but it is also an intellectualised and symbolic one. Language, act and image supported an ideology wherein the king's body and the body politic were joined to one another in an earthly manifestation of the Body of Christ through the agency of the virtues. The texts, ceremonies, symbols and images that propagated this ideology were every bit as instrumental to the growth and regulation of state power as any administrative office or source of finances. Still, when it came to what Peter Lewis has called the 'dirty-work' of politics, those more material underpinnings of the state were absolutely necessary, and it is to these and to those equally material factors that resisted and limited state power that we now turn.[89]

Notes

1 Menut 1970: 44 (my translation).
2 Coleman 2000: 59–69.
3 Black 1992: 12; Reinhard 1996: 1–18.
4 Canning 1996: 135–37.
5 Guenée 1985: 23.
6 Verger 2000b.
7 Verger 2000b: 31.
8 Verger 2000b: 33.
9 Black 1992: 7–12.
10 Dyson 2004: 37.
11 Watt 1971: 88.
12 Genet 1977: 56.
13 Riley 1863–64: vol. 2, 32.
14 Harding 1984: 166.
15 Lusignan 2003: 51–70; Canning 1996: 153.
16 Briggs 2012: 397–98.
17 Barlow 1950.
18 Watts 1990.
19 Witt 2003: 124–29.
20 Gamberini 2012: 409.
21 Nederman 1990: 31, 67.
22 Menut 1970: 44.
23 Coleman 2000: 56.

24 Canning 1996: 35–36, 99–100.
25 Dyson 2004: 173, 181.
26 Quillet 1995.
27 Watt 1971: 76–82.
28 Canning 1996: 147.
29 Dunbabin 1998: 166.
30 Blythe 1997: 36–37.
31 Dunbabin 1998.
32 Canning 1996: 170–71.
33 Kay 1998: xxvi–xxxi.
34 Kay 1998: 303–5.
35 Brett 2005: 22–23, 34–35.
36 Brett 2005: 557.
37 Brett 2005: 273.
38 Nederman 2002: 181.
39 McGrade, Kilcullen and Kempshall 2001: 590.
40 Briggs 1999.
41 Williams 2003.
42 Blythe 1992: 280–83.
43 Ubl 1994.
44 Briggs 2007.
45 Nederman 1998.
46 Storey 1972; Nejedlý 2000.
47 Sears 1952; Beltrán 1971.
48 Hankins 1996.
49 Willard 1989: 106–9.
50 Pearsall 1994: 410.
51 Bergen 1923: pt. 1, 11.
52 Bergen 1923: pt. 3, 682.
53 Strohm 2005: 89–109.
54 Coleman 2000: 247.
55 Wootton 1995: 79–80.
56 Najemy 2000: 80
57 Najemy 2000: 80
58 Watts 2002: 43.
59 Beaune 1991: 4.
60 Burckhardt 1958.
61 Beaune 1991: 10.
62 Stow 1977: 138.
63 Watts 2002.
64 Paravicini and Paravicini 2000; Lassalmonie 2000.
65 Pryds 1993.
66 Birdsall and Newhall 1953.
67 Pryds 1993.
68 Sandquist 1969: 332.
69 Given-Wilson 1997: 242–43.
70 Guenée 1985: 27–28.
71 Barker 2005: 331–36.
72 Lewis 1995: 122.
73 Guenée 1998: 644.
74 Rigaudière 2000: 375.
75 Bertelli 2001: 203; Huizinga 1996: 305–7.
76 Genet 1995: 103–4.
77 Brown and Famiglietti 1994: 24.
78 Jones 1995.
79 Muir 2004: 232.

80 Muir 2004: 237–8.
81 Ricciardelli 2015: 129; Muir 2004: 229–30, 242.
82 Klaniczay 2002: 308–9.
83 Rosario 2000: 91–92.
84 Scheifele 1999: 264–65.
85 Russo 1995.
86 Skinner 1986.
87 Pascucci 2001; Barron 2004.
88 Kinser and Cazeaux 1973: vol. 2, 590–94.
89 Lewis 1995.

5

THE LINEAMENTS AND
LIMITS OF STATE POWER

The person who gains whatever he desires seems to be perched at the very top of the wheel of Fortune, who, acting as God's chamberlain for the punishment of their sins, sometimes raises up and other times casts down men and women without discretion or advice and without regard for the quantity of men's merits, but according to a confused manner whose causes are evident to God. But men, being ignorant of divine ordinances, cannot know such causes. . . . All are participants in the mockeries of Fortune, who amuses herself by elevating and ruining men.[1]

French magnate Jean, duke of Berry, probably took cold comfort from these monitory words which Laurent de Premierfait addressed to him c. 1409 in the dedication of his second translation of Boccaccio's *De casibus virorum illustrium* ('Fall of Famous Men', 1358, first translated by Premierfait c. 1400). The history of Duke Jean's own lineage provided ample evidence of Fortune's mockeries. Just under a century before, Capetian King Philip IV died after a long and successful reign. He left behind a strong and, for its time, united realm and three healthy adult sons. Then, between 1314 and 1328 the Capetian line, which had reliably produced legitimate male heirs for over three centuries, ran through four kings. Louis X died having sat less than two years on the throne; his infant son, John I, followed him to the grave just a few days later. Louis's younger brothers, Philip V and Charles IV each reigned six years, neither producing a viable male heir, even though Charles was on his fourth wife at the time of his demise. The monarchy survived the extinction of the line by turning to Philip of Valois, Duke Jean's grandfather and the son of Philip IV's younger brother. Although the first three Valois kings had better fortune in so far as having sons was concerned, the first two suffered grave defeats in battle against the English: Philip VI at Crécy in 1346 and John II at Poitiers ten years later. King John indeed spent several years after the battle as a prisoner of his enemies. If his son Charles V fared better at war and the business of governance than his Valois predecessors, his weak physical constitution drove him to an early grave in 1380, leaving a child heir who, as King Charles VI, would descend into madness in 1392. Jean of Berry was one of the three royal uncles who worked to steer the ship of state during the uncertain years at the turn of the century. But Fortune's wiles conspired to create enmity between two of Jean's nephews, John the Fearless of Burgundy and Charles VI's younger brother Louis of Orléans. So poisoned did their relationship become, that in 1407 John conspired in his cousin Louis's murder, an act that would plunge France into civil war. Jean, then, was very well acquainted with the mysterious machinations of Fortune. Perhaps he turned again for consolation to Boccaccio's tragic stories of famous men when, shortly before his death, he lamented the slaughter of the flower of French chivalry on the fields of Agincourt.

The late medieval fascination (if not obsession) with Fortune is evidenced by the popularity of works dedicated to the theme. Boccaccio's book was frequently copied (83 manuscripts survive). Premierfait's translation was even more popular and served as the basis for Pedro López de Ayala's Castilian translation (c. 1400) and John Lydgate's versified *Fall of Princes* (c. 1438). John the Fearless even went so far as to cite Boccaccio/Premierfait in defence of his sanguinary actions in 1407, while just over a half-century later his grandson's court historian, Georges Chastelain dedicated his continuation of Boccaccio, the *Temple de Bocace*, to Margaret of Anjou after her fall from power as queen of England in 1461. In this work Chastelain had no trouble whatsoever coming up with forty fallen kings and nobles since the time of Crécy.[2] The late medieval popularity of this theme, like the contemporary taste for mirrors of princes, can perhaps be explained by a growing awareness of the fragility and contingency of political order in a time when state power was at once increasingly present in people's lives and yet still so dependent on imperfect, passible, mortal bodies. Politics, after all, continued to be fundamentally dynastic and personal, even as the institutional foundations of the modern and impersonal national state were in the process of being laid. Thus political fortunes depended not only on such perennial variables as weather and war, but also on marriage, childbirth (or failure thereof), sickness, madness and sudden, unlooked-for death. Little wonder that so many thought it prudent to take account of Boccaccio's doleful counsel:

> [F]ix this in your mind: Whenever anyone's situation seems to be taken for granted by ever-turning Fortune, then in the midst of this unfortunate credulity, she is preparing a trap. Far as we seem to be carried up to the stars, in the same way our hopes are very carefully planted in the depths.[3]

Few contemporary historiographical discourses are as vexed and contentious as that concerning the genesis of the modern national state. This results in part from a tendency to see the modern state as a kind of natural and perfect entity, one that necessarily *had* to come into being and is the final product of inexorable and rational historical forces. According to this way of thinking, European states like France or Spain are the result of a teleological progression, whereby a people and territory who share a natural affinity gradually articulate the institutions and realise the natural bonds that unite them. This tendency, however, is itself an outgrowth of what can be called the 'myth of modernity', the idea that out of the declining, decadent morass of the Middle Ages, modern Western civilisation emerged thanks to the regenerative and purgative movements of the Renaissance and Reformation. According to this way of thinking, the kernel of the modern national state, like those of rational thought, enlightened secularism and reformed religion, lay germinating in the late Middle Ages, finally springing forth at the dawn of the modern era. The most extreme form of the modernist argument denies the very existence of the 'state' in the Middle Ages, preferring terms like 'regime', and sees the birth of the nation as being coeval with that of the state. Responding to this challenge, medievalists have asserted the genesis of both states and nations in the Middle Ages, although sensibly conceding that medieval polities were of a different order from the modern national state.

The quest for the roots of the 'modern' in the medieval has, on the whole, been a salutary one. If a nationalist ideology lay far in the industrial capitalist future, in several of these polities one can nonetheless find plenty of evidence for a growing sense of collective consciousness and sentiment, as in late medieval France, England, Bohemia or Hungary, as well as in city-states like Florence and Venice. Even in the fractious and fragmented political topographies of northern Italy and Germany, some sense of an Italian people and a German *natio* is clearly discernible. Chronicles and romances promoted notions of a nation's common and ancient ancestry, a genetic heritage that in dynastic states found its purest expression in the persons of the royal family. National saints, like George and Edward the Confessor in England, or Denis and Michael in France, served as loci for shared veneration, and the sense of a common language played an important role in the articulation of Castilian, English, German and Italian national sentiment. Likewise if a polity only merits the designation 'state' with the coming of absolutism and 'reason of state' pragmatics, or once it has achieved the territorial sovereignty, monopoly of the legitimate use of force and 'homogenous mass of subjects each of whom has the same rights and duties' with which today we are familiar, then surely there were no medieval states worthy of the name.[4] But looked at in another way, late medieval polities had many of the attributes of states. They developed increasingly sophisticated and competent bureaucracies at both the central and local level, they exercised justice in the name of the king, prince or commune, they taxed their subjects with the consent of some sort of representative body, they waged war with publicly financed armies of paid soldiers, and they at least dreamed of territorial boundaries that roughly conform to those of several contemporary states. Yet the trajectories of these late medieval states were neither simple nor straightforward; nor were they all alike. If the origins of some modern European states, and of the modern national state as a type, can be traced to the Middle Ages, the outcome was hardly preordained and the course was very much subject to the contingencies of Lady Fortune. This chapter will first describe the common structural and relational aspects of state power and its limits. It will then trace some of the more salient political developments in the histories of different regions and polities. Because war played such an important role in the development and fortunes of states, it merits further discussion in the next chapter.

The structures of rule: monarchic states

The states of the late Middle Ages were inheritors of a machinery of government developed and refined over the course of the twelfth and thirteenth centuries. They also inherited, for the most part, fairly modest expectations on the part of the governed of the place of government in their lives. Basically, that role was conservative and consisted of rendering justice, defending the realm, protecting the Church and true religion, and keeping the peace and preserving the social order. For the governed, innovation was not normally a good thing. Rulers, for their part, felt entitled to exercise and enforce their will. However absolute princes might have wished their rule to be – and some wanted this more than others – successful and sustained rule was nonetheless dependent on an ongoing dialogue and give-and-take with the political community. The reason for this was, quite simply, that the power of medieval states and rulers was limited in every way. It was limited by such factors as local and regional particularism and the competing interests of the political elites, as well as by the modest potentialities of its administrative apparatus and finances. Still, innovation and experimentation certainly did occur, largely in response to the financial demands of warfare, so that by the start of the fifteenth century, the states of Europe and their governments were beginning to look more like what we think of as 'modern' rather than 'feudal' polities.

In terms of their form and level of complexity, the polities of late medieval Europe exhibited a striking diversity, ranging from the very limited capacities of the Scandinavian and

Scottish monarchies, to the internally sophisticated but militarily constrained Italian city-states, to the great dynastic national monarchies of England and France, to such transnational entities as the dominions of the Aragonese royal family. In what follows, attention will first be given to the common structures of states ruled by dynastic monarchies (with some reference to the peculiar features of the Empire) and then of some of the city-states of northern Italy. This will be followed by a discussion of the less formal, but nonetheless critically important channels through which state power was exercised.

The typical national monarch of 1300 presided over a government administered, at both the central and local level, by offices and officials responsible for communication, finance and justice. Although the central institutions of government had their origins in the royal household, there was a tendency for them to move 'out of court' and become free-standing offices, staffed by salaried professionals. Royal correspondence was the province of a writing office, called the chancery, whose chief official, the chancellor, was also often the chief minister of state. Given the high level of literacy required, chancellors tended to be ecclesiastics, usually drawn from the episcopate, although laymen held the office with increasing frequency as the fifteenth century progressed. The staff of clerks who did the actual work of drafting documents and keeping records could number from the less than half-dozen in the Scandinavian kingdoms of the early fourteenth century to the fifty or so clerks drafting and sealing some 300 documents a day in early fifteenth-century England. All states, large and small, had chanceries, but the more advanced the machinery of government, the more writing offices there were. So, English kings relied on two secretariats besides the Chancery, these being the office of the Privy Seal, with its Keeper and six clerks, who drafted various kinds of warrants, and the office of the Signet, whose Secretary and clerks travelled with the king and handled his personal correspondence. In France, too, a second writing office, of the *clercs du secret*, was established in the early fourteenth century to handle the king's personal letters; the necessity of this personal secretariat can be gleaned from the fact that by the mid-fifteenth century the French chancery was sealing some 18,000 to 35,000 letters each year.

As the financial demands of states grew in the course of the late Middle Ages, so too did the kinds of income as well as the machinery for the granting, receipt, issue and accounting of funds. Late medieval monarchs continued to draw on their traditional sources of ordinary income: these being the proceeds from the royal domain (income from rents, mills, forests, tolls, etc.) and royal mints, the profits of justice (court fees and fines), rights of hospitality (particularly helpful when the court peregrinated) and various 'feudal' revenues. These last consisted of payments associated with the inheritance or vacancy of fiefs in the royal domain (known as relief, wardship and escheat), those aids paid by royal vassals on the occasion of the marriage of an eldest daughter or knighting of an eldest son, and the payments of cash in lieu of military service in the feudal host. Such revenues had the advantage of being entirely in the monarch's control. They tended, however, to render scarcely enough funds for just the ordinary business of government in peacetime (especially as the size of bureaucracies increased and as kings and princes dispensed ever greater sums on the magnificence of their courts), and they were entirely insufficient when it came to covering the costs of war. This is not to say, however, that no strategies of augmentation were tried. One of the most common (and effective in the short term), was to manipulate the coinage, either by increasing the base-metal content of coins, clipping them or changing their face value. Such strategies were employed repeatedly in France and Castile and by several of the German princes. The problem with these 'mutations' is that they devalued the currency, thus wreaking havoc on the economy and creating tremendous resentment among the ruler's subjects. A monarch might also exercise much greater care in the management of his domain and in the enforcement of feudal dues; this strategy was employed to great effect by Henry VII of England, for example. Again, though, the result was seething resentment: so much so that his successor, Henry VIII abandoned these practices at his accession and had their chief agents executed. Finally, sometimes monarchs had the good fortune of being able to benefit from some particularly lucrative windfall. This might come in the form of several vacancies and forfeitures of estates in the royal gift or, as happened in fourteenth-century Bohemia and fifteenth-century Hungary, when new seams of precious metals were uncovered in royally controlled mines. Such turnovers of property, however, were not a regular occurrence and mines, of course, eventually petered out.

Needless to say, in order to cover the increasing costs of government it was necessary to levy taxes, either indirect or direct, and to incur public debt. Indirect taxation was of two principal kinds, sales taxes and customs. One of the most commonly employed sales taxes was the gabelle on salt. The gabelle was initiated in Angevin Naples in 1259 and later adopted in Castile and France, in 1338 and 1341 respectively. Because salt was cheap, it could be taxed at a high rate, and because it was necessary for all manner of purposes, from kitchen use, to food preservation, to certain manufacturing processes, it could bring considerable profit to monarchs, as it did, especially, in France. Under pressure to pay King John II's ransom after the battle of Poitiers, France in 1360 imposed a sales tax (the *aide*) on wine and other commodities; this tax became more or less permanent. In Castile a heavy tax was imposed on all sales in the recently conquered Muslim lands of Andalusia and Murcia, while various taxes were levied as well on the transhumance of the great flocks of sheep that were constantly on the move between summer and winter pastures. The kings of Castile also benefited from customs on both imports and exports. Customs on exports of raw wool and wool cloth were the most important source of funds for the English state of the fourteenth and fifteenth centuries. Since 1275 native merchants had paid the 'ancient custom' of 6s. 8d./sack of raw wool, while foreigners paid 10s. The exigencies of war compelled Parliament in 1337 to begin granting an additional customs of 40s./sack for specified periods, a tax that became virtually permanent from 1362. As long as raw wool exports remained high, these two customs yielded impressive sums (an average of £70,000 per year in 1360–75). But they declined starting in the last quarter of the fourteenth century, owing to the high rate of customs and the lowball prices that the monopoly of the wool staple was willing to pay growers. So, by 1430 only some £30,000 was being collected each year; and although this loss was partly offset by the customs on exports of wool cloth, an industry that grew impressively in the course of the later fourteenth and fifteenth centuries, the rate on cloth was much lower than that on raw wool, and remained so in order not to depress this native industry.[5]

Still, neither traditional sources of revenue nor indirect taxation could keep up with the exploding costs of government – largely the result of war – starting in the late thirteenth century. These shortfalls could only be made up with direct taxation, either in the form of capitation or property taxes. For rulers and their servants, the advantage of direct taxation was its capacity to tap considerable reserves of cash in private and institutional hands. There was, however, a catch: requests for direct taxation forced rulers into a dialogue with the political community. On the one hand, this dialogue could be advantageous to the ruler, since it gave him the opportunity to mould public opinion in his favour. On the other, it inevitably carried with it demands for concessions on his part and had the potential to strengthen the solidarity of the representatives of the political community in ways that were not always beneficial for government in accordance with the sovereign's will. In England and France, war and the need for taxes to pay for it necessitated frequent summoning of representative assemblies, although with rather different results. In the former, Parliament became a true institution of national government. The greater nobility, prelates and representatives of the towns and shires met annually or even more often and granted taxes on moveable property in towns and the countryside, known as tenths and fifteenths. Representatives of the clergy would meet concurrently in an assembly known as Convocation, in order to grant a tenth on their moveables. As the fourteenth century progressed, the representatives of town and country began to meet separately as the Commons, and in 1376 began choosing a Speaker to represent their views to the Lords (nobles and prelates) and the king. The great size and regional diversity of France, coupled with a certain wariness on the part of monarchs, led there to the practice of summoning regional Estates, with only very rare recourse made to calling a national Estates General. These Estates, representing nobles, clergy and the towns, granted clerical tenths and a form of tax on households, known as *fouage*. At the end of the fourteenth century the *fouage* was replaced by a tax known as the *taille*, which operated much like the old *fouage* in the north of the country but as a property tax in the south. In Castile and the Crown of Aragon, the demands of war prompted the monarchs to call their nations' representative assemblies, the *Cortes*, where they made concessions in return for subsidies. The most important of these subsidies in Castile was the *alcabala*, a sales tax on towns, which by the fifteenth century became an annual tax, no longer under the control of the *Cortes*. In the Crown of Aragon, the greater strength of representative institutions (the three *Cortes* of Catalonia, Aragon and Valencia, and the *Generalitat* of Barcelona) ensured that their assent continued to be necessary for grants of *monedaje* and *bovatge*.

Rulers of smaller kingdoms, like Scotland and the Scandinavian realms, also had recourse to representative assemblies, but received little from them in the way of grants of taxation, obliging them to depend largely on the income they could collect from their domains and other traditional sources of ordinary revenue. The German emperors also fared poorly when it came to levying direct taxation on their realm. True, in response to the Hussite wars, the imperial Diet (*Reichstag*) meeting in Nuremberg in 1422 granted a one per cent tax on individuals, a grant that was renewed by the Diet of Basle in 1433–34. But the tax ceased to be collected once the war ground to a halt later in the 1430s, and although there was some talk of an imperial tax during the 1480s and 1490s, this came to nothing. Instead, the rulers of the Empire had to satisfy themselves with taxes levied on cities and towns, each of which negotiated separate terms, and with income from their personal lands (*Hausgut*) and from the imperial domain (*Reichsbereiche*). During the second half of the fourteenth century, Charles IV granted away much of the *Reichsbereiche* to secure the imperial election of his son Wenceslas. Thus, with little income from either taxes or lands, the emperors of the fifteenth century were constantly cash-strapped, debt-ridden and looking for ways to augment their personal property.

Debt was not limited to the rulers of Germany. In fact, loans backed by the security of future taxes provided much of the ready cash that funded the wars of the late Middle Ages. Edward III leaned heavily on the Florentine banking firms of the Bardi and Peruzzi at the very start of the Hundred Years War, only to default on his loans. Thereafter, Edward and his successors turned to English creditors, a practice which contributed to the growth of a national political dialogue. Florentine bankers, this time Dino Rapondi and the Medici, also bankrolled much of the expansionist activities of the fifteenth-century dukes of Burgundy. The kings of France looked to their subjects for multiple small loans, although for a time Charles VII relied particularly heavily on a single creditor, the wealthy merchant of Bourges,

Jacques Coeur. By the later fifteenth century, the practice of receiving loans from government officials was developing into the institution of venality of office (i.e. the sale of offices), a fixture of French government throughout the early modern period. Jews were also an important source of credit, especially in the Empire and in the Mediterranean and Iberian kingdoms. This, rather than enlightened toleration, is what compelled late medieval monarchs to protect them. When other sources of revenue and credit became more abundant, those same rulers were not slow to withdraw this protection, or worse. In Castile, Ferdinand and Isabella began selling annuities (*juros*) in the same years when they rejected the long-standing close relationship between royal finances and Jewish and *converso* financiers, and ordered the expulsion of the entire Jewish population.

As in the case of secretariats, the more centralised and advanced the bureaucracy, the more articulated the offices of finance. In smaller, less complex governments finances were handled in the chamber or even the chancery, but in the most developed of dynastic states, financial administration was far more complex. Beginning with the reign of Philip IV of France, a central financial office, the *chambre des comptes*, oversaw the receipt, disbursing and accounting of royal income. At the local level, the responsibility for collecting revenue was in the hands of officials known as receivers. The growth of national taxation occasioned by the war with England brought with it the need for local tax assessors, known as *élus* (first appointed in 1355). In the fifteenth century, reports of corruption on the part of *élus* and receivers prompted the creation of inspectors, called *généraux des finances*, and Louis XI's desire to control finance led him to create a new household financial office (itself based on models already established in the duchies of Brittany and Burgundy), the *épargne*. Under French influence, Castile also expanded its central administration of finance, with the creation in the later 1300s of officers in charge of receipts and accounts, the *contador mayor de hacienda* and *contador mayor de cuentas*. Already by 1300, finances in the Crown of Aragon were overseen by the *maestre racional*, who was assisted in his task by a staff of clerks in the central office and by financial officers, known as *battles generales*, in Catalonia, Aragon and Valencia. In so far as financial management was concerned, however, England was the most precocious of national monarchies. Already in the early twelfth century, a central accounting office, the Exchequer, had received and audited the funds collected by local royal officials known as sheriffs. Some of these funds were disbursed to the household offices of the Chamber and Wardrobe, each of which managed the king's daily expenses, a job which in wartime required considerable expertise. In the localities, several offices came into being during the late Middle Ages which complemented the sheriffs' role in assessing and collecting revenues, including assessors, purveyors, escheators and collectors of the customs. At the end of the fifteenth century, in a similar move to that of Louis XI in France, Henry VII sought to increase his control over royal finances by transferring some of the oversight and management of finances from the Exchequer to the Chamber.

Justice was the virtue most often associated with kings. 'Justice', wrote the English royal clerk Walter of Milemete c. 1327, 'pertains to the greatest extent to the king'.[6] According to a mid-fourteenth-century French poem, translated into English a century later as *The III Consideracions Right Necesserye to the Good Governaunce of a Prince*, 'a king or prince should chiefly and principally do two things. The first is that he should make sure justice is properly kept throughout the lands obedient to him. The second is that he should especially and principally love the common profit of his people and subjects'.[7] This piece of advice points up the inextricable connection between justice and the common good in medieval attitudes toward government. But justice was also believed to be the glue that held the state together and maintained the proper relationship between the members of the body politic, a concept given forceful expression by Giles of Rome, who concluded that 'just as the soul preserves the body, since by leaving it the body dissolves and withers, so justice preserves cities and realms, because without it cities fall apart and no realms can endure'.[8]

In the real, imperfect world, of course, justice was the province of the law, and law was administered by government officials. In monarchic states, justice was the king's justice, and he was, technically and sometimes actually, the highest judge of cases adjudicated in his realm (unless they fell under the jurisdiction of ecclesiastical courts). The vast majority of cases came, however, under the ordinary jurisdiction of both central and local courts staffed by judges and lawyers. Again, the states with the most developed bureaucracies in the areas of correspondence and finance also operated the most complex legal apparatus. By the fourteenth century, the English central courts sat in the Palace of Westminster. Here in the Great Hall met the common law courts of King's Bench, which dealt with felonies and breaches of the king's peace, and Common Pleas, which was the chief court in the realm for civil litigation. Judges also occasionally met in the adjoining hall of the Exchequer to discuss particularly difficult cases referred to them from lower courts. As the century progressed, a court of equity and arbitration, presided over by the Chancellor, and hence called the court of Chancery, joined the common law courts in the Great Hall. In the time of the first Tudors this work of arbitration was augmented by an informal court of royal counsellors meeting in the Star Chamber and making decisions under the aegis of the royal prerogative. Parliament, too, could act in the capacity of a court, as it was famously to do with the Commons' impeachments of royal officials in 1376 and 1386, and in the Lords' appeal of treason against some of Richard II's closest associates in 1388.

Late medieval England experienced major developments in the area of local jurisdiction as well. What had largely been the province of sheriffs and itinerant justices in the twelfth and thirteenth centuries became at once more specialised and articulated. Sheriffs, who continued to deliver writs and make arrests, were joined by coroners, who conducted inquests into homicides, and royally appointed justices of the peace, who both acted as magistrates in cases of misdemeanour and minor felonies and heard indictments for serious felonies. All these officers were drawn from the ranks of local minor nobility, known in England as the 'gentry'. The judgement of serious felonies and breaches of the king's peace was, however, still the business of professional judges and lawyers, who twice yearly conducted local assizes. Local free men whose property was valued at more than £5 also participated in the legal system, making accusations during inquests and delivering judgements at trial. Thus English justice became not just the affair of the king and the great men of the realm but of a substantial number of participants and a broad cross-section of English society, making it at once an instrument of state centralisation and of national dialogue.

France too saw important developments in the area of justice. Owing to the flood of appeals that started making their way to the king's court in the time of Louis IX (d. 1270), a central court, known as the *Parlement*, came into being. Meeting in the Palais de la Cité on the Île de la Cité in Paris, its *Chambre des requêtes* heard litigants' appeals while the *Chambre des enquêtes* had investigative functions; judgements were made in the *Grande Chambre*. Local jurisdiction was in the hands of royal officials called *prévôts* (*juges-mages* in the Midi). As the fourteenth century progressed, the Paris *Parlement* became increasingly professionalised. In the fifteenth, several regional *parlements* were established to handle increasing litigation and in recognition of the practicalities involved in providing justice in such a large and regionally varied country. The late Middle Ages was also the time when the customary law of northern France gradually made inroads into the traditionally Roman law-dominated south. Thus if the law in France, in contrast to England, continued to be more under the control of royal government and in the hands of professionals, there too it acted as a conduit for some level of dialogue between state and nation. Also, in a move contemporary with that in England, a French royal prerogative court came into being, known as the *Grand Conseil*.

Over the course of the fourteenth century in Castile, royal control over the administration of justice increased thanks to two important developments. The first was the gradual replacement of local customary law (*fueros*) by the strongly pro-royal Roman law system of the *Siete Partidas*, first promulgated by Alfonso X in the 1260s. Royal jurisdiction was further assisted by the creation of a central court of appeal, called the *audiencia*, in 1371, and, in the fifteenth century, by the establishment of three *audiencias* in Valladolid, Ciudad Real and Santiago. Contrastingly, in the Crown of Aragon, the highest judicial officer, the *justicia*, represented the interests not of the monarch but, rather, of the *Cortes*. Nor was the monarch able to impose any distinctly royal law there, having rather to abide by traditional *fueros* that favoured the nobility. Little wonder, then, that when Alfonso V 'the Magnanimous' of Aragon gained control over the kingdom of Naples in the 1440s, he made his own privy council the final court of appeal, enjoying there, at least, some measure of jurisdictional sovereignty.

In the German-speaking lands, as well, the emperors had no monopoly on justice, which remained the property of towns and territorial princes, for the most part. There, local ordinary jurisdiction was administered by judges, called *Richter*; they were assisted by jurors (*Schöffen*), who were free men of property familiar with customary law. But what in 1300 was the work of part-time amateurs became, over the course of the next two centuries, a job for university-educated legal professionals, learned in Roman law. Frequent and widespread outbreaks of feuds and private war and the depredations of robber knights demanded more than could be provided by local judges. Typically these problems were resolved either by arbitration – and here the emperor at times played an important role – or by the intervention of temporary, regional leagues, which, by means of tribunals, arbitration and outright military intervention, sought to impose the public peace (*Landfriede*).

In small, less centralised realms with fairly limited administrative machinery, like Scotland and the Scandinavian kingdoms, courts of justice played an important role as instruments of royal power. In Scotland, the influence of English practices can be seen in the fact that the king's law was administered by two itinerant justiciars, aided in the localities by sheriffs and 'crownars' (coroners). In Scandinavia, royal judges, assisted by bailiffs, began in the late Middle Ages to record their decisions (first in Latin and then, increasingly, in the vernacular), thereby creating some common standards and routine procedures of justice, where before there had been substantial local variation.

Whatever the extent of their power and control, the governments of late medieval national monarchies underwent certain common developments. First, there was a trend toward greater size and complexity, with more offices and officials, and a proliferation of documentation, both in the form of written instruments and in the way of records. Second, the tendency was toward staffs that were at once more professionalised and less ecclesiastical, reflecting the rise of an educated and literate laity and the broadening of the political community. This broadening, however, was, like the growth of government, the result of a growing need for money: a need born largely from war. It was this need that stimulated the dialogue between monarch and community in representative assemblies. Yet if this dialogue tightened the bonds between ruler and ruled and between ruled and ruled, it also limited the monarch's unfettered exercise of power. By the end of the fifteenth century, some monarchs drew on the strength of their administrative apparatus in order to assert their prerogative and will as divinely appointed heads of state.

The structures of rule: Italian city-states

The governing structures of the Italian city-states were different enough from those of monarchic national states that they require separate treatment here. Owing to a complex of economic and political factors, including precocious and vibrant growth of trade and industry, and being situated between the competing forces of the Empire and papacy, several of these cities had developed republican forms of government and won for themselves considerable autonomy over the course of the twelfth and thirteenth centuries. Here it should be noted that urban government was hardly unique to central and northern Italy. Cities and towns throughout Latin Christendom had established communal governments, with mayor and city council drawn from an oligarchy of merchants and, frequently, the masters of major guilds. In areas of strong urban economies and relatively weak or distant royal/aristocratic control, like Catalonia, Flanders, the Swiss Confederation, southern Germany and the Rhenish and Baltic-facing cities of the Hanse, these urban governments continued to exercise considerable freedom in the late Middle Ages. Nonetheless, Italy knew no rivals when it came to the ubiquity, scale and sophistication of its urban polities.

Just as no national monarchy's government was exactly like another's, so too was there diversity in the particulars of each city republic's institutions of government. Nonetheless, certain commonalities can be perceived in the cities which maintained, with greater or lesser consistency and permanence, republican government in the late Middle Ages: namely Florence, Venice, Lucca, Siena, Pisa, Perugia, Genoa and Bologna. First, in all city republics the functions of government were carried out by a combination of representative legislative councils and a plethora of standing and *ad hoc* executive committees charged with such responsibilities as justice, tax assessment and collection, public works and defence. The membership of these councils and committees was determined either by election or lot, and frequently by some combination of the two, and the terms of service tended to be short (frequently as little as two months), with some delay imposed before one could serve another term. Such procedures were designed not only to broaden participation but also to keep any one person or faction from gaining too much power. Still, the franchise in these republics was hardly democratic, since membership was invariably limited to adult male citizens of means. In some cases the business of government might be confined to the elite of aristocrats and merchant bankers (*magnati*) and in others it might include the middle class (*popolo*) of guild masters and a host of businessmen, artisans and professionals. For brief moments, as after the revolt of the Ciompi in Florence in 1378, even labourers might have a hand in governance (though never for long). It was the norm for these councils and committees to avail themselves of the expert assistance of professional lawyers and notaries; these same professionals also found work in the city's chancery.

A common feature of republics and *signorie* was their dependence upon and efforts to control the surrounding countryside, or *contado*, drawing on it as a source of tax revenue, provender and soldiers. All city-states also sought not only to exploit their *contado* with greater and greater efficiency but also to expand the area of their control, thereby not only absorbing countryside with its rural communities and feudal lords but also what had previously been independent towns. This process led at times to considerable friction within both city and *contado*, and to competition and conflict with other city-states or territorial rulers, like, for example, the pope or the kings of Naples. The city-states that in the long run were most successful in these ventures, Milan, Venice, and Florence, created what were, in effect, territorial states.

City republics were not known for their stability. They were habitually at war with neighbours, foreign invaders and economic competitors, and were riven by family rivalries and vendettas, inter-class hostilities and the party politics of Guelfs and Ghibellines (although these parties originated in the papal-imperial conflicts of the thirteenth century, with Ghibellines supporting the emperors and the Guelfs backing the popes and their Angevin allies, 'by the middle of the fourteenth century Guelfs and Ghibellines no longer signified the partisans of church and empire'[9]). Thanks to all this strife and faction, already by the early fourteenth century several communal governments had fallen permanently under the control of a local strong-man who exercised personal lordship, the *signore*. But even cities that preserved republican governing structures were no strangers to rebellion (see Chapter 1) and the occasional loss of freedom either from foreign occupation (as happened repeatedly to Genoa, especially during the fifteenth and early sixteenth century) or by temporarily ceding power to, or having it seized by a *signore* (even Florence ceded its power to Angevin *signori* on three occasions in the first half of the fourteenth century, and Lucca famously came under the control of the bellicose Castruccio Castracani during the 1320s). Nor was it unusual for these cities to experiment and tinker with their constitutions, prompting Dante in the sixth Canto of his *Purgatorio* to complain of his native Florence:

> If thou remember'st well and canst see clear,
> Thou wilt perceive thyself like a sick wretch,
> Who finds no rest upon her down [bed], but oft
> Shifting her side, short respite seeks from pain.[10]

By the late fourteenth century, moreover, there was also a tendency for the reality of power in the republics to become more oligarchic, or even, in the case of Florence under the Medici, princely. Siena, for example, which was ruled by an oligarchic council of nine magistrates (the *Nove*) from 1287 to 1355, thereafter broadened its political franchise in the 1360s through the mid-1380s, but then went back to what amounted to oligarchic rule for over a century before coming under the despotic rule of Pandolfo Petrucci at the end of the fifteenth century. Florence, for its part, continued, officially, to be ruled by its elected officers, the priors, magistrates and standard-bearer of justice, or *gonfaloniere di giustizia*. In reality, however, the membership of these offices came to be restricted and controlled by a process of scrutiny, while real power was in the hands, from 1387, of the merchant-banking family of the Albizzi and their allies, and, after 1434, of Cosimo de' Medici and his successors. Venice was the one republic that maintained both its independence and the reality of republican government after the middle of the fifteenth century. This was not only the result of its being a great maritime and, beginning in the fifteenth century, territorial power, but also of the fundamentally conservative nature of its government structure. From 1297 eligibility for service on the Great Council (*Maggior Consiglio*) was restricted to those 100–150 patrician families whose members had previously served. From among their own number the members of the Great Council elected (through a tortuously complicated process) a chief executive, the doge, who held office for life. And because the Great Council itself met only for elections and to discuss especially great and weighty matters, the day-to-day business of governance was in the hands of the doge, a senate of some 160, and later 300 members, and a ten-member council of justice, the *Dieci*.

Whereas republican government was the rule in northern Italian cities throughout most of the thirteenth century, by the early 1300s several city-states had become *signorie*, subject to the lordship of wealthy and powerful *signori*, who established what amounted to dynastic rule. This was the case in Milan (ruled by the Visconti and, after 1450, the Sforza), Verona (della Scala), Ferrara (Este), Mantua (Gonzaga), Padua (Carrara) and Urbino (Montefeltro), as well as several smaller cities like Rimini (Malatesta) and Parma (Correggio). Later, in the mid-fifteenth century, the republics of Bologna and Perugia became 'para-*signorie*' under the control of the Bentivoglio and Baglioni. Typically, it was a combination of fractious local politics (often that of Ghibellines versus Guelfs) coupled with some external threat that drove the citizens of what had been communal republics to give extraordinary powers temporarily to a local magnate, who then found ways to make his power first permanent and then hereditary. In order to legitimate and shore up their power, the *signori* adopted a number of tactics. They turned to experts in Roman law, who made the case for the *signore*'s fullness of power (*plenitudo potestatis*) over jurisdiction, in imitation of the legal authority enjoyed by the emperor and national monarchs. From emperors and popes they purchased the title of vicar, thereby giving them authority to act in the emperor's or pope's name in temporal affairs. Then, beginning with Giangaleazzo Visconti of Milan in 1396, they began to sport the hereditary title of imperial duke or marquis. When it came to the more mundane affairs of city government, *signori* might from time to time behave like out-and-out despots, but more often they ruled as a kind of senior controlling partner, hand-picking the staff of their chanceries and the members of councils and committees, but giving them some latitude when it came to decision-making and administration. So we find the administration of government in Milan being handled by a secret council and council of justice, by two committees of finance, and by the Office of Provisions. In fifteenth-century Ferrara, the Este not only ruled through a hand-picked chancery and financial office, but also relied on an elected body of twelve senators, called the *savi*, overseen by an official, the *giudice*, and assisted by a group of professional experts, the *adiuncti*. If, then, a formal division can be made between those city-states that were republics and those that were *signorie*, in reality the governance of these states tended not to be so very different, especially in the fifteenth century.

Certain practices and institutions of these central and northern Italian governments can also be compared to those of national monarchies. The prerogative courts set up in late fifteenth-century England and France had their counterparts in the courts of the *capitani di giustizia* ('captains of justice') in Milan, Ferrara and Mantua, as well as in the secretive courts of the Eight on Security and the Council of Ten in Florence and Venice. And just as the turn to arbitrary justice was a common feature of monarchies, *signorie* and republics, so too, for all the talk of republican values from humanists like Coluccio Salutati (1331–1406) or Leonardo Bruni (1370–1444), there is clear evidence of familial and dynastic interests at work in the city-states, whether of the monarchic stripe found in the *signorie* and Medici Florence or the oligarchic manoeuvres so readily visible in republics like Genoa, Siena and Lucca. The demands of public finance, stimulated by the cost of war and defence, were also met in the Italian states, as they were in monarchic ones, by a combination of direct and indirect taxation, and public debt. Still, it must be said that public debt played a larger role in the financing of some of the city republics. Florence, Genoa, Venice and Pisa were particularly reliant on public debt financing, since the wealthy citizens that tended to control their governments preferred levying forced loans to direct taxation, thereby becoming themselves creditors of the state and profiting from the interest, which at times could be as high as 15 per cent, although usually hovering between 5 and 10 per cent. The interest was funded by a combination of direct taxation on the *contado* and regressive consumption taxes (for example, the *gabelle* on salt) that hit the poorer segments of society especially hard, leading to resentment and the occasional uprising. State debt was managed by public banks, like the *monti communi* of Venice and Florence, and the Casa di San Giorgio in Genoa, which paid out the interest on what became, in effect, publicly traded bonds. Public debt could reach quite extraordinary levels. Genoa's debt in 1339 was almost fifteen times its annual revenue, while in both mid-fifteenth-century Florence and Venice the public debt stood at about 6,000,000 florins. Chronic deficits forced the public banks to pay out lower interest and eventually led to the institution of direct taxation on citizens in Florence (1427), Pisa (1428) and Venice (1463). Even this was not enough for Florence, however, which began to rely on short-term loans from particularly wealthy citizens. One important reason for Cosimo de' Medici's rise to power was his ability to bankroll the state with his considerable fortune.

Relationships of rule: courts, councils and patronage

The informal, extra-constitutional means through which the Medici gained and maintained political power reminds us that such power was not only based on ideology and formal, institutional structures, but also on relationships. In an age when the personal and the public were intimately intertwined, the role of personal relationships was fundamental. Relations between states were created and nurtured through dynastic marriages and induction into chivalric orders, all done in the hopes of fostering ties of kinship, mutual affection and obligation. Within states, the webs of relationships were far more complex, multi-layered and overlapping, linking rulers with political elites, and the members of those elites with one another and with their own bases of power. Both hierarchical and mutual, these ties were at once an abundant source of power for rulers and a potent curb on the limitless and arbitrary exercise of it. Prudent management of these relationships made for successful reigns, whereas fecklessness, profligacy and favouritism eventually led to problems. This explains why two of the qualities especially praised in rulers were magnanimity and largesse, the virtues governing freely dispensed, but properly measured and even-handed, affection, mercy and benefaction: 'There is no doubt', said Christine de Pizan, 'that nothing profits a prince as much as discreet generosity'.[11] If the ruler was the fount of largesse, the principal site of this fountain was the court and the water that flowed therefrom was patronage. Connected to the court but also occupying a separate, semi-autonomous place, was the ruler's council.

Defining the court is more difficult than might at first appear, although, perhaps, not so difficult as the twelfth-century courtier Walter Map jokingly asserted: 'I can say that I am in the court, and speak of the court and know not – God alone knows – what the court is'.[12] For the court, in addition to being where the king and his *familia* resided, was also an occasion, as in 'the king held his court', but it could additionally be, and was in the late Middle Ages increasingly associated with, a place, as with the English royal palace of Windsor, completely refurbished by Edward III, or the Valois royal court at the Louvre, updated by Charles V. Likewise, the court was an assemblage of people, both 'courtiers' and those functionaries that made up the household; and it was an institution, in the sense of comprising such offices as a chancery, chamber and various councils. The court has also received considerable attention as a centre of cultural patronage – even as the generator of 'courtly literature' or 'courtly music' – and has, at times, been characterised as a faction or 'party', as in 'court versus country'. I suppose one could say that medieval courts were at various times and in different ways all these things (and less, or more). Their role as a site for the display and performance of power has already been discussed (in Chapter 4), while their place in the history of cultural patronage awaits treatment in a later chapter. Here we will confine ourselves to the court as the normative setting wherein ruler and ruled achieved proximity with one another and thus as a site for the creation and nurturing of personal bonds, the exercise of influence, and the exchange of information, service and favour.

Just as government administration expanded and became more articulated in the late Middle Ages, so too did the personnel and structure of royal and princely courts. Not yet the great, stationary palace court of the early modern absolutist state, and no longer the small and mobile military retinue of earlier times, the court of the late Middle Ages still peregrinated to some extent, even if by this time there was a tendency for the court to spend most of its time in or near the centre of government administration. At a time when princes were still expected to lead the army, the peripatetic court was a necessity in wartime. But it also behoved monarchs to move about their realms on occasion just to keep tabs on regions distant from the capital as well as to renew bonds with regional elites and to show themselves to their subjects. Still it must be said that the court of 1500 looked much more like that of the early modern era than had the court of two hundred years earlier. The number of officials serving the most magnificent of fifteenth-century courts, that of Burgundy, grew from 234 officials in 1426 to 1,030 a half-century later.[13] At the start of the fourteenth century in England, the royal household comprised some 150 members, and had increased to some 400 members, with an additional 120 belonging to the queen's household, by 1390; by 1450 it had swelled to some 875 members, although including the queen's household it may have numbered as many as 1,200. A smaller court, like that of Portugal, more than doubled in size between 1405 and 1462, going from 130 to 265, and it is reckoned that in 1476 Duke Galeazzo Maria Sforza of Milan lavished 200,000 ducats on court expenses, that is, roughly half the state's budget.[14] But courts also became more stratified and specialised, dividing, for example, into an upper and lower court and the prince's private chamber, and applying strict rules of hierarchy and comportment, functioning thereby: 'as a microcosm of society at large, in which hierarchical structures – which were difficult (or indeed impossible) to maintain or enforce outside – were more effectively kept in place. Furthermore, the court could express, admittedly in heightened form, perceptions of social position and status which were also prevalent far outside its boundaries.'[15]

Still, the court was very much the prince's place; he was both its subject and its centre, and it acted, principally, as 'the channel for his political will'.[16] This will expressed itself most forcefully and patently through such formal means as ordinances, statutes, edicts and legal judgements. But such acts were really only punctuations in an ongoing exercise of power and authority through the medium of patronage. Princes practised patronage in everything from the appointment of counsellors and officials of state, to provision to ecclesiastical benefices, to grants of pensions, annuities, privileges and titles, to the arrangement of suitable marriages among the nobility. Recipients of the prince's good will (*benevolentia*) were thus bound to him by ties of gratitude and loyalty, but also of dependence and duty, since what the royal will had bestowed it could also take away. Still, prudent princes had to take great care in the management of patronage. First, too much largesse soon diminished the considerable but nonetheless finite resources of available offices, lands and revenues, as happened in England during the late 1440s, thanks to Henry VI's imprudent patronage, coupled with spending on the war in France. Sometimes, however, what seemed profligate might mask shrewd calculation, as when Emperor Charles IV granted away enormous tracts of imperial lands to secure the succession of his son, Wenceslas, to the imperial throne. Second, nothing raised the ire of the political community more quickly and thoroughly than the appearance of favouritism. Nobles expected their due when it came to access to the prince's person, opportunities to serve and counsel him, and princely recognition and support of their own authority. In part this was simply a validation of the nobility's 'status within the hierarchy of honour', but even-handed patronage also had the effect of balancing competing interests in the localities, acting as a 'device for modifying the natural pattern of lordship to suit the vagaries of the common interest'.[17] Favouritism upset the balance, both in court and country, unduly raising the status and influence of some and undercutting the position and political activity of others.

Among the most jealously guarded privileges of the great was their role as counsellors. Giles of Rome's admonitions that princes should seek out the advice of 'the eldest wise barons who love the realm' and avoid the blandishments of flatterers surely struck a chord with those great nobles and prelates who regarded themselves as the prince's 'natural counsellors'.[18] The institutional setting for this giving and taking of advice was the council, and it comes as no surprise that the membership of the council and the method of choosing those councillors were among the most contentious issues of late medieval politics. Just as princes had to steer a careful course when it came to doling out patronage, so too did they have to exercise great care in the choice of councillors, looking out at once for their own interest while also staying on good terms with the magnates. In skilled hands, the council (or councils), was the prince's most valuable asset. Those princes, however, who took counsel only from a small coterie of favourites, were often branded as tyrants. On the other hand, faction could also arise when princes were unable to exercise proper control over council membership, thus letting undue power and influence fall into the hands of self-interested magnates. A properly regulated court and council, then, together with proper exercise of patronage maintained the complex networks of personal relationships on which government both at the national and local level was built.

The fall (and rise) of princes

A properly directed will, guided by virtue, learning and the love of God, supported by the good counsel of wise men who loved the realm: this was, according to the writers of mirrors of princes, the best guarantee of a fortunate and enduring regime. Of course, this was the ideal, not the reality, and the plentiful evidence of messy reality prompted writers of mirrors like Christine de Pizan ever to remind their readers that 'one must never believe a person to be happy who lives in this world, because, until our last day we are subject to fortune, who is untrustworthy and changeable, and change takes the name "happy" away from human creatures'.[19] The reality of late medieval politics was certainly messy, not to mention too often violent and changeable; but attention to its unfolding also allows us to observe the functioning and development of those structures and the interplay of those relationships discussed earlier. The narrative of political developments that follows seeks to elucidate important aspects of that unfolding; those needing more comprehensive and detailed narrative and analysis of national and regional histories will find more guidance below in Selected Further Readings.

Map 5.1 Map of Europe in around 1360, taken from *Gothic Europe, 1200–1450* by Derek Pearsall, © 2001, Routledge. Reproduced by permission of Taylor & Francis books UK

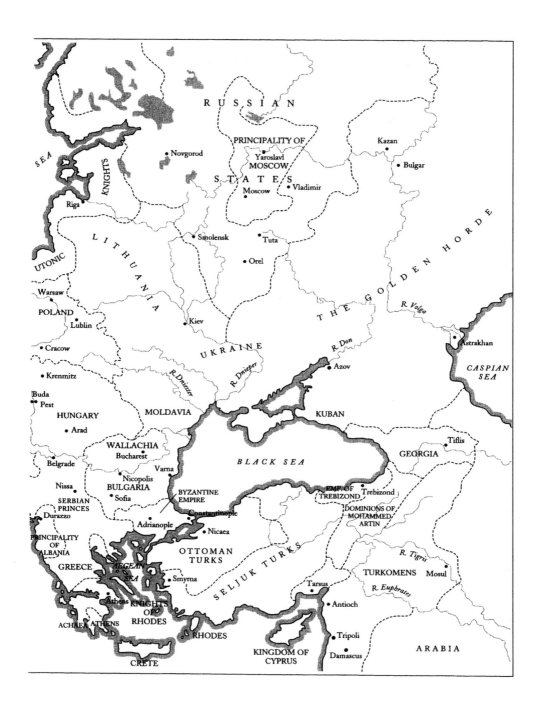

R U S S I A N

PRINCIPALITY OF
MOSCOW

S T A T E S

Kazan

• Novgorod

• Yaroslavl

• Bulgar

• Moscow   • Vladimir

• Smolensk   • Tuta

• Orel

SEA

KNIGHTS

• Riga

L I T H U A N I A

UTONIC

• Warsaw

POLAND
• Lublin

• Cracow

• Krenmitz

Buda
Pest

HUNGARY
• Arad

Belgrade

Nissa

SERBIAN
PRINCES
Durazzo

PRINCIPALITY
OF
ALBANIA

GREECE

ACHAEA ATHENS

CRETE

• Kiev

U K R A I N E

T H E   G O L D E N   H O R D E

R. Volga

• Astrakhan

R. Don

CASPIAN
SEA

R. Dniester   R. Dnieper

• Azov

MOLDAVIA

KUBAN

WALLACHIA
Bucharest

• Varna
• Nicopolis
BULGARIA
• Sofia

BLACK SEA

GEORGIA

• Tiflis

EMP. OF
TREBIZOND   • Trebizond

BYZANTINE
EMPIRE

Constantinople

• Adrianople

• Nicaea

OTTOMAN
TURKS

AEGEAN
SEA

Athens

KNIGHTS
OF
RHODES

• Smyrna

SELJUK TURKS

DOMINIONS OF
MOHAMMED
ARTIN

R. Tigris

TURKOMENS
Mosul

• Tarsus

R. Euphrates

• Antioch

• RHODES

KINGDOM OF
CYPRUS

• Tripoli

• Damascus

ARABIA

The British Isles

In 1300, the English king, Edward I, bestrode Britain like a colossus. Endowed with an indomitable will, political shrewdness and military acumen, he had mastered his own kingdom through the application of Roman legal principles, the augmentation of royal administration and the cultivation of that great council of the realm called Parliament. He had also made Wales his own, conquering it by military force and pacifying it with castles and new towns bustling with English settlers. It was only a matter of time before Scotland, too, would be his. Having made and unmade its king, John Balliol, in 1291–96, he had recently turned the tables on the hero of Scottish resistance, William Wallace, defeating his forces at Falkirk in 1298. England seemed set for strong royal rule and the rest of the island to overwhelming English dominance. Ireland, although not a major preoccupation of Edward, was nonetheless technically under his overlord-ship as well, and its south and east had long been under the control of Anglo-Norman nobles and English settlers. No wonder an Irish annalist referred to Edward as 'King of England, Wales and Scotland, Duke of Gascony and Lord of Ireland'.[20] Edward, however, was not to be the founder of an 'English empire' in the British Isles. Wales, although conquered, hardly became culturally or politically assimilated, a state of affairs forcefully expressed in the rebellion of Owain Glyn Dŵr in the first decade of the fifteenth century. Ireland, if anything, drifted further from English control in the late Middle Ages, with the Gaelic-Irish kings maintaining considerable freedom of action and the Anglo-Irish nobility tending to identify less with their ancestral homeland and more with their own interests in Ireland. Nor did fortune smile on Edward's designs in Scotland, since the conquest that seemed a *fait accompli* in 1305 was jeopardised a year later when Robert Bruce, earl of Carrick, assumed the Scottish throne and proclaimed his realm's independence. When the English king died in 1307, Scotland still eluded his grasp. And in England itself, the royal power which Edward I had so assiduously crafted was soon dealt a severe blow by his politically and personally inept son and heir Edward II. By the time of his forced abdication (and murder a short time thereafter) in 1327, Edward had thoroughly alienated his wife, Isabella of France, and a greater part of the nobility on account of his feckless favouritism, first for the Gascon parvenu Piers Gaveston (executed in 1312) and, then, for the brutally acquisitive father-and-son team of nobles, Hugh Despenser the elder and the younger. It certainly did not help his cause that he had also presided over the disastrous defeat at the hands of the Scots at Bannockburn (June 1314), a battle which secured Scotland's claim of independence, proudly declared in the Declaration of Arbroath of 1320 and recognised by England in the Treaty of Edinburgh–Northampton of 1328.

When it came to the practice of politics, Edward III was as skilled as his father was incompetent. He seems to have learned a great deal from the negative examples of his father's reign and of the equally unpleasant rule of his mother and her lover, Roger Mortimer, from September 1326 till October 1330. By temperament and design, Edward III was the paragon of chivalrous kingship, taking great care to cultivate good relations with the aristocracy and pressing his claims to overlordship in Scotland and sovereign control of England's holdings in France. The natural corollary to this belligerent programme was war; and Edward and his nobles got to enjoy war in abundance, against both the French and their Scottish allies (owing to the 'Auld Alliance' of 1295), starting in 1333 and continuing until 1360, then reviving in 1369. These wars, which demanded tremendous resources in the way of money, provisions and materiel, compelled Edward to seek out and cultivate the support of an expanded political community which included not only the great men of the realm but also

Table 5.1 Rulers of England and Scotland

England	
Edward I	1272–1307
Edward II	1307–27 (deposed and killed)
Edward III	1327–77
Richard II	1377–99 (deposed and killed)
Henry IV (L)	1399–1413
Henry V (L)	1413–22
Henry VI (L)	1422–61 (restored Oct. 1470; killed Apr. 1471)
Edward IV (Y)	1461–83 (exiled Oct. 1470–Apr. 1471)
Edward V (Y)	1483 (killed)
Richard III (Y)	1483–5 (killed in battle)
Henry VII (T)	1485–1509
Henry VIII (T)	1509–47

L=Lancaster	T=Tudor	Y=York

Scotland	
Robert I (Bruce)	1306–29
David II	1329–71 (captive of the English 1346–57)
Robert II (Stewart)	1371–90
Robert III	1390–1406
James I	1406–37 (captive of the English 1406–24; assassinated)
James II	1437–60 (killed by exploding cannon at siege of Roxburgh)
James III	1460–88 (killed after the battle of Sauchieburn)
James IV	1488–1513 (killed at battle of Flodden)
James V	1513–42

those of more modest means, the rural gentry and urban merchants and artisans, as represented in Parliament by the Commons. Parliament's consent to taxation, however, came with conditions, prompting an ongoing conversation between the monarch and this broadened political nation. This conversation was further enriched by a kind of partnership, enacted in war through military contracts and subcontracts, and in peace by empowering the gentry in their new role as justices of the peace.

Despite great successes in the French and Scottish wars of the 1330s through 1350s and a decade of peace in the 1360s, the reign did not end well. First, England was unable to prosecute with any success the renewed war with France and its new ally, Castile. Worse, the king slid into a shabby senility, surrounding himself with a small group of favourites, including his mistress Alice Perrers; meanwhile a wasting disease incapacitated and finally killed (in 1376) the heir to the throne and hero of the battle of Poitiers, Edward the Black Prince.

The power vacuum of Edward III's declining years continued into the reign of his grandson, Richard II, whose tender age of eleven at his accession necessitated several years of government by council. Intelligent, morally upright and courageous when he needed to be, Richard was nonetheless badly suited to his job. Rather than seeking to restore the spirit of respectful partnership between crown and political nation that characterised the reign of Edward III, Richard increasingly came to insist on the absolute majesty of his office and the imperative of an untrammelled royal will. In practice this meant an unwillingness to seek compromise, a lack of sensitivity toward the greater nobles and their claim of being the king's natural counsellors, a preference for counsel from a small, hand-picked group of friends, and a tendency to exercise patronage in such a way as to encourage faction rather than standing above it. In 1386 and 1388 Parliament was the site of efforts to curb the king and his favourites. On the first occasion the Commons impeached several of the king's 'evil counsellors' and imposed on him a council of Parliament's own choosing; on the second, a group of magnates which included the king's uncle, Thomas of Woodstock, duke of Gloucester, and cousin, Henry Bolingbroke, earl of Derby, brought an 'appeal' of treason against several of Richard's closest associates, several of whom were executed. This severe blow to his power only seems to have stiffened Richard's resolve to exercise the royal prerogative and he spent the next decade carefully building up his power-base and converting a theory of absolute power into practice by eventually destroying or exiling his enemies in 1397–98. Seemingly triumphant, however, Richard could not erase the suspicion and resentment created by his heavy-handed rule. Even his efforts to initiate a lasting peace with France were regarded by many as a shameful abandonment of English rights abroad and a pretext for imposing autocratic rule at home.

By the spring of 1399 Richard felt confident enough to lead a military expedition to Ireland, a move which expressed the king's desire to rule over a greater 'British empire' rather in the mode of Edward I. Instead his absence left the door open for his old enemy Henry Bolingbroke's return from exile in France. Bolingbroke's original intent seems only to have been to claim the inheritance rightly due him after the decease earlier in the year of his father, John of Gaunt, but so far denied him by Richard. Fortune's wheel, however, quickly turned, making Richard, hurriedly returned from Ireland, Bolingbroke's captive, and prompting the latter to lay claim to the English throne as King Henry IV. The founder of the new Lancastrian dynasty never could, however, lay to rest the ghost of the deposed and murdered Richard, and spent much of his troubled reign battling rebellions in Wales and the north, and dispensing money and patronage in an effort to shore up the crumbly foundation of his usurped throne.

Strikingly different was the reign of Bolingbroke's son, Henry V. Already experienced in the arts of governance and war at the time of his accession in 1413, Henry reactivated the war with France which had been in suspension since Richard II's peace efforts of the 1380s, and resurrected the dignity of the English crown through a carefully executed policy of good government at home and successful war abroad. The remarkable victory at Agincourt in October 1415 opened the way for Henry to pursue a strategy of territorial conquest in Normandy and, ultimately, make a successful bid to be named the rightful heir to the French throne, in the Treaty of Troyes of 1420. Henry also restored, and strengthened, the spirit of partnership initiated by Edward III. Parliament readily granted generous subsidies to fund the war, and the aristocracy benefited richly from the profits flowing from military contracts and the grants of lands and privileges in English-controlled France. The English Church, too, regarded Henry as a true defender of orthodoxy in the wake of his suppression of the Lollard conspiracy of Sir John Oldcastle in 1413–14.

Henry never got to wear two crowns, however, dying instead of dysentery just a few weeks before his father-in-law, Charles VI of France in 1422. His infant son, Henry VI (whose mother, Queen Catherine was Charles VI's daughter), inherited the English throne but none of his father's abilities, and his putative French inheritance proved to be an ongoing irritant in English domestic politics throughout his unfortunate reign. Parliament proved far less willing to fund an overseas war they no longer believed was their affair, it now being, they reckoned, the responsibility of Henry's presumptive French subjects. Matters there only got worse, with the coronation of the Valois Charles VII in 1429, following French victories, inspired by Joan of Arc, at Orléans and Patay. At home, bitter divisions developed in the council governing England during Henry's minority, with a pro-war party, led by Henry's uncle Humphrey, duke of Gloucester, pitted against a peace party dominated by his great uncle Henry Cardinal Beaufort. The young king did not help matters by showing clear favouritism for Beaufort and his allies William de la Pole, duke of Suffolk, and John Beaufort, duke of Somerset. When Henry reached his majority in 1437, he began to demonstrate stunning incompetence when it came to the business of kingship, behaving more as the tool of his favourites than ruler of England in matters of policy, while also practising lavish and feckless patronage, granting away crown lands and expending vast sums of money on his pet projects, Eton College and King's College Cambridge, during a time of expensive (and losing) warfare, falling revenues from the customs and economic depression.

Diplomatic efforts in the 1440s to make the best of a bad situation in France, which included Henry's marriage to Charles VII's niece, Margaret of Anjou in 1445 along with some territorial concessions, led only to the loss of Normandy in 1450 and of the last Gascon holdings in 1453. Public disorder was also on the rise in the 1440s thanks to a breakdown of proper policing and justice, with justices of the peace and royal judges frequently acting more as accomplices in, than obstacles to, aristocratic feuds. Much of the blame for problems at home and abroad fell on the duke of Suffolk, whom Henry rescued from Parliamentary impeachment only to lose him to a shipboard lynching. Popular discontent continued to grow, however, leading to Jack Cade's rebellion in the summer of 1450, whose aim was the restoration of good government by freeing the king from the influence of his greedy counsellors. This set the stage for the rise to political prominence of Richard, duke of York, who sought to dislodge Henry's chief surviving favourite, the duke of Somerset, from power. York briefly attained his ends when, in 1453, Henry was stricken with a bout of madness, perhaps sparked by the final disastrous loss of the Hundred Years War, at Castillon. Richard was named protector of the realm and embarked on a programme of reform, imprisoning Somerset in the Tower of London and trying to improve the provision of justice and the finances of the crown. Henry's return to his senses in 1455, however, plunged England into a period of civil war (the first of the so-called Wars of the Roses) that left both Somerset and York dead, but propelled York's heir, Edward to the throne in 1461.

As king, Edward IV faced the dual problem of restoring peace and order and of establishing the legitimacy of his rule in the face of an exiled and mentally incapacitated (Henry's madness returned, permanently, in late 1455) but nonetheless very much alive king under the protection of James III of Scotland. Still, Edward showed himself well suited to the task, reducing or reconciling his enemies and bringing royal finances under control. One serious misstep during the early years of Edward's reign, however, did precipitate his temporary removal from power, and the restoration in 1470–71 of Henry VI, his queen Margaret and son Edward. This was his ill-advised marriage to Elizabeth Woodville, a widow thought by many to be of too humble lineage for a queen. Resentment at her perceived inferiority, coupled with Edward's too lavish patronage of her sizeable immediate and extended family, alienated the king's most powerful and influential supporter, Richard Neville, earl of Warwick, who then backed the return of the Lancastrian regime. By spring of 1471, however, Edward had regained the throne, killing Warwick and Prince Edward of Lancaster in battle and unceremoniously murdering Henry. With no more legitimate threat to his own hereditary claim to the throne and having learnt important lessons from his earlier mistakes, Edward made a great success of the rest of his reign. His renewal of the Anglo-Burgundian alliance, originally secured by Henry V but broken in 1435, was the basis for a military expedition in 1475 which prompted Louis XI of France to buy Edward off with a pension of 50,000 gold crowns per year. This, along with closely managed policies of patronage and fiscality, allowed the king to fund a lavish and magnificent court life and engage actively in foreign policy without having to go cap in hand to Parliament.

None could have predicted how swiftly Edward's legacy would be abased after his unexpected death in April 1483. By high summer the dead king's heretofore steadfastly loyal brother, Richard, duke of Gloucester seized the throne after deposing his nephew, Edward V and imprisoning him in the Tower of London along with his younger brother, Richard, duke of York. The usurpation, and his subsequent murdering of the child princes, alienated many avid supporters of the Yorkist regime while also opening wounds barely healed or still festering of former supporters of the Lancastrians. The result was almost immediate rebellion, culminating in Richard III's death in battle at Market Bosworth in 1485. Bosworth's victor, Henry Tudor, presented himself as the champion of Lancastrian interests and the legitimate successor of that lineage, through his mother, Margaret Beaufort (an extremely weak claim, given that the Beaufort line originated in an adulterous relationship of John of Gaunt). With little experience of English methods and traditions of governance, having himself lived most of his life in Wales, France and the duchy of Brittany, Henry VII was a quick study; he held on to power in the face of a major rebellion in Cornwall (1497) and repeated challenges to his rule by the royal pretenders Lambert Simnel and Perkin Warbeck, who received their backing from disaffected Yorkists and Continental princes who saw them as useful counters to English ambitions. He also developed and refined certain government practices of his Yorkist predecessors, operating an incredibly tight fiscal programme to fill the royal coffers, thereby freeing himself from dependence upon the broad political community, and delegating authority to hand-picked household bureaucrats at the level of central government while maintaining the loyalty of the nobility through the judicious parcelling out of lands, offices and titles. At his death in 1509 he left a strong, united realm, an overflowing treasury and an extremely effective administrative machinery to his heir, Henry VIII.

The new king shared his father's strong sense of the royal prerogative, but had far grander ambitions on the European stage. While Henry VII had been content to make threats against France in return for cash, Henry VIII intended to make good on the old English claim to the throne of France originally made by Edward III. His pursuit of this goal reactivated the ancient alliance between the French and Scots, leading to the horrendous bloodbath of the Scots at the battle of Flodden in September 1513, where King James IV and more than 10,000 others, including the flower of the Scottish nobility met their deaths. Surely, if the motif of Fortune's wheel applied to the monarchs of Britain's southern kingdom, it did equally to the rulers of its northern neighbour. From the accession of Robert Bruce in 1306 through the disaster of Flodden, two of Scotland's eight kings spent long years as captives of the English, four met violent ends and four left behind minor heirs. Partly as a consequence of this, late medieval Scotland never developed a strong, centralised monarchy, and its kings had, on the whole, to content themselves with ruling in partnership with the nobility. Still, if the Scots seem to have liked their kingship fairly weak, there was never any question of abandoning monarchy or the line of Robert Bruce. His successor, David II, came to the throne at the age of five in 1329 and later spent eleven years in captivity after the Scottish loss at Neville's Cross in 1346. Yet at no time was his kingship seriously challenged. And when he died childless, the crown passed smoothly to the next in line of succession, Robert Stewart, whose lineage continued through his grandson James I's eighteen years as a captive of the English and assassination in 1437, through his great grandson James II's demise owing to an unfortunate proximity to an exploding cannon, through the killing of James III shortly after the battle of Sauchieburn in 1488 and the death in battle of James IV at Flodden, and on to the final ascendance of the Bruce-Stewart line to the English throne in the person of James VI (James I of England) in 1603. Like the English, whose apparent affinity for killing their kings has been amply shown, the Scots also could not contemplate an alternative to dynastic kingship. And, like the English, they only demanded that their kings respect the web of limitations, expressly defined or implied, that made them kings and not tyrants. The Scots, however, also refused to be tyrannised by their much larger, wealthier and more populous neighbour to the south, and after coming within a hair's breadth of being conquered at the beginning of the fourteenth century, they not only successfully asserted their independence from England but acted as a valuable ally to its enemy France for better than two centuries.

France and Burgundy

As the fourteenth century opened, the triumphal story of royal dominance over the realm of France, as narrated in the official organ of Capetian historiography, the *Grandes chroniques de France*, seemed to have just about been realised in the powerful rule of Philip IV 'the Fair'. Autocratic by nature, like his English rival Edward I, Philip asserted his royal will through a rapidly developing administrative machinery, staffed by loyal, efficient and ruthless servants. His capital city, Paris was the largest in Latin Christendom and the home of its intellectual centre, the University of Paris, and the realm over which he held sway was the largest and wealthiest in Europe. Before his death in 1314, Philip had managed to break the power of the pope, Boniface VIII, to destroy the international military order of the Templars, to expel the Jews from his realm, and to keep in check two of what had traditionally been the most independent and troublesome of the territories over which he exercised suzerainty, Flanders and Gascony. But instead of his reign marking the start of the final stage of a smooth process of centralisation and unification leading to the formation of a modern state, it was, instead, 'the culmination of the medieval French monarchy. . . . a point that was not surpassed, and often not equaled, during the rest of the fourteenth century'.[21] Only in the second half of the fifteenth century would the kings of France again be able to exercise the kind of control over their realm that Philip IV had. The reasons for this were partly structural, for the underlying reality which Philip obscured by the force of his personality and will was a France that was still very much divided into more or less autonomous regions, each with its own identity, culture, customs and institutions of governance. The rulers of the duchy of Brittany, for example, still thought of themselves as being independent of France, while Maine, Anjou and Provence were controlled by the Angevin kings of Naples (who were themselves members of a cadet branch of the Capetian family); and the Flemish towns, although momentarily quiescent, were hardly pacified. It was the southwestern duchy of Gascony, however, that turned out to be the greatest cause of grief for the rulers of France: a grief brought on by the wars waged against them by Gascony's dukes, the kings of England. The Hundred Years War would, in its turn, exacerbate many of France's internal divisions, helping to spark off the Jacquerie of 1358 as well as the several civil wars that plagued the realm, especially in the fifteenth century.

Both dynastic and territorial issues lay at the heart of the Hundred Years War. With the extinction of the direct male Capetian line in 1328, three serious candidates for the succession put themselves forward: Philip, the thirty-five-year-old count of Valois, who was the son of Philip IV's younger brother; Philip, the young count of Evreux, son of Philip IV's

Table 5.2 Rulers of France and of Valois Burgundy

Philip IV	1285–1314			
Louis X	1314–16			
John I	1316			
Philip V	1316–22			
Charles IV	1322–28			
Philip VI of Valois*	1328–50			
John II	1350–64	–>	Philip the Bold (son of John II)	1363–1404
Charles V	1364–80		John the Fearless	1404–19
Charles VI	1380–1422		Philip the Good	1419–67
Charles VII	1422–61		Charles the Bold	1467–77
Louis XI	1461–83			
Charles VIII	1483–98			
Louis XII	1498–1515			
Francis I	1515–47			

*The accession of Philip VI marks the end of the Capetian and beginning of the Valois dynasty.

youngest brother and husband of Louis X's daughter, Joan; and the recently crowned boy king of England, Edward III, whose claim derived from his being the grandson of Philip IV, through his mother, Isabella. Although the decision in favour of Philip of Valois initially elicited little complaint, Edward III would resurrect his claim after the outbreak of war in 1337; and this dynastic claim continued to motivate the English kings' belligerence toward France throughout the remainder of the Middle Ages. Moreover, later, the son of Philip of Evreux and Joan, King Charles II of Navarre, would prove to be a serious irritant to the Valois. Still, there can be no doubt that the war's initial spark was the territorial dispute over Gascon sovereignty. Simply put, did the English king hold Gascony as a feudal vassal of the king of France, as the Valois claimed (and with good reason, since this relationship had been enshrined in the Treaty of Paris of 1259), or did he, as he insisted, possess it in full sovereignty (on the grounds that Henry III's homage to Louis IX in 1259 was a personal one that was not binding upon his successors)? Needless to say, such a dispute could not satisfactorily be adjudicated by lawyers; only trial by battle could determine the outcome.

The terrible losses at Crécy and Poitiers had dire effects on the reigns of Philip VI and of his son John II. The years immediately after Poitiers were particularly trying. While John II, captured at Poitiers, was a prisoner in England, his eldest son, the dauphin Charles, duke of Normandy tried to govern in his stead. But resentment at the inability of the crown and nobility to defend the realm from the depredations of English soldiers and mercenary bands prompted several of the representatives of the Estates General, which had been called to meet in Paris directly after Poitiers, to ally themselves in 1358 with Charles of Navarre and with the rebellious commune of Paris (led by the provost of merchants, Etienne Marcel) and challenge the duke of Normandy's regency government. The same resentment sparked the Jacquerie, whose violence engulfed the north French countryside in the same year. The duke of Normandy soon regained control of things, however, and succeeded his father, as King Charles V, in 1364. Under his intelligent rule, France gained the upper hand over its English enemies after the renewed outbreak of war in 1369, now assisted by its new ally, the usurper of the Castilian throne, Enrique of Trastámara. Victories against the English (and against their Flemish allies at Roosebeke in 1382) continued into the reign of Charles VI, who succeeded to the throne as a minor in 1380. These victories, coupled with Richard II's disinclination to pursue the war, resulted in a series of truces, starting in 1389, that suspended open war between the two countries until the accession of Henry V in 1413.

Charles V, though, was also a tough advocate of strong bureaucratic government, and resentment at his policies flared up soon after his death in several rebellions, the most serious of which were the *Harelle* at Rouen and the seizure of control in Paris by the *Maillotins* (Hammer-Men) in 1381–82. Throughout the 1380s Charles VI seemed on track to continue and develop the policies of his father, but starting in 1392 he began to suffer lengthy fits of madness, which rendered him largely incapable of effective rule throughout the remainder of his troubled reign. Into the vacuum created by Charles VI's 'absence' strode the great princes of the blood, the royal uncles Louis of Anjou, Jean of Berry and Philip the Bold of Burgundy, and Charles's brother, Louis of Orléans. Their acquisition of power was partly a logical extension of the growth in power of the territorial principalities in France that the Anglo–French war had promoted through the alliances of mutual advantage forged between Edward III and such powerful nobles as the duke of Brittany and the *vicomte* of Béarn. This centrifugal process was only exacerbated by Charles V's willingness to grant extensive privileges, like the power to collect taxes and the holding of regional *parlements* in the apanages of his brothers. Such tendencies might have been directed and controlled by a strong monarch, but got totally out of hand during the madness of King Charles. A strong rivalry developed at court, moreover, between Louis of Orléans and Philip the Bold, with each vying for control of the king and government. This rivalry turned into live hatred between Louis and Philip's heir, John the Fearless, who engineered Louis's murder in 1407.

Civil war soon followed between the Burgundian faction and the supporters of Louis's heir, Charles, the chief among whom was Bernard, count of Armagnac. This clash between Burgundians and Armagnacs helped precipitate the renewal of the Hundred Years War, with Henry V taking advantage of a divided France and gaining the, at least tacit, support of the dukes of Brittany and Burgundy to facilitate his invasion of Normandy in the late summer of 1415. The slaughter at Agincourt did nothing to quell the civil war, leaving the way open to Henry's reduction of Normandy in 1417–19. Paris was the scene of slaughter in May 1418, when the Burgundians gained entry, killed Bernard of Armagnac, and took control of Charles VI. The dauphin, Charles, fled south of the Loire to the lands he had inherited upon the death of his great uncle Jean of Berry. His active involvement in the murder of John the Fearless the following year gave the new duke of Burgundy, Philip the Good, all the political ammunition he needed to secure the dauphin's legal removal from the royal succession, replacing him with Henry V in the Treaty of Troyes. France was now truly divided, with Paris and the north and east (as well as Gascony) controlled by the Anglo-Burgundian alliance and the south, the so-called 'Kingdom of Bourges', loyal to the dauphin (proclaimed Charles VII by his supporters on the death of his father).

Things might have gone very badly indeed for the House of Valois – and certainly seemed headed in that direction, thanks to the dedicated and competent direction of the English 'regent' in France, John, duke of Bedford – but then, in 1429, fortune again smiled on the dynasty, in the form of Joan of Arc (see Chapter 8). Charles's official coronation at Reims, on the heels of the victories at Orléans and Patay, turned what had been a civil war into a war of liberation from the English. Shortly thereafter, relations began to cool between Philip the Good and the English, and in 1435 he was reconciled with Charles VII and the Armagnac faction at Arras. This was not the end of France's troubles, however. Frustration with the king's apparent inability to suppress the depredations of roving bands of brigands and the resentment of several of the great princes of the realm against what they saw as Charles's high-handedness and favouritism, led to a rebellion in 1440 (the 'Praguerie') and the threat of one in 1442. Still, the king maintained the upper hand, restoring some order in the countryside and instituting military reforms which played a hand in driving the English out of Normandy and Gascony in 1449–53. And although princely factions still troubled the realm thereafter, Charles secured the rule of his dynasty, passing it on at his death in 1461 to his son, Louis XI.

Louis, who himself had plotted with the territorial princes during the reign of his father, now showed his former co-conspirators no mercy. Continuing his father's policies of military reform and juridical and bureaucratic expansion, Louis successfully countered their ambitions in the War of the Public Weal in 1465 and, again, in 1475, when the dukes of Burgundy and Brittany supported Edward IV's invasion. The ever-looming threat of Burgundy was removed in 1477, with Duke Charles the Bold's death in battle at Nancy; and a series of wars with his successor, Maximilian of Habsburg, led by 1493 to the restoration to France of Artois and the duchy of Burgundy. Also the extensive territorial complex in France of the dukes of Anjou, which included Anjou, Maine, Bar and Provence along with their claim to the kingdom of Naples, passed to the French crown with the extinction of the line of Anjou in 1481. Upon Louis's own death in 1483, the accession of his young son, Charles VIII, brought on the noble factionalism typical of a minority. The boy king's sister, Anne and her husband Pierre de Beaujeu, gained the upper hand, destroying the power of the duke of Orléans and then that of Brittany, whose heiress, Anne, then married Charles, in 1491. On reaching his majority, the king felt comfortable enough with his hold on power to launch a war of conquest in Italy, trying to make good on his dynastic claim to the kingdom of Naples, then ruled by the Aragonese Ferrante I. His successor Louis XII could continue to dabble in Italian affairs, for by the time of his accession in 1498 the era of the great territorial princes in France was effectively over. France, although still a nation of regions, had become the sort of monarchic state that Philip IV could only have dreamed of forging two centuries earlier.

Throughout most of the fifteenth century, Burgundy was the French principality whose ambitions had affected the course of politics more than any other. Its rise to power had been built on the fortunes of death and marriage. The duchy of Burgundy had returned to the royal patrimony on the death of its duke without an heir in 1361. Two years later, John II granted it as an apanage to his youngest son, Philip the Bold, who in 1369 married Margaret, heiress to the count of Flanders, Louis de Male. Thanks to this most lucrative of unions, the dukes of Burgundy, after Louis de Male's death in 1384, ruled over a discontinuous but enormous and wealthy principality that included not only Burgundy and Flanders, but also Artois, Revel, Nevers and Franche-Comté. Rulers of a vast principality, whose lands spanned both the eastern parts of France and the west of the Empire, the fifteenth-century dukes behaved accordingly, building up what was, in effect, a state, with a large and sophisticated bureaucracy, magnificent court and order of chivalry (the Golden Fleece, founded in 1431), and pursuing its own foreign policy. What the dukes were unable to overcome, however, was the essentially heterogeneous character of their far-flung holdings, each with its own history, institutions and interests. Political geography also stood in the way of a unified state, since a vast swath of territory, including Champagne, Alsace and Lorraine, separated their lands in eastern France from those in the Low Countries. Charles the Bold's efforts at gaining control of these lands involved him in ruinously expensive wars with France in 1473–75. His efforts at territorial expansion also aroused the hostility of the Swiss Confederation, and it was this war which proved the undoing of the Burgundian state. In the immediate aftermath of Charles's death, only the hastily arranged marriage of his heiress, Mary, to Maximilian, son of the Habsburg Emperor Frederick III, staved off the total partition of the Burgundian territorial agglomeration. Thanks to this marriage, the Burgundian lands, with the exception of Artois and the duchy of Burgundy itself, were to form part of the inheritance of Mary and Maximilian's grandson, Emperor Charles V.

The Iberian kingdoms

The marriage in 1469 of Charles V's other set of grandparents, Isabella of Castile and Ferdinand of Aragon, in effect united the largest of the Christian kingdoms of the Iberian Peninsula. Ferdinand and Isabella's reign, however, marked other important changes in the composition and character of what would henceforth be called Spain. Their conquest of the Muslim Nasrid kingdom of Granada in 1492, which completed the centuries-long Christian *reconquista* of the peninsula, initiated the expulsions and forced conversions of Muslims and Jews in what had formerly been a religiously pluralistic (if hardly harmonious) land. Their rule also witnessed, on the one hand, a westward shift of focus, with the 'Catholic Monarchs' committing themselves to the same decidedly Atlantic perspective that had occupied their neighbours of Portugal throughout the fifteenth century, and, on the other, a re-commitment to Italian affairs, with Ferdinand's invasion and occupation of the kingdom of Naples in 1503.

Table 5.3 Rulers of Aragon, Castile and Portugal

Aragon	
Jaume II	1291–1327
Alfonso IV	1327–36
Pere IV 'the Ceremonious'	1336–87
Joan I	1387–95
Marti	1395–1410
Fernando I	1412–16 (new dynasty: Trastámara)
Alfonso V 'the Magnanimous'	1416–58
Joan II	1458–79
Ferdinand 'the Catholic'	1479–1516 (marries Isabella of Castile 1469)
Castile	
Fernando IV	1295–1312
Alfonso XI	1312–50
Pedro I 'the Cruel'	1350–69
Enrique II 'of Trastámara'	1369–79 (new dynasty: Trastámara)
Juan I	1379–90
Enrique III	1390–1406
Juan II	1406–54
Enrique IV	1454–74
Isabella 'the Catholic'	1474–1504 (marries Ferdinand of Aragon 1469)
Portugal	
Dinis	1279–1325
Afonso IV	1325–57
Pedro I	1357–67
Fernando	1367–83
João I 'of Avis'	1385–1433 (new dynasty: Avis)
Duarte	1433–38
Afonso V	1438–81
João II	1481–95
Manuel I	1495–1521

Things had been rather different c. 1300. Then the gaze of the king of the Crown of Aragon, Jaume II, was directed very much to the east. Besides ruling the three territories of Barcelona, Aragon and Valencia, which formed the Crown of Aragon, he also controlled the Balearic Islands and Sicily, and laid claim to Corsica and Sardinia. This interest in what has been called a Mediterranean Arago-Catalonian 'empire', occupied a considerable amount of the attention of Jaume and his successors throughout the fourteenth and much of the fifteenth century.[22] Nonetheless, the Aragonese monarchs also had concerns on the Iberian mainland. Aragonese expansion south into Murcia eventually helped spark a war between King Pere IV 'the Ceremonious' and his eponymous rival of Castile, Pedro I 'the Cruel'. Starting in 1356, with fighting off and on until the late 1360s, this 'War of the Two Pedros' took on a more European-wide character, when Pedro's brother, Enrique of Trastámara and a group of French mercenaries under the command of Bertrand du Guesclin (and supported by Charles V of France) allied with Pere against a coalition of Pedro the Cruel and an Anglo-Gascon force under the command of Edward the Black Prince. The war did not, on the whole, go well for Aragon, but Enrique's ascent to the Castilian throne, after capturing and murdering his brother in 1369, brought some recompense. Pere had greater success in the Mediterranean, bringing Majorca, which had become an independent kingdom ruled by a branch of the house of Barcelona, under his rule in 1349. More difficult was asserting his control over Sardinia, Corsica and Sicily, tasks which involved him and then his younger son, Marti, in a series of wars from about 1350 until Marti's death in 1410.

Marti's death without a living heir brought an end to his dynasty, the house of Barcelona. The Crown of Aragon, with its strong traditions of noble and urban government through the *Cortes*, chose to fill the empty throne by appointing a commission of nine electors, three selected from each of the territories, to settle on a successor. Their choice, Fernando of Trastámara, the younger brother of Enrique III of Castile, took up the Mediterranean policies of his predecessors and succeeded in gaining control of affairs in both Sardinia and Sicily. The range of this western Mediterranean empire was further extended by Fernando's heir, Alfonso V 'the Magnanimous', who set out to conquer the Angevin kingdom of Naples after the death of its queen, Joanna II, in 1435. His efforts, which brought him into conflict with Joanna's presumptive heir, René, duke of Anjou, finally met with success in 1442. Not satisfied with this, Alfonso sought control over northern Italy as well, thereby contributing to the endemic warfare there that was only finally settled by the Peace of Lodi in 1454.

Alfonso's Italian adventures meant both heavy taxation and absentee rule for the Crown of Aragon. The resentment this caused, especially in Catalonia, led to the civil war that plagued the middle years of the reign of Alfonso's successor, his brother Joan II. Into this (1462–72) stepped René of Anjou, now asserting his claim to the Crown of Aragon. It was in part owing to hopes of gaining Castilian support in this war that Joan married his son Ferdinand to Isabella, half-sister of King Enrique IV. Although the marriage did not bring much aid, since Isabella and her supporters were themselves locked in conflict with Enrique, its future consequences were to be significant, leading eventually to the union of the crowns and the rise of Spain as a European and world power in the sixteenth century.

The kingdom to which Isabella succeeded, on the death of Enrique IV in 1474, had been rocked by political turmoil since the late thirteenth century. Lightly populated, especially in the aftermath of the Black Death, and politically fragmented thanks to a combination of regionalism, noble faction, and considerable autonomy on the part of many of its towns, it had not proved easy to govern, a situation not helped by the poor quality of several of its monarchs. The bright spot, as far as it went, came in the reign of Alfonso XI, who succeeded between c. 1325 and 1340, with the help of administrators learned in the law, called *letrados*, in bringing some degree of peace and unity to his realm. After years of hostile relations with his neighbours of Portugal and Aragon, Alfonso enlisted their aid to defeat the combined forces of Yusef I of Granada and the Marinids of Morocco at Salado, not far from Gibraltar, in 1340. This inspired him to renew the *reconquista*, taking Algeciras in 1344 and then making an unsuccessful attempt on Gibraltar, where he died of plague in 1350. During his nineteen-year reign, Alfonso's only legitimate son, Pedro I, distinguished himself by rank cruelty in an age of brutal politics. He also, however, dominated his neighbours and countered the bid to the throne of his illegitimate half-brother, Enrique of Trastámara, for much of his reign. Yet Enrique had the last laugh in 1369, when he had the personal pleasure of stabbing Pedro to death after defeating him in battle at Montiel.

As king, Enrique II honoured the alliance he had formed with France in 1366, thus drawing Castile into the renewed Hundred Years War, and prompting John of Gaunt to invade Castile on two occasions on behalf of his bride, Constanza, daughter of Pedro the Cruel. Enrique also returned to the old Castilian policy of hostility against Portugal, whose king, Fernando I, responded by making an alliance with England. The war with Portugal was taken up with alacrity by Enrique's heir, Juan I, who claimed the Portuguese throne on the death of Fernando I, in 1383. His invasion, however, only served to unite much of the divided Portuguese nobility behind João, the master of Avis, who ascended the throne as João I after defeating Juan at the battle of Aljubarrota in 1385.

The modicum of peace that came to the Iberian Peninsula with the cessation of hostilities in the Hundred Years War in 1389 was shattered two years later in the savage pogroms against Jews and *conversos* in 1391. And if in the decades that followed the realms of Portugal and Aragon both occupied themselves with overseas adventures – in North Africa and the Atlantic, in the case of the former, and in the Mediterranean, in that of the latter – Castile instead descended into a long era of noble faction and internecine strife. Matters only truly began to improve in 1479, after Isabella and Ferdinand had triumphed in the civil wars that had broken out at her accession five years previously. The co-rulers worked to build a strong monarchy in Castile as well as to unite the interests, if not the administrations, of their two kingdoms. And, inspired by crusading ideals and apocalyptic prophecy, they had by the end of 1492 conquered Granada (after a decade-long war), ordered the expulsion of all Jews from their realms, and backed Columbus's voyage. This last act, which had been billed in part as a bid to bring the 'Grand Khan' of China into an alliance with the Catholic Monarchs against Islam, worked instead to increase Spain's interest in the Atlantic, as a competitor of Portugal. It was this united Spain, purged of its last Muslims in 1502, fortified by the acquisition of the tiny Pyrenean kingdom of Navarre in 1512 and possessor of an incipient New World empire, to which the Habsburg Charles V (Charles I of Spain) acceded in 1516.

Italy and the Empire

In his person Charles V exemplified the workings of Fortune in dynastic politics. He was heir to the Spanish kingdoms and had a claim on Aragon's western Mediterranean holdings through his mother, Juana 'the Mad' (Ferdinand and Isabella's daughter), and was endowed with the Austrian and Burgundian inheritance of his father, Philip of Habsburg (son of Emperor Maximilian I and Mary of Burgundy). His power and prestige were further amplified by his election to the imperial throne in 1519. There was, of course, no real unity to this disparate collection of polities, territories and peoples. Italy and the German lands were particularly fragmented, and had been throughout the late Middle Ages. The Italian peninsula divided itself into three main parts: the southern kingdoms of Sicily and Naples; the Papal States, running in a band from the region of Lazio south of Rome up through Umbria and the Marche to the Adriatic and north to Bologna in the Romagna; and the centre-north of multiple city-states as well as various feudal principalities, the chief of which was the duchy of Savoy. Sicily was, throughout this period, ruled either directly by the kings of Aragon or by a branch of the Aragonese royal family. For its part, Naples (or the *Regno*) belonged to a branch of the Capetian dynasty of France, the house of Anjou. Masters of both the practical and symbolic aspects of kingship, the first Angevin kings, Charles I, Charles II and Robert 'the Wise', established a powerful state that, especially under Robert, frequently dominated Italian affairs. This position of strength disintegrated during the unfortunate reign of Robert's heiress, Joanna I, a monarch particularly subject, it seems, to the wiles of Lady Fortune. Her first marriage, to her Angevin cousin Andrew of Hungary, was not a good one. Joanna bridled at Andrew's insistence on ruling as king, rather than accepting his designated role as consort. Her adultery, complicity in Andrew's defenestration and seeming abandonment to death of her and Andrew's daughter, brought down on her the wrath of Andrew's elder brother, Louis the Great, king of Hungary. Worse still, her several succeeding marriages produced no living heir and left the realm open to the political manoeuvring of the greater nobility. Near the end of her reign, in 1378, she got on the wrong side of papal politics by opposing the Roman pope Urban VI in the Schism, thus opening the way for her cousin Charles of Durazzo, to claim the throne with the help of Urban and his supporter Louis the Great of Hungary. In a bid to save herself, she turned to one of the Avignonese pope Clement VII's chief allies, Louis of Anjou, the brother of Charles V of France, naming Louis as her adopted heir. Joanna's bid failed, and after a reign characterised by civil war and the depredations of armies and mercenary bands she was imprisoned and murdered by her cousin, who in 1382 succeeded to Naples' throne as King Charles III (d. 1386). The new king's claim, however, was disputed by Louis of Anjou (d. 1384), whose claim would be taken up by his son, Louis II (d. 1417), and grandsons, Louis III (d. 1434) and René (d. 1480). Joanna's lands of the Neopolitan kingdom and county of Provence thus ended up being, effectively, divided between Louis's line, which succeeded after a brief but nasty civil war to the county Provence, and the Durazzo line in Naples, represented by Charles, followed by his son Ladislas (d. 1414) and daughter Joanna II (d. 1435). Louis's heirs continued to press their claim to the kingdom of Naples, leading to repeated conflict in the Italian peninsula. Moreover, both Charles and Ladislas made a bid for the throne of Hungary, left vacant on the death of Louis the Great in 1381. Here, however, their efforts were stymied by Sigismund of Luxemburg, son of Emperor Charles IV and husband of Louis's eldest daughter, Maria.

In the dozen years preceding his death, Louis the Great must have felt that Fortune had by and large favoured him. He had inherited strong royal power from his father, the Angevin Charles-Robert (r. 1309–42), and tremendous riches from the royal monopoly on the gold mines at Kremnica. Secure in generally warm relations with his royal neighbours, the emperor Charles IV of Bohemia and Casimir III 'the Great' of Poland, and having gained the good will of his nobility by granting them considerable concessions, he was able to turn his attention to wars of acquisition in the Balkans and along the Dalmatian coast (thus bringing him into conflict with both the Ottomans and the republic of Venice), and a war of revenge against his cousin and former sister-in-law Joanna of Naples. In 1370 he added the kingdom of Poland to his patrimony, having been named heir to his childless uncle Casimir (r. 1333–70). In the last dozen years of his life, however, he faced diminishing yields from his gold mines and an uncertain succession to both his kingdoms. In 1370, being still child-less after almost eighteen years of marriage, he was ready to name Charles of Durazzo as his heir (who might, had this occurred, have eventually been ruler of Naples, Hungary, and Poland!). However, the birth of three daughters in rapid succession to his queen, Elizabeth of Bosnia, put Charles out of the running. Louis now hatched a plan to make his eldest daughter, Catherine, queen of Naples, and to secure the succession of the younger daughters, Maria and Jadwiga, to Hungary and Poland. The death of Catherine in 1378 prompted Louis to again back the interests of Charles of Durazzo in Naples, while making arrangements for Maria's future marriage to Sigismund of Luxemburg and Jadwiga's to Leopold III of Austria. Louis's death left his two young daughters with rightful but precarious claims to their inher-itances. Maria, despite having been crowned 'king' of Hungary at her mother's instigation, faced several years of peril before she and Sigismund (they married in 1385) succeeded in defeating the forces of the Durazzo claimants and their supporters. Meanwhile, Jadwiga had to forgo her planned marriage to Leopold owing to considerable Polish opposition to him. In return for their accepting her rule, it was agreed that she would marry the grand duke of pagan Lithuania, Jagiello, on condition that he convert to Catholicism (r. 1386–1434 as King Władisław II). There had been a moment when Louis the Great could imagine himself the emperor of a great realm that stretched from the Adriatic to the Baltic. In the end, the most fortunate inheritors of his legacy were his sons-in-law, Sigismund and Jagiello, who added the bits of his partitioned patrimony to their own imperial agglomerates.

Back in the *Regno*, things became unstuck under Charles of Durazzo's truly incompetent daughter, Joanna II, whose fecklessness and favouritism were only matched by her inabil-ity to control her nobility. At her death, the kingdom became a battleground, contested by René of Anjou and the Aragonese Alfonso V 'the Magnanimous', both of whom Joanna had designated at different times as her successors. The victories of Alfonso brought Naples and Sicily under his control. On his death in 1458, Naples passed to his illegitimate son, Ferrante (d. 1494), while Sicily remained in the orbit of the kings of Aragon. War again afflicted the *Regno* in 1494–1503, when the kingdom and its short-reigning kings, Alfonso II, Ferrante II and Federigo, endured the successive invasions of Charles VIII and Louis XII of France, who both pressed the old Angevin claim, and then of Ferdinand 'the Catholic', who, in 1503, reunited Naples and Sicily under Aragonese rule, and joined them to his Iberian dominions.

Although Rome and much of central Italy were technically under papal lordship, the absence of the popes from Italy during the Avignon papacy of 1309–77, followed by the Great Schism of 1378–1415 favoured the genesis of powerful *signorie*. A weakened Empire promoted a similar trend in the north, although there considerable power also rested in the great republics of Venice, Florence and Genoa. By the late 1300s, the politics of the north were dominated by the competition of Florence, Venice and Visconti Milan, all of which were engaged in the enterprise of creating territorial states. The Genoese, meanwhile, continued their long-standing competition with Venice for control of Mediterranean trade while also com-ing into increasing conflict with the Aragonese over control of Sardinia. Genoa's ultimately unsuccessful struggle for Sardinia lasted for the better part of a century, between c. 1330 and c. 1420, while a ruinous war with Venice (the War of Chioggia, 1378–81) severely compro-mised Genoa's trade network in the eastern Mediterranean. The resolution of the Schism at the Council of Constance opened the door to (the new) Pope Martin V's attempts to reassert papal control in Rome and central Italy. His and his successors' efforts not only poured fuel on the flames of the murderous rivalry between the powerful noble families of Colonna and Orsini, but complicated the already very complicated international politics of Italy. So much conflict

Table 5.4 Rulers of the kingdom of Naples

Charles II (of Anjou)	1285–1309
Robert	1309–43
Joanna I	1343–82
Charles III	1382–86
Ladislas	1386–1414
Joanna II	1414–35
Alfonso I (V of Aragon)	1442–58
Ferrante I	1458–94
Alfonso II	1494–95
Ferrante II	1495–96
Federigo	1496–1502
Ferdinand 'the Catholic'	1503–16

involving so many players made Italy a veritable playground for mercenary armies and their captains, the *condottieri*. One of these, Francesco Sforza, who had learned his trade under the tutelage of his father in the wars in southern Italy and then commanded the forces of Milan under its duke, Filippo Maria Visconti, engineered his own accession to rule there three years after Filippo Maria's death without a legitimate heir in 1447 (Sforza had wed his illegitimate daughter, Bianca Maria, in 1441).

The decade of the 1450s brought with it some degree of peace as well as a realignment of political alliances in Italy. First, the traditional alliance of the republics of Florence and Venice against Milan dissolved, owing, on the one hand, to growing concern on the part of both Florence and Milan regarding Venice's expansion into the interior (the *terraferma*) during the previous several decades, and, on the other, to the threat faced by Florence from Alfonso of Naples, and by Milan from Charles VII of France. Second, alarm at the fall of Constantinople, especially on the part of Venice and Pope Nicholas V, prompted the talks that led to the general peace made at Lodi in 1454. The provisions of Lodi recognised the primacy of five territorial states in the peninsula – Milan, Venice, Florence, the Papal States and Naples – and created a peninsular military alliance, the 'Italian League'. Lodi did not end warfare in Italy. A partially botched effort in 1478 to assassinate Lorenzo de' Medici and his brother, Giuliano (Lorenzo survived) by the Pazzi family and Pope Sixtus IV, led to a brief war (the Pazzi War, 1478–80) between Florence and its allies Venice and Milan against the pope and King Ferrante of Naples; and Venice's attempt to invade the neighbouring duchy of Ferrara was the occasion of the War of Ferrara (1482–84), which brought all the other members of the Italian League together against Venice to assist Duke Ercole d'Este of Ferrara. Nonetheless, in the four decades after Lodi, warfare and mayhem were considerably reduced.

The remainder of the century was to see a growing Turkish threat to Italy, leading to Venice's loss of its substantial territorial holdings on the Dalmatian coast and, ultimately, to an Ottoman attack in 1480 on Otranto in the kingdom of Naples. Finally, a kind of entente even arose between the papacy and Florence. Then, in 1494, the relative peace that had reigned since Lodi was shattered by the decision in 1494 of Charles VIII of France to invade Italy to press his claim on the kingdom of Naples. Five years later, Italy again suffered from the invasion of Charles's successor, Louis XII. These invasions were the beginning of a new era in Italian politics, in which the peninsula became the battleground and subject of great powers. The great Lombard state ruled by the Sforza of Milan fell, first to Louis XII in 1499, who pressed an old and rather questionable claim based on his grandfather Louis of Orléan's marriage to Valentina Visconti. After again being occupied by the French in 1515, Milan eventually became subject to the rule of Emperor Charles V in 1525. Venice, although it maintained its independence, nonetheless temporarily lost dominion over its territorial state after being defeated at Agnadello in 1509 by Pope Julius II and the League of Cambrai. Moreover, its dominance of eastern Mediterranean trade was severely curtailed by the rise of the Ottoman empire. As for Florence, the arrival of Charles VIII ushered in a tumultuous period of republican rule, first under the populist-reformist government of the Observant Dominican friar Girolamo Savonarola (1494–98) and then under Piero Soderini. In 1512, however, Florence fell again under the dominance of the Medici, who had the backing of Ferdinand of Spain. It was this chastened Italy that Soderini's former colleague Niccolò Machiavelli tried to rouse against the foreign 'barbarians' with the publication of his *Il Principe*. Shortly before his death in 1527, Machiavelli may well have received news that these barbarians, that is, the Spanish and German troops of Charles V, had sacked Rome and slaughtered as many as 10,000 of its inhabitants.

Although the Italian north had been nominally under the authority of the German emperors since the time Otto I in the 900s, whatever real power they exercised there had been effectively broken with the destruction of the Hohenstaufen after the death of Frederick II in 1250. Moreover, imperial power north of the Alps, tenuous and discontinuous in the age of the Hohenstaufen, had devolved to a considerable degree to the territorial princes and urban leagues after their demise. These tendencies only continued after 1300. Nonetheless, the desire to revive the Empire remained and the elected German king-emperors of the late Middle Ages remained a force to be reckoned with. Yet if their *authority* inhered largely in their status as the elected emperor, their *power*, their capacity for action and manoeuvre, rested more on the resources they acquired and dispensed through the dynastic mechanisms of inheritance and marriage. Three princely dynasties entirely dominated the office of emperor at the end of the Middle Ages, the Habsburgs, Luxemburgs and Wittelsbachs.

Albert I of Habsburg's power-base ran discontinuously from his family's lands in parts of Switzerland and the upper Rhine in the west to Austria and Styria in the east. He was an extremely canny political operator, facing down opposition from the Rhenish electors and turning Pope Boniface VIII's initial hostility to support early in his reign and later, in 1307, installing his son Rudolf as king of Bohemia, when that kingdom reverted to imperial hands on the death without an heir of its last Přemysl king, Wenceslas III. Fortune, however, did not continue to smile on Albert. Bohemia was lost to him on Rudolf's death without an heir just a few months after becoming king. Albert followed him to the grave a short time later, murdered by a nephew. Now the imperial crown passed to Henry VII of Luxemburg. Being neither a Habsburg nor the king of France (Philip IV had put himself forward as a candidate), and without a strong dynastic base, he seemed the perfect choice of electors favouring a weak emperor. And so he was, on the whole; but the future of his dynasty was assured owing to the acquisition by his line of Bohemia and Moravia through the marriage of his son John to Elizabeth Přemysl in 1311. This was the signal achievement of Henry's reign, since he followed it up by getting mired in the morass of northern Italian politics. His decision to reassert imperial authority south of the Alps, after a long hiatus, is certainly understandable. But instead of managing to stay above the fray of Guelf/Ghibelline and Angevin/Aragonese factionalism (as Dante had hoped he would do), he instead came down on the side of Ghibelline Milan and the Aragonese, thus raising the ire of the Guelf cities of Tuscany, led by Florence, and of Pope Clement V. He died of malaria while besieging Siena in 1313.

Table 5.5 Rulers of Germany and the Empire

Albert I of Habsburg (H)	1298–1308
Henry VII of Luxemburg (L)	1308–13
Ludwig IV of Bavaria (W)	1314–47
Charles IV of Luxemburg (L)	1346–78
Wenceslas (L)	1378–1400 (deposed). King of Bohemia 1378–1419
Rupert of the Palatinate (W)	1400–10
Sigismund (L)	1411–37. King of Hungary 1387–1437 and of Bohemia 1419–37
Albert II (H)	1438–39
Frederick III (H)	1440–93
Maximilian I (H)	1493–1519

Imperial claimants as a result of disputed elections:
Frederick, duke of Austria (H), 1314–22
Jost, margrave of Moravia and Brandenburg (L), 1410–11

H=Habsburg   L=Luxemburg   W=Wittelsbach

His Wittelsbach successor, Ludwig IV of Bavaria, also spent several years in Italy (1327–30), although to greater effect, conferring imperial vicariates on several of his Ghibelline supporters in return for considerable sums of money. Still, Ludwig never achieved his final goal there, which was to supplant the power of that most imperious of fourteenth-century popes, John XXII, despite installing an anti-pope in Rome and having the support of those intellectual heavyweights Marsilius of Padua, Jean of Jandun and William of Ockham. The emperor's luck was also spotty in Germany. Ludwig's victory at Mühldorf in 1322 over the Habsburg Frederick of Austria put an end to this rival's claim to the imperial throne. Frederick, however, was still a force to be reckoned with, so Ludwig offered him Carinthia (thus creating an enormous power-block in the east for the Habsburgs) in return for Frederick's tacit support of Ludwig making his own son margrave of the large northeastern principality of Brandenburg. In 1338, his authority still shaky on account of ongoing papal hostility, Ludwig worked out a deal with the imperial electors at Rhense, whereby he recognised their fundamental juridical autonomy in return for their assertion that the imperial office was conferred by their election alone, without needing papal approval.

In 1346 the spadework of Henry VII paid off in the imperial election of his grandson, Charles IV, king of Bohemia. Charles wisely maintained good relations with the papacy and largely kept out of Italian affairs; the tremendous power he derived from his kingdom meant he could afford to. For Charles, the imperial office was mostly a means to the end of aggrandising his lineage and supporting his ambitions in central and eastern Europe. So confident was he of his own position and so desirous of guaranteeing the imperial succession of his son, Wenceslas, that he promulgated the Golden Bull of 1356, which codified and strengthened the power and privileges of the seven elector princes: these being the archbishops of Cologne, Mainz and Trier, the king of Bohemia, the count Palatine, the duke of Saxony and the margrave of Brandenburg. The Golden Bull also reiterated the principle of imperial election first mooted at Rhense. Interestingly, other German princes began to imitate the privileges granted to the electors in 1356, and this annoyed many German towns, whose sense of political and legal victimisation at the hands of the territorial princes was only exacerbated by confidence in their own economic strength. Their response was to form, or join, urban leagues, like the Hanse and the Swabian League. Despite the defeat in battle of the Swabian League in 1388 and Wenceslas's efforts to undercut the power of urban leagues through the imposition of regional public-peace associations (*Landfrieden*) in which power was shared by towns and nobles, such urban leagues, as well as the Swiss Confederation of forest cantons and towns, continued to operate in the late Middle Ages.

For all Charles IV's carefully laid plans, however, the imperial career of his son Wenceslas was essentially a failure which ended in his deposition as emperor in 1400. He fared little better as king of Bohemia, whose nobles imprisoned him on a few occasions and where he spent his last years countering the rising threat of the Hussites, who were infuriated at the underhanded treatment and execution of their leader, Jan Hus at the Council of Constance in 1415. The prince chosen to replace Wenceslas as emperor, the Wittelsbach Rupert of the Rhineland, met with little more good fortune than his predecessor. His ill-conceived Italian expedition of 1402 was a complete flop, while his efforts to enforce the *Landfriede* policy started by Wenceslas met with the insurmountable opposition of a league of imperial electors and towns (the League of Marbach). When Rupert died in 1410, the Empire passed again to a Luxemburg, this being Wenceslas's younger brother, Sigismund, king of Hungary.

More politically astute and energetic than his brother, Sigismund paid dearly for his active role in the martyrdom of Hus, inheriting the Hussite problem from his brother in 1419 and spending the rest of his reign in unsuccessful crusades against them. The Hussite war virtually impoverished him, and the need for support within the Empire forced him to aggrandise his imperial vassals, including Frederick of Hohenzollern (to whom he gave the margravate of Brandenburg) and Philip the Good of Burgundy. Upon Sigismund's death without an heir in 1437 the power of the Luxemburgs was terminated and their great eastern power-block broken up. For a time Bohemia and Hungary remained united under the rule of the emperor Albert II of Habsburg and then of his son Ladislas 'Posthumous'. But with the death of Ladislas at a young age in 1457, Bohemia and Hungary both passed to separate 'native' rulers, the former to George Podebrady (1457–71), and the latter to John Hunyadi (1457–58) and then to his son Mathias Corvinus (1458–90).

The empire had now returned to the Habsburg line, where it was to remain. After the very brief reign of Albert II, who died in battle against the Turks in 1439, there followed the extremely long period of Frederick III's rule. At one level, his reign can be judged a success. He held on to power, despite repeated challenges, in the west from Burgundy and a renewed Swabian League, and in the east from Mathias Corvinus. He also secured the marriage of his son Maximilian to Charles the Bold's heiress, Mary of Burgundy, and then paved the way to Maximilian's succession to the imperial throne in 1493. Still, it must be said that what was left of the Empire itself at the time of Maximilian's accession was a poor thing indeed compared to what it had been at its late medieval apogee during the reign of Charles IV. Maximilian, always short of money and men, spent his reign fighting the Swiss and some of his fellow German princes, while also facing the threat of Turks in the east and the French in the west. Particularly galling was his inability to counter the moves of both Charles VIII and Louis XII in Italy. And yet he consolidated his hold over Austria and died knowing his grandson Charles was ruler of Spain, Sicily, Naples and the Netherlands, as well as of a burgeoning overseas empire in the Americas. Charles, of course, also soon followed his grandfather onto the imperial throne and would eventually dominate all of Italy

The political history of late medieval Europe is dizzying in its complexity. How could it be otherwise, given the extremely fragmented, atomised and fissile state of Latin Christendom's body politic, on the one hand, and, on the other, the almost mind-blowing variety of political actors, each with their own agenda. It comes as no surprise that contemporary observers tended to invoke Fortune's wheel as the chief (mis-)directive force in history. Today we call fortune 'contingency', and contingency certainly played a determinant role in late medieval politics, thanks to its essentially personal and dynastic character. Still, one can discern the undercurrent of some broad trends beneath the seemingly incomprehensible activities of Lady Fortune. The most important is the movement toward consolidated territorial states, whether large monarchies like France and Spain or smaller states like Milan and Venice. Within these states rulers had to engage in dialogue with broad political communities while also relying upon increasingly sophisticated and professionalised bureaucracies to enhance their own autonomy and power. The great 'international' polities of the Church and the Empire, their universal power diminished by the rise of principalities, began themselves to behave in the manner of princes. At the same time, small polities, whether the duchies and counties of France or the territorial states of northern Italy, were increasingly threatened by the great monarchies. In the sixteenth century, political power became the province of the great dynastic monarchies. That power came largely from their ability to fund and field large standing armies.

Notes

1 Bergen 1923: pt. 1, lvi (my translation).
2 Hall 1962; Mortimer 2005.
3 Hall 1965: 242.
4 Reinhard 1996: 1.
5 Harriss 2005: 59.
6 Nederman 2002: 51.
7 Genet 1977: 197.
8 Fowler, Briggs and Remley 1997: 57–60.
9 Gentile 2012: 313.
10 Cary 1883: 31.
11 Forhan 1994: 26.
12 James 1983: 3.
13 Paravicini 1991: 76.
14 Harriss 2005: 16; Costa Gomes 2003: 243; Muir 2004, 243.
15 Vale 2001: 95.
16 Harriss 2005: 14.
17 Harriss 2005: 22; Watts 1996: 98.
18 Fowler, Briggs and Remley 1997: 53, 355.
19 Forhan 1994: 34.
20 Davies 1994: 121.
21 Strayer 1980: xii.
22 Fernández-Armesto 1987.

6

WAR, CHIVALRY AND CRUSADING

But now that I have got this far, I should examine my work's subject-matter. . . .
I make at the beginning of my book a vision which came to me of a tree of sor-
row, on the top of which you will be able to see, firstly, that those who rule over
Holy Church are in more cruel disorder than ever before, as will be well known
to those who pay heed to this book. Afterwards you will be able to see the great
discord at this time between Christian kings and princes. You will then be able
to see the great anguish and discord between communities.[1]

At the time Honoré Bouvet dedicated his *L'Arbre des batailles* ('Tree of Battles') to Charles
VI of France in 1387, the Benedictine doctor of canon law had good reason to believe that
all Christendom was in a state of war. War and rebellion had been frequent occurrences over
the course of the previous decades, and his native Provence had just suffered through the
civil war between the supporters of Louis of Anjou and Charles of Durazzo; moreover, the
Church was in schism and there was a new threat in the east, the Ottoman Turks. So common
was war, that Bouvet found ridiculous the very notion of anything like an enduring and widespread peace in the world: 'At this stage I would like to put a question . . . namely, whether
this world can by nature be without conflict, and at peace? I reply that it can by no means be
so'.[2] Since wars and conflict were, then, inevitable, the best one could hope for was to regulate and conduct them according to law and reason, a programme best overseen by legitimate
authorities, like the king of France. What was taking shape in the minds of professionals like
Bouvet and his chief source, the Bolognese jurist, John of Legnano (d. 1383), was the legal
basis of what was to become one of the most important characteristics of the modern state,
the monopoly on the legitimate exercise of violence. It is understandable that this concept
was being worked out in an era when warfare had become so prevalent, enduring, expensive
and destructive, and in a time of growing state power.

Several of the social and political factors contributing to the ubiquity of warfare and insurrection in late medieval Latin Christendom have already been discussed earlier (especially
in Chapters 1 and 5). At the root of all these was the growing ambitions of states and rulers,
ambitions that almost invariably entailed compulsion and required force. Likewise, as the
proliferation of mercenary companies amply attests, war could be a lucrative, if risky, source
of pay and profit. There was, however, also an important cultural element at play, which
might be called the valorisation of violence. This valorisation is apparent in clerical culture,
which naturalised warfare as a legitimate, indeed desirable, means for the pursuit of justice.
We have just seen this in Bouvet's *Arbre des batailles*; in the same work, he even answers the

question 'From what law does war come?' with 'Thus we must understand that war comes from God, and not merely that He permits war, but that He has ordained it. . . . Further we say that our Lord God Himself is lord and governor of battles'.[3] Clerics were also avid war propagandists, whether leading prayers and processions in support of war or in thanksgiving for victory, preaching pro-war sermons or, in the case of chroniclers like Jean Le Bel and Jean Froissart, lauding 'honourable enterprises, noble adventures and deeds of arms . . . so that brave men should be inspired thereby to follow such examples'.[4] Pacifism might even be taken as a sign of heresy, as was certainly the view of the Cambridge theologians who in 1393 condemned the anti-war doctrines of the Lollard William Swynderby: 'To fight in the defence of justice, against both unbelievers and Christians, is in itself holy and permissible: to hold the opposite is to be in error'.[5]

Chivalry, however, was the cultural force which most valorised violence. This complex web of beliefs, values and habits that promoted deeds of prowess in pursuit of honour guided the behaviour of not only knights but of all men-at-arms. According to this bellicose 'code', as eloquently expressed by the French knight Geoffroi de Charny in his *Livre de chevalerie* (c. 1350), although the individual warrior could licitly win honour in the joust or tournament, he nonetheless should regard them as only practice and preparation for the ultimate expression of chivalrous activity, war:

> Their [i.e. aspiring men-at-arms'] knowledge increases until they see and recognize that the men-at-arms who are good in war are more highly prized and honored than any other men-at-arms. It therefore seems to them from their own observation that they should immediately take up the practice of arms in war in order to achieve the highest honor in prowess, for they cannot attain this by any other form of armed combat. And as soon as they realize this, they give up participating so frequently in exercising their skill at arms in local events and take up armed combat in war.[6]

Simply stated, men like Charny enjoyed 'a privileged practice of violence' and 'found in their exhilarating and fulfilling fighting the key to identity'.[7] It just so happens that men like Charny included almost all those kings, princes and nobles who constituted the chief political class. For these men and those who aspired to be like them, the waging of war was their *raison d'être*. Kings and princes satisfied their honour by waging war and cemented ties of loyalty with their nobility by calling on them for service; nobles expected to serve their rulers in war but also practised warfare for their own ends, seeing the wars of rulers as 'only one of the guises which the profession of arms could wear'.[8]

War and bellicosity, then, are inextricably intertwined with the political history of the late Middle Ages. In this chapter we will look first at the relationship between war and the state, examining the characteristics of the 'war state' and pondering the question of the 'medieval military revolution'. Next we will turn to the matter of chivalry, both as an aspect of warfare and as a cultural and political form. The practice of chivalry was essentially the art of war, an art whose growing sophistication inspired a large and varied production of war literature. Finally, the issue of crusading will be addressed, since this not only constituted an important kind of warfare in the late Middle Ages but was also one of the principal ways in which European Christians encountered their non-Christian neighbours, and the forces of orthodoxy confronted both heretics and schismatics within Latin Christendom.

War and the state

The single most important enterprise of the late medieval state was the waging of war.[9] The states of the fourteenth and fifteenth centuries devoted, on average, at least half their resources to war and defence, and considerably more so during actual conflicts. So, for example, whereas the ordinary peacetime revenues of the government of Edward III of England amounted to somewhere between £30,000 and £40,000, soldiers' pay alone during a single two-month siege in 1340 ran to £60,000; the entire Low Countries campaign of 1338–40 cost somewhere in the range of £400,000, of which almost 95 per cent was funded by debt. By the 1370s, when the English had learned to conduct less expensive campaigns and after the dramatic decline in population brought about by plague, a typical six-month expedition still cost somewhere between £60,000 and £75,000, and the total cost of war in 1369–75 amounted to about £670,000.[10] In Charles of Valois's crusade proposal of 1323, the estimated annual cost of funding a force of 5,000 mounted men-at-arms and 15,000 infantry came to the rough equivalent of £267,000 (1,600,000 *livres tournois*).[11] War, then, was the single most important motivator of fiscal innovation and expansion in the late Middle Ages. Mobilisation and provisioning of armies and navies, and construction, maintenance and garrisoning of defences also placed considerable demands on the administrative machinery of states. In 1325 Florence mobilised something like 15–20 per cent of its adult population and something like 5 per cent of England's adult male population fought in the army raised for the Scottish campaign of 1298. And even if armies did not typically comprise such a large proportion of the populace, it is also true that efforts were made to field more efficient and effective forces; the business of recruiting, mustering and adequately arming such a force, then transporting, supplying and paying it over a period of several months or longer was no mean administrative feat. The composition and armaments of armies had to be determined, indentures and contracts drawn up, horses and wagons (and sometimes ships) secured and paid for, and munitions and provisions obtained and monitored.

Was, then, the late medieval state a 'war state' like its early modern successor, and did the fourteenth and fifteenth centuries experience a 'military revolution' akin to that of the sixteenth through eighteenth centuries? Here the answer to both questions must be a qualified 'yes'. The arguments made in favour of a military revolution in early modern Europe centre on: (1) the growth in size of armies; (2) a shift from heavy cavalry to infantry as the most effective part of an army – a shift which contributed to the aforementioned growth; (3) the introduction and growing importance of gunpowder weapons, which in turn necessitated innovations in the architecture of fortifications; and (4) the duration of time these armies spent in the field and the new and more complex challenges they faced encouraged greater professionalism (including regular pay) and a more scientific approach to warfare. These developments increased the costs of war considerably, forcing states to increase taxation and bureaucratic efficiency, thereby behaving in a more absolutist way, and to devote the preponderance of their revenues and resources to their militaries: they became, in short, war states.[12]

Most of these factors can, however, be extended back to the fourteenth century, and some, even earlier. The first half of the fourteenth century witnessed several battles (Courtrai, Bannockburn, Morgarten and Laupen) in which highly disciplined contingents of infantry, armed with long pikes and shorter spears and poleaxes, inflicted a terrible toll on mounted opponents (see Chapter 1). The Swiss, victors at Morgarten and Laupen, continued to refine their tactics and weaponry, using them to devastating effect against the Austrians at Sempach in 1386 and against Charles the Bold of Burgundy at Grandson and Morat in 1476. Feared and admired, the Swiss were in high demand as mercenaries in the fifteenth and early six-teenth centuries, and provided the model for the mercenary companies of German infantry called *Landsknechte*. English armies in the time of Edward III also perfected a method of infantry warfare, the highly mobile mounted companies of men-at-arms and archers that spread destruction and terror during their *chevauchées* in the French countryside, but then dismounted for battle, as at Crécy (1346) and Poitiers (1356). This 'English system' proved its worth beyond the fields of France, being employed by the Black Prince against the forces of Enrique of Trastámara at Nájera (1367) and by John Hawkwood's mercenary companies in northern Italy during the later decades of the fourteenth century. Henry V relied on it again (minus the destruction of the countryside) during the Agincourt campaign of 1415.

If fourteenth-century English armies demonstrated the battlefield effectiveness of artillery in the form of massed units of highly trained archers armed with the longbow, during the 1420s the Hussites of Bohemia under the command of Jan Žižka first realised the potential of gunpowder weapons in pitched battle. Protected by the defences of their *Wagenburg* – mobile war wagons chained together into a kind of fortress – the Hussites employed cannon and primitive handguns, called culverins, as well as crossbows to break up cavalry charges; soldiers armed with pikes and halberds would then sally forth from behind the wagons to finish off the disordered knights and men-at-arms. Later, gunpowder artillery proved deci-sive in the French victories over the English at Formigny (1450) and Castillon (1453), and handgunners also played an increasingly important part in the armies of Burgundy. By the end of the century, the culverin had been superseded by the more accurate and reliable arque-bus, a weapon whose deadly force was applied by the Spanish against the French and Swiss at Cerignola in 1503. In 1515 at Marignano French field artillery destroyed the formations of Swiss pikemen in the employ of Milan, and a decade later, at Pavia, Spanish arquebusiers laid low the army of Francis I of France: the age of the gun had truly arrived.

Long before the firearm ruled the field of battle it had become the indispensible weapon of siegecraft. Gunpowder, a blend of saltpetre, sulphur and charcoal invented by the Chinese, had been brought westwards by the Mongols in the thirteenth century. By 1267 it had come to the notice of Europeans, as evidenced by the gunpowder recipe of the English Franciscan Roger Bacon. Better than half a century was to pass, however, before gunpowder weapons came into use in Latin Christendom, and their first serious application seems to have occurred in the 1340s, most notably in the use made of cannon by the English at the siege of Calais in 1346–47. Prior to 1400 cannon tended to be fairly small, made from copper or from strips of iron hammered together, and firing either lead or stone projectiles. Their rate of fire was slow and they propelled their projectiles with little force or accuracy. There were several reasons for this rather disappointing state of affairs. First, prior to the early 1400s, gunpowder's rate of combustion was slow and irregular and projectiles fitted fairly loosely in the barrel. These factors in turn necessitated a complicated, multi-step process prior to firing, wherein the powder was poured into a separate, plugged chamber that was hammered into place behind the breech, while wooden wedges and a bung were used to hold the ball in place: all this so that at the time of ignition sufficient pressure could build in the breech to propel the projectile. The need to bung the projectile also necessitated a short barrel, which contributed to these guns' poor accuracy and low muzzle-velocity. These deficits help explain why the counterweight siege engines called trebuchets, with their faster rate of fire and reasonable accuracy, continued in use throughout the fourteenth and well into the fifteenth century.

Still, cannon were used in greater and greater numbers throughout the latter half of the fourteenth century, and during the fifteenth century the accumulated weight of experience

Figure 6.1 Fifteenth-century siege with cannon. Photograph: Lebrecht Music & Arts / Alamy Stock Photo

and experimentation led to truly revolutionary modifications. First, in the early 1400s, large bombards of forged iron and cast bronze began to be fashioned, which could pulverise fortress walls with great stone projectiles weighing 300 to 560 pounds. Then, in the 1420s, a process was developed whereby gunpowder was 'corned' or granulated, thereby greatly improving its rate of combustion. Now longer-barrelled guns could be made of a single piece and loaded with powder and shot at the muzzle. This and improvements in the casting of lead and cast-iron shot, meant that smaller and medium-sized cannon could be loaded and fired rapidly and deliver an accurate, high-velocity shot. By 1428 some English cannons at Orléans were delivering 124 shots every twenty-four hours. The problem of transporting and aiming cannon was ameliorated mid-century, when barrels sporting trunnions began to be mounted on two-wheeled gun carriages. Thus in the fifteenth century the long-held advantage of the besieged shifted to the besiegers. This is already apparent in Henry V's Normandy campaign of 1417–19, where instead of launching a *chevauchée* to draw the French out of their fortifications and get them to engage in pitched battle, as his predecessors had done, he instead reduced one fortified town after another with his siege train. So improved had these weapons and the skill of their operators become by the middle of the century, that the forces of Charles VII reconquered Normandy in a much shorter time than it had taken Henry to conquer it. At the same time, at the opposite corner of Christendom, the great bombards of the Ottoman Turks pulverised the hitherto unbreachable walls of Constantinople.

All this firepower came at a staggering cost. Ingredients for powder had to be purchased and the powder milled, cannon and shot had to be forged and cast and wagons built, draft animals needed to be purchased and trained gunners paid. And the size of arsenals kept growing. Charles the Bold may have had as many as 300 cannon in the 1470s and in 1489 Charles VIII of France had five bands of artillery, each with some 150 pieces. For the siege of Tournai in 1513, Henry VIII of England brought 180 artillery pieces and 510 tons of powder. Of course, field pieces only represented a portion of a state's artillery, since towns and fortresses had to build up substantial arsenals for their defence. The city of Rennes in Brittany obtained 343 pieces of varied size between 1450 and 1492; by 1479 Ghent had 486 pieces. The most impressive figure comes from Nuremberg, which in 1468 housed 2,230 pieces. The great artillery trains and arsenals greatly drove up military costs; for example, the government of France devoted 8 per cent of its military budget to artillery in 1489. Eventually the cost of fortifications increased in response to the new threats posed by cannon, with the building of thicker, angled walls and angle-bastions, beginning in the later 1400s.

Size was one area in which early modern armies distinguished themselves from their late medieval predecessors. No European armies of the fourteenth through early sixteenth centuries approached the magnitude of the 200,000 men under arms in late sixteenth-century Spain or the 280,000 soldiers serving Louis XIV's France in 1678. Compared to these great forces, even the largest mobilisations, like the 44,700 men-at-arms and foot soldiers called to defend France in 1340 or the 1,656 cavalry and 31,000 infantry assembled for the crusade against the Hussites in 1422, seem modest. Throughout most of the period field armies were considerably smaller than this, however. Most English armies of the Hundred Years War numbered from 6,000 to 10,000, and the armies of fifteenth-century Milan typically ranged between 10,000 and 25,000. Particularly during the period 1340–1440, the small army was the rule, but then from the middle of the fifteenth century armies began to expand. Charles VII of France began c. 1450 to keep armies of some 20,000–25,000 in the field for extended periods and the Swiss could, and frequently did, muster some 20,000. In 1486 Mathias Corvinus of Hungary fielded an army of 28,000, two-thirds of which was composed of light and heavy cavalry, while his contemporaries Ferdinand and Isabella called up armies of between 11,000 and 13,000 light horse and 40,000–45,000 infantry in their war of conquest against Granada. Such forces compare well with those of the later period, especially when one recalls the diminished population of the late medieval period.

Extended campaigns like those launched by the English against France and the demands of continuous defence occasioned by endemic warfare, especially in France and the Italian peninsula, encouraged the professionalisation of soldiering, including, in the second half of the fifteenth century, the genesis of standing armies. The story of military professionalisation is neither simple nor straightforward, but the general trend was a movement away from unpaid obligatory service, whether feudal or militia, toward paid, contractual service. The length of these contracted terms tended, in turn, to grow longer, beginning with indentures lasting through a single campaigning season to contracts of several years' duration. Two basic types of paid soldier can be distinguished in the fourteenth century: the indentured retainer, a phenomenon especially associated with the English armies serving in France; and the (usually foreign) mercenary, a soldier especially common in Italy. The system of indentures (written contracts) used by the English in wartime was itself an outgrowth of the peacetime practice of royal and aristocratic patronage known as 'retaining', whereby lords formed networks of loyalty and service in return for various kinds of remuneration and favour. When organising an expedition to the Continent in 1373, John of Gaunt, the duke of Lancaster, brought his own sizeable indentured retinue but also made indentures of war with twenty-eight captains (thirteen Englishmen and fifteen foreigners), who in their turn subcontracted soldiers into their own retinues. One of the members of John of Gaunt's retinue in 1369, John Neville, lord of Raby, agreed to bring along on campaign twenty men-at-arms and twenty mounted archers. Each member of a retinue, from the greatest lord to the least infantryman, agreed to assemble at a certain time and place, to serve for a certain term and to come armed in a certain fashion; in turn he could expect a daily wage and some pre-determined cut of whatever spoils and ransoms might be gathered. Transport costs were covered by the king, who also guaranteed compensation for horses killed on campaign. The English continued to rely on the indenture system throughout the remainder of the Middle Ages, although they did adapt it to meet the long-term demands of defending lands in English-held Normandy. Something similar to the English indenture, the *lettre de retenue*, was also employed in France, prior to the 1440s.

Large mercenary armies were the spawn of the many wars which ravaged fourteenth-century Italy. The so-called Catalan Company which formed during the Angevin-Aragonese conflict over the control of Sicily in the late 1200s, thereafter entered Byzantine service when peace was made between those warring parties in 1302. The Angevin and papal wars of the 1340s through 1360s encouraged companies largely made up of Germans, Hungarians and Provençals to seek their fortune in Italy, after which companies of demobilised English and Bretons, like the White Company of John Hawkwood, fought under contract for several northern Italian city-states. Over the course of the fourteenth century, the early 'democratic' organisation of these mercenary companies, in which the soldiers elected their leaders and chose representatives to negotiate contracts with employers, changed into a more 'monarchic' one in which a company was under the singular command of a military contractor, the *condottiero*. By the end of the century the terms of these contracts tended to lengthen, from what had originally been only a few weeks or a season to a year or more, in order to contain the ravaging carried out by these companies during the winter months and times of peace. Likewise, the composition and leadership of these armies became more and more Italian, like the companies led by the *signori* Ludovico Gonzaga, marquis of Mantua, and Federigo da Montefeltro, duke of Urbino. These latter two trends continued into the fifteenth century, a time that also saw greater control being exercised over the mercenary companies through officers of state in charge of overseeing the contracts and conduct of the *condottieri*, so that by the mid-1400s, the mercenary armies of the Italian states looked more like professional standing armies than like the predatory bands of freebooters that had plagued the peninsula in the early and mid-fourteenth century.

The problem of under-employed mercenaries, this time the scourge of the *écorcheurs* in France after the decline in hostilities attendant on the Peace of Arras in 1435, prompted Charles VII a decade later to initiate the first truly professional standing army of the late Middle Ages, the *compagnies de l'ordonnance*, which by the second half of the century kept some 20,000 to 25,000 in their permanent employ. At the start of the 1470s, Charles the Bold of Burgundy followed suit with the formation of his troops of the ordinance, a permanent force of some 10,000 professionals, which constituted the core of his armies. Further east, in Hungary, Mathias Corvinus recruited a permanent force of 28,000 to counter the severe threat posed by the vast armies of the Ottomans, which could number close to 100,000 by the end of the century. In Italy during the third quarter of the fifteenth century, both Venice and Naples organised standing armies, in part to weaken the power of the *condottieri* in their employ. The Catholic Monarchs of Spain were not far behind, having created their own standing contingents by the end of the century. Although these new permanent armies were extremely expensive to maintain, their advantages in terms of greater centralised control and effectiveness in combat made them more than worth it.

Pay, long-term service and centralised control were not the only markers of the new professionalised armies of the late Middle Ages. They also demonstrated considerable sophistication in their composition and a high degree of discipline. Likewise they engendered in their soldiery some sense of service in the interest of the national common weal and the opportunity for them to rise up through the ranks to become the precursors of the professional officer class of the early modern period. The ongoing evolution of battlefield technology and tactics meant that the late medieval army was, increasingly, a force of specialists. We have already discussed the role played by massed infantry and archers, and then of the specialists in charge of gunpowder weapons. But the growing influence of artillery and infantry on the battlefield did not render the mounted man-at-arms impotent. The deadliness of the longbow, crossbow and pike stimulated significant improvements in armour composition and design for both horse and rider. The chainmail armour of the thirteenth century, which could so easily be penetrated by hardened steel points, gave way to increasingly sophisticated articulated plate-armour whose reinforced, angled surfaces neutralised or at least diminished the effect of hardened point and sharpened edge. More effective cavalry units and tactics were also brought into play, with the formation of 'lances', squads made up of, usually, one man-at-arms accompanied by one or two mounted squires and anywhere from three to six infantry specialists who fought together in battle. Light cavalry also made its appearance in some regions, like the mounted archers used by the Hungarians to fight the Turks, the Balkan stradiots employed in Italian armies, and the Castilian *jinetes*. Heavy and light cavalry greatly improved the effectiveness of late medieval armies, since the shock-force of a well-disciplined charge of men-at-arms could still break the cohesion of infantry units, while both heavy and light cavalry could harry the enemy and cut off its retreat.

If the imposition of discipline, order and control reduced the opportunities for brigandage and improved the combat effectiveness of armies, it also hardened men to the horrors of the battlefield. Needless to say, hand-to-hand fighting with edged weapons is a brutal business, and the terror inspired in infantry by a cavalry charge or among horsemen moving at breakneck speed toward a hedge of sharpened spikes and pikes manned by infantry who thought nothing of slitting throats and cutting out hearts (the latter was a practice in which the Swiss apparently engaged), must have been considerable. If death was omnipresent, injuries, too, could be grisly. One example will suffice. In 1403 at Shrewsbury, the young Prince of Wales, the future Henry V, while leading a charge against the forces of the rebelling Percy family was struck full in the face by an arrow. Despite the shaft's barbed point having shattered his nasal cavity just to the left of his nose and then driven itself a further six inches to lodge in the base of his skull, Prince Henry fought throughout the remainder of the day until the battle was won. He then was subjected to what must have been a frightful remedy, beginning with the removal of the shaft and proceeding to the extraction of the barbed head by the physician John Bradmore, who achieved this feat thanks to the application of an ingenious mechanism rather like an elongated cork-screw.

But the late medieval battlefield was also more deadly than its high medieval predecessor. The typical battle of the twelfth and thirteenth centuries in which mounted knights fought mounted knights was one in which the taking of hostages was preferred to killing. However, the non-aristocratic infantry who made up such a considerable proportion of late medieval armies had a different agenda. Their goal was simply to kill and avoid being killed; nor, conversely, did knights feel any compunction when it came to killing infantry. Battlefields north of the Alps were especially blood-soaked, with the vanquished always suffering far greater mortality than the victors. The Flemish infantry slaughtered 40 per cent of the French

Figure 6.2 Fifteenth-century articulated plate armour. Photograph: © The Wallace Collection

knights at Courtrai and the French in their turn wiped out half the Flemings at the battle of Cassel. At Halidon Hill the English killed 55 per cent of the Scottish cavalry; the English went on to kill 40 per cent of the French cavalry at Poitiers and again at Agincourt. On the battlefields of fifteenth-century Italy, death and injury were certainly very real threats, but less pressing than in the north, thanks to the preference of the *condottieri* to rely primarily on contingents of cavalry. Death rates there ballooned, however, whenever large contingents of foreign infantry were involved. For those who survived, soldiering increasingly became a career in which one could both serve one's prince and nation, and make a living. This was not only true for men of humble origin but also for those aristocrats who were on their way to becoming the core of the early modern officer corps.

War's relationship with the growth of the state and nation would have been far more limited had its burdens not been shared by non-combatants. Certainly they frequently were the victims of war. But they also contributed to the war effort by paying their taxes

163

and providing supplies (often less than willingly). War also created a substantial military economy: horses had to be bred for war, armour and weapons forged, cannons cast, fortifications constructed and repaired, ships built and refitted both for transport and navies, provisions gathered and transported, and loans made at interest. Combatants were also very conscious of strategy's economic component. This, after all, was one of the principal reasons for the devastation which the Scots visited upon the countryside of the north of England and which the English wrought in the fair fields of northern France. It was economics first and foremost that lay behind the almost incessant naval warfare and piracy in the Mediterranean, and that frequently broke out in the Bay of Biscay, the English Channel and the Baltic. *Chevauchées* and coastal raids were also a form of psychological warfare designed to increase the frustration of the populace with rulers incapable of performing their fundamental duty of defence. Such a strategy was needed because rulers also devoted considerable energy to disseminating propaganda favourable to their war aims and policies. This could come in the form of newsletters, like Edward III's letter informing his subjects of the progress of his campaign in Normandy in July 1346:

> Our lord the king, to the honour of God and of Our Lady, St Mary, and for the comfort of all his faithful and liege subjects in England, announces to them the success and prosperity of his undertakings, granted to him by God, since the time of his coming to la Hougue, near Barfleur, in Normandy. [The letter then describes the royal host's progress from la Hogue to Caen.] Then, soon afterwards, our men began the assault upon the town which was heavily reinforced and defended by about 1,600 men-at-arms, afforced by about 30,000 of the people, also armed. . . . But, let us thank God for it, the town was finally captured by assault without loss to us. . . . And the naval squadron which remained with the king burned and destroyed all the sea coast from Barfleur to Colleville near Caen. And also burned were the town of Cherbourg and the ships in the harbour: and more than 100 or more large ships and other enemy vessels were burned by our lord the king and his people. For all this our lord king asks his loyal subjects of England to tender devout thanks to God for what he has thus made possible, and that they ask God fervently that he may continue to grant the king his favour.

The letter goes on to explain the means through which this propaganda will be disseminated:

> [H]e has ordered his chancellor to write letters, under his great seal, to the prelates and clergy of his kingdom of England that they exhort the people to do the same; and the chancellor and other members of the royal council are to inform the people and citizens of London of what has happened, for their comfort.[13]

Edward's letter makes plain the strong religious content of official war propaganda and the role of the Church in its propagation. The forms taken by this religious devotion in support of successful war are nicely described in the so-called *Journal d'un Bourgeois de Paris* for the year 1412. 'As soon as the Parisians knew that the king [Charles VI] was in the lands belonging to his enemies, by common consent they called for processions which were the most devout to have been seen in living memory'. The processions occurred daily throughout the week and involved people of all social ranks and condition. In the final, Sunday, procession, those from Saint-Denis came to Paris, all bare-footed, bearing the bodies of seven holy men, the holy *oriflamme* [i.e. the sacred war-banner of the kings of France] . . . the sacred nail and the holy crown, which was borne by two abbots, accompanied by thirteen processional banners; and there went out to meet them the parish[ioners] of Saint-Eustache, to take their saint's body, which was in one of the reliquaries; and they all went directly to the Palace in Paris. There they very devoutly sang high Mass, and then all departed.[14]

In fourteenth-century England the clergy, both seculars and monks, even took up arms to protect the realm from the Scots in the north and from French and Castilian naval raids along the Channel coast. At the close of the Middle Ages, the wars of states had become a very public affair, solidifying the bonds of state and nation. Intimately connected to this development were those changes in the composition, arms, tactics and strategies of armies. These changes amounted to as much of a 'military revolution' as that which some early modern historians have asserted for their period. But what really was happening, of course, was a long, though accelerated, evolution over the course of several centuries spanning both what we call the 'late medieval' and the 'early modern' eras.

Chivalry and the literature of war

It used to be fashionable to see the late Middle Ages as a time during which knighthood and chivalry entered a long period of decadence and decline. Infantry and artillery turned the mounted knight into an anachronism. Knights, deprived of any real significance on the battlefield, engaged increasingly in symbolic and costly display, continuing to perform the over-determined forms of a chivalry emptied of its content. As Johan Huizinga baldly stated in the second decade of the twentieth century, 'the period of genuine feudality and the flourishing of knighthood ended during the thirteenth century', to be replaced by 'the great game of the beautiful life played as the dream of noble courage and fidelity'.[15] Now, it is true that the actual number of knights – defined as men who had in fact been knighted – fighting in the armies of late medieval Europe was indeed rather small. By the late fourteenth century, the percentage of knights in the cavalry contingents of English armies stood at less than 5 per cent; by the time of the duke of Somerset's expedition to France in 1443, it had fallen to 1.3 per cent. Such low numbers were not confined to the English, as bannerets and knights made up only 2.2 per cent of French armies in 1418–20.

Scholarship of the last two and a half decades has, however, modified the dismissive judgement of late medieval chivalry, replacing the metaphor of decadence with one of transformation. Yes, the proportion of knights in armies had declined from its height in the High Middle Ages, but, as we have discussed earlier, the function of the man-at-arms remained vital, whether fighting dismounted in the English forces at Crécy and Agincourt, or on horseback in the cavalry contingents of late fifteenth- and early sixteenth-century armies. Certainly most men-at-arms were not technically knights, just as there were certainly knights, like those derided by the early fourteenth-century Italian jurist Cino da Pistoia, who did not practise the art of war:

many are found who do not know how to arm themselves and who have exercised the most base crafts, and yet they are belted with a sword, bathed in water, have precedence in drinking and in the honour of [wearing] squirrel-fur and beautiful spurs, and are greeted with some prerogative of reverence.[16]

Likewise, any nice distinction between an aristocratic knight and a mercenary horse-soldier could easily become blurred. Geoffroi de Charny, that paragon of chivalry, recommended mercenary employment to knights in search of war abroad:

> Now we must consider yet another category of men-at-arms who deserve much praise. That is those who, for various compelling reasons . . . leave their locality, perhaps for the profit they might expect to get from this. . . . and go to Lombardy or Tuscany or Pulia [i.e. Apulia] or other lands where pay or other rewards can be earned. . . . where they can witness and themselves achieve great deeds of arms. . . . And when God has by His grace granted them honor for their great exploits in this military activity, such men deserve to be praised and honored everywhere, provided that they do not, because of the profits they have made, give up the exercise of arms too soon.[17]

Charny here does not much care about whether this man-at-arms came from a knightly aristocratic family or if he hailed from more humble origins. His chivalry would be a product of the renown he was to win through acts of prowess on the field of battle. Mercenary service, especially in Italy, 'blurred traditional societal markers and distinctions and forced soldiers into the unique position of re-creating themselves'.[18] No small part of this re-creation was the adoption of a chivalric persona, 'a chivalry which persisted in glorifying the individual who made his skills available to political masters in return for recognition and reward'.[19]

Chivalry, which at its heart had always been the expression of a bellicose individuality in search of honour, renown and advancement through deeds of arms and service, continued to be just that at the end of the Middle Ages. Chivalry had not decayed; rather it fitted itself to changing military and political contexts. In the military sphere, the knight on campaign was becoming a military commander. As such, he acted in concert with other commanders in a hierarchical structure of command, with the prince, or state, at the top. This points to the changing political situation: the shift from the feudal polity in which nobles viewed themselves as autonomous agents, toward the centralised state wherein an aristocrat's position and welfare was tied and essentially subordinated to the interests of the polity. The old spirit of independence did not shuffle off without a fight, however: witness the many civil wars and the widespread problems of aristocratic crime that are such ubiquitous features of the fourteenth and fifteenth centuries. Nor did it wholly die out, being, rather, co-opted. Those princely chivalric orders, like the Band, the Garter, the Star and the Golden Fleece, which were so common to the period, were just such institutions of co-optation. On the one hand they reinforced the sense of equality as well as 'class pride in the social ethic of chivalry' among their inductees.[20] On the other, these orders were the political instruments of their founders, 'the only formal means whereby chivalric values might be enlisted and harnessed to the service of a sovereign'.[21] In both senses, however, the late medieval chivalric orders confirm the ongoing vitality of chivalry.

Knights and other practitioners of war were engaged in what was becoming a more and more complicated business that demanded a high level of sophistication from successful commanders. Military science then as now was mostly learned from experience, beginning with training in the handling of arms and, for men-at-arms, equitation, and advancing to an apprenticeship in arms through participation in campaigns. Still, the last centuries of the Middle Ages also witnessed the composition of a substantial canon of war literature. The military manual, a genre originating in antiquity, made a comeback. The ancient models

Figure 6.3 Charles the Bold of Burgundy presides over a chapter of the Order of the Golden Fleece. Photograph: ART Collection / Alamy Stock Photo

inspiring these works were the *Strategemata* of Frontinus, written in the first century AD, and the *De re militari* ('On Warfare') of the late Roman writer Flavius Vegetius Renatus (c. AD 400). Although the first work found its way into some royal and noble libraries, far more popular was the work of Vegetius, which circulated during the late Middle Ages in over 200 Latin manuscripts as well as in numerous vernacular translations. Many readers of the fourteenth to early sixteenth centuries also got their Vegetius from the tenth and last book of Giles of Rome's *De regimine principum*; it is virtually lifted from Vegetius, although adding some original material regarding the use of trebuchets, a siege engine unknown to antiquity. Also very popular was Christine de Pizan's *Livre de fais d'armes et de chevalerie* ('Book of Deeds of Arms and Chivalry', c. 1410), a military manual which borrowed and adapted material from Vegetius, Giles of Rome and Honoré Bouvet's *Arbre des batailles*. Although the real practical impact of these works on late medieval warfare is debatable, certain writers of the time certainly *thought* some military commanders applied their lessons. João I of Portugal was credited with having drawn on Giles's *De regimine principum* during the siege of Ceuta in 1415, and the author of the *Gesta Henrici Quinti* ('Deeds of Henry V') relates how in the same year, during the siege of Harfleur, Thomas, duke of Clarence,

> in accordance with the theory of Master Giles and by order of the king, had a ditch of good depth and breadth dug between him and the enemy, and the soil that had been excavated, following the same Master Giles, thrown up on the inside towards his men.[22]

Several decades later, when Charles the Bold of Burgundy was laying siege to Neuss in 1474–75, one of his knights, inspired 'by Vegetius and other venerable writers who were very highly recommended and authoritative for the art of war', recommended the duke construct a moveable siege tower equipped with a kind of draw bridge called a 'crane'. Sadly for the besiegers, the engine got stuck in the mud far from the city's walls.[23]

Seasoned soldiers also began to write military handbooks, drawing on their own experience. Geoffroi de Charny is the first of these, having not only composed his *Livre de chevalerie* in the mid-fourteenth century but also two other treatises, one on the manners and qualities of a knight and the other a series of questions debated on the proper conduct of jousts, tournaments and war. Just over a century later, another French knight, Jean de Bueil, wrote down his recollections in a semi-fictionalised account of his own education and life as a soldier, *Le Jouvencel*. Then, around the turn of the fifteenth and sixteenth centuries, an even more practical kind of manual appeared, the first written during the 1490s by the French courtier and military veteran Robert de Balsac, entitled *La nef des princes et des batailles de noblesse* ('The Ship of Princes and of the Nobility's Battles'). A few short years later, Béraud Stuart, lord of Aubigny, borrowed from and augmented Balsac's work. Stuart's long and distinguished service had included service in the French king's Scottish company and Scottish guard, as well as fighting in England (he served with a French contingent supporting Henry Tudor at Bosworth in 1485), Spain and Italy. Knowledge of the art of war without the experience of it is of little worth, Stuart admits, but he still thinks it valuable to write about 'the form, manner and experience of the conduct and exercise of military discipline, for the formation and instruction of all noble, virtuous and chivalrous men, just as I myself practised and experienced it in several realms, lands, countries and lordships'.[24]

The practical, functional aspects of warfare were also addressed by several technical treatises. Early examples were produced in concert with plans for the re-conquest of the Holy Land, whose last crusader outpost, Acre, had fallen to the forces of the Egyptian Mamluks in 1291. In his *Liber secretorum fidelium crucis* ('Book of Secrets of the Faithful of the Cross'), completed by 1321, Marino Sanudo Torsello, a Venetian merchant born in Acre, provided detailed plans for the re-conquest, which included estimates of the number and kinds of troops and armaments, descriptions of war machines and maps. In 1335, Guido da Vigevano, the Pavian physician of Queen Jeanne of France, prepared his *Texaurus*, an illustrated book of complicated and ingenious war machines and engines, designed to be transported by sea to the Holy Land and appropriate for the conditions and obstacles which the crusaders would meet once they had arrived:

And since it will be necessary to break suddenly into towns, cities and castles both by night and by day, and to cross with horse and foot rivers both great and small, without delays, I . . . will so compose all the devices for the conquest of the Holy Land both by sea and by land that they can be easily borne by horses, and disposed without delay for the actual work of conquest.[25]

Sometime around 1400, another physician, the German Konrad Kyeser, produced a similar work, minus the crusading intent, called the *Bellifortis* ('Strong in War'), perhaps for the benefit of Wenceslas of Bohemia. Like the *Texaurus*, the *Bellifortis* describes in words and illustrations an impressive assortment of ingenious war wagons, siege engines and machines. It also, however, incorporates recent advances in gunpowder weaponry and some inventions designed for civilian use, including a heated bathhouse and a chastity belt. Several works of this kind followed during the fifteenth century, like Mariano di Jacopo Taccola's *De machinis libri X* ('Ten Books on Machines', 1449), Roberto Valturio's *De re militari* (1450s), and anonymous treatises with titles like *L'Art de l'artillerie et cannonerye* and *L'Art d'archerie*. The production of so many manuals and technical treatises and the avid readership for them, as evidenced by the many surviving manuscript copies and, in some cases, early printed editions, makes clear the degree to which the art of war was becoming a true military science.

War was also turning into a matter of governance, with the organisation and conduct of armies regulated by published statutes and ordinances. So, in 1352 King John II of France issued an ordinance stipulating that 'wars concerning the people of France should take precedence over all (private) conflicts, since the king's wars were fought for the interest of the common good'.[26] In 1369, the Florentine republic produced its *Codice degli stipendiarii* ('Book of the Paid Soldiers') and in England Richard II (1385) and Henry V (1419) both issued lists of ordinances. Ordinances were regularly drawn up by the Swiss cantons, as well. Valois France and Burgundy, however, produced the most elaborate of these published ordinances, beginning with Charles V's great ordinance of 1374, and proceeding to the many ordinances promulgated by Charles VII and Louis XI, and, in Burgundy, by Charles the Bold. The latter, in 1473, even sent a copy of his book of ordinances to each of his captains. These ordinances, like much of the literature of war, promoted an ideology of state power and legitimacy wherein the only legitimate war was that waged for the prince, the fatherland (*patria*) and the common good, and by a trained, disciplined and regulated army.

Still, the ethos of the chivalric knight waxed strong, for this was also an age in which chivalric biography proliferated. The Black Prince was the hero of the *La vie du Prince Noir*, a verse biography composed in the 1380s by the herald of one of the Prince's companions in arms, Sir John Chandos. Also celebrated in a biography were the deeds of one of the Black Prince's greatest rivals, the sometime mercenary and constable of France, Bertrand du Guesclin. Lionised in the same fashion was du Guesclin's successor as France's paragon of chivalry, Jean le Maingre, the Marshal Boucicault. These accounts celebrate individual prowess, loyalty and honour, as well as the soldier's rough and ready trust in a God who favours those fighting in a just cause. The dirty business of warfare is transformed into something beautiful and good, and the noble participants, who suffer mightily the hardships of campaign, still find time to treat themselves to lavish feasts and entertainments before and after battle. Even the life of a noble Castilian naval captain and part-time pirate, Don Pero Niño, found its promoter in his own standard-bearer, Gutierre Diaz de Gamez. A campaign of raids on the south coast of England in 1405 (in support of the Welsh rebellion) becomes, in *El Vitorial* ('The Victorious One'), a grand chivalric undertaking. After the Castilian fleet, with the assistance of two French galleys commanded by Charles de Savoisy, sacked St Ives, they by-passed Dartmouth where 'they saw fair troops of soldiers and archers coming up on all sides to defend the shore', then burnt several boats in the harbour of Plymouth and engaged in some fierce fighting at Portland. The chief armed encounter of this particular adventure, however, occurred at Poole, which the Castilians especially targeted because 'it belonged to a knight called Harry Paye, a Corsair who . . . had many times come to the coasts of Castille, whence he had carried off many boats and ships'. Don Pero sent several men ashore to set fire to the town, but after doing so, 'so many English came against them, that they could not make a stand against them, but withdrew slowly and in good order towards the sea'. The fighting, however, continued to escalate as more English defenders arrived, prompting Don Pero himself finally to make a landing:

> He recognised that the issue hung in the balance; he left his galley with the small company that had stayed there and landed. . . . When the Castillians saw the captain they took fresh courage. He, encouraging all he met, reached his standard. He who bore it [i.e. Gutierre Diaz de Gamez] was alone and in great jeopardy. . . . And Pero Niño said to Gutierre Diaz . . . 'Friend, take heed when you hear the trumpets sound; then march forward with the standard and go forward up to the English. There make your stand and leave it not'. The captain, very well armed, as soon as he had arrayed his men, started shouting with a loud voice: 'Saint James! Saint James!' The trumpets sounded, the standard advanced and all rushed after it. Then was it time for every man to do his duty and to shew his worth, for no man lacked an adversary.

After a good deal of hard and close fighting, victory went to the Castilians and French, and:

> When all was over, Pero Niño invited Messire Charles [de Savoisy] to dine with him that day, he and his knights; and so was it done. . . . And then Messire Charles said to the captain: 'My lord, you must forgive me, for these knights were overlong in arming themselves and while I awaited them I did not bring you aid in this battle; wherefore the honour is all yours, and I have no part in it'. The captain answered: 'My lord, another time you will do better; and if were mine to give, I would give you all the honour of this battle, for I know you to be so good a knight that you can do no wrong wheresoever you may be.'[27]

Such noble deeds and fine words! This was the stuff of romantic chivalry, a code whose ethic and aesthetic continued to motivate the very men whose role on the battlefield an earlier generation of historians dismissed as obsolete.

Crusading

Like the chivalry of the late Middle Ages, crusading in the aftermath of the fall of Acre has often been characterised as an anachronistic lost cause, emptied of the vital content that had inhabited it from the time of Pope Urban II's preaching at Clermont in 1095 which had inspired the First Crusade, down to the glorious, if unsuccessful, Egyptian and Tunisian expeditions of St Louis in the thirteenth century. Using hindsight it is easy to dismiss the frequent late medieval plans for crusades to the Holy Land as just so much talk, cynical political manoeuvring posing as pious intention. Some have also been tempted to disregard the many internal crusades, those against heretics, schismatics and 'enemies of the Church', as perversions of the true spirit of the armed pilgrimage in defence of the Holy Places. Some medieval critics of the Church, like the English John Wyclif and many of his Lollard followers, would have shared this point of view. But for the great majority of those living in the fourteenth through early sixteenth centuries, such talk was not only nonsense but heresy. For them, these attacks on foes of the Body of Christ, both within Latin Christendom and at the frontiers against Moors, Turks and the pagans of the eastern Baltic, were every bit as much crusades as those destined for the Levant. Indeed these wars were justified (if not always universally regarded) as necessary precursors to the reestablishment of Christian control in the East. Their definition of a crusade should be ours as well: 'papal validation, the granting of crusade status, preaching, and . . . recruitment'.[28] This is not to say that the later crusades lacked strong political motivations, for they certainly had them; but in this they were no different from the expeditions of crusading's golden age. Nor did the ongoing failure to retake the Holy Land lead to the terminal cooling of crusader zeal, since at times there is evidence of considerable excitement among both the participants in and supporters of all manner of wars waged in defence of the Faith.

The later crusades took several forms, though these can roughly be divided into three categories: (projected) expeditions to regain the Holy Land; crusades waged within Latin Christendom itself; and expansionist and defensive frontier wars. Planning for the recovery of Jerusalem was particularly intense in the decades immediately following the Mamluks' conquest of Acre in 1291. Thanks to the continued existence of the Latin kingdom of Cyprus and, in 1309, the conquest of the island of Rhodes by the Order of St John of Jerusalem (the Hospitallers), some hope remained of regaining what had been lost. For a time there was even serious talk of forming a strategic alliance against the Mamluks with the Mongol Il-Khans (who themselves had recently converted to Islam), although any real possibility of effecting this seems to have ended with the death of the Il-Khan Ghazan in 1304. Active planning continued, led by the kings of France, until the mid-1330s, when Philip VI relocated the crusading fleet he was assembling on the Mediterranean coast to his kingdom's Atlantic ports in preparation for war with England. The nearly thirty crusade treatises composed between 1291 and 1336, including those of Marino Sanudo Torsello and Guido da Vigevano, bear ample witness to the seriousness of intentions during these years. Even Philip IV's suppression of the military order of the Templars can be read as an expression of that king's genuine, albeit self-serving and predatory, zeal, since he had come to see the Templars' alleged corruption and perversion as dangerous obstacles to the business of recovery.[29]

The outbreak of the Hundred Years War in 1337 and the ravages of pestilence starting in the late 1340s put a temporary halt to crusading schemes. Then in the early 1360s, the new king of Cyprus, Peter I, fired with a crusading ardour that owed some of its heat to the prompting of his chancellor, Philippe de Mézières, initiated talk of a new expedition. What began as a crusade to retake the Holy Land soon turned into a targeted attack on Mamluk Alexandria, which Peter's force had the good fortune to capture in 1365. After looting the city, however, Peter and his army returned to Cyprus, prudently abandoning their prize before the Mamluk sultan could organise a retaliatory response. Peter continued to engage in warfare against the Mamluks until his murder in 1369, immediately after which his successor arranged a peace with his Muslim enemies. No other expeditions to the Holy Land ever went beyond the planning stages for the remainder of the Middle Ages. Nonetheless the dream stayed alive. Philippe de Mézières made the realisation of the dream his life's work. He came closest to achieving his goal in the 1390s, when the common purpose of a crusade fitted in nicely with the efforts of Richard II and the pro-peace counsellors of Charles VI to bring an end to the Anglo-French war and appealed to those reformers in the Church who sought a resolution of the Great Schism. Mézières's allegorical *Songe du vieil pèlerin* ('Dream of the Old Pilgrim', 1389) and *Epistre au Roi Richart* ('Letter to King Richard', 1395), as well as his attempts to create a new chivalric order, the Order of the Knighthood of the Passion of Jesus Christ, all focused on the restoration of peace and concord within Christendom and the recovery of the Holy Land. Such an undertaking, led by the kings of England and France, would heal the 'open and mortal wound . . . full of poison', which was the Hundred Years War, and would repair the Church, the 'Bride of Christ' who 'lies in her bed, sick, wounded, in fragments, divided in two'.[30] As it so happened, France and England did temporarily take time out from their hostilities, but this had little to do with Mézières's proposed crusade; and although a crusade was indeed launched, in 1396, it was led neither by Richard nor Charles, and its destination was Nicopolis in Bulgaria, not the Holy Land.

Hopes for the Holy Land's recovery were not abandoned, however, being voiced by Christine de Pizan in her *Ditié de Jehanne d'Arc* ('Song of Joan of Arc'). Christine, full of enthusiasm in the immediate aftermath of the French victories at Orléans and Patay in 1429, predicts that after casting out the English, Joan will:

> restore harmony in Christendom and the church. She will destroy the unbelievers people talk about, and the heretics and their vile ways, for this is the substance of a prophecy that has been made. Nor will she have mercy on any place which treats faith in God with disrespect. She will destroy the Saracens, by conquering the Holy Land. She will lead Charles [VII] there, whom God preserve! Before he dies he will make such a journey. He is the one who is to conquer it. It is there that she is to end her days and that both of them are to win glory. It is there that the whole enterprise will be brought to completion.[31]

Joan ended her days in Rouen two years later, abandoned by her monarch, tied to a stake and burned as a heretic by the English and Burgundians; Charles VII kept his hands full fighting the English and his own rebellious subjects. The prophets of a renewed crusade were not finished, however, and at the end of the century they placed their most earnest hopes in the Catholic Monarchs of Spain. Thus we find Christopher Columbus in 1501 calling on Ferdinand and Isabella to recover Jerusalem in accordance with a prophecy made in the early fourteenth century by the Catalan Arnau de Vilanova, that 'he who will rebuild the [Holy] House upon Mount Zion will come from Spain'.[32] This blend of apocalyptic expectation and crusading enthusiasm had by now combined with the Castilians' belief in themselves as a Chosen People destined to heal the wounds of Christendom. In this they were not alone, for the French had long identified themselves with God's special elect, a sentiment increasingly shared as well by the supporters of the German emperors. Ironically, at the end of the Middle Ages, visions of a unified and purified Body of Christ found their sincerest expression in the fervent hopes of exclusive national primacy.

Such dynastic and national aspirations were not restricted to crusades *ad Terram Sanctam*. French royal propagandists depicted the wars against the Flemings in the first decades of the fourteenth century as the equivalent of a crusade. In an anonymous sermon written shortly after the French defeat at Courtrai in 1302, the Flemish 'rebels' are warned that: 'He who wages war against the King [of France] works against the whole Church, against Catholic doctrine, against holiness and justice, and against the Holy Land'.[33] Later, in the 1330s and 1340s, they made the same case against the English. The popes, to their credit, resisted French royal pressure to place their imprimatur on these dynastic struggles. This all changed with the outbreak of the Great Schism in 1378. Pope Urban VI almost immediately granted crusade status to any belligerent attacks by the English on his rival pope Clement VII and any of his supporters. Five years later Henry Despenser, the bishop of Norwich, led a crusade to Flanders in support of Ghent and against the pro-French count, Louis de Male. This holy war against fellow Christians but national foes received avid support in England. That it achieved little besides wasting huge sums of pious donations probably explains why the English responded coolly three years later, when John of Gaunt led a crusade to make good on his claim to the throne of Castile (whose king, Juan I, was a supporter of Clement and the French). Several popes, it should be mentioned, had no qualms about elevating to the status of crusades their own wars against political rivals in the Italian peninsula, like Visconti Milan in the fourteenth century and Ladislas of Naples in the early fifteenth.

One important by-product of the Great Schism was the rise of a radical religious reform movement in Bohemia which would itself become the target of several crusades in the 1420s and 1430s. What began as a generalised call for a reform of the Church in the late fourteenth century took on an increasingly nationalist and heretical aspect under the leadership of the Czech theologian, Jan Hus, in the first decade and a half of the 1400s. Hus and other Czechs on the faculty of the University of Prague found themselves increasingly at odds with their German colleagues over the Czech professors' support for the teachings of John Wyclif. The key tenets of the Hussites, as Hus and his adherents came to be called, were the belief in the overriding authority of Scripture and a Christian's duty to devote himself to close study of God's unmediated Word, as well as the insistence upon the laity's frequent partaking of communion in both kinds (*in utraque specie*). These doctrines threatened the pre-eminence of the clergy, whose privilege it was to preach God's Word to the laity and for whom the second element of the Eucharist, the wine, was reserved. What began as a Czech–German split in the university quickly spread to the nobility, who seized upon Hus's teachings as ammunition against a German influence in Bohemian politics which they deeply resented. Interestingly, what finally brought matters to a head was Hus's opposition to Pope John XXIII's crusade against Ladislas of Naples, and what kindled the Hussite revolt were the fires that in 1415 incinerated Hus at Constance, the very Council that ended the Schism. Now a reunited Latin Christendom faced the threat of a national heretical movement which in 1419 erupted in riots in Prague that included the defenestration of several Catholic city councillors. The response was the crusade led by Bohemia's (and Hungary's) king, the emperor Sigismund, which suffered a serious defeat at Kutná Hora late in 1420. Four more crusades followed, which enlisted many of the great German princes and nobles as well as chivalric adventurers and mercenaries from throughout Europe. All were equally unsuccessful. What finally defused the Hussite movement was internal divisions between the moderate 'Utraquists', whose membership included most of the Czech nobles, and the more radical Taborites. This gave an opening to those in the Church who favoured a diplomatic solution, and in the 1430s talks opened between representatives of the Catholic reformist Council of Basle and the Utraquists. A movement that withstood a decade and a half of assaults from crusading armies finally acquiesced to a compromise in 1437, which allowed for communion in both kinds but skirted the other three doctrinal demands of the Hussites, embodied in their basic creed, the Four Articles: unrestricted lay preaching; divesting of clerical wealth; and the public punishment of sins.

Where crusading occurred most frequently, however, was on the frontiers of Latin Christendom. These frontier wars were both expansionist, as was the case in the Iberian Peninsula and in the eastern Baltic, and also defensive, as happened in the Balkans and eastern Mediterranean. The chief threat to southeast Europe came from the Turks of Anatolia. In the second quarter of the fourteenth century, these crusades were conducted largely by navies and sea-borne forces which attempted to secure sea-lanes and coastal ports. Their greatest success came in 1344, when a fleet organised by Pope Clement VI, the Hospitallers of Rhodes, the Cypriots and the Venetians attacked and seized the chief Anatolian port of the Turkish emir Umur Bey. By the second half of the 1300s, however, a new and more potent Turkish threat was waxing in the East, the Ottomans. Originating in the successful campaigns of territorial acquisition in north-central Anatolia of the Turkish tribal leader, Osman Bey (d. 1326) and his son and successor Orhan Bey (d. 1362), the first Ottomans were the beneficiaries of the power vacuum created in Anatolia by the declining strength of both the Seljuk Sultanate of Rum and the Mongol Il-Khanate in the first decades of the 1300s. Participation on the side of John VI Kantakouzenos against his rival claimant to the Byzantine throne, John V Palaeologus, gave the Ottomans their first purchase on the European side of the Dardanelles in the 1350s. From their new base at Gallipoli the Ottomans continued their expansion into the Balkans under Orhan's and his son Murad Bey's (d. 1389) leadership; simultaneously they extended their control over most of Anatolia, including the lands immediately across the Bosphorus from Constantinople.

In 1387 Murad effectively completed his drive to conquer Bulgaria, gaining its last stronghold at Nicopolis on the Danube. Turning his attention westwards, he first met with defeats at the hands of the allied forces of the Serbians and Bosnians. But in 1389, at Kosovo, fortune granted his forces a decisive victory against this same Christian alliance, though he himself met his death there. His successor Bayezid, the first of the true Ottoman sultans, had by 1391 secured Serbian, Bulgarian, Albanian and Byzantine recognition of his overlordship. When, three years later, he began a blockade of Constantinople and led a campaign against Sigismund's kingdom of Hungary, the powers of Latin Christendom finally determined to destroy this Muslim threat and launched a crusade. It was in this crusade that Philippe de Mézières put his hopes for concord between England and France. The English, however, backed out, and the enterprise became a largely Franco-Burgundian affair, under the leadership of Philip the Bold's eldest son, John of Nevers (the future John the Fearless), but also boasting the flower of French knighthood, including the great Marshal of France, Boucicault. Meeting up with Sigismund's German and Hungarian forces at Buda in 1396, the expedition marched on the Ottoman stronghold of Nicopolis. There the Christians were annihilated by Bayezid's army. Sigismund escaped, but many French knights were captured, including John of Nevers and Marshal Boucicault. Oddly enough, this disaster bathed John of Nevers in the glow of Christian knighthood and secured for the dukes of Burgundy a leading role in the crusading movement during the fifteenth century.

There was little now to stop Bayezid from tightening the noose around Constantinople and strangling what little life remained in the etiolated Byzantine state. What saved it for

Figure 6.4 Massacre of prisoners at Nicopolis. Paris Bibliothèque nationale de France, ms. fr. 2646, fol. 255v

another half century was not a crusading army but rather the wrath of the great central-Asiatic ruler, Timur (Tamerlane), whose army dealt a crushing blow to the Ottomans at Ankara in 1402 and captured Bayezid, who died in prison shortly thereafter. Relief from Ottoman attacks was only temporary, as Turkish raids resumed in the Balkans during the 1410s. However, it was only in the 1430s, after the Ottoman state had managed fully to reconstitute itself, that Sultan Murad II (r. 1421–51) set his sights on renewed expansion in the Balkans. Although he quickly regained control over Bosnia and Serbia, to the north he faced the effective resistance of the Hungarian governor of Transylvania, John Hunyadi. Impressed by Hunyadi's deft deployment of cannon and handgun troops, Murad II started building up his own arsenal of siege artillery and began arming his Janissary corps with handguns. Despite Hunyadi's successes, the Ottoman threat continued to grow in the Balkans, compelling the Byzantine emperor John VIII Palaeologus to agree to put the Greek Church under the spiritual leadership of Pope Eugenius IV in 1439. Now Latin Christendom began enthusiastically planning a crusade to rescue Constantinople and crush the Ottomans. The result was two crusades, the first of which, led by Hunyadi, King Władisław of Poland and Hungary and Cardinal Cesarini, enjoyed considerable success in 1443. A follow-up crusade the next year, however, met with a decisive defeat at Varna. After this, despite continuing resistance by the Hungarians and the spirited assistance of Venice and Philip the Good of Burgundy, Constantinople fell in 1453 to the crushing assault of ships, manpower and artillery gathered by Sultan Mehmed II. For the remainder of the century and into the 1500s, the Ottomans, from their new capital of Istanbul, sent out armies to fight the forces of Hungary and Poland, while their navies sought to control the waters of the Aegean and eastern Mediterranean. Although Hungary held out against the Ottoman threat through the reigns of Mathias Corvinus and Wladislas II, the forces of Suleiman I 'the Magnificent' dealt the Hungarians a crushing blow at Mohács in 1526 and killed their young king, Louis II. Three years later, the sultan's forces laid siege to Vienna.

The eastern Baltic and the southern extremity of the Iberian Peninsula provided zones of what amounted to permanent crusading. In the first half of the thirteenth century, the Teutonic Knights, a military order originally formed in 1189 to fight in the Holy Land, began operations against the pagans of Prussia. Crusading in the Baltic became the Teutonic Order's sole *raison d'être* after the fall of Acre and in 1309 they transferred their headquarters to their base at Marienburg in Prussia. The Order now created what amounted to a state (the *Ordensstaat*) in Prussia and Livonia, and actively encouraged colonisation and trade. What continued to give their baldly expansionist and economic activities the legitimacy of a crusade was the avowed paganism of their chief rivals, the Lithuanians. Twice yearly, the Order mounted expeditions against the Lithuanians, military exploits which became a popular destination for chivalric crusader 'tourists' like the English Henry Bolingbroke in 1390–91. Oddly enough, the period of greatest activity for these foreign adventurers occurred *after* the Lithuanian grand duke Jagiello had converted to Roman Catholicism as a condition of his becoming king of Poland (as King Władisław II) in 1386. This activity continued in earnest until the Polono-Lithuanian victory over the Teutonic Knights in 1410 at Tannenberg/Grunwald. Thereafter, although the *Ordensstaat* continued, it lost much of its steam as a crusading venture.

In Iberia, the persistent presence of the Muslim principality of Granada and the activities of Moorish pirates along the Barbary Coast created an ongoing opportunity for expansionist militancy under the guise of crusading. Like Prussia, it became a *de rigueur* destination for crusade tourism, attracting the likes of the earls of Derby and Salisbury in 1340 and being one of the places visited by Chaucer's Knight:

> At Alexandria was he when it was won.
> Often he sat at the head of the table
> Before all the nations [of knights] in Prussia.
> In Lithuania he had journeyed, and in Russia,
> More often than any other Christian of his status.
> In Granada he had been at the siege
> Of Algeciras and had ridden in Benmarin.[34]

The atmosphere of crusade enthusiasm reached its height during Ferdinand and Isabella's war against Granada in 1482–92; and the success there stoked the zeal for holy war that fuelled the ambitions of the Spanish empire in the 1500s. Other successes preceded this age of pious self-satisfaction. João I of Portugal conceived of the attack on Ceuta as a kind of crusade, and crusade ideology helped motivate the African and Atlantic adventures sponsored by his son, Henrique. Similar motives, supported by crusade privileges, can be discerned behind the plans of the Castilian nobleman Louis de la Cerda's plans to conquer the Canaries in 1344–45, the Castilian-backed Canary adventure of the French knights Gadifer de la Salle and Jean de Béthencourt at the start of the fifteenth century, and Ferdinand and Isabella's own conquest of the islands in 1478–96. There in the Canaries, the sordid business of slaughtering and enslaving an indigenous stone-age people who was guilty of nothing more than minding its own business was dressed up in the fine phrases of chivalric deeds and the propagation of the Faith.[35]

Notes

 1 Nys 1883: 2–3 (my translation).
 2 Coopland 1949: 118.
 3 Coopland 1949: 125.
 4 Brereton 1968: 37.
 5 Allmand 1973: 20.
 6 Kaeuper and Kennedy 2005: 56–57.
 7 Kaeuper 1999: 143.
 8 Contamine 1972: 187.
 9 Kaeuper 1988.
10 Rogers 1999: 148; Harriss 2005: 62; Prestwich 1996: 339.
11 Contamine 1984: 118.
12 Kaeuper 1988; Ayton and Price (1995): 1–22.
13 Allmand 1973: 146–47.
14 Allmand 1973: 143–44.
15 Huizinga 1996: 61, 91.
16 Dean 2000: 150.
17 Kaeuper and Kennedy 2005: 51–52.
18 Caferro 2006: 334.
19 Allmand 1998: 166.
20 Keen 1984: 197.
21 Vale 1981: 62.
22 Taylor and Roskell 1975: 43.

23 Contamine 1984: 211–12.
24 Contamine 1976: 117.
25 Hall 1976: 16.
26 Allmand 2011: 264.
27 Evans 1928: 115–28.
28 Housley 1992: 2.
29 Barber 2006: 297–98.
30 Coopland 1975: 6, 21.
31 Allen and Amt 2003: 408–9.
32 Housley 1998: 123.
33 Housley 1991: 185–86.
34 Wright 1853: 14.
35 Fernández-Armesto 1987: 175–85.

Part III

RELIGION AND DEVOTION

THE BRIDE OF CHRIST

The institutional Church

Urged on by faith, we are compelled to believe and to hold that there is one holy Catholic and apostolic Church, and this we firmly believe and plainly confess, that outside it there is neither salvation nor the remission of sins, as the bridegroom proclaims in the Song of Solomon [6:9]: 'My dove is one, my perfect one. Her mother's only one, chosen by her that bore her'; by which is meant the one mystical body whose head is Christ, and God is Christ's [head], in which there is one Lord, one faith, one baptism. . . . This [Church] alone do we venerate, as the Lord, speaking through the Prophet [Psalm 22:20] [says], 'Deliver my soul from the sword, God, and my only one from the power of the dog!' He prayed for the soul, that is, for himself, and also for the body, which body he called his 'only one', namely the Church, on account of the unity of the pledge, faith, sacraments and love of the Church. It is that seamless tunic of the Lord, which was not torn but rather assigned by lot. There is, then, one body of this one and only Church, and one head – not two (like a monster) – namely Christ, and Peter the vicar of Christ, and Peter's successor, as the Lord said to Peter [John 21:17]: 'Feed my sheep'. . . . Henceforth we declare, assert, determine and pronounce it to be entirely necessary for human salvation that every human creature be subject to the Roman pontiff. . . . For, according to blessed Dionysius, it is the law of divinity that the lowest is brought to the highest through intermediaries. Thus it is not in keeping with the order of the universe that all things be brought to order equally and immediately but rather the lowest by intermediaries and the lower by the higher.[1]

When Boniface VIII promulgated these words in the constitution *Unam sanctam* in November 1302, the immediate target of his righteous anger was Philip IV of France, who in contravention of canon law had recently arrested, tried, convicted and imprisoned one of the bishops of his kingdom, Bernard Saisset of Pamiers, on charges of treason, heresy and blasphemy. Boniface was right to be alarmed at Philip's actions, since they imperilled the pope's longstanding sole jurisdiction over the episcopate and, by extension, the very liberty of the Church. Instead of forcing Philip to amend his ways, however, *Unam sanctam* achieved the exact opposite effect. In the summer of 1303, the irate monarch dispatched his trusted servant Guillaume Nogaret to Italy. At the head of a band of soldiers and accompanied by one of the pope's most implacable Roman foes, Sciarra Colonna, Nogaret tracked down and accosted Boniface at his palace at Anagni, near Rome. Although subsequently rescued, the elderly pontiff never recovered from the shock of being robbed of his possessions, verbally abused, and threatened with arrest and murder; broken in body and spirit, he died a few weeks later, in October.

As a practical instrument of policy *Unam sanctam* was doubtless a failure. Not only did it precipitate the events at Anagni, but those responsible for laying violent hands on the Vicar of Christ were never brought to justice and within two years a new, French pope, Clement V, set up residence not in Rome, but in Lyons in the French Midi. From there, in 1309 the centre of papal government moved a few miles down the river Rhône to Avignon, where it remained until 1377 under a succession of French popes. The papacy's return to Rome and the subsequent troubled election of an Italian pope, Urban VI, in 1378 rapidly led to a fragmentation of the Latin Church into two and then three divisions under rival popes, the Great Schism of 1378–1415. When unity was finally restored, at the Council of Constance (1414–18), it was not through the agency of a pope but rather owing to the promptings of princes, bishops and university masters. And although the new pope, Martin V, and his successors ruled ostensibly over a single Church, in reality the members of that body operated in an increasingly independent fashion down to the time of the final fission brought about by the Protestant reformations of the sixteenth century.

It must be kept in mind, however, that at the time of *Unam sanctam*'s publication these events had not yet come to pass and that from the perspective of someone living at the time its bold claims were as true as they ever had been or were ever going to be. Thirteen centuries after the birth of Jesus, a millennium after the emperor Constantine legalised Christianity in 313, and almost a century after the crafting of Latin Christendom's most comprehensive body of legislation for the guidance, correction and care of its flock in the canons of the Fourth Lateran Council (1215–17), the Church had attained an admirable level of institutional maturity. The governance of the Church was relatively centralised in terms of the ability to transmit, receive and record information, collect revenue, appoint to ecclesiastical offices and impose its jurisdiction. There was, moreover, considerable conformity in worship and official belief among a laity that by and large participated in religion. Given the apparent structural solidity, operational efficiency and universality of his Church, then, perhaps Boniface believed his own rhetoric, even down to the inflammatory and audacious assertion of papal sovereignty over people's souls in *Unam sanctam*'s final sentence.

One must also avoid the temptation of reading the history of the late medieval Church backwards from Martin Luther to Anagni, and thus of seeing 1303 as a turning point and 1517 as its necessary corollary. According to this perspective, common among earlier generations of historians and still curiously prevalent in the classroom, the monolithic, clerically controlled Church reached the apex of its authority and power during the age of Thomas Aquinas in the latter half of the thirteenth century, but then faltered and lost its vitality after 1300, entering an era of gradual but inevitable decline, in which corruption reigned in the ecclesiastical hierarchy, the laity became disaffected and all efforts at reform failed. For those of a Protestant persuasion Luther finally brought much-needed relief to the faithful, while for Roman Catholics, the outbreak of Protestantism provided the lamentable goad that forced the True Church to get its act together in the reforms of the Council of Trent in the middle years of the sixteenth century. Either way, the fourteenth and fifteenth centuries were a time of missed opportunities at best and of hopeless decrepitude at worst.

Two generations of historical scholarship have done much to discredit this tale of woe, however. The tendency now is to read the history forwards, rather than backwards, and thus to see the Church of the fourteenth and fifteenth centuries as the successor of the thirteenth-century Church. Research has also shifted from the prescriptive approach, which weighed the late medieval Church in the scales of an ideal and found it sorely wanting, to a more descriptive one, which tries, on the one hand, to explain how the Church as an institution functioned and responded to challenges and, on the other, to reconstruct the myriad attitudes, experiences and expressions of religious life. This and the following chapter examine these two sides of the coin of late medieval Latin Christianity. First we will consider the theory, organisation and personnel of the Church, and trace its institutional developments; then, in Chapter 8, the focus will shift to 'lived religion', that is the complex of devotional practices, attitudes and relationships that formed the religious life of the denizens of Latin Christendom.

Incorporating the Body of Christ: theory, organisation and personnel

By the end of the thirteenth century, the basic theory, structure and *modus operandi* of the Church had been firmly established. In so far as theory is concerned, one need look no further than the text of *Unam sanctam*, which in a few words sums up the ideology and aspirations of the medieval Latin Church. The Church (*ecclesia*) is one, both in the inclusive sense of being a unity and in the exclusive one of there being no other legitimate church and no hope for salvation outside it; it is holy in that from the time of the Pentecost recorded in the Book of Acts, the Holy Spirit began to dwell in the Church, ensuring thereby its unfailing doctrinal correctness and the ability of its members to live in conformity with God's will; just as it is one, it is also catholic, or universal; and finally, the Church is apostolic in the sense that it embodies an unbroken tradition, extending from the time of the original followers of Jesus down to the end of time. This Church is both the Bride of Christ and his mystical body, of which he is the head and whose members are all the faithful, unified in their worship of Christ/God as Lord, their faith and their participation in the sacraments administered through the Church, beginning with baptism. On earth, the head of the Church is the pope, who is Christ's vicar on account of being the successor of Peter, the chief of the apostles and first bishop of Rome.

The earthly Church only constituted a portion of the Body of Christ, however. It was called the Church Militant, whose living faithful were in communion as well with the faithful departed of the Church Dormant (or Expectant) who awaited God's final judgement, and the saints of the Church Triumphant whose exceptionally meritorious lives and deaths earned them the reward of dwelling with God and gazing upon his face. Alongside this broad definition of the Church was another more technical and institutional one, which identified the Church specifically with the clergy of the ecclesiastical hierarchy. According to this definition, the broader Church Militant consisted of an ecclesiastical, or spiritual order – the clergy – and of a secular, or temporal one – the laity. Like the Priests and Levites of the Old Testament, the clergy were dedicated to the service of God, and by analogy with the Gospel story of the sisters Martha and Mary (Luke 10:38–42), they played the role of Mary, 'who sat at the Lord's feet and listened to what he was saying' and thus had 'chosen the better part', to that of the laity, who like Martha were 'distracted by . . . many things'.

The clergy, then, were set apart from the laity (Gr. *kleros*, 'the chosen' vs. *laos*, 'the crowd'), at once ministering to them (from *minister*, 'servant'), yet also guiding them, as a shepherd (*pastor*) guides his flock, and they were in some sense more pleasing to God, as Martha's sister Mary was to Jesus. Their distinctiveness was symbolised and expressed in a number of ways. Most obvious to the casual observer was their distinctive dress and wearing of the tonsure. These superficial signs could deceive, however. Youthful students received the tonsure as a sign of their *intention* to enter clerical orders, although many, if not most of them never ended up making a formal ecclesiastical profession. As far as the law was concerned, however, the tonsured student was every inch the cleric and therefore subject to ecclesiastical jurisdiction and protection. Some confusion also arose from the common practice of using the terms *clericus* ('cleric' or 'clerk') and *litteratus* ('one who is learned' or 'who can read and write') as synonyms, so that a literate layman frequently was called clerk and an ignorant clerk branded as *laicus*, that is a layman or ignoramus.[2] One disturbing outcome of this practical ambiguity and terminological fuzziness was the not uncommon recourse of career criminals to don the clerical habit and take the tonsure in order to avoid the harsh penalties of secular law. Even the demonstration of a smattering of literacy proved sufficient at times to get a criminal's case transferred from a secular to a Church court.[3]

At a more profound level, however, a cleric was one who had received the sacrament of ordination, a ceremony wherein a bishop laid hands on and said a prayer of ordination over the recipient. In this sacramental sense, there were seven 'orders' of clergy, although the most important were the so-called major orders of sub-deacon, deacon, priest and bishop, the first two of which were normally conferred as a preliminary to becoming a priest. The priests and bishops were the true linchpins of the medieval Church, the 'real' clergy in a functional sense, since only they had the 'cure of souls', the ability and duty to act as necessary inter-mediaries between God and humankind through correct teaching and the administration of the seven sacraments, those visible signs of divine grace which included baptism, commun-ion (Eucharist), confession, marriage, last rites, confirmation and ordination. Although lay people could baptise in an emergency – for instance midwives were instructed to administer baptism to newborns in peril of death – and the sacrament of marriage needed only the mutual vows of a man and woman, there was an expectation that priests should perform bap-tisms under normal circumstances, and priests officiating at weddings was gradually being accepted (although it was not at all the norm in much of Italy, where a notary was the only official personage required at a wedding). At the end of one's life it was also desirable to receive the last rites of a final confession, communion and anointing from a priest. Again, however, the intercession of a priest was not absolutely required for this sacrament, since a dying person could confess in an emergency to any layperson or even repent directly to God at the moment of death. Two sacraments, ordination and confirmation, could only be performed by bishops. Most of the faithful never received confirmation, a sacrament which conferred the gift of the Holy Spirit on the already baptised, and it was not considered abso-lutely necessary to salvation.

All Christians were baptised and all who reached adulthood participated in the sacra-ments of confession and communion. Yet if baptism was the fundamental act in an individual Christian's life since it *made* someone a Christian by casting out the Devil and washing away the original sin of Adam and Eve, confession and communion in fact played a far more impor-tant role in the life of the Church and in Christian society. Baptism was a non-repeatable act and infant baptism was the universal rule. It was frequently done immediately after birth without the intercession of a priest; and when done in church by a priest, it was more a pri-vate, familial ceremony than a public one. Communion and confession were, on the contrary, meant to be repeated, at least once a year according to the twenty-first canon of the Fourth Lateran Council. Their administration was, moreover, strictly controlled by the priesthood. The same canon stipulated that confession to a priest should precede taking communion:

> Every Christian of either sex after reaching the years of discretion shall confess all his sins at least once a year privately to his own priest and try as hard as he can to perform the penance imposed on him; and receive with reverence the sacrament of

the eucharist at least at Easter. . . . As for the priest, he should be discerning and prudent so that like a practised doctor he can pour wine and oil on the wounds of the injured, diligently enquiring into the circumstances both of the sinner and of the sin, from which to choose intelligently what sort of advice he ought to give him and what sort of remedy to apply.[4]

And only in the hands of a priest (or bishop, since they remained priests after their episcopal consecration) could the awesome miracle of the Eucharist be enacted whereby the communion elements of bread and wine changed ('transubstantiated') into the body and blood of Christ sacrificed: 'This sacrament no one can perform but a priest, who has been duly ordained, according to the keys of the church, which Jesus Christ Himself granted to the apostles and their successors'.[5]

By 1300 an elaborate pastoral and liturgical machinery of confession and communion was fully in place, giving the late medieval Church its peculiar sacramental and sacerdotal character. The clergy's exclusive control of these two sacraments was both symptom and motivator of the ideology of clerical distinctiveness. It added force to the proscription of clerical marriage. This ban, which was based in part on Paul's counsel –

> To the unmarried and the widows I say that it is well for them to remain unmarried as I am. . . . I want you to be free from anxieties. The unmarried man is anxious about the affairs of the Lord, how to please the Lord; but the married man is anxious about the affairs of the world, how to please his wife, and his interests are divided (1 Corinthians 7:8, 32–34)

– had been enforced with some degree of effectiveness since the Church reform movement associated with Pope Gregory VII (1073–85). But Lateran IV's assertion of the mystery of transubstantiation and of the priest's unique ability to confect the True Body and Blood of the Lord gave added support to the clergy's celibacy, a status that set them apart from, and in some sense above, the laity. For how could the very hands in which created matter was transformed into the Holiest of Holies be in any way sullied by something as base as sexual congress? Likewise, the new stress on periodic private confession demanded a higher standard of clerical education, since in addition to being equipped with at least the rudiments of Latin literacy and familiarity with the liturgy, creeds and a smattering of scripture, now a priest was also expected to be a skilled confessor. Although many a parish priest of the thirteenth through early sixteenth centuries never attained a very high level of intellectual formation, the overall level of clerical education does seem to have risen. More importantly, the clergy's role in confession reinforced their image as specialists whose services were absolutely essential for one's salvation.

The clerical order was itself divided into several distinct orders. The most basic division was that between the 'secular' and the 'regular' clergy. To the former belonged all those whose principal ministry was in the world (*saeculum*) and directed toward the laity. First and foremost in this group was the pope, who as bishop of Rome was the successor of St Peter and head of the Church. Next were the archbishops and bishops, whose authority came from being the successors of the apostles. Finally, and most numerous, were the priests, who derived their authority from having been ordained at the hands of a bishop. Secular priests performed many different ministries, including those of cathedral clergy, parish rectors and stipendiary priests working in private foundations such as family chapels and chantries.

Those who had turned away from the world and submitted themselves to the rigours of a monastic rule (*regula*) together constituted the 'regular' clergy, also known as the 'religious' (*religiosi*). By 1300 this was a very diverse group indeed. Those religious with the longest history were the cloistered monks who lived according to the rule of the sixth-century Italian abbot Benedict. Before the mid-tenth century these monks, living in many autonomous monasteries, each under the rule of an abbot and subject to the oversight of the local bishop, were *the* monastic order. Then over the course of the tenth through the mid-thirteenth centuries the one monastic order became several religious *orders*. It began with the reformed Benedictine monasticism of the Cluniacs and Cistercians; the popularity of these new orders ensured that they encompassed scores of houses located throughout Latin Christendom. The Cluniac houses were all under the monarchic rule of the abbot of Cluny, whereas the even more numerous houses of the Cistercians were semi-autonomous and united into what amounted to a federal structure. Both orders were exempt from the jurisdiction of local bishops. A desire to return to the extreme asceticism of the first monks, as exemplified by the life of St Anthony of Egypt (d. 356), inspired the Carthusians and Camaldolese, while new kinds of challenges growing out of urbanisation and a market economy, the crusades and heresy gave rise to several kinds of mixed orders. The twelfth century saw the formation of the canons regular (Augustinians, Premonstratensians, Victorines), priests with some pastoral duties but living according to a monastic rule, and the military orders (Templars, Hospitallers, Teutonic Knights) of soldier-monks, priest-chaplains and, in the case of the Hospitallers, carers for the sick and infirm. Then, in the early thirteenth century, Francis of Assisi and Dominic de Guzmán founded orders of mendicant friars ('begging brothers') who were subject to a form of monastic discipline but also dedicated to pursuit of the apostolic life (which they interpreted to mean living solely from the proceeds of their work, begging and charity, rather than from lands and rents) and whose principal charge was that of pastoral care: preaching, teaching, caring for the poor, acting as confessors and rooting out heretics. The Franciscans and Dominicans (officially known as the Order of Friars Minor and Order of Preachers) were instrumental in promoting the goals of the 'pastoral revolution' initiated by Lateran IV, and in the course of the thirteenth century they were joined by two more orders of friars, the Carmelites and Augustinians.

To be a monk or friar one did not necessarily have to receive ordination. Indeed, among the monks of the first several centuries of Christianity ordination was quite rare. By the end of the eleventh century, however, monks in priestly orders were the norm. Motivating this shift was the growing importance of the sacrament of the Eucharist and the complementary belief in the salvific efficacy of the mass, especially when said by a monk. The more monks in priestly orders, the more masses celebrated for the souls of founders and patrons, and for their families and friends. Ordination became even more necessary when regulars took on pastoral duties, as in the case of the canons regular and friars. The pressure for 'sacerdotal professionalism' of the religious orders had become so strong by the thirteenth century that from the start St Dominic envisioned his order as one made up principally of priests; and although St Francis himself advocated lay ministry and never became a priest, his order became fully clericalised shortly after his death.[6] Thus what had started as an order of laity devoted to a life of prayer, work and contemplation, became specialised orders of regular clergy.

These developments had a profound effect on the status of women religious. Barred from clerical orders on account of their sex, their inability to officiate at mass or act as pastors relegated them to an inferior status and denied them the opportunity to develop specialised forms of religious life, as, for example, the Cluniacs, canons regular and friars had. As a consequence, fewer monasteries for women were founded and those that were tended to be less generously endowed. Also, despite the fact that many of the orders instituted complementary foundations for women, the form of life in these convents was uniformly cloistered, on the Benedictine model, even in the case of Dominican and Franciscan nuns. Given the limited opportunities for especially pious women, it comes as no surprise that they frequently expressed their devotion in uniquely individual fashion or on the margins of officially sanctioned religion.

Although not constituting a separate order, university masters of theology and canon law formed a distinct branch of the late medieval Church. The opinions of the theology faculty at the University of Paris carried especially heavy weight in matters of doctrine, and both theologians and canonists continued to exercise special authority in matters of Church governance. And although laymen frequently occupied the faculty chairs of arts, law and medicine, the disciplines of theology and canon law were the property of the priesthood. The religious orders also maintained a conspicuous presence at the universities, and the many secular masters and scholars alike who dwelt in university colleges were also subject to a way of life modelled on that of collegiate churches or religious houses, since the colleges were not only places of study but also pious foundations.

Such complexity and diversity in ecclesiastical order as well as the many problems that beset the late Middle Ages prompted many learned reflections on the structure of the Church. According to these musings, the Church, because it had been instituted by Christ, was structured in such a way that it reflected the architecture of the heavenly hierarchy which had been so carefully described and explicated by Dionysius the Pseudo-Areopagite in the sixth century. In one section of *Unam sanctam*, Boniface VIII employed the hierarchical model in order to assert the clergy's power over the laity and the pope's over the whole Church Militant:

> For, according to blessed Dionysius, it is the law of divinity that the lowest is brought to the highest through intermediaries. Thus it is not in keeping with the order of the universe that all things be brought to order equally and immediately but rather the lowest by intermediaries and the lower by the higher. . . . For, with truth bearing witness, the spiritual power has to establish the earthly power, and has to judge it, if it has not been good. . . . Therefore if the earthly power deviates, it will be judged by the spiritual power; but if a lesser spiritual [power] deviates, it will be judged by its superior; if, however, the supreme [spiritual power] deviates, it can be judged by God alone.[7]

A decade and a half later, the Paris theologian Thomas of Ireland argued that the contemporary ecclesiastical hierarchy expressed both the structure of the heavenly host and the form of the primitive Church, with the pope representing Christ, in the upper tier, the cardinals, archbishops and bishops taking the place of the apostles, in the middle, and, in the lowest grade, priests being the living manifestation of the seventy-two disciples. When, in the first years of the following century, another Paris theologian, Jean Gerson, devoted his energies to ending the Great Schism, he returned to the theme of three grades of hierarchy, saying that ideally the Church on earth consisted of a top grade of pope and cardinals, a middle one of patriarchs, archbishops, bishops and priests, and a bottom rank of laity and religious. Gerson, who was a secular priest, quite specifically relegated members of religious orders to the status of the laity, for by rights, he thought, religious had no business performing pastoral functions. In fact, to his mind

> the Church consists more principally of the first and second [grades] than of the third, which is the order of lay people and especially of women, to whom belong no acts of hierarchy or sacred orders, no public or solemn preaching, according to the prohibition of the Apostle.[8]

Such frequent and repeated efforts to liken the earthly Church to the City of God betray an anxiety arising from the fact that the Church Militant was to the contrary a very mundane, human and imperfect institution, whose structure had more to do with the practicalities of governance than the divine mysteries of the celestial hierarchy. In many ways the terrestrial Church was organised, managed and even thought of as an empire, and one with a particularly Roman cast to it. The Latin Church had a single supreme ruler, based in Rome, who was not only the heir of St Peter but also claimed to be the successor of the Roman emperors in the West (a power which they then delegated to the Holy Roman Emperor). Although the claim to imperial succession was in fact spurious, being based on a late eighth-century forgery known as the Donation of Constantine, advocates for papal supremacy continued to insist on its veracity until the humanist scholar Lorenzo Valla decisively proved it false in 1440. Besides, the popes' losing bid for temporal sovereignty did not nullify their traditional monarchical authority in the spiritual realm, their status as final judge in cases of canon law, a legal system that was itself modelled on Roman law, or their considerable political power, exercised as leader of the Church and territorial prince of the Papal States.

The popes governed through a central administration called the *curia*, whose business was overseen by the College of Cardinals, which one of their number, Pierre d'Ailly (d. 1420) referred to as the 'sacred college or senate of the apostles'.[9] Beneath the level of the popes, the government of the medieval Church had many other elements that harkened back to the late Roman Empire. It was divided into territorial units of jurisdiction that bore the very Roman name of province (*provincia*), each overseen by an archbishop; within each province were several dioceses (also the name of a late Roman territorial division), ruled by bishops – the archbishop, too, had a diocese, called an archdiocese. Together with the cardinals, the archbishops and bishops formed what amounted to an ecclesiastical aristocracy, with some prelates, like the bishop of Winchester, commanding vast wealth and others, like the bishop of Durham or the German ecclesiastical imperial electors, exercising true princely powers in the secular sphere. The diocese was, in turn, divided into parishes (*parochiae*), each staffed by one or more priests. Thus ideally, from the pope on down to the priests, power and authority were distributed hierarchically, with all prelates (i.e. cardinals, archbishops and bishops) being appointed by the pope and recognising his direct jurisdiction, all bishops in a province according a special respect to their archbishop, and all priests in a diocese being subject to the discipline of their bishop.

This basic hierarchy was only the skeleton of the earthly manifestation of the Body of Christ, however. Enfleshed, the body was much more varied and complex. First, in the diocese, which constituted the most fundamental unit of ecclesiastical jurisdiction, oversight involved not only the bishop but also numerous clerical personnel. Performance of the liturgy in and day-to-day administration of the diocese's principal church (called a cathedral, because it housed the bishop's throne or *cathedra*) were the responsibility of a dean, precentor, treasurer and chancellor, as well as several canons. In the diocese at large, the bishop's spiritual, legal, disciplinary and financial responsibilities required a staff of officials who both assisted him and could be empowered to act in his name. In addition to having his own chancellor and staff of clerks, the bishop appointed an 'official' to act as judge in the diocesan canon-law court, the consistory; he might also appoint vicars-general to carry out a variety of duties including visitations, receivers-general to collect taxes and 'suffragan bishops' – bishops consecrated to dioceses no longer in Christian hands (*in partibus infidelium*) and thus without jurisdiction – to perform ordinations and confirmations. As a general rule, the bigger and richer a diocese was the more personnel it had. In Italy many of its nearly 300 dioceses were quite small and poor, being only coterminous with the town in which the bishop's cathedral was situated. Beyond the Alps, however, dioceses tended to be larger (there were some 55 in the Empire, for example), incorporating not only the bishop's city but surrounding rural areas and towns as well. These larger dioceses in addition to having more of the staff already mentioned often were divided into smaller units administered by archdeacons and rural deans.

Second, another ecclesiastical map overlay that of provinces and dioceses. This was crowded with monasteries and friars' convents, most of which belonged to international orders which were exempt from episcopal jurisdiction and had their own leadership, policies and jurisdiction. Likewise there were universities, university colleges and various private foundations, including collegiate churches (endowed churches staffed by several canons), hospitals, almshouses, chapels and chantries, all of which were partially or entirely free from episcopal interference. The activities and interests of these many and varied institutions at times conflicted or worked at cross-purposes with those of the bishop as well as with those of one another.

Further complicating matters were three related issues which also did the most to anchor the Church Militant firmly in the dirt of human affairs: property, patronage and privilege. Christ may have been poor, but his Bride was collectively the largest property owner in Christendom. This property was, moreover, intimately and inextricably tied to a cleric's ability to perform his duties, on the one hand, and to the privilege and interests of a patron, on the other. Every ecclesiastical office was connected to a benefice (*beneficium*, 'reward'). Much like the feudal fief, for which the term *beneficium* was also used, it was a form of property that provided an income to the office-holder but also carried with it some sort of dependency on the patron who had conferred it. Frequently the patron was some ecclesiastical person or foundation. Bishops had the right of provision to several of the benefices in their diocese and many a parish church was in the 'gift' of an abbot or monastery. Very often, however, the office/benefice was conferred by a lay entity, whether individual or corporate. The greatest of these lay patrons were kings and princes, who used benefices to provide incomes to their servants and as rewards for services rendered. Even greater, however, was the patronage of the pope, who used benefices in much the same way his secular counterparts did.

On the whole, the system worked. Benefices provided the means that enabled clerics to perform their offices. They also enabled the functioning of universities and of government and ecclesiastical administration. They opened up ecclesiastical careers to men of talent from modest backgrounds, being used, for example, as scholarships for study at university. More profoundly, they encouraged a close association of lay and clerical society, thereby forestalling widespread mutual alienation. That being said, the system left plenty of room for abuse. There was always the temptation for patrons to use their right purely for self-interest without any regard for the suitability of their preferred candidate. Moreover, clerics (and often their patrons as well) often saw benefices merely as sources of income, rather than as offices with duties and responsibilities. This was particularly problematic when a benefice carried with it cure of souls, since incumbents often were non-resident. Worse, the problem of falling revenues from real estate which plagued the aristocracy also affected ecclesiastical property, thereby compelling clerics to hold several benefices at once, a practice known as pluralism. A non-resident incumbent was supposed to appoint a vicar to act in his stead in return for a stipend. And although doubtless many vicars performed their duties conscientiously, even the best were usually poorly remunerated, and many, frankly, were not of the highest calibre. Some non-residents failed to appoint vicars, moreover, and even those who did often showed little interest in either the physical upkeep of real property or the spiritual health of their parishioners.

The governance of the Church under the Avignon popes

Certainly abuses associated with benefices generated complaints and occasionally inspired efforts at reform, as when in 1317 John XXII prohibited the holding of multiple benefices with cure of souls and prescribed that anyone holding a benefice with cure of souls could only hold one other benefice without cure (*sine cura*). The ban, however, was honoured as much in the breach as in the observance because in fact John XXII and the other popes residing in Avignon during the first three quarters of the fourteenth century made control and exploitation of the provision of benefices the central mission of their financial administration. They did so chiefly because their major customary sources of income were shrinking at the same time as the expense of running their government was growing. Having retreated from Italy, they no longer could access the considerable revenue streams from the Papal States to which they had traditionally been entitled. Indeed repeated attempts to re-establish control of these lands and of Rome itself were one of the largest drains on the papal treasury during the Avignon years. Likewise the crusade subsidies (usually a tax on a tenth of clerical income) which had been such an abundant source of cash during the thirteenth century became less frequent and lucrative. The popes also exploited the provision of benefices, however, because their new situation in Avignon allowed them to develop a bigger, and more efficient, government there. First, Avignon offered stability. Instead of being in thrall to factional politics and popular unrest as Rome was, it belonged to the Angevin rulers of Naples, who were friendly to the papacy, as well as being papal vassals. Also its salubrious situation on the banks of the Rhône did not require the pope and much of the curia to vacate during the summer, as they were regularly forced to do by the malarial conditions that prevailed along the Tiber. Second, its position north of the Alps and on major north–south and east–west trade routes made it more easily accessible than Rome to more of Europe. Thus at Avignon a larger bureaucracy – eventually more than twice as big as that of Boniface VIII – was able to cater to much more business than had been the case when it had been based in Rome.

Starting already with Clement V, the popes reserved the right to provide to more and more classifications of major benefices, so that by 1363 this included all episcopal sees valued at 200 florins per year and all abbacies of over 100 florins per year. Provision to lesser benefices increased as well through the creation of a host of general categories of reservation and because individual clerics were encouraged to petition the curia for entry into vacant benefices as well as those that would eventually become vacant, through the granting of something known as an expectancy. To get some sense of the success of this programme of expansion into the benefice market one need only look at the 4,002 provisions and expectancies granted during the eight years of Benedict XII's pontificate (1334–42) and then consider

Table 7.1 The Popes

Boniface VIII (Benedetto Caetani)	1294–1303
Benedict XI (Niccolò Boccasini)	1303–04
Clement V (Bertrand de Got)	1305–14
John XXII (Jacques Duèze)	1316–34
Nicholas V (Pietro de Corvaro)	*1328–33**
Benedict XII (Jacques Fournier)	1334–42
Clement VI (Pierre Roger I)	1342–52
Innocent VI (Étienne Aubert)	1352–62
Urban V (Guillaume de Grimoard)	1362–70
Gregory XI (Pierre Roger II)	1370–78
Rome	
Urban VI (Bartolomeo Prignano)	1378–89
Boniface IX (Pietro Tomacelli)	1389–1404
Innocent VII (Cosimo Migliorati)	1404–06
Gregory XII (Angelo Correr)	1406–15 (resigned)
Avignon	
Clement VII (Robert of Geneva)	1378–94
Benedict XIII (Pedro de Luna)	1394–1417 (deposed)**
Clement VIII (Gil Sanchez Muñoz)	*1423–29*
Benedict XIV (Bernard Garnier)	*1425–30*
Pisa	
Alexander V (Peter Philarges)	1409–10
John XXIII (Baldassare Cossa)	1410–15 (deposed)
Post-Schism	
Martin V (Oddone Colonna)	1417–31
Eugenius IV (Gabriele Condulmer)	1431–47
Felix V (Amadeus of Savoy)	*1439–49*
Nicholas V (Tommaso Parentucelli)	1447–55
Callixtus III (Alonso Borja/Borgia)	1455–58
Pius II (Enea Silvio Piccolomini)	1458–64
Paul II (Pietro Barbo)	1464–71
Sixtus IV (Francesco della Rovere)	1471–84
Innocent VIII (Giovanni Battista Cibo)	1484–92
Alexander VI (Roderigo Borja/Borgia)	1492–1503
Pius III (Francesco Piccolomini)	1503
Julius II (Giuliano della Rovere)	1503–13
Leo X (Giovanni de' Medici)	1513–21
Adrian VI (Adriaan Florensz)	1522–23
Clement VII (Giulio de' Medici)	1523–34***

*The names of anti-popes are italicised.

**Benedict XIII maintained his claim to be the rightful pope until his death in 1423.

***This is the second pope of that name.

that this pope is noted for his relative modesty in making these grants.[10] One can add to this the considerable trade in translations (i.e. transfers) of incumbents from one benefice to another in which the popes engaged with ever greater frequency.

Commerce in benefices offered substantial financial rewards. Entry into major benefices required the payment of 'common services' (one-third of the first year's income), while annates (the first year's income) were paid by those who had received minor benefices through papal provision. During the period when a reserved benefice was left vacant, the popes had access to all its income. They also had right of spoils (*ius spolii*) to the moveable property of any benefice that fell vacant owing to the death of the incumbent while visiting the papal court, or who died intestate or in debt to the curia (this had the added benefit of being a major source of books for the papal library).[11] It has been calculated that by the 1370s papal income amounted to some 300,000 florins per year, of which roughly half came directly from services, annates and the *ius spolii*. To these major sources of income can be added the fees paid by petitioners for benefices. As if these were not enough, there was also the hail of fees and other expenditures that were generated by the legal disputes that almost invariably arose between competing petitioners (since benefices and expectancies were usually granted to multiple petitioners) and between petitioners and those whose claim to a benefice came from having been canonically elected (say, by a cathedral or monastic chapter) or appointed by a patron other than the pope or curia.

The successful centralisation of control over benefices also gave the popes political leverage with secular rulers and enabled them to bargain as effective equals over such matters as the appointment of prelates. Directing the largest and most sophisticated bureaucracy in Christendom, they had in effect become monarchs. And yet, like other monarchs of the late Middle Ages, their expenditures almost invariably outran their revenues. Ongoing efforts to regain control of the Papal States and Rome through war and diplomacy sucked up most of the money. But a great deal of it never left Avignon, being spent on building and furnishing the great papal palace, started in 1336, funding a papal library and university, and supporting lavish court ceremonial – Clement VI's coronation alone cost 15,000 florins.[12] The cardinals also benefited from papal largesse, receiving an equal share of some revenues and being paid a gift by each incoming pope that could amount to as much as 100,000 florins. Enriched as well by the income of multiple benefices held in plurality and exercising considerable powers of patronage in their own right, the College of Cardinals had become what amounted to an oligarchy governing in partnership with the papal monarch.

That this partnership was amicable on the whole had much to do with the fact that the Avignon popes habitually appointed relations and friends to the cardinalate. In this they were not so different from their Roman predecessors. Now, however, French popes chose French cardinals. Immediately upon becoming pope, Clement V (the former Bertrand de Got, archbishop of Bordeaux) appointed ten cardinals, nine of whom were French and four of whom were his nephews. By 1378, of 134 cardinals appointed by the seven Avignon popes, 112 were French. The next largest group was the Italians, with fourteen appointees. The English were a distant third, with two. Not surprisingly, curial personnel were drawn largely from France as well, with some 70 per cent being French.[13] The overwhelmingly French complexion of the curia probably would on its own have caused resentment in all those quarters of Europe which felt slighted. What made the resentment far worse, however, was the perception, largely justified, of contemporaries that the Avignon papacy favoured the political ends of the French monarchy. Clement V, after all, not only supported Philip IV's persecution of the Templars (albeit with deep misgivings) but also lifted the sentence of excommunication against Boniface VIII's nemesis Guillaume Nogaret. His successors regularly granted crusade subsidies to the Capetians and Valois, which they used for their wars against the English. Clement VI even went so far as to loan the king of France 620,000 florins with no expectation that he would be repaid, and Urban V derailed a proposed marriage alliance between Edward III's son Edmund of Langley and Margaret of Flanders, insuring that she instead would wed the Valois Philip the Bold of Burgundy.

In hindsight we can recognise that the Avignon papacy's dependence on France for almost half its income from benefices provided most of the stimulus for this favouritism. It is also now readily apparent that these popes genuinely desired peace between France and England (after all, the war devastated the countryside of their south French homeland) and that the overall direction of their policies was determined far more by a desire to regain the patrimony of St Peter in Italy than to further the ends of the French kings. Even had they known all this, however, one doubts the English Lords and Commons in Parliament would have relented from drafting the Statutes of Provisors (1351) and Praemunire (1353), which respectively sought to curtail papal provisions in favour of royal ones and to direct disputes involving the patronage of benefices to royal courts rather than to the papal curia. That their king, Edward III, approved of these statutes owed less to his resentment against the papacy than to his desire to increase his own powers of patronage and jurisdiction over the English Church. It helped that he could do so under cover of sharing his subjects' patriotic anger at the French popes, as expressed in this little ditty that English soldiers scrawled in various places in France: 'Now has the pope become French, and Jesus become an Englishman. Now it will be seen who strikes the hardest, the pope or Jesus'.[14]

The papacy's Italian policy was itself the source of growing alienation within Germany. John XXII's alliance with the Angevin Robert of Naples pitted him against the German emperor Ludwig of Bavaria. Among the spiritual weapons employed by the pope was an interdict on all regions supporting the emperor. Where observed, this ban, which remained in effect up till Ludwig's death in 1347, suspended all worship services, baptisms, burials and church weddings. Those churches which did not observe it grew comfortable over time with ignoring papal authority. Whether observed or not, the interdict inspired disgust with the papacy and left the door open to princes and municipal authorities to strengthen their control of their local clergies. The fact that no Avignon pope appointed a German cardinal further alienated the German churches.

Despite the advantages of Avignon as a seat of government, the popes continued to dream of a return to the Eternal City. In 1353 Innocent VI, inspired by the success of the jubilee year pilgrimage to Rome three years earlier, commissioned Cardinal Gil Albornoz to lead a military expedition to pacify the Papal States. After fourteen years of hard fighting, fortress building and diplomacy, Albornoz's efforts paved the way for Urban V's return to Rome in 1367. Although circumstances forced Urban's retreat to Avignon in 1370, his successor, Gregory XI had better luck, and died in Rome in 1378, surrounded by most of his cardinals and the majority of curial personnel. The papacy's persistent pursuit of and eventual success in returning to Rome warn us not to be entirely taken in by the commonly held condemnatory assessment of the Avignon years as a hopelessly corrupt and decadent 'Babylonish captivity', and thus as the first phase of the inevitable decline that set in after Anagni. Most of the popes of the Avignon era were reasonably competent and conscientious, with only one of their number, Clement VI, being notably corrupt. They had a genuine interest in expanding the boundaries of Christendom through crusade and mission, and cannot be blamed for the disappointing overall results of crusading or the fact that the initial successes of the missions in China and central Asia during the first decades of the fourteenth century dissolved along with Mongol rule. Moreover, the powerful bureaucratic machinery developed at the curia was a creative response to the threats to papal sovereignty posed by secular governments and declining revenue from customary sources. Judged purely on its administrative muscle and ability to control ecclesiastical appointments and revenues from the universal Church, then, papal government reached the height of its power at Avignon.

The Great Schism and its aftermath

Had the disputed election of 1378 not occurred, the papacy may have continued to build upon the administrative base developed at Avignon. When, however, the cardinals who had accompanied Gregory XI to Rome began the work of choosing his successor, the Roman populace saw to it that their deliberations were carried out in an atmosphere of intimidation and fear. The commune, distrustful of the French cardinals and curia in their midst, were not content merely to have the pope back in Rome; they wanted a Roman pope and threatened to kill the cardinals if they did not elect 'A Roman or at least an Italian!'[15] In the end, the Sacred College chose the Neapolitan Bartolomeo Prignano, a veteran curial bureaucrat who took the name Urban VI. Instead of exercising the caution and moderation called for after being elected in such highly charged and irregular circumstances, the new pontiff immediately alienated the cardinals by chastising them for their luxurious lifestyle, threatening to end the longstanding Avignon practice by which pope and cardinals shared governance and income, and promising to replace French cardinals with Italian ones.

Convinced now that the election they so recently had hailed as legitimate had instead been a grave error, the cardinals promptly abandoned the pope and Rome, declared Urban's election null and void and, before returning with the bulk of the curia to Avignon, elected the cardinal Robert of Geneva as pope Clement VII. Latin Christendom was now faced with the dilemma of there being two popes, neither of whose claims to legitimacy clearly trumped those of the other. Queen Joanna of Naples took the side of Clement from the start and within weeks the French king Charles V announced his support for Clement, with France's Scottish and Iberian allies in the war against England soon following suit. England and its allies as well as the emperor Charles IV, Louis the Great of Hungary and most of Italy declared for Urban. Adherence thus became a matter of politics rather than of conscience and the Great Schism, whose longevity was largely the result of the choices of princes, would only be solved when those same princes decided their mutual interest lay in ending it.

For nearly two decades there was little real political will to end the schism by any means other than force. The greatest proponents of this so-called *via facti* were the French royal princes of Anjou and Orléans. Louis of Anjou, who exercised considerable influence over the French court in the aftermath of his brother Charles V's death in 1380, wedded his militant support of Clement VII with his own ambitions to make good on his Italian inheritance as the adopted successor of Joanna of Naples (against the Urbanist Charles of Durazzo). To sweeten the pot further, Clement promised much of the Papal States to Anjou as a fief if he could conquer it, a pledge repeated in the 1390s to King Charles VI's brother, Louis of Orléans. Between them, the houses of Anjou and Orléans brought war on several occasions to the peninsula but failed to destroy or dislodge the Roman popes. Clement and his successor, Benedict XIII spent lavishly on these fruitless campaigns, exerting tremendous strain on a treasury whose revenues amounted to just over half those of Gregory XI. Raising these funds obliged the Avignon popes of the schism to resort to an even more predatory fiscalism than that pursued by their predecessors. Now benefices and papal goodwill were put up for sale and failure to pay services and annates promptly invited excommunication. It did not help the cause of the Avignonese popes that these abuses fell almost entirely on that part of the Church which should have been their greatest advocate: the French clergy.

Stripped of the fiscal machinery of Avignon and the fat revenues of France, while receiving little from England thanks to the Statutes of Provisors and Praemunire, the Roman popes resorted to even more deplorable measures. They milked what they could from the Papal

States and engaged avidly in the selling of benefices, offices, favours and indulgences. Having to create a College of Cardinals virtually *de novo*, they made most of their choices from among a claustrophobic coterie of closely related Neapolitan noble clans. Urban VI displayed such mental unbalance that several of his cardinals considered removing him from power. Informed of their intentions, Urban only confirmed their assessment of him by having them tortured and put to death. If Urban's successor, another Neapolitan Boniface IX, was more competent, his ruthless fiscality and bellicose reduction of the Papal States to his over-lordship alienated many of those living in the Roman 'obedience', with some even labelling him as Antichrist.

There is no denying the withering blow to papal prestige dealt by the Great Schism. But the split in the Church initiated and nurtured other, and arguably more fundamental and transformative developments. First, it accelerated a process whereby the universal Church saw itself become increasingly divided into national churches under secular control. This had first been signalled by Philip IV's successes against Boniface VIII and was to some extent encouraged by the Avignon popes' willingness to concede to princes a good deal of *de facto* control over clerical taxation and many kinds of ecclesiastical patronage. Still, the relative weakness and poverty of the rival popes left them less able to assert their claims to patronage and jurisdiction while compelling them to make further concessions to princes. These same princes and their governments also benefited from the tendency of their clerical subjects to turn to them for protection against the arbitrary impositions and grasping exactions of popes about whose legitimacy they had some doubts. The practical turn to a greater degree of national autonomy found justification in theory, with the argument that Christ delegated equal authority to all his apostles, rather than mediating it through St Peter and his successors.

The second development arose from the clergy's desire to reunify the broken Body of Christ. Initially this was largely an academic matter, with theologians, especially at the University of Paris, debating the best means to resolve the problem of two rival claimants to the papal throne. To their minds what made the problem especially grave and intractable was not only that neither claimant had a decisive advantage over the other in terms of legitimacy but that the only personage who might have been able to act as a universally recognised arbiter, the emperor Charles IV, died in 1378 and his successor Wenceslas' personal failings and precarious hold on his office denied him the necessary authority. Failing a decisive outcome from the *via facti*, the intellectuals proposed that each pope abdicate, the so-called *via cessionis*, so that a single new pope could be elected. In 1398, after their calls for mutual abdication fell on deaf ears, the theologians of the University of Paris convinced Charles VI and his uncles the dukes of Burgundy and Berry to agree to 'subtract' the obedience of the French realm and Church from Benedict XIII. When this too failed, the only way left open to resolve the crisis in their minds was to call a general council of the Church, which on its own authority could depose the rival popes and elect a successor. But on whose authority was this council to be called? Since custom dictated that only the pope could call a council, this forced the advocates for recourse to the *via concilii* to rethink the very nature of the Church, replacing the long-held conception of ecclesiastical authority as *descending* from Christ to the pope, who as Christ's vicar was the *head* of the Church Militant, and then from the pope to the cardinals, bishops and clergy, with one in which Christ's authority *ascended* from the congregation of the faithful *members* of the Body of Christ. This corporatist ideology of the Church has come to be known as 'conciliarism'. Drawing some of its inspiration from the earlier political writings of John of Paris, Marsilius of Padua and William of Ockham, the conciliarist programme began to be developed by two German theologians at the University of Paris, Conrad of Gelnhausen and Henry of Langenstein, but was later given its clearest and most mature expression by their younger French colleagues Pierre d'Ailly and Jean Gerson.

In 1409 conciliarist theory conjoined with enough political goodwill to produce the Council of Pisa. In the previous year France, under the effective leadership of the duke of Burgundy, had again subtracted its obedience from Avignon and pushed for the council. Likewise several other European monarchs, as well as a majority of cardinals of both obediences had decided enough was enough and called on the rival popes either to abdicate voluntarily or face the prospect of deposition. In response, Benedict XIII and his Roman competitor Gregory XII called their own councils, at Perpignan in the Crown of Aragon and Cividale in the Papal States. This left the participants at Pisa with no other option than to depose the contumacious popes and elect their own, the Greek-born cardinal Peter Philarges, as Alexander V. Unfortunately, despite having been judged criminals, 'schismatics, fosterers of schism, notorious heretics deviating from the faith . . . and notorious scandalisers of the Church' and thus 'ipso facto deposed and deprived of all right to rule or preside', Benedict and Gregory ignored the decrees of Pisa, leaving Latin Christendom with three popes.[16]

Five years later the political environment again facilitated the meeting of a general council, in the imperial city of Constance; only this time there was to be a successful result. If the French had been the driving force behind Pisa, it was the emperor Sigismund who called the Council of Constance (1414–18) and worked tirelessly to ensure it bore fruit. When the council began at the end of 1414, it already had the support of the Empire, most of Italy, France, England, Poland and Denmark; and over the course of the next two years he convinced the rulers of Castile, Aragon and Scotland to cancel their obedience to Benedict XIII and support the goals of the council. After inviting the rival popes to resign voluntarily (which all refused to do), in the spring of 1415 the council arrested and detained the pope of the Pisan line, John XXIII and then published a decree, entitled *Haec sancta*, which laid out in no uncertain terms the superiority of general councils over errant popes:

> This sacred synod of Constance . . . declares . . . that it forms a general council, legitimately assembled in the Holy Spirit and representing the Catholic Church Militant, that it has its powers immediately from Christ, and that all men, of every rank and position, including even the pope himself, are bound to obey it in those matters that pertain to the faith, the extirpation of the said schism, and to the reformation of the said Church in head and members. It declares also that anyone, of any rank, condition or office – even the papal – who shall contumaciously refuse to obey the mandates, statutes, decrees or instructions made by this holy synod or by any other lawfully assembled council on the matters aforesaid or on things pertaining to them, shall, unless he recovers his senses, be subjected to fitting penance and punished as is appropriate.[17]

Empowered by *Haec sancta* and enabled by the rulers of Latin Christendom, the cardinals, bishops, clerical representatives and scholars assembled at Constance deposed John XXIII, compelled the Roman pope, Gregory XII, retroactively to convoke the council (as added insurance for the council's legitimacy) and immediately resign, and, once the support of the former adherents of the Avignonese pope had been secured, deposed Benedict XIII. Now the way lay open for a special commission composed of the cardinals and of representatives of the council to elect a new pope, Martin V, in November 1417. So ended the Great Schism.

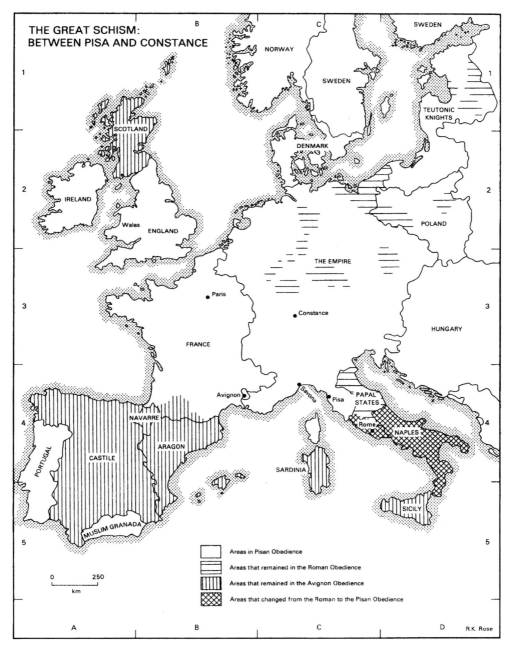

Map 7.1 The Great Schism: between Pisa and Constance, taken from *The Atlas of Medieval Europe*, 2nd Edition, © 2007, Routledge. Reproduced by permission of Taylor & Francis books UK

Haec sancta reveals, however, a third important development growing out of the schism and the second part of the conciliarist programme: a strong desire to reform the Church 'in head and members'. Periodic calls for reform (*reformatio*) were nothing new to the Church. Monastic reform had been a signal aspect of the ninth through twelfth centuries; it was joined by the reform of the clergy so ardently advocated by Pope Gregory VII and his twelfth-century successors, and the reformation of Christian society aimed at by the Fourth Lateran Council. Early in the fourteenth century at the Council of Vienne (1311–12) convoked by Clement V, the bishop of Mende, Guillaume Durand had even urged a reform 'in head and members', a plea to which the Avignon popes paid little heed. The Great Schism, however, lent a new note of urgency to a reform impulse already quickened by the anxiety sparked by the social ills of plague, war and insurrection. It is readily apparent among the religious orders. Alarmed at the laxity of their leadership and fellow friars, rigorist groups within the Franciscan, Dominican and Augustinian Orders initiated 'Observant' movements to recreate the apostolic life prescribed by their founders; a call for the return to the purity of the monastic ideal also occurred in some houses of the Cistercian and Benedictine Orders and inspired the foundation of the reformed house of Augustinian canons at Windesheim. The new Brigittine Order (founded by St Bridget of Sweden (d. 1373)) aimed at extreme monastic simplicity while the uncompromising asceticism of the Carthusians experienced a renewed appeal at the end of the fourteenth and in the early fifteenth century. Desire for a reformed Christian life also motivated the laymen and women in the Netherlands and Rhineland who flocked to the congregations of the Brethren and Sisters of the Common Life which sought to implement Geert Grote's (d. 1384) *Devotio moderna* (Modern Devotion). Even the heretical movements of the Lollards and Hussites were at their inception nothing other than attempts at the programmatic reform of the Church and Christian society. It is surely one of the signal tragic ironies of history that the reformist Council of Constance condemned the Czech reformer Jan Hus of heresy and burned him at the stake.

The reforms approved at Constance were programmatic and institutional in nature and applied more to the head of the Church than to its members. Besides *Haec sancta*, the other major decree of the council, *Frequens*, was designed to limit papal power, in this case by stipulating the convocation of general councils at regular intervals, with the next council scheduled in five years, followed by another after seven years, after which councils would occur every ten years. Other decrees tried to limit the practice of episcopal translation and to abolish certain financial exactions, like spoils. The new pope was also instructed to begin reforming such practices as the reservation of benefices, the charging of annates and the granting of indulgences and dispensations. For the conciliar reformers, Constance was, then, just the first step on the long road toward significant and fundamental reform. Unfortunately for them, their creation Martin V was by no means their creature. Scion of the ancient noble Roman lineage of the Colonna and bent on restoring the wealth and power formerly associated with his office, the new pope expressed nothing but distaste for the limits on papal *plenitudo potestatis* ('fullness of power') envisioned by the conciliarists. Martin also had his hands full imposing some modicum of order in central Italy, first contending with the great *condottiero* Braccio da Montone (d. 1424) and then, with considerable military assistance from his Colonna kin, reducing the Papal States to his obedience while also reconstituting a curial administration and finances. By his death in 1431, papal revenues almost equalled those of the Avignon popes of the Great Schism, but now more than half came from the Papal States. Constance may have put the Church once again under a single pope but it could not restore the previous territorial extent of his authority. Henceforth the popes were more Renaissance Italian princes than medieval universal monarchs.

Compelled by the provisions of *Frequens*, Martin V reluctantly convoked a council at Pavia in 1423, which achieved virtually nothing, unless one counts its moving for a time to Siena, before being dissolved. By the time the next general council convened at the imperial city of Basle, in 1431, those of a conciliar bent were determined to make good on the unfulfilled promises of Constance. Martin V died shortly after calling the council, but his opposition to conciliarism was shared by his successor, the Venetian Eugenius IV, who precipitously dismissed the council in December. Yet the council refused to disband, even promulgating a decree saying that only a council had the authority to move, suspend or terminate itself. Pope and conciliarists officially reconciled at the end of 1433, and over the next three and a half years the council helped smooth the way to the Peace of Arras (1435) between the Armagnac and Burgundian factions in France and worked out a compromise peace with the moderate Utraquist Hussites (1437). These positive developments did little, however, to soothe the growing hostility between the, mostly French, conciliarists (and their peninsular supporters Milan and Savoy) and, mostly Italian, supporters of papal supremacy. The council's outright abolition of annates and papal provisions were two important practical results of a theory that made of the pope a mere executor of legislation enacted by general councils which truly embodied the mystical Body of Christ.

The radicalism and intractability of the committed conciliarists at Basle proved to be the downfall of their programme. They frightened off reformers like Johannes Nider, a Dominican Observant who rejected the notion that the Church could be reformed from the top down, advocating instead a general reform, beginning with the religious orders who, once reformed, would lead the effort to root out witchcraft and heresy and preach the moral renewal of Christian society.[18] They also drove away the influential conciliarists Cardinal Giulio Cesarini and Nicholas of Cusa when they refused to move the council to Italy in order to facilitate talks with representatives of the Greek Orthodox Church who held out the hope of ending the longstanding Latin–Greek schism. Finally, and perhaps most critically, they gradually lost the support of many secular princes by refusing to take their interests into consideration.

The council's refusal to cross the Alps in order to meet with the Greek representatives gave Eugenius IV and his supporters the opportunity to abandon Basle and call a council at Ferrara, which subsequently moved to Florence (1437–39). There the Byzantine acknowledgement of papal primacy restored papal prestige and spelled the doom of the conciliarist cause. Until 1449 the Council of Basle continued to deliberate; indeed, in 1439 it had even gone so far as to declare the deposition of Eugenius IV and elect its own anti-pope (the former duke of Savoy, Amadeus, who took the name Felix V). But for all intents and purposes the initiative was now with Eugenius IV and his successor Nicholas V, who between 1438 and 1447 worked out separate deals with those European states which had either continued to support Basle or had declared their neutrality in the aftermath of the papal move to Ferrara. Yet although Basle had failed to overhaul the system of Church governance, the influence of its reformist programme was not entirely without effect. Many of those same ecclesiastics who attended the council were also civil servants and thus had the ear of princes attracted to conciliarist efforts to weaken papal supremacy and give greater autonomy to local churches. In 1438 Charles VII of France issued the Pragmatic Sanction of Bourges which recognised the superiority of general councils over popes, banned annates and drastically curtailed appeals to Rome and papal provisions. Secular control over the Gallican Church now had the force of law. Similar statements of secular control were made by the German princes and by the duke of Milan, Filippo Maria Visconti in 1439. As much as these moves irritated the popes, they had to give tacit recognition to them in their efforts to pry these same rulers away from Basle while making similar concessions of their own to secure the adherence of the rulers of the Iberian kingdoms. Between 1450 and 1453 Pope Nicholas V made official concordats with Milan, Savoy, Venice and Genoa.

After the middle of the fifteenth century the popes expended most of their energy on Italian affairs. Thus they brokered the Peace of Lodi in 1454, patronised the arts and engaged in impressive building projects in Rome, and dealt with threats from the Ottoman Turks and from the kings of France and Spain. They would not have been able to achieve any of this, however, had it not been for each pope's assiduous efforts to aggrandise his own temporal power, as well as that of the papal office. This meant, firstly, managing the ambitions of the Roman nobility and imposing control over and financially exploiting the Papal States. No pope after Martin V belonged to one of the great Roman noble families (the Orsini, Colonna, Savelli, and Caetani) so the normal course of action was to find ways to negotiate power with them, while also relying on one's own kinship network to partially contain them. Control of the Papal States was effected either by establishing direct governance over cities and towns or by working out deals with *signori*, who were given appointments as 'apostolic vicars' in return for recognising papal overlordship. Secondly, the popes had to look for ways to have as much influence as possible within the Italian church. Much of this was achieved through the popes' careful cultivation of good relations with the religious orders in Italy, and especially by promoting the activities of the Observant mendicant friars. Equally essential, though less savoury to those of a reformist cast of mind, was, on the one hand, the popes' shameless promotion of family members to all manner of ecclesiastical posts and curial offices (called 'nepotism', from the Latin *nepos*, 'nephew') and, on the other, the growing practice of selling ecclesiastical offices ('venality'). Whatever one may think of these expedients, it must be remembered that the post-Schism pontiffs were, effectively, Italian territorial princes. And yet their princely rule posed unique challenges. Popes were elected, celibate (at least in the legal sense) and usually elderly. Thus, in addition to their reigns being necessarily of short duration, 'There was no lasting bond between the sovereign, his dynasty, a territorially defined power and the local elites. . . . Nor was it possible to count on strong kinship networks, marriage alliances or feudal loyalty'.[19] To rule effectively, therefore, each pope on assuming office had to move swiftly and decisively to install a loyal and pliant support network. Moreover, being princes, there was an expectation that their court and capital city should be magnificent. Paying for all this ostentatious display encouraged the selling of benefices and ecclesiastical offices, and this was a price the members of the Italian elites were willing to pay in return for having family members and clients with access to and influence on what happened at the curia.

The demands of governing the Italian church and Papal States coupled with the practices of nepotism and venality encouraged the explosive growth of the number of cardinals and the staff of the curia. The number of cardinals increased during the fifteenth century from twenty-four to thirty-five, and then, in 1517, the Medici pope Leo X added a further thirty-one to their number. Likewise, by the early sixteenth century the curia's staff of 560 was double that of the Avignon papacy at its height. And just as the popes, cardinals and curia of the Avignon papacy had been overwhelmingly French, now the centre of the Church's government was thoroughly Italianised. Of the fourteen popes, from the Roman Martin V to the Florentine Clement VII (Giulio de' Medici), all but three were Italians. Moreover, two of the three foreigners, Callixtus III and Alexander VI (Alonso and Roderigo Borja/Borgia) were Aragonese and thus closely connected to the rulers of Naples, and an Italian connection can also be made with the Dutch Adrian VI (Adriaan Florensz), who was a client of the Habsburg king of Naples and Sicily, Charles V. The cardinalate too became a veritable preserve of the Italian ruling class, since the popes appointed their own relations as well as the sons of their princely and oligarchic supporters. Thus in 1461, in return for his support of a planned crusade against the Turks that the Sienese nobleman and pope Pius II (Enea Silvio Piccolomini) was trying to organise, Ludovico Gonzaga of Mantua got his seventeen-year-old son Francesco made cardinal. More strikingly, Leo X (Giovanni de' Medici) started his ecclesiastical career virtually at the top, when in 1489, at the tender age of thirteen, his father, Lorenzo 'the Magnificent' prevailed upon the stepfather of Giovanni's illegitimate half-sister, Pope Innocent VIII (the Genoese Giovanni Battista Cibo), to raise the boy to the cardinalate. Innocent VIII was closely connected through patronage to his fellow Genoese Sixtus IV, whose nephew became Pope Julius II, while Leo X and Clement VII were first cousins. So too was the Venetian Paul II the nephew of Eugenius IV, the Sienese Pius III the nephew of Pius II and Alexander VI the nephew of Callixtus III. Nepotism indeed!

The character and composition of the late-fifteenth and early sixteenth-century papacy and Italian church influenced the political and religious fortunes of Latin Christian Europe in a number of ways. First, the overwhelmingly Italian membership and focus at the universal Church's centre encouraged certain centripetal and centrifugal trends. In Italy itself, the policies and preeminence of the papal court fostered ever-closer ties between itself and the secular and clerical elites throughout the peninsula. Beyond Italy, however, these same factors further accelerated the movement toward national and regional churches that had begun in the time of the Avignon papacy and Schism, and then gained steam from papal grants of concessions and concordats in the conciliar and post-conciliar years. On the other hand, the prospect of greater influence over pope and curia raised the stakes in the contest for Italian supremacy waged between the monarchs of France and Spain. Paradoxically, these trends encouraged both Protestant reform and Catholic loyalty. For Protestant reformers and those princes who supported them, there would be little love lost for a Church that was not only patently mired in corruption but also distant, detached, meddlesome and foreign. Conversely, in Italy, Rome could be regarded at one and the same time as a den of corruption and the nerve-centre of an interdependent web of strong and deeply rooted local religious and civic institutions and identities. The situation was much the same in Iberia and France, where 'national' Catholic churches were already taking hold, and whose monarchs and ruling elites were deeply invested in maintaining the religious status quo.

None of this is to say that reformist ideals were moribund within the Church of c. 1500. Indeed, the longing to reform the head and members of the Body of Christ that had inspired the conciliarists and the Observants in the first half of the fifteenth century began to catch fire again near its end. It is readily observable in the programme of moral puritanism and republican populism which the Dominican Observant friar Girolamo Savonarola led in Florence between 1494 and his death at the stake in 1498, and in the passionate calls of the Dutch humanist priest Desiderius Erasmus (d. 1536) for the Church's return to the simplicity of that early apostolic Church which had promoted the pure love of Christ. The popes themselves, however, were deeply suspicious of anything that smacked of conciliar ideals (indeed, Pius II had condemned all the tenets of conciliarism in the bull *Execrabilis* of 1460) and they gave very low priority to reforms of any stripe. That their priorities lay elsewhere, in the realm of mundane power-politics, need hardly surprise us. For just as the papacy was managing to establish a fairly stable base of support for itself, Italy was overrun by the invading forces of French and Spanish monarchs. This political reality may not excuse either the sanguinary politics of Alexander VI and his son Cesare Borgia or Julius II's delight in personally commanding armies of conquest, but it does help explain it.

Interestingly, one milieu within which reformist ideals found some traction was the College of Cardinals. Certainly, some of its members were lacklustre time-servers or toadies of the current pope. But others were the appointees of former popes or owed their positions to the influence of national monarchs, and this gave the cardinalate as a whole something of an international and independent cast. In 1511, having become deeply offended by the rampant simony and nepotism of the curia and by the high-handedness of Pope Julius II, five of the cardinals, with the backing of Louis XII of France, called a 'council' (the so-called *conciliabulum* of Pisa, 1511–12). Although itself a dismal failure, the *conciliabulum* did compel Julius II to call his own council, which met at the Lateran in Rome from 1512 to 1517. At this Fifth Lateran Council Julius II and his successor, Leo X, categorically condemned the proceedings at Pisa and convinced Louis XII's successor, Francis I to revoke the Pragmatic Sanction of Bourges (the Concordat of Bologna, 1516) in return for papal recognition of the king's right of appointment to major benefices. Shortly before the Lateran Council concluded, Leo published the bull *Pastor Aeternus* (1516) which confirmed the provisions of the Concordat of Bologna and stated the pope's unique authority over councils. Having pounded the last nail into the coffin of the late medieval conciliar reform movement and then insured the cardinalate's pliability by installing 31 compliant new members, it comes as little surprise that Pope Leo regarded the German Martin Luther's reformist challenge of 1517 as nothing more than a distant 'monastic squabble'.[20] As for Luther himself, in 1518 he appealed against papal authority to that of a future general council. At the time neither he nor the pope envisioned the imminent and permanent breaking apart of *Unam sanctam*'s 'one holy, Catholic and apostolic church'.

Notes

1 Friedberg 1881: cols 1245–46 (my translation).
2 Clanchy 1993: 226–30.
3 Geremek 1987: 136–47.
4 Geary 2003: 452.
5 Geary 2003: 443–44.
6 Lawrence 1984: 202.
7 Friedberg 1881: cols 1245–46 (my translation).
8 Luscombe 1991: 195.
9 Oakley 1979: 307.
10 Oakley 1979: 50.
11 Zutshi 2000: 663–64.
12 Schimmelpfennig 1992: 207.
13 Oakley 1979: 42.
14 Pantin 1980: 82.
15 Kaminsky 2000: 675.
16 Kaminsky 2000: 695.
17 Oakley 1979: 65–66.
18 Bailey 2003.
19 Carocci 2012: 80.
20 Schimmelpfennig 1992: 258.

8

DEVOTION

Catholic and dissenting beliefs and practices

Questioned about where she was baptised, she answered that it was in the church of Domremy.

Questioned as to who her godparents were, she said one of her godmothers was called Agnes, another Jeanne, and another Sibille; as for godfathers, one was called Jean Bavant and the other Jean Barrey; from what her mother told her, she had several other godmothers.

Questioned regarding who had baptised her, she responded that she believed it was Father Jean Minet. . . .

Questioned regarding her age, she answered that it seemed to her that she was around nineteen. She went on to say that she had learned from her mother the Our Father, Hail Mary and Creed, and she had not learned any beliefs from anyone other than her mother. . . .

Questioned whether she confessed her sins each and every year, she responded, yes, and to her own priest; and when he was not able to do so, she confessed to another priest whom her own priest had authorised. She also had confessed a few times – two or three, she reckoned – to the friars, and that this had happened at Neufchâteau. And she received the sacrament of the Eucharist every Easter.

Questioned whether she ever received that same sacrament on feasts other than Easter, she told the questioner that he should proceed to the next question.[1]

In many ways, there was little of the conventional in the short life of Joan of Arc. Nevertheless, according to the responses she gave her interrogators during her trial for witchcraft and heresy in 1431, her early formation in the Christian religion and practice of the faith was utterly unremarkable. She could recite the most basic prayers and the words of the Apostles' Creed, taught her by her mother; she only confessed to her parish priest, except in cases of necessity and with his permission; and took communion once a year, at Easter, as stipulated in the canons of the Fourth Lateran Council. This was lay religion at its most basic and orthodox.

But the lived religion of later medieval Europeans was almost invariably richer, more complex and more complicated than that outlined at Lateran IV. The questions and answers at Joan's trial give ample evidence of this. When queried if she took communion at feasts other than Easter, she refuses to respond. By the fifteenth century, frequent communion had become the fashion among some pious members of the aristocracy and urban patriciate, and with lay people who had dedicated their lives to God in officially sanctioned communities of lay devout, like those of the Third Order Franciscans and Dominicans and of the *Devotio moderna*. The nineteen-year-old peasant girl was none of these and so her frequent partaking of the Eucharist could have been a sign of heterodox belief, like that of the Hussites. Two days after being questioned about her habits of confession and communion, Joan talked about a set of beliefs and practices in her village that smacked of paganism:

> She was questioned about a certain tree that stood in that village [of Domremy]; to which she responded that there is a certain tree rather near Domremy called the 'Tree of the Ladies', and others call it the 'Tree of the Fates', which, in French, is the 'Tree of the Fairies', nearby which is a spring; and she heard it said that those who are sick with fever drink from that spring and go in search of its waters in order to be cured. And she saw this herself, but does not know whether they were cured or not. She also says she heard that the sick, when they are able to get up [from their beds], go to the tree in order to take a walk there. . . . And she said that sometimes she went there with the other girls to take a walk, and at that tree they would make garlands for the image of Our Lady of Domremy. And on several occasions she heard from the old people (though none of them was of her own family) that the lady fairies were wont to assemble there. And she had heard it said by a woman named Jeanne, who was her godmother and the wife of Aubri, the mayor of Domremy, that she herself had seen the lady fairies there, but Joan said she did not know whether or not this was true. [Joan] also said that she had never seen these fairies at the tree, that she knew of. But whether she had seen them elsewhere, she did not know if she had or not. . . . [S]he had heard her brother say that it was being said in the countryside that she herself, Joan, had received her revelations at the Tree of the Lady Fairies; but she says that she did not, and she told him she did not.[2]

Such popular traditions were common and did not, in themselves, threaten Christian orthodoxy. They serve as a reminder, however, that the belief systems of many laypeople incorporated elements that were not, strictly speaking, Christian. In the charged atmosphere of her trial, Joan made certain to distance herself from the happenings at the tree of the fairies (though she does mention how she made wreaths there to honour the Virgin Mary) and to deny that she had first received divine instructions (i.e. 'her message') there, since in the minds of the inquisitors, fairies and demons were fellow travellers.

Those messages and what Joan did with them were the whole point of the trial. At the age of thirteen she began to receive messages from God, either through the agency of St Michael the Archangel or from St Catherine of Alexandria and St Margaret of Antioch. The voices directed her to dress as a man, take up arms and engage personally in warfare against the English and their Burgundian allies and to support the cause of Charles VII and the Armagnacs. It was not conversing with heavenly denizens *per se* that was the problem, since Joan and her enemies all believed that saints, like the souls of the departed in Purgatory, were as real, and in some senses as present, as the flesh-and-blood living. Even the prophetic holy woman was a well-recognised, if problematic type by the time Joan started hearing her voices. Rather, it was the militantly political content of the messages, the identity of the messengers, and the status of the messages' recipient that so disturbed Bishop Pierre Cauchon of Beauvais and the learned lawyers and theologians of the University of Paris who sat on the inquisitorial tribunal. Earlier female prophets, like Bridget of Sweden (d. 1373), Catherine of Siena (d. 1380), Marie Robine (d. 1399) and Jeanne-Marie of Maillé (d. 1414), had largely confined their pronouncements to the reform of the Church or healing of the Great Schism.[3] Joan instead had enlisted God and his saints on the side of the French in the Hundred Years

War and now found herself among those who were adherents of, or at least sympathetic to the Anglo-Burgundian alliance. As for the messengers, two of them, St Michael and St Catherine, had both recently been adopted as the chief heavenly patrons of the Armagnac faction, and St Margaret spoke to Joan in French, for 'how would she speak in English, since she is not on the English side?'[4]

But Joan's choice of heavenly messengers probably worried her interrogators for other, more fundamental reasons as well. Margaret was usually invoked along with Catherine as a protector of women who were pregnant or giving birth, and Catherine was also considered a protector of young girls.[5] With the benefit of very long hindsight, we can appreciate that these would have been just the sort of saints who would have been particularly familiar and comforting to a teenage girl. However, viewed from the perspective of the 'university scholars and the great clerics, masters of the Church during the years of the Council of Basel', Joan's choice of saints, which blended the national and masculine with the domestic and feminine, must have exemplified the transgressive role and identity she had assumed. For in the end there was the problem posed for the authority of the Church by Joan herself. Here was an ignorant peasant girl, who not only claimed to be a privileged instrument of God's will but had achieved widespread recognition as such. Honoured by nobles, followed by soldiers, revered by simple folk – indeed it was even reported that moved by her prayers God had restored a dead infant to life – Joan had the makings of a popular saint whose authority derived not from the Church and the guardians of its doctrinal orthodoxy, but rather from the workings of the Holy Spirit 'received through the grace of baptism'.[6] More generally, she represented, albeit in an extreme form, the growing self-confidence and autonomy of lay religion in the final centuries of the Middle Ages.

In a very real sense, the laity's avid participation in religion was the great success story of the late medieval Church. It has been reckoned that by the fifteenth century, the

> willingness, and indeed the desire to sanctify worldly life within the framework of the institutions created by the Church and with the help of the treasures of grace she offered were hardly as generally widespread at any other time in the Middle Ages and have never been more clearly visible.[7]

After what had amounted, in effect, to centuries of missionary activity on the part of the ecclesiastical hierarchy – with the encouragement and support of secular authorities, to be sure – the long struggle to Christianise Latin Christendom was over. By 1300, for all intents and purposes, all lay people who were not 'infidels' (i.e. Jews, Muslims or 'pagans') or notorious heretics now participated in the sacraments and rites of Christian worship. More than that, a great deal of public, communal life had become sacralised in the context of institutional structures like the parish and (in towns) mendicant churches, public events like open-air sermons, liturgical celebrations and processions, and convivial and charitable organisations like guilds and confraternities. But increased involvement in religion by the laity also meant a greater sense of 'ownership' on their part, and the clergy had to recognise and respond to their sensibilities, desires and demands while also endeavouring to channel and contain them. This same process is evident in the sphere of private devotion, where trends of interiorised, contemplative, affective lay piety whose origins lay in the late twelfth and thirteenth centuries developed and ramified into new and varied forms. At times in some places this dynamic moved beyond the clergy's control or even in opposition to it. Labelled as heretics, the adherents of these dissident religious groups became targets of suppression and persecution. Around the year 1520, a German friar from an order renowned for its orthodoxy and commitment to the cause of papal supremacy, the Augustinians, was branded with the label of heterodoxy. Unlike earlier heresiarchs, however, Brother Martin Luther rejected several of the paradoxes which gave life and meaning to the medieval Church and successfully exposed the fiction of a unified Latin Christendom.

Christianity: belief, faith, and practice

At the outset, certain terms are in need of definition. The first of these are 'belief' and 'faith'. At one level they can be construed doctrinally as the intellectual acceptance of some 'Truth' or 'truths'. Thus the 'truths' of the creeds (from *credo*, 'I believe') of the Church were in the Middle Ages, and still are for Christians today, objects of belief, 'Articles of the Faith'. Modern-day fundamentalists make the same claim for the words of Scripture, whose objectifiable 'Truth' has to be believed. However, belief and faith can also be defined more broadly as what might be called 'trust' (*fides*), and thus as something belonging to the realm of the emotions and of 'common sense', something felt and practised more than thought. Thus, with few exceptions it seems, medieval Christians believed in miracles and put their faith in the salvific agency of Jesus, Mary and the sacraments, the salutary effects of prayer, and the healing power of the saints and their relics. These were as real to them as science and its benefits are real to us. With varying intensity depending on the individual, the faithful cultivated 'spirituality', which has been defined as 'a conscious relationship with God, in Jesus Christ, through the indwelling of the Spirit and in the context of the community of believers'.[8] People expressed their spirituality in acts of 'devotion' or 'piety', which included both participation in public worship and private practices like prayer, meditative reading, contemplation and mortification of the flesh.

Once upon a time historians were in the habit of calling the Middle Ages 'the Age of Faith'. At the time they assumed an unproblematic and unified single faith, propagated by the clergy and shared by all, as revealed most especially in such monumental works of scholasticism as Thomas Aquinas's *Summa theologica* and in the canons of Church councils. Although more recent work has thoroughly discredited this old view, the notion of an age of faith has some validity if medieval Christianity is seen, on the one hand, as a common set of cultural practices –

> baptism at birth and last rites at death . . . rudimentary knowledge of the Apostles' Creed and Lord's Prayer, rest on Sunday and feast days . . . with attendance at mass, fasting at specified times, confession once a year . . . communion at Easter, the payment of various fees and tithes at specified times, and alms for the needy

– and, on the other, as a 'mentality . . . a group of representations and mental images common to all the people'.[9] Beyond this, however, one might more fruitfully speak of the variety and dynamism of religious life. Just as a fully uniform and unified institutional Church remained a dream in the minds of the most assiduous apologists for papal sovereignty, so too was '"western Christianity" . . . a generalisation encompassing an almost infinite variety of regional, parochial, familial, and individual Christianities which were subject to constant change and development in response to a wide range of forces'.[10] One of the most pervasive of those forces was the interplay between various doctrines and observances sponsored by the ecclesiastical hierarchy and the attitudes and practices of various groups within the laity and, indeed, the clergy. All responded in complex ways to one another, giving late medieval Christianity its authoritarian aspect, in which 'salvation implied sameness: obeying the rules, conforming in behaviour, fitting into place', but also its popular, varied and 'demand-led' character.[11]

Sacred time and space

In the highly secularised Western world today, only the rare, unobtrusive legacy or trace reminds us of what had, in the Middle Ages, been the all-pervasive presence of the sacred along the basic temporal and spatial axes which orientate everyday life. Years are still reckoned according to the Incarnation (Before Christ/Anno Domini) and the week begins on the Sunday Sabbath, but hardly anyone pays this any mind, and if they do it is to eschew the terminology (although not the arithmetic) of the BC/AD system for that of BCE/CE. Churches, although they remain meaningful as places of worship for their parishioners, for the broader public only the odd church still retains significance as either a landmark or historical monument, and some of these have even ceased to be places of worship. As for names of streets and districts like Charing Cross or Saint-Germain, they retain not even a vestige of holiness.

The feasts of the ecclesiastical calendar ordered time. In most of Latin Christendom, the year began on 25 March, the feast of the Annunciation of the Blessed Virgin Mary (Lady Day), although there were some variants on this, like the French chancery starting the year at Easter and the fourteenth-century English monastic chronicler Adam Murimuth insisting instead on the feast of St Michael Archangel (Michaelmas, 29 September). As for 1 January, it signified little besides the feast of the Circumcision of the Lord. The days and months of the year were those of the Roman calendar, but it was the liturgical feasts of the ecclesiastical calendar that gave them meaning and made them memorable. Likewise medieval Europeans were quite cognisant of the four solar seasons with which we are familiar, but they also ordered their lives according to the liturgical ones of Advent, Christmas, Lent, and Easter. The feasts and seasons of the Church calendar ran, actually, along two tracks, obeying the rules of two *different* kinds of time. One of these, called 'temporal' time, respected the annual cycle of Sundays based on the date of the most important feast of the liturgical year: Easter. Because Easter's position migrated each year (and still does), falling anywhere between 22 March and 25 April owing to its being celebrated on the Sunday following the first full moon occurring on or after 21 March, the dates of all the religious feasts connected with the Lenten and Easter seasons (Ash Wednesday, Palm Sunday, Maundy Thursday, Good Friday, Ascension, Pentecost, Trinity and Corpus Christi) also moved. Thus, for example, Ash Wednesday was forty days before Easter and Pentecost (Whit Sunday) fell on the seventh Sunday after Easter. Temporal time also encompassed the seasons of Advent (beginning the fourth Sunday before Christmas) and Christmas (from 25 December till Epiphany on 6 January).

Running alongside the time of Sundays and movable feasts was 'sanctoral' time. Sanctoral time took its name from the multitude of 'immovable' feasts celebrating the 'birthdays' of saints (i.e. the dates of their deaths and entry into heaven), but also included an ever-growing number of feasts associated with the 'translation' from one location to another of a saint's body or relics, and with the life and Passion of Christ and life of the Virgin Mary. The result was a calendar crowded with days infused with sacred meaning. This can be demonstrated by looking at the sanctoral calendar for June in late medieval England (Table 8.1).

Almost every day, then, belonged to a particular saint or saints, and in churches throughout Christendom stories about them (*legenda*) were recited during the daily office and their intercession was called on during the mass. Several of these saints had a particularly national or local cult (and so comprised different saints in different parts of Europe), whereas others, like the apostles and early martyrs, were venerated throughout Christendom. Some, like the feasts of John the Baptist and of Peter and Paul, had special significance and might be accompanied by fasting on the preceding day (the vigil), a holiday from work, obligatory attendance at mass, public processions and dramatic re-enactments.

June also often fell in the latter part of the Easter season and so in many years included such major feasts as Pentecost, Trinity and Corpus Christi. The last of these was a relative latecomer to the liturgical round, having only been instituted as a feast in 1264 but not gaining wide acceptance before the early 1300s. Then, however, it became the most popular and elaborated of feasts, with the exception of the great Holy Week cycle running from Palm Sunday to Easter. Both Corpus Christi and Holy Week were occasions for masses, public sermons and processions whose central feature was the showing of the Body of Christ in the form of the consecrated host, or in some locales on Palm Sunday an effigy of Christ. The guilds of many towns also staged play-cycles during Corpus Christi that re-enacted Bible stories and the events of the Passion, told the tale of human sin and redemption, explored elements of the Creed or celebrated Eucharistic miracles, often with some anti-Semitic message.[12] Drama, too, was an important feature of the church services from Maundy Thursday to Easter morning. Following the Maundy Thursday mass, which commemorated the Last Supper, the altars of the church were ritually stripped of all cloths and ornaments – symbolising the stripping of Christ before the Crucifixion – while the story of the Passion was read aloud; this was followed in some churches by the ritual washing of feet. On Good Friday priest and parishioners mourned the death of Christ. No mass was celebrated, but the Passion story from the Gospel of John was read. After this, a cross was unveiled, which parishioners crept to on their knees and kissed. The cross and a small container called a 'pyx', containing a single host consecrated the preceding day, were then shrouded in linen cloth and 'buried' in a model of Christ's sepulchre. There they remained until Easter morning, guarded by a relay of parishioners who kept a constant vigil at the 'tomb'. On Easter day, the pyx with its host and the cross were 'resurrected' from the sepulchre and the cross borne around the church in triumph, accompanied by the hymn 'Christ, Rising Again from the Dead'. After another episode of creeping to the cross, high mass was celebrated.[13]

In the late fourteenth and fifteenth centuries, devotion to the awesome divinity of Christ, on the one hand, and to his human suffering, on the other, inspired new feasts dedicated to his Transfiguration and Holy Name (6 and 7 August, respectively), and to the Crown of Thorns (4 May in Germany and 11 August in France) and Five Wounds (4th Friday in Lent). Events in the life of Mary also afforded plenty of opportunity for liturgical observance in an age when devotion to Jesus' mother rivalled that to the Son himself (Table 8.2).

Assumption and Purification were the Marian feasts of greatest importance, if gauged by the amount of public ritual they generated. The feast of the Assumption celebrated the doctrine that when Mary had finished her time on earth her living soul and body were taken up into heaven where she now reigned as Queen; it also was a festival marking the beginning of the harvest. Purification commemorated Mary and Joseph's presentation of the infant Jesus in the Temple. It was the occasion for a procession in which parishioners offered candles at the altar; these were then lit before an image of the Virgin. Like Corpus Christi, Candlemas became a popular time for dramatic re-enactments of the Holy Family's visit to the Temple; interestingly, in these plays Mary and Joseph, sometimes accompanied by Mary's mother, St Anne, behave like good parishioners and offer candles at the altar. Mary had become the

Table 8.1 English 'sanctoral' calendar for June

1	–
2	Marcellinus and Petrus, martyrs; Odo, abp. of Canterbury
3	–
4	Petroc of Cornwall
5	Boniface, martyr
6	–
7	Trans. Wulfstan, bp. of Worcester
8	Medard and Gildard, bps.; trans. Alphege, abp. of Canterbury; William, abp. of York
9	Trans. Edmund, abp. of Canterbury; Primus and Felicianus, martyrs
10	–
11	Barnabas, apostle
12	Basilidis, Cyrinus and Nabor, martyrs
13	Anthony of Padua, Franciscan friar
14	Basil, bp. of Caesarea
15	Vitus, Modestus and Crescentius, martyrs; Eadburh of Bicester, nun
16	Trans. Richard, bp. of Chichester; Cyril and Julitta, martyrs
17	Botolf, abbot
18	Marcus and Marcellianus, martyrs
19	Gervasius and Protasius, martyrs
20	Trans. Edward, martyr
21	Leufred, abbot
22	Alban, protomartyr
23	Etheldreda, nun; vigil of Nativity of John the Baptist
24	Nativity of John the Baptist
25	2nd day of Nativity of John the Baptist; Eloi, bp. of Noyon
26	John and Paul, martyrs; Salvius, bp. of Valenciennes
27	4th day of Nativity of John the Baptist
28	Leo, pope; vigil of Peter and Paul, apostles
29	Peter and Paul, apostles
30	Commemoration of Paul, apostle

Sources: Pfaff 2007: 58–9; Cheney 2000.

locus of such intense affective piety by the end of the Middle Ages, that several new feasts were established celebrating the apocryphal story of the infant Mary's own Presentation at the Temple (introduced in the 1370s), her Visitation to her cousin Elizabeth, mother of John the Baptist (1380s), and her own Compassion for the suffering and death of Jesus at the Crucifixion (early 1400s). Even her mother, Anne became the focus for a cult. Observance

Table 8.2 Feasts of the Blessed Virgin Mary

Conception	8 December
Nativity	8 September
Presentation*	21 November
Annunciation (Lady Day)	25 March
Visitation*	2 July
Purification (Candlemas)	2 February
Compassion*	Friday before Passion Sunday or Wednesday of Holy Week
Assumption	15 August

*Late medieval additions

Figure 8.1 Corpus Christi procession. Paris, Bibliotheèque nationale de France, ms. lat. 865a, p. 340

of her feast (26 July) had become widespread by the end of the fourteenth century. It too inspired plays, like for example the St Anne pageants staged by the guilds of Lincoln.[14]

Like feasts, fasts constantly reminded the laity of the presence of the holy in their lives. Most important were the great fasts of Advent and Lent. Because they were times of penance, throughout their duration no marriages could be solemnised – nor, technically, was sex permitted between spouses. Laypeople began Lent, the most important of the penitential seasons, with the annual sacrament of confession to their parish priest; then, as an act of penance and in order to purify themselves prior to partaking of the Eucharistic host at Easter, they refrained from eating meat and animal products. Much shorter periods of fasting were compulsory at several other specified times throughout the year, including the vigils of Christmas, All Saints (1 November) and several saints' days. The annual cycle of feasts and fasts complemented the rhythm of the seasons, with the liturgical seasons largely corresponding to winter and spring, and summer and autumn being punctuated by the observance of feasts from St John's Day through St Anne's, St Peter's Chains (Lammas, 1 August), Assumption, Holy Cross (15 September), St Michael Archangel, and All Saints.

Space too had its sacred points of orientation. Parish churches were the most ubiquitous of these, as well as being the most frequented by the laity. England had some 9,500 parishes in 1300 and 8,800 in 1535.[15] By 1500, the great metropolis of London counted 107 parishes with another ten in its suburbs, while York and Norwich each had some forty parishes; the medium-sized town of King's Lynn (pop. 4,691 in 1377) had the very large parish church of St Margaret as well as the suburban parish of All Saints and two chapels, St James and St Nicholas, which carried out certain parochial functions.[16] In Paris, twelve parishes crowded the Île de la Cité, with another twenty-five churches serving the populace of the Right and Left Banks.[17] The mid-sized cities of Liège and Dijon had twenty-six and nine parish churches respectively.[18] Fifty-five non-collegiate churches, the overwhelming majority of which were parishes, were packed into the city and suburbs of Florence, with some 500 more parishes in the countryside of its *contado*.[19] In these churches parishioners confessed their sins and attended mass, had their marriages blessed, baptised their children, and, within the church or in its cemetery, buried their dead. Women came to church to be ritually purified after giving birth and all heard sermons preached in the church or outside in the churchyard. Many cities and towns, including London, Paris, Liège and Florence, were also the seat of a bishop's church, or cathedral. Often large and ornate, and normally repositories of important saints' relics, the cathedrals were centres of almost continuous liturgical activity.

Added to the warp of parochial and cathedral churches in the rich tapestry of the ecclesiastical landscape was the diverse weft of pious foundations, including religious houses for men and women, mendicant convents, hospitals, almshouses, colleges, collegiate churches and chapels. Early fourteenth-century Florence had fifteen collegiate churches (endowed churches staffed by several canons), thirty-one male and sixty-six female monasteries and convents, thirty-seven hospitals (these had increased to roughly fifty by 1500), and two hermitages. Seven collegiate churches and five monasteries, as well as convents for each of the four orders of mendicant friars (Franciscans, Dominicans, Augustinians and Carmelites) could be found in contemporary Liège. The friars, and especially the Franciscans and Dominicans, demonstrated a particularly strong vocation for offering pastoral care to the laity, and by the fourteenth century they had colonised all large cities and most towns of at least medium size, like for example King's Lynn, where all four orders had established convents before the end of the thirteenth century. Places of worship, education and charity, churches and other ecclesiastical foundations were some of the most important landmarks in both urban and rural space. Many of them, and especially parish and mendicant churches, also acted as what we might today call community centres, since they frequently provided meeting space for guilds and confraternities, and lay people gathered in them to conduct all manner of public and private business.

The activities of the faithful were only a part of what made places holy, however. More important was what – or more accurately in the late medieval context *who* – resided in or at them: the countless relics and images of Christ and the saints found in profusion throughout Christendom. Relics could be bodies or body parts (e.g. hair, bones, scraps of skin), or 'contact relics', including instruments of martyrdom or pieces of clothing once worn by, or objects touched by the saint. Even the most humble of parish churches had a saint's relic buried in its altar stone as well as several sacred images, like those of the cross with the Virgin Mary and St John, of the Trinity, of Mary, again, and of 'Sts Margaret, Anne, Nicholas, John the Baptist, Thomas Becket, Christopher Erasmus, James the Great, Katherine, Petronella, Sythe, and Michael the Archangel' at the country church of Stratton Strawless in Norfolk.[20] Larger and better endowed churches had correspondingly more, and more impressive relics, as well as more, and more ornate images. At the shrine of St Cuthbert in Durham Cathedral, one of England's most important pilgrimage sites, dozens of reliquaries were arrayed on the steps leading up to the saint's tomb in the cathedral's Chapel of the Nine Altars. On one of these steps were:

> a small gilded and jeweled silver cross containing a piece of the Lord's Cross. Next, a piece from the Lord's manger in a blue silk purse. Next, four saints' bones in a small silver cross. Next, a piece of St. Godric's beard. Next, a little wooden box with some of the wood with which St. Lawrence was beaten and some tiny bones from the martyr St. Concordius, and pieces from St. Bernard the abbot's rib and from his hair, and a joint of St. Lawrence, partly burned by fire, in a crystal vial decorated with silver. Also bones from the holy martyrs Nereus and Achilleus and a bone of St. Felix the martyr, and one bone of St. Germanus the bishop, and a piece of the bishop St. Acca's chausable, and one bone of St. Balbina in a silk purse with four pockets with white castles on it.

Among the treasures on the next step was 'a crystal pyx containing milk of the Blessed Virgin Mary'.[21]

These sacred images and bits of holy matter were more than objects of devotion: they were points of contact between the faithful and the divine, portals between this world and the next, with power to heal bodies in this life and convey remission of sins in the next. As such, they were landmarks of sacred geography and desirable destination points for pilgrimages. Most holy places had only local significance and drew visitors from fairly close by. Florence had the shrines of its local saints: Zenobius (d. c. 429), in the cathedral; Umiliana dei Cerchi (d. 1246), at the Franciscan church of Santa Croce; and Villana dei Botti (d. 1361), at the Dominican convent of Santa Maria Novella.[22] In England, if the north had its shrine of St Cuthbert in Durham, the West Midlands had the relics of St Thomas Cantilupe (d. 1282) at Hereford, and East Anglia the miracle-performing remains of St Etheldreda (d. 679) at Ely.[23] After his death in 1391, Bishop Nicholas of Linköping in Sweden became the focus of a local cult there.[24] Nor were local shrines confined to churches. Various places became sites of spontaneous popular veneration. In 1292 and for a while thereafter, people sought, and found, miracles before a small tabernacle containing an image of the Virgin at the open-air grain market of Orsanmichele in Florence; in 1389 at All Saints church just outside King's Lynn something very similar happened before an image of the Trinity.[25] These expressions of piety could provoke the displeasure of ecclesiastical officials, as when in the 1290s Bishop Oliver Sutton of Lincoln sought to ban pilgrims from flocking to the private chapel of the earl of Cornwall in Hambledon and to 'a certain well situated in a field at Linslade', since 'no profane place should be visited by people for the sake of veneration on account of a brash claim of miracles which have not been approved by the church'.[26] A century later, another bishop of Lincoln, John Buckingham, failed to keep pilgrims away from a rural cross in Rippingale, a popular shrine that to his mind was no more than a fraud perpetrated by the local parish priest.[27]

Other places drew pilgrims from far and wide. Jerusalem, the centre of the sacred universe and a pilgrimage site since antiquity, continued to attract a large number of visitors, as did the next two most holy sites for Latin Christians, Rome and Santiago de Compostela. The shrine of St Thomas Becket at Canterbury remained a popular destination as well. To these older sites were added several newer ones, many of them expressing the late Middle Ages' particularly strong devotion to the Virgin Mary and the Passion of Christ. Statues of the Virgin were everywhere, but some, like those at Walsingham in Norfolk and at Rocamadour in central France attained special significance; added attractions at Walsingham included a reliquary full of the Virgin's milk and a miniature reproduction of the Holy House at Nazareth, scene of the Annunciation.[28] Several Passion relics, chief among them the Crown of Thorns, were housed in the Sainte-Chapelle in Paris. Even more impressive according to late medieval tastes, however, were relics of Christ's blood. Hailes in Gloucestershire boasted a relic of the Holy Blood which performed several miracles including, when a Lollard priest attempted to say mass there, boiling up 'unto the chalyce brynke'.[29] Wilsnack in northern Germany attained enormous popularity at the end of the fourteenth century thanks to its miraculous bleeding hosts.[30]

Most pilgrims confined their sacred tourism to local and regional sites, but a not inconsiderable number took it upon themselves at some time in their lives to travel quite long distances, always at considerable cost and often at substantial personal risk. We are particularly well informed about the prodigious pilgrimages of Margery Kempe. In 1413–15 she travelled to the Holy Land and back, stopping on the way to visit shrines in Bologna, Assisi and Rome. Not satisfied with this, she headed off to Santiago de Compostela in 1417 and, once back in England, made her way to Hailes and to the shrine of St John of Bridlington. Then, in 1433–34, after going 'to Walsyngham and offeryn in worschep of owr Lady', she set off on a northern European junket, which included stops at Wilsnack and at Aachen, whose Marienkirche housed a relic of the Virgin's cloak.[31] Safely landed at Dover, she made sure to seek the benefits conferred by the shrine of St Thomas at Canterbury and by some relics of St Bridget of Sweden at Syon Abbey in Middlesex. No doubt the number and extent of Margery's wanderings were exceptional, but she always had plenty of company on her journeys. Nearly 150,000 pilgrims are said to have visited Aachen during a single week in 1496, while two million reported to have swamped Rome in the papal Jubilee year of 1300. Even children got in on the act, with what seem to have amounted to periodic 'virtual exoduses' of them to Mont-Saint-Michel in Normandy.[32]

Movements of devotion

Doubtless people as often as not had mixed motives for going on pilgrimage. Merchants could do double-duty, combining pious visits to shrines with the quest for lucre. Likewise, suitors to the papal curia in Rome would reap whatever spiritual benefits they could from a trip necessitated by litigation. Pilgrimages were also occasions for sociability and social posturing, as Chaucer and the readers of the *Canterbury Tales* clearly appreciated. Nor should fascination with the marvellous and a hankering after novelty and adventure be disconnected from belief in miraculous power and intercession. The church of Boxley in Kent became a popular destination for miracle seekers and gawkers thanks to its mechanical cross; St Patrick's Purgatory at Lough Derg in Ireland tempted visitors with visions of ghosts and a view down into the Underworld; and readers of the miraculous saints' lives recorded in James of Voragine's *Golden Legend* also thrilled to the tales of distant wonders in *The Travels of Sir John Mandeville*.

Still, the principal reasons for pilgrimage and visits to local holy places were certainly spiritual and included: (1) the search for divine assistance, usually to remedy physical or mental ailments or impairments; (2) giving thanks for previously rendered aid; (3) fulfilling the conditions of a penance; and (4) seeking indulgences for the good of one's own soul and intercession for the souls of one's family and friends, both living and in Purgatory. In a world where medical science offered little in the way of relief for the miseries arising from physical deformities, disease, injury, insanity and accidental death, Christ and the saints offered hope of remedy and recovery. In the 1300s a blood relic came to the aid of a haemorrhaging nun at Mariengarten in Lower Saxony, while in the early 1400s, the blood-host relic at Wilsnack was credited with straightening withered limbs and resurrecting the dead.[33] On the same day in the late 1400s, two crippled visitors to the shrine at Windsor of the somewhat unlikely popular (although never canonised) saint, King Henry VI, regained the use of their legs and left their crutches behind as proof.[34] More often, however, the saints worked their miracles telekinetically, in response to prayer or a heartfelt invocation. Such favours frequently elicited a visit to the saint's shrine, to give thanks, bear witness and leave a gift. In 1318, in return for her having healed his brother, Pucpus of Spoleto vowed to make an annual pilgrimage, barefoot, to the tomb of St Clare of Montefalco (d. 1308)

> to offer there a wax image the weight of his brother . . . and a twisted candle weighing two pounds, and to provide 50 livres in Cortona pennies for the marriage of a young girl or the construction of a fine tomb to St Clare, whichever the nuns [of her convent] wished.[35]

In the 1450s, Thomas Lake, the vicar of Dunton St Mary in Bedfordshire travelled a considerable distance to the shrine of St Osmund of Salisbury (d. 1099), 'and there made an offering, telling of a great miracle revealed in the person of John Gregory, a stonemason of Biggleswade, on the left side of his face'. According to Lake, he and several others had witnessed John being struck dead in the face by a 'rafter 12 feet in length and 4 inches square' falling thirty feet from a scaffold. The priest first entreated God and St Mary 'to demonstrate a miracle of life', then prayed 'to St Thomas of Canterbury and afterwards to St William, bishop of York'. When these imprecations failed to produce a positive result, Lake thought of St Osmund, 'of whose translation he had heard this year; and straight away, by prayers extended to God, to St Mary, and to St Osmund, the said dead man began to vomit, and thus more and more he began to draw breath' and was revived.[36]

Even images of the saints might effect cures, as happened in 1389 when the duchess of Bourbon during a particularly difficult birth told her confessor to dedicate her to Peter of Luxemburg (bp. of Luxemburg and cardinal, d. 1387). While he was doing so, 'the lady had

Figure 8.2 Thick gold ring with figures of saints on inside: fifteenth-century. © Museum of London

an image of the Lord Cardinal placed upon her stomach'; soon afterwards the duchess safely gave birth to a healthy child. And, in turn, people began to visit images, rather than shrines, to give thanks, like the woman from Macerata in Italy who at a local church left one of her son's shirts before a painting of St Nicholas of Tolentino (d. 1305) in return for the saint's healing intercession; she deposited the shirt there 'because she had been unable to travel to Tolentino owing to the very poor state of the roads'. More often than not, the gifts (known as 'ex-votos') which pilgrims gave to saints were also images, made of wax or silver and depicting the body part healed or referring to the infirmity repaired or catastrophe averted. Thus the following list of objects left before the tomb of Charles of Blois (claimant to the duchy of Brittany, killed at the Battle of Auray in 1364) in Guincamp: 'ships, images [of people?], feet with lower legs, hands, arms, heads, fortresses, houses, animals, birds, fetters, forms or figures of money, casks of wine, and wax figures of eyes, breasts, genitals, and litters . . . staffs, or crutches'.[37]

Pilgrimage was as closely tied to penance as it was to healing. Often ecclesiastical and civil courts imposed visits to shrines as a form of punishment, as when, in 1491, Bishop Thomas Langton of Salisbury sentenced the fuller Thomas Tailour to walk barefoot and with head uncovered, carrying a bundle of faggots, to his own parish church and to several other churches and Reading Abbey. Convicted of heresy for having impugned the practice of pilgrimage to Santiago de Compostela, Tailour carried the faggots to symbolise the means of his own execution, by burning, should he lapse again into heresy. Two centuries earlier, a civil court imposed a pilgrimage to Canterbury and to Saint-Gilles in the south of France on Jan Uttensacke for having acted fraudulently as executor of a will.[38]

More generally, however, the faithful regarded pilgrimage as an especially effective vehicle for obtaining remission of sins. According to the doctrine of the sacrament of confession, human nature, although created perfect by God, had been corrupted when Adam and Eve, at the prompting of the devil, committed the primordial crime of disobedience in the Garden of Eden. God in His infinite mercy had rescued human souls from eternal damnation by sacrificing Himself, in the person of Jesus Christ, in expiation of this Original Sin. Yet despite the way of heaven having thereby been opened and the opportunity of eternal salvation having been offered to all Christians who participated in the sacraments, the fact of humanity's imperfection and tendency to sinfulness remained. The Church provided remedy for these sins in the form of the sacrament of confession, whereby Christians, moved by true contrition, confessed their sins to a priest, who offered them absolution on condition of their subsequently fulfilling the punishment, or penance which he assigned. Typically a penance involved some combination of prayers and charitable activity, but it very often also included pilgrimage. The penitential efficacy of pilgrimage resulted partly from the hardship it inflicted on the penitent and the danger to which he or she was exposed, thus eliciting God's mercy. But the virtuous power of the relics and images visited by pilgrims was just as important, if not more so. This power could even work through intermediaries, which explains the not-uncommon recourse to proxies. Queen Elizabeth of York, wife of Henry VII, paid surrogates to visit several shrines throughout southern England on her account, and plenty of less elevated people did so as well.[39]

As added incentive and assurance, ecclesiastical authorities regularly awarded indulgences to pilgrims. Much maligned by Luther and other Protestant reformers, the practice of granting indulgences was a reasonable outgrowth of what would become another Protestant bugbear, the doctrine of Purgatory. According to this doctrine, which had been worked out by theologians over the course of the twelfth and thirteenth centuries and then given its most eloquent expression in Dante's *Divine Comedy*, there were three places to which the souls of the dead were consigned immediately after exiting this life. A few notably virtuous souls, those of the saints, went directly to heaven, while those of the damned (infidels, heretics, and un-confessed and unrepentant evil-livers of various stripes) plunged straight down into hell. Purgatory was the place between hell and heaven where the souls of Christians went who had merited salvation but were nonetheless weighed down or stained with sin. Contributing to this weight/stain of sin was a combination of penances which had not been completed, of minor 'venial' sins which had not been pardoned and of grave 'mortal' ones which had been forgiven but whose 'effect' still needed to be worked off. It was commonly assumed that Purgatory was the temporary destination for the departed souls of conventionally devout Christians who had accepted the authority of the Church and its doctrines and had availed themselves of the sacraments. There they would go and be subject to painful punishment, akin to the torments of hell; and there they would remain suffering but comforted in the knowledge of their eventual ascent into Paradise.

Once dead and in Purgatory, a soul had no power to shorten its stay there or diminish its suffering. The living Christian could, however, take a sizeable chunk out of this mountain of future pain by acquiring indulgences. An indulgence pardoned Purgatorial punishment for some stated period of time, ranging from the forty days granted by bishops to the severwal thousand years sometimes offered by popes. Popes also, on occasion, granted full (plenary) remission of punishment. From 1343, and perhaps earlier, indulgences could also be obtained by the living *for* the dead. An indulgence could be secured in a number of ways. Very often it was purchased with cash, the money then ostensibly being directed to some charitable end. But an even greater, though impossible to calculate, number was obtained through pious acts, including pilgrimage and crusade, prayer, and attendance at mass. Indulgences worked by drawing on the super-abundant merit of Christ and the saints contained in the Church's 'Treasury of Merit'. This storehouse's inexhaustible supply of grace was held in common by the entire mystical Body of Christ, which explains why its benefits could be shared by the living and the dead, since the souls in Purgatory were as much a part of the Church as the living.

Fear of hellfire and the desire to shorten one's time in Purgatory and diminish the pains suffered there were, therefore, chief motivators of the pious activity of the living. Concern for the welfare of the community was, however, of equal importance. Broadly conceived, this community encompassed all the faithful of Christendom. The prayers and other pious works of the Dominican nun of Engelthal in Franconia, Adelheid Langmann (1306–75) were credited with having released 30,000 souls from Purgatory; this impressive feat was dwarfed by another sister of Engelthal, Christina Ebner (1277–1356), who managed to free another 23,710,200![40] In practice, however, rank-and-file Christians lavished their pious attentions on the more restricted community of family, friends and neighbours, a fact nicely expressed in a prayer in the liturgy of the requiem mass: 'for father and mother, for relations and bene-factors, for friends, for male and female neighbours'.[41] Indeed, the living had an obligation to the familiar dead in Purgatory, as Bishop John Fisher of Rochester made clear in a sermon of the early sixteenth century: 'Every one of us hath some of his friends and kinfolk there . . . or some of his alliance . . . to whom he had in this world before some favour and friendship' and to whom we must 'do like friends . . . let us be loving unto them as we pretended love before unto them'.[42] A popular story much used by preachers even recounted how a loving and dutiful son rescued his recently deceased mother from the clutches of the devil, to whom she had sold her soul, by offering a post-mortem confession on her behalf and carrying out a seven-year penance of fasting.[43] Though fantastic, this story expressed a perfectly orthodox position, as stated by the German theologian Gabriel Biel (c. 1420–95):

> The suffrages which are made for the living and the dead can be said to be the works of those for whom they are done. . . . For the work is appropriated to [the recipient] (i) by the intention of him who does it, and (ii) because that which is his who is one with me, is in a certain sense also mine. Whence it is not against divine justice if one man receives the fruits of works done by another who is one with him in charity, particularly when they are done specifically on his behalf.[44]

This is the other reason why surrogate pilgrimages were such a common feature of late medieval devotion. Margery Kempe, for example, financed her pilgrimages largely with donations provided to her by family, friends and other sponsors, on the understanding that she would conduct her pilgrimage in a suitably pious fashion and be sure to pray for them at all the shrines she visited.[45] True to her word, when she visited the shrine of St Francis in the Portiuncula Chapel outside Assisi on the feast of St Peter's Chains, 'when there is great pardon of plenary remission', she made sure 'to purchase grace, mercy, and forgiveness for herself, for all her friends, for all her enemies, and for all the souls in Purgatory'.[46]

The logic of substitution also functioned in another way: in the increasingly common practice of granting indulgences, for a fee, to those who visited surrogate pilgrimage sites, which would temporarily stand in for such major destinations as Rome in a Jubilee year, the Portiuncula Chapel, Jerusalem and Aachen. In the 1390s, Boniface IX extended the Roman Jubilee indulgence to several individuals and institutions, promising those who vis-ited the surrogate sites, 'the indulgence of the Jubilee as if they had come to Rome in the year appointed and visited the basilicas and churches, the toil and cost of the journey being commuted by their confessors into other works of piety'.[47] In 1450 Nicholas V established Glasgow Cathedral as an alternative Roman Jubilee pilgrimage site for all the denizens of Scotland. Each pilgrim was to make a gift to the cathedral of what was calculated to be a quarter of what it would have cost them to journey to Rome; this sum was then evenly divided between the cathedral, the rest of the churches of Scotland, and the papacy.[48]

Complementing this mathematical calculus of exchange in late medieval piety was another, of addition and multiplication. This arithmetic logic was especially applied to the mass and to prayers. The number of masses celebrated multiplied exponentially during the last two centuries of the Middle Ages; so too did the ancillary altars that came to crowd the naves of churches. This was partly a response to the belief in the power of the mass to assist souls in Purgatory. Not only was it commonly held 'that each mass will cause a poor soul to be freed from purgatory and a sinner to repent', but individuals and collective entities such as guilds and confraternities also endowed chantries and chapels, where masses were to be said for the express purpose of easing the passage through Purgatory of the endowed foundations' patrons, families and friends.[49] The arrangements made by the wealthy could be quite elaborate. In 1348 the surgeon Angelo of Arezzo arranged for requiem masses to be said every year in perpetuity for his soul and those of his ancestors on six of the Marian feasts and on the feast of Our Lady of the Snows (5 August), and this was to be done not only at the private altar he had endowed in his own parish church, but also at each of the four mendicant friaries in Arezzo; Archbishop William Courtenay of Canterbury (d. 1396) made arrangements for 15,000 masses for his soul.[50] More commonly the stipulation was for the celebration of a mass on the thirty days following one's death (called a 'trental') and/or a perpetual annual commemorative mass. A closely related phenomenon was the proliferation of special 'votive' masses, designed to aid the sick, avoid sudden death or avert the plague, and dedicated to various cults, like the Name of Jesus, the Five Wounds, Holy Cross, the Crown of Thorns, the Virgin or the Holy Spirit. The repetition of particular votive masses had special significance. So, for example, if one commissioned the celebration of the Name of Jesus mass on thirty consecutive days, one received 3,000 years of pardon for *each* of those thirty masses.[51]

Just as lay demand motivated this proliferation of occasions and kinds of masses, so too did these masses provide multiple opportunities for the laity to benefit from participation. True, few lay people actually took communion more than once or at most three times a year. But each time they attended mass they could *gaze* upon the living Christ in the consecrated host and chalice. The key moment in the mass came at the consecration of the Eucharistic bread and wine, when the priest uttered the words 'For This is My Body' and then elevated the host. Now the priest held God in his hands, and merely by looking upon Him the participants received spiritual benefits. When c. 1393 an elderly bourgeois of Paris wrote a book of instruction, the so-called *Ménagier de Paris*, for his teenage wife, his treatment of how she is supposed to comport herself during mass makes it quite clear that what really counts is seeing the host. After the priest says 'lift up your hearts' and the congregants answer 'we lift them up to the Lord':

> Then we ought to prepare ourselves and have our eyes on the priest. After this are sung the praises of the angels, namely *Sanctus, Sanctus, Sanctus*, at which the angels come down and make ready and surround the table where God will descend and by his look alone feed his friends. And then we hope to see his coming . . . when the king enters his city. We ought lovingly and with great joy of heart to look upon him and receive him, and looking upon him, to be grateful for his coming, and give praise and blessing, and in our hearts and with a low voice beseech to grant us remission and pardon for our past errors.[52]

By the late fourteenth century, prayer books for the laity, also called primers, were full of suggestions for just what sorts of things people were supposed to say in their heart and with a low voice during mass. These 'elevation prayers', which were believed to augment the benefits of gazing upon Christ, invariably began with a greeting followed by a request, and sometimes included a brief statement of doctrine. The most common was the *Ave verum corpus* (mid-1300s):

Hail! true Body,
Of the Virgin Mary born,
Which for humankind did suffer,
And on the cross was sacrificed;
Whose pierced side
Poured out true blood,
Be for us upon the tongue
A foretaste of our death.[53]

Not surprisingly, these prayers usually came replete with indulgences, like the prayer 'Lord Jesus Christ Who This Most Sacred Flesh' with its 2,000 years (or in some versions 10,000 years), the 'Spirit of Christ Sanctify Me' with its 30,000 years, and the plenary remission of 'I Beseech Thee, Dearest Lord Jesus Christ'.[54] Hungry to see repeat performances of Christ descending and to pile up as many indulgences as possible both for themselves and for the dead, mass-goers in towns habitually hurried from altar to altar and from church to church, a practice which prompted the sixteenth-century English Protestant reformer, Thomas Cranmer to ask,

What made the people to run from their seats to the altar, and from altar to altar, and from sacring [i.e. consecration] (as they called it) to sacring, peeping, tooting and gazing at that thing which the priest held up in his hands, if they thought not to honour the thing which they saw?[55]

Prayer too was governed increasingly by the principle of multiplication. A popular series of prayers called the 'Fifteen Os', if recited daily over the course of a year, would rescue fifteen souls from Purgatory, save fifteen relations from being consigned to hell and strengthen the faith of fifteen more.[56] Another, particularly elaborate programme was connected to the 5,490 wounds of Christ:

[T]here were 5,490 wounds on my body; if you wish to venerate them, then repeat the Lord's Prayer fifteen times daily with the English salutation [Hail Mary] in memory of my suffering; after a year has passed you will have saluted each wound reverently.[57]

Such complicated repetitive sequences encouraged the adoption of aids, the most important of which were prayer books and rosaries. The use of these aids served, in turn, to augment the spiritual benefits of prayer. A copy of a prayer in a fifteenth-century book belonging to the Dominican nuns of Strasbourg promised:

Whoever reads the psalter of Our Lady [a series of 150 short prayers to the Virgin] with zeal daily, [gains] 34 years, 30 weeks and 3 days indulgence; and that is 174 years and 80 days for each week; and whoever reads it daily for an entire year has 8,949 years of indulgence.[58]

Such prayers were usually said while counting off the beads on a rosary, which acted as a kind of abacus. The full rosary was a string of 150 beads, each of which was counted while saying a prayer to the Virgin, although other prayers and invocations were also often added. Common was the sequence of 150 Hail Marys, punctuated by an Our Father after every ten beads and a Creed after each fifty, with sometimes the name of Jesus added at the end, for good measure. Frequently the 150 prayers of the Lady Psalter took the place of the Hail Marys, meaning that the person praying did so holding both rosary and book. Almost invariably, indulgences fortified these rosary prayers. One indulgence awarded twenty-four years, thirty weeks and three days for every recitation of the Lady Psalter with beads. Done every day over the course of a year, this sequence gave 9,300 years and 140 days of pardon. One can only wonder how many purgatorial years were erased by the reported 700,000 Hail Marys that the 5,000 members of Cologne cathedral's rosary confraternity were saying every week in 1475.[59] Depending on who had blessed them, some rosaries were better than others. This led to the development of a lively trade in indulged rosaries over the course of the fifteenth century. Prayers said on a rosary obtained from the Carthusians of Coventry secured 700 days of pardon for each *word* of prayer uttered.[60]

Prayer before images also carried hefty indulgences. Especially popular were a number of stereotyped images of the suffering or risen Christ. One, called the 'Veronica', showed the face of Christ suffering on his way to Calvary. Three closely related images, of the Mass of St Gregory, Man of Sorrows and Image of Pity, all showed Christ at the moment of his resurrection, displaying his wounds, still fresh and bleeding in a clear reference to the Real Presence in the Eucharist. Prayers before images of Mary and St Anne also often came freighted with indulgences. All these images were ubiquitous, appearing as panel and wall paintings and as statues and reliefs in churches, and depicted either in prayer books or on printed broadsides. And it mattered not by what medium they were conveyed, as the most humble rendering, like that of the Man of Sorrows 'on a piece of vellum nailed to an oak board', conveyed the same indulgence as the most exquisite altar triptych. Nor did one have to exhaust oneself in prayer to rack up quite impressive tallies of pardon. Simply saying five Our Fathers, five Hail Marys and a Creed before the Image of Pity earned one a remission of 32,750 years. Again with image prayers the logic of multiplication came into play: a 56,000-year pardon for a series of five prayers before the Image of Pity claimed its sum was derived from two 14,000-year indulgences, by Gregory I and Nicholas V, which had then been doubled by Sixtus IV.[61]

It is easy for us today to criticise these pious practices and the motivations behind them. The counting of prayers and multiplication of indulgences seems baldly mechanical and opportunistic, and the use of images naive if not downright idolatrous. Certainly this was the view of the Protestant reformers and even Catholic humanists like Erasmus. Criticism can even be found much earlier, however. In the early fourteenth century, the Dominican mystic Meister Eckhart (c. 1260–1327) said that only by joining one's will to that of God did one earn salvation. All the rest was meaningless and could even get in the way of true spirituality. Regarding the kinds of practices we have just been discussing, Eckhart likened them to the merchant's quest for profit:

> Look, all of these men are merchants who shun gross sins and would like to be good men and perform their good works in honor of God, such as fasting, vigils, praying, and the like, every sort of good work, and yet do it so that our Lord may give them something in return or something that would please them: they are all merchants.[62]

Figure 8.3 Mass of Saint Gregory, by Master of the Lübeck Bible. 83.ML.114, folio 272v.
Image: © The J. Paul Getty Museum

Later both the Lollard and Hussite heretics derided such practices, and even the eminently orthodox theologian Jean Gerson found the arithmetic mentality distasteful.

Yet the fact remains that during the late Middle Ages these critics belonged to a small minority, while the vast majority of Christians were reasonably content with, and more often than not avidly committed to, the status quo. Thus it is incumbent on us to suspend our own disbelief and try to understand the system and its adherents. It is easy to dismiss as illogical the heaping up of pardons on top of pardons, with multiple plenary indulgences being

Figure 8.4 Man of Sorrows, by Hans Memling. Photograph: classicpaintings / Alamy Stock Photo

fortified by tens of thousands if not hundreds of thousands of additional years, especially when we recall that it was commonly assumed at the time that all of world history from the Creation until the end of the world and Last Judgement was only likely to encompass some six thousand years. The practice of accumulation was, however, a reasonable response to the considerable uncertainty surrounding the adequacy of one's own confession and penance. A lifetime provided considerable opportunity for incomplete confessions and overly lenient penances; and at the moment of one's death, there were all those unconfessed sins and unfulfilled penances to think of. Added to this was anxiety over the validity of any given indulgence (people, after all, were quite cognisant of the large number of bogus indulgences in circulation). Moreover, did one ever truly know the mind of God? Better, then, to accept as much ostensible grace as possible, before it was too late.

Other motivations as well inspired Christians to participate in pilgrimages, masses and prayers, to venerate images and to seek indulgences. Love of family and friends and concern for the cohesion and welfare of the community were powerful motivators. Pious practices were demonstrations of affection, but more than that they protected the living members of the community from harm and preserved the memory of the dead; they demonstrated the triumph over suffering and death and the transcendent permanence of the individual and the community, despite the evident changeableness of human affairs and transitory nature of mortal existence. Just as important, however, devotional acts expressed love for God and the saints and the heartfelt desire to imagine, to recall, the suffering of Christ and the compassion of his mother. This goes a long way toward explaining the enormous popularity of blood relic and blood-host sites like Hailes and Wilsnack, and of the images of the Passion and Resurrection. The same mentality inspired the *Obsecro te domina* (1300s), a prayer to 'Mary sweetest virgin, Mother of God and of mercy', commonly found in primers and Books of Hours, which beseeches her aid and intercession:

> [T]hrough that holy, great compassion and that most bitter sorrow in your heart that you had when you saw your Son, our Lord Jesus Christ, nude and lifted up on the cross, hanging crucified, wounded, thirsty but served gall and vinegar, and you heard him cry 'Eli' and you saw him dying; and through the five wounds of your Son and through the collapse of his flesh because of the great pain of his wounds; and through the sorrow that you had when you saw him wounded; and through the fountains of his blood and through all his suffering; and through all the sorrow of your heart and through the fountains of your tears.[63]

In the same manner, people thrilled to stories of bleeding hosts, crowded about to see the elevation of the host at mass and touched the relics of the saints because they were seeking material, physical confirmation of the mysteries of the faith and because they longed for a direct personal contact with the divine. A prayer to be said when taking communion, from an early fifteenth-century primer, implores:

> that when my heart stirs with the sweetness of your blessed presence, there may be complete cleansing of my spiritual languor, there may be washing away of my sins. . . . Let my heart be enflamed with your love. Let my soul taste now how sweet you are, Lord, tasting you so completely that the voluptuousness of the flesh not deceive it. O delectable bread! O sweetest food! O desirable meal! O sweet feast restoring all things, and in you never failing![64]

The culture of affective, empathic spirituality also led to a certain feminisation of sainthood, especially in Italy and with the avid sponsorship of the Franciscan and Dominican Orders. St Clare of Montefalco, a Franciscan nun, devoted her entire being to reproducing 'in her body the principal stages in [Christ's] agony, from the Garden of Olives to Golgotha'. Her repeated assertion that Christ had placed a cross in her heart, inspired the sisters of her convent to take the gruesome initiative just after her death of cutting open her chest, where they found the instruments of the Passion, including the cross, the sponge, the lance, the scourge and the crown of thorns.[65] Events from the life of St Catherine of Siena, a lay woman associated with the Dominicans, reveal the same blend of the visceral and spiritual. In a letter written to her confessor in 1375, she tells of how she came to the spiritual assistance of a young man named Niccolò da Toldi, who had been sentenced to death by execution in Siena:

> I waited for him at the place of execution. . . . Then he arrived like a meek lamb. . . . He knelt down very meekly; I placed his neck [on the block] and bent down and reminded him of the blood of the Lamb. His mouth said nothing but

'Gesiù!' and 'Caterina!' and as he said this, I received his head into my hands, saying, 'I will!' with my eyes fixed on divine Goodness. Then was seen the God-Man as one sees the brilliance of the sun. [His side] was open and received blood into his own blood – received a flame of holy desire . . . into the flame of his own divine charity. After he had received his blood and his desire, [Jesus] received his soul as well and placed it all-mercifully into the open hostelry [i.e. the wound] of his side. . . . With what tenderness and love he awaited that soul when it came to enter into his side bathed in its own blood, which found its worth in the blood of God's Son! . . . Now that he was hidden away where he belonged, my soul rested in peace and quiet in such a fragrance of blood that I couldn't bear to wash away his blood that had splashed on me. Ah, poor wretch that I am, I don't want to say any more. With the greatest envy I remained on earth![66]

A heightened concern about death and dying also seems to have accompanied the strong strain of emotionalism in late medieval spirituality. No doubt the theology of Purgatory had much to do with this, though some historians have also stressed the contributions of repeated visitations of the plague. Several artistic conventions certainly convey this impression. In funerary art, the late fourteenth century witnessed the development of a fashion for cadaver tombs and shroud brasses, and for the more elaborate sepulchres called *transi* tombs, which depict a serene, composed and unblemished effigy of the deceased above and a horrific, rotting, worm-infested corpse below. In the visual arts a common theme was that of the Three Living and the Three Dead, which showed three young aristocrats out on a hunt confronted by their own reanimated corpses. Also popular, in both art and theatre, was the theme of the *Danse Macabre*, in which Death dances with a host of people representing different social groups, from peasants to royalty. Likewise, books on *The Art of Dying Well* were among the most widely disseminated of the late Middle Ages. Compiled at the Council of Constance and based on a treatise by Jean Gerson, *The Art of Dying Well* was a step-by-step (and almost invariably illustrated) guide to making a good death. The key thing was to be prepared:

[E]veryone thinks that he is going to live longer than he does, never believing that he is about to die suddenly – a belief surely inspired by the Devil. Consequently, many people, through such vain hope, have neglected themselves, and so they die unprepared. Thus, one should never give a sick person too much hope that he will regain his physical health. For . . . because of such false consolation and the unrealistic hope of recovery, a man often incurs damnation.[67]

Commenting on the late Middle Ages' preoccupation with death, dying and the afterlife, Johan Huizinga saw only decadence and morbidity:

No other age has so forcefully and continuously impressed the idea of death on the whole population as did the fifteenth century, in which the call of memento mori ["reminder of death"] echoes throughout the whole of life. . . . It seems as if the late medieval mind could see no other aspect of death than that of decay.[68]

While there is evidently some truth in this assessment, recent scholarship has been more sympathetic, stressing, on the one hand, the communal and commemorative aspects of the cult of death, and, on the other, its essentially hopeful and therapeutic function in the face of 'the four apocalyptic horsemen of Famine, War, Plague, and Death'.[69]

Figure 8.5 Transi tomb of John Fitzalan, 17th earl of Arundel. Reproduced with kind permission of the Conway Library, The Courtauld Institute of Art, London

Intolerance of difference

Late medieval Christians' fear of damnation and purgatorial punishment, their emotionally charged focus on the crucified Christ and his dolorous mother, and their earnest striving for community and unity made them very unsympathetic to those who did not share their religion or who they thought threatened the welfare of Christian society. Such thinking had much to do with the rampant anti-Semitism of the period (see also Chapters 1 and 2). Several Corpus Christi and blood-host miracle stories cast the Jews in the role of the villain. Such tales seem to have begun circulating in the 1290s and typically involved a Jew or group of Jews managing through nefarious means to obtain a consecrated host, to then defame Christ and Christians with a statement like 'Aren't the Christians who believe in this host stupid?' and then to torture the host/Body of Christ by cutting it with knives, pounding nails into it and/or throwing it in boiling water. The host in response would, of course, start to bleed, often breaking into three pieces in imitation of the priest breaking the host into three pieces after the elevation; sometimes it also turned into a hunk of bloody flesh.[70]

Sometimes the willingness of Christians to propagate and believe these stories led to tragic consequences. In 1298 rumours of host desecration resulted in the murder of some 3,500 Jews during the Rintfleisch persecutions in Germany; almost twice that number perished there four decades later.[71] In 1421, rumours of an alliance of the Hussites and the Jews led to accusations of host desecration against the Jews of Vienna which resulted in the burning of some 240 members of their community.[72] Another outbreak of similarly inspired persecutions occurred in northern Germany around the turn of the sixteenth century.[73] Over the course of the fifteenth century, the preaching campaigns of the Observant mendicant friars encouraged a related conjunction of anti-Semitism and affective devotion to the Body of Christ, this being accusations of ritual murder of Christian children. Ritual murder accusations had fallen off after the thirteenth century, but they reappeared in southern Germany, starting in the 1430s.

Likely the preaching campaigns of the Observant mendicants had something to do with this. Anti-Semitic sermons were the stock-in-trade of the two earliest firebrands of the Dominican and Franciscan Observants, St Vincent Ferrer (c. 1350–1419) and St Bernardino of Siena (1380–1444). St Vincent preached that 'he will never be a good Christian, who is neighbour to a Jew' and sought to remove the Jews from Christian society, preferably through their conversion; St Bernardino, who labelled the Jews as the 'chief enemies of Christians' also advocated a programme of either conversion or segregation. Neither friar explicitly accused the Jews of ritual child-murder, and yet devotion to each saint helped lend credence to such accusations. Vincent's most remarkable miracle was having restored to life and made whole a small boy who had been butchered by his insane mother. Although the miracle tale itself said nothing of Jews, by the middle of the century, and perhaps aided by the anti-Semitic rants of Observants like John of Capistrano, some artistic representations of the miracle began associating the mother with Judaism and the little boy with the Christ child and Eucharist. During Holy Week of 1475, in the Alpine Italian town of Trent, the murder of a little Christian boy named Simon lit a match to this toxic blend of affective piety and anti-Semitism thereby obliterating the small Jewish community there and inspiring a rash of pogroms and further accusations of Jewish child murder in Germany and Italy. As for Simon, thanks to the efforts of the local bishop, the preaching of the friars and the recently invented printing press, his cult spread like wildfire, leading in short order to over a hundred miracles being credited to him. Enough doubts were expressed by some at the curia to stave off Simon's official canonisation (and in 1965 the Catholic Church categorically denied his eligibility for sainthood). But this did nothing to dampen Simon's popularity, especially in Italy and southern Germany.[74] As for the relationship between Bernardino and Simon, this was pushed by Franciscan Observants like Bernardino da Feltre, who connected his saintly fellow friar (canonised in 1450) with the boy martyr as a way to encourage towns in Italy to shut down Jewish money-lending and instead set up low-interest loan institutions for the poor, the *monti di pietà* (see Chapter 3).[75]

In the eyes of ecclesiastical authorities, heretics, with their divergent doctrines and practices and their denial of the authority of the clergy, threatened the unity and homogeneity of Christendom; princes considered them a threat to public order. Consequently, they were subject to inquisition and persecution at the hands of Church and state. The Cathars and Waldensians, who had suffered so at the hands of ecclesiastical authorities in the thirteenth century, continued to be targeted by ecclesiastical authorities in the fourteenth and fifteenth. In the early fourteenth century, the inquisitors in Languedoc, already busy mopping up the remnants of Catharism and Waldensianism, added the Spiritual Franciscans and their lay Third Order Franciscan followers, commonly referred to as Beguins, to their list of victims.[76] Meanwhile, to the north, communities of beguines (a group totally unrelated to the Beguins of Languedoc) which had flourished in the southern Low Countries and Rhineland Germany during the thirteenth century began to arouse the suspicions of Church authorities at the turn of the fourteenth century. It was feared that these pious women, dedicated to a life of simplicity, work and devotion but neither cloistered nor subject to a monastic rule, were secret followers of the 'heresy of the Free Spirit', a group whose adherents were supposed to believe themselves incapable of sinning. Such anxieties were the product of ecclesiastical authorities' over-active imagination and discomfort with female mystical spirituality, since the Free Spirit movement never really existed.[77] However, in 1310, one of these beguines, Marguerite Porète, was executed in Paris after having been found guilty of preaching this 'heresy' in her *Mirror of Simple Souls*, a mystical tract which advocated a regimen of physical austerity and meditation in order to achieve the soul's union with God. This spiritual union, once established, freed the individual from the need any longer to participate in the sacraments. Much of what Marguerite counselled is found in other perfectly orthodox mystical writings, and it seems likely that she was the victim of the Church's fear of overly independent holy women and of the fraught political environment in France in the later years of Philip IV's reign.[78] Other beguines continued to be investigated throughout the first half of the fourteenth century, leading to the eventual closure of most of their communities.[79]

The teachings of the Oxford theologian John Wyclif (c. 1330–84) presented a more real and serious challenge to the institutional Church. Wyclif placed the authority of the Bible before all else, including that of the pope and Church councils. He also advocated the Bible's translation from Latin into the vernacular, so that lay people might have direct access to the Word of God rather than having to rely solely on what they could glean indirectly through such avenues as works of instruction or the preaching of the clergy. Convinced of the worldliness and corruption of the ecclesiastical hierarchy, he argued in favour of the transfer of ecclesiastical property into the hands of secular rulers. Most radical of all, however, was his denial of the doctrine of transubstantiation, the teaching that the bread and wine of communion physically and essentially changed into the true flesh and blood of Christ at the moment of consecration:

> [T]he feigned miracle of the sacrament of bread induces almost all men to idolatry, for they believe that God's body, that shall never depart from heaven, should, by virtue of the priests' words, be enclosed, in its essence, in a little bit of bread which they show to the people.[80]

Wyclif substituted for this a kind of spiritual infusion of Christ's body and blood into the communion bread and wine and shifted the focus away from the miracle of the host itself to the morally regenerative effect which the communion had on those who partook of it. Wyclif gained some disciples among the student body at Oxford, including John Aston, Philip Repingdon and Nicholas Hereford – his writings also made their way to the Continent and influenced the thought of theologians at the University of Prague, chief among them being Jan Hus.[81] Moreover, his puritanical bent, anticlericalism and privileging of the laity appealed to some in English society, who came to be labelled Lollards by their enemies. Lollardy began to establish itself during the troubled years of Richard II's reign, inspiring at least some of the participants in the Peasants' Revolt of 1381 and being adopted in the 1380s and 1390s by several influential knights associated with the court; but it then retreated in the first decades of the fifteenth century, thanks to the concerted efforts of Archbishop Thomas Arundel of Canterbury (d. 1414) and of the scrupulously orthodox King Henry V, especially after a botched uprising by some Lollards in 1414. The Lollards remained a persecuted minority until the time of the Protestant Reformation, subject to occasional local inquisitions, like that carried out by Bishop William Alnwick of Norwich in 1428–31.[82] Nurtured by very different political and cultural circumstance in Bohemia, Wyclif's legacy had far deeper and more lasting influence, although in the modified form developed by Hus (see Chapter 6).

As anxious as the clergy was to stamp out heresy, though, their fears do not appear to have inspired the same fervour for persecution among the laity. Witches, however, were altogether another matter. Heretics damned themselves to hell but they did not threaten the souls of proper Christians, whereas witches could cast harmful spells and help the devil deceive the faithful. Fear of sorcerers and sorceresses was not new to the late Middle Ages, but there is no doubt that it began to be an obsession starting in the second quarter of the fifteenth century. Although the reasons for this are somewhat obscure, it seems likely that the roots of the witch craze that gripped Europe from the late fifteenth through the seventeenth century were planted by two of the most important movements of the early fifteenth century: Church reform and the Observant friars. In addition to preaching against the Jews, Vincent Ferrer was also among the first pioneers of the witch craze, setting off a spate of witch persecutions in the Dauphiné and western Switzerland.[83] A few years later, during the 1420s, Bernardino of Siena in a series of fiery sermons preached throughout central Italy and Tuscany whipped up enthusiasm for hunting down and burning witches:

> I don't know how better to tell you: To the fire! To the fire! To the fire! *Oimmè!* Do you want to know what happened in Rome when I preached there? If I could only make the same thing happen here in Siena! Oh, let's send to the Lord God some of the same incense here in Siena![84]

Accusing witches of committing atrocities ranging from infanticide to host desecration, he cautioned his audience not to be lenient on witches:

> Do as I say, so that you will not be held to account on the Judgment Day for not preventing so much evil by denouncing it. And I tell you as well, that once a man or a woman is accused [of witchcraft], if anybody goes to give them help, then the curse of God will come upon their house, and they will see its effects in both their body and their possessions, and then, even in their soul.[85]

The Observants were motivated by the same concern as the theologians and canonists of the conciliar movement: the reform of the Church in head and members. Faced with the reality of schism, the rise of the Hussite heresy, and the ongoing devastation of war and plague, many of these reformers increasingly came to see all these ills as manifestations of a diabolical plot. From here it was a small step to seeing the hand of a very real and present Satan and his minions in any and all moral failings and perceived deviations from the faith. All this came to a head during the Council of Basle, which in addition to focusing on bringing the papacy to heel and defeating the Hussites, also acted as a forum for discussions on witchcraft. The description of witches that evolved there borrowed elements from earlier descriptions of heretics, Jews and necromancers, but combined these with clerical suspicion of women and folk-medicine. The fruits of these discussions can be read in two treatises of the 1430s, the *Errores Gazariorum* ('Errors of the Heretics'), by an anonymous clerk, and the *Formicarius* ('Anthill') by Johannes Nider (c. 1380–1438), an erudite Observant Dominican and prior of the Dominican convent in Basle at the time of the council. A half-century after Nider completed the *Formicarius*, two fellow Dominicans, the German inquisitors Heinrich Kramer and Jakob Sprenger published the *Malleus Maleficarum* ('Hammer of Witches', 1486–87), which for the next two centuries became the standard manual for rooting-out, prosecuting and punishing witches.[86]

It was not by chance that the trial and burning of Joan of Arc coincided with the time of the first full formulation of the characteristics of witches. Her accusers and persecutors interpreted her eccentricities as evidence of witchcraft, although in the end it was the charges of heresy that brought her down. Johannes Nider mentioned in the *Formicarius* that Joan was not alone, and that three other cross-dressing sorceresses, Piéronne the Breton, an unnamed woman, and Claudia of Cologne, had been put on trial in France during the 1430s.[87] Joan's case should also remind us that religious conviction was hardly the only motivator of ostensibly religious persecution. Joan's trial was as much about the politics of the Hundred Years War as it was about religion. A decade later, the political ill will between Duke Humphrey of Gloucester and Cardinal Beaufort and his supporters also lay behind the trial and conviction for necromancy of Humphrey's wife, Eleanor Cobham.[88]

Laity, clergy and reformation

As has already been mentioned, trials like those of Marguerite Porète and Joan of Arc demonstrate clerical unease over the growing involvement in religion of the laity in general and of women more particularly. This worry manifested itself in other ways as well. Many Church authorities were uncomfortable about making full translations of the Bible available to an unrestricted lay audience (especially in England, owing to Lollardy), and all sought to exclude the laity from the sort of in-depth speculation and disputation about doctrine which was practised in university faculties of theology.[89] Heightened lay religiosity was, however, precisely the outcome for which the Church had strived, especially since the time of the Fourth Lateran Council and the institution of the orders of friars in the thirteenth century. Virtually all people were served by a parish church and those in towns also developed close ties to the churches of the mendicant friars. They participated in the mass and other religious occasions, and internalised the lessons of the Creed, of sermons, of the confessional, and of religious art. Increasingly literate, the laity consumed works of religious instruction and devotion which clerics and an ever-growing number of lay authors wrote in response to a seemingly inexhaustible demand (see Chapter 10).

Ownership was also expressed in more practical and programmatic ways. Many churches had long had lay patrons who exercised the right of appointment to benefices. The proliferation of chantries and private chapels, most of which were endowed by individual lay patrons or by lay confraternities and guilds exponentially increased the number of clerics in lay employ. Serving two masters, these stipendiary clerks were subject to the ecclesiastical discipline of the local bishop but were in the pay and service of their lay patrons. Countless clerics supplemented their incomes by working as notaries or school tutors, or served the state in the capacity of bureaucratic clerks. In short, most secular clerks had one foot in the Church and the other very much in the lay world.

Lay people, for their part, played an increasingly active role in religious life. More and more of the day-to-day management and upkeep of parish churches was taken over by lay churchwardens. The laity also created and joined all manner of guilds and confraternities. These voluntary organisations took many different forms. Some were affiliated with different trades and thus had more to do with the regulation and sponsorship of business. Most, however, were primarily pious and charitable in orientation. There were parish guilds, civic guilds, guilds of flagellants and a dizzying assortment of confraternities dedicated to the propagation of all kinds of devotional cults: Corpus Christi, the Name of Jesus, the Five Wounds, Our Lady of Pity, St Anne, the Trinity, Holy Cross etc. The city of Florence had some forty-five confraternities and guilds by the 1340s with another fourteen in the surrounding countryside; roughly 150 guilds with a primarily religious orientation operated in late medieval London.[90] The guilds and confraternities maintained chantries and chapels (and paid the wages of their priests), supplied candles and ornaments to their local parishes and other churches with which they were affiliated, organised processions on religious feast days, wrote and staged devotional dramas, and distributed alms. The members of guilds and confraternities also staged a certain number of convivial gatherings every year and maintained a fund to help pay for the burial and requiem masses of their members and provide some death benefits to their widows and children.

The laity was also responsible for the foundation of many of the hospitals and almshouses that proliferated in the last centuries of the Middle Ages (there may have been as many as fifty-eight hospitals in fourteenth-century Florence, for example). These institutions had a charitable function, caring for the sick and disabled, or giving room and board to the poor and displaced, to orphans and the elderly. They also imposed a strict moral code on their inmates, who were also expected to perform devotional exercises for the benefit of their patrons' souls. In some foundations the expectations of the inmates could be quite rigorous. At the almshouse in Ewelme established by Alice Chaucer, duchess of Suffolk, c. 1440, the thirteen inmates (called 'bedesmen') went to the nearby parish church several times a day to recite a total of thirty-nine Our Fathers, 177 Hail Marys and seven Creeds, several of which had to be said around the tomb of Alice's father and mother.[91]

For those called to a religious vocation above and beyond what the parish and guild could provide, the options were no longer restricted to entering the priesthood or joining a religious order. Some opted to lead a solitary life as hermits and anchoresses. Such was the choice of the English mystics Richard Rolle of Hampole (c.1300–49) and Julian of Norwich (c. 1342–after 1413). Others, and mostly women, attached themselves to the mendicant orders as tertiaries, continuing to live in the world but subject to a quasi-monastic rule and the spiritual guidance of the friars. Starting in the late fourteenth century, many women and men in the Low Countries and Germany dedicated themselves to the *Devotio moderna*. In 1380, the founder of the movement, Geert Grote (1340–84), a cleric from Deventer in the Low Countries, began to preach a message of repentance and moral regeneration. He urged his audience to adopt a communal life of material simplicity, prayer and contemplation, inspired by the life of the apostles and early desert monks and by the teachings of the great fourteenth-century mystics Henry Suso (c. 1295–1366) and Jan van Ruysbroeck (1293–1381). Grote died only four years into his preaching mission, but his disciples formed themselves into communities of lay men and women, called the Brethren and Sisters of the Common Life, and into a clerical order of canons, the Windesheim Congregation. The ideals of the *Devotio moderna* found their clearest expression in *The Imitation of Christ*, likely written by one of the Windesheim canons, Thomas à Kempis (c. 1380–1471). Initially greeted with suspicion by civil and ecclesiastical authorities, the adherents of the *Devotio moderna* earned the respect of the former by supporting themselves through useful labour, primarily by making textiles and copying books, and they established a reputation among the latter for impeccable orthodoxy and esteem for the clergy and the sacraments of the Church.

Still, it must be said that the mystical spirituality of the *Devotio moderna* had at its core an overwhelming desire to establish direct contact with Christ and to be Christ-like. Grote said:

I always and nearly everywhere teach that the passion of our Lord Jesus Christ is ever to be before our minds. Reflect upon it as often as possible, for in this way no adversity can strike that will not be borne with an even-tempered soul. Nor should we grasp it in our minds only through meditation but even more through the desire of our affections. By imitating his suffering, abuse, and labors we may come to be configured to Christ in work and in effect. For through desire and affection the mind is moved, as it finds opportunity, toward Christ's crucifixion, suffering, and rejection. And this is the end to which meditation upon Christ's passion is finally and principally directed; remembrance of the passion alone avails little, if it is not accompanied by an overpowering desire to imitate Christ.[92]

Grote's yearning for unmediated contact with the Christ of the Passion was, of course, but one more expression of the intensely affective and dramatic Passion-centred spirituality characteristic of late medieval Christianity. What *The Imitation of Christ*, the mysticism of Marguerite Porète and Julian of Norwich, the Eucharistic visions of St Catherine of Siena, the reformist zeal of the Observants, and the popularity of the feast of Corpus Christi and the pilgrimage to Wilsnack all had in common was:

a wide-sweeping attempt toward the 'normative centering' of theology and piety – 'normative', in that it involved standards, rules, and orientation aids for leading a Christian life; 'centering', in that a reduction of themes and concepts occurred at the pivotal discursive level of what ensured salvation, a reduction that emphasized above all else the Passion of Christ and the co-redeemer Mary, the mercy of God and the repentance of man.[93]

The point about this 'normative centering' which put the individual into direct contact with the redeeming Christ, is that it left the door open to the possibility that the mediation of the ecclesiastical hierarchy was not *essential* to the Christian life and eternal salvation. It was precisely this essentialist way of seeing that prompted Wyclif and the Lollards to put the authority of the Word of God before that of the Church. Just under a century and a half later, Luther came to the same conclusion in his doctrine of 'justification by faith alone'.

Yet Luther's compelling alternative to priest-controlled sacramental religion needed more than a receptive devotional aesthetic to succeed. To take root, it also required a receptive populace, as well as the right network of communications and political environment. It initially found these in his native Germany. Many average Germans shared Luther's sense of alienation from what he believed to be a corrupt and out-of-touch clergy. In 1476, at Niklashausen near Würzburg, a young shepherd named Hans Behem preached to many thousand avid followers the good news he had received from the Virgin Mary. She assured him that he and his fellow peasants and other simple folk were the true body of Christ. As for the clergy, the priests and bishops, the learned theologians, they were greedy and grasping wolves who oppressed their flocks; they were also worthless and ineffectual. Behem recommended their destruction. His violent movement, however, was violently suppressed and he ended his days on the stake. Yet many in late medieval Germany shared Behem's sentiments, if not his bloodthirsty prescriptions. Several decades later, this same sentiment meant both a receptive audience for Luther's teachings and the appropriation of his ideas in the bloody Peasant War of 1525. More broadly, Luther's ideas spread through the media of printed words and images. Printers flocked to his city of Wittenberg, and between 1520 and 1525 they published some 600 editions, almost all them being of Luther's works. Many of those editions were adorned with laudatory images of Luther engraved by the brilliant artist Lucas Cranach.[94] Also, Luther's message of *cuius regio, eius religio* ('whose region, his religion'), which made the local ruler the final authority in matters of religion, encountered a warm reception among some princes and city governments in Germany and in the Swiss Confederation. In the 1530s, the same message offered Henry VIII of England a way out of his marital predicament. That Protestantism quickly ramified into several different 'confessions' (e.g. Lutheran, Calvinist, Anglican) in the three decades after 1517, and that Catholicism continued to thrive is a reminder of the complex and powerful local factors that conditioned religious adherence in the sixteenth century. Catholicism remained genuinely popular in Italy and Spain, as well as in parts of the Empire, for example, whereas in France and England, deep religious divisions made the imposition of uniformity a messy and violent business indeed. And even in those regions where Christianity of the Roman Catholic stamp would continue to hold sway, the real authority in matters of religion rested more with princes than with the pope. Monarchs like Emperor Charles V and King Francis I of France became the new champions of a universal Church which was in fact no longer universal.

Notes

1 Tisser 1960: 40–47 (my translation).
2 Tisser 1960: 65–67 (my translation).
3 Vauchez 1993: 219–29, 258–60.
4 Tisser 1960, 84; Beaune 1991: 127–32, 156–60.
5 Rawcliffe 2003.
6 Vauchez 1993: 264.
7 Moeller 1971: 53.
8 Swanson 1993: 3.
9 Van Engen 1986: 546; Vauchez 1997: 537.
10 Swanson 1995: 8–9.
11 Arnold 2005: 22; Swanson 1995: 9.
12 Rubin 1991: 271–87; Beckwith 1992.
13 Duffy 2005: 28–31.
14 Pfaff 1970; Duffy 2005: 15–22, 48.
15 Swanson 1989: 4–5.
16 Barron 1985; Goodman 2002: 78–81, 137–38.
17 Géraud 1837.
18 Lemarignier, Gaudemet and Mollat 1962: 199–203; Rubin 1991: 164.
19 Dameron 2005: 36–37.
20 Duffy 2005: 155.
21 Shinners 1997: 197.
22 Dameron 2005: 202–5; Vauchez 1997: 239–42.
23 Duffy 2005: 165.
24 Vauchez 1997: 139.
25 Dameron 2005: 1–2; Goodman 2002: 152.
26 Shinners 1997: 463–65.
27 Swanson 1989: 248.
28 Goodman 2002: 155.
29 Duffy 2005: 104.
30 Bynum 2007.
31 Windeatt 2004: 393.
32 Swanson 1995: 165–66; Moeller 1971: 54.

33 Bynum 2007: 30, 291.
34 Duffy 2005: 199.
35 Vauchez 1997: 458.
36 Swanson 1993: 196.
37 Vauchez 1997: 452, 457.
38 Arnold 2005: 2–3, 183–84.
39 Swanson 1994: 168.
40 Lentes 2001: 57.
41 Bossy 1983: 43.
42 Duffy 2005: 349.
43 Duffy 2005: 353.
44 Bossy 1983: 43.
45 Goodman 2002: 164–65.
46 Windeatt 2004: 180–81.
47 Webb 2006: 255–56.
48 Webb 2006: 265.
49 Lentes 2001: 59.
50 Cohn 1992: 207; Swanson 1989: 298.
51 Swanson 2006: 234.
52 Shinners 1997: 252.
53 Blume and Bannister (1915): 257 (my translation).
54 Swanson 2006: 223–26.
55 Duffy 2005: 98.
56 Swanson 2006: 227.
57 Lentes 2001: 59.
58 Lentes 2001: 56.
59 Wunderli 1992: 14.
60 Swanson 2006: 236–38.
61 Swanson 2006: 233.
62 Lentes 2001: 69.
63 Shinners 1997: 142–43.
64 Fassler 2004: 22.
65 Vauchez 1997: 353.
66 Noffke 1988: 109–11.
67 Shinners 1997: 526.
68 Huizinga 1996: 156.
69 Duffy 2005: 301–37; Aberth 2001: 256.
70 Langmuir 1996: 299–300; Rubin 1995.
71 Langmuir 1996: 302.
72 Hsia 1992: 13.
73 Bynum 2007: 68–73.
74 Hsia 1992.
75 Rusconi 2004.
76 Burnham 2008; Lambert 2002: 225–35.
77 Lerner 1972; Lambert 2002: 201–7.
78 Field 2012.
79 Simons 2001: 130–37.
80 Aston 1994: 42.
81 Catto 1992.
82 Tanner 1977.
83 Bailey 2003: 121.
84 Mormando 1999: 52.
85 Mormando 1999: 106.
86 Russell 1972: 228–33.
87 Vauchez 1993: 262–63.
88 Harriss 2005: 609.

89 Hasenohr 1994.
90 Dameron 2005: 52–53; Barron 1985.
91 Richmond 2001.
92 Van Engen 1988: 87–88.
93 Hamm 2004: 21–22.
94 Pettegree 2010: 91–106.

Part IV

CULTURAL CHANGE

9

SCHOOLS, SCHOOLING AND INTELLECTUAL DEVELOPMENTS

> Oh well-counselled people! Oh well-favoured people! I speak to you, Wisdom's dedicated disciples, who, by God's grace, and either good fortune or nature are engaged in investigation of the loftiness of the bright, delightful star, which is to say, knowledge. Partake diligently of this treasure; drink from this secret and healthful spring; fill yourself up on that pleasing meal which can improve and elevate you. For what is more worthy to man than learning and the eminence of knowledge. You who seek after and dedicate yourself to this have chosen a glorious life, by which you can understand the choice of virtue and the shunning of vice, as it encourages the former and forbids the latter. Thus nothing is more perfect than knowing and understanding the truth and clearness of the things which learning teaches. There is therefore no treasure of Fortune's goods that one who has had a taste of this noble learning would prefer to gain in return for the loss of scarcely the smallest of crumbs left by Wisdom. And truly I dare to maintain something that others do not say: there is no joy or treasure comparable to that of understanding. You would thus not wish to spare any labour, you champions of Wisdom, to acquire it. For if you have it and use it properly, you are noble, you are rich, you are all perfect. And this is made clear by all the doctrines of the philosophers who teach and instruct the path to travel by way of Wisdom to the treasure of pure and perfect sufficiency.[1]

Christine de Pizan's lavish praise of 'students, whether at the University of Paris or elsewhere' states a key social value of the late Middle Ages: the importance of knowledge and learning. Similar thoughts are given voice to again and again, from many different quarters. In the *Romance of the Rose* (c. 1275), Jean de Meun tells of the nobility conferred by learning:

> Learned men have a greater opportunity than have princes or kings, who know nothing of what is written, to be noble, courteous, and wise. . . . In short, [the clerk] sees written in books whatever one should flee or follow. Thus all learned men, disciples or masters, are noble or should be.[2]

The foundation charters of universities insisted on their public utility in words akin to these of Pope Clement VII for the University of Erfurt (1379): 'that in this place faith shall be spread, the simple-minded be educated, justice be preserved at court, reason be strengthened, the spirits illuminated, and the minds of men enlightened'.[3] And humanists like Pier Paolo Vergerio and Battista Guarino assured the readers of their educational treatises, *De ingenuis moribus et liberalibus adulescentiae studiis* ('The Character and Studies Befitting a

Free-Born Youth', c. 1402) and *De ordine docendi et studendi* ('A Programme of Teaching and Learning', 1459), that 'parents can provide their children with no more lasting resources, no more dependable protection in life than instruction in honorable arts and liberal education', and 'no possession is more honorable or stable than learning'.[4] The value which fourteenth- through early sixteenth-century Latin Christendom placed on education was also expressed more palpably in the proliferation of schools of many different kinds, catering to the needs of a growing and increasingly diverse clientele.

The spread of education as well as the prestige, and even power, which it imparted to those who mastered the more advanced subjects of the curriculum were the result of several factors. At a practical level, the growth and growing complexity of affairs connected with Church and state, as well as with commerce of all kinds, demanded the services of notaries and clerks to perform contractual and administrative tasks, of surgeons and physicians to heal the sick, of pastors and preachers to care for souls, of theologians to guard the doctrinal purity of the faith, and last, but certainly not least, of lawyers to protect and further the interests of all parties, from popes and emperors down to the most humble of husbandmen. In turn, the more sophisticated practices and messages of institutions raised the overall level of discourse – think, for example, of the sermons of the friars or the references to history and mythology in civic pageants – as well as the extent of literate and numerate ways of doing things. But the growth of education also had an attitudinal and ideological dimension. Thanks to the Church's long dominance, and indeed virtual monopoly over literacy and learning of a bookish kind during the early and High Middle Ages, a close connection had developed between being learned and having privileged access to the holy, as exemplified most concretely in the clergy's command of the Latin liturgy and text of the Bible; so close was this connection, in fact, that the common Old French word for learning was *clergie*. Learning to read then, and especially learning to read Latin, put someone one step closer to God.

Being learned, however, also made one in some way *noble*. This was so in two senses. First, from antiquity the Middle Ages had inherited a respect for the dignity of knowledge for its own sake. Instruction in the liberal arts was also a means to a more virtuous character. Even an elementary knowledge of grammar informed a child's character through the discipline of study and the moral lessons contained in instructional texts. At the more advanced level, we find that by the second half of the thirteenth century the masters of arts at the University of Paris had begun to claim for themselves the title of 'philosopher' with its aura of ancient and quasi-mystical authority. Such assertions of authority were voiced even more strongly by the practitioners of the higher disciplines of law, theology and medicine, on the grounds that 'the mastery of such lofty sciences could not be possessed by unworthy or even merely ordinary men; they naturally ennobled those who had made the effort to complete long and difficult courses of study to acquire the sacred store of knowledge'.[5] Second, the functions performed by the 'nobility' of the learned in the service of Church and state, on account of their intellectual competence gained from long study, was likened to the military service and counsel provided by the nobility of birth. Already in 1299, the Majorcan missionary Ramon Llull likened the professors at Paris to 'knights armed with wisdom and devotion to Christ' and in the fourteenth century holders of degrees in civil law began to refer to themselves as 'knights', and even as 'lords' and 'counts' of law.[6] In the mid-fourteenth century a German student at Paris likened the conferring of degrees to the dubbing of knights and crowning of 'lords of sciences', and his contemporary at Bologna, the law professor, and later cardinal, Simone da Borsano, said the holders of doctorates 'ought to have precedence over knights' and that professors who had taught law for twenty years or more should be considered the peers of counts and dukes.[7] In 1389 the University of Vienna gave public expression to these claims in a statute which assigned places for its members in the city's great Corpus Christi procession. The masters of arts were ranked with the petty nobility, the holders of doctorates in law with the middle nobility, and the theologians with the counts and dukes.[8] Some men of humble origins even managed through the exercise of their learning to join the ranks of the aristocracy or at least to lay the foundation for the ennoblement of their heirs. Such was the story of the Paston family of Norfolk, which managed in three generations to rise to the status of knighthood through the practice of the common law. In late fifteenth-century France a new category of nobility, the *noblesse de robe*, was established to reward educated men, most of them lawyers, who had distinguished themselves for their loyalty and competence in royal service.

Conversely, one of the key reasons for the success of the humanists in the fifteenth century was their ability to convince aristocrats that learning was a desirable, even necessary, adjunct to nobility. Learning thus not only conveyed gentility, it was also, as the humanist architect Leon Battista Alberti (1404–72) asserted, proof of it:

> And who does not know that the first thing useful for children are Latin letters? And this is so important that someone unlettered, however much a gentleman, will be considered nothing but a country bumpkin. . . . If there is anything which goes with gentility or which gives the greatest distinction to human life or adds grace, authority and name to a family, it is surely letters, without which no one can be reputed to possess gentility.[9]

A broadly literate and learned society, the presence of those institutions of learning that give rise to it, the state's patronage of these institutions, and the active and essential part played by educated professionals in the functioning of the state are often considered marks of modernity. Yet these characteristics were already in the process of formation during the last two centuries of the Middle Ages. This chapter will begin by describing the different occasions and institutional settings of education, from the most elementary to the most advanced. It will then turn to a discussion of some of the key intellectual developments, debates and controversies that played themselves out in the universities. Attention will also be given to the new educational and cultural programme of humanism.

Schooling outside school

Much learning, if not most, happens outside school. In the late Middle Ages, just as now, children acquired most of their 'life skills' from imitating their elders and competing with their peers. The daughters and sons of peasants learned by doing chores suitable to their age, in the household and out of doors, and they and their counterparts in towns often continued their practical education in their teens by going into service for a time (see Chapter 2). Trades were taught by apprenticeship, usually beginning in the early teens and lasting for some seven years. When it came to the instruction of the young, the households of princes and nobles functioned in the way of schools. Non-noble children learned all manner of skills working in kitchen, bakery, laundry, larder, cellar and stables, while those of the lesser nobility began to acquaint themselves with their own future of service, as cup-bearers, sewers, henchmen and ladies in waiting. Noble households also educated the sons of the aristocracy in military arts, teaching them to ride, hunt and handle weapons (see Chapter 6), and noble children of both sexes learned to dance, sing and play games. Archery was a noble pastime learned in youth by boys and girls; but what was a game for them was, in England at least, also an essential skill for the sons of commoners, as preparation for service in the companies of archers that fought at Crécy and Agincourt. Finally, noble and non-noble girls alike were expected to learn various skills related to the production of textiles: spinning, needlework, silk work and weaving.[10]

Church too was a kind of school for the laity. Sermons reinforced the basic tenets of the faith (Creed, Ten Commandments, seven sacraments, seven works of mercy) and prescribed a moral code based on avoiding the seven capital vices (pride, wrath, envy, greed, sloth, gluttony and lechery) and practising the seven virtues. The virtues were either grouped according to the scheme of the counteracting 'remedial' virtues (humility, patience, love, poverty/generosity, spiritual zeal, sobriety and chastity) or, more commonly, were a combination of the three 'theological' virtues of faith, hope and charity, and the four 'cardinal' ones of prudence, justice, fortitude and temperance. To help them prepare their sermons, preachers of the late Middle Ages had available for their use a vast array of preaching aids. These included manuals on how to construct and deliver sermons, like the *De modo componendi sermones* ('How to Compose Sermons' c. 1342) by the English Dominican Thomas Waleys and the *Ars praedicandi* ('Art of Preaching') written c. 1372 by the Paris theologian and abbot of Pontigny, Jean de Châlons; collections of model sermons like the *Festial* (c. 1400) of John Mirk; and a plethora of summaries (*summae*) of the virtues and vices, and of alphabetised collections of passages from the Bible and from Christian and pagan authors (*auctoritates*, 'authorities'), of similes drawn from nature (*similitudines*, 'likenesses') and of brief stories meant to illustrate particular points, called *exempla*.[11]

Confession has also been characterised as 'an occasion to send – or return – adults to "school"', since in addition to being a sacrament it was also an opportunity for the priest to instruct the penitent in morals.[12] As was the case with sermons, so too was there a plentiful practical literature on confession. The summaries of virtues and vices, most of them modelled on the *Summa de vitiis et virtutibus* (1249) of the Dominican Guillaume Peyraut, were as useful to the priest in his function as confessor as they were to him as preacher. In addition to these he had recourse to two other sorts of text. First there were the manuals which explained the method of confession, one of the most influential of which was the *Oculus sacerdotis* ('Priest's Eye', 1320s) by the English priest William of Pagula. Then there was the battery of encyclopaedic reference books which treated all conceivable subjects and variables that might have a bearing on the efficacy of any given confession. The *Summa confessorum* (c. 1298) of the Dominican John of Freiburg was the most popular and important of these practical aids, though several members of his order sought to improve upon it during the course of the fourteenth through early fifteenth centuries.[13] Bartolomeo da San Concordio, for example, converted John's topical ordering of contents – sins against God, sins against neighbour, holy orders and the administration of penance, and marriage – into alphabetical order in the *Summa de casibus conscientiae* ('Summary on Cases of Conscience', 1338). Several works on confession which closely followed the format of the manuals for confessors were also written for the laity (Bartolomeo's *Summa*, for example, circulated widely in vernacular form under the title *Pisanella*). What all these works, for priests and penitents, had in common was: (1) a concern for completely and correctly identifying sins; (2) assigning the proper weight to those sins corresponding to the type of sin (mortal or venial), the status of the sinner (according to social rank, occupation, age and sex) and the 'circumstance' of the sin (who, what, where, with what help, why, how and when); (3) and then, on the basis of the preceding factors, assigning a proper penance.

If one might continue the analogy of church and classroom, the sermon performed the function of lecture, the confession that of seminar. In both cases the priest asserted his authority on the grounds of his clerical order, knowledge and wisdom. But if the communication of the sermon was one-way, confession, like the seminar, involved discussion, with the priest frequently having to find ways to elicit the proper responses from the penitent, the penitent crafting answers that were truthful but also perhaps modified to conform to the priest's expectations, and both sizing the other up. Penitents – rather like university students shopping for teachers – sought out the priest they thought made the best confessor, despite diocesan injunctions against making confession to anyone save one's own parish priest. Because the mendicant friars often surpassed their parochial counterparts in the art of confession they tended to lure parishioners away from their local priests, and this became a major contributor to the frequently prickly relations between the friars and the secular clergy. Sometimes, too, penitents proved especially recalcitrant during confession, rather like the student bargaining for a higher mark, prompting the archbishop of Pisa Federigo Visconti (d. 1277) to observe: 'For the sinner says, "I will do all you wish; but I will on no account give up such-and-such a mistress – or usury, or my hatred or envy for such-and-such people."'[14]

Preaching and confession, then, were two of the most important means whereby the priesthood and the Church declared their authority over the laity. The sermons, with their standardised format and contents drawn from a common stock of sources, instructed the faithful in normative Christianity and exhorted them to behave in a certain way. Confession was an even more powerful agent of discipline because as a sacrament it gave the confessor sole power to offer absolution and impose penance, while the counselling offered by priest to penitent inculcated a specific moral code. Because confession had this unique blend of the sacramental, educative and disciplinary, some historians have regarded it as a crucial agent of 'social control . . . predicated on an ecclesiastical authority's theology of law, guilt, and absolution' during which 'the priest-confessor, as teacher, instructs and examines the penitent, to produce in him or her an internalized system of self-regulation'.[15] Others, however, have given greater autonomy to the penitent and stressed a more mutual relationship in which confessor and penitent influenced one another.[16] Both sermon and confession also contributed to the formation of a lay culture of learning which took many of its cues from the clergy but was hardly controlled by it. The pulpit and confessional transferred to their audience, albeit in mediated form, some of the information, habits of thought and methods of discourse of learned clerical culture. In short, the Church did more than indoctrinate its flock, it also educated; but what the flock chose to do with that education did not always conform to the desires or expectations of its pastors.

Primary and secondary schools

Schooling of the more conventional type often began in the home, with a parent, and probably not infrequently the mother, teaching her child the alphabet. Primary schooling was also the responsibility of the parish priest or some other local cleric, who might well have several children under his tutelage at a time, or it might happen in the more formal setting of a 'reading' school under the direction of a reading master or mistress. With the ABC committed to memory the small pupil usually advanced to learning how to pronounce the Latin words of the Our Father, Hail Mary and Creed. The alphabet and these Latin prayers were frequently written on parchment or paper attached to both sides of a wooden tablet, the ancestor of the 'hornbook' of the early modern era. Around 1300 this most elementary material also began to be put at the beginning of prayer books and Books of Hours; this is why in England these books of devotion were commonly referred to as 'primers', i.e. 'first books'. Reading thus began, curiously enough, with sounding out and memorising words in a language one did not understand; it also trained Christian readers invariably to associate the written word with the Latin language and the Christian religion. This relationship of literacy, Latinity and the sacred helps explain why the vernacular was so slow to replace Latin as the language of devotion and learning. Something similar happened in European Jewish education, with children first reciting the Hebrew alphabet and then learning to read Hebrew, beginning around the age of three.

Virtually all Jewish boys in late medieval Europe went on to be fluent readers of Hebrew, as did many Jewish girls. Such was not the case for their Christian counterparts. Many children, especially those of the rural peasantry, never even learned the ABC, and of those who did learn to sound out Latin words and prayers, only a tiny fraction of the girls and a minority of the boys continued their Latin education. This does not mean that all those who stopped their formal Latin schooling at this stage remained functionally illiterate, since many went on to be adept readers of the written word in their mother tongues. They were, however, formally 'illiterate', since to be *litteratus* (fem. *litterata*) in the Middle Ages meant being literate in Latin.

Learning to read and write Latin constituted the next, or 'secondary', level of education. The notable exception to this rule occurred in central and northern Italy, where parents could choose between two tracks of secondary schooling for their sons. Urban merchants more often than not preferred to send their sons to *abbaco* (i.e. abacus) schools in order to have them taught the business skills of arithmetic and bookkeeping; only those boys destined to become priests or notaries, or to study at university went on to learn their Latin at grammar school. In 1338, the historian Giovanni Villani estimated that in Florence: '8,000 to 10,000 boys and girls are learning to read [at the elementary level]. There are 1,000 to 1,200 boys learning abbaco in six schools. And those who study grammar and logic in four large schools are 550 to 600.'[17] What Villani failed to mention were the many sons of Florence's patrician elite who were tutored in Latin at home.

Latin instruction varied from region to region and even from school to school. However, some basic commonalities can be discerned. Normally, the first Latin reader was the 'Donatus', a text based in part on the *Ars minor* ('Lesser Art') of Aelius Donatus, a Roman grammarian who lived c. AD 400. The pupil learned the contents of 'Donatus' by rote, then set about actually understanding what it had to say about the basic noun declensions and verb conjugations. This accomplished, one moved on to a series of texts, eventually called the *Auctores octo* ('Eight Authors'), whose canon varied with place and time but which almost invariably began with a collection of brief maxims in verse called the *Disticha Catonis*. Ascribed to the great Roman statesman and orator Cato the Censor (234–149 BC) but in fact a compilation dating to late antiquity and the early Middle Ages, the verses of the *Disticha Catonis* were also, like 'Donatus', committed to memory. Teacher and students then submitted the language in the sayings to grammatical analysis while simultaneously discussing their moral import, especially in so far as they provided instruction in the four cardinal virtues; the same mix of Latin and moral instruction was applied to other texts in the *Auctores octo*.[18] Eventually, pupils advanced to the more complex material of the *Doctrinale* (c. 1200) of Alexandre de Villedieu and Évrard de Béthune's *Graecismus* (1212), as well as a sampling of such classics as Virgil's *Aeneid*, *Eclogues* and *Georgics*, the *Ars amatoria* and *Metamorphoses* of Ovid, and Boethius's *Consolation of Philosophy*. Advanced students might even get an introduction to logic and some mathematics, and to the *ars dictaminis*, that is the art of writing official letters and documents in Latin.[19]

Responding to the needs of their students and to current fashions, late medieval grammar masters also tried their hand at composing textbooks and books of exercises. During the fifteenth century the Italian humanists Agostino Dati and Niccolò Perotti wrote grammars, and at Exeter High School the grammar master John Boryngton penned a collection of Latin exercises, which required pupils to translate the Latin of such moral precepts as, 'I have been accepted among men of honor and virtue, which accords well with my character, being that of a benign, humble, and well mannered young man', as well as passages that reveal the brutal realities of grammar instruction:

> I have acquired three hard beatings on the buttocks this cold morning to warm me before I get completely cold, hoping that a gracious fortune will strike me on this day: it is a good omen to receive at the beginning of my labor, which may God perfect and finish![20]

Schoolmasters did not only beat schoolboys to assert their authority; the rod, it was generally assumed, disciplined the body and improved memory. Good behaviour as well as parts of speech, declensions, conjugations and rules of style were literally beaten into boys' bodies and brains. In 1348, immediately after the first onslaught of the Black Death, the city council of Lucca looked forward to the services of a salaried grammar teacher, under whose 'rod boys might achieve the glory of learning'.[21] Such practice, however, did not sit well with at least one fourteenth-century 'expert' on pedagogy, a certain 'Guillaume' who in the course of translating Giles of Rome's *De regimine principum* into French (c. 1330) sympathised with parents' worries that their young boys might be beaten savagely and 'in dangerous places like around the temples and on top of the head' by evil-tempered or alcoholic schoolmasters. Besides, children learnt far better when treated kindly:

> for I have seen in my own time a nine-year-old child named Alexius who was from the city of Bergamo in Lombardy . . . who never was beaten nor had to cover his head, who learned his grammar completely and his syllogisms excellently and the algorism perfectly as far as the tenth place, for he had been duly and kindly instructed without any coercion having been applied if he did not immediately start learning something.[22]

Guillaume also sheds light on another aspect of grammar instruction: regional differences in the use of the vernacular for teaching Latin. In fourteenth-century northern France boys were commonly forbidden to speak French while learning Latin.[23] Guillaume remarks that in England, on the contrary, boys were instructed in both French and Latin. There, of course, French was, like Latin, a second language that had to be learned through schooling. It was also, like Latin, a language of official culture in England. After the middle of the fourteenth century, however, the medium of Latin instruction in England shifted to English.[24] During the course of the fifteenth century in France several Latin-French glossaries and dictionaries appeared, suggesting that the vulgar tongue was becoming the preferred medium for teaching Latin there as well.[25] Italy followed a similar trend.[26]

Despite the intrusion of the vernacular into Latin instruction, however, the elites and those who wished to join them in late medieval society continued to believe that learning Latin grammar was both desirable and valuable. Their stubborn adherence to a secondary curriculum whose sole purpose was mastering a 'dead' language may appear wrong-headed or, at the very least, overly conservative to us today; but such an assessment misses the multi-layered utility of such an education. First, grammar instruction gave pupils mastery over a fixed, rule-governed written language with a standardised orthography, lexicon, grammatical structure and style. In 1300 no European vernacular could lay claim to this and it was only thanks to the influence of Latin on the vernaculars that they gradually acquired these characteristics over the course of the late thirteenth through early sixteenth centuries. Thus the grammar schools taught a common, international, written code. Second, grammar schools laid bare to pupils the structure and function of language. In other words, they taught the principle that language could be analysed; that it was a subject of intellectual inquiry. It was this very consciousness, in fact, that made possible the development of standardised written vernaculars. Third, grammar schools introduced their students to a certain kind of discipline that was at once an interior habit of thought and an exterior comportment. The product of a grammar school education thought and acted in distinctive ways: his education made him a kind of clerk, whether or not he was destined for holy orders. A retentive, well-ordered and accessible memory was among the most important disciplines acquired in grammar school.[27] Another was a strong moral character, although then, as now, one suspects such an outcome was hardly guaranteed. Finally, the grammar school was a necessary step on the ladder to higher education and the professions.

Two trends stand out in the history of primary and secondary education in late medieval Europe: the first is that the number of schools grew considerably; the second is that they ramified in kind. Both trends originated in the thirteenth century but accelerated during the fourteenth through early sixteenth centuries. In the diocese of York, the number of confirmed or probable grammar schools grew from thirteen before 1300, to fifteen by 1350, nineteen by 1400, twenty by 1450, twenty-five by 1500, and sixty-eight by 1548; a similar trend is observable for the rest of England as well.[28] Genoa's guild of grammar teachers had thirteen members c. 1300 and twenty-two c. 1500. The number of grammar teachers paid by the city of Bologna held relatively steady at about four from 1384 to 1439; by the early 1480s the number had risen to eight, then to twelve by the end of that decade and then to fifteen by 1500.[29] Indeed, if the appointment of salaried elementary, grammar and *abbaco* teachers by communes is anything to go by, schools multiplied throughout central and northern Italy during the late Middle Ages.[30] Demand for teachers grew so much that many smaller communes had to offer higher salaries to attract qualified teachers and were often still unsuccessful; meanwhile high demand in larger, wealthier towns like Ferrara (in 1443) encouraged unqualified teachers to set up shop:

Our citizens desire to instruct their sons and their adolescents in good letters, and they are sunk in I know not what pit from which they can never extricate themselves. That is, certain barbarous teachers – who, far from knowing, never even saw any good literature – have invaded our city, opened schools, and professed grammar. Citizens ignorant of these men's ignorance entrust their sons to them to be educated. They want them to learn and to graduate learned, but they learn those things which later they must unlearn. Lest this calamity and pest progress further, [the governing board of the Twelve Wise] decree that no one take scholars to train, nor hold a school, unless first he shall have demonstrated that he is acquainted with good literature or has been approved by the board . . . as suited to open a school.[31]

Although it is likely that not all regions of Europe were as blessed with new schools as were England and Italy, and that urban centres were better served than rural areas, the overall trend seems likely to have been one of growth. Here it should be recalled that the proliferation of schools began during a time of demographic decline and stagnation.

The late Middle Ages also witnessed the development of new kinds of school as well as innovations in funding, regulation and curriculum. Traditionally, primary and secondary schooling had been the province of cathedral and collegiate churches, monasteries, parish priests and private tutors supported by pupils' fees. Some locales in southern Europe first began to move beyond this system in the second half of the thirteenth century with the founding of schools that were at once secular and state-funded. The *abbaco* schools of the Tuscan communes were all about training boys to be businessmen, and primary and grammar education also came to be dominated by laymen, first in Italy and later in southern France. State-supported teaching was also an innovation of the Italian communes, beginning in university towns in the second half of the thirteenth century and spreading to nearly all municipalities over the course of the next two centuries. The practice also spread to several towns in southern France. Thus in many locales of southern Europe teachers became, in effect, servants of the state and, as a consequence, subject to government regulation and control. The next step was to abolish all student fees for the sons of citizens, something done in several Italian communes over the course of the fifteenth century. Not surprisingly, the practice of civic education encouraged the view that schools contributed to the welfare and defence of the state. This idea, first pithily expressed in Francesco Petrarca's (Petrarch) letter to a Florentine grammar teacher in 1352, 'You teach children; you perform a task for the state', reached its full development in the official statement of the commune of Treviso in 1524: 'Nothing so ennobles and exalts a city as the study of good letters, which make men learned and wise, honorable to their city, useful to the republic, and capable of every civic enterprise.'[32]

Northern Europe never adopted the practice of state-funded education. There primary and secondary schooling maintained closer ties with the Church and grammar instruction continued to be carried out in cathedrals, monasteries and parishes. This by no means ruled out innovations in response to increasing demand for educational opportunities, however. There a new kind of institution emerged, the endowed school. Endowed schools were founded and funded by pious bequests and donations, offered for the good of one's soul. Support of education, then, answered to the same spiritual need (and, in many cases, to the same desire to display one's wealth and power of patronage) as the endowment of chantries, chapels, hospitals, almshouses and orphanages. In England, where the practice has been studied with particular thoroughness, some 114 schools were endowed between 1382 and 1530.[33] These schools fell into two categories, the larger collegiate type and the smaller chantry version. The first of the new schools was of the large variety, the creation of William Wykeham, bishop of Winchester, who endowed a combined collegiate chapel and grammar school in his cathedral city to complement his recent university college foundation at Oxford, New College (1379). The second, founded in 1384 by Lady Katherine Berkeley at Wotton-under-Edge in Gloucestershire, was a small chantry school. There the endowment supported two poor pupils and a schoolmaster who was to teach grammar to the pupils and anyone else who desired instruction. The schoolmaster also had to be a priest since his other obligation was to celebrate a daily mass at Wotton parish church for the souls of Lady Katherine and her relations. For the next several decades the foundation of endowed schools continued at a slow pace, but then accelerated after, and under the influence of, Henry VI's creation of Eton College in the 1440s.

The sentiment behind the foundation of these schools appears to have been more universal and ecclesiastical than that which prompted the creation of municipal schools in Italy. In his foundation charter for Winchester College, Wykeham said 'by the knowledge of letters justice is cultivated and the prosperity of the human condition is increased'.[34] Just over half a century later, a priest named William Bingham beseeched Henry VI to support the foundation of a college at Cambridge for the training of grammar masters in order to strengthen 'the clergy of this your realm' which according to Bingham was 'impaired and enfeebled by the defect and lack of schoolmasters of grammar'.[35]

A strong religious and devotional impulse also inspired adherents of the *Devotio moderna* to create grammar schools in association with some communities of the Brethren of the Common Life and the canons of Windesheim. In keeping with the ideals of the movement, the curriculum combined grammar and logic with prayer and Bible reading. Several of these schools came into being in the course of the fifteenth century, first at Deventer and Zwolle in the Low Countries and then throughout the lands of the dukes of Burgundy. Near the end of the century one of the Brethren, Jan Standonck brought the curriculum to Paris when he reformed the Collège de Montaigu. These schools encouraged both a commitment to spiritual renewal and a respect for textual purity, as evidenced by the careers of three of their most famous former pupils, the ecclesiastical reformer and cardinal Nicholas of Cusa (1401–64), and the great humanists Rudolf Agricola (1444–85) and Desiderius Erasmus (1467–1536). They were also the first schools to develop a system of progressive class levels in which the prescribed material became increasingly difficult the further along a pupil advanced.[36] Another religious movement, that of the Observants, had a notably salutary effect on education in the convents of Dominican nuns in German lands. The convent schools aimed at teaching their charges so well that they were not only able to read Latin texts but also to write it and even translate from Latin into the vernacular. One nun, Sister Regula of Lichtenthal (d. 1478) wrote of having translated a work called *The Life of Jesus* 'from the Latin of the Holy Gospel into German in the briefest form, out of affection and love for those who are not educated to understand Latin and therefore are sometimes frustrated when they have too much to read'. Another nun, of Ebstorf, discussed her education (c. 1490):

> [Our teacher] explained to us declination, the 'Donatus', and the 'glossed Donatus' word for word completely. . . . And she proposes soon to explain to us the first part of Alexander [de Villa Dei, *Doctrinale*]. . . . She makes every effort toward the goal that we may properly understand the declination of words, cases, and tenses.

She also urged her sisters to 'with all vigor apply ourselves to the study of grammar until we have arrived at the knowledge of rightly reading, understanding and composing prose or verse.'[37]

Probably the most important innovations in the theory and practice of pedagogy, however, were those introduced by the Italian humanists. Nonetheless humanism's influence on the teaching of grammar at the primary level was virtually non-existent, and at the secondary level was slow to penetrate. Even in such centres of Quatrocento humanism as Florence and Padua, traditional texts of the reading list, from 'Donatus' through the *Doctrinale* and *Graecismus*, continued to command the field. Likewise, the earliest 'humanist' grammar textbook, the *Regulae grammaticales* ('Grammatical Rules', 1418) of Guarino da Verona, looked much like its medieval predecessors and made no substantive changes to the method of instruction. Gradually, however, humanist influence began to make itself felt. Initially there was the insertion of more works of classical authorship into the advanced secondary curriculum: first Seneca's *Tragedies*, and Cicero's *De amicitia* ('On Friendship') and *De officiis*, and by the middle of the fifteenth century Cicero's *Orator* and *De oratore*. Then, in the last third of the century, grammar textbooks stressing rules and usage based on the writings of classical authors, like Niccolò Perotti's *Rudimenta grammaticales* (1468), Agostino Dati's *Elegantiolae* (1471) and Giovanni Sulpizio's *Opus grammaticum* (c. 1475) began to circulate in manuscript and print, first in Italy and, by the end of the century, in northern Europe, including England.[38] At this time, too, grammar schools devoted to the humanist curriculum began to be established, like Magdalen College School, Oxford (founded 1480). By 1520, grammar schools all over Europe were teaching a purified, classical Latin.

Higher education

When applied to the realities of the time, the term 'higher education' is a bit problematic since it implies, inaccurately, a clear categorical distinction between schooling at the secondary and higher levels where one often did not exist, and some sort of formal equivalency between the different kinds of more advanced schooling, when in fact those relationships were only casual. These caveats borne in mind, however, 'higher education' seems as apt a generic label as any since it has the advantage of being vague enough to encompass the several kinds of places that offered learning above the grammar school level in the late Middle Ages. These included not only universities but also university colleges, places of advanced

Table 9.1 Universities active in 1300

Salerno* (before 1200; not officially recognised as *studium generale* until 1592)
Bologna (late 1100s)
Paris (c. 1200)
Oxford (c. 1200)
Montpellier (c. 1200)
Cambridge (1209–25)
Salamanca (before 1218–19)
Padua (1222)
Naples (1224)
Vercelli (1228; disappeared by mid-14th cent.)
Toulouse (1229)
Orléans (c. 1235; not officially recognised as *studium generale* until 1306)
Studium of the Roman curia (1245)
Siena (1246; imperially chartered 1357)
Angers (c. 1250; not officially recognised as *studium generale* until 1337)
Valladolid (end of 13th cent.; not officially recognised as *studium generale* until 1346)
Lisbon-Coimbra (1290)

Sources: Verger 1992: 62–5; Grendler 2002; Rashdall 1936.

*University status not established before 1500.

professional training like the 'business schools' of Oxford or the Inns of Court and Inns of Chancery in London, the schools of the mendicant friars and the academies of the humanists.

Like schools at the primary and secondary levels, places of higher education proliferated, diversified and innovated between 1300 and the early 1500s. The most visible evidence of these trends is the multiplication of universities, from seventeen active in 1300 (if one counts Salerno, Orléans, Siena, Angers and Valladolid), to almost forty in 1400, to nearly seventy in 1500 (see Tables 9.1 and 9.2; it should be noted that foundation dates sometimes preceded the initiation of instruction by many years). In Germany, where the increase was most dramatic in the late fourteenth and fifteenth centuries, the annual enrolment of students grew from roughly 300 per year in 1385, to some 3,000 per year a century later. Other signs of growth are the addition of faculties, especially of theology, at several already established universities, beginning in the 1360s, and the swelling enrolment of students at some of the oldest and most prestigious universities. In England, the student population of Oxford seems to have remained relatively constant at about 1,100 students enrolled per year between 1300 and 1380, despite the ravages of plague, and then to have grown to around 1,500 between 1380 and 1399. The growth trend continued up to the middle of the fifteenth century, when some 2,000 students seem to have been enrolled.[39] At Cambridge the student population seems to have doubled in the fifteenth century from about 700 to roughly 1,400. During the fourteenth and early fifteenth century Paris held its own at around 4,000 in the face of war and demographic decline; by the 1480s the number of students had more than trebled, even with increasing competition from new universities.[40]

Table 9.2 University foundations, 1300–1500

Lérida (1300)
Avignon (1303)
Rome* (1303)
Perugia (1308)
Treviso (1318; disappeared by 1407)
Cahors (1332)
Grenoble (1339; disappeared mid-14th cent.)
Verona (?) (1339; university status doubtful, disappeared 15th cent.)
Pisa (1343)
Prague (1347)
Florence (1349; most of the university transferred to Pisa in 1472/3)
Perpignan (1350)
Cividale (?) (1353; granted imperial charter, but no evidence of studies ever being initiated)
Huesca (1354)
Pavia (1361)
Cracow (1364)
Orange (1365)
Vienna (1365)
Pécs (1367; disappeared after 1376)
Lucca (?) (1369; university status doubtful)
Erfurt (1379)
Heidelberg (1385)
Cologne (1388)
Buda (1395; disappeared c. 1460)
Ferrara (1391; little activity until after the university's re-foundation in 1442)
Würzburg (1402; disappeared after 1413)
Turin (1404)

Leipzig (1409)
Aix-en-Provence (1409)
St Andrews (1411)
Parma (?) (1412; claimed to be a university during 1410s)
Rostock (1419)
Dôle (1422)
Louvain (1425)
Poitiers (1431)
Caen (1432)
Bordeaux (1441)
Catania (1444)
Gerona (?) (1446; royally chartered but no papal recognition until 16th cent.)
Barcelona (1450)
Glasgow (1451)
Valence (1452)
Trier (1454)
Greifswald (1456)
Freiburg-im-Breisgau (1457)
Basle (1459)
Ingolstadt (1459)
Nantes (1460)
Bourges (1464)
Pozsony (1465; disappeared end of 15th cent.)
Venice (?) (1470; college of physicians only authorised to grant degrees)
Genoa** (founded 1471; opened 1513)
Saragossa (1474)
Copenhagen (1475)
Mainz (1476)
Tübingen (1476)
Uppsala (1477)
Palma, Majorca (1483)
Sigüenza (1489)
Aberdeen (1495)
Frankfurt-am-Oder** (founded 1498; opened in 1506)
Alcalá (1499)
Valencia (1500)
Universities in *italics* no longer active in 1500.
(?) University status unclear or doubtful.

Sources: Verger 1992: 62–5; Grendler 2002; Rashdall 1936.

*Foundation of *studium urbis*; the papacy had conferred degrees through the curia since 1245.

**Foundation before 1500 but not active until after 1500.

The proliferation and expansion of universities was the result of growing demand for the benefits they bestowed upon those who studied there and for the services they provided to Church, polities and localities. Although intellectual curiosity no doubt motivated a minority to pursue higher learning, most primarily saw it as a way to get ahead. Degrees conferred status and graduates, especially those from the higher faculties, had marketable knowledge and skills. But even those who never completed their degree requirements – and they seem to have constituted a substantial majority of those who matriculated – often could put what they had learned to advantage. Moreover, relationships formed with friends, colleagues and patrons proved useful in later life. For those of the clerical estate this might mean the acquisition of benefices and perhaps even prelacies; others moved into lucrative careers as lawyers, notaries and physicians, and both clerics and laymen often filled posts within the bureaucracies of Church and state. Interestingly, very few of these 'men of learning', as they have been aptly called, planned on a career as professional teachers.[41] Teaching at university was, rather, an obligation that went along with study for the higher degrees; life-long professors like Jean Buridan in the arts faculty at Paris or the Oxford theologian John Wyclif were a rarity (though they became more common from the late fourteenth century) and arts graduates consigned to a lifetime of grammar teaching tended to be looked upon as unfortunate, or worse yet, as failures.

By 1300 the university had become a fixture of European society. Many, indeed, had come to see the universities as a 'third power', the *Studium*, which stood between but also supported the powers of Church (*Sacerdotium*) and State (*Regnum*).[42] The universities, and especially the oldest and most prestigious of them, were also thought to fulfil a universalising mission. Thus the civilians and canonists of the law faculty at Bologna were credited with defending the unity of both the Roman Empire and Roman Catholic Church, and the theologians of Paris and Oxford with guarding the purity of the Christian faith. The universities' universality also came from them sharing enough institutional characteristics in common to be seen thereby as belonging to a single generic category. To begin with, each university had been recognised by a legitimate public authority as a place of advanced teaching and learning which had a reputation that extended beyond, and drew teachers and students from beyond, its locality: the Latin term for this was *studium generale*. Next, students who matriculated at a *studium generale* followed a prescribed curriculum (in arts, medicine, civil or canon law, or theology) that culminated, for those who stayed the course, with a set of exams followed by the granting of a degree. The degree guaranteed that its recipient was competent to teach his subject at any university in Christendom. This right, called the *ius ubique docendi* ('the right to teach anywhere'), was conferred by the papacy. Finally, a university was a sworn association of voluntary members who collectively constituted a fictive legal person – a *universitas* – in other words an autonomous, self-regulating entity, recognised by law as being deathless and possessing an identity separate from the membership of its individual members. The word *universitas* was also applied to guilds and business corporations, however, and thus the more specific terms *universitas scholarium* ('university of students'), *universitas magistrorum et scholarium* (university of masters and students') or, simply, *studium* were those most commonly used in the Middle Ages to designate what we now call 'university'.

Beyond these basic similarities, however, diversity was the rule. In terms of organisation and the main concentration of studies, Bologna and Paris provided two very different archetypes of university, which most other universities resembled to a lesser or greater degree. The 'university' at Bologna was really a federation of three *universitates* of students, those of law students from Italy and from outside Italy, and of students of arts and medicine. Within each university the students were grouped into several 'nations' corresponding roughly to their members' geographic origins. The professors too had their own collective bodies, the 'colleges' of doctors of law and of doctors of arts and medicine. In the late twelfth through mid-thirteenth centuries the students ran the university, since they not only governed themselves through elected rectors and councillors, but also determined the material to be taught and had the power to appoint, discipline and set the salaries of professors. After this, however, the colleges of doctors gained more control over academic affairs, including the curriculum, arrangement of courses and degree requirements. Bologna's communal government began to encroach upon the power of the students as well, first taking over the right to pay lecturers

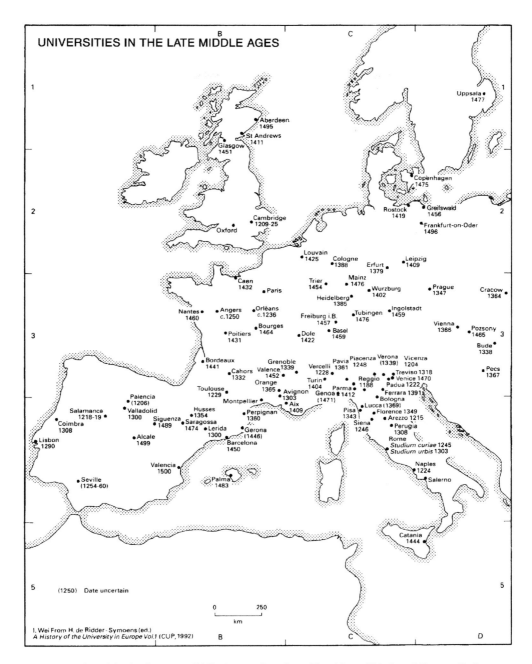

UNIVERSITIES IN THE LATE MIDDLE AGES

Uppsala 1477

Aberdeen 1495
St Andrews 1411
Glasgow 1451

Copenhagen 1475
Rostock 1419
Greifswald 1456
Frankfurt-on-Oder 1496

Cambridge 1209-25
Oxford

Louvain 1425
Cologne 1388
Erfurt 1379
Leipzig 1409

Caen 1432
Paris
Trier 1454
Mainz 1476
Wurzburg 1402
Prague 1347
Cracow 1364

Heidelberg 1385
Nantes 1460
Angers c.1250
Orléans c.1236
Freiburg i.B. 1457
Tubingen 1476
Ingolstadt 1459
Vienna 1366
Pozsony 1465

Bourges 1464
Poitiers 1431
Dole 1422
Basel 1459
Bude 1338

Bordeaux 1441
Cahors 1332
Grenoble 1339
Valence 1452
Vercelli 1228
Pavia 1361
Piacenza 1248
Verona (1339)
Vicenza 1204
Treviso 1318
Pecs 1367

Toulouse 1229
Orange 1365
Turin 1404
Reggio 1188
Venice 1470
Padua 1222

Palencia (1206)
Montpellier
Avignon 1303
Aix 1409
Genoa 1412
Parma
(1471)
Ferrara 1391
Bologna

Valladolid 1300
Husses 1354
Perpignan 1360
Lucca (1369)
Florence 1349
Salamanca 1218-19
Siguenza 1489
Saragossa 1474
Lerida 1300
Gerona (1446)
Pisa 1343
Arezzo 1215
Perugia 1308
Coimbra 1308
Alcale 1499
Barcelona 1450
Siena 1246
Rome
Studium curiae 1245
Studium urbis 1303
Lisbon 1290

Valencia 1500
Naples 1224
Salerno

Seville (1254-60)
Palma 1483

Catania 1444

(1250) Date uncertain

0   250
km

I. Wei From H. de Ridder - Symoens (ed.)
A History of the University in Europe Vol.1 (CUP, 1992)

Map 9.1 Universities in the Late Middle Ages, taken from *The Atlas of Medieval Europe*, 2nd
Edition, © 2007, Routledge. Reproduced by permission of Taylor & Francis books UK

and then, after 1350, appointing them. Throughout the Middle Ages, however, Bologna retained its essentially lay and civic character. In keeping with its origins, law was Bologna's main focus of study, with medicine being the next most important discipline. Theology was not a university discipline at all until its institution by papal bull in 1360, and even then the college of theology doctors remained jurisdictionally separate from the rest of the university, with most of the teaching being left to the mendicant convents. As for arts subjects, these had a strictly subordinate status, being studied primarily in association with medicine and, in a limited way, as preparation for legal studies.[43]

In contrast with Bologna, the University of Paris had a distinctly ecclesiastical character and was dominated by the faculties of arts and theology. Paris too, though, was a product of its origins, it being the descendant of the schools of theology, logic and grammar that sprang up in the twelfth century on the Île-de-la-Cité under the jurisdiction of the chancellor of the cathedral of Notre Dame, and on the Left Bank thanks to the fame of teachers like Peter Abelard (d. 1142/44) and Hugh of Saint-Victor (d. 1141). The clerical status of masters and students resulted from their efforts to obtain immunity from municipal jurisdiction. As for the university itself, a long-running conflict between the chancellor and the masters during the late twelfth and early thirteenth century compelled the latter to form a *universitas*, which in 1231 gained papal recognition. Because the great majority of masters and students (something like two-thirds) belonged to the four 'nations' of the arts faculty, the arts masters were the predominant power at Paris and their elected rector was the chief representative of the university. This did not mean, however, that the masters of the higher faculties of theology, canon law (Paris had no faculty of civil law) and medicine had no power, since the deans of each faculty also had representation on the university's general council. Of the higher faculties theology reigned supreme, owing to its well-earned and long-standing reputation for excellence and orthodoxy. By 1300 a good bit of that reputation rested on the brilliant contributions of mendicant theologians like the Dominicans Albert the Great (d. 1280) and Thomas Aquinas (d. 1274), the Franciscans Alexander of Hales (d. 1245) and Bonaventure (d. 1274), and the Augustinian Giles of Rome (d. 1316). Somewhat ironically, had the thirteenth-century masters of arts and the secular masters of theology had their way, the mendicants would never have been allowed to teach at Paris; their presence there was the result of a combination of heavy-handed papal interference and academic compromise.[44]

As a general rule, the universities of northern Europe conformed more closely to the Parisian archetype whereas those of Mediterranean Europe looked more like Bologna. Nonetheless no two universities were identical. Although Oxford and Cambridge were similar in many ways to Paris, unlike Paris both taught civil law. The University of Montpellier for all its commonalities with Bologna was a medical school first and foremost, while Orléans and Angers taught only law prior to the fifteenth century. The only function of the Universities of Naples and of the Roman curia was to train specialists to serve their respective royal and papal masters, and students at the Scottish universities of St Andrews, Glasgow and Aberdeen could only complete an arts course.[45] It is also the case that prior to the mid-1300s only Paris, Oxford and Cambridge (and in a much more limited way Naples and the Roman curia) boasted a theological faculty. Then theological faculties proliferated owing to the pressure exerted by princes and by the papacy's own discomfort with Paris's virtual monopoly over theology and the subsequent taint of Wyclifism in Christendom's second most prestigious theology faculty at Oxford.[46]

Broad similarity punctuated by local diversity also characterised the method, content and structure of teaching and learning at the universities. At its most basic, a university education was designed to instil a distinct way of thinking about the world derived from a discrete body of written (and mostly ancient) texts referred to as the 'authorities' (*auctoritates*), and to develop a ready ability to organise, manipulate, interrogate and communicate ideas in a rational, systematic way: an outlook and approach to knowledge commonly referred to as 'scholasticism'. The foundation of higher education was the seven liberal arts as taught in the faculty of arts. Students preparing for the first degree of bachelor of arts spent most of their time attending lectures on the first three liberal arts of grammar, logic and rhetoric, known as the *Trivium*; of these, logic (also called 'dialectic'), as contained in the so-called Old and New Logic of Aristotle, received the most attention by far. They would also be exposed to the *Quadrivium* of arithmetic, music, geometry and astronomy. The other subjects of the arts curriculum belonged to the 'three philosophies' – natural, moral and metaphysical – which appear to have been reserved mostly for bachelors fulfilling the requirements for the master of arts. Here again Aristotle was the chief authority. The most important distinction between the course of studies of undergraduates and bachelors was not what they read but rather what they *did*: the former were only expected to study, the latter to study *and* assist with teaching, in the manner of an apprentice. Those who successfully completed this second stage were then examined by a committee of the faculty and by whatever external authority oversaw the university (whether cathedral chancellor, local ruler or some municipal committee). Assuming a candidate passed over these hurdles, he then 'incepted' into the faculty, thereby becoming a 'master' (*magister artium*) and received a teaching licence (*licentia ubique docendi*). Now he was obligated to teach for some length of time, usually two years. In universities of the northern variety the whole process, from matriculation to conclusion of teaching stint took from seven to ten years.[47] Universities of the southern type had a more streamlined curriculum, since there the whole goal was to move students quickly into the medical and law courses.

The mainstay of power in both the ecclesiastical and secular sphere, law was correspondingly the most popular destination of those students who decided to pursue studies in one of the three higher faculties. Most universities had law faculties, and some, like Montpellier, Angers and Orléans in France, Salamanca in Castile, Perugia, Pavia and Padua in Italy, and Prague, Vienna, Heidelberg and Cologne in the Empire, attracted students from beyond their own regions. Nonetheless, Bologna, the earliest centre of legal studies in Latin Christendom, continued to dominate the field throughout the Middle Ages. At Bologna and the other Italian universities, most of the students were not in clerical orders and dedicated themselves primarily to the study of civil law. These 'civilians' focused attention on the great body of Roman law compiled under the emperor Justinian in the sixth century, entitled the *Corpus iuris civilis*, and the later addendum of constitutions of the German emperors, called the *Libri feudorum*. Outside Italy, however, most of the law students were clerics who concentrated on canon law. Here the chief textual authorities were the *Decretum*, a summary of conciliar and papal decrees compiled by the monk Gratian in the middle of the twelfth century, and several subsequent collections of 'Decretals' issued by various popes of the thirteenth and early fourteenth century. Both collections came equipped with extensive glosses and commentary, all of which gave the masters of civil and canon law plenty of material to lecture upon and ample opportunity for forming the contrary opinions which fuelled university disputations and arguments in the law courts. After four or five years of study, a student lectured for a year as a bachelor and then was eligible for examination and the licence. An interesting feature of legal studies is that whichever kind of law a student chose to specialise in, he would also be expected to familiarise himself with the other form, since many of the underlying principles and most of the terminology and methods of civil and canon law were related.[48]

More often than not people in the Middle Ages sought their medical cures from sources other than university-trained physicians. The consecrated host and the shrines of saints promised healing to the sick, and herbalists, surgeons, midwives and medics without degrees (including highly skilled Jewish physicians) all provided services that promised as much success as those of their more learned competitors. It comes as no surprise then, that faculties of medicine attracted the smallest number of students. Nonetheless those who did obtain the doctorate in medicine were highly sought-after experts and became increasingly so over the course of the late Middle Ages. Owing in part to the relatively small number of students attracted to the discipline, the faculties of only four universities, Bologna, Padua, Montpellier and Paris, stood out as superior and produced the lion's share of graduates and medical treatises. More than any other men of learning, the university-trained physicians had to prove their worth and set themselves apart from their non-academic competitors. They did this by creating a kind of medical practice guided by the rational scientific principles of Aristotelian logic and natural philosophy combined with the superior knowledge of the ancient Greek authorities Hippocrates and Galen and the great Muslim physicians Avicenna, Al-Razi and Haly Abbas. The strong Aristotelian component of their discipline explains the very close ties between the study of arts and medicine, as exemplified in the combined faculties of arts and medicine at both Bologna and Padua. Medical students attended lectures running between five and eight years, depending on the university, that treated both the theory and practice of medicine. But what really set the candidate for the licence in medicine apart from his colleagues in the other higher disciplines is that prior to receiving his degree he also had to spend about a year as an apprentice practitioner actually treating patients.[49]

Theology may have attracted fewer students than law and its graduates may not have achieved as much worldly success and wealth as the lawyers and physicians; yet, because it delved into the truths of sacred Scripture and the mysteries of the faith, theology of all the disciplines was accorded the greatest respect and created the most controversy. Throughout the fourteenth century academic theology was virtually synonymous with the faculty at Paris, although Oxford, which at times could claim the more innovative minds, was a close competitor. Despite this monopoly being brought to an end by the proliferation of theology faculties in the late fourteenth and fifteenth centuries, the scheme of theological instruction and the schools of thought established at Paris and Oxford set the pattern of theological study throughout the remainder of the Middle Ages. Unlike in the higher faculties of civil law and medicine, where secular clerks and laymen predominated, in the faculties of theology laymen were absent and seculars had to share the stage with a large contingent of mendicants as well as many members of the monastic orders. On the one hand this created the conditions for lively debate and innovation; on the other, it left the door open to rivalry between seculars and mendicants and between members of the different orders – rivalry which at times turned quite bitter. Theologians also had to be on their guard against interference from ecclesiastical authorities since their pursuit of certain lines of inquiry and the application of the logical and philosophical tools they had learned while studying the arts could look from the outside like dabbling in dangerous error or even advocating heresy.

The theology curriculum rested on two core texts, the first being the Bible, with the great mass of commentary that had accreted to it over the centuries. The second authority was the *Sentences* of the twelfth-century Paris theologian Peter Lombard. Respectively treating in its four books the topics of God, creation, Christ and the sacraments, the *Sentences* takes up one proposition after another in the form of questions, and lines up authorities which appear to argue for or against the proposition, the goal being for the reader to resolve the dispute. Over time the *Sentences* gathered its own freight of weighty commentary. The course in theology was divided into three lengthy parts. In the first students attended five to seven years of lectures on the Bible and *Sentences*. Next the student gave cursory lectures on the Bible and then moved on to more analytical lectures on the same topic while simultaneously participating in disputations as a 'bachelor of the Bible'. After some three years of this the bachelor was ready to give a series of lectures, over the span of about a year, on the *Sentences* (at Oxford students first lectured on the *Sentences* then on the Bible). Having successfully completed this he became a *baccalarius formatus* (something akin to today's junior lecturer), who for between three and four years lectured, disputed and delivered sermons. Finally after nearly a decade and a half of training the bachelor, who had to have attained at least the clerical order of deacon, was admitted into the guild of masters and received the licence.[50]

In all faculties and at all levels, then, students were habituated to a highly technical, Latinate, philosophy-based and heavily Aristotelian 'scholastic' body of knowledge whose principal modes of communication in the classroom were the lecture (*lectio*) and the disputed question (*quaestio disputata*). Lectures were of two kinds, the 'ordinary' lecture, delivered by a member of the faculty licensed to teach (i.e. a master) on the core texts of the curriculum, and the 'extraordinary' lecture, given by either a master or his bachelor assistant on a text of secondary importance. Ordinary lectures consisted of a summary of the main divisions of a text, followed by reading the text, sentence by sentence, each sentence being commented upon as need be, after which the master returned to what he thought was notable in the text and discussed any questions he or the students might have. Extraordinary lectures, on the contrary, treated texts in a more cursory fashion (which accounts for why they also went by the name of 'cursory' lectures). Adjuncts to the lecture were: the *dictatio*, when a bachelor read a full or abbreviated text to students outside normal lecture hours so that they might take detailed notes; the *repetitio* (sometimes also called a *collatio*), which was a kind of evening tutorial; and the *reportatio*, a written transcript of a master's course of lectures distributed for copying. Lectures fulfilled several functions. In a manuscript culture marked by a relatively constrained access to the written word, lectures communicated to students in a memorable way the material contained in authoritative texts; the master's comments facilitated the comprehension of difficult and confusing material while giving him room to add his own thoughts; in theological studies, in particular, the lecture was also a means of imposing doctrinal orthodoxy; finally, the raising of questions, by both master and students, helped introduce students to the other chief method of teaching, the disputation.

Disputed questions were also of two kinds. The first took their cue from topics currently being treated in ordinary lectures and as such were invariably devoted to subjects chosen by the masters. The others, called *quaestiones quodlibetales* (from *quodlibet*, 'whatsoever you please') were on any topic whatsoever and could be proposed by any member of the university community. Because the topics of quodlibets usually reflect the 'hot-button' issues of the time, both within the faculties and in society at large, they are an invaluable source to historians studying intellectual culture. As weighty and important as many quodlibetal questions were, however, it is also the case that there were those who could not resist the urge to propose rude or silly topics, prompting, for example, the dean of arts at Heidelberg in 1518 to forbid bringing forward 'shameful, lascivious and impudent' questions, 'which by their allurements may attract or provoke the religious and innocent youth ignorant of sexual matters, or any others, to unseemly or illicit lust'.[51]

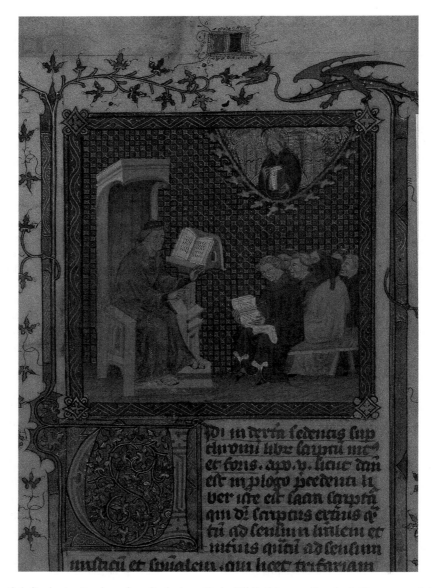

Figure 9.1 Students attend a university lecture. Paris, Bibliothèque nationale de France, ms. lat. 14247, fol. 2r

Underlying all the oral give-and-take of the university classroom was an enormous and ever-expanding body of written texts. Lectures were, after all, oral 'readings' (*lectiones*) of written authorities which had to be consulted by masters and students alike. Lectures and disputations were themselves often recorded by skilled note-takers so that they could circulate in the written form of the *reportatio*, and bachelors and masters were in the habit of composing more formal commentaries, some of which attained an authoritative status of their own. Getting access to these texts and being able quickly to find what one needed and to make sense of abstruse concepts written in highly technical Latin stimulated a number of ingenious responses. One was the compilation of study aids, many of which had originally been developed by the friars during the thirteenth century to assist them in their pastoral duties. Long works were abridged (*compendia*) and passages from many different authorities were gathered together into collections known as *florilegia* ('picked flowers'); one of the most popular of these *florilegia* was the *Parvi flores* ('Little Flowers', c. 1300) of the Montpellier Franciscan Johannes de Fonte, a collection of passages from the works of Aristotle and other ancient authorities. Other handy tools like alphabetical indexes, tables of contents (sometimes arranged schematically to facilitate memorisation), and lists of subjects called variously *notabilia*, *propositiones*, *sententiae* or *conclusiones* also facilitated teaching and learning.[52].

The heavy demand for books meant that the major university towns supported a lively industry of commercial book production. Booksellers (*librarii*) sold new books made to order. During the late thirteenth and early fourteenth-century at Paris, Oxford and Bologna, specially licensed booksellers, called stationers (*stationarii*), developed an ingenious way to make accurate exemplars of texts available at once for copying to multiple academic buyers. The stationers divided sought-after texts into a number of booklets (usually consisting of eight leaves), which were called *peciae*, 'pieces'. These were then rented out separately, so that professional copyists working for as many buyers, potentially, as there were booklets could reproduce the text. Because new manuscript books were such an expensive commodity, however, there was also a thriving second-hand trade. Used books could either be bought from booksellers or obtained from 'loan chests' – essentially pawn brokers who provided loans to strapped students and masters in return for their books. Many books also found their way into institutional libraries. Although the first university libraries came into being during the late Middle Ages – Oxford's was founded in 1412 – they were not to flourish until the modern era. Far better equipped were the libraries of mendicant convents and monastic houses, whose members' books were held in common, and of the growing number of university colleges enriched by the pious donations of fellows' books. Finally many students simply borrowed books and copied what they needed from them, writing in the highly current and abbreviated script that so frustrates modern-day researchers.[53]

An assortment of higher professional schools grew up in connection with the universities as well as independently of them. University colleges, the first of which were founded in the later thirteenth century, proliferated in the fourteenth and fifteenth. Like endowed grammar schools, the colleges were pious charitable foundations with an educational function. Between 1300 and 1500, forty-nine colleges were founded in Paris, twenty-one at Oxford and Cambridge (as well as one at each of the three fifteenth-century Scottish universities), thirty-six in Italy, and twenty-seven in the German Empire.[54] Although most medieval university colleges never amounted to anything more than places of residence with some tutorial functions, many others, like the Sorbonne (founded 1257) and Collège de Navarre (1304) in Paris, Oxford's All Souls (1438) and Magdalen (1448), and the Spanish College (1367) in Bologna, became renowned and prestigious centres of learning in their own right, building up substantial libraries and attracting many of the best and brightest. Some offered their own selection of lecture courses (a practice which was the norm at Oxford and Cambridge colleges) and a few colleges, like the Sorbonne and Magdalen College, eventually provided what amounted to full courses, especially in arts. The colleges were of great importance in the development of universities, creating relatively stable communities of scholars with a shared identity, living according to statutory rules and funded by endowed fellowships for masters and scholarships for students.

Individual monasteries, like the cathedral priories of Durham and Canterbury, also established residential colleges at university, as did consortia of several monasteries. Far more important for the intellectual life of the universities, however, were the schools (*studia generalia*) set up by the mendicant orders to house friars studying for advanced degrees, especially in theology. These schools were themselves only the most advanced of whole networks of provincial mendicant *studia* teaching everything from arts to pastoral theology. Several university towns also were home to professional 'business' schools teaching the arts of letter-writing (*ars dictaminis*) and the drafting of legal documents (*ars notaria*). Oxford was an important centre for this in England as were Bologna and Padua in Italy. In the fifteenth century, Venice too established schools at the Rialto and San Marco to train its young patricians for state service. And because both England and northern France were governed by customary rather than Roman law, legal and professional schools separate from the universities came into being at the Inns of Court and Chancery in London and in association with the *Parlement* and *chancellerie* of Paris. Even some cathedrals continued to play a role in the professional education of their diocesan clergy by giving lectures on theology on a regular, if rather limited, basis. The flourishing of so many and varied institutions of higher learning bears eloquent testimony to the phenomenal growth of demand for educated professionals during what used to be called the 'waning' of the Middle Ages.

Intellectual developments

Research over the last few decades has entirely discredited the old characterisation of late medieval scholasticism as the sterile and decadent interlude between the brilliance of the thirteenth-century Thomistic synthesis of faith and reason and the flowering of Renaissance humanism. Despite the strictures imposed on scholastic thought by conservative adherence to a relatively stable body of textual authorities, scholars of the fourteenth and early fifteenth centuries continued to innovate, to engage in creative reassessments of their predecessors' ideas, and to contribute and respond to developments outside the precincts of the schools. And although trends within late medieval scholasticism and forces both within and without the universities diminished their intellectual vitality and freedom as the fifteenth century wore on, the universities and the kind of education they offered continued to be valued commodities. Likewise their curriculum remained open to innovation, adopting, for example, some aspects of the humanist programme.

Although the universities had something of the ivory tower about them, they and their members were nonetheless engaged with the larger world. Located in the heart of cities and lacking any sort of campus, universities were wholly integrated into urban life. Masters, because they tended to move out of and into the university milieu throughout their lives, also acted as conduits between the classroom and the world. In Chapters 4, 5 and 7 we saw how men of learning contributed to political theory and ideology, government administration and Church reform; their role as translators of learned works for lay audiences will be discussed in Chapter 10. Theologians brought their experience as preachers and confessors, missionaries and inquisitors to their teaching. After the first onslaught of the Black Death professors of medicine composed plague tracts, drawing on what they had learned treating patients. It has even plausibly been argued that arts masters' contact with money and the marketplace inspired 'the shift toward quantification, geometric representation, multiplication, relativity, probability, mechanistic order, and dynamic equilibrium'[55] that occurred in the teaching of natural philosophy at Oxford and Paris during the fourteenth century. As responsible for administration as they were for teaching, the teaching masters had to assess, collect and keep up with the accounting of many and varied kinds and amounts of student fees while also having to go into the marketplace and deal with merchants, money-lenders and bankers.[56] The intellectual habits nurtured by these activities stimulated novel approaches to the physics of horizontal and vertical motion, thereby enabling Thomas Bradwardine (d. 1349) at Oxford and Jean Buridan (d. after 1358) and Nicole Oresme (d. 1382) at Paris to improve drastically upon Aristotle's explanations.

The most important and persistent issues with which late medieval scholasticism grappled were those having to do with the limits of human knowledge, on the one hand, and the freedom of divine and human will, on the other. These problems were the legacy of efforts in the thirteenth century to make sense of the great flood of new Latin translations of Greek and Arabic philosophical writings. Awestruck by the intellectual prowess and complex architecture of knowledge they found in the works of Aristotle, Avicenna and Averroës, the arts masters Siger of Brabant (d. 1284) and Boethius of Dacia (fl. 1270s) confidently asserted the philosopher's ability to access all truth and to know the causes and ends of all things, *without* the aid of divine revelation. Also impressed but more circumspect were the Dominicans Albert the Great and Thomas Aquinas who sought to harmonise the teachings of the philosophers with the truths of Christian doctrine. The first approach had the serious drawback of advocating many propositions that were profoundly un-Christian, some of the most troubling being the eternality of the world, the impossibility of there being a void, a universe ruled by determinism, and the existence of a universal soul as opposed to individual souls. As for the second approach, its attempt to explain divine mysteries in a way that accorded with logic and human reason ran afoul of the traditional Augustinian strain in theology, derived from the writings of St Augustine of Hippo (d. 430), that stressed the limits of human knowledge and the infinite power, incomprehensible mind and unconstrained will of God.

Faced with such incompatible strains of thought, the Franciscan John Duns Scotus (d. 1308), who studied at both Oxford and Paris, argued that human knowledge of God cannot approach God's knowledge of Himself but that human will can be perfected by God's grace since it participates in God's perfect will. Scotus also disagreed with Aristotle and Aquinas on the relationship between the intellect and the will, saying that the will alone directed one to do what was good in accordance with God's commandments, rather than that the intellect directed the will to act in accordance with human nature, leading as a consequence to good actions. Scotus's younger confrere William of Ockham (d. 1347/9) attacked the problem of human knowledge differently. He rejected the commonly held philosophical position of 'realism', which posited that individual things sharing some perceivable likeness with one another, say for example two chairs, are conceived by the intellect as chairs because they are singular expressions of an eternal transcendent 'universal' entity, 'The Chair'. He substituted for this a 'nominalist' epistemology that severed any 'real', essential connection between individual things. For him instead the commonalities we see between things are simply a result of our mind's attempt to make sense of the world by grouping things together based on similar characteristics and assigning names (*nomina*) to them. Thus the concepts in our minds are either instrumental, conventional 'signs' we use to make sense of what would otherwise be a chaotic plurality of things, or they are divine truths revealed to us by God through faith. It follows from this that the human intellect cannot use reason to prove either the existence of God or the validity of Christian doctrine. Scotus's voluntarism and Ockham's nominalism were to have important implications for the future of scholastic theology, encouraging the gradual abandonment of Aristotelian rational speculation and much greater emphasis on either moral and pastoral or mystical theology.[57] Nominalism also became a school of thought, called the *via moderna* ('new way'), taking its place beside and in competition with the realist *via antiqua* ('old way'), which was itself divided into Thomist and Scotist factions.

Disturbed by the efforts of some scholars, most notably Adam Wodeham (d. 1358) and Jean de Mirecourt (fl. 1340s), to assign an autonomous role to human free will in meriting salvation, the Augustinian friar Gregory of Rimini (d. 1358) and the Oxford theologian Thomas Bradwardine denied any role whatsoever to human volition, instead assigning all power of salvation to an infinitely gracious God who had predestined all souls to either salvation or damnation. In the same vein, John Wyclif (d. 1384) railed against the institutional Church's possession of property on the grounds that because only those living in a state of grace could lawfully have dominion over property, the Church, being mired in sin, had forfeited that privilege. He also said that the only source of authority in the Christian religion was the Word of Scripture, since neither the earthly Church nor human reason possessed full and immediate authority in matters of religion.

There is some truth to the old characterisation of Renaissance humanism as an intellectual movement independent of and antithetical to the universities. Although scholars are mostly in agreement that its origins can be traced to the university town of Padua at the turn of the thirteenth and fourteenth century, where the lawyers Lovato dei Lovati (1241–1309) and Albertino Mussato (1261–1329) penned an especially classical form of Latin verse, it was not until well into the fifteenth century that the humanist educational program began being adopted at the universities. Instead, following a humanist course of studies was throughout the remainder of the fourteenth century a matter of individual motivation and effort by the likes of the Avignon clerk and notary of Florentine parentage Petrarch (1304–74) and the Florentine chancellor Coluccio Salutati (1331–1406). Only in the early 1400s were the first humanist 'schools' – these being really more along the lines of private tutorials for the sons (and a few daughters) of the well-born – which Vittorino da Feltre (1378–1446) offered at Mantua, and Guarino da Verona (1374–1460) at Venice, Verona, Florence and Ferrara. Likewise, Petrarch, who was the first self-conscious promoter of humanism (which was then called the *studia humanitatis*), conceived of his cultural and educational program as something new and in contradistinction to that of the universities. Petrarch's principal aim was to resurrect ancient Roman virtue, especially in his native Italy, and thus banish the 'dark age' in which he thought Christendom had been trapped since the fall of Rome. Achieving this would first require rejecting the 'barbarous' Latin of the universities, and replacing it with the elegant Latinity of classical Rome, as exemplified in the orations and letters of Cicero. Secondly, he espoused a course of studies that favoured the study of poetry, rhetoric, history and moral philosophy as found in the literature of Roman antiquity, rather than the arid dialectic and Aristotelianism of the university's arts course, and its vocationally directed legal and medical studies. As for the pointless metaphysical speculations of its theologians, one should reject them and turn instead to the teachings of the early Church Fathers, chief among them St Augustine.

Petrarch and his humanist acolytes lavished scorn on both university learning and on the intellectual achievements of the several centuries that had intervened between antiquity and their own present day (what in the fifteenth century the humanists started calling the 'Middle Ages'). Pretty typical are the following disparaging comments. In his imagined dialogue with St Augustine in the *Secretum* (c. 1350), Petrarch has Augustine blurt out, 'Against this breed of men [i.e. university educated scholastics], with their cultivated ignorance and useless curiosity, it is good to protest, "why do you labor endlessly for nothing, you miserable creatures; why exercise your mind on inane subtleties?'[58] Some seventy-five years later, in his treatise on education (*De studiis et litteris*) for Lady Battista Malatesta di Montefeltro, Leonardo Bruni writes that when he speaks of 'learning', he does 'not mean that confused and vulgar sort such as is possessed by those who nowadays profess theology [i.e. scholastics], but a legitimate and literary kind'.[59] As for the state of learning before humanism, Lorenzo Valla wrote in 1444:

> But when I wish to say more, sorrow hinders and torments me, and forces me to weep as I contemplate the state which eloquence had once attained [in antiquity] and the condition into which it has now fallen. . . . Indeed, for many centuries not only has no one spoken in the Latin manner, but no one who has read Latin has understood it.[60]

Fortunately, in very recent times the liberal and other arts have been restored, so that 'as wretched as were those former times in which no learned man was found, so much the more this our age should be congratulated'![61]

This theme of the death and resurrection of learning became a trope for the humanists. 'It was shameful how little the men of Ferrara knew of letters before the arrival of Guarino' said Ludovico Carbone in praise of his recently deceased former teacher.[62] According to Matteo Palmieri, in his *Della vita civile* ('On the Civil Life', c. 1435), prior to the new learning:

> Of letters and liberal studies at large it were best to be silent altogether. For these, the real guides to distinction in all the arts, the solid foundation of all civilization, have been lost to mankind for 800 years and more. It is but in our own day that men dare boast that they see the dawn of better things.[63]

Writing in 1492, the German Johannes Sanstritter expressed hope that learning, which now flourished in Italy, would soon come to his native land: 'But even in Italy proper Latin was once forgotten . . . and I hope that it will not be long before eloquence, the queen of all things, will attain perfection in our own country as well'.[64] Of course these statements are more expressions of an ideology than descriptions of a true state of affairs. Several aspects of this ideology stand out. The first is that education is more a matter of style than substance: the principal practical aim of a humanist education was 'for the student to read and write classical Latin like a "native"'.[65] Secondly, the learning conveyed by humanism was not only far superior to that of the 'scholastics', but it was also the only one that conferred true nobility and virtue. As Carbone put it, 'No one was considered noble, no one as leading a blameless life, unless he had followed Guarino's courses'.[66] And thirdly, as Sanstritter makes clear, the cultural resurrection of Roman antiquity was a particularly *Italian* affair. The barbarians had not only destroyed the glory that was Rome, they had also imported their barbaric 'Gothic' culture and scholastic learning. Now the Italians, true inheritors of Rome, were ready to tame that barbarism.

Although the humanists certainly exaggerated the superiority of their brand of learning, humanism's intellectual achievements were considerable. Their immersion in the language, literature and culture (including material culture) of antiquity made them far more sensitive to nuances of usage and meaning in their sources, while their imitation of ancient language and culture paradoxically enhanced their awareness of its difference from their own. Also the humanists' recovered a treasure trove of ancient texts which had lain hidden and forgotten for centuries in monastic and cathedral libraries: works like Cicero's oration *Pro Archia*, found by Petrarch, or Poggio Bracciolini's discovery of Lucretius' long poetic rendering of Epicurean philosophy, *De rerum natura*. They thus vastly expanded what had long been essentially a fixed and limited canon of Roman literature. And, finally, that same love of antiquity and appetite for a neglected cultural legacy inspired the humanists' programme of Greek language learning (see Chapter 10) and the subsequent recovery of works like Ptolemy's *Geographia* and Plato's *Republic*.

At the institutional level, humanist antipathy for the teaching and curriculum of the universities led, on the one hand, to the creation of a new kind of educational setting, the humanist academy. Among the earliest and most famous of these academies were those established by Marsilio Ficino (1433–99) in Florence, Giovanni Pontano (1426–1503) in Naples and Pomponio Leto (1425–98) in Rome. The academies substituted public readings of literature followed by amicable conversation among their members for the authoritative lectures and combative disputations of the university classroom.[67] It is also the case, however, that during the fifteenth century many universities, especially in Italy, grafted courses in the *studia humanitatis* onto their arts curriculum and that there was no shortage of university men open to humanistic studies or of humanists teaching in universities. For example, Gasparino Barzizza (1360–1431) lectured on Ciceronian rhetoric and moral philosophy at Pavia and Padua and Francesco Filelfo (1398–1481) taught rhetoric and poetry at Florence. Outside Italy, the University of Cracow became a major centre of humanistic studies during the fifteenth century, and it was in part due to the arts education he received there in 1491–95 that Nicholas Copernicus went on to challenge the Aristotelian geocentric model of the cosmos.[68] Humanism's influence even began to be felt at such venerable institutions as the University of Oxford and its colleges, which were the recipients of substantial gifts of humanist books from such influential patrons as Humphrey of Gloucester and alumni like William Gray (d. 1478), bishop of Ely, Robert Flemmyng (d. 1483), and James Goldwell (d. 1499), bishop of Norwich. Another bishop, Richard Fox of Winchester, founded Oxford's first humanist college at Oxford, Corpus Christi, in 1517. But just as the universities were not nearly so resistant to the humanist programme as one might assume, given the anti-scholastic diatribes of some humanists, so too could humanists at times express admiration for the teaching methods of scholasticism, as when Coluccio Salutati lauded the scholastic practice of disputation:

> For what is there, by the immortal gods, that is of more avail in learning and discussing subtle matters than disputation, in which man's eyes view from all directions the subject placed in the midst, as it were, so that there is nothing in it that can be camouflaged or hidden or that escapes the gaze of all? What is there that more refreshes and restores the mind, tired and exhausted . . . from long sittings and close reading, than discussions carried on in assembly and company, where you are strongly incited to reading or learning either by glory, if you have overcome the others, or by shame if you have been defeated? What is there that sharpens the ingenuity more . . . than disputation. . . . Nay more, how it polishes our speech, how it trains us in extemporaneous utterance. . . . For you can see this in many persons, who, although they profess that they know literature and read books, nevertheless, because they have abstained from this exercise, are not able to talk Latin except with their books.[69]

Conclusion: universities and external authorities

When viewed as a whole the story of education in the late Middle Ages is one of expansion and innovation, and of creative responses to contemporary needs. But alongside this narrative of success there is, in the case of the universities, another, less upbeat tale of fragmented authority and the abdication of autonomy and liberty. Despite their claims to independence and academic freedom, universities were founded, supported, and protected by ecclesiastical and secular political authorities. This was mostly to the benefit of universities and scholars, of course, since it was thanks to the patronage of Church and state that universities spread throughout Europe, and that scholars funded their long years of study and masters made a living, whether from benefices or salaries. Also, had it not been for the intervention of princes and municipal governments, the universities would have been much slower to accept the new humanist curriculum which injected new life into higher studies during the fifteenth and sixteenth centuries.[70]

A price had to be paid for this generosity, however. The proliferation of universities deprived the law faculty at Bologna and even more the arts and theology faculties at Paris of their near universal magisterium. Paris in the early fourteenth century could with some justification claim to be the third power in Christendom. It attracted talented minds from all Latin Christendom and its theology faculty had such great authority that it was able in the 1330s to force the imperious Pope John XXII to admit the error of his teaching on the Beatific Vision.[71] As the century wore on, however, its fruitful connections with England and the German lands were severed, first by the Hundred Years War and then by the Great Schism, an event which also stimulated the creation of new German universities. Its prestige sunk yet further when it sided with the Anglo-Burgundian faction in the 1420s and early 1430s, even going so far as to give its imprimatur to the trial and execution of Joan of Arc. No longer a truly international entity and having shown itself to be party to political interests, in 1446 it bowed to its new subservient title of 'eldest daughter of the king' and was deprived of its long-cherished immunity from royal jurisdiction. It had officially become a servant of the state.[72] Meanwhile the other great ancient theology faculty, at Oxford, also lost much of its freedom at the turn of the fourteenth and fifteenth century as a consequence of its having tolerated the heretical teaching of John Wyclif and his followers. It had done so out of respect for the privilege of its masters and students to formulate and defend daring propositions so long as they were willing to recant them when challenged by ecclesiastical authorities. All this changed in 1407 when the archbishop of Canterbury, Thomas Arundel abolished this privilege in his *Constitutiones* against the Lollard heresy. Now, instead of a scholar's statements being subject to charges of heresy, he himself was. The chilling effect of this constitution was augmented by a Parliamentary statute of 1401 making heresy an offence punishable by burning at the stake. No longer free to speculate, the theologians turned to less controversial matters.[73] With the great universal *studia* domesticated, it comes as no surprise that lesser centres also felt bound to bow down and serve their ecclesiastical and political masters.

Notes

1 Paris, Bibliothèque nationale de France, ms. fr. 12439, fols 200v–201v (my translation).
2 Dahlberg 1983: 308–9.
3 Miethke 2000: 221.
4 Kallendorf 2002: 5, 263.
5 Verger 2000b: 160.
6 Menache 1982: 308.
7 Thorndyke 1972: 215.
8 Verger 2000b: 159–60.
9 Black 1998: 276.
10 Orme 1984; Orme 2001.
11 Rouse and Rouse 1979.
12 Woods and Copeland 1999.
13 Mulchahey 1998: 527–52.
14 Murray 1998: 75.
15 Tentler 1974: 124; Woods and Copeland 1999: 377.
16 Murray 1998; Haren 1998.

17 Grendler 1989: 71.
18 Hazelton 1957; Gehl 1993: 43–81.
19 Grendler 1989: 111–15; Verger 2000b: 44.
20 Orme 1995: 277–79.
21 Grendler 1989: 13.
22 Paris, Bibliothèque de l'Arsenal 2690, fol. 120r (my translation).
23 Ouy 1986: 90.
24 Lusignan 1987: 97–100.
25 Grondeux 1998: 12.
26 Black 2004: 22.
27 Carruthers 1990.
28 Moran 1985: 96; Orme 2006: 347–71.
29 Verger 2000b 40–41; Grendler 1989: 26.
30 Denley 1990.
31 Thorndyke 1972: 337.
32 Grendler 1989: 1, 14.
33 Orme 2006: 225–40.
34 Orme 1973: 88.
35 Orme 2006: 222–23.
36 Verger 2000b: 61.
37 Winston-Allen 2004: 54, 169, 176.
38 Black 1998: 158–62; Jensen 1996.
39 Evans 1992: 491–95.
40 Verger 2007: 3.
41 Verger 2000b.
42 Le Goff 1980: 144.
43 Cobban 1975: 48–74; Leff 1992: 309; Siraisi 1992: 375.
44 Cobban 1975: 75–95.
45 Gieysztor 1992: 109–13.
46 Verger 1992: 59–60; Catto 1992: 175–261.
47 Leff 1968: 138–60; Fletcher 1984: 369–99; Fletcher 1992: 315–45.
48 García y García 1992: 388–408.
49 Siraisi 1992: 360–87.
50 Asztalos 1992: 409–41.
51 Thorndyke 1972: 372.
52 Hamesse 1974; Hamesse 1994; Rouse and Rouse 1991; Briggs 1993.
53 Parkes 1992: 407–83; Rouse and Rouse 2000.
54 Cobban 1975; Denley 1991; Verger 1998; Verger 2000a.
55 Kaye 1998: 2
56 Kaye 1998.
57 Catto 2000; Knowles 1962: 301–36.
58 Quillen 2003: 62.
59 Kallendorf 2002: 95.
60 Kelley 1991: 249
61 Kelley 1991: 249.
62 Grafton and Jardine 1986: 34.
63 Hay 1976: 12.
64 Jensen 1996: 65.
65 Grafton and Jardine 1986: 14.
66 Grafton and Jardine 1986: 34.
67 Witt 2003; Furstenberg-Levi 2006.
68 Rüegg 1992: 442–68.
69 Thorndyke 1972: 266–67.
70 Rüegg 1992.
71 Menache 1982; Wei 1995.
72 Verger 1972.
73 Larsen 2008.

10

LANGUAGE, LITERACY
AND THE ARTS

Since Babel was built men have spoken divers tongues, so that divers men are strange to one another and know not each other's speech. Speech is not known unless it is learned; common learning of speech is by hearing. . . . So men of different countries and lands which have different speech, if neither of them has learned the other's speech, neither of them knows what the other means though they meet and have great need of information and lore, of talking and of speech. . . . This is a great mischief which now accompanies mankind; but God of his mercy and grace has ordained a double remedy. One is that some men learn and know many different languages, so that between men who are strange to one another and do not understand one another's speech, such a man may be between them and tell each what the other wants to say. The other remedy is that one language is learned, used and known in many nations and lands. And thus Latin is learned, known and used especially on this side of Greece in all the nations and lands of Europe. Therefore clerks of their goodness and courtesy make and write their books in Latin so that their writing and books should be understood in divers nations and lands. And so Ranulf, monk of Chester, wrote in Latin his books of chronicles. . . . And so therein is noble and great information and lore to them that can read and understand. Therefore I would have these books of chronicles translated out of Latin into English, so that more men should understand them and derive thereof knowledge, information and lore.[1]

Thus does John Trevisa begin the *Dialogue between a Lord and a Clerk on Translation*, a short work which introduces Trevisa's English translation (1387) of the *Polychronicon*, a history of the world from the Creation until the middle of the fourteenth century, written, in Latin, by a monk from St Werburgh's, Chester named Ranulf Higden. The dialogue pits a 'Lord' – modelled on Trevisa's patron, Thomas Lord Berkeley – who advocates the practice of translating learned works out of Latin into the vernacular against a pedantic 'Clerk' whose views represent those of the ecclesiastical hierarchy and of many 'men of learning'. According to the Lord, Latin's role is purely functional, that of a *lingua franca* used by an international body of educated clerics. It has value so long as it facilitates communication but should be abandoned in favour of the vernacular when it impedes the free exchange of information. The Clerk, on the contrary, thinks Latin is a sacred and restricted code of 'holy writ . . . holy doctors . . . and philosophy' whose books 'should not be translated into English'; and if any translating is to be done, it should only happen orally in the manner of sermons, where 'they that understand no Latin may ask and be informed and taught by them that understand Latin'. After several more exchanges which leave the Clerk no more ready to accept the merit of the Lord's sensible arguments, the latter in exasperation finally bursts out:

> It is a wonder that you make such feeble arguments [when you] have gone so long to school! Aristotle's books and other books of logic and of philosophy were translated out of Greek into Latin. Also holy writ [i.e. the Bible] was translated out of Hebrew into Greek and out of Greek into Latin, and then out of Latin into French. Then how has English trespassed that [the Bible] might not be translated into English?[2]

Trevisa's *Dialogue* expresses a number of important and interrelated themes in the cultural history of the late Middle Ages. First there is the theme of the broken inheritance of Babel: of the manifest diversity of peoples and nations who stubbornly resisted the Church's claims of universal authority; of the many tongues that had begun to assert their own authority over and against that of the Latin of the clergy; and of the rich harvest of diverse architectural and artistic styles that ramified from the more unitary forms of the high medieval Gothic. The second theme is that of translation, in the semantically rich sense of the Latin word *translatio*. More often than not *translatio* simply meant 'transfer': thus the translation of a saint's relics from one place to another or of a bishop from one diocese to another. However, translation was also believed at the time to be a historical process; chronicles like Higden's taught that over the course of world history authority and power had moved from one empire to another (*translatio imperii*) and knowledge had migrated from one centre to another (*translatio studii*), starting in the east with the ancient Babylonians and moving westwards until eventually settling in Latin Christendom. And, of course, translation had the meaning most familiar to us, that of language translation. But as the *Dialogue* makes clear, the issue of Latin to vernacular translation was hardly ideologically neutral, since it too involved a transfer of authority and power from a mostly Latinate and clerical sphere to one that was vernacular and lay. The third theme is that of new publics for, and new makers and patrons of, literary and artistic culture. Provincial nobles like Thomas Berkeley wanted access to the learned culture which had long been the preserve of university-educated clerks; women and men of middling rank wanted to read works of religious devotion and instruction, including the Bible, in their own tongues; Italian merchants wrote histories and memoirs; and princes, urban patricians and rural gentry alike sponsored the work of authors, artisans and artists. A concomitant of these new publics was an expansion of literacy and increased demand for the written word. Thus, the fourth theme is that of increased output of texts, whether inscribed by hand or in the form of printed books.

Language, literacy and literature

Until 1300 the Latin language was virtually synonymous with literacy and dominated almost every field of written culture. It was the language of religion and learning, of contracts and wills, of government correspondence and records. It was the international language of learned elites whose mastery of it was a means to power. This was most certainly not the case just over two centuries later, however, for by the early sixteenth century, an ascendant vernacular culture of literacy, on the one hand, and the humanists' recovery of ancient languages (Greek and Hebrew, but also the Latin of antiquity), on the other, had broken Latin's monopoly.

Some of the factors contributing to this shift had already got under way during the thirteenth century. The translation into Latin of the vast corpus of ancient Greek and Arabic scientific and philosophical works that became the core of the university arts curriculum presented challenges to the hitherto unquestioned primary and sacred status of the Latin language. First, it made plain to many scholars that Latin was not always the *original* language of wisdom and knowledge. Second, the translations introduced the notion that the Latin tongue was not always able to express adequately and easily the ideas and exact sense of the Greek and Arabic originals. Annoyed by the evident inferiority of many of these translations, the English Franciscan Roger Bacon (d. 1292/4) advocated learning Greek, Arabic and Hebrew. He also removed Latin from the place it had traditionally shared with Greek and Hebrew among the holy trinity of 'sapiential' languages (i.e. the primal languages of ancient wisdom) and ranked it instead with contemporary, spoken vernacular tongues, like English and French. After all, said Bacon, the Latin of clerks and scholars like himself was a living, spoken language learned in childhood. It even had national dialects: '[I]n fact in many cases Italians pronounce and write [Latin] in one way, the Spanish in another, and the French, Germans and English each in their own way'.[3]

Although no one took up Bacon's radical education programme during his lifetime, his ideas gained traction for very different reasons in the early fourteenth century among those sponsoring the crusade to regain the Holy Land (see Chapter 6). Ramon Llull in a sermon to the University of Paris (1299) and Pierre Dubois in his crusade tract *De recuperatione terrae sanctae* ('On the Recovery of the Holy Land', 1309) both pointed out that the long-term prosperity of such an enterprise depended on the equally successful conversion of the infidel Muslims, Jews and Mongols, and of the heretical Greeks to Catholic Christianity. Since this could only be done by missionaries schooled in the languages of these potential flocks, the Council of Vienne in 1312 decreed that courses in 'the languages which the infidels chiefly use' were to be taught 'wherever the Roman curia happens to reside, also in the universities of Paris, Oxford, Bologna, and Salamanca'.[4]

Old ways die hard, however, and these first stirrings of a more nuanced and inclusive conception of language within the academic and clerical elites would likely have been insufficient to topple Latin from its pedestal. Thus the recommendation of the Council of Vienne was not acted upon and Latin remained the sole language of instruction in higher education. The real motivators of change occurred outside the schools and at those points where clerical and lay culture intersected. By the end of the thirteenth century writing had become the most important instrument of both government and commerce and this meant, in turn, that most people had at least some familiarity with literate modes of communication. Writing was used by great ministers of state and the most petty of government officials alike. Merchants and bankers kept diaries and drafted letters to their agents in other towns, while landlords and their servants maintained accounts of estate business and jealously guarded property rights by means of legal documents. In early fourteenth-century England even peasants had their own seals for authenticating official documents like contracts and charters.[5] Religion too played an important role, since most parishioners gained some familiarity with Latin through repeated contact with it in the liturgy, the more pious and well-off among them following the order of the service in their prayer books. Preachers quoted Scripture in Latin and used various Latin tags in sermons.[6] Starting in the fourteenth century there even was a vogue among clerical and lay audiences alike for 'macaronic' sermons that artfully blended Latin and vernacular.[7]

Vernacular tongues also intruded more and more into the sphere of written culture. History was one of the first areas colonised by vernacular writing, first in Anglo-Norman

French verse in the middle of the twelfth century and then, in the thirteenth century, in northern French, Castilian and Italian prose.[8] Furthermore, in the second half of the thirteenth century, as part of his efforts to increase royal power in Castile, Alfonso X promoted the vernacular as a language of government administration and formal learning.[9] Meanwhile, in northern Italy French joined Latin as a high-status language of culture. The Florentine Brunetto Latini chose to write his great encyclopaedic *Livre dou tresor* ('Book of the Treasure', 1260s) in French since it was 'the most delightful as well as the most commonly known of all languages', and some four decades later Marco Polo and Rustichello wrote the account of Polo's travels in Asia in French as well.[10] The language spoken by literate people in England in the early 1300s was such a mix of French, Latin and English, with the first two of these being so dominant in written discourse, that one historian has speculated that had it not been for the efforts of Wyclif, Trevisa, Chaucer, Langland and Gower in the latter part of the century, 'the language of the British Isles might before long have become an autonomous form of French, with a strong superstratum of Latin terms and an extensive substratum of a few dying, and eventually extinct, north-west Germanic insular dialects'.[11]

These thirteenth-century trends accelerated as the fourteenth century progressed. Latin to vernacular translation of both learned and religious works played an especially important role. In the France of John II (1350–64) and even more during the reign of his son Charles V (1364–80), many translators contributed to a programme whose goal was to transfer the learning of Latin clerical culture to the French court. The most important among them, Nicole Oresme, brought all his vast erudition to bear on his translations of several key texts of the university arts curriculum, Aristotle's *On the Heavens*, *Nicomachean Ethics* and *Politics*, and the pseudo-Aristotelian *Economics*, as well as of his own scholarly treatises *On Money*, *On Divination*, and *On the Sphere*. Together these translators and their royal and noble patrons transformed French into a language suitable for philosophy and theology. The task of translation itself also made them acutely conscious of two very important things about Latin and about language more generally. The first was the tremendous difference between the 'laborious and strange' classical Latin of ancient Roman authors like Seneca, Valerius Maximus and Livy and the ecclesiastical and scholastic Latin with which they were more comfortable. There was, then, a historical gulf separating the Latin they wrote and spoke from that used by the classical authors. The second realisation, first made by Nicole Oresme in the 1370s, was that just as the French language was the vernacular of the French, so too had Latin once been the vernacular of the ancient Romans. As obvious as this might seem to us, it was a revelation at the time. The prevailing view prior to that time had been nicely stated by Giles of Rome: 'Philosophers, seeing that no vulgar idiom was complete and perfect enough for them to be able to express the nature of things, the affairs of men, the courses of the stars, and other matters they wished to dispute upon, decided to fashion for themselves a sort of idiom appropriate for these ends, which is Latin, or the literal idiom, which they would make so broad [*latum*] and copious that through it they could sufficiently express everything they thought of'.[12] Compare this with what Oresme says in his preface to the translation of the *Ethics*:

> to translate [the books of Aristotle] into French and bring the arts and sciences [of the university curriculum] into French is a very profitable labour, for it is a noble language common to a people of great intelligence and prudence. And as Cicero in his *Academics* said, weighty matters of great authority are more delightful and

agreeable to people when they are in the language of their country. And . . . against the opinion of some [in his own time] he said that it was good to translate the sciences from Greek into Latin and to appropriate them and treat of them in Latin. Well, at that time Greek had a relationship to Latin among the Romans that Latin now has to French among us. And at that time students at Rome and other places learned Greek, and all the sciences were in Greek; and in that country the common and mother tongue was Latin.[13]

Contained in this is an implied critique of the contemporary situation wherein students had to learn Latin in order to pursue higher studies. For Oresme, Latin has served its purpose: it is time to move on and make French the language of learning in France.[14]

Only a few years later, in the *Dialogue*, Trevisa outlined a strikingly similar programme for English in England. There, however, English had to share the field with French and Latin, both of which were the preferred languages of literate culture. Nonetheless this situation began to change in the second half of the fourteenth century, thanks in large part to the growing literacy of the middle classes, in whose own conversation English dominated. First English began to take the place of French as the medium through which Latin was taught in grammar schools. Then in the 1360s Parliament started opening its sessions in English, rather than French and tried, albeit unsuccessfully, to displace the French of the common law courts with English. In 1370s Oxford, Wyclif and several of his disciples, one of whom was probably John Trevisa, initiated a project of English Bible translation. Under Berkeley's tutelage, Trevisa then went on in the next two decades to translate several learned Latin works, including Higden's *Polychronicon*, Bartholomeus Anglicus's great encyclopaedia of learning, *De proprietatibus rerum* ('On the Properties of Things', 1245), and Giles of Rome's *De regimine principum*.[15] Meanwhile, Trevisa's contemporary, William Langland, a cleric from Worcestershire but with ties to London, composed and then repeatedly revised his great poetic dream-vision, *Piers Plowman*.

The association of English translation with Lollardy and of Langland's poetry with the Peasants' Revolt of 1381 seems temporarily to have stymied the progress of English as a language appropriate for Biblical translation or the written expression of doctrine. Still, English remained a suitable medium for mystical contemplation, owing to the unimpeachable orthodoxy of Walter Hilton's *Scale of Perfection* and Julian of Norwich's *Revelations of Divine Love*, both written c. 1393, and of Nicholas Love's *Mirror of the Blessed Life of Jesus Christ*, composed some fifteen years later. Yet what seems more than anything else to have assured the future dominance of English as a national literary and official language came from the pens of several London writers connected with the royal court. Comfortable reading Latin and French, and writing for a coterie of courtly readers who were writers as well (including Thomas Usk and John Clanvowe, who were poets in their own right), John Gower and Geoffrey Chaucer proceeded in a highly self-conscious way to create an English poetic language of admirable subtlety and fineness. Gower wrote works in French and Latin as well as in English, but seems to have acknowledged the association of the English tongue with the English nation in the prologue to his second version of the English-language *Confessio Amantis* ('The Lover's Confession', 1387/93), where he called it 'a bok for Engelondes sake'. From c. 1370 till his death in 1400, Chaucer ingeniously combined the material and language drawn from French, Italian and Latin literature with the cadences of English speech to create an illustrious English poetry, whose brightest achievements were the courtly *Troilus and Criseyde* and the satirical *Canterbury Tales*.[16]

Inspired by Chaucer's example, the Privy Seal clerk Thomas Hoccleve (d. 1426) turned English verse to the high task of counselling the future king, Henry V, in his *Regiment of Princes* (1411) and the Benedictine monk and royal courtier John Lydgate (d. c. 1450) became what amounted to England's first poet laureate.[17] Much credit can also be given to Henry V himself for the rapid rise of English to the status of England's 'official' tongue. In 1417, during his second invasion of France, Henry suddenly abandoned French as his language of private correspondence and began writing and dictating letters in a straightforward, no-nonsense style, like this one to Sir John Tiptoft: 'Tiptoft. I Charge yow by the Feith that ye owe to me that ye kepe this Matere, her after Writen, from al Men secre save from my Brother Th'Emperor [Sigismund's] owne Persone; that never Creature have Wittyng thereof, withowt myn especial Commandement, of myn owne Mouthe, or els Writen with myn owne Hand'.[18] The king's precedent and example opened the door to the use of written English in all manner of situations, both personal and public, and it was not long before what amounted to a 'standard' written English developed, based on that of the king himself and of Privy Seal scribes like Thomas Hoccleve. By the 1420s a clear identity had been formed between the English tongue and realm.[19]

Italy's fragmented politics, commercial precocity and peculiar past as the centre of the Roman Empire of antiquity together gave birth to a rich literature in the vernacular and inspired the 'rebirth' (Renaissance) of classical Latin and Greek letters. Just as in France and England, translation played an important role in the transfer of the authority of ancient texts from a Latin to a vernacular context. A notary by profession and passionately involved in the politics of his native Florence, the author of the French *Tresor*, Brunetto Latini (d. 1294) devoted himself to translating the rhetorical eloquence of the ancient Romans into his native Italian. Turning to the greatest of the Roman orators, Cicero, Latini translated three of his orations, and began a translation of and commentary on his rhetorical treatise, *De inventione*. An interest in the ethical formation of a politically active citizen compelled Latini's contemporary Taddeo Alderotti (d. 1295), a professor of medicine at Bologna, to translate an abridged Latin version of Aristotle's *Ethics*. Moral and ethical concerns also lay at the heart of the Pisan Dominican friar Bartolomeo da San Concordio's translations, while resident at the convent of his order in Florence, of the Roman historian Sallust's *Conspiracy of Catiline* and *Jugurthan War* (both c. 1302). Other important translations, all by Florentines, followed: Seneca's *Moral Letters* (c. 1310), Boethius's *Consolation of Philosophy* (c. 1332), the *Facta et dicta memorabilia* ('Memorable Deeds and Sayings') of Valerius Maximus (1330s), Livy's history of Rome (1340s), and Cicero's *On Friendship* (before 1350).[20]

These translations evince a heightened interest in and appreciation of the moral and political value for contemporaries of the legacy of (mostly pagan) antiquity. The affinity of these Tuscan city-state dwellers with the ancient Romans, whom they regarded as their ancestors, was strengthened at the same time as their language was enriched through the appropriation of classical Latin's rhetorical constructions and philosophical lexicon. Already in the first decade of the fourteenth century the great Florentine poet Dante Alighieri (d. 1321) glimpsed Italian's potential as a poetic and philosophical language. The *Convivio*, which Dante started c. 1300 and abandoned writing in 1307, is a philosophical disquisition on his own poetry; framed as a discussion during a banquet between himself and a group of guests who are ignorant of Latin, the *Convivio* is both an attempt to import Aristotelian philosophy into Dante's native idiom and an act of literary self-promotion. While working on the *Convivio*, Dante began to formulate an ambitious plan to craft Italian into an illustrious, standardised and rule-governed poetic language that would both take Latin's place as the dominant language of literacy and help unite a politically fractured Italy. In *De vulgari eloquentia* ('On Vernacular Eloquence', c. 1305), which, interestingly, Dante wrote in Latin, he says that Latin is currently superior to the vernacular only because, unlike the vernacular, it functions according to a universally agreed-upon set of grammatical rules (indeed Dante's term for Latin is *gramatica*) as well as having its own fully developed system of rhetoric and poetics. Yet in spite of these advantages, Latin really is less *noble* than the vernacular,

> first, because [the vernacular] was the language originally used by the human race; second, because the whole world employs it, though with different pronunciations and using different words; and third, because it is natural to us, while the other [i.e. Latin] is, in contrast, artificial.[21]

Of the vernaculars, Italian is superior to all others,

> because those who have written vernacular poetry more sweetly and subtly, such as Cino da Pistoia and his friend [i.e. Dante], have been its intimates and faithful servants; and second because they seem to be in closest contact with the *gramatica* which is shared by all.[22]

Standing in the way of the Italian vernacular taking its rightful place as a great language of literary culture was the absence of a universally accepted poetic language. In other words, there were numerous competing dialects and no codified set of rules for poetic composition. At first Dante tried to fix these problems prescriptively in the *De vulgari eloquentia* itself, by drafting a manual of poetic technique. Perhaps overwhelmed by the complexity of the task, Dante abandoned *De vulgari eloquentia* and devoted himself to the far more fruitful endeavour of crafting his poetic masterpiece, the *Divine Comedy* (c. 1307–18). Paradoxically, in the magnificent and magisterial example of his *Divine Comedy* Dante achieved the ends he had originally intended to accomplish through the arid precepts of *De vulgari eloquentia*. In the next few decades, his countrymen Petrarch and Giovanni Boccaccio built on his achievement, Petrarch crafting beautiful sonnets to his (imaginary) love, Laura, and Boccaccio authoring the brilliant tales of the *Decameron*.

Driving the ingenious endeavours of Dante, Latini and the translators was the demand of a substantial lay audience. That Florence was the centre of these activities owes much to the precocious development of a large, wealthy and literate mercantile class. These hard-headed merchants transacted business by means of written correspondence and a battery of account books that were meticulously organised and constantly updated and cross-referenced. However, turning over the responsibility of writing to functionaries just would not do for these highly competitive men, jealous of their company secrets and wanting to maintain strict control over all aspects of their family, business and political interactions. So instead of relying on notaries and clerks schooled in Latin, the merchants did their own correspondence and kept their own records in the vernacular. And because their public, commercial and personal affairs were so closely intertwined, many of the merchants also began to write what were, in effect, personal memoirs and histories. We have already touched on one of these personal histories, Gregorio Dati's, in Chapters 2 and 3. In another Florentine family history, the *Ricordi* of Giovanni Morelli (d. 1444), the merchant advises his children:

make sure that all you do is written down extensively in your books, and never spare your pen, and dedicate yourself to knowing what is in the book; and from this it will follow that you will profit without too much peril . . . and you will live at ease, feeling secure and solid in your net worth and without anxiety.[23]

Stirred by momentous political events and strong devotion to their city, the merchants Dino Compagni (d. 1324), and Giovanni (d. 1348) and Matteo Villani (d. 1363) embarked on histories of a more public kind. These merchant-historians had little or no direct contact with literature in Latin, but they read fluently and wrote skilfully in their native tongue.[24]

Like merchants, notaries were laymen whose professional lives were intimately tied to reading and writing. Unlike merchants, however, the notaries (who also often had some training in civil law) conducted business in the highly formalised rhetorical Latin of the *ars dictaminis* ('art of letter writing'). For reasons still not fully understood, in the decades on either side of 1300, several lawyer-notaries in Padua, Bologna and Arezzo started showing great interest in Roman antiquity and tried to emulate the classical style of the ancient authors. Following their lead, Petrarch, a resident at the papal curia in Avignon and son of an exiled Florentine notary, dedicated his life to the revival of classical culture (see Chapter 9). He and his younger friend, the notary Boccaccio, hunted down manuscripts of hitherto lost or incomplete works of such ancient authors as Cicero, Terence and Livy, and tried to perfect their own skill at writing Latin verse and prose in flawless imitation of their ancient models. Petrarch even showed a novel awareness of these ancient authors' humanity, the fact that they had once been living, breathing, and yes, even flawed individuals, rather than simply being the sources of sententious precepts.[25]

Petrarch was not content to emulate the ancients, however. He also attacked the educational programme of the universities and scholasticism's 'barbarous' Latin, tried (albeit without much success) to revive the study of ancient Greek, and expressed a desire to abandon the entire 'Gothic' system of handwriting and develop a script more appropriate for the expression of classical and classicising literature. Here in a nutshell, then, are most of the features that came to characterise Italian Renaissance humanism. In the decades following his death, Petrarch's vision was developed and refined. Thorough searches of monastic and cathedral libraries throughout Europe uncovered more and more classical texts, usually in manuscripts written in the Caroline minuscule script of the ninth through early twelfth centuries. These books' clear legible script and single-column page format, which contrasted sharply with the crowded, highly abbreviated script and double-column layout of Gothic manuscripts, became the model for the new humanist script and book pioneered by Coluccio Salutati (d. 1406), Poggio Bracciolini (d. 1459) and Niccolò Niccoli (d. 1437), and popularised by the enterprising bookseller, Vespasiano da Bisticci (d. 1498).[26]

The rich harvest of manuscripts also meant that humanists could examine several copies of the same text or place one work of a classical author next to another to compare their language and determine the 'best' version. One of the most astute practitioners of what was eventually to be known as 'philology', Lorenzo Valla (d. 1457) proved that the 'Donation of Constantine', a document which the popes had for centuries used to back up their claims to temporal sovereignty in Latin Christendom, was in fact a forgery (see Chapter 7). He also applied himself to the textual criticism of the New Testament, comparing the original Greek version to the Latin of the Vulgate and finding serious flaws in the latter. Valla's facility with Greek was owed in large part to the establishment of classical Greek studies in Italy, first taught in 1397, at the University of Florence, by the Byzantine diplomat Manuel

Chrysoloras.[27] The revival of Greek learning and the influx of Greek texts from Byzantium, many of them brought to Italy by refugees from Constantinople prior to its fall to Ottoman Turks in 1453, led among other things to the gradual displacement of the medieval Latin corpus of Aristotle that had formed the backbone of the university arts curriculum.

Somewhat paradoxically, the revival of classical Latin helped bring about the demise of Latin as a living language.[28] This resulted partly from the scorn that humanism heaped on the 'barbarous' but user-friendly Latin that for so long had been taught in grammar schools and partly from the humanists' own realisation that they would never be able fully to recover a language that had died with its ancient Roman speakers. Sapped of its strength by the vernacular languages' growing prestige and sophistication, on the one side, and the difficulty and anachronism of the new humanist Latin, on the other, the Middle Ages' universal language of learning and literacy slowly but inexorably gave way to a culture of linguistic pluralism.

Script and print

Johannes Gutenberg's invention of the moveable-type printing press at Mainz c. 1450 has rightly been heralded as a signal turning-point in the history of communications technology. However, Gutenberg would not have devoted the preceding decade and a half of his life to working out the intricacies of his method, nor would his wealthy merchant backers have risked their capital investment on something they did not think would secure a healthy return. In other words, print did not just happen; rather, it was the outcome of several factors, including growing demand for the written word (and for painted or printed images), technological developments, the growth of commerce and the refinement of business techniques.

By 1300 few activities were carried out without the aid of writing. Bureaucracies and businesses of all kinds kept records and drafted copious quantities of written instruments and correspondence, law courts and representative assemblies recorded their proceedings, and people from many walks of life needed books, whether they were pious laywomen, nuns, students, preachers, learned professionals or princes. Moreover, in spite of demographic decline and stagnation, individual and institutional demand grew substantially over the next two centuries, requiring a number of innovations to speed production, keep down costs, facilitate distribution and satisfy the exigencies and tastes of consumers.

Written texts, whether documents or books, were physical objects produced by hand: besides needing a scribe to write them, they required a writing surface, a writing implement, ink and, in the case of illuminated books, pigments of assorted colours. Book production was labour intensive and time-consuming. It took some twenty-six ten-hour days for a professional scribe to complete a typically sized book of 80 leaves (160 pages) in high-quality 'textualis' script. In fourteenth-century Paris he would be paid £3 (in *livres parisis*) for his pains. This same professionally produced book no doubt also had at least one illuminated border and several decorated initials (large capital letters marking chapters or other divisions in the text) at a cost of about 1s. 8d. for a standard border and 5d./initial. Then there was the cost of materials. Although quills and inks were inexpensive and plentiful, the cost of parchment was hardly negligible. The parchment for our hypothetical book would cost £1 10s., bringing the total price of the finished manuscript to some £5. To purchase such a book, our scribe would have to hand over almost two months of his hard-earned wages.[29]

This being said, the normal price differential of new books in parchment was enormous, ranging from the £55 paid for a luxury illuminated missal commissioned from the Paris stationer Thevenin de l'Angevin in 1382 to about £2 for a book of inexpensive parchment, devoid of decoration and copied by an amateur scribe writing in an informal cursive script. Even cheap books were not cheap, however, which explains the flourishing second-hand book trade and the frequent recourse taken by those who could to copying their own books. It also explains the growing preference for paper. Before the middle of the thirteenth century the use of paper, imported from the Muslims of North Africa and the Iberian Peninsula, had been quite limited in Europe. But in mid-century, at Fabriano, a town in central Italy noted for its iron-working, some artisans turned their skills to the making of paper. Already before 1300 the paper-makers of Fabriano had introduced several efficiencies and improvements, including using water-driven machinery to make pulp from cotton and linen rags, fashioning forms of fine brass wire and watermarks to identify paper stocks, and smoothing the writing surface with sizing made from animal gelatine. In the early decades of the fourteenth century the technology of paper-making spread throughout Italy, after which it made its way to France in the mid-1300s, and then to Germany and the southern Low Countries in the 1390s. By 1500 scores of paper mills operated throughout Europe.[30]

As production increased and networks of distribution improved and ramified, the cost of paper dropped while that of parchment remained fixed. It took time, however, for the makers and buyers of books to accept paper as a suitable alternative to the smoother and more durable medium of parchment. Indeed, parchment remained the chosen medium for luxury books throughout the late Middle Ages. But at one-eighth the cost of parchment in 1400 and one-sixteenth a century later, paper drove down the cost of books and became the preferred writing surface for almost all other purposes.

Although cheaper books stimulated demand, several other forces were at work as well. Increased demand for books was a necessary corollary to the growth of education and proliferation of educational institutions. In addition there were the new religious sensibilities that privileged both the written word and the devotional image, thus fuelling the desire for primers, books of hours and a raft of instructional and devotional works such as the *Lay Folks' Mass Book*, James of Voragine's *Golden Legend* and Guillaume de Deguilleville's *Pèlerinage de vie humaine* ('Pilgrimage of Human Life'). The same desire prompted production, starting in the early fifteenth century, of cheap, mass-produced books of woodcut prints, the most popular of which were the *Ars moriendi* ('Art of Dying') and *Biblia pauperum* ('Bible of the Poor'). The *Devotio moderna* played an especially important role as well, since it not only cultivated a taste for private reading as a spiritual exercise but also made book copying a chief source of income for the Brethren of the Common Life and canons of Windesheim, who sought to produce accurate, standardised texts in clear, easy-to-read script. Institutional organisation of book production also became a distinctive feature of the reformed religious orders in the fifteenth century. Carthusians, Brigittines, Observant mendicants and reformed Benedictines alike set out to stock their libraries with accurate, well made copies, many produced in-house, of all manner of religious texts, from the Bible and St Augustine to such new works as the *Imitation of Christ*.

Humanism was also a movement predicated on books. Every work by a humanist and every new humanist edition of a classic appeared in multiple copies, some in the scores or even hundreds. Although there was an active trade in inexpensive humanist editions costing only two or three florins, much of the demand for humanist books came from wealthy patrons who wanted cartloads of deluxe books to furnish the shelves of well-appointed libraries that were both expressions of cultivation and symbols of power. Already in the second decade of the fifteenth century, the future unofficial ruler of Florence Cosimo de' Medici and his brother Lorenzo recognised the cultural capital of humanist books. Not content to build up his own library, Cosimo (d. 1464) also patronised humanist book collections at the monastery of San Marco in Florence and at his new monastic foundation of La Badia in nearby Fiesole. For the latter, he commissioned the bookseller Vespasiano da Bisticci to arrange the production of the books:

> He was anxious that I should use all possible despatch, and, after the library was begun, as there was no lack of money, I engaged forty-five scribes and completed two hundred volumes in twenty-two months, taking as a model the Vatican library of Pope Nicholas V [Tommaso Parentucelli, a noted humanist] and following directions which Pope Nicholas had given to Cosimo, written in his own hand.[31]

Later, in the 1470s and 1480s, Bisticci oversaw the purchasing and copying of books for the lavishly decorated library of Federigo da Montefeltro, duke of Urbino, who

> had a mind to do what no one had done for a thousand years or more; that is, to create the finest library since ancient times. He spared neither cost nor labour, and when he knew of a fine book, whether in Italy or not, he would send for it. Over a period of fourteen or more years he always employed, in Urbino, in Florence and in other places, thirty or forty scribes in his service.[32]

By 1482, Montefeltro's library contained 900 volumes, almost all manuscripts.

The taste for libraries was not confined to Renaissance Italian princes, however. By 1420, the library in the French royal palace of the Louvre included almost 1,000 books; forty years later the library of the duke of Burgundy, Philip the Good contained 900 books.[33] Before his death in 1447, Humphrey, duke of Gloucester had already donated more than 280 of his books, both humanist and non-humanist, to the University of Oxford. The remainder of his library, which he had also willed to Oxford, was seized by the crown at his death and granted to his nephew Henry VI's new foundation at Cambridge, King's College.[34] Such collections were dwarfed, however, by the great library of the humanist-inspired king of Hungary, Mathias Corvinus (d. 1490). Most of its more than 2,500 volumes were manuscripts purchased in Florence, though many were printed scientific treatises and Greek manuscripts seized from the Ottomans.[35]

Less impressive, but far more numerous were the smaller libraries of nobles, merchants and professionals. Mechthild of Rottenburg, countess of Palatine, owned more than 100 books by the middle of the fifteenth century, and the countess of Montpensier, Gabrielle de la Tour had collected some 200 books at the time of her death in 1474.[36] In fourteenth- and fifteenth-century Sicily personal libraries of twenty or more books were not uncommon among wealthy urban patricians and rural aristocrats, while the collections of professional men of learning tended to number in the forties or more; there even artisans and lesser merchants often owned a few books.[37] Some scholar-clerics put together book collections that rivalled those of princes. It was thanks to a generous gift of 627 books from the physician and dean of Mainz Cathedral Amplonius Ratinck (d. 1435) that the University of Erfurt had the largest institutional book collection in northern Germany. Ratinck's contemporary, the canon lawyer Heinrich Neithart left his 300 books to Ulm Cathedral, while in 1446, the priest Albrecht Fleimann bequeathed 200 books to his parish of St Sebald's, Mainz.[38]

Clearly, book collecting was a widespread practice by the fifteenth century. It had also become big business, supplied by countless paper-makers, parchmeners, scribes and illuminators and organised by international publishing firms, among the largest of which were Bisticci's in Florence, and Jean Wauquelin's and David Aubert's in the Low Countries. These great merchants were so confident of the demand for books that they had even begun to engage in speculative publishing, thus anticipating and shaping demand.[39] It was in this environment that enterprising artisans like the goldsmith Johannes Gutenberg, working in Strasbourg and then in Mainz, and the silversmith Prokop Waldfoghel and clockmaker Girard Ferrose, in Avignon, began experimenting with mechanical writing techniques. Gutenberg's eventual success was mostly due to the ingenuity of the process he developed. Working from the analogy of woodblock printing and applying recent innovations in metallurgy and copperplate engraving, Gutenberg created the technology of moveable metal type. Each block of type was manufactured in a four-step process in which: (1) a soft steel 'punch' on the end of which was carved a raised sign or character; (2) was pressed with great force into a softer copper 'matrix'; (3) which was then placed at the base of a 'type-mould'; (4) into which was poured an alloy of lead, tin and the hardening agent antimony. These completed type blocks were stored in 'founts', each of which contained all the necessary upper and lower case letters, numerals, punctuation marks, spaces etc. Printing itself was simply a matter of arranging these type-blocks in a frame to form a page of text; after the application of an oil-based ink, a sheet of paper (or parchment) was imprinted with the text by means of a press very much like those used in wine-making.[40]

The new technology alone might not have succeeded, however, had it not been for the application of sound business practices. Cost containment was essential, hence the decision to shrink margins and increase the amount of space filled by text, and the preference for paper over parchment. Then there was the crucial role played by Gutenberg's partners, the scribe Peter Schoeffer, who designed types that mimicked the look of a Gothic manuscript (including all the ligatures and abbreviation signs), and the businessman Johann Fust, who provided the financial backing for what was an extremely capital-intensive project. Making the right choices about what to print also mattered. Their first publication, the so-called 42-line Bible (Mainz, c. 1453), was an immediate success because it met the needs of churches and reformed monasteries. The same market was served by their other early major publications: two large-format psalters (1457 and 1459). In between they did smaller jobs, including the printing of school grammars and indulgences, cheap products meant for wide distribution.

In no time at all, several printers had set up shop in Mainz and in nearby Strasbourg and Bamberg. When Mainz was sacked by the forces of Adolf of Nassau in 1462, the printers there scattered to other cities in Germany and to the monastery of Subiaco not far from Rome. Once the technology arrived in Italy, ties were immediately forged between humanists and printers, and the Germans at Subiaco, Conrad Sweynheym and Arnold Pannartz, set about making printed books that looked like humanist manuscripts, even crafting Greek characters.[41] Over the next few decades the technology continued to spread, so that by 1500 there were more than 250 centres of printing operating throughout Europe. Many small operations failed, while other modest enterprises satisfied local demand of a university or group of religious houses. Where trade already flourished, however, great international publishing houses came into being, like the syndicate of Nicholas Jensen, Johannes de Colonia and Johannes Manthen in Venice, and the Koberger company of Nuremberg.[42] With printing becoming big business, demand for large quantities of low-cost type founts moved type manufacturing out of the printer's shop and into specialised type foundries which disseminated standardised, uniform founts.

In the first five decades of printing, a confirmed 27,000 editions were published in some fifteen million copies: a number of books perhaps equal to the total number of manuscript books produced in the entire Middle Ages. There is no doubt that printing made exponentially more books available at a more affordable price to a larger and more diverse readership. But it should not be assumed that printing immediately changed everything. First, these early printed books, called 'incunabula', adopted the conventions of manuscripts, borrowing their script forms and even leaving spaces for decorated initials (hence the spaces we now use to mark the beginning of paragraphs), rubrics and painted miniatures. Second, manuscript production if anything increased in the last decades of the fifteenth century, with scribes sometimes even copying their texts *from* printed books. Third, the frequently made assertion that print radically improved the accuracy of texts can no longer be accepted. Late medieval scribes were already making standardised copies before the advent of print, and although printing made possible the exact replication of the same text, the quality of that text depended on the accuracy of the edition from which it was made and the care taken by the person who composed the frames of type. In other words, when printers made inaccurate texts, they did so on an industrial scale. As the sixteenth century got under way, however, the printed book developed its own look (title page, small margins, few or no abbreviations, monochrome text in standardised typefaces, engraved illustrations) and hand-written books started being abandoned in favour of printed ones. Writing was hardly dead, since it was still the only means available for making records and drafting documents and correspondence, but the centuries-old identity of scribes and books was permanently severed.

Music, architecture and the visual arts

In 1471, Borso d'Este, *signore* of Ferrara, made his way to Rome to receive the title of duke from Pope Paul II. To complement the solemnity of the occasion and show off his own lofty status he brought along a great hoard of precious items, the most impressive of which was an enormous and lavishly illustrated two-volume Bible, for which Borso had paid the princely sum of 2,200 florins. Because the Bible itself as well as the contract between its makers and the *signore* survive, we know that it took six years for the master illuminators Taddeo Crivelli and Franco dei Rossi along with their team of three assistant illuminators and several scribes to adorn the two volumes' thirty (or so) pounds of parchment with exquisite script and over a thousand miniatures. The Bible's original binding was evidently not ostentatious enough for Borso, since he had it rebound just before leaving for Rome.[43] Borso's Bible was but one small expression of his cultural patronage, however, since he also spent considerable sums to secure the services of artists to paint the frescoes of his Palazzo Schifanoia. Even more glittering was the reputation of Borso's half-brother, Ercole, who seized the duchy on Borso's death shortly after his Roman holiday. Under Ercole, the Este's family chapel gained renown for the inventiveness of its choir's music, composed by such resident luminaries as Johannes Martini (d. 1497/8), Jacob Obrecht (d. 1505) and the incomparable genius Josquin Desprez (d. 1521).[44]

There is no way to know how impressed Pope Paul II was by Borso's artistic fireworks; suffice it to say that during his lifetime, which ended a few weeks before Borso's, this occupant of the see of St Peter was not particularly renowned for his cultural patronage. One imagines, however, that the duke's efforts would have been appreciated by Paul's successor, Sixtus IV (Francesco della Rovere), who after ascending to the papal throne embarked on his own programme of cultural patronage. He completed building the Vatican Library and appointed

Figure 10.1 A humanist book for Matthias Corvinus, king of Hungary. Photograph: Classic Image / Alamy Stock Photo

the great humanist Bartolomeo Platina as librarian. To accompany the increasingly elaborate liturgical rituals performed in St Peter's Cathedral and his new Sistine Chapel, the pope hired an international assortment of noted musicians, and to adorn its walls he employed such sought-after painters as Botticelli, Ghirlandaio and Perugino.[45] A Franciscan friar, Sixtus IV as pope nonetheless behaved very much like any prince, using cultural patronage as a means to aggrandise himself, his office, his principality and his family. Nor was this strategy limited to princes in the late Middle Ages, since it was also employed by nobles and urban patricians, as well as by such collective bodies as municipal governments and guilds.

278

Prior to the late thirteenth century, artistic patronage on a grand scale, whether of architecture, music, or the visual and decorative arts, had largely been confined to a few royal courts and wealthy ecclesiastical institutions. From then on, however, the number, kinds and geographic diversity of patrons grew tremendously, as did the amount of money and favours they were willing to expend. This in turn encouraged experimentation and competition on the part of artists, builders and musicians who sought to satisfy and shape the demand of patrons. Together these factors helped initiate a period remarkable for its diversity and creativity.

Music was omnipresent in late medieval life. In religious worship psalms and hymns were set to music, and in even the humblest of churches the priest intoned the words of the mass. In more secular settings, minstrels were fixtures of court life and few public events took place without music. Never having been written down, little of this day-to-day music is extant. What does survive, however, are the subtle compositions written down by clerk musicians employed by great churches and princely chapels. When it came to this sort of music, the fourteenth century saw the development of a musical style called the *Ars Nova* ('New Art'), which reached its perfection in the exquisite motets, *virelais* and *ballades* of the poet/composer Guillaume de Machaut (d. 1371) at Reims Cathedral and in the *ballate* of Francesco Landini (d. 1397) at the church of San Lorenzo, Florence.[46] In the fifteenth century the *Ars Nova*'s intricate polyphony, achieved through the interlacing of several semi-independent vocal lines, gave way to a more disciplined and unified polyphony, which has been called 'a series of events spaced in time'.[47] Here the pioneers were the Englishman John Dunstable (d. 1453), who spent much of his professional life in the employ of John, duke of Bedford, and the chorister and canon of Cambrai Cathedral Guillaume Dufay (d. 1474).[48]

Dufay's influence was most keenly felt in his native Low Countries, where musical expertise flourished thanks to the professional choral training provided by several cathedrals there and by the patronage of the dukes of Burgundy and many wealthy urban merchants. But the competition of princes assured the spread of the 'Franco-Flemish' style throughout Europe and especially to Italy. Dufay himself found employment in several cities in northern and central Italy, including Rome, and at the court of the dukes of Savoy. The greatest composer of the generation after Dufay, Johannes Ockeghem (d. 1497) of Antwerp was employed by three successive French kings to compose for the royal chapel. Ockeghem's imprint on younger Franco-Flemish composers was memorialised by the Hainaulter Josquin Desprez in his haunting tribute, *La déploration de la mort de Johannes Ockeghem* ('Lamentation at the Death of Johannes Ockeghem'):

> For the harsh molestations of Atropos
> Have inescapably ensnared your Ockeghem,
> Music's very treasure and master,
> Who henceforth no longer escapes death. . . .
> Dress yourselves in clothes of mourning,
> Josquin, Brumel, Pierchon, Compère;
> And weep great tears from your eyes,
> Who have lost your good father.[49]

Josquin's own fame secured him positions not only at the Este court but also with Cardinal Ascanio Sforza of Milan and at the papal chapel under Popes Innocent VIII and Alexander VI, before ending his days as provost of the church of Notre Dame in Condé.

The basic rule governing musical composition for great cathedrals, princely courts and chapels was simple: the more important the occasion, the more impressive the music. Thus important liturgical feasts or occasions were supplied with the most impressive mass or office settings, while great occasions of state called forth such tours de force as Josquin's *Missa Hercules Dux Ferrarie*, composed to honour Ercole d'Este during a state visit to Ferrara by Cardinal Sforza in 1480–81. And although clerk musicians saved their heaviest artillery for liturgical compositions, they also produced a steady stream of profane songs for courtly entertainment. The subject matter of the bulk of Machaut's and Landini's work, for example, seems to have been secular, while Dufay set to music several French poems of Christine de Pizan and Alain Chartier.

Music at cathedral, court and chapel served a number of purposes. As sonic decoration, its excellent quality confirmed a patron's lofty status. When performed on special occasions, like the dedication of a cathedral or during a royal entry or coronation, it reinforced hierarchy and strengthened corporate identity; when sung on liturgical occasions it magnified the Lord and stimulated devotion. Many of the same motivations can be seen at play in the patronage of architecture and works of visual and decorative art. In architecture, the two most important stylistic developments were the dissemination and fragmentation into regional variants of the Gothic during the fourteenth and fifteenth centuries, and the neo-classical experimentation that got under way in Italy during the fifteenth century. A style mostly associated with the great cathedrals of northern France and England prior to the late thirteenth century, the Gothic became the common architectural language throughout most of Europe for the next two and a half centuries. Although it continued to be the default setting for cathedral-building, the patrons and builders of those churches experimented with variations on the Gothic theme, from the preference for broad and colourful mural surfaces at Siena and Orvieto Cathedrals, to the textural richness of the vaulting in Wells and Ely Cathedrals (built in the so-called 'Decorated' style) and the fan vaulting and structural horizontality of Gloucester Cathedral (the earliest example of the 'Perpendicular' style), to the dizzyingly tall spires of Ulm, Strasbourg and Vienna Cathedrals.[50]

More importantly, however, the Gothic style was adapted to suit many different kinds of buildings, most of them commissioned by lay patrons or destined for secular uses. Kings and great lords built great castle-palaces, like Edward III's Windsor (1348, for the staggering amount of £51,000), Emperor Charles IV's Karlstein (begun 1348) or Jean, duke of Berry's Mehun-sur-Yèvre (begun 1367). Designed to express lordship and power in their exterior and public aspects, such buildings were also statements of cultural refinement that delighted the eye and catered to the creature comforts of their inhabitants. Proud republics and trading cities like Florence, Siena, Venice, Bruges and Stralsund sponsored the construction of town halls whose magnificence rivalled that of princely palaces. Meanwhile merchant guilds everywhere built splendid halls which combined commercial function with Gothic finery. Princes, nobles and merchants also funded the construction of all manner of churches, from private chapels to collegiate and parish churches (see Figure 10.3). Some of these, like the brick-faced Marienkirche of Lübeck (early 1300s) surpassed the local cathedral in magnificence.[51]

In fifteenth-century Italy patrons and architects started translating the classicism of humanism into building design. In Florence, Filippo Brunelleschi revived forms of ancient Roman architecture in his great dome for the cathedral of Santa Maria del Fiore (1418–34) and the chapel of the Pazzi family (begun 1429). More antiquarian still were Leon Battista Alberti's Tempio Malatestiano in Rimini (c. 1454) and basilica of Sant'Andrea, Mantua (begun shortly before his death in 1472). By the late years of the century, neo-classicism was the defining characteristic of Italian architecture.

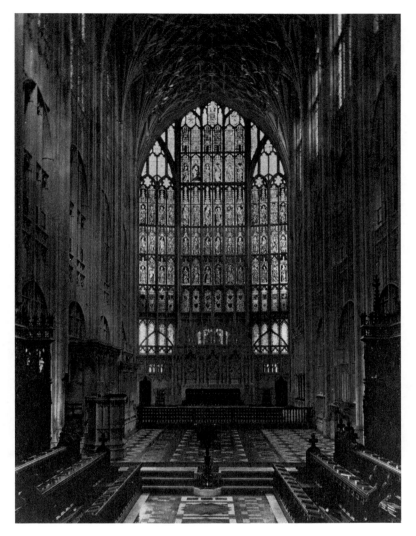

Figure 10.2 Gloucester Cathedral, choir, begun after 1330. Photograph: Bygone Collection / Alamy Stock Photo

According to Huizinga, art in the late Middle Ages

> had the task of embellishing the forms in which life was lived with beauty. . . . In contrast to later ages, one did not step outside a more or less indifferent daily routine in order to enjoy art in solitary contemplation for the sake of solace or edification; rather, art was used to intensify the splendor of life itself . . . art was not yet perceived as beauty *per se*. It was for the most part applied art, even in cases where we could consider the works to be their own reason for being. That is to say . . . the reason for desiring a given work of art rested in its purpose, rested in the fact that artworks are the servants of any one of the forms of life.[52]

Figure 10.3 Aerial photograph of Salle Church, Norfolk. Image © Norfolk County Council and Derek A. Edwards

The visual arts, just like music and architecture, fulfilled practical functions and conveyed meaning. Devotional images on the pages of books or painted on and carved into altarpieces and reliquaries were at one and the same time precious objects in their own right, meaningful symbols, and supports for prayer and penance. Tomb sculpture and painting commemorated the dead but also glorified the family (and in some cases, the city or realm). Mural programmes like those painted by Simone Martini (1315) and Ambrogio Lorenzetti (1337–39) on the interior walls of the Palazzo Pubblico in Siena, expressed the commune's collective pride, corporate solidarity and mutual responsibility for the common good.[53] Portraits both commemorated their subjects and advertised their wealth, social standing and good taste. Art, in short, was a necessary expression of and complement to virtually all aspects of life and, as such, was produced and consumed in prodigious quantities.

The heavy and varied demand for art from a multiplicity of patrons helps explain the astonishing variety and creativity of late medieval and Renaissance art. No brief account

Figure 10.4 Florence Cathedral with Brunelleschi's dome. Photograph: Sergey Borisov / Alamy Stock Photo

can do justice to what is no doubt one of, if not *the* most decisive eras in the history of Western art. Here it must suffice to delineate some of the most important developments. First, there was a growing interest in the individual. Subjects began to be portrayed with recognisable, individualised features, rather than as conventional types. The trend is already apparent in the presentation scene of a manuscript produced in 1361 for the future Charles V of France. This realistic (and not particularly flattering) depiction must have pleased the prince, however, since painters of later images of him – and most successfully the Flemish artist Jean Bondol – continued the practice and worked to improve it.[54] The same attention to individualised features can also be seen in contemporary portraits produced by artists in Prague, like the portrait of Rudolf IV of Austria painted by the Prague Master c. 1365.[55] After these early efforts, the artists of the fifteenth century perfected the individualised portrait. In such portraits as Jan van Eyck's of Chancellor Nicholas Rolin of Burgundy (c. 1435), Jean Fouquet's of Charles VII of France (1450s), and Pedro Berruguete's of Federigo da Montefeltro (c. 1475) the individual patron/subject seems a living presence.[56] Individual artists, too, emerged from their accustomed anonymity and became notable personages, not only to us today but during their own lifetimes. In the fifteenth century they even began to paint portraits of themselves and their lives were memorialised in biographies, like Antonio Manetti's (d. 1497) *Life of Brunelleschi*. Art even aimed at the eternal welfare of the individual soul; thus the enormous popularity of all those devotional images and memento moris that have for so long been mistaken as evidence of the late Middle Ages' excessive morbidity and decadence.[57]

Art also had a notably international character. This was thanks in large part to the mobility of artists and patrons. Simone Martini, for example, worked on commissions not only in his native Siena, but also in Naples, Assisi and Avignon, and members of the Parler workshop of masons and sculptors worked throughout central Europe in the middle and later fourteenth century. As for patrons, many of them were no doubt influenced by the art and architecture they observed during their travels. Nor should it be forgotten that artworks themselves also travelled, especially in the form of illuminated manuscripts and small panel paintings. This movement of patrons, artists and art gave rise to the so-called 'International Gothic' style during the decades around 1400. One sees unmistakeable similarities in style, whether looking at the *Wilton Diptych*, painted for Richard II of England c. 1390, or the *Trinity and Scenes from the Life of Saint Denis* by the Burgundian court painter Henri Bellechose (1416), or the *Adoration of the Magi* painted in 1423 by Gentile da Fabriano for the Florentine banker Palla Strozzi.[58]

The third development was a heightened naturalism (or realism) in both painting and the plastic arts. Although the move toward naturalism can already be seen in Giotto's (d. 1337) facial modelling and attempts at perspective, it was only at the start of the fifteenth century that Brunelleschi's discovery of linear perspective and Flemish artists' adoption of oil as a medium radically enhanced painting's capacity for realistic representation. So convincing is the combined illusion of space, distance, volume, light and surface in such works as van Eyck's *Arnolfini Wedding Portrait* (1434) and Rogier van der Weyden's *Altarpiece of the Seven Sacraments* (before 1450, see Figure 10.5), that their images might even be called hyper-real. In sculpture, naturalism is already apparent by the later fourteenth-century in Peter Parler's and Claus Sluter's careful sculpting of facial features. Then, in fifteenth-century Florence, Donatello combined naturalism and classicism to bring to life the naked male form of his bronze masterpiece, the *David* (1433). Classicism, the fourth development, was pioneered in the early 1400s by several Florentines working under humanist inspiration, including Donatello, Brunelleschi and Lorenzo Ghiberti (d. 1455). Their classicising project and interest in antiquity was developed further by Domenico Ghirlandaio (d. 1494), Andrea Mantegna (d. 1506) and Rafael Sanzio (d. 1520): an especially fine example of full-blown classicism is Ghirlandaio's fresco of six heroes of the Roman Republic in Florence's Palazzo Vecchio.[59] Prior to the sixteenth century, classicism in the visual arts, as in architecture, remained an almost exclusively Italian phenomenon. One can, however, already see its influence beyond Italy in the work of the French Jean Fouquet (d. 1481), especially in the programme of miniatures he executed for the manuscript of Josephus' *Jewish Antiquities* (early 1470s) destined for his patron Jacques d'Armagnac, duke of Nemours. Fouquet travelled to Italy in the early 1440s, where he, reportedly, admired the work of several of its artists and painted a portrait of Pope Eugenius IV.

Fifthly, one cannot help but be struck by the commercialisation of artistic production in the late Middle Ages and Renaissance. Although the artists of this time, like their earlier medieval forebears, remained artisans dependent on patronage, their business practices and interaction with patrons became increasingly contractual and money-driven. On the classical portico of Florence's Hospital of the Innocents (designed by Brunelleschi), are a series of glazed terracotta medallions turned out from the production line of the della Robbia workshop, while indoors one can view Ghirlandaio's painting, the *Adoration of the Magi*. It was completed in the early months of 1488 in fulfilment of a contract:

This day 23 October 1485 the reverend Messer Francesco di Giovanni Tesori, presently Prior of the Spedale degli Innocenti at Florence, commits and entrusts to Domenico di Tomaso di Ghirlandaio the painting of a panel which the said Francesco has had made and has provided; the which panel the said Domenico is to make good, that is, pay for; and he is to colour and paint the said panel all with his own hand in the manner shown in a drawing on paper with those figures and in that manner shown in it, in every particular according to what I, Fra Bernardo, think best; not departing from the manner and composition of the said drawing; and he must colour the panel at his own expense with good colours and with powdered gold . . . and the blue must be ultramarine of the value about four florins the ounce; and he must have made and delivered complete the said panel within thirty months from today; and he must receive as the price of the panel as here described . . . 115 large florins if it seems to me, the abovesaid Fra Bernardo, that it is worth it.[60]

Figure 10.5 Altarpiece of the Seven Sacraments, by Rogier van der Weyden. Photograph: Historic Images / Alamy Stock Photo

Figure 10.6 Adoration of the Magi, Florence, by Domenico Ghirlandaio. Photograph: MARKA / Alamy Stock Photo

One can almost hear the haggling that had gone on previously between the prior, his agent Fra Bernardo, and the artist. Today Ghirlandaio's finished product is considered a 'masterpiece'; at the time it was executed it was meant to be an expression of religious devotion and civic pride (the cult of the Magi was an important civic cult in fifteenth-century Florence). It was, however, also a commercial product, the result of a business transaction. So commercialised had art become in the fifteenth century, that when van Eyck painted *Man in a Turban*, a work which is believed to be his self-portrait, he portrayed himself in the guise of a merchant.[61]

Notes

1 Waldron 1988: 289–90 (my modernisation).
2 Waldron 1988: 291–92 (my modernisation).
3 Lusignan 1987: 72.
4 Thorndyke 1972: 125–27, 147, 149–50.
5 Clanchy 1993: 49–51.
6 Coleman 1983: 42–43.
7 Wenzel 1994.
8 Briggs 2012.
9 Wright 2002: 262–73.
10 Carmody 1948; Larner 1999: 46–67.
11 Catto 2003: 36.
12 Briggs 2003: 101.
13 Menut 1940: 100–1 (my translation).

14 Lusignan 1989.
15 Fowler 1995; Hanna 1989.
16 Catto 2003.
17 Harriss 2005: 36–40.
18 Richardson 1980: 732.
19 Allmand 1992: 420–22.
20 Witt 2003: 174–90.
21 Botterill 1996: 3.
22 Botterill 1996: 23.
23 Robins 2003: 118–19; Trexler 1980: 159–86.
24 Bornstein 1986; Bagge 1997; Witt 2003: 191–93.
25 Witt 2003: 230–91; Reeve 1996: 20–29.
26 Davies 1996: 47–53; Vale 1998: 281.
27 Reeve 1996.
28 Black 1998: 255.
29 Bozzolo and Ornato 1983; Lemaire 1989; Camille 1996: 34–38.
30 Martin 1994: 208–10.
31 Jardine 1996: 190.
32 Jardine 1996: 188.
33 Vale 1998: 282.
34 Parkes 1992: 473–74.
35 Vale 1998: 284; Jardine 1996: 202, 366.
36 Bell 1982: 750–51.
37 Martin 1994: 195.
38 Martin 1994: 204–05.
39 Vale 1998: 281.
40 Martin 1994: 216; McKitterick 1998: 290.
41 Davies 1996: 53–54.
42 Vale 1998: 293–94.
43 Jardine 1996: 205; Alexander 1992: 53, 127, 140.
44 Lockwood 1981.
45 Schimmelpfennig 1992: 239–44; Zuffi 2005: 200–02.
46 Seay 1975: 125–67.
47 Curtis 1998: 323.
48 Strohm 1993: 127–35.
49 Hillier and James 1996.
50 Crossley 2000.
51 Crossley 2000.
52 Huizinga 1996: 296.
53 Skinner 1986; Starn and Partridge 1992: 11–80; Boucheron 2018.
54 Sherman 1971.
55 Baragli 2007: 185.
56 Zuffi 2005: 151, 235, 366.
57 Binski 2000: 232–33.
58 Baragli 2007: 133; Zuffi 2005: 144–45, 285.
59 Hope and McGrath 1996: 172.
60 Jardine 1996: 22–23.
61 Jardine 1996: 31–32.

CONCLUSION

A new Europe?

The year 1525 did not mark the end of the Middle Ages any more than it heralded the end of the Italian Renaissance or announced the beginning of the Modern Age. No one living in Europe at the time would have been conscious of having passed from one period to another, because the periods themselves are wholly artificial, mere inventions of historians looking for shorthand ways to make sense of the past. Still, a reasonably well-informed person whose life spanned the decades on either side of 1525 probably would have noted some important events and developments in and around that year. The coming together of the great Habsburg political complex in the inheritance of Emperor Charles V would have been impressive enough had it only comprised the European assets of Spain, the kingdoms of Sicily and Naples (and growing hegemony over much of central and northern Italy), the Low Countries, Burgundy and its many holdings within the Empire. That it also included Spain's Atlantic and New World possessions made it even more imposing, especially after the conquests of the Aztec empire by Hernán Cortés in 1519–21 and of the empire of the Inca in 1533 by Francisco Pizarro. A few years after the fall of the Inca, the discovery of vast seams of silver-bearing ore at Zacatecas in Mexico and Potosí in what is now Bolivia, enriched the new Spanish empire and ended Europe's long dearth of precious metals. The westward shift of the centre of trade from the Mediterranean to the Atlantic, stimulated on the positive side by the overseas exploits of the Portuguese and Spanish (with help from their Genoese and Florentine partners), was also compelled on the negative side by Ottoman hegemony over the eastern Mediterranean. The reign of Sultan Suleiman the Magnificent (1520–66) marked the apex of Ottoman power in the Mediterranean and Eastern Europe. His forces seized the Hospitallers' military base at Rhodes in 1522 and conquered most of the kingdom of Hungary in 1526. Only the need to respond to a threat on the eastern frontier of his empire kept Suleiman's armies from taking the city of Vienna in 1529.

Another result of Portuguese and Spanish expansionism was a changing perspective of the world and Europe's place in it. Until 1513, despite the evidence to the contrary, the new lands on the western edge of the Atlantic could be rationalised as being in close proximity to China and the Indies. Vasco Nuñez de Balboa's discovery of the Pacific in that year and the subsequent circumnavigation of the globe by Ferdinand Magellan's expedition in 1519–22 proved that the world was a much bigger place, and Asia much further away, than Columbus and the first European explorers of the New World could have imagined. This world was very different and much more diverse than the one previously imagined by Europeans, who had assumed a world of Ocean in the middle of which floated a single land-mass, divided into its three segments of Europe, Africa and Asia, all gathered around the sacred centre of Jerusalem.

Now they had to account for another great land-mass on the other side of the world, full of strange peoples, beasts and plants.

Although it would take time for the import of these discoveries to sink in and for their effects to play themselves out, our observer, informed by the accounts of books and the graphics of world maps – both widely disseminated by means of the printing press – would likely have experienced a shift in perspective. In one sense, Christendom had become much smaller, owing to the incursions of the Ottomans and the expansion of the globe. But in another, its province had grown substantially, although it had done so in strange and unsettling ways. The Portuguese, in their quest for the legendary kingdom of Prester John, had indeed found fellow Christians at Goa in western India and in Ethiopia; but the beliefs and practices, not to mention the culture and appearance, of these notional co-religionists were disturbingly alien to those of Catholic Christians. Likewise the success of Portuguese missionaries in converting the equatorial West African state of Kongo to Christianity in the 1480s sat uncomfortably with the acquisitiveness of Portuguese merchants engaged in the slave trade. The denizens of the Kingdom of Kongo were fellow Christians, but this fact did not square well with the growing perception on the part of Europeans that black Africans were savages and thus rightly subject to enslavement.

From the 1520s on our observer would also have had a much harder time equating Europe with a single, unified Body of Christ. Much of this had to do with Martin Luther having made public his doubts about the myth of Christendom, starting in 1517. But the success of Luther's challenge rested on political and cultural movements of long gestation. Long before Luther, as we have seen, the real sovereignty over the Church had been shifting away from the papacy to dynastic monarchies. What made Luther's challenge to Rome so appealing, after all, to those German princes and councils of imperial free cities who initially supported him, was his assurance that religion should be a matter of state, just as it had already largely become in the national monarchies of France, Spain and, to a somewhat lesser degree, England. Also, the general direction of Christian devotion over the course of the fifteenth century had been toward a more personal, individual relationship with God, while even the old corporate bonds encouraged by the Eucharist were often experienced by believers as uniting friends, family and neighbours more than some notional body of all Christian believers.

In the wake of Luther, Europe embarked on a new age of divided faith, between Catholics and Protestants, and of doctrinally incompatible – and more often than not mutually hostile – national churches. With this was extinguished whatever feeble validity still remained of the myth of Latin Christendom. Still, it must be said that up until then the edifice of Latin Christendom had had a long go. Certainly much of its endurance can be credited to the institutional framework of the Church itself. But it was the attendant metaphor of the mystical and sacralised Body of Christ, with its promise of unity, community, permanence and immutability, which vivified and legitimated that structure. In the end, though, it was only a metaphor, an artificial construct used to naturalise and reify what was 'out there', but which in and of itself was not real. The inherent fragility of the metaphor of Christ's broken yet whole body had long been recognised. It was, after all, fantastic, incredible. This fact had been discussed in countless sermons on the Eucharist, like that of the Dominican Remigio de' Girolami in the early fourteenth century:

> that the bread and wine become Christ's true body and blood. . . . It is a big thing to think of, that it should be in so many places, on all the altars, in heaven and on earth, in over 100,000 places. . . . But God is there to help our faith.[1]

The metaphor's incredibleness was what gave it its tremendous symbolic power. It was also what made it so susceptible to scepticism and doubt.[2] As long as the sceptics, doubters and unbelievers could be inscribed outside the circle, as heretics, Jews, pagans and infidels, the unity of Christendom could be preserved. As a popular English carol put it:

> Heretics wonder at this thing most:
> How God is put in the holy host,
> Here and at Rome and on every coast.[3]

But when a substantial number of *believers*, of those inside the circle, no longer valued the metaphor or felt that it described their world, once they could no longer connect the Eucharist to the real Body of Christ, or the real Body of Christ to the one, holy, Catholic and apostolic Church of Rome, that's when the edifice all started tumbling down.

The end of Latin Christendom was not the end of Europe, of course. It lived on; and it continued to change and develop just as it had always done. In this sense, the Europe of 1525 was no more 'new' than the Europe of 1300. However, as should have been made apparent in the preceding pages, the Europe of 1525 was also a very different place from what it had been in 1300. Myriad factors saw to that, with some of the most notable being the destabilising but also transformative effects of famine, plague and war, the acquisitiveness of merchants, the inventiveness and at times resentment of workers, the ambitions of elites, the inquisitiveness of intellectuals, the growth of literacy and of lay vernacular culture, the rise of states, and (as has just been suggested) the accumulation of doubts. It was also in some ways a bigger Europe than it had been in 1300, if one takes this to mean the integration of areas on Latin Christendom's periphery like Finland, Poland and Lithuania, and increased, though not always friendly, relations with the rising eastern power of Muscovy. After the fall of Constantinople in 1453, the princes of Muscovy, a culturally distinct Orthodox Christian polity which had, prior to the late fifteenth century maintained closer relations with the Byzantine state and the Mongol Khanates of central Asia than with Latin Christendom, adopted the title of *tsar* ('caesar') and claimed to be the legitimate successors of the Roman and Byzantine emperors. In time, this Russian empire came to be seen as part of Europe as well.

Other myths of identity and unity soon filled the void left behind when the Body of Christ shuffled off the scene. There was the historical myth of nations, which stated that the people of a nation shared a common descent from some ancient tribe. According to this way of thinking, the French were the descendants of the barbarian Franks, who were themselves a branch of the ancient Trojans, while the Florentines were direct descendants of the ancient Romans of the time of the Republic (who, again, were descendants of Trojan exiles who had been led to Italy by Aeneas). This myth with its venerable roots stretching back through the works of medieval historians all the way to Virgil's *Aeneid*, had the advantage of explaining national divisions while at the same time positing a common European identity.[4] The second powerful myth also appealed to history; this was the idea that civilisation had, over time, moved inexorably from the ancient Near East to its final destination in the West (i.e. Latin Christian Europe). This idea, which had first been formulated in the twelfth century by Bishop Otto of Freising in his universal chronicle, *The Two Cities*, was taken up with alacrity by all subsequent medieval authors of universal histories. Like the myth of nations, this myth – expressed in the terms *translatio imperii* and *translatio studii* ('transfer of empire' and 'transfer of learning') – tied the Europeans to ancient Greece and Rome, since civilisation had to pass through them on its peregrination from Assyria to Europe.[5] These myths fit in well with the humanists' historically inspired efforts to reconnect with and emulate antiquity. They also provided Europeans with all the ideological ammunition they needed to distinguish themselves from other people with whom they came into contact, whether Ottoman Turks, Jewish *conversos*, African Christians or enslaved American Indians.

Notes

1 Arnold 2005: 222–23.
2 Rubin 1991: 347–61.
3 Aston 1994: 45.
4 Geary 2002; Guenée 1985: 58–63.
5 Mierow 1966; Smalley 1974.

CHRONOLOGY

The following list of some key dates is no more than a rough guide, meant for quick reference. It is heavy on events and sequences of events that are easily dateable but it has little to say about long-term developments. Events under a single year are not necessarily listed in the order in which they happened that year. The dates for the reigns of monarchs and popes, and the foundation dates of universities can be found in the tables in Chapters 5, 7 and 9.

1302	Battle of Courtrai
1302	Boniface VIII promulgates constitution, *Unam Sanctam*
1303	Boniface VIII seized at Anagni
1304	Collège de Navarre founded at Paris
1306	Expulsion of Jews from France
1307–14	Trial of the Templars
1309	Clement V takes up residence in Avignon
1310	Trial and execution of Marguerite Porète
1311–12	Council of Vienne
1314	Battle of Bannockburn
1315	Battle of Morgarten
1315–17	Great Famine
1316	Death of Giles of Rome
1320	Declaration of Arbroath
1320	Pogroms against Jews in France, Navarre and the Crown of Aragon
1321	The Pastoureaux
1321	Death of Dante Alighieri
1323	John XXII promulgates bull, *Cum inter nonnullos* against Spiritual Franciscans
1323–28	Flemish Revolt
1324	Marsilius of Padua composes *Defensor pacis*
1327	Death of Meister Eckhart
1328	Battle of Cassel
1329	Death of Albertino Mussato
1330	Battle of Posada
1333	Battle of Halidon Hill
1336	Lanzarotto Malocello has first sighting of Canary Islands
1337	Death of Giotto
1337	Beginning of Hundred Years War
1337–39	Ambrogio Lorenzetti paints frescoes in Sala dei Novi, Palazzo Pubblico, Siena

1339	Battle of Laupen
1340	Battle of Sluys
1340s	Bankruptcies of the Florentine 'super-companies'
1341	Portuguese discoveries of Madeira and the eastern Azores
1346	Battle of Crécy
1346	Battle of Neville's Cross
1347	Famine in much of southern Europe
1347–51	Black Death
1348	Pogroms against Jews in Germany
1356	Battle of Poitiers
1356	Golden Bull of Charles IV
1356–69	War of the Two Pedros
1358	Étienne Marcel and the uprising of the Paris commune
1358	The Jacquerie
1367	Battle of Nájera
1367	Spanish College founded at Bologna
1371	Death of Guillaume de Machaut
1374	Death of Petrarch
1375–77	Cluster of revolts against papal lordship in central and northern Italy
1377	Slaughter of civilians in Cesena
1377	Gregory XI returns to Rome
1378	Revolt of the Ciompi in Florence
1378	Outbreak of the Great Schism
1378–81	War of Chioggia
1379	William Wykeham founds New College, Oxford
1380	Death of St Catherine of Siena
1381	English Peasants' Revolt
1381–82	The *Harelle* in Rouen and *Maillotins* in Paris
1382	William of Wykeham founds school, Winchester College
1382	Battle of Roosebeke
1382	Death of Nicole Oresme
1384	Blast Furnace invented
1384	Death of John Wyclif
1384	Death of Geert Grote
1388	English 'Merciless' Parliament
1388	Defeat of Swabian League
1389	Battle of Kosovo
1391	Pogroms against Jews and *conversos* in Spain
1396	Battle of Nicopolis
1396	Giangaleazzo Visconti of Milan gains title of imperial duke
1397	Manuel Chrysoloras begins teaching Greek in Florence
1398	French subtraction of obedience from Avignon pope Benedict XIII
1400	Death of Geoffrey Chaucer
1402	Conquest of Canary Islands begins under Gadifer de la Salle and Jean de Béthencourt
1402	Battle of Ankara
1406	Death of Coluccio Salutati
1407	Murder of Louis of Orléans

1409	Council of Pisa
1410	Battle of Tannenberg/Grunwald
1413–15	Margery Kempe's pilgrimage to Jerusalem and Rome
1414–18	Council of Constance and resolution of Great Schism (1415)
1415	Jan Hus burned at Constance
1415	Battle of Agincourt
1415	Portuguese take Ceuta
1417–19	English conquest of Normandy
1419	Murder of John the Fearless
1419	Death of St Vincent Ferrer
1420	Treaty of Troyes
1420	Battle of Kutná Hora
1420–34	Hussite wars
1421	Burning of 240 members of Jewish community in Vienna
1424	Battle of Verneuil
1429	French under Joan of Arc relieve Orléans
1429	Battle of Patay
1431	Trial and execution of Joan of Arc
1431–49	Council of Basle
1433	Donatello casts statue of David
1434	Christine de Pisan dead by this year
1434	Jan van Eyck paints *Arnolfini Wedding Portrait*
1434	Brunelleschi's dome on the cathedral at Florence completed
1435	Peace of Arras
1437	Council of Basle works out compromise with moderate Hussites
1437–39	Council of Ferrara/Florence
1438	Charles VII issues Pragmatic Sanction of Bourges
1438	All Souls College, Oxford founded
1439	Byzantine acknowledgement of papal supremacy
1440	Lorenzo Valla proves falsity of 'Donation of Constantine'
1440	Henry VI founds school, Eton College
1441	Henry VI founds King's College, Cambridge
1444	Death of St Bernardino of Siena
1447	Death of Filippo Maria Visconti
1448	Magdalen College, Oxford founded
1449–50	French reconquest of Normandy
1450	Battle of Formigny
1450	Jack Cade's Rebellion
1453	Battle of Castillon
1453	End of Hundred Years War
1453	Constantinople falls to Ottoman Turks
1453	Gutenberg and associates publish 42-line Bible
1454	Peace of Lodi
1455	Ottomans seize alum mines at Phocaea
1455–85	English Wars of the Roses
1459	Death of Poggio Bracciolini
1460	Alum mines discovered at Tolfa

1460s	African slaves first used for growing sugarcane in Cape Verde Islands
1464	Death of Cosimo de' Medici
1465	War of the Public Weal
1471	Death of Borso d'Este
1472	Death of Leon Battista Alberti
1473	Pogroms against Jews and *conversos* in Andalusia
1475	Ritual murder trials at Trent
1476	Battles of Grandson and Morat
1478–80	Pazzi War
1480	Magdalen College School, Oxford founded
1482–84	War of Ferrara
1485	Battle of Market Bosworth
1486	Battle of Sempach
1486–87	Heinrich Kramer and Jakob Sprenger publish the *Malleus Maleficarum*
1487–88	Bartolomeu Dias reaches Cape of Good Hope
1488	Domenico Ghirlandaio completes *Adoration of the Magi*
1492	Granada falls to forces of Ferdinand and Isabella
1492	First voyage of Christopher Columbus
1492	Expulsion of Jews from Spain begins
1494	Charles VIII of France invades Italy
1496–98	Expeditions of John Cabot
1497	Cornish Rebellion
1497–99	Expedition of Vasco da Gama to India and back
1498	Death of Girolamo Savonarola
1500	Pedro Alvarez de Cabral makes landing in Brazil
1502	Last Muslims expelled from Spain
1503	Ferdinand the Catholic conquers Naples
1509	League of Cambrai defeats Venice at Agnadello
1512–17	Fifth Lateran Council
1513	Battle of Flodden
1514	Hungarian Revolt
1515	Battle of Marignano
1515	Machiavelli writes *Il Principe*
1516	Concordat of Bologna
1517	Martin Luther posts *Ninety-Five Theses*
1517	Foundation of humanist Corpus Christi College at Oxford
1519	Charles V elected to imperial throne
1519–21	Hernán Cortés conquers Aztec empire
1519–22	Ferdinand Magellan's expedition of global circumnavigation
1521	Death of Josquin Desprez
1521	Diet of Worms
1525	Battle of Pavia
1526	Ottoman victory over Hungarians at Mohács
1527	Charles V's forces sack Rome
1527	Death of Niccolò Machiavelli

SUGGESTED FURTHER READING

Reference

For general reference, see J.R. Strayer (ed.) (1982–89), *Dictionary of the Middle Ages*, 13 vols (New York: Scribner). Atlases to consult are R. McKitterick (ed.) (2004), *Atlas of the Medieval World* (Oxford: Oxford University Press) and D. Ditchburn, S. MacLean and A. MacKay (eds) (2007), *Atlas of Medieval Europe*, 2nd ed. (London: Routledge). Also useful are F.L. Cross and E.A. Livingstone (eds) (1997), *The Oxford Dictionary of the Christian Church*, 3rd ed. (Oxford: Oxford University Press), C.R. Cheney (2000), *A Handbook of Dates for Students of British History*, new ed., revised by M. Jones (Cambridge: Cambridge University Press) and D.H. Farmer (2003), *The Oxford Dictionary of Saints*, 5th ed. (Oxford: Clarendon Press).

General

The best, most recent and thorough general history of late medieval Europe is found in M. Jones (ed.) (2000) and C. Allmand (ed.) (1998), *The New Cambridge Medieval History*, vols 6 and 7 (Cambridge: Cambridge University Press); these volumes will be cited hereafter as *NCMH* 6 and *NCMH* 7. Single volume surveys of the period are W.K. Ferguson (1962), *Europe in Transition, 1300–1500* (New York: Houghton Mifflin), S.E. Ozment (1980), *The Age of Reform (1250–1550): An Intellectual and Religious History of Late Medieval and Renaissance Europe* (New Haven, Ct: Yale University Press), R. Fossier (ed.) (1986), *The Cambridge Illustrated History of the Middle Ages*, vol. 3, *1250–1520*, tr. S.H. Tenison (Cambridge: Cambridge University Press), D. Hay (1989), *Europe in the Fourteenth and Fifteenth Centuries*, 2nd ed. (London: Longman) (originally 1966), D. Nicholas (1999), *The Transformation of Europe, 1300–1600* (London: Arnold), G.A. Holmes (2000), *Europe, Hierarchy and Revolt, 1320–1450*, 2nd ed. (Oxford: Blackwell) (originally 1975) and D. Waley and P. Denley (2001), *Later Medieval Europe, 1250–1520*, 3rd ed. (London: Longman) (originally 1964). See also the stimulating chapters on late medieval Europe in C. Wickham (2016), *Medieval Europe* (New Haven, Ct: Yale University Press). For Italy, see J.M. Najemy (ed.) (2004), *Italy in the Age of the Renaissance 1300–1550* (Oxford: Oxford University Press) and K.R. Bartlett (2013), *A Short History of the Italian Renaissance* (Toronto: University of Toronto Press).

For some interesting recent thoughts about the traditional historical periodisation of the Middle Ages (and especially, late Middle Ages), Renaissance and modern, read J.L. Watts (ed.) (1998), *The End of the Middle Ages? England in the Fifteenth and Sixteenth Centuries* (Stroud: Sutton Publishing) (especially Watts's 'Introduction', 1–22), E. Peters and

W.P. Simons (1999), 'The New Huizinga and the Old Middle Ages', *Speculum*, vol. 74, 587–620, H. Kaminsky (2000), 'From Lateness to Waning to Crisis: The Burden of the Later Middle Ages', *Journal of Early Modern History*, vol. 4, 85–125, J. Le Goff (2005), 'A Long Middle Ages', in his *My Quest for the Middle Ages*, tr. R. Veasey (Edinburgh: Edinburgh University Press), 23–44, M.D. Bailey (2009), 'A Late-Medieval Crisis of Superstition?' *Speculum*, vol. 84, 633–61 and W. Caferro (2011), 'The Renaissance Question', in his *Contesting the Renaissance* (Oxford: Wiley-Blackwell), 1–30.

Part I

Chapter 1

The most thorough and up-to-date general treatment of the crises of the late Middle Ages in English is J. Aberth (2010), *From the Brink of the Apocalypse: Confronting Famine, War, Plague, and Death in the Later Middle Ages*, 2nd ed. (London: Routledge). Efforts to identify and understand the causes of population stagnation and decline in the first decades of the fourteenth century, especially in Britain and northwest Europe can be found in G. Bois (1984), *The Crisis of Feudalism: Economy and Society in Eastern Normandy c. 1300–1550* (Cambridge: Cambridge University Press), T.H. Aston and C.H.E. Philpin (eds) (1985), *The Brenner Debate: Agrarian Class Structure and Economic Development in Pre-Industrial Europe* (Cambridge: Cambridge University Press) and B.M.S. Campbell (ed.) (1991), *Before the Black Death: Studies in the 'Crisis' of the Early Fourteenth Century* (Manchester: Manchester University Press). For a critique of the demographic and subsistence crisis theory, based on evidence from France, see J.L. Goldsmith (1995), 'The Crisis of the Late Middle Ages: The Case of France', *French History*, vol. 9, 417–50. On climate and demography, consult E. Le Roy Ladurie (1972), *Times of Feast, Times of Famine: A History of Climate since the year 1000*, tr. B. Bray (London: George Allen and Unwin), L.R. Poos (1989), 'The Historical Demography of Renaissance Europe: Recent Research and Current Issues', *Renaissance Quarterly*, vol. 42, 794–811 and M. Livi-Bacci (1992), *A Concise History of World Population*, tr. C. Ipsen (Oxford: Blackwell). The Great Famine has been thoroughly studied by W.C. Jordan (1996), *The Great Famine: Northern Europe in the Early Fourteenth Century* (Princeton, NJ: Princeton University Press).

War's effects on society are the subject of C.T. Allmand (1971), 'The War and the Non-Combatant', in *The Hundred Years War*, ed. K.A. Fowler (London: Macmillan), 163–83, N. Wright (1998), *Knights and Peasants: The Hundred Years War in the French Countryside* (Woodbridge: Boydell Press) and C.T. Allmand (1999), 'War and the Non-Combatant in the Middle Ages', in *Medieval Warfare: A History*, ed. M. Keen (Oxford: Oxford University Press), 253–72. For other aspects of late medieval warfare, see the suggested readings for Chapter 6.

The extensive scholarship on plague is surveyed in the bibliography of J. Aberth (2010), mentioned earlier. Some works I found especially useful, in addition to Aberth, are W.P. Blockmans (1980), 'The Social and Economic Effects of Plague in the Low Countries, 1349–1500', *Revue belge de philologie et d'histoire*, vol. 58, 833–63, L.R. Poos (1991), *A Rural Society after the Black Death: Essex, 1350–1525* (Cambridge: Cambridge University Press), J. Hatcher (1994), 'England in the Aftermath of the Black Death', *Past & Present*, vol. 144, 1–35, C. Platt (1996/1997), *King Death: The Black Death and Its Aftermath in Later Medieval Europe* (London: UCL Press; Toronto: University of Toronto Press),

S.K. Cohn (2002), *The Black Death Transformed: Disease and Culture in Early Renaissance Europe* (London: Arnold), J. Theilmann and F. Cate (2007), 'A Plague of Plagues: The Problem of Plague Diagnosis in Medieval England', *Journal of Interdisciplinary History*, vol. 37, 371–93 and L.K. Little (2011), 'Plague Historians in Lab Coats', *Past & Present*, vol. 213, 267–90. A vivid, though partially fictionalised, reconstruction of life in an English village during the Black Death is J. Hatcher (2008), *The Black Death: A Personal History* (Philadelphia, Pa: Da Capo Press).

General treatments of insurrection in the late Middle Ages are M. Mollat and P. Wolff (1973), *The Popular Revolutions of the Late Middle Ages*, tr. A.J. Lytton-Sells (London: George Allen and Unwin), G. Fourquin (1978), *The Anatomy of Popular Rebellion in the Middle Ages*, tr. A. Chesters (Amsterdam: North-Holland Publishing) and S.K. Cohn (2006), *Lust for Liberty: The Politics of Social Revolt in Medieval Europe, 1200–1445, Italy, France, and Flanders* (Cambridge, Ma: Harvard University Press). On individual rebellions, see: for Flanders, W.H. TeBrake (1993), *A Plague of Insurrection: Popular Politics and Peasant Revolt in Flanders, 1323–1328* (Philadelphia, Pa: University of Pennsylvania Press); for Germany and Hungary, A. Laube (1975), 'Precursors of the Peasant War: "Bundschuh" and "Armer Konrad" – Popular Movements on the Eve of the Reformation', *Journal of Peasant Studies*, vol. 3, 49–53, P. Blickle (1979), 'Peasant Revolts in the German Empire in the Late Middle Ages', *Social History*, vol. 4, 223–39, W. Rösener (1994), *The Peasantry of Europe*, tr. T.M. Barker (Oxford: Blackwell), 83–103 and N. Housley (1998), 'Crusading as Social Revolt: The Hungarian Peasant Uprising of 1514', *Journal of Ecclesiastical History*, vol. 49, 1–28; for Spain, A. MacKay (1972), 'Popular Movements and Pogroms in Fifteenth-Century Castile', *Past & Present*, vol. 55, 33–67 and A. MacKay (1990), 'Faction and Civil Strife in Late Medieval Castilian Towns', *Bulletin of the John Rylands Library*, vol. 70, 119–31; for England, R.H. Hilton and T.H. Aston (eds) (1984), *The English Rising of 1381* (Cambridge: Cambridge University Press) is still the best place to start. See also M. Aston (1994), 'Corpus Christi and Corpus Regni: Heresy and the Peasants' Revolt', *Past & Present*, vol. 143, 3–47, S. Justice (1994), *Writing and Rebellion: England in 1381* (Berkeley, Cal: University of California Press) and M. Bush (1999), 'The Risings of the Commons in England, 1381–1549', in *Orders and Hierarchies in Late Medieval and Renaissance Europe*, ed. J. Denton (Basingstoke: Macmillan), 109–25.

Excellent collections of translated primary sources are R.B. Dobson (ed.) (1983), *The Peasants Revolt of 1381*, 2nd ed. (London: Macmillan), R. Horrox (ed.) (1994), *The Black Death* (Manchester: Manchester University Press) and S.K. Cohn (2004), *Popular Protest in Late Medieval Europe: Italy, France and Flanders* (Manchester: Manchester University Press).

Chapter 2

On the ranks and orders of society and on social groups, see the essays in J. Le Goff (ed.) (1990), *Medieval Callings*, tr. L.G. Cochrane (Chicago, Il: University of Chicago Press), S.H. Rigby (1995), *English Society in the Later Middle Ages: Class, Status, and Gender* (New York: St Martin's Press), J. Denton (ed.) (1999), *Orders and Hierarchies in Late Medieval and Renaissance Europe* (London: Macmillan) and O.G. Oexle (ed.) (2001), *Ordering Medieval Society: Perspectives on Intellectual and Practical Modes of Shaping Social Relations*, tr. P. Selwyn (Philadelphia, Pa: University of Pennsylvania Press). More information on the nobility, in particular, can be found in the essays by P. Contamine (1998), 'The European Nobility', in *NCMH* 7, 89–105 and M. Keen (2000), 'Chivalry and the Aristocracy', in *NCMH* 6, 209–21.

There is now a very rich and varied body of literature on the history of women, gender and the family. Some good places to start are: S.M. Stuard (ed.), *Women in Medieval Society* (Philadelphia, Pa: University of Pennsylvania Press, 1976), D. Herlihy (1985), *Medieval Households* (Cambridge, Ma: Harvard University Press), J.M. Bennett (1987), *Women in the Medieval English Countryside: Gender and Household in Brigstock before the Plague* (Oxford: Oxford University Press), M. Erler and M. Kowaleski (eds) (1988), *Women and Power in the Middle Ages* (Athens, Ga: University of Georgia Press), D. Herlihy, *Opera Muliebria: Women and Work in Medieval Europe* (Philadelphia, Pa: Temple University Press), P.J.P. Goldberg (ed.) (1992), *Woman is a Worthy Wight: Women in English Medieval Society c. 1200–1500* (Stroud: Sutton), J.C. Brown and R.C. Davis (eds) (1998), *Gender and Society in Renaissance Italy* (London: Longman), C. Klapisch-Zuber (2000), 'Plague and Family Life', in *NCMH* 6, 124–54, J. Ward (2002), *Women in Medieval Europe 1200–1500* (London: Longman), S. Shahar (2003), *The Fourth Estate: A History of Women in the Middle Ages*, revised ed., tr. C.Galai (London: Routledge) (originally published 1983) and W. Caferro (2011), 'Gender: Who Was the Renaissance Woman?' in his *Contesting the Renaissance* (Oxford: Wiley-Blackwell), 61–97.

On rural communities, B. Hanawalt (1986), *The Ties That Bound: Peasant Families in Medieval England*, R. Fossier (1988), *Peasant Life in the Medieval West*, tr. J. Vale (Oxford: Blackwell), W. Rösener (1992), *Peasants in the Middle Ages*, tr. A. Stützer (Cambridge: Polity) and (1994), *The Peasantry of Europe*, tr. T.M. Barker (Oxford: Blackwell), C. Dyer (1998), 'Rural Europe', in *NCMH* 7, 106–20 and P. Freedman (2000), 'Rural Society', in *NCMH* 6, 82–101. Urban and rural communities are studied in D. Herlihy and C. Klapisch-Zuber (1985), *Tuscans and Their Families: A Study of the Florentine Catasto of 1427* (New Haven, Ct: Yale University Press), T. Dean and C. Wickham (eds) (1990), *City and Countryside in Late Medieval Italy: Essays Presented to Philip Jones* (London: Hambledon Press), T. Scott (2002), *Society and Economy in Germany 1300–1600* (Basingstoke: Palgrave), C. Dyer (2002), *Making a Living in the Middle Ages: The People of Britain, 850–1520* (New Haven, Ct: Yale University Press) and C. Dyer (2005), *An Age of Transition? Economy and Society in England in the Later Middle Ages* (Oxford: Clarendon Press). For more on urban communities, see M. Kowaleski (1988), 'The History of Urban Families in Medieval England', *Journal of Medieval History*, vol. 14, 47–63, D.M. Nicholas (1997), *The Later Medieval City, 1300–1500* (London: Longman), J.-P. Leguay (1998), 'Urban Life', in *NCMH* 7, 102–23 and B. Dobson (2000), 'Urban Europe', in *NCMH* 6, 121–44. Crime and the margins of society are discussed in M. Mollat (1986), *The Poor in the Middle Ages: An Essay in Social History*, tr. A. Goldhammer (New Haven, Ct: Yale University Press), B. Geremek (1987), *The Margins of Society in Late Medieval Paris*, tr. J. Birrell (Cambridge: Cambridge University Press) and T. Dean (ed. and tr.) (2001), *Crime in Medieval Europe, 1200–1550* (Harlow: Longman).

Source collections of particular value for the study of late medieval communities include G. Duby (1968), *Rural Economy and Country Life in the Medieval West*, tr. C. Postan (London: Edward Arnold), M. Bailey (2002), *The English Manor, 1200–1500* (Manchester: Manchester University Press) and M. Kowaleski (ed.) (2006), *Medieval Towns: A Reader* (Toronto: Broadview).

Chapter 3

On trade and commerce, consult: R.S. Lopez (1976), *the Commercial Revolution of the Middle Ages, 950–1350* (Cambridge: Cambridge University Press), J. Day (1987), *The Medieval Market Economy* (Oxford: Blackwell), P. Spufford (1988), *Money and Its Use in Medieval Europe* (Cambridge: Cambridge University Press), J.L. Abu-Lughod (1989), *Before European Hegemony: The World System AD 1250–1350* (Oxford: Oxford University Press), R.H. Britnell (1993), *The Commercialisation of English Society 1000–1500* (Cambridge: Cambridge University Press), C. Cipolla (1993), *Before the Industrial Revolution: European Society and Economy, 1000–1700*, 3rd ed. (London: Routledge), W. Childs (1998), 'Commerce and Trade', in *NCMH* 7, 145–60, E.S. Hunt and J. Murray (1999), *A History of Business in Medieval Europe, 1200–1550* (Cambridge: Cambridge University Press), P. Spufford (2000), 'Trade in Fourteenth-Century Europe', in *NCMH* 6, 155–208, P. Spufford (2002), *Power and Profit: The Merchant in Medieval Europe* (London: Thames and Hudson) and S.A. Epstein (2009), *An Economic and Social History of Later Medieval Europe, 1000–1500* (Cambridge: Cambridge University Press).

Since the pioneering publication of L. White (1962), *Medieval Technology and Social Change* (Oxford: Clarendon Press), several excellent contributions have been made to the history of medieval technology, including: B.S. Hall and D.C. West (eds), *On Pre-Modern Technology and Science: A Volume of Studies in Honor of Lynn White, Jr.* (Malibu, Cal: Undena Publications), R.W. Unger (1980), *The Ship in the Medieval Economy, 600–1600* (London: Croom Helen; Montreal: McGill-Queen's University Press), E. Ashtor (1989), 'The Factors of Technological and Industrial Progress in the Later Middle Ages', *Journal of European Economic History*, vol. 18, 7–36, F. Gies and J. Gies (1994), *Cathedral, Forge, and Waterwheel: Technology and Invention in the Middle Ages* (New York: Harper Collins) and E.B. Smith and M. Wolfe (eds) (1997), *Technology and Resource Management in Medieval Europe: Cathedrals, Mills, and Mines* (Aldershot: Ashgate). See also the essays on time and labour in J. Le Goff (1980), *Time, Work, and Culture in the Middle Ages*, tr. A. Goldhammer (Chicago: University of Chicago Press).

On European expansion and exploration, the early work of P. Chaunu (1979), *European Expansion in the Later Middle Ages*, tr. K. Bertram (Amsterdam: North Holland Publishing), has been added to substantially in publications by F. Fernández-Armesto (1987), *Before Columbus: Exploration and Colonisation from the Mediterranean to the Atlantic, 1229–1492* (London: Macmillan), F. Fernández-Armesto (1998), 'Exploration and Discovery', in *NCMH* 7, 175–201, J.R.S. Phillips (1998), *The Medieval Expansion of Europe*, 2nd ed. (Oxford: Clarendon Press) and J. Larner (1999), *Marco Polo and the Discovery of the World* (New Haven, Ct: Yale University Press). For a longer and broader view, see F. Fernández-Armesto (2006), *Pathfinders: A Global History of Exploration* (New York: W.W. Norton).

A useful collection of translated documents is R.S. Lopez and I.W. Raymond (eds) (1990), *Medieval Trade in the Mediterranean World: Illustrative Documents Translated with Introductions and Notes* (New York: Columbia University Press) (originally 1955).

Part II

Chapter 4

The two indispensible introductions to all aspects of late medieval politics are B. Guenée (1985), *States and Rulers in Later Medieval Europe*, tr. J. Vale (Oxford: Blackwell) and, now, J. Watts (2009), *The Making of Polities: Europe, 1300–1500* (Cambridge: Cambridge University Press); Guenée's generous bibliography in *States and Rulers* has also been updated repeatedly in the supplements to subsequent French editions of *States and Rulers*, under the title *L'occident aux XIVe et XVe siècles: les états*. Late medieval political thought is surveyed in J.H. Burns (ed.), *The Cambridge History of Medieval Political Thought, c. 350–c. 1450* (Cambridge: Cambridge University Press), A. Black (1992), *Political Thought in Europe, 1250–1450* (Cambridge: Cambridge University Press), J. Canning (1996), *A History of Medieval Political Thought, 300–1450* (London: Routledge) and J. Coleman (2000), *A History of Political Thought: From the Middle Ages to the Renaissance* (Oxford: Blackwell). On this see also the essays of J.-P. Genet (1998), 'Politics: Theory and Practice', in *NCMH* 7, 3–28 and A. Rigaudière (2000), 'The Theory and Practice of Government in Western Europe', in *NCMH* 6, 17–41, K. Green and C.J. Mews (eds) (2005), *Healing the Body Politic: The Political Thought of Christine de Pizan* (Turnhout: Brepols) and C.J. Nederman (2009), *Lineages of European Political Thought: Explorations along the Medieval/Modern Divide from John of Salisbury to Hegel* (Washington D.C.: Catholic University of America Press).

More on books of political instruction (mirrors of princes) can be found in R.F. Green (1980), *Poets and Princepleasers: Literature and the English Court in the Late Middle Ages* (Toronto: University of Toronto Press), M. Viroli (1992), *From Politics to Reason of State: The Acquisition and Transformation of the Language of Politics, 1250–1600* (Cambridge: Cambridge University Press), C.F. Briggs (1999), *Giles of Rome's 'De regimine principum': Reading and Writing Politics at Court and University, c. 1275–c. 1525* (Cambridge: Cambridge University Press) and P. Strohm (2005), *Politique: Languages of Statecraft between Chaucer and Shakespeare* (Notre Dame, Ind: University of Notre Dame Press). The propagation of political ideology is treated in E.H. Kantorowicz (1957), *The King's Two Bodies: A Study in Medieval Political Theology* (Princeton, NJ: Princeton University Press), Q. Skinner (1986), 'Ambrogio Lorenzetti: The Artist as Political Philosopher', *Proceedings of the British Academy*, vol. 72, 1–56, C. Beaune (1991), *The Birth of an Ideology: Myths and Symbols of Nation in Late-Medieval France*, tr. S.R. Huston, ed. F.L. Cheyette (Berkeley, Cal: University of California Press), D.L. d'Avray (1994), *Death and the Prince: Memorial Preaching before 1350* (Oxford: Clarendon Press), I. Rosario (2000), *Art and Propaganda: Charles IV of Bohemia, 1346–1378* (Woodbridge: Boydell Press), S. Bertelli (2001), *The King's Body: Sacred Rituals of Power in Medieval and Early Modern Europe*, tr. R.B. Litchfield (University Park, Pa: Pennsylvania State University Press), E. Muir (2004), 'Representations of Power', in *Italy in the Age of the Renaissance 1300–1550*, ed. J.M. Najemy (Oxford: Oxford University Press), 226–45 and P. Boucheron (2018), *The Power of Images: Siena, 1338*, tr. A. Brown (Cambridge: Polity Press).

Collections of translated political writings can be found in R. Lerner and M. Mahdi (eds) (1963), *Medieval Political Philosophy: A Sourcebook* (New York: The Free Press of Glencoe), C.J. Nederman and K.L. Forhan (eds) (1993), *Medieval Political Theory – A Reader: The Quest for the Body Politic, 1100–1400* (London: Routledge) and A.S. McGrade, J. Kilcullen and M. Kempshall (eds) (2001), *The Cambridge Translations of Medieval Philosophical Texts*, vol. 2, *Ethics and Political Philosophy* (Cambridge: Cambridge University Press).

Chapter 5

There is a vast body of scholarship on the structures of government and on the event-history of late medieval politics. Here, the best place to start is with the numerous contributions in *NCMH* 6 and 7 and the indispensible treatment by J.L. Watts (2009), *The Making of Polities: Europe, 1300–1500* (Cambridge: Cambridge University Press). In addition to these studies, some works on structures and relationships that I found especially useful are R.G. Asch and A.M. Birke (eds) (1991), *Princes, Patronage, and the Nobility: The Court at the Beginning of the Modern Age, c. 1450–1650* (London and Oxford: German Historical Institute and Oxford University Press), W. Reinhard (ed.) (1996), *Power Elites and State Building* (Oxford: Clarendon Press) and M. Vale (2001), *The Princely Court: Medieval Courts and Culture in North-West Europe* (Oxford: Oxford University Press). Additional information on specific regions is in: for the British Isles, M. Keen (2003), *England in the Later Middle Ages: A Political History*, 2nd ed. (London: Routledge), L. Clark and C. Carpenter (eds) (1994), *The Fifteenth Century*, vol. 4, *Political Culture in Late Medieval Britain* (Woodbridge: Boydell Press), G. Harriss (2005), *Shaping the Nation: England 1360–1461* (Oxford: Oxford University Press) and M. Brown (2013), *Disunited Kingdoms: Peoples and Politics in the British Isles 1280–1460* (London: Routledge); recent stimulating comparative essays on England and France are in C. Fletcher, J.-P. Genet and J. Watts (eds) (2015), *Government and Political Life in England and France, c. 1300–c. 1500* (Cambridge: Cambridge University Press); for France and Burgundy, P.S. Lewis (1968), *Later Medieval France: The Polity* (London: Macmillan), P.S. Lewis (1985), *Essays in Later Medieval French History* (London: Hambledon) and G. Small (2009), *Late Medieval France* (Basingstoke: Palgrave Macmillan); for the Iberian and western Mediterranean kingdoms, J.N. Hillgarth (1976–78), *The Spanish Kingdoms, 1250–1516*, 2 vols (Oxford: Clarendon Press), A. MacKay (1977), *Spain in the Middle Ages: From Frontier to Empire, 1000–1500* (London: Macmillan) and D. Abulafia (1997), *The Western Mediterranean Kingdoms, 1200–1500* (London: Longman); on Italy, S. Kelly (2003), *The New Solomon: Robert of Naples (1309–1343) and Fourteenth-Century Kingship* (Leiden: Brill), J.M. Najemy (ed.) (2004), *Italy in the Age of the Renaissance 1300–1550* (Oxford: Oxford University Press), A. Gamberini and I. Lazzarini (eds) (2012), *The Italian Renaissance State* (Cambridge: Cambridge University Press), E. Casteen (2015), *From She-Wolf to Martyr: The Reign and Disputed Reputation of Johanna I of Naples* (Ithaca, NY: Cornell University Press) and F. Ricciardelli (2015), *The Myth of Republicanism in Renaissance Italy* (Turnhout: Brepols); for a comparative study of European city-states, see now T. Scott (2012), *The City-State in Europe, 1000–1600* (Oxford: Oxford University Press); and on Germany, J. Leuschner, *Germany in the Later Middle Ages*, tr. S. MacCormack (Amsterdam: North-Holland Publishing), F.R.H. Du Boulay (1983), *Germany in the Later Middle Ages* (London: Athlone Press) and P.H. Wilson (2016), *Heart of Europe: A History of the Holy Roman Empire* (Cambridge, Ma: The Belknap Press).

Chapter 6

Anyone wishing to approach the history of war in the late Middle Ages should begin by consulting P. Contamine (1984), *War in the Middle Ages*, tr. M. Jones (Oxford: Blackwell), M. Prestwich (1996), *Armies and Warfare in the Middle Ages: The English Experience* (New Haven, Ct: Yale University Press), C. Allmand (1998), 'War', in *NCMH* 6, 161–74 and M. Keen (ed.) (1999), *Medieval Warfare: A History* (Oxford: Oxford University Press). Additional places to look for information on war and the state and on technological, tactical and strategic advances are R.W. Kaeuper (1988), *War, Justice, and Public Order: England and France in the Later Middle Ages* (Oxford: Clarendon Press), A. Ayton and J.L. Price (eds) (1995),

302

The Medieval Military Revolution: State, Society, and Military Change in Medieval and Early Modern Europe (London: I.B. Tauris Publishers) and B.S. Hall (1997), *Weapons and Warfare in Renaissance Europe: Gunpowder, Technology, and Tactics* (Baltimore, Md: Johns Hopkins University Press). The subject of mercenaries can be accessed through the works of M. Mallet (1974), *Mercenaries and Their Masters: Warfare in Renaissance Italy* (Totowa, NJ: Rowman and Littlefield), K.A. Fowler (2001), *Medieval Mercenaries*, vol. 1, *The Great Companies* (Oxford: Blackwell) and W. Caferro (2006), *John Hawkwood: An English Mercenary in Fourteenth-Century Italy* (Baltimore, Md: Johns Hopkins University Press).

Of all the armed conflicts of the late Middle Ages, none has received more attention than the Hundred Years War; consequently, the works devoted to it are legion. A few of the more recent ones are J. Sumption (1990–2015), *The Hundred Years War*, 4 vols (London: Faber and Faber; Philadelphia, Pa: University of Pennsylvania Press), C.J. Rogers (2000), *War Cruel and Sharp: English Strategy under Edward III, 1327–1360* (Woodbridge: Boydell Press), C.T. Allmand (2001), *The Hundred Years War: England and France at War, c. 1300–c. 1450*, rev. ed. (Cambridge: Cambridge University Press), A. Curry (2003), *The Hundred Years War*, 2nd ed. (Basingstoke: Palgrave Macmillan) and D. Green (2014), *The Hundred Years War: A People's History* (New Haven, Ct: Yale University Press).

The subject of late medieval chivalry is masterfully explored in M. Keen (1984), *Chivalry* (New Haven, Ct: Yale University Press). On chivalry, see also R.W. Kaeuper (1999), *Chivalry and Violence in Medieval Europe* (Oxford: Oxford University Press) and R.W. Kaeuper (intro.) and E. Kennedy (tr.) (2005), *A Knight's Own Book of Chivalry: Geoffroi de Charny* (Philadelphia, Pa: University of Pennsylvania Press). The late medieval crusades have been studied by N. Housley (1992), *The Later Crusades, 1274–1580: From Lyons to Alcazar* (Oxford: Oxford University Press) and N. Housley (2001), *Crusading and Warfare in Medieval and Renaissance Europe* (Aldershot: Ashgate) and A.V. Murray (ed.) (2001), *Crusade and Conversion on the Baltic Frontier, 1150–1500* (Aldershot: Ashgate).

For translations of texts related to warfare, see C.T. Allmand (ed.) (1998), *Society at War: The Experience of England and France during the Hundred Years War*, new ed. (Woodbridge: Boydell Press), A. Curry (ed.) (2000), *The Battle of Agincourt: Sources and Interpretations* (Woodbridge: Boydell Press), T.A. Fudge (ed.) (2002), *The Crusade against Heretics in Bohemia, 1418–1437: Sources and Documents for the Hussite Crusades* (Aldershot: Ashgate) and N. Housley (ed.) (2004), *Crusading in the Fifteenth Century: Message and Impact* (Basingstoke: Palgrave Macmillan).

Part III

Chapter 7

F. Oakley (1979) *The Western Church in the Later Middle Ages* (Ithaca, NY: Cornell University Press) remains the best and most approachable survey of the late medieval Church. This can be supplemented with B. Schimmelpfennig (1992), *The Papacy*, tr. J. Sievert (New York: Columbia University Press), and with the contributions of P.N.R. Zutshi (2000), 'The Avignon Papacy' and H. Kaminsky (2000), 'The Great Schism', both in *NCMH* 6, 653–96, of A. Black (1998), 'Popes and Councils', in *NCMH* 7, 65–86, and for the papacy and Italian politics, see S. Carocci (2012), 'The Papal State' and G. Chittolini (2012), 'The Papacy and the Italian States', both in *The Italian Renaissance State*, ed. A. Gamberini and I. Lazzarini (Cambridge: Cambridge University Press), 69–89, 467–89. The history of the religious orders can be found in C.H. Lawrence (1984), *Medieval Monasticism: Forms of Religious Life in Western Europe in the Middle Ages* (London: Longman) and C.H. Lawrence (1994), *The Friars: The Impact of the Early Mendicant Movement on Western Society* (London: Longman). On the role of the universities in the Great Schism and the origins of conciliarism, see R.N. Swanson (1979), *Universities, Academics and the Great Schism* (Cambridge: Cambridge University Press).

Chapter 8

The last forty years has seen a flood of publications on religious practice, devotion and spirituality. Especially useful surveys are found in R.N. Swanson (1995), *Religion and Devotion in Europe, c. 1215–c. 1515* (Cambridge: Cambridge University Press), J.H. Arnold (2005), *Belief and Unbelief in Medieval Europe* (London: Arnold), and in the essays of J. Catto (2000), 'Currents of Religious Thought and Expression', in *NCMH* 6, 42–65 and F. Rapp (1998), 'Religious Belief and Practice', in *NCMH* 7, 205–19; see also the pertinent essays in M. Rubin and W. Simons (eds) (2009), *The Cambridge History of Christianity*, vol. 4, *Christianity in Western Europe, c. 1100–c. 1500* (Cambridge: Cambridge University Press). For Joan of Arc, see D. Hobbins (tr.) (2005), *The Trial of Joan of Arc* (Cambridge, Ma: Harvard University Press). The feasts of the liturgical calendar are discussed in R.W. Pfaff (1970), *New Liturgical Feasts in Later Medieval England* (Oxford: Clarendon Press) and R.W. Pfaff (2007), 'Telling Liturgical Times in the Middle Ages', in *Procession, Performance, Liturgy, and Ritual*, ed. N. van Deusen (Ottowa: Institute of Mediaeval Music), 43–64. The cultural relevance of the feast of Corpus Christi has been examined with particular sensitivity by M. Rubin, *Corpus Christi: The Eucharist in Late Medieval Culture* (Cambridge: Cambridge University Press). The pilgrimages of Margery Kempe and other aspects of her religious life are the subject of A. Goodman (2002), *Margery Kempe and Her World* (London: Longman). A still very good introduction to some of the historiographical problems and debates associated with lay religion and devotion is J. Van Engen (1986), 'The Christian Middle Ages as an Historiographical Problem', *American Historical Review*, vol. 91, 519–52.

Many aspects of lay religion and devotion are specific to localities and the amount of published scholarship on these is enormous. Some studies that I found especially helpful were: for England, E. Duffy (2005), *The Stripping of the Altars: Traditional Religion in England 1400–1580*, 2nd ed. (New Haven, Ct: Yale University Press) and R.N. Swanson (1989), *Church and Society in Late Medieval England* (Oxford: Blackwell); for Germany, B. Moeller (1971), 'Piety in Germany around 1500', in *The Reformation in Medieval Perspective*, ed. S.E. Ozment (Chicago: Quadrangle Books), 50–75, B. Hamm (2004), *The Reformation of the Faith in the Context of Late Medieval Theology and Piety: Essays of Berndt Hamm*, ed. R.J. Bast (Leiden: Brill) and C.W. Bynum (2007), *Wonderful Blood: Theology and Practice in Late Medieval Northern Germany and Beyond* (Philadelphia, Pa: University of Pennsylvania Press); for Italy, S.K. Cohn (1992), *The Cult of Remembrance and the Black Death: Six Renaissance Cities in Central Italy* (Baltimore, Md: Johns Hopkins University Press), D. Bornstein (1993), *The Bianchi of 1399: Popular Devotion in Late Medieval Italy* (Ithaca, NY: Cornell University Press), J. Henderson (1994), *Piety and Charity in Late Medieval Florence* (Oxford: Clarendon Press) and G.W. Dameron (2005), *Florence and Its Church in the Age of Dante* (Philadelphia, Pa: University of Pennsylvania Press).

Late medieval saints and sainthood are the topic of A. Vauchez (1997), *Sainthood in the Later Middle Ages*, tr. J. Birrell (Cambridge: Cambridge University Press). Women's spirituality has been the subject of considerable attention of the last few decades; on this, see C.W. Bynum (1987), *Holy Feast and Holy Fast: The Religious Significance of Food to Medieval Women* (Berkeley, Cal: University of California Press), A. Vauchez (1993), *The Laity in the Middle Ages: Religious Beliefs and Devotional Practices*, ed. D.E. Bornstein, tr. M.J. Schneider (Notre Dame, Ind: University of Notre Dame Press), D. Bornstein and R. Rusconi (eds) (1996), *Women and Religion in Medieval and Renaissance Italy*, tr. M.J. Schneider (Chicago: University of Chicago Press), W. Simons (2001), *Cities of Ladies: Beguine Communities in the Medieval Low Countries, 1200–1565* (Philadelphia: University of Pennsylvania Press) and D. Wood (ed.) (2003), *Women and Religion in Medieval England* (Oxford: Oxbow Books). For more information about specific aspects of religious practice, like the mass, confession, Purgatory, indulgences and a mathematical sensibility, see the following: J. Bossy (1983), 'The Mass as a Social Institution 1200–1700', *Past & Present*, vol. 100, 29–61; T.N. Tentler (1974), 'The Summa for Confessors as an Instrument of Social Control', in *The Pursuit of Holiness in Late Medieval and Renaissance Religion*, ed. C. Trinkaus and H.A. Oberman (Leiden: Brill), 103–37 (the pagination here includes the responses to Tentler by L.E. Boyle and W.J. Bouwsma) and P. Biller and A.J. Minnis (eds) (1998), *Handling Sin: Confession in the Middle Ages* (York: York Medieval Press); J. Le Goff (1984), *The Birth of Purgatory*, tr. A. Goldhammer (Chicago, Il: University of Chicago Press); R.N. Swanson (ed.) (2006), *Promissory Notes on the Treasury of Merits: Indulgences in Late Medieval Europe* (Leiden: Brill); T. Lentes (2001), 'Counting Piety in the Late Middle Ages', in *Ordering Medieval Society: Perspectives on Intellectual and Practical Modes of Shaping Social Relations*, ed. B. Jussen, tr. P. Selwyn (Philadelphia, Pa: University of Pennsylvania Press), 55–91. Many studies try to take into account the influence of the pestilence on attitudes toward death. For an introduction to the subject, look at J. Delumeau (1990), *Sin and Fear: The Emergence of a Western Guilt Culture, 13th–18th Centuries*, tr. E. Nicholson (New York: St. Martin's Press) and J. Aberth (2010), *From the Brink of the Apocalypse: Confronting Famine, War, Plague, and Death in the Later Middle Ages*, 2nd ed. (London: Routledge).

In their quest for unity, doctrinal purity and normative practice, Christians of the fourteenth through early sixteenth centuries defined, excluded and often persecuted those who did not convert or conform. There is an extremely rich body of scholarship on the history of the Jews in medieval Europe. For a recently published introduction, see R. Chazan (2006), *The Jews of Medieval Western Christendom, 1000–1500* (Cambridge: Cambridge University Press); also especially apposite to the topic of Christian attitudes toward Jews are R. Po-Chia Hsia (1992), *Trent 1475: Stories of a Ritual Murder Trial* (New Haven, Ct: Yale University Press), M. Rubin (1995), 'Imagining the Jew: The Late Medieval Eucharistic Discourse', in *In and Out of the Ghetto: Jewish-Gentile Relations in Late Medieval and Early Modern Germany*, ed. R. Po-Chia Hsia and H. Lehmann (Cambridge: Cambridge University Press), 107–208, D. Nirenberg (1996), *Communities of Violence: Persecution of Minorities in the Middle Ages* (Princeton, NJ: Princeton University Press), M. Rubin (1999), *Gentile Tales: The Narrative Assault on Late Medieval Jews* (Philadelphia, Pa: University of Pennsylvania Press) and several of the essays collected in W.C. Jordan (2001), *Ideology and Royal Power in Medieval France: Kingship, Crusades and the Jews* (Aldershot: Ashgate).

Heresy, heretics and their persecution at the hands of the Church and secular rulers generate no end of fascination. For medieval heresies, in general, go first to M. Lambert (2002), *Medieval Heresy: Popular Movements from the Gregorian Reform to the Reformation*, 3rd ed. (Oxford: Blackwell). J.B. Given (1997), *Inquisition and Medieval Society: Power,*

Discipline, and Resistance in Languedoc (Ithaca, NY: Cornell University Press) is an especially interesting look at the inquisition of the late medieval Cathars and Waldensians in the south of France, while L.A. Burnham (2008), *So Great a Light, so Great a Smoke: the Beguin Heretics of Languedoc* (Ithaca, NY: Cornell University Press) examines the fate of the proscribed followers of Peter John Olivi; several heresies receive attention in P. Biller and A. Hudson (eds) (1994), *Heresy and Literacy, 1000–1530* (Cambridge: Cambridge University Press). The most authoritative treatment of Wyclif and the Lollards is A. Hudson (1988), *The Premature Reformation: Wycliffite Texts and Lollard History* (Oxford: Clarendon Press), although G. Harriss (2005), *Shaping the Nation: England, 1360–1461* (Oxford: Clarendon Press), 376–402, also provides a splendid overview. The best place to start for the history of the Hussites is still H. Kaminsky (1967), *A History of the Hussite Revolution* (Berkeley, Cal: University of California Press), though J. Klassen (1998), 'Hus, the Hussites and Bohemia', in *NCMH* 7, 367–91, should be consulted for a more recent assessment.

The early history of Europe's obsession with witches and witchcraft is traced in J.B. Russell (1972), *Witchcraft in the Middle Ages* (Ithaca, NY: Cornell University Press), N. Cohn (1975), *Europe's Inner Demons: An Enquiry Inspired by the Great Witch-Hunt* (New York: Basic Books), R. Kieckhefer (1976), *Witch Trials: Their Foundations in Popular and Learned Culture, 1300–1500* (Berkeley, Cal: University of California Press) and M.D. Bailey (2003), *Battling Demons: Witchcraft, Heresy, and Reform in the Late Middle Ages* (University Park, Pa: Pennsylvania State University Press).

Some good places to start when trying to understand the background to and causes of the Protestant Reformation are S.E. Ozment (ed.) (1971), *The Reformation in Medieval Perspective* (Chicago: Quadrangle Books), C. Harper-Bill (1989), *The Pre-Reformation Church in England, 1400–1530* (London: Longman), H.A. Oberman (1992), *The Dawn of the Reformation: Essays in Late Medieval and Early Reformation Thought* (Edinburgh: T&T Clark), A. Levi (2002), *Renaissance and Reformation: The Intellectual Genesis* (New Haven, Ct: Yale University Press), B. Thompson (2004), 'Prelates and Politics from Winchelsey to Warham', in *Political Culture in Late Medieval Britain*, ed. L. Clark and C. Carpenter (Woodbridge: Boydell and Brewer), 69–95 and P.G. Wallace (2004), *The Long European Reformation: Religion, Political Conflict, and the Search for Conformity, 1350–1750* (Basingstoke: Palgrave Macmillan).

Three excellent collections of primary sources in translation are J. Van Engen, (tr.) (1988), *Devotio Moderna: Basic Writings* (New York: Paulist Press). R.N. Swanson (ed.) (1993), *Catholic England: Faith, Religion, and Observance before the Reformation* (Manchester: Manchester University Press) and J. Shinners (ed.) (1997), *Medieval Popular Religion, 1000–1500* (Toronto: Broadview Press).

Part IV

Chapter 9

J. Verger (2000), *Men of Learning in Europe at the End of the Middle Ages*, tr. L. Neal and S. Rendall (Notre Dame, Ind: University of Notre Dame Press) is the best and most thorough treatment on scholars' self-perception, status and careers. On this see also J. Le Goff (1980), *Time, Work, and Culture in the Middle Ages*, tr. A. Goldhammer (Chicago: University of Chicago Press), 122–49, J. Le Goff (1993), *Intellectuals in the Middle Ages*, tr. T.L. Fagan (Oxford: Blackwell) and I.P. Wei (1995), 'The Self-Image of Masters of Theology at the

University of Paris in the Late Thirteenth and Early Fourteenth Centuries', *Journal of Ecclesiastical History*, vol. 46, 398–431.

Several studies on schools and the education of children and adolescents in England and Italy have appeared over the last several years. For England, see J.A.H. Moran (1985), *The Growth of English Schooling, 1340–1548: Learning, Literacy, and Laicization in Pre-Reformation York Diocese* (Princeton, NJ: Princeton University Press), N. Orme (1984), *From Childhood to Chivalry: The Education of the English Kings and Aristocracy, 1066–1530* (London: Methuen), N. Orme (2001), *Medieval Children* (New Haven, Ct: Yale University Press) and N. Orme (2006), *Medieval Schools: From Roman Britain to Renaissance England* (New Haven, Ct: Yale University Press). For Italy, see P.F. Grendler (1989), *Schooling in Renaissance Italy: Literacy and Learning, 1300–1600* (Baltimore, Md: Johns Hopkins University Press), P. Denley (1990), 'Governments and Schools in Late Medieval Italy', in *City and Countryside in Late Medieval Italy and Renaissance Italy: Essays Presented to Philip Jones*, ed. T. Dean and C. Wickham (London: Hambledon Press), 93–107, P.F. Gehl (1993), *A Moral Art: Grammar, Society, and Culture in Trecento Florence* (Ithaca, NY: Cornell University Press) and R. Black (2004), 'Education and the Emergence of a Literate Society', in *Italy in the Age of the Renaissance 1300–1550* , ed. J.M. Najemy (Oxford: Oxford University Press), 18–36. Humanism's impact on schooling is the subject of K. Jensen (1996), 'The Humanist Reform of Latin and Latin Teaching', in *The Cambridge Companion to Renaissance Humanism*, ed. J. Kraye (Cambridge: Cambridge University Press), 63–81 and R. Black (2001), *Humanism and Education in Medieval and Renaissance Italy: Tradition and Innovation in Latin Schools from the Twelfth to the Fifteenth Century* (Cambridge: Cambridge University Press).

Far more numerous are studies devoted to all aspects of university education. Good general introductions are A.B. Cobban (1975), *Medieval Universities: Their Development and Organization* (London: Methuen) and H. de Ridder-Symoens (ed.) (1992), *A History of the University in Europe*, vol. 1, *Universities in the Middle Ages* (Cambridge: Cambridge University Press), though also still of some value is the venerable survey of H. Rashdall (1936), *The Universities in Europe in the Middle Ages*, 3 vols, ed. F.M. Powicke and A.B. Emden (Oxford: Oxford University Press). Worthwhile too are the articles on late medieval universities that appear regularly in the periodical, *History of the Universities*. Studies of individual universities or universities by country are: for France, G. Leff (1968), *Paris and Oxford Universities in the Thirteenth and Fourteenth Centuries: An Institutional and Intellectual History* (New York: John Wiley and Sons) and J. Verger (1972), 'The University of Paris at the End of the Hundred Years' War', in *Universities in Politics: Case Studies from the Late Middle Ages and Early Modern Period*, ed. J.W. Baldwin and R.A. Goldthwaite (Baltimore, Md: Johns Hopkins University Press), 47–78; for England, W.J. Courtenay (1987), *Schools and Scholars in Fourteenth-Century England* (Princeton: Princeton University Press), J.I. Catto (ed.) (1984), *The History of the University of Oxford*, vol. 1, *The Early Oxford Schools* (Oxford: Clarendon Press), J.I. Catto and R. Evans (eds) (1992), *The History of the University of Oxford*, vol. 2, *Late Medieval Oxford* (Oxford: Clarendon Press), D.R. Leader (1988), *A History of the University of Cambridge*, vol. 1, *The University to 1546* (Cambridge: Cambridge University Press); for Italy, P.F. Grendler (2002), *The Universities of the Italian Renaissance* (Baltimore, Md: Johns Hopkins University Press); for Bohemia, H. Kaminsky (1972), 'The University of Prague in the Hussite Revolution: The Role of the Masters', in *Universities in Politics: Case Studies from the Late Middle Ages and Early Modern Period*, ed. J.W. Baldwin and R.A. Goldthwaite (Baltimore, Md: Johns Hopkins

University Press), 79–106. Also useful are the essays in W.J. Courtenay and J. Miethke (eds) (2000), *Universities and Schooling in Medieval Society* (Leiden: Brill) and J. Van Engen (ed.) (2000), *Learning Institutionalized: Teaching in the Medieval University* (Notre Dame, Ind: University of Notre Dame Press).

For education in the schools of the mendicants, see C.T. Davis (1984), 'Education in Dante's Florence', in his *Dante's Italy and Other Essays* (Philadelphia: University of Pennsylvania Press), M.M. Mulchahey (1998), *'First the Bow is Bent in Study . . .': Dominican Education before 1350* (Toronto: Pontifical Institute of Mediaeval Studies), B. Roest (2000), *A History of Franciscan Education (c. 1210–1517)* (Leiden: Brill) and several of the essays in R.B. Begley and J.W. Koterski (eds) (2005), *Medieval Education* (New York: Fordham University Press).

Intellectual developments at the universities are treated in the studies of universities mentioned earlier and in N. Kretzmann, A. Kenny and J. Pinborg (eds) (1982), *The Cambridge History of Later Medieval Philosophy* (Cambridge: Cambridge University Press). On humanism, consult A. Grafton and L. Jardine (1986), *From Humanism to the Humanities: Education and the Liberal Arts in Fifteenth- and Sixteenth-Century Europe* (Cambridge, Ma: Harvard University Press), J. Kraye (ed.) (1996), *The Cambridge Companion to Renaissance Humanism* (Cambridge: Cambridge University Press), R. Black (1998), 'Humanism', in *NCMH* 7, 243–77, R.G. Witt (2003), *In the Footsteps of the Ancients: The Origins of Humanism from Lovato to Bruni* (Leiden: Brill) and C.G. Nauert (2006), *Humanism and the Culture of Renaissance Europe*, 2nd ed. (Cambridge: Cambridge University Press).

Two translated source collections on medieval education are L. Thorndyke (tr.) (1972), *University Records and Life in the Middle Ages* (New York: Norton) and C.W. Kallendorf (ed. and tr.) (2002), *Humanist Education Treatises* (Cambridge, Ma: Harvard University Press).

Chapter 10

A large and diverse body of scholarship has appeared in the last few decades on the processes by which vernacular languages became high-status, textualised, literary languages. On this, see the essays in F. Somerset and N. Watson (eds) (2003), *The Vulgar Tongue: Medieval and Postmedieval Vernacularity* (University Park, Pa: Pennsylvania State University Press) and M. Goyens and W. Verbeke (eds) (2003), *The Dawn of the Written Vernacular in Western Europe* (Leuven: Leuven University Press). See also A.J. Minnis (1988), *Medieval Theory of Authorship: Scholastic Literary Attitudes in the Later Middle Ages*, 2nd ed. (Philadelphia, Pa: University of Pennsylvania Press), R. Copeland (1991), *Rhetoric, Hermeneutics and Translation in the Middle Ages: Academic Traditions and Vernacular Texts* (Cambridge: Cambridge University Press), C.F. Briggs (2000), 'Literacy, Reading, and Writing in the Medieval West', *Journal of Medieval History*, vol. 26, 397–420, J.I. Catto (2003), 'Written English: The Making of the Language 1370–1400', *Past & Present*, vol. 179, 24–59, A.J. Minnis, '"I speke of folk in seculer estaat": Vernacularity and Secularity in the Age of Chaucer', *Studies in the Age of Chaucer*, vol. 27, 25–58 and C.F. Briggs (2006), 'Translation as Pedagogy: Academic Discourse and Changing Attitudes toward Latin in the Thirteenth and Fourteenth Centuries', in *Frontiers in the Middle Ages*, ed. O. Merisalo (Louvain-la-Neuve: Fédération Internationale des Instituts d'Études Médiévales), 495–505.

For late medieval literature, see D. Wallace (ed.) (1999), *The Cambridge History of Medieval English Literature* (Cambridge: Cambridge University Press), S. Gaunt and S. Kay (eds) (2008), *The Cambridge Companion to Medieval French Literature* (Cambridge:

Cambridge University Press) and L. Scanlon (ed.) (2009), *The Cambridge Companion to Medieval English Literature, 1100–1500* (Cambridge: Cambridge University Press). For works that discuss humanism's impact on attitudes toward language and writing, see the relevant suggested readings for Chapter 9 earlier.

There are a number of good, approachable introductions to the making of manuscript books. These include B.A. Shailor (1991), *The Medieval Book* (Toronto: University of Toronto Press), C. de Hamel (1992), *Medieval Craftsmen: Scribes and Illuminators* (London: The British Museum) and J.J.G. Alexander (1992), *Medieval Illuminators and Their Methods of Work* (New Haven, Ct: Yale University Press). On the book trade in particular, J. Griffiths and D. Pearsall (eds) (1989), *Book Production and Publishing in Britain 1375–1475* (Cambridge: Cambridge University Press), R.H. Rouse and M.A. Rouse (2000), *Manuscripts and Their Makers: Commercial Book Producers in Medieval Paris 1200–1500*, 2 vols (Turnhout: Harvey Miller) and M. Vale (1998), 'Manuscripts and Books', in *NCMH* 7, 278–86. For the transition from script to print, see H.-J. Martin (1994), *The History and Power of Writing*, tr. L.G. Cochrane (Chicago: University of Chicago Press), D. McKitterick (1998), 'The Beginning of Printing', in *NCMH* 7, 287–98, and the essays in S. Hindman (ed.) (1991), *Printing the Written Word: The Social History of Books, circa 1450–1520* (Ithaca, NY: Cornell University Press), J. Crick and A. Walsham (eds) (2004), *The Uses of Script and Print, 1300–1700* (Cambridge: Cambridge University Press) and A. Pettegree (2010), *The Book in the Renaissance* (New Haven, Ct: Yale University Press).

More information on late medieval and early Renaissance music can be found in A. Seay (1975), *Music in the Medieval World*, 2nd ed. (Englewood Cliffs, NJ: Prentice-Hall), I. Fenlon (ed.) (1981), *Music in Medieval and Early Modern Europe: Patronage, Sources and Texts* (Cambridge: Cambridge University Press), T. Knighton and D. Fallows (eds) (1992), *Companion to Medieval and Renaissance Music* (London: Orion Publishing Group), R. Strohm (1993), *The Rise of European Music, 1380–1500* (Cambridge Cambridge University Press) and G. Curtis (1998), 'Music', in *NCMH* 7, 319–33.

On architecture, in addition to the contributions of P. Crossley (2000), 'Architecture', in *NCMH* 6, 234–56 and (1998), 'Architecture and Painting', in *NCMH* 7, 299–318, see P. Frankl (2000), *Gothic Architecture*, revised by P. Crossley (New Haven, Ct: Yale University Press) and R. Recht (2008), *Believing and Seeing: The Art of Gothic Cathedrals*, tr. M. Whittall (Chicago: University of Chicago Press). Introductions to the vast field of the history of Gothic and Renaissance art can be found in M. Baxandall (1972), *Painting and Experience in Fifteenth-Century Italy: A Primer in the Social History of Pictorial Style* (Oxford: Clarendon Press) and P. Binski (2000), 'Court Patronage and International Gothic' in *NCMH* 6, 222–33. Useful handbooks are S. Zuffi (2005), *European Art of the Fifteenth Century*, tr. B.D. Phillips (Los Angeles, Cal: J. Paul Getty Museum) and S. Baragli (2007), *European Art of the Fourteenth Century*, tr. B.D. Phillips (Los Angeles, Cal: J. Paul Getty Museum). On connections between cultural production and patronage in the Renaissance, the indispensible guide is L. Jardine (1996), *Worldly Goods: A New History of the Renaissance* (London: Macmillan).

BIBLIOGRAPHY

Abbreviations

NCMH 6 M. Jones (ed.) (2000), *The New Cambridge Medieval History*, vol. 6, *c. 1300–c. 1415* (Cambridge: Cambridge University Press).

NCMH 7 C. Allmand (ed.) (1998), *The New Cambridge Medieval History*, vol. 7, *c. 1415–c. 1500* (Cambridge: Cambridge University Press).

Texts

Aberth, J. (2001), *From the Brink of the Apocalypse: Confronting Famine, War, Plague, and Death in the Later Middle Ages*, 1st ed. (London: Routledge).

—— (2010), *From the Brink of the Apocalypse: Confronting Famine, War, Plague, and Death in the Later Middle Ages*, 2nd ed. (London: Routledge).

Alexander, J.J.G. (1992), *Medieval Illuminators and Their Methods of Work* (New Haven, Ct: Yale University Press).

Allen, S.J. and E. Amt (eds) (2003), *The Crusades: A Reader* (Toronto: Broadview).

Allmand, C.T. (1992), *Henry V* (Berkeley, Cal: University of California Press).

—— (1998), 'War', in *NCMH* 6, 161–74.

—— (2011), *The 'De re militari' of Vegetius: The Reception, Transmission and Legacy of a Roman Text in the Middle Ages* (Cambridge: Cambridge University Press).

Allmand, C.T. (ed.) (1973), *Society at War: The Experience of England and France during the Hundred Years War* (Edinburgh: Oliver and Boyd).

Anderson, B. (1991), *Imagined Communities: Reflections on the Origin and Spread of Nationalism*, revised ed. (London: Verso).

Arnold, J.H. (2005), *Belief and Unbelief in Medieval Europe* (London: Arnold).

Ashtor, E. (1989), 'The Factors of Technological and Industrial Progress in the Later Middle Ages', *Journal of European Economic History*, vol. 18, 7–36.

Aston, M. (1994), 'Corpus Christi and Corpus Regni: Heresy and the Peasants' Revolt', *Past & Present*, vol. 143, 3–47.

Aston, T.H. and C.H.E. Philpin (eds) (1985), *The Brenner Debate: Agrarian Class Structure and Economic Development in Pre-Industrial Europe* (Cambridge: Cambridge University Press).

Asztalos, M. (1992), 'The Faculty of Theology', in *A History of the University in Europe*, vol. 1, *Universities in the Middle Ages*, ed. H. de Ridder-Symoens (Cambridge: Cambridge University Press), 409–41.

Ayton, A. and J.L. Price (eds) (1995), *The Medieval Military Revolution: State, Society, and Military Change in Medieval and Early Modern Europe* (London: I.B. Tauris Publishers).

Bagge, S. (1997), 'Medieval and Renaissance Historiography: Break or Continuity?' *The European Legacy*, vol. 2, 1336–71.

Bailey, M. (1991), '*Per impetum maris*: Natural Disaster and Economic Decline in Eastern England, 1275–1350', in *Before the Black Death: Studies in the 'Crisis' of the Early Fourteenth Century*, ed. B.M.S. Campbell (Manchester: Manchester University Press), 184–208.

Bailey, M.D. (2003), *Battling Demons: Witchcraft, Heresy, and Reform in the Late Middle Ages* (University Park, Pa: Pennsylvania State University Press).

—— 'A Late-Medieval Crisis of Superstition?' *Speculum*, vol. 84, 633–61.

Baragli, S. (2007), *European Art of the Fourteenth Century*, tr. B.D. Phillips (Los Angeles, Cal: J. Paul Getty Museum).

Barber, M. (2004), *The Two Cities: Medieval Europe 1050–1320*, 2nd ed. (London: Routledge).

—— (2006), *The Trial of the Templars*, 2nd ed. (Cambridge: Cambridge University Press).

Barker, J. (2005), *Agincourt: Henry V and the Battle That Made England* (London: Little, Brown).

Barlow, C.W. (ed.) (1950), *Martini Episcopi Bracarensis Opera Omnia* (New Haven, Ct: American Academy in Rome).

Barron, C.M. (1985), 'The Parish Fraternities of Medieval London', in *The Church in Pre-Reformation Society: Essays in Honour of F.R.H. Du Boulay*, ed. C.M. Barron and C. Harper-Bill (Woodbridge: Boydell Press), 13–37.

—— (2004), 'The Political Culture of Medieval London', in *The Fifteenth Century*, vol. 4, *Political Culture in Late Medieval Britain*, ed. L. Clark and C. Carpenter (Woodbridge: Boydell Press), 110–33.

Beaune, C. (1991), *The Birth of an Ideology: Myths and Symbols of Nation in Late-Medieval France*, tr. S.R. Huston, ed. F.L. Cheyette (Berkeley, Cal: University of California Press).

Beckwith, S. (1992), 'Ritual, Church and Theatre: Medieval Dramas of the Sacramental Body', in *Culture and History 1350–1600: Essays on English Communities, Identities and Writing*, ed. D. Aers (Detroit, Mich: Wayne State University Press), 65–89.

Bell, S.G. (1982), 'Medieval Women Book Owners: Arbiters of Lay Piety and Ambassadors of Culture', *Signs*, vol. 7, 742–68.

Beltrán, L. (1971), 'The Poet, the King, and the Cardinal Virtues in Juan de Mena's *Laberinto*', *Speculum*, vol. 46, 318–32.

Bennett, J.M. (1987), *Women in the Medieval English Countryside: Gender and Household in Brigstock before the Plague* (Oxford: Oxford University Press).

—— (1996), *Ale, Beer, and Brewsters in England: Women's Work in a Changing World, 1300–1600* (Oxford: Oxford University Press).

Bergen, H. (ed.) (1923), *Lydgate's Fall of Princes*, pts 1–3 (Washington, DC: Carnegie Institution of Washington).

Bertelli, S. (2001), *The King's Body: Sacred Rituals of Power in Medieval and Early Modern Europe*, tr. R.B. Litchfield (University Park, Pa: Pennsylvania State University Press).

Biller, P. (1991), 'Aristotle's *Politica* and "Demographic" Thought in the Kingdom of Aragon in the Early Fourteenth Century', *Annals of the Archive of 'Ferran Valls I Taberner's Library'*, vols 9/10, 249–64.

—— (1992), 'Marriage Patterns and Women's Lives: A Sketch of a Pastoral Geography', in *Woman is a Worthy Wight: Women in English Medieval Society c. 1200–1500*, ed. P.J.P. Goldberg (Stroud: Sutton), 60–107.

—— (1998), 'Confessor's Manuals and the Avoiding of Offspring', in *Handling Sin: Confession in the Middle Ages*, ed. P. Biller and A.J. Minnis (York: York Medieval Press), 165–90.

Binski, P. (2000), 'Court Patronage and International Gothic', in *NCMH* 6, 222–33.

Birdsall, J. (tr.) and R.A. Newhall (ed.) (1953), *The Chronicle of Jean de Venette* (New York: Columbia University Press).

Black, A. (1992), *Political Thought in Europe, 1250–1450* (Cambridge: Cambridge University Press).

Black, R. (1998), 'Humanism', in *NCMH* 7, 243–77.

—— (2004), 'Education and the Emergence of a Literate Society', in *Italy in the Age of the Renaissance 1300–1550*, ed. J.M. Najemy (Oxford: Oxford University Press), 18–36.

Blamires, A. (ed.) (1992), *Woman Defamed, Woman Defended: An Anthology of Medieval Texts* (Oxford: Clarendon Press).

Blickle, P. (1979), 'Peasant Revolts in the German Empire in the Late Middle Ages', *Social History*, vol. 4, 223–39.

Blockmans, W.P. (1980), 'The Social and Economic Effects of Plague in the Low Countries (1349–1500)', *Revue belge de philologie et d'histoire*, vol. 58, 833–63.

Blume, C. and H.M. Bannister (eds) (1915), *Liturgische Prosen des Übergangsstiles und der zweiten Epoche insbesondere die dem Adam von Sanct Victor zugeschriebenen*, Analecta Hymnica Medii Aevi, vol. 54 (Leipzig: O.R. Reisland).

Blume, C. and G.M. Dreves (eds) (1907), *Lateinische Hymnendichter des Mittelalters*, Analecta Hymnica Medii Aevi, vol. 50 (Leipzig: O.R. Reisland).

Blythe, J.M. (1992), *Ideal Government and the Mixed Constitution in the Middle Ages* (Princeton, NJ: Princeton University Press).

Blythe, J.M. (tr.) (1997), *On the Government of Rulers: Ptolemy of Lucca, with Portions Attributed to Thomas Aquinas* (Philadelphia, Pa: University of Pennsylvania Press).

Böhmer, J.F. (ed.) (1868), *Fontes Rerum Germanicarum*, vol. 4, *Heinricus de Diessenhofen und andere Geschichtsquellen Deutschlands im späteren Mittelalter* (Stuttgart: Cotta).

Bornstein, D.E. (ed. and tr.) (1986), *Dino Compagni's Chronicle of Florence* (Philadelphia, Pa: University of Pennsylvania Press).

Bossy, J. (1983), 'The Mass as a Social Institution 1200–1700', *Past & Present*, vol. 100, 29–61.

Botterill, S. (ed. and tr.) (1996), *Dante, 'De vulgari eloquentia'* (Cambridge: Cambridge University Press).

Boucheron, P. (2018), *The Power of Images: Siena, 1338*, tr. A. Brown (Cambridge: Polity Press).

Bozzolo, C. and E. Ornato (1983), *Pour une histoire du livre manuscrit au Moyen Age: trois essais de codicologie quantitative* (Paris: Éditions du CNRS).

Brereton, G. (ed. and tr.) (1968), *Froissart, Chronicles* (Harmondsworth: Penguin).

Brett, A. (ed. and tr.) (2005), *Marsilius of Padua, 'The Defender of the Peace'* (Cambridge: Cambridge University Press).

Briggs, C.F. (1993), 'Late Medieval Texts and *Tabulae*: The Case of Giles of Rome, *De regimine principum*', *Manuscripta*, vol. 37, 253–75.

—— (1999), *Giles of Rome's 'De regimine principum': Reading and Writing Politics at Court and University, c. 1275-c. 1525* (Cambridge: Cambridge University Press).

—— (2003), 'Teaching Philosophy at School and Court: Vulgarization and Translation', in *The Vulgar Tongue: Medieval and Postmedieval Vernacularity*, ed. F. Somerset and N. Watson (University Park, Pa: Pennsylvania State University Press).

—— (2007), 'Aristotle's *Rhetoric* in the Later Medieval Universities: A Reassessment', *Rhetorica*, vol. 25, 243–68.

—— (2012), 'History, Story, and Community: Representing the Past in Latin Christendom, 1050–1400', in *The Oxford History of Historical Writing*, vol. 2, *400–1400*, ed. S. Foot and C.F. Robinson (Oxford: Oxford University Press), 391–413.

Brown, E.A.R. and R.C. Famiglietti (1994), *The Lit de Justice: Semantics, Ceremonial, and the Parlement of Paris, 1300–1600* (Sigmaringen: Jan Thorbecke Verlag).

Brucker, G. (ed.) and J. Martinas (tr.) (1967), *Two Memoirs of Renaissance Florence: The Diaries of Buonaccorso Pitti and Gregorio Dati* (New York: Harper and Row).

Burckhardt, J. (1958), *The Civilization of the Renaissance in Italy*, vol. 1, tr. S.G.C. Middlemore (New York: Harper and Row) (originally 1860).

Burnham, L. (2008), *So Great a Light, So Great a Smoke: The Beguin Heretics of Languedoc* (Ithaca, NY: Cornell University Press).

Butcher, A.F. (1984), 'English Urban Society and the Revolt of 1381', in *The English Rising of 1381*, ed. R.H. Hilton and T.H. Aston (Cambridge: Cambridge University Press), 84–111.

Bynum, C.W. (2007), *Wonderful Blood: Theology and Practice in Late Medieval Northern Germany and Beyond* (Philadelphia, Pa: University of Pennsylvania Press).

312

Caferro, W. (2006), *John Hawkwood: An English Mercenary in Fourteenth-Century Italy* (Baltimore, Md: Johns Hopkins University Press).

Camille, M. (1996), *Master of Death: The Lifeless Art of Pierre Remiet, Illuminator* (New Haven, Ct: Yale University Press).

Canning, J. (1996), *A History of Medieval Political Thought, 300–1450* (London: Routledge).

Carmody, F.J. (ed.) (1948), *Li livres dou tresor de Brunetto Latini* (Berkeley, Cal: University of California Press).

Carocci, S. (2012), 'The Papal State', in *The Italian Renaissance State*, ed. A. Gamberini and I. Lazzarini (Cambridge: Cambridge University Press), 69–89.

Carruthers, M.J. (1990), *The Book of Memory: A Study of Memory in Medieval Culture* (Cambridge: Cambridge University Press).

Cary, H.F. (tr.) (1883), *Dante's Purgatory and Paradise* (New York: Cassell, Petter, Galpin & Co.).

Catto, J.I. (1992), 'Wyclif and Wycliffism at Oxford 1356–1430', in *The History of the University of Oxford*, vol. 2, *Late Medieval Oxford*, ed. J.I. Catto and R. Evans (Oxford: Clarendon Press), 175–261.

—— (2000), 'Currents of Religious Thought and Expression', *NCMH* 6, 42–65.

—— (2003), 'Written English: The Making of the Language 1370–1400', *Past & Present*, vol. 179, 24–59.

Cheney, C.R. (2000), *A Handbook of Dates for Students of British History*, new ed., revised by M. Jones (Cambridge: Cambridge University Press).

Childs, W. (1998), 'Commerce and Trade', *NCMH* 7, 145–60.

Cipolla, C.M. (1993), *Before the Industrial Revolution: European Society and Economy, 1000–1700*, 3rd ed. (London: Routledge).

Clanchy, M.T. (1993), *From Memory to Written Record: England 1066–1307*, 2nd ed. (Oxford: Blackwell).

Cobban, A.B. (1975), *Medieval Universities: Their Development and Organization* (London: Methuen).

Cohn, S.K. (1992), *The Cult of Remembrance and the Black Death: Six Renaissance Cities in Central Italy* (Baltimore, Md: Johns Hopkins University Press).

—— (2002), *The Black Death Transformed: Disease and Culture in Early Renaissance Europe* (London: Arnold).

—— (2004), *Popular Protest in Late Medieval Europe: Italy, France and Flanders* (Manchester: Manchester University Press).

—— (2006), *Lust for Liberty: The Politics of Social Revolt in Medieval Europe, 1200–1445, Italy, France, and Flanders* (Cambridge, Ma: Harvard University Press).

Coleman, J. (1983), 'English Culture in the Fourteenth Century', in *Chaucer and the Italian Trecento*, ed. P. Boitani (Cambridge: Cambridge University Press), 33–63.

—— (2000), *A History of Political Thought: From the Middle Ages to the Renaissance* (Oxford: Blackwell).

Contamine, P. (1972), *Guerre, état et société à la fin du Moyen Age: études sur les armées de France 1337–1494* (Paris: Mouton).

—— (1976), 'The War Literature of the Late Middle Ages: The Treatises of Robert de Balsac and Béraud Stuart', in *War, Literature and Politics in the Late Middle Ages: Essays in Honour of G.W. Coopland*, ed. C.T. Allmand (Liverpool: Liverpool University Press), 102–21.

—— (1984), *War in the Middle Ages*, tr. M. Jones (Oxford: Blackwell).

—— (1998), 'The European Nobility', in *NCMH* 7, 89–105.

Coopland, G.W. (tr.) (1949), *The Tree of Battles of Honoré Bonet* (Liverpool: Liverpool University Press).

—— (1975), *Letter to King Richard II: A Plea Made in 1395 for Peace between England and France* (Liverpool: Liverpool University Press).

Costa Gomes, R. (2003), *The Making of a Court Society: Kings and Nobles in Late Medieval Portugal*, tr. A. Aiken (Cambridge: Cambridge University Press).

Crossley, P. (2000), 'Architecture', in *NCMH* 6, 234–56.

Curtis, G. (1998), 'Music', in *NCMH* 7, 319–33.

Dahlberg, C. (tr.) (1983), *The Romance of the Rose by Guillaume de Lorris and Jean de Meun* (Princeton, NJ: Princeton University Press).

Dameron, G.W. (2005), *Florence and Its Church in the Age of Dante* (Philadelphia, Pa: University of Pennsylvania Press).

Davies, M. (1996), 'Humanism in Script and Print in the Fifteenth Century', in *The Cambridge Companion to Renaissance Humanism*, ed. J. Kraye (Cambridge: Cambridge University Press), 47–62.

Davies, R.R. (1994), 'The Failure of the First British Empire? England's Relations with Ireland, Scotland and Wales, 1066–1500', in *England in Europe, 1066–1453*, ed. N. Saul (London: Collins and Brown), 121–32.

Dean, T. (ed. and tr.) (2000), *The Towns of Italy in the Later Middle Ages* (Manchester: Manchester University Press).

Dean, T. (2001), *Crime in Medieval Europe, 1200–1550* (Harlow: Longman, 2001).

Denley, P. (1990), 'Governments and Schools in Late Medieval Italy', in *City and Countryside in Late Medieval and Renaissance Italy: Essays Presented to Philip Jones*, ed. T. Dean and C. Wickham (London: Hambledon Press), 93–107.

—— (1991), 'The Collegiate Movement in Italian Universities in the Late Middle Ages', *History of the Universities*, vol. 10, 29–91.

Dobson, R.B. (ed.) (1983), *The Peasants' Revolt of 1381*, 2nd ed. (London: Macmillan).

Duby, G. (1980), *The Three Orders: Feudal Society Imagined*, tr. A. Goldhammer (Chicago, Il: University of Chicago Press).

Duffy, E. (2005), *The Stripping of the Altars: Traditional Religion in England 1400–1580*, 2nd ed. (New Haven, Ct: Yale University Press).

Dunbabin, J. (1998), 'Hervé de Nédellec, Pierre de la Palud and France's Place in Christendom', in *Political Thought and the Realities of Power in the Middle Ages*, ed. J. Canning and O.G. Oexle (Göttingen: Vandenhoeck & Ruprecht), 159–72.

Dyer, C. (1998), 'Rural Europe', in *NCMH* 7, 106–20.

—— (2002), *Making a Living in the Middle Ages: The People of Britain 850–1520* (New Haven, Ct: Yale University Press).

Dyson, R.W. (ed. and tr.) (2004), *Giles of Rome's 'On Ecclesiastical Power': A Medieval Theory of World Government* (New York: Columbia University Press).

Epstein, S.A. (2009), *An Economic and Social History of Later Medieval Europe, 1000–1500* (Cambridge: Cambridge University Press).

Evans, J. (tr.) (1928), *The Unconquered Knight: A Chronicle of the Deeds of Don Pero Niño, Count of Buelna, by His Standard Bearer Gutierre Diaz de Gamez (1431–1449)* (London: Routledge).

Evans, T.A.R. (1992), 'The Number, Origin and Careers of Scholars', in *The History of the University of Oxford*, vol. 2, *Late Medieval Oxford*, ed. J.I. Catto and R. Evans (Oxford: Clarendon Press), 485–538.

Fassler, M. (2004), 'Psalms and Prayers in Daily Devotion: A Fifteenth-Century Devotional Anthology from the Diocese of Rheims: Beineke 757', in *Worship in Medieval and Early Modern Europe: Change and Continuity in Religious Practice* (Notre Dame, Ind: University of Notre Dame Press), 15–40.

Fernández-Armesto, F. (1987), *Before Columbus: Exploration and Colonisation from the Mediterranean to the Atlantic, 1229–1492* (London: Macmillan).

—— (1998), 'Exploration and Discovery', in *NCMH* 7, 175–201.

Field, S.L. (2012), *The Beguine, the Angel, and the Inquisitor: The Trials of Marguerite Porete and Guiard of Cressonessart* (Notre Dame, Ind: University of Notre Dame Press).

Fletcher, J.M. (1984), 'The Faculty of Arts', in *The History of the University of Oxford*, vol. 1, *The Early Oxford Schools*, ed. J.I. Catto (Oxford: Clarendon Press), 369–99.

—— (1992), 'Developments in the Faculty of Arts 1370–1520', in *The History of the University of Oxford*, vol. 2, *Late Medieval Oxford*, ed. J.I. Catto and R. Evans (Oxford: Clarendon Press), 315–45.

Forhan, K.L. (tr. and ed.) (1994), *Christine de Pizan: The Book of the Body Politic* (Cambridge: Cambridge University Press).

Fossier, R. (ed.) (1986), *The Cambridge Illustrated History of the Middle Ages*, vol. 3, *1250–1520*, tr. S.H. Tenison (Cambridge: Cambridge University Press).

Fossier, R. (1988), *Peasant Life in the Medieval West*, tr. J. Vale (Oxford: Blackwell).

Fourquin, G. (1978), *The Anatomy of Popular Rebellion in the Middle Ages*, tr. A. Chesters (Amsterdam: North-Holland Publishing).

Fowler, D.C. (1995), *The Life and Times of John Trevisa, Medieval Scholar* (Seattle, Wa: University of Washington Press).

Fowler, D.C., C.F. Briggs and P.G. Remley (eds) (1997), *The Governance of Kings and Princes: John Trevisa's Middle English Translation of the 'De regimine principum' of Aegidius Romanus* (New York: Garland).

Fowler, K.A. (1998) 'Sir John Hawkwood and the English Condottieri in Trecento Italy', *Renaissance Studies*, vol. 12, 131–48.

Fowler, K.A. (2001), *Medieval Mercenaries*, vol. 1, *The Great Companies* (Oxford: Blackwell).

Franceschi, F. (2004), 'The Economy: Work and Wealth', in *Italy in the Age of the Renaissance 1300–1550*, ed. J.M. Najemy (Oxford: Oxford University Press), 124–44.

Friedberg, E. (ed.) (1881), *Corpus Iuris Canonici*, pt. 2, *Decretalium Collectiones* (Leipzig: Bernhard Tauchnitz).

Furstenberg-Levi, S. (2006), 'The Fifteenth-Century Accademia Pontaniana—An Analysis of its Institutional Elements', *History of the Universities*, vol. 21, no. 1, 33–70.

Gamberini, A. (2012), 'The Language of Politics and the Process of State-Building: Approaches and Interpretations', in *The Italian Renaissance State*, ed. A. Gamberini and I. Lazzarini (Cambridge: Cambridge University Press), 406–24.

García y García, A. (1992), 'The Faculties of Law', in *A History of the University in Europe*, vol. 1, *Universities in the Middle Ages*, ed. H. de Ridder-Symoens (Cambridge: Cambridge University Press), 388–408.

Geary, P.J. (2002), *The Myth of Nations: The Medieval Origins of Europe* (Princeton, NJ: Princeton University Press).

—— (2003), *Readings in Medieval History*, 3rd ed. (Toronto: Broadview Press).

Gehl, P.F. (1993), *A Moral Art: Grammar, Society, and Culture in Trecento Florence* (Ithaca, NY: Cornell University Press).

Genet, J.-P. (1995), 'La monarchie anglaise: une image brouillée', in *Répresentation, pouvoir et royauté à la fin du Moyen Age*, ed. J. Blanchard (Paris: Picard), 93–107.

Genet, J.-P. (ed.) (1977), *Four English Political Tracts of the Later Middle Ages*, Camden Fourth Series, vol. 18 (London: Royal Historical Society).

Gentile, M. (2012), 'Factions and Parties: Problems and Perspectives', in *The Italian Renaissance State*, ed. A. Gamberini and I. Lazzarini (Cambridge: Cambridge University Press), 304–24.

Géraud, H. (ed.) (1837), *Paris sous Philippe-le-Bel, d'après un manuscrit contenant le rôle de la Taille imposée sur les habitants de Paris en 1292* (Paris: Crapelet).

Geremek, B. (1987), *The Margins of Society in Late Medieval Paris*, tr. J. Birrell (Cambridge: Cambridge University Press).

Gewirth, A. (tr.) (2001), *Marsilius of Padua, Defensor Pacis* (New York: Columbia University Press) (originally 1956).

Gies, F. and J. Gies (1994), *Cathedral, Forge, and Waterwheel: Technology and Invention in the Middle Ages* (New York: Harper Collins).

Gieysztor, A. (1992), 'Management and Resources', in *A History of the University in Europe*, vol. 1, *Universities in the Middle Ages*, ed. H. de Ridder-Symoens (Cambridge: Cambridge University Press), 108–43.

Given-Wilson, C. (ed. and tr.) (1997), *The Chronicle of Adam of Usk* (Oxford: Clarendon Press).

Goldberg, P.J.P. (2001), 'Coventry's "Lollard" Programme of 1492 and the Making of Utopia', in *Pragmatic Utopias: Ideals and Communities, 1200–1630*, ed. R. Horrox and S. Rees Jones (Cambridge: Cambridge University Press), 97–116.

Goldsmith, J.L. (1995), 'The Crisis of the Late Middle Ages: The Case of France', *French History*, vol. 9, 417–50.

Goodman, A. (2002), *Margery Kempe and Her World* (London: Longman).

Grafton, A. and L. Jardine (1986), *From Humanism to the Humanities: Education and the Liberal Arts in Fifteenth- and Sixteenth-Century Europe* (Cambridge, Ma: Harvard University Press).

Grendler, P.F. (1989), *Schooling in Renaissance Italy: Literacy and Learning, 1300–1600* (Baltimore, Md: Johns Hopkins University Press).

—— (2002), *The Universities of the Italian Renaissance* (Baltimore, Md: Johns Hopkins University Press).

Grondeux, A. (1998), *Anonymi Montepessulanensis Dictionarius. Le glossaire latin-français du Ms. Montpellier H236* (Turnhout: Brepols).

Guenée, B. (1985), *States and Rulers in Later Medieval Europe*, tr. J. Vale (Oxford: Blackwell).

—— (1998), 'Le prince en sa cour: des vertus aux usages (Guillaume de Tyr, Gilles de Rome, Michel Pintoin)', *Comptes-rendus des séances de l'Academie des Inscriptions et Belles-Lettres*, vol. 142, 633–46.

Hall, A.R. (1976), 'Guido's *Texaurus*, 1335', in *On Pre-Modern Technology and Science: Studies in Honor of Lynn White, Jr.*, ed. B.S. Hall and D.C. West (Malibu, Cal: Undena Publications), 11–52.

Hall, L.B. (ed.) (1962), Giovanni Boccaccio, *De casibus illustrium virorum: A Facsimile Reproduction of the Paris Edition of 1520* (Gainesville, Fla: Scholars' Facsimiles and Reprints).

Hall, L.B. (tr.) (1965), *Giovanni Boccaccio, 'The Fates of Illustrious Men'* (New York: F. Ungar Publishing).

Hamesse, J. (1974), *Les 'Auctoritates Aristotelis': un florilège médiéval* (Louvain: Publications Universitaires; Paris: Béatrice-Nauwelaerts).

—— (1994), 'Les manuscrits des "Parvi flores": une nouvelle liste de témoins', *Scriptorium*, vol. 48, 299–332.

Hamm, B. (2004), *The Reformation of the Faith in the Context of Late Medieval Theology and Piety: Essays of Berndt Hamm*, ed. R.J. Bast (Leiden: Brill).

Hanawalt, B. (1986), *The Ties That Bound: Peasant Families in Medieval England* (Oxford: Oxford University Press).

Hankins, J. (1996), 'Humanism and the Origins of Modern Political Thought', in *The Cambridge Companion to Renaissance Humanism*, ed. J. Kraye (Cambridge: Cambridge University Press), 118–41.

Hanna, R. (1989), 'Sir Thomas Berkeley and His Patronage', *Speculum*, vol. 64, 878–916.

Harding, A. (1984), 'The Revolt against the Justices', in *The English Rising of 1381*, ed. R.H. Hilton and T.H. Aston (Cambridge: Cambridge University Press), 165–93.

Haren, M. (1998), 'Confession, Social Ethics and Social Discipline in the *Memoriale presbiterorum*', in *Handling Sin: Confession in the Middle Ages*, ed. P. Biller and A.J. Minnis (York: York Medieval Press), 109–22.

Harriss, G. (2005), *Shaping the Nation: England 1360–1461* (Oxford: Oxford University Press).

Harvey, B.F. (1991), 'Introduction: The "Crisis" of the Early Fourteenth Century', in *Before the Black Death: Studies in the 'Crisis' of the Early Fourteenth Century*, ed. B.M.S. Campbell (Manchester: Manchester University Press), 1–24.

Hasenohr, G. (1994), 'Religious Reading amongst the Laity in France in the Fifteenth Century', in *Heresy and Literacy, 1000–1530*, ed. P. Biller and A. Hudson (Cambridge: Cambridge University Press), 205–21.

Hatcher, J. (1994), 'England in the Aftermath of the Black Death', *Past & Present*, no. 144, 1–35.

Haverkamp, A. (1995), 'The Jewish Quarters in German Towns during the Late Middle Ages', in *In and Out of the Ghetto: Jewish-Gentile Relations in Late Medieval and Early Modern Germany*, ed. R. Po-Chia Hsia and H. Lehmann (Cambridge: Cambridge University Press), 13–28.

Hay, D. (1976), *The Italian Renaissance in Its Historical Background*, 2nd ed. (Cambridge: Cambridge University Press).

Hazelton, R. (1957), 'The Christianization of Cato: The *Disticha Catonis* in the Light of Late Medieval Commentaries', *Mediaeval Studies*, vol. 19, 157–73.

Herlihy, D. (1985), *Medieval Households* (Cambridge, Ma: Harvard University Press).

—— (1990), *Opera Muliebria: Women and Work in Medieval Europe* (Philadelphia: Temple University Press).

—— (1997), *The Black Death and the Transformation of the West*, ed. S.K. Cohn (Cambridge, Ma: Harvard University Press).

Herlihy, D. and C. Klapisch-Zuber (1985), *Tuscans and Their Families: A Study of the Florentine Catasto of 1427* (New Haven, Ct: Yale University Press).

Hillier, P. and P. James (trs) (1996), brochure notes for *Josquin Desprez, Motets and Chansons*, The Hilliard Ensemble, EMI CDC 7 49209 2.

Hilton, R.H. (1975), *The English Peasantry in the Later Middle Ages* (Oxford: Clarendon Press).

Hilton, R.H. and T.H. Aston (eds) (1984), *The English Rising of 1381* (Cambridge: Cambridge University Press).

Hope, C. and E. McGrath (1996), 'Artists and Humanists', in *The Cambridge Companion to Renaissance Humanism*, ed. J. Kraye (Cambridge: Cambridge University Press), 161–88.

Horrox, R. (ed.) (1994), *The Black Death* (Manchester: Manchester University Press).

Housley, N. (1991), 'France, England, and the National Crusade, 1302–86', in *France and the British Isles in the Middle Ages and Renaissance: Essays by Members of Girton College, Cambridge, in Memory of Ruth Morgan*, ed. G. Jondorf and D.N. Dumville (Woodbridge: Boydell Press), 183–98.

—— (1992), *The Later Crusades, 1274–1580: From Lyons to Alcazar* (Oxford: Oxford University Press).

—— (1998), 'The Eschatological Imperative: Messianism and Holy War in Europe, 1260–1556', in *Toward the Millennium: Messianic Expectations from the Bible to Waco*, ed. P. Schäfer and M.R. Cohen (Leiden: Brill), 123–50.

Howell, M.C. (1986), *Women, Production, and Patriarchy in Late Medieval Cities* (Chicago: University of Chicago Press).

Hsia, R. Po-Chia (1992), *Trent 1475: Stories of a Ritual Murder Trial* (New Haven, Ct: Yale University Press).

Hudson, A. (1994), '*Piers Plowman* and the Peasants' Revolt: A Problem Revisited', *The Yearbook of Langland Studies*, vol. 8, 85–106.

Hughes, D.O. (1986), 'Distinguishing Signs: Ear-Rings, Jews and Franciscan Rhetoric in the Italian Renaissance City', *Past & Present*, no. 112, 3–59.

—— (2004), 'Bodies, Disease, and Society', in *Italy in the Age of the Renaissance 1300–1550*, ed. J.M. Najemy (Oxford: Oxford University Press), 103–23.

Huizinga, J. (1996), *The Autumn of the Middle Ages*, tr. R.J. Payton and U. Mammitzsch (Chicago: University of Chicago Press) (originally 1919).

Hunt, E.S. and J. Murray (1999), *A History of Business in Medieval Europe, 1200–1550* (Cambridge: Cambridge University Press).

James, M.R. (ed. and tr.) (1983), Walter Map, *De nugis curialium – Courtiers' Trifles*, revised by C.N.L. Brooke and R.A.B. Mynors (Oxford: Clarendon Press).

Jardine, L. (1996), *Worldly Goods: A New History of the Renaissance* (London: Macmillan).

Jensen, K. (1996), 'The Humanist Reform of Latin and Latin Teaching', in *The Cambridge Companion to Renaissance Humanism*, ed. J. Kraye (Cambridge: Cambridge University Press), 63–81.

Jones, M. (1995), '"En son habit royal": le duc de Bretagne et son image vers la fin du Moyen Age', in *Répresentation, pouvoir et royauté à la fin du Moyen Age*, ed. J. Blanchard (Paris: Picard), 253–78.

Jordan, W.C. (1996), *The Great Famine: Northern Europe in the Early Fourteenth Century* (Princeton, NJ: Princeton University Press).

Kaeuper, R.W. (1988), *War, Justice, and Public Order: England and France in the Later Middle Ages* (Oxford: Clarendon Press).

—— (1999), *Chivalry and Violence in Medieval Europe* (Oxford: Oxford University Press).

Kaeuper, R.W. (intro.) and E. Kennedy (tr.) (2005), *A Knight's Own Book of Chivalry: Geoffroi de Charny* (Philadelphia, Pa: University of Pennsylvania Press).

Kallendorf, C.W. (ed. and tr.) (2002), *Humanist Educational Treatises* (Cambridge, Ma: Harvard University Press).

Kaminsky, H. (2000), 'The Great Schism', in *NCMH* 6, 674–96.

Karlsson, G. (1996), 'Plague without Rats: The Case of Fifteenth-Century Iceland', *Journal of Medieval History*, vol. 22, 263–84.

Kay, R. (tr.) (1998), *Dante's 'Monarchia'* (Toronto: Pontifical Institute of Mediaeval Studies).

Kaye, J. (1998), *Economy and Nature in the Fourteenth Century: Money, Market Exchange, and the Emergence of Scientific Thought* (Cambridge: Cambridge University Press).

Keen, M. (1984), *Chivalry* (New Haven, Ct: Yale University Press).

—— (2000), 'Chivalry and the Aristocracy', in *NCMH* 6, 209–21.

Kelley, D.R. (ed.) (1991), *Versions of History from Antiquity to the Enlightenment* (New Haven, Ct: Yale University Press).

Kinser, S. (ed.) and Cazeaux, I. (tr.) (1973), *The Memoirs of Philippe de Commynes*, vol. 2 (Columbia, SC: University of South Carolina Press).

Klaniczay, G. (2002), *Holy Rulers and Blessed Princesses: Dynastic Cults in Medieval Central Europe*, tr. E. Pálmai (Cambridge: Cambridge University Press).

Klapisch-Zuber, C. (1990), 'Women and the Family', in *Medieval Callings*, ed. J. Le Goff, tr. L.C. Cochrane (Chicago: University of Chicago Press), 285–311.

—— (2000), 'Plague and Family Life', in *NCMH* 6, 124–54.

Knowles, D. (1962), *The Evolution of Medieval Thought* (New York: Vintage Books).

Kowaleski, M. (ed.) (2006), *Medieval Towns: A Reader* (Toronto: Broadview).

Lambert, M. (2002), *Medieval Heresy: Popular Movements from the Gregorian Reform to the Reformation*, 3rd ed. (Oxford: Blackwell).

Langmuir, G.I. (1996), 'The Tortures of the Body of Christ', in *Christendom and Its Discontents: Exclusion, Persecution, and Rebellion, 1000–1500*, ed. S.L. Waugh and P.D. Diehl (Cambridge: Cambridge University Press), 287–309.

Larner, J. (1999), *Marco Polo and the Discovery of the World* (New Haven, Ct: Yale University Press).

Larsen, A.E. (2008), 'Academic Condemnation and the Decline of Theology at Oxford', *History of the Universities*, vol. 23, no. 1, 1–32.

Lassalmonie, J.-F. (2000), 'Un discours à trois voix sur le pouvoir: le roi et les états généraux de 1484', in *Penser le pouvoir au Moyen Age (VIIIe–XVe siècle)*, ed. D. Boutet and J. Verger (Paris: Éditions rue d'Ulm), 127–55.

Lawrence, C.H. (1984), *Medieval Monasticism: Forms of Religious Life in Western Europe in the Middle Ages* (London: Longman).

Leff, G. (1968), *Paris and Oxford Universities in the Thirteenth and Fourteenth Centuries: An Institutional and Intellectual History* (New York: John Wiley and Sons).

—— (1992), 'The *Trivium* and the Three Philosophies', in *A History of the University in Europe*, vol. 1, *Universities in the Middle Ages*, ed. H. de Ridder-Symoens (Cambridge: Cambridge University Press), 307–36.

Leguai, A. (1982), 'Les révoltes rurales dans le royame de France, du milieu du XIVe siècle à la fin du XVe', *Le moyen âge*, vol. 88, 49–76.

Leguay, J.-P. (2000), 'Urban Life', in *NCMH* 6, 102–23.

Le Goff, J. (1980), *Time, Work, and Culture in the Middle Ages*, tr. A. Goldhammer (Chicago: University of Chicago Press).

Lemaire, J. (1989), *Introduction à la codicologie* (Louvain-la-Neuve: Publications de l'Institut d'Études Médiévales).

Lemarignier, J.-F., J. Gaudemet and G. Mollat (1962), *Histoire des institutions française au Moyen Age: Tome III – Institutions ecclésiastiques*, gen. ed. F. Lot and R. Fawtier (Paris: Presses universitaires de France).

Lentes, T. (2001), 'Counting Piety in the Late Middle Ages', in *Ordering Medieval Society: Perspectives on Intellectual and Practical Modes of Shaping Social Relations*, ed. B. Jussen, tr. P. Selwyn (Philadelphia: University of Pennsylvania Press), 55–91.

Lerner, R.E. (1972), *The Heresy of the Free Spirit in the Later Middle Ages* (Berkeley, Cal: University of California Press).

—— (1983), *The Powers of Prophecy: The Cedar of Lebanon Vision from the Mongol Onslaught to the Dawn of the Enlightenment* (Berkeley, Cal: University of California Press).

Le Roy Ladurie, E. (1972), *Times of Feast, Times of Famine: A History of Climate since the Year 1000*, ed. B. Bray (London: George Allen and Unwin).

Lewis, P.S. (1995), 'Pourquoi aurait-on voulu réunir des états généraux, en France, à la fin du Moyen Age?' in *Réprésentation, pouvoir et royauté à la fin du Moyen Age*, ed. J. Blanchard (Paris: Picard), 119–30.

Little, L.K. (2011), 'Plague Historians in Lab Coats', *Past & Present*, no. 213, 267–90.

Lockwood, L. (1981), 'Strategies of Music Patronage in the Fifteenth Century: The *cappella* of Ercole I d'Este', in *Music in Medieval and Early Modern Europe: Patronage, Sources and Texts*, ed. I. Fenlon (Cambridge: Cambridge University Press), 227–48.

Lopez, R.S. and I.W. Raymond (eds) (1990), *Medieval Trade in the Mediterranean World: Illustrative Documents Translated with Introductions and Notes* (New York: Columbia University Press) (originally 1955).

Lumby, J.R. (ed.) (1895), *Chronicon Henrici Knighton vel Cnitthon Monachi Leycestrensis*, vol. 2 (London: Rolls Series).

Luscombe, D. (1991), 'Gerson and Ideas of Hierarchy', in *Church and Chronicle in the Middle Ages: Essays Presented to John Taylor*, ed. I. Wood and G.A. Loud (London: Hambledon Press), 193–200.

Lusignan, S. (1987), *Parler vulgairement: les intellectuels et la langue française aux XIIIe et XIVe siècles*, 2nd ed. (Paris: Librairie philosophique J. Vrin; Montreal: Les Presses de l'Université de Montréal).

—— (1989), 'La topique de la *translatio studii* et les traductions françaises de textes savants au XIVe siècle', in *Traduction et traducteurs au Moyen Age*, ed. G. Contamine (Paris: Éditions du CNRS), 303–15.

—— (2003), 'L'administration royale et la langue française aux XIIIe et XIVe siècles', in *The Dawn of the Written Vernacular in Western Europe*, ed. M. Goyens and W. Verbeke (Leuven: Leuven University Press), 51–70.

MacKay, A. (1972), 'Popular Movements and Pogroms in Fifteenth-Century Castile', *Past & Present*, no. 55, 33–67.

Martin, H.-J. (1994), *The History and Power of Writing*, tr. L.G. Cochrane (Chicago: University of Chicago Press).

Martindale, A. (1967), *Gothic Art* (London: Thames and Hudson).

McGrade, A.S., J. Kilcullen and M. Kempshall (eds) (2001), *The Cambridge Translations of Medieval Philosophical Texts*, vol. 2, *Ethics and Political Philosophy* (Cambridge: Cambridge University Press).

McKitterick, D. (1998), 'The Beginning of Printing', in *NCMH* 7, 287–98.

McWilliam, G.H. (tr.) (1972), *Giovanni Boccaccio, The Decameron* (Harmondsworth: Penguin).

Menache, S. (1982), 'La naissance d'une nouvelle source d'autorité: l'université de Paris', *Revue historique*, vol. 258, 305–27.

Menut, A.D. (ed.) (1940), *Maistre Nicole Oresme, Le livre de Ethiques d'Aristote* (New York: G.E. Stechert and Co.).

—— (1970), *Maistre Nicole Oresme, Le livre de Politiques d'Aristote*, Transactions of the American Philosophical Society, n.s. vol. 60, pt. 6 (Philadelphia, Pa: American Philosophical Society).

Mierow, C.C. (tr.) (1966), Otto of Freising, *The Two Cities: A Chronicle of Universal History to the Year 1146 A.D.*, ed. A.P. Evans and C. Knapp (New York: Octagon).

Miethke, J. (2000), 'Practical Intentions of Scholasticism: The Example of Political Theory', in *Universities and Schooling in Medieval Society*, ed. W.J. Courtenay and J. Miethke (Leiden: Brill), 211–28.

Moeller, B. (1971), 'Piety in Germany around 1500', in *The Reformation in Medieval Perspective*, ed. S.E. Ozment (Chicago: Quadrangle Books), 50–75.

Mollat, M. (1986), *The Poor in the Middle Ages: An Essay in Social History*, tr. A. Goldhammer (New Haven, Ct: Yale University Press).

Mollat, M. and P. Wolff (1973), *The Popular Revolutions of the Late Middle Ages*, tr. A.J. Lytton-Sells (London: George Allen and Unwin).

Moran, J.A.H. (1985), *The Growth of English Schooling, 1340–1548: Learning, Literacy, and Laicization in Pre-Reformation York Diocese* (Princeton, NJ: Princeton University Press).

Mormando, F. (1999), *The Preacher's Demons: Bernardino of Siena and the Social Underworld of Early Renaissance Italy* (Chicago: University of Chicago Press).

Morsel, J. (2001), 'Inventing a Social Category: The Sociogenesis of the Nobility at the End of the Middle Ages', in *Ordering Medieval Society: Perspectives on Intellectual and Practical Modes of Shaping Social Relations*, ed. B. Jussen, tr. P. Selwyn (Philadelphia, Pa: University of Pennsylvania Press), 200–240.

Mortimer, N. (2005), *John Lydgate's 'Fall of Princes': Narrative Tragedy in Its Literary and Political Contexts* (Oxford: Clarendon Press).

Muir, E. (2004), 'Representations of Power', in *Italy in the Age of the Renaissance 1300–1550*, ed. J.M. Najemy (Oxford: Oxford University Press), 226–45.

Mulchahey, M.M. (1998), *'First the Bow is Bent in Study . . .': Dominican Education before 1350* (Toronto: Pontifical Institute of Mediaeval Studies).

Müller, J.R. (2004), *'Erez gezerah* – "Land of Persecution": Pogroms against the Jews in the *Regnum Teutonicum* from c. 1280 to 1350', in *The Jews of Europe in the Middle Ages (Tenth to Fifteenth Centuries)*, ed. C. Cluse (Turnhout: Brepols), 245–60.

Murray, A. (1998), 'Counselling in Medieval Confession', in *Handling Sin: Confession in the Middle Ages*, ed. P. Biller and A.J. Minnis (York: York Medieval Press), 63–77.

Najemy, J.M. (2000), 'Civic Humanism and Florentine Politics', in *Renaissance Civic Humanism: Reappraisals and Reflections*, ed. J. Hankins (Cambridge: Cambridge University Press), 75–104.

Nederman, C.J. (1998), 'The Mirror Crack'd: The *Speculum Principum* as Political and Social Criticism in the Late Middle Ages', *The European Legacy*, vol. 3, 18–38.

Nederman, C.J. (ed. and tr.) (1990), *John of Salisbury, Policraticus: Of the Frivolities of Courtiers and the Footprints of Philosophers* (Cambridge: Cambridge University Press).

—— (2002), *Political Thought in Early Fourteenth-Century England: Treatises by Walter of Milemete, William of Pagula, and William of Ockham* (Tempe, Az: Arizona Center for Medieval and Renaissance Studies).

Nejedlý, M. (2000), 'L'idéal du roi en Bohême à la fin du XIVe siècle: remarques sur le *Nouveau Conseil* de Smil Flaška', in *Penser le pouvoir au Moyen Age (VIIIe–XVe siècle)*, ed. D. Boutet and J. Verger (Paris: Éditions rue d'Ulm), 247–60.

Noffke, S. (tr.) (1988), *The Letters of St. Catherine of Siena*, vol. 1 (Binghamton, NY: Medieval and Renaissance Texts and Studies).

Nys, E. (ed.) (1883), *L'Arbre des batailles d'Honoré Bonet* (Brussels and Leipzig: Librairie européenne C. Muquardt, Merzbach & Falk).

Oakley, F. (1979), *The Western Church in the Later Middle Ages* (Ithaca, NY: Cornell University Press).

Oexle, O.G. (2001), 'Perceiving Social Reality in the Early and High Middle Ages: A Contribution to a History of Social Knowledge', in *Ordering Medieval Society: Perspectives on Intellectual and Practical Modes of Shaping Social Relations*, ed. B. Jussen, tr. P. Selwyn (Philadelphia, Pa: University of Pennsylvania Press), 92–143.

Orme, N. (1973), *English Schools in the Middle Ages* (London: Methuen).

—— (1984), *From Childhood to Chivalry: The Education of the English Kings and Aristocracy 1066–1530* (London: Methuen).

—— (1995), 'An English Grammar School ca. 1450: Latin Exercises from Exeter (Caius College MS 417/447, Folios 16v–24v)', *Traditio*, vol. 50, 261–94.

—— (2001), *Medieval Children* (New Haven, Ct: Yale University Press).

—— (2006), *Medieval Schools: From Roman Britain to Renaissance England* (New Haven, Ct: Yale University Press).

Ormrod, W.M. (1991), 'The Crown and the English Economy, 1290–1348', in *Before the Black Death: Studies in the 'Crisis' of the Early Fourteenth Century*, ed. B.M.S. Campbell (Manchester: Manchester University Press), 149–83.

Otis, L.L. (1985), *Prostitution in Medieval Society: The History of an Urban Institution in the Languedoc* (Chicago, Il: University of Chicago Press).

Ouy, G. (1986), 'Bilinguisme ou trilinguisme? Latin commun, latin savant et français aux XIVe et XVe siècles', in *État et Église dans la genèse de l'État moderne*, ed. J.-P. Genet and B. Vincent (Madrid: Casa de Velásquez), 85–101.

Paget, V. (tr.) (1908), *More's Millenium: Being the Utopia of Sir Thomas More Rendered into Modern English* (New York: The John McBride Company).

Pantin, W.A. (1980), *The English Church in the Fourteenth Century* (Toronto: University of Toronto Press) (originally 1955).

Paravicini, A. and W. Paravicini (2000), 'L'arsenal intellectuel d'un homme de pouvoir: les livres de Guillaume Hugonet, chancelier de Bourgogne', in *Penser le pouvoir au Moyen Age (VIIIe–XVe siècle)*, ed. D. Boutet and J. Verger (Paris: Éditions rue d'Ulm), 261–325.

Paravicini, W. (1991), 'The Court of the Dukes of Burgundy: A Model for Europe?', in *Princes, Patronage, and the Nobility: The Court at the Beginning of the Modern Age, c. 1450–1650*, ed. R.G. Asch and A.M. Birke (London and Oxford: German Historical Institute and Oxford University Press).

Parkes, M.B. (1992), 'The Provision of Books', in *The History of the University of Oxford*, vol. 2, *Late Medieval Oxford*, ed. J.I. Catto and R. Evans (Oxford: Clarendon Press), 407–83.

Pascucci, I. (2001), 'L'iconografia delle virtù nella Sala Vecchia degli Svizzeri in Vaticano', *Studi romani*, vol. 48, 26–35.

Pearsall, D. (1994), 'Hoccleve's *Regement of Princes*: The Poetics of Royal Self-Representation', *Speculum*, vol. 69, 386–410.

Pettegree, A. (2010), *The Book in the Renaissance* (New Haven, Ct: Yale University Press).

Pfaff, R.W. (1970), *New Liturgical Feasts in Later Medieval England* (Oxford: Clarendon Press).

—— (2007), 'Telling Liturgical Times in the Middle Ages', in *Procession, Performance, Liturgy, and Ritual*, ed. N. van Deusen (Ottawa, Ont: Institute of Mediaeval Music), 43–64.

Phillips, J.R.S. (1998), *The Medieval Expansion of Europe*, 2nd ed. (Oxford: Clarendon Press).

Platt, C. (1996/1997), *King Death: The Black Death and Its Aftermath in Later-Medieval Europe* (London: UCL Press; Toronto: University of Toronto Press).

Postan, M.M. (1966), 'Medieval Agrarian Society in its Prime: England', in *The Cambridge Economic History of Europe*, vol. 1, *The Agrarian Life of the Middle Ages*, 2nd ed., ed. M.M. Postan (Cambridge: Cambridge University Press), 548–632.

Potthast, A. (ed.) (1859), *Liber de rebus memoriabilioribus sive Chronicon Henrici de Hervordia* (Göttingen: Dieterich).

Prestwich, M. (1996), *Armies and Warfare in the Middle Ages: The English Experience* (New Haven, Ct: Yale University Press).

Prevenier, W. (1983), '*La démographie des villes du comté de Flandre aux XIIIe et XIVe siècles*', *Revue du Nord*, vol. 65, 255–75.

Pryds, D. (1993), '*Rex praedicans*: Robert d'Anjou and the Politics of Preaching', in *De l'homélie au sermon: histoire de la prédication médiévale*, ed. J. Hamesse (Louvain-la-Neuve: Université Catholique de Louvain), 239–62.

Quillen, C.E. (ed. and tr.) (2003), *The Secret, by Francesco Petrarch, with Related Documents* (Boston and New York: Bedford/St Martin's).

Quillet, J. (1995), 'Remarques sur les théories politiques du XIVe siècle', in *Les philosophies morales et politiques au Moyen Age*, vol. 3, ed. B. Carlos Bazán, E. Andújar and L. Sbrocchi (New York and Ottawa: Legas), 1571–81.

Rashdall, H. (1936), *The Universities in Europe in the Middle Ages*, 3 vols, ed. F.M. Powicke and A.B. Emden (Oxford: Oxford University Press).

Rawcliffe, C. (2003), 'Women, Childbirth, and Religion in Later Medieval England', in *Women and Religion in Medieval England*, ed. D. Wood (Oxford: Oxbow Books), 91–117.

Rees Jones, S. (2001), 'Thomas More's *Utopia* and Medieval London', in *Pragmatic Utopias: Ideals and Communities, 1200–1630*, ed. R. Horrox and S. Rees Jones (Cambridge: Cambridge University Press), 117–35.

Reeve, M.D. (1996), 'Classical Scholarship', in *The Cambridge Companion to Renaissance Humanism*, ed. J. Kraye (Cambridge: Cambridge University Press), 20–46.

Reinhard, W. (1996), 'Introduction: Power Elites, State Servants, Ruling Classes, and the Growth of State Power', in *Power Elites and State Building*, ed. W. Reinhard (Oxford: Clarendon Press), 1–18.

Ribordy, G. (2004), *'Faire les nopces': le marriage de la noblesse française (1375–1475)* (Toronto: Pontifical Institute of Mediaeval Studies).

Ricciardelli, F. (2015), *The Myth of Republicanism in Renaissance Italy* (Turnhout: Brepols).

Richardson, M. (1980), 'Henry V, the English Chancery, and Chancery English', *Speculum*, vol. 55, 726–50.

Richmond, C. (2001), 'Victorian Values in Fifteenth-Century England: The Ewelme Almshouse Statutes', in *Pragmatic Utopias: Ideals and Communities, 1200–1630*, ed. R. Horrox and S. Rees Jones (Cambridge: Cambridge University Press), 224–41.

Rigaudière, A. (2000), 'Le bon prince dans l'oeuvre de Pierre Salmon', in *Penser le pouvoir au Moyen Age (VIIIe–XVe siècle)*, ed. D. Boutet and J. Verger (Paris: Éditions rue d'Ulm), 365–84.

Riley, H.T. (ed.) (1863–64), *Thomas Walsingham, 'Historia Anglicana'*, 2 vols (London: Rolls Series).

Robins, W. (2003), 'Vernacular Textualities in Fourteenth-Century Florence', in *The Vulgar Tongue: Medieval and Postmedieval Vernacularity*, ed. F. Somerset and N. Watson (University Park, Pa: Pennsylvania State University Press).

Rocke, M. (1998), 'Gender and Sexual Culture in Renaissance Italy', in *Gender and Society in Renaissance Italy*, ed. J.C. Brown and R.C. Davis (London: Longman), 150–70.

Rogers, C.J. (1999), 'The Age of the Hundred Years War', in *Medieval Warfare: A History*, ed. M. Keen (Oxford: Oxford University Press), 136–60.

Rosario, I. (2000), *Art and Propaganda: Charles IV of Bohemia, 1346–1378* (Woodbridge: Boydell Press).

Rösener, W. (1994), *The Peasantry of Europe*, tr. T.M. Barker (Oxford: Blackwell).

Ross, C. (1974), *Edward IV* (Berkeley, Cal: University of California Press).

Rossiaud, J. (1990), 'The City-Dweller and Life in Cities and Towns', in *Medieval Callings*, ed. J. Le Goff, tr. L.C. Cochrane (Chicago: University of Chicago Press), 139–79.

Rouse, M.A. and R.H. Rouse (1991), *Authentic Witnesses: Approaches to Medieval Texts and Manuscripts* (Notre Dame, Ind: University of Notre Dame Press).

Rouse, R.H. and M.A. Rouse (1979), *Preachers, Florilegia and Sermons: Studies on the 'Manipulus florum' of Thomas of Ireland* (Toronto: Pontifical Institute of Mediaeval Studies).

Rouse, R.H. and M.A. Rouse (2000), *Manuscripts and Their Makers: Commercial Book Producers in Medieval Paris 1200–1500*, 2 vols (Turnhout: Harvey Miller).

Rubin, M. (1991), *Corpus Christi: The Eucharist in Late Medieval Culture* (Cambridge: Cambridge University Press).

—— (1995), 'Imagining the Jew: The Late Medieval Eucharistic Discourse', in *In and Out of the Ghetto: Jewish-Gentile Relations in Late Medieval and Early Modern Germany*, ed. R. Po-Chia Hsia and H. Lehmann (Cambridge: Cambridge University Press), 107–208.

Rüegg, W. (1992), 'Epilogue: The Rise of Humanism', in *A History of the University in Europe*, vol. 1, *Universities in the Middle Ages*, ed. H. de Ridder-Symoens (Cambridge: Cambridge University Press), 442–68.

Rusconi, R. (2004), 'Anti-Jewish Preaching in the Fifteenth Century and Images of Preachers in Italian Renaissance Art', in *Friars and Jews in the Middle Ages and Renaissance*, ed. S.J. McMichael and S.E. Myers (Leiden: Brill), 225–37.

Russell, J.B. (1972), *Witchcraft in the Middle Ages* (Ithaca, NY: Cornell University Press).

Russo, D. (1995), 'Les modes de représentation du pouvoir en Europe dans l'iconographie du XIVe siècle', in *Représentation, pouvoir et royauté à la fin du Moyen Age*, ed. J. Blanchard (Paris: Picard), 177–98.

Saak, E.L. (2002), *High Way to Heaven: The Augustinian Platform between Reform and Reformation, 1292–1524* (Leiden: Brill).

Sandquist, T.A. (1969), 'The Holy Oil of St. Thomas of Canterbury', in *Essays in Medieval History Presented to Bertie Wilkinson*, ed. T.A. Sandquist and M.R. Powicke (Toronto: University of Toronto Press), 330–44.

Scheifele, E. (1999), 'Richard II and the Visual Arts', in *Richard II: The Art of Kingship*, ed. A. Goodman and J.L. Gillespie (Oxford: Clarendon Press), 255–71.

Schimmelpfennig, B. (1992), *The Papacy*, tr. J. Sievert (New York: Columbia University Press).

Scott, S. and C. Duncan (2004), *Return of the Black Death: The World's Greatest Serial Killer* (Chichester: Wiley).

Scott, T. (2002), *Society and Economy in Germany 1300–1600* (Basingstoke: Palgrave).

Sears, H.L. (1952), 'The *Rimado de Palaçio* and the "De regimine principum" Tradition of the Middle Ages', *Hispanic Review*, vol. 20, 1–27.

Seay, A. (1975), *Music in the Medieval World*, 2nd ed. (Englewood Cliffs, NJ: Prentice-Hall).

Shahar, S. (2003), *The Fourth Estate: A History of Women in the Middle Ages*, revised ed., tr. C. Galai (London: Routledge) (originally published 1983).

Sherman, C.R. (1971), 'Representations of Charles V of France (1338–80) as a Wise Ruler', *Medievalia et Humanistica*, new series vol. 2, 83–96.

Shinners, J. (ed.) (1997), *Medieval Popular Religion, 1000–1500: A Reader* (Toronto: Broadview Press).

Simons, W. (2001), *Cities of Ladies: Beguine Communities in the Medieval Low Countries, 1200–1565* (Philadelphia, Pa: University of Pennsylvania Press).

Siraisi, N. (1992), 'The Faculty of Medicine', in *A History of the University in Europe*, vol. 1, *Universities in the Middle Ages*, ed. H. de Ridder-Symoens (Cambridge: Cambridge University Press), 360–87.

Skinner, Q. (1986), 'Ambrogio Lorenzetti: The Artist as Political Philosopher', *Proceedings of the British Academy*, vol. 72, 1–56.

Smalley, B. (1974), *Historians in the Middle Ages* (London: Thames and Hudson).

Smith, R.M. (1991), 'Demographic Developments in Rural England, 1300–348: A Survey', in *Before the Black Death: Studies in the 'Crisis' of the Early Fourteenth Century*, ed. B.M.S. Campbell (Manchester: Manchester University Press), 25–77.

—— (1992), 'Geographical Diversity in the Resort to Marriage in Late Medieval Europe: Work, Reputation, and Unmarried Females in the Household Formation Systems of Northern and Southern Europe', in *Woman is a Worthy Wight: Women in English Medieval Society c. 1200–1500*, ed. P.J.P. Goldberg (Stroud: Sutton), 16–59.

Spufford, P. (2000), 'Trade in Fourteenth-Century Europe', in *NCMH* 6, 155–208.

—— (2002), *Power and Profit: The Merchant in Medieval Europe* (London: Thames and Hudson).

Starn, R. and L. Partridge (1992), *Arts of Power: Three Halls of State in Italy, 1300–1600* (Berkeley, Cal: University of California Press).

Storey, W.G. (1972), *The 'De quatuor virtutibus cardinalibus pro eruditione principum' of Michael the Carthusian of Prague: A Critical Text and Study*. Analecta Cartusiana 6 (Salzburg: Dr. James Hogg).

Stow, G.B. (ed.) (1977), *Historia Vitae et Regni Ricardi Secundi* (Philadelphia, Pa: University of Pennsylvania Press).

Strayer, J.R. (1980), *The Reign of Philip the Fair* (Princeton, NJ: Princeton University Press).

Strohm, P. (2005), *Politique: Languages of Statecraft between Chaucer and Shakespeare* (Notre Dame, Ind: University of Notre Dame Press).

Strohm, R. (1993), *The Rise of European Music, 1380–1500* (Cambridge: Cambridge University Press).

Surtz, E. (ed.) (1964), *St. Thomas More, Utopia* (New Haven, Ct: Yale University Press).

Swanson, R.N. (1989), *Church and Society in Late Medieval England* (Oxford: Blackwell).

—— (1994), 'Literacy, Heresy, History and Orthodoxy: Perspectives and Permutations for the Later Middle Ages', in *Heresy and Literacy, 1000–1530*, ed. P. Biller and A. Hudson (Cambridge: Cambridge University Press), 279–93.

—— (1995), *Religion and Devotion in Europe, c. 1215–c. 1515* (Cambridge: Cambridge University Press).

—— (2006), 'Praying for Pardon: Devotional Indulgences in Late Medieval England', in *Promissory Notes on the Treasury of Merits: Indulgences in Late Medieval Europe*, ed. R.N. Swanson (Leiden: Brill), 215–40.

Swanson, R.N. (ed.) (1993), *Catholic England: Faith, Religion, and Observance before the Reformation* (Manchester: Manchester University Press).

Symcox, G. and B. Sullivan (2005), *Christopher Columbus and the Enterprise of the Indies: A Brief History with Documents* (Boston: Bedford/St. Martin's).

Tanner, N.P. (ed.) (1977), *Heresy Trials in the Diocese of Norwich, 1428–31*, Camden Fourth Series, vol. 20 (London: Royal Historical Society).

Taylor, F. and J.S. Roskell (trs) (1975), *Gesta Henrici Quinti—The Deeds of Henry the Fifth* (Oxford: Clarendon Press).

Tentler, T.N. (1974), 'The Summa for Confessors as an Instrument of Social Control', in *The Pursuit of Holiness in Late Medieval and Renaissance Religion*, ed. C. Trinkaus and H.A. Oberman (Leiden: Brill), 103–37.

Thorndyke, L. (tr.) (1972), *University Records and Life in the Middle Ages* (New York: Norton).

Tisser, P. (ed.) (1960), *Procès de condamnation de Jeanne d'Arc*, vol. 1 of 3 (Paris: Librairie C. Klincksieck).

Trexler, R.C. (1980), *Public Life in Renaissance Florence* (Ithaca, NY: Cornell University Press).

Tuchman, B.W. (1978), *A Distant Mirror: The Calamitous 14th Century* (New York: Alfred A. Knopf).

Twigg, G. (1984), *The Black Death: A Biological Reappraisal* (London: Batsford Academic and Educational).

Tyrrell, E. and N.H. Nicolas (eds) (1827), *A Chronicle of London: From 1089 to 1483* (London: Longman, Rees, Orme, Brown and Green).

Ubl, K. (ed.) (1994), *Die Schriften des Alexander von Roes und des Engelbert von Admont, pt. 2, Engelbert von Admont, Speculum virtutum* (Hannover: Hahnsche Buchhandlung).

Unger, R.W. (1980), *The Ship in the Medieval Economy, 600–1600* (Montreal: McGill University Press).

Vale, M. (1981), *War and Chivalry: Warfare and Aristocratic Culture in England, France and Burgundy at the End of the Middle Ages* (London: Duckworth, 1981).

—— (1998), 'Manuscripts and Books', in *NCMH* 7, 278–86.

—— (2001), *The Princely Court: Medieval Courts and Culture in North-West Europe, 1270–1380* (Oxford: Oxford University Press).

Van Engen, J. (1986), 'The Christian Middle Ages as an Historiographical Problem', *American Historical Review*, vol. 91, 519–52.

Van Engen, J. (tr.) (1988), *Devotio Moderna: Basic Writings* (New York: Paulist Press).

Vauchez, A. (1993), *The Laity in the Middle Ages: Religious Beliefs and Devotional Practices*, ed. D.E. Bornstein, tr. M.J. Schneider (Notre Dame, Ind: University of Notre Dame Press).

—— (1997), *Sainthood in the Later Middle Ages*, tr. J. Birrell (Cambridge: Cambridge University Press).

Verger, J. (1972), 'The University of Paris at the End of the Hundred Years' War', in *Universities in Politics: Case Studies from the Late Middle Ages and Early Modern Period* (Baltimore, Md: Johns Hopkins University Press), 47–78.

—— (1992), 'Patterns', in *A History of the University in Europe*, vol. 1, *Universities in the Middle Ages*, ed. H. de Ridder-Symoens (Cambridge: Cambridge University Press), 35–74.

—— (1998), 'Schools and Universities', in *NCMH* 7, 220–42.

—— (2000a), '*Ad prefulgidum sapiencie culmen prolem regis inclitam provehere*: L'initiation des dauphins de France à la sagesse politique selon Jean Gerson', in *Penser le pouvoir au Moyen Age (VIIIe–XVe siècle): études d'histoire et de littérature offertes à Françoise Autrand*, ed. D. Boutet and J. Verger (Paris: Éditions rue d'Ulm), 427–40.

—— (2000b), *Men of Learning in Europe at the End of the Middle Ages*, tr. L. Neal and S. Rendall (Notre Dame, Ind: University of Notre Dame Press).

—— (2007), 'Landmarks for a History of the University of Paris at the Time of Jean Standonck', *History of the Universities*, vol. 22, no. 2, 1–13.

Waldron, R. (1988), 'Trevisa's Original Prefaces on Translation: A Critical Edition', in *Medieval English Studies Presented to George Kane*, ed. E.D. Kennedy, R. Waldron and J.S. Wittig (Woodbridge: D.S. Brewer), 285–95.

Ward, J. (2002), *Women in Medieval Europe, 1200–1500* (Harlow: Longman).

Watkins, R.N. (tr.) (1969), *The Family in Renaissance Florence* (Columbia, SC: University of South Carolina Press).

Watt, J.A. (tr.) (1971), *John of Paris, 'On Royal and Papal Power'* (Toronto: Pontifical Institute of Mediaeval Studies).

Watts, J.L. (1990), '*De consulatu Stiliconis*: Texts and Politics in the Reign of Henry VI', *Journal of Medieval History*, vol. 16, 251–66.

—— (1996), *Henry VI and the Politics of Kingship* (Cambridge: Cambridge University Press).

—— (2002), '*The Policie in Christen Remes*: Bishop Russell's Parliamentary Sermons of 1483–84', in *Authority and Consent in Tudor England: Essays Presented to C.S.L. Davies* (Aldershot: Ashgate), 33–59.

Webb, D. (2006), 'Pardons and Pilgrims', in *Promissory Notes on the Treasury of Merits: Indulgences in Late Medieval Europe*, ed. R.N. Swanson (Leiden: Brill), 241–75.

Wei, I.P. (1995), 'The Self-Image of the Masters of Theology at the University Paris in the Late Thirteenth and Early Fourteenth Centuries', *Journal of Ecclesiastical History*, vol. 46, 398–431.

Wenzel, S. (1994), *Macaronic Sermons: Bilingualism and Preaching in Late-Medieval England* (Ann Arbor, Mich: University of Michigan Press).

White, L. (1962), *Medieval Technology and Social Change* (Oxford: Clarendon Press).

Willard, C.C. (ed.) (1989), *Christine de Pizan, 'Le livre des trois vertus'* (Paris: H. Champion).

Williams, S.J. (2003), *The Secret of Secrets: The Scholar Career of a Pseudo-Aristotelian Text in the Later Middle Ages* (Ann Arbor, Mich: University of Michigan Press).

Windeatt, B. (ed.) (2004), *The Book of Margery Kempe* (Cambridge: D.S. Brewer).

Winston-Allen, A. (2004), *Convent Chronicles: Women Writing about Women and Reform in the Late Middle Ages* (University Park, Pa: Pennsylvania State University Press).

Witt, R. G. (2003), *In the Footsteps of the Ancients: The Origins of Humanism from Lovato to Bruni* (Leiden: Brill)

Wolff, P. (1986), *Automne du Moyen Age ou printemps des temps nouveaux? L'économie européenne aux XIVe et XVe siècles* (Paris: Aubier).

Woods, M.C. and R. Copeland (1999), 'Classroom and Confession', in *The Cambridge History of Medieval English Literature*, ed. D. Wallace (Cambridge: Cambridge University Press), 376–406.

Wootton, D. (ed. and tr.) (1995), *Niccolò Machiavelli, 'The Prince'* (Indianapolis, Ind: Hackett Publishing).

Wright, R. (2002), *A Sociophilological Study of Late Latin* (Turnhout: Brepols).

Wright, T. (ed.) (1853), *The Canterbury Tales of Geoffrey Chaucer: A New Text, with Illustrative Notes* (London: N. Cooke).

Wunderli, R. (1992), *Peasant Fires: The Drummer of Niklashausen* (Bloomington, Ind: Indiana University Press).

Zuffi, S. (2005), *European Art of the Fifteenth Century*, tr. B.D. Phillips (Los Angeles, Cal: J. Paul Getty Museum).

Zutshi, P.N.R. (2000), 'The Avignon Papacy', in *NCMH* 6, 653–73.

INDEX